*Near Callander is Balquhidder Church, containing the 8th-century St. Angus Stone, a 17th-century bell, and some Gaelic Bibles. But most people come here to see the grave of Robert "Rob Roy" MacGregor. See chapter 8. © Catherine Karnow Photography.*

*The first Saturday of September brings the Royal Highland Gathering to Braemar. The highlights are bagpiping and dancing competitions and performances of great strength like the hammer throw. See chapter 9. © Churchill & Klehr Photography.*

*The lochs and moors of the West Highlands are irresistibly beautiful spots where you'll want to linger and shoot a few rolls of film. This is Rannoch Moor off Loch Laidon, as viewed from A82. See chapter 10. © Kindra Clineff Photography.*

*Near Kyle of Lochalsh is Eilean Donan Castle, built in 1214 as a defense against the Danes. In ruins for 200 years, it was restored by Colonel MacRae of Clan MacRae in 1932 and is now a memorial/museum. See chapter 11. © Catherine Karnow Photography.*

On Skye and the other Hebridean Islands are thatch-roofed "black houses," built without mortar. Though some houses have chimneys, the smoke from the fires inside passes through the thatch, making it "black." See chapter 11. © Art Wolfe Photography.

On the Isle of Lewis, you can marvel at the Standing Stones of Callanish, only one of many such prehistoric formations in the Hebrides. From a circle of 13 stones, a road of 19 monoliths leads north. See chapter 11. © Greg Gawlowski/Photo 20-20.

*The oldest (1128) and probably largest of the Borders abbeys, Kelso Abbey has lain in ruins since the late 16th century, when it suffered its last and most devastating attack by the English. See chapter 5. © Andrea Pistolesi/The Image Bank.*

With more than 440 courses, Scotland is synonymous with golf. The famous golfing center/sports complex at Gleneagles boasts several 18-hole courses: The King's and Queen's are among the best in the country. See chapters 3 and 9. © Macduff Everton Photography.

Loch Awe is Scotland's longest lake. Along its banks are many ruins, including those of Kilchurn Castle, once a stronghold of the Campbells of Glen Orchy and still spectacularly intact. See chapter 7. © John Lawrence/Tony Stone Images.

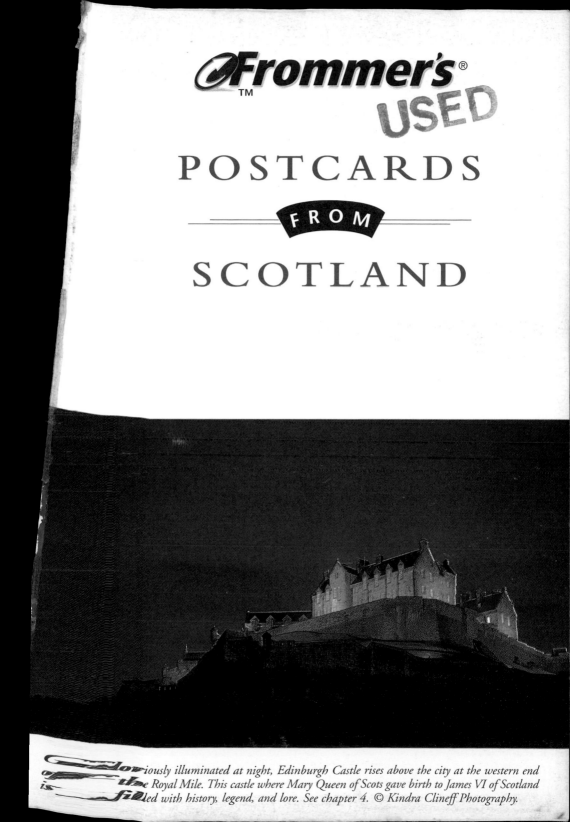

# *Frommer's*®
™

USED

# POSTCARDS

FROM

# SCOTLAND

Gloriously illuminated at night, Edinburgh Castle rises above the city at the western end of the Royal Mile. This castle where Mary Queen of Scots gave birth to James VI of Scotland is filled with history, legend, and lore. See chapter 4. © Kindra Clineff Photography.

Edinburgh Castle's early history is vague, though it's known that in the 11th century Malcolm III and his Saxon queen (later St. Margaret) founded a castle here. The only fragment left is St. Margaret's Chapel. See chapter 4. © Kindra Clineff Photography.

Old Town's Royal Mile stretches from Edinburgh Castle all the way to the Palace of Holyroodhouse and bears four names along its length—Castlehill, Lawnmarket, High Street, and Canongate. See chapter 4. © Catherine Karnow Photography.

*When should I travel to get the best airfare?*
*Where do I go for answers to my travel questions?*
*What's the best and easiest way to plan and book my trip?*

# frommers.travelocity.com

**Frommer's**, the travel guide leader, has teamed up with **Travelocity.com**, the leader in online travel, to bring you an in-depth, easy-to-use resource designed to help you plan and book your trip online.

At **frommers.travelocity.com**, you'll find free online updates about your destination from the experts at Frommer's plus the outstanding travel planning and purchasing features of Travelocity.com. Travelocity.com provides reservations capabilities for 95 percent of all airline seats sold, more than 47,000 hotels, and over 50 car rental companies. In addition, Travelocity.com offers more than 2,000 exciting vacation and cruise packages. Travelocity.com puts you in complete control of your travel planning with these and other great features:

**Expert travel guidance from Frommer's** - over 150 writers reporting from around the world!

**Best Fare Finder** - an interactive calendar tells you when to travel to get the best airfare

**Fare Watcher** - we'll track airfare changes to your favorite destinations

**Dream Maps** - a mapping feature that suggests travel opportunities based on your budget

**Shop Safe Guarantee** - 24 hours a day / 7 days a week live customer service, and more!

Whether traveling on a tight budget, looking for a quick weekend getaway, or planning the trip of a lifetime, Frommer's guides and Travelocity.com will make your travel dreams a reality. You've bought the book, now book the trip!

## Other Great Guides for Your Trip:

*Frommer's England*

*Frommer's England from $70 a Day*

*Frommer's London*

*Frommer's Ireland*

*Frommer's Best-Loved Driving Tours: Scotland*

## Here's what the critics say about Frommer's:

"Amazingly easy to use. Very portable, very complete."
—*Booklist*

♦

"The only mainstream guide to list specific prices. The Walter Cronkite of guidebooks—with all that implies."
—*Travel & Leisure*

♦

"Complete, concise, and filled with useful information."
—*New York Daily News*

♦

"Hotel information is close to encyclopedic."
—*Des Moines Sunday Register*

♦

"Detailed, accurate, and easy-to-read information for all price ranges."
—*Glamour Magazine*

# Scotland

## 2001

### by Darwin Porter & Danforth Prince

IDG Books Worldwide, Inc.
An International Data Group Company
Foster City, CA • Chicago, IL • Indianapolis, IN • New York, NY

## ABOUT THE AUTHORS

Although this is only the fifth edition of this guide devoted to Scotland, **Darwin Porter** has covered the country since the beginning of his travel-writing career as author of *Frommer's England & Scotland*. Since 1982, he has been joined in his efforts by **Danforth Prince,** formerly of the Paris bureau of the *New York Times*. Together, they've written numerous best-selling Frommer's guides—notably to England, France, and Italy.

## IDG BOOKS WORLDWIDE, INC.

An International Data Group Company
909 Third Avenue
New York, NY 10022

Find us online at **www.frommers.com**

Copyright © 2001 by IDG Books Worldwide, Inc.
Maps © 2001 by IDG Books Worldwide, Inc.

ISBN 0-7645-6168-5
ISSN 1055-5390

Editor: Lisa Renaud/Dog-Eared Pages
Production Editor: Donna Wright
Photo Editor: Richard Fox
Design by Michele Laseau
Cartographer: John Decamillis
Production by IDG Books Indianapolis Production Department

## SPECIAL SALES

For general information on IDG Books Worldwide's books in the U.S., please call our Consumer Customer Service department at 1-800-762-2974. For reseller information, including discounts, bulk sales, customized editions, and premium sales, please call our Reseller Customer Service department at 1-800-434-3422.

Manufactured in the United States of America

5  4  3  2  1

# Contents

v

## 5  The Borders & Galloway Regions   129

## 6  Glasgow & the Strathclyde Region   173

## 7  Argyll & the Southern Hebrides   226

# List of Maps

## An Invitation to the Reader

In researching this book, we discovered many wonderful places—hotels, restaurants, shops, and more. We're sure you'll find others. Please tell us about them, so we can share the information with your fellow travelers in upcoming editions. If you were disappointed with a recommendation, we'd love to know that, too. Please write to:

*Frommer's Scotland 2001*
IDG Books Worldwide, Inc.
909 Third Avenue
New York, NY 10022

## An Additional Note

Please be advised that travel information is subject to change at any time—and this is especially true of prices. We therefore suggest that you write or call ahead for confirmation when making your travel plans. The authors, editors, and publisher cannot be held responsible for the experiences of readers while traveling. Your safety is important to us, however, so we encourage you to stay alert and be aware of your surroundings. Keep a close eye on cameras, purses, and wallets, all favorite targets of thieves and pickpockets.

## What the Symbols Mean

### ✪ Frommer's Favorites

Our favorite places and experiences—outstanding for quality, value, or both.

The following abbreviations are used for credit cards:

| | | | |
|---|---|---|---|
| AE | American Express | DISC | Discover |
| CB | Carte Blanche | MC | MasterCard |
| DC | Diners Club | V | VISA |

## Find Frommer's Online

**www.frommers.com** offers up-to-the-minute listings on almost 200 cities around the globe—including the latest bargains and candid, personal articles updated daily by Arthur Frommer himself. No other Web site offers such comprehensive and timely coverage of the world of travel.

# The Best of Scotland

**S**cotland is permeated with legend and romance. Its ruined castles standing amid fields of heather and bracken speak of a past full of heroism and struggle and events that still ring across the centuries. Its two great cities—the ancient seat of Scottish royalty, Edinburgh, and the even more ancient Glasgow, boasting Victorian splendor—are among Europe's most dynamic cities. The country's other side is its awesomely beautiful outdoors, with highlands, mountains, lakes, lochs, salmon-filled rivers, incomparable golf courses, and more.

## 1 The Best Travel Experiences

- **Checking Out the Local Pub:** You're in a Scottish pub, talking to the bartender and choosing from a dizzying array of single-malt whiskies. Perhaps the wind is blowing fitfully outside, causing the wooden sign to creak above the battered door, and a fire is flickering against the blackened bricks of the old fireplace. This is the best place in town to quaff a wee dram and to get a real one-on-one taste of what the Scots are like. If you head here to ward off the chill of a cold damp night, you certainly won't be alone. As the evening wanes and you've established common ground with the locals, you'll realize you're having one of your most authentic Scottish experiences.
- **Sailing off the Coast of Argyll:** Eons ago, glaciers carved the west coast of Scotland into one of Europe's most spectacularly jagged shorelines. Warmed by the Gulf Stream and dotted with sheltered estuaries and channels, it offers challenging sailing and rugged scenery. If you're a qualified sailor, you can rent a vessel from virtually any fisherman along the coast for a watery overview of terrain made famous by the Lowland clans. Or, you can rent a boat from the **Linnhe Marine Watersports Centre,** Lettershuna, Appin (☎ **01631/730-401**).
- **Visiting Edinburgh at Festival Time:** The Edinburgh Festival has become one of Europe's most prestigious arts festivals. During 3 weeks in August and September, a host of performers descends on the city, infusing it with a kind of manic creative energy. If you're planning to sample the many offerings, get your tickets well in advance, and make your hotel and flight reservations early. Contact the **Edinburgh International Festival Box**

# Scotland

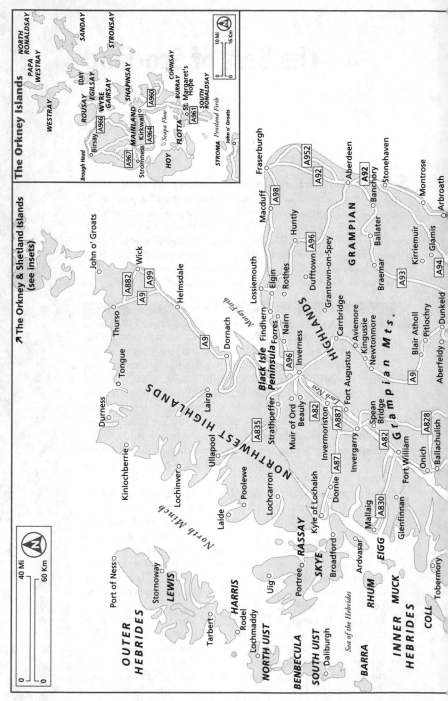

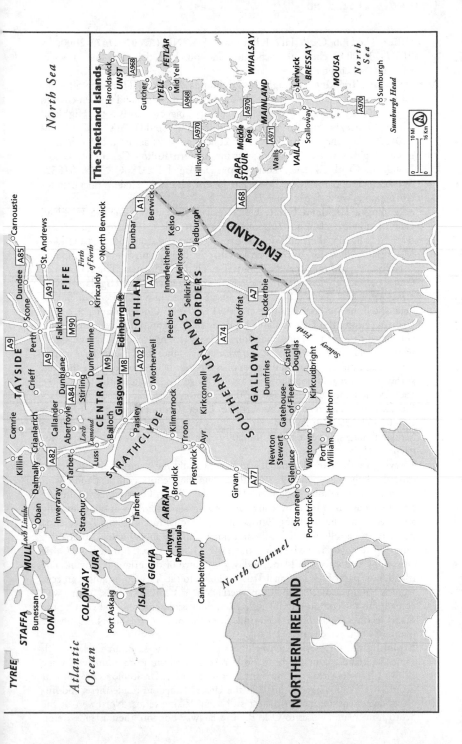

The Shetland Islands

North Sea

UNST · A968
YELL · FETLAR · WHALSAY
Haroldswick
Gutcher
Mid Yell · A968
MAINLAND · A970 · Lerwick · BRESSAY
Hillswick · A970
Muckle Roe
PAPA STOUR · A971 · MOUSA
Walls · VAILA · Scalloway · A970
Sumburgh
Sumburgh Head
North Sea

10 Mi
16 Km

North Sea

TYREE
STAFFA
MULL · Loch Linnhe
IONA
Bunessan
Oban
Dalmally
Inveraray
Strachur
Tarbert
COLONSAY
JURA
ISLAY
Port Askaig
GIGHA
Kintyre Peninsula
Campbeltown
ARRAN
Brodick
Tarbert
Atlantic Ocean
North Channel

Carnoustie
Dundee · A85
St. Andrews
Scone · A91 · FIFE
Perth · Kirkcaldy
Falkland · M90 · Dunfermline
A9
Crieff · TAYSIDE
A9
Comrie
Killin
Crianlarich
Callander
Aberfoyle · A84
Dunblane
Stirling · CENTRAL
Loch Lomond
Luss
Balloch
Paisley · Glasgow · M8 · A702 · Motherwell
STRATHCLYDE
Kilmarnock
Troon
Prestwick
Ayr
Girvan · A77
M9
Edinburgh
LOTHIAN
North Berwick
Dunbar · A1
Berwick
Innerleithen · Kelso
Peebles · A7 · Melrose · Jedburgh · A68
Selkirk · BORDERS
SOUTHERN UPLANDS
Moffat · A7 · A74
Lockerbie
ENGLAND
Newton Stewart
Gatehouse-of-Fleet
Castle Douglas
Dumfries
GALLOWAY
Kirkcudbright
Glenluce · Wigtown
Stranraer · Port William · Whithorn
Portpatrick
Solway Firth
Kirkconnell

NORTHERN IRELAND

3

**Office,** The Hub, Castle Hill, Edinburgh EH1 7ND (☎ 0131/473-2000; fax 0131/473-2003), check the schedule, and purchase tickets online at www. eif.co.uk. See chapter 4.

- **Horseback Trekking Through the Highlands & Argyll:** There's nothing like riding one of the country's sturdy ponies through the Highland's lichen-covered rocks and fragrant heather. One of the country's biggest stables is the **Highland Riding Centre,** Borlum Farm, Drumnadrochit, Highland IV3 6XN (☎ 01456/450-220). See chapter 10. For scenic equestrian treks across the Argyll area's moors, highlands, and headlands, try the **Ardfern Riding Centre** (Appaloosa Holidays), Croabh Haven, Loch Gilphead, Argyll PA31 8QR (☎ 01852/500-632). Proprietor Nigel Boase has lots of ideas for suitable itineraries for cross-country treks. See chapter 7.

- **Attending a Highland Game:** Unlike any other sporting event, a Highland Game emphasizes clannish traditions rather than athletic dexterity, and the centerpiece is usually the exhibition of brute strength (tossing logs and the like). Most visitors show up for the men in kilts, the bagpipe playing, the pomp and circumstance, and the general celebration of all things Scottish. The best-known (and most widely televised) of the events is the **Braemar Royal Highland Gathering,** held near Balmoral Castle the first Saturday in September. For further details, call the local tourist office at ☎ 013397/416-00. See chapter 9.

- **Cruising Along the Caledonian Canal:** In 1822, a group of enterprising Scots connected three of the Highland's longest lakes (Lochs Ness, Lochy, and Oich) with a canal linking Britain's east and west coasts. Since then, barges have hauled everything from grain to building supplies without having to negotiate the wild storms off Scotland's northernmost tips. If you'd like a waterborne view of the countryside tamed centuries ago by the Camerons, the Stewarts, and the Mac-Donalds, you can rent a cabin cruiser. **Caley Cruisers,** based in Inverness (☎ 01463/236-328; fax 01463/714-879; www.caleycruisers.co.uk), maintains Scotland's largest inventory (45) of 60-horsepower diesel-powered cruisers. See chapter 10.

- **Ferrying to the Isle of Iona:** It's an otherworldly rock, one of Europe's most evocative holy places, anchored solidly among the Hebrides off Scotland's western coast. St. Columba (Columcille) established it as a Christian center in 563 and used it as a base for converting Scotland. In the Dark Ages, it saved learning and literacy for the emerging European world. You'll find a ruined Benedictine nunnery and a fully restored cathedral (known as the abbey) where 50 Scottish kings opted to be buried during the early Middle Ages. Hundreds of Celtic crosses once adorned the island; today, only three of the originals remain. The island, now part of the National Trust, is home to the Iona Community, an ecumenical group dedicated to the perpetuation of Christian ideals. You're welcomed into the community for reflection, discussion, and prayer. Reaching the island requires a 10-minute ferry ride from the hamlet of Fionnphort, on the island of Mull. See chapter 11.

- **Exploring the Orkneys:** Archaeologists say the Orkneys, an archipelago with some 70 islands, contain the richest trove of prehistoric monuments in the British Isles—an average of three sites per square mile. Ornithologists claim that about 16% of all winged animals in the United Kingdom reside there, and linguists document an ancient dialect still using Viking terms. Northwest of the Scottish mainland, closer to Oslo than to faraway London, these islands are on the same latitude as St. Petersburg but much more exposed to the raging gales of the North Sea. The sunsets here during late spring and the aurora borealis have been called mystical, and in midsummer the sun remains above the horizon for 18 hours per day. In winter, the islands are plunged into an equivalent twilight or total darkness. Only 19 of the Orkneys are inhabited; the others seem to float above primordial seas, drenched with rains and the weak sunlight of these northern climes. See chapter 12.

## 2 The Best Golf

For full details about golfing in Scotland, see chapter 3.

- **Royal Troon Golf Club,** Ayrshire (☎ **01292/311-555;** fax 01292/318-204): Laid out along lines paralleling the Firth of Clyde, this club fills a flat lowland terrain whose fairways are almost breathtakingly green despite their foundations on sandy soil. This is Lowland Scotland at its most seductive, a 7,097-yard (6,458m) course (one of Scotland's longest) with an SSS of 74 and a par of 71. See chapter 6.
- **Turnberry Hotel Golf Courses,** Ayrshire (☎ **01655/331-000;** fax 01655/ 331-706): Established in 1902, this is one of the world's most sought-after courses. It's not for the faint of heart—although some of the links are verdant, others are uncomfortably paired with the sands, the salt-resistant tough grasses, and the powerful winds blasting in from the nearby sea. See chapter 6.
- **The Old Course, St. Andrews,** Fife (☎ **01334/466-666**): Sometime during the late 14th century, a group of bored aristocrats started batting a ball around the nearby meadows. By the time their activities were officially recorded in 1552, the bylaws of the game were well on the way to being part of Scotland's lore. The Old Course is the world's most legendary temple of golf, one whose difficulty is shaped by nature and the long-ago paths of grazing sheep. See chapter 8.
- **Carnoustie Golf Links,** Tayside (☎ **01241/853-789;** fax 01241/852-720): Site of six British Open tournaments, Carnoustie is much more difficult than most players anticipate at first glance. U.S. champions Tom Watson and Gary Player have referred to it as their favorite, and much of the town of Carnoustie (incorporated as late as 1880) was built because of the stream of world-class golfers who migrated here. See chapter 9.
- **Royal Dornoch Golf Club,** Sutherland (☎ **01862/810-219**): This is the most northerly of the world's great golf courses, set in the underpopulated province of Sutherland, only 6° south of the Arctic Circle. Despite its northern isolation, Royal Dornoch enjoys a microclimate more akin to the fens around Norfolk, England, than to the Arctic. See chapter 10.

## 3 The Best Fishing

For more details about fishing in Scotland, see chapter 3.

- **The Borders & Galloway Regions:** Sea fishing is pure heaven in the Solway Firth; it's best near Port William and Portpatrick villages, in the vicinity of Loch Ryan, and along the shore of the Isle of Whithorn. The elusive salmon is best pursued along the River Tweed, and the lesser-known hill lochans are ideal for trout fishermens. Local tourist offices distribute two helpful guides: *A Comprehensive Guide to Scottish Borders Angling* and *Castabout Anglers Guide to Dumfries and Galloway.* See chapter 5.

- **Argyll & the Southern Hebrides:** This much-visited area in western Scotland is split in two by the long peninsula of Kintyre. It's definitely a northern Atlantic ecology, filled with open sea and loch and separated by the Firth of Clyde from the islands of the Inner Hebrides. There are some 50 prime sites on rivers and lochs for freshwater fishing, and some two dozen villages with fantastic sea fishing. See chapter 7.
- **Tayside:** The northeast section of Scotland is filled with major rivers—the Don, Dee, Ythan, and Deverson—plus smaller rivers like the Ugie, all ideal for salmon fishing. When estuary and loch fishing are considered, this becomes one of the country's best areas for game fishing. Local tourist offices keep abreast of all the details about boat rentals and permit prices, and some country hotels offer fishing packages. See chapter 9.
- **The Great Glen:** From all over the world, anglers flock to the Great Glen, with its many lochs and rivers, to cast their flies in search of Scottish trout and salmon. Sea angling from boat or shore is also permitted. Salmon season is February to September; brown trout season is mid-March to early October. Anglers can catch rainbow trout here year-round. See chapter 10.
- **Northern Highlands:** There are endless possibilities for fishing here, since Sutherland is riddled with lochs. Trout fishing is the big lure, and local tourist offices will tell you all about boats and permits. Not only is the fishing great, but your hotel cook will often prepare your catch for you. See chapter 10.
- **The Orkney Islands:** These far northern islands are major fishing grounds. At least seven outfitters offer charters, and you can rent fishing equipment. Loch fishing is also a popular pastime in the Orkneys, especially in Loch of Stenness and Loch of Harray, where hopeful anglers go after salmon, trout, sea trout, and salmon trout, although porbeagle shark, cod, halibut, bass, hake, skate, and turbot also turn up. See chapter 12.

# 4  The Best Countryside Drives

- **The Valley of the Tweed:** The waters originate in Scotland, define the border with England for part of their length, and are noted for some of Britain's best salmon fishing. Ruins of once-wealthy abbeys dot the landscape like beacons of long-lost power and prestige. Most travelers begin in Kelso and move west through Dryburgh, Selkirk, Melrose, Innerleithen, and Peebles. Although the total distance is less than 50 miles (80.5km), with a bit of backtracking en route, the many historic sites call for at least a full day's exploration. See chapter 5.
- **The Isle of Arran:** Anchored off Scotland's southwestern edge, Arran combines radically different climates and topographies into a relatively small (10 miles/16km wide by 20 miles/32km long) space. You'll find a rich trove of prehistoric monuments, a red sandstone pile (Brodick Castle) beloved by medievalists, nostalgic ruins (Lochranza Castle), and sweeping panoramas as far away as Northern Ireland. Its southern tier, warmed by the Gulf Stream, contains a lush temperate vegetation, while the moors and hills of its northern edge are as wild and craggy as the Highlands. Allow half a day, not including stopover times, for the 56-mile (90km) circumnavigation of the island's coastal road. See chapter 7.
- **The Lochs & Mountains South of Oban:** This area is lonely, but its drama includes views of the longest freshwater lake (Loch Awe), one of the longest saltwater fjords (Loch Fyne), some of the most historic buildings (Kilchurn Castle, Carnasserie Castle, and the Kilmartin Church), and one of the most crucial battlefields (the slopes of Ben Cruachan) in Scotland. Locals refer to it as

the Hinterlands near Oban, but the 87-mile (140km) route follows an excellent network of highways inscribing a large oval along the jagged coast. Major towns you'll traverse en route are Dalmally, Inveraray, Lochgilphead, and Oban, all offering opportunities for refueling, food, and drink. See chapter 7.

- **The Trossachs:** At the narrowest point of the mainland, just north of Glasgow, the Trossachs have been famous for their scenery since Queen Victoria decreed them lovely in 1869. Mystery seems to shroud the waters of Lochs Lomond and Katrine. According to legend, the region's highest mountain, Ben Venue, is the traditional meeting point for Scotland's goblins. Ruled for generations by the MacGregor clan, this is the countryside of Sir Walter Scott's *Rob Roy* and *The Lady of the Lake.* A tour through the region, beginning at Callander and meandering through Aberfoyle, Stronachlacher, and Inversnaid, should take about half a day, unless you opt to extend it with boat rides along Loch Katrine. Expect lots of traffic in summer, often from tour buses. See chapter 8.

- **The Road to the Isles (Hwy. A830):** It begins in Fort William, western terminus of the Caledonian Canal, and ends at Mallaig, the departure point for ferries servicing several offshore islands, including Mull, 46 miles (74km) northwest. En route, it passes the highest mountains in Britain. Along the way, you can see one of the Victorian Age's most dramatic engineering triumphs—Neptune's Staircase, a network of eight locks that raise the level of the canal 64 feet (19m) in less than 500 yards (455m). Although summer traffic can be dense, services en route are scarce, so start with a full tank of gas. See chapters 10 and 11.

## 5 The Best Bike Rides

For details on bike rentals around the country, see chapter 3.

- **The Galloway Region:** Scotland's southwestern region is one of the least visited but one of the most beautiful. A land of fields, verdant forests, and mist-shrouded hills, Galloway offers endless biking possibilities. All tourist offices in the area sell *Cycling in Dumfries and Galloway* for £1 ($1.70), describing the best biking routes. A free leaflet published by the Scottish Forest Enterprise gives trail routes through the various forests. See chapter 5.

- **The Isle of Arran:** The largest of the Clyde Islands, the Isle of Arran has been called "Scotland in miniature." If you don't have time to see the whole country, you can get a preview of its various regions by biking this island. The northern part is mountainous like the Highlands, but the southern part is more typically Lowland, like the scenery in the Borders. The full circuit around the island takes about 9 hours, but you can do only a part of it. The tourist office distributes the free *Cycling on Arran,* giving the best routes. See chapter 7.

- **The Trossachs:** Scotland's most beautiful stretch for biking is the Trossachs (also the loveliest for driving or country walks), famed as Rob Roy MacGregor country. The best spot for biking is along Loch Katrine, 10 miles (16km) long and 2 miles (3km) at its widest. See chapter 8.

- **Glencoe:** Site of a famous 1692 massacre, Glencoe is called the Glen of Weeping. Rent a bike in Glencoe village and set out on an adventure, although you're likely to get rained on, as some 100 inches of rain a year are recorded. But as one local said, "Biking through Glencoe in the rain is when it's at its most mystical— we Scots have done that for years." As you bike along, stark and grandiose mountain scenery rises around you. The glen is about 11 miles (18km) long, but you can settle for seeing only a part of it. See chapter 10.

- **The Isle of Skye:** One of the most evocative of the Hebrides, Skye is the land of the Cuillins, a brooding mountain range you'll see at every turn as you pedal along. The island's most unusual place to bike is the 20-mile (32km) Trotternish Peninsula north of Portree, the island's capital and boating center. Trotternish is known for its odd rock formations, and its coastal road passes an area of beautiful but often rocky seascapes, opening onto Loch Snizort and the Sound of Raasay. See chapter 11.

# 6  The Best Hikes

- **The Southern Upland Way:** Rivaling the West Highland Way (see below), this is the second of Scotland's great walks. The footpath begins at Portpatrick and runs 212 miles (341km) on the southwest coast to Cockburnspath on the eastern coast. Along the way, it passes through some of the most dramatic scenery in the Borders, including Galloway Forest Park. Contact the Scottish Tourist Board (see below). See chapter 5.
- **The Trossachs:** The Trossachs Trail stretches from Loch Lomond in the west to Callander in the east and also from Doune to Aberfoyle and the Lord Ard Forest to the south. In the north, it's bounded by the Crianlarich Hills and Balquhidder, the site of Rob Roy's grave. Ever since Sir Walter Scott published *The Lady of the Lake* in 1810 and *Rob Roy* in 1817, the area has attracted hikers in search of its unspoiled natural beauty. Our favorite start for walks is the village of Brig o' Turk, between Lochs Achray and Venachar at the foot of Glen Finglas. From here you can set out in all directions, including one signposted to the Achray Forest. There's also the Glen Finglas circular walk, and many hikers leave Brig o' Turk heading for Balquhidder via Glen Finglas. See chapter 8.
- **East Neuk:** Directly south of St. Andrews lies some of Scotland's loveliest fishing villages, collectively known as East Neuk (see chapter 8). The most enchanting walk is between the villages of Pittenweem and Anstruther. The day is likely to be breezy, with wind from the sea, so dress accordingly. The path begins at the bottom of West Braes, a cul-de-sac off the main road in Anstruther.
- **The West Highland Way:** This is one of Scotland's great walks. Beginning north of Glasgow in Milngavie, the long-distance footpath stretches for 95 miles (153km) north along Loch Lomond, going through Glencoe to Fort William and eventually to Ben Nevis, Britain's highest mountain. Even if you walk only part of this path, you need to make plans in advance. Contact the **Scottish Tourist Board,** 23 Ravelston Terrace, Edinburgh (☎ **0131/352-2433**). See chapters 8 and 10.
- **Ben Nevis:** At the point 4 miles (6km) southeast of the town of Fort William looms Ben Nevis, Britain's highest mountain at 4,406 feet (1,336.5m). The snow-capped granite mass dominates this entire region of Scotland. This trip can be done in a day, but you'll need to massage your feet in the evening at a local pub. See chapter 10.

# 7  The Best Castles & Palaces

- **Edinburgh Castle:** Few other buildings symbolize the grandeur of an independent Scotland as clearly as this one. Begun around A.D. 1000 on a hilltop high above the rest of Edinburgh, it witnessed some of the bloodiest and most treacherous events in Scottish history, including its doomed 1573 defense by Scottish patriot Grange in the name of Mary Queen of Scots. See chapter 4.

- **Palace of Holyroodhouse** (Edinburgh): Throughout the clan battles for independence from England, this palace served as a pawn between opposing forces, being demolished and rebuilt at the whim of whomever held power at the time. In its changing fortunes, it has housed a strange assortment of monarchs involved in traumatic events: Mary Queen of Scots, Bonnie Prince Charlie, James VII (before his ascendancy to the throne), and French king Charles X (on his forced abdication after an 1830 revolution). The building's present form dates from the late 1600s, when it was rebuilt in a dignified neo-Palladian style. Today, Holyroodhouse is one of Queen Elizabeth's official residences. See chapter 4.
- **Drumlanrig Castle** (Dumfries): Begun in 1679, this castle required 12 years to build and so much money that its patron, the third earl and first duke of Queensbury, complained to anyone who would listen how deeply he resented its existence. Later, it was embroiled in dynastic inheritance scandals worthy of a gothic novel. One of the most prestigious buildings in Scotland, it contains the family antiques and artwork of four illustrious genealogies: the Douglas, Montagu, Scott, and Buccleuch families. See chapter 5.
- **Culzean Castle** (4 miles/6.5km west of Maybole): Designed for comfort and prestige, this castle was built in the late 1700s by Scotland's most celebrated architect, Robert Adam, as a replacement for a dark, dank, and fortified tower that had stood for longer than anyone could remember. It was donated to the National Trust for Scotland just after World War II. A suite was granted to General Eisenhower for his lifetime use, in gratitude for his role in staving off a foreign invasion of Britain. See chapter 6.
- **Stirling Castle:** Stirling is a triumph of Renaissance ornamentation, a startling contrast to the severe bulk of many other Scottish castles. Despite its beauty, after its completion in 1540 the castle was one of the most impregnable fortresses in the British Isles, thanks partly to its position on a rocky crag. See chapter 8.
- **Scone Palace:** As early as A.D. 900, Scottish kings were crowned here, on a lump of granite so permeated with ancient magic the English hauled it off to Westminster Abbey in the 13th century, where it remained until 1995. The building you see today was rebuilt in 1802 from ruins that incorporated a 1580 structure and stones laid during the dim early days of Scottish and Pictish union. See chapter 9.
- **Glamis Castle:** This castle's core was built for defense against rival clans during the 1400s, but over the centuries it evolved into a luxurious dwelling. The seat of the same family since 1372, Glamis is said to be haunted by the ghost of one of its former owners, Lady Glamis, who James V had burnt as a witch when she resisted his annexation of her castle. It figured into the ambitions of Macbeth, thane of Glamis, as well. See chapter 9.
- **Braemar** (Grampian): Built by the earl of Mar in 1628 as a hunting lodge, Braemar was burned to the ground, then rebuilt by Farquharson of Invercauld, the ancestor of the present owner. It's often photographed as a symbol of Scottish grandeur and the well-upholstered aristocratic life. See chapter 9.
- **Crathes Castle and Gardens** (Grampian): Crathes evokes the severe luxury of a 15th- and 16th-century Scottish laird. The style focuses on high heraldry, with frequent references to the persistent Scottish hope of an enduring independence. The gardens contain massive yew hedges originally planted in 1702. See chapter 9.
- **Balmoral Castle** (Ballater): Scotland offers far greater castles to explore, but Balmoral, the rebuilt castle of Prince Albert and Queen Victoria, draws the visiting hordes, hoping to get a glimpse of Prince William, no doubt. That's because it's still the Scottish residence of the queen. Although you can visit only its ballroom, the sprawling manicured grounds and gardens also await you. See chapter 9.

- **Cawdor Castle:** From its heavily fortified origins in the 1300s, Cawdor evolved into the Campbell clan's luxurious seat. According to legend and Shakespearean plot lines, three witches promised this castle to Macbeth to tempt him into the deeds that led to his destruction. See chapter 10.

## 8  The Best Cathedrals

- **Melrose Abbey** (the Borders): If it weren't for the abbey's location in the frequently devastated Borders, this would be one of the world's most spectacular ecclesiastical complexes. Founded in the 1100s, Melrose acquired vast wealth and was the target of its covetous enemies; it was burned and rebuilt several times before the Protestant takeover of Scotland. Today, this is one of the world's most beautiful ruins, a site immortalized by Robert Burns, who advised people to visit it only by moonlight. See chapter 5.
- **Cathedral of St. Kentigern** (Glasgow): In the 7th century, St. Mungo built a wooden structure here, intending it as his headquarters and eventual tomb. It burned down but was rebuilt in the 1300s. St. Kentigern is mainland Scotland's only complete medieval cathedral, with a form based extensively on the pointed arch. In the 1600s, the Calvinists stripped it of anything hinting at papist idolatry, although a remarkable set of sculptures atop its stone nave screen, said to be unique in Scotland, still represent the seven deadly sins. See chapter 6.
- **Dunfermline Abbey** (Fife): During the 1100s, in its role as Scotland's Westminster Abbey, Dunfermline became one of Europe's wealthiest churches. Three kings of Scotland were born here, and 22 members of the Scottish royal family were buried here. In the early 1800s, its ruined premises were partially restored to what you see today. Several years later, a different kind of benefactor, Andrew Carnegie, was born within the cathedral's shadow. See chapter 8.
- **Dunblane Cathedral:** Partly because the site had been holy since the days of the Celts, David I founded a church here in 1150. Despite later alterations and additions, Dunblane is still one of the country's best examples of Gothic architecture from the 1200s. See chapter 8.
- **St. Magnus Cathedral** (the Orkney Islands): The most spectacular medieval building in the Orkneys, St. Magnus features an odd imposition of the Norman Gothic style on a territory administered during the time of its construction (the 1100s) by the Norwegians. The bodies of St. Magnus, patron saint of the Orkneys, and his nephew, Earl Rognvald, the church's builder, are buried inside. See chapter 12.

## 9  The Best Ruins

- **Linlithgow Palace** (Lothian): These ruins brood over an island in a loch, an unhappy vestige of what was the most glamorous royal residence during Scotland's golden age of independence in the early 1500s. Mary Queen of Scots was born here, but tragedy seemed to permeate the place, as roofs collapsed from lack of maintenance and early deaths in the royal family hastened an inevitable union of Scotland with England. In 1745, after it was occupied by Bonnie Prince Charlie and his troops, a mysterious fire swept over it. See chapter 4.
- **Dryburgh Abbey** (the Borders): Begun in 1150 against a meandering curve of the River Tweed, Dryburgh was once home to thousands of monks who transformed the surrounding forests into arable fields and drained many local swamps. The abbey's position astride the much-troubled border with England resulted in

its destruction in three episodes (1322, 1385, and 1544), the last of which included the burning of the nearby village (Dryburgh) as well. Today, the red sandstone rocks are dim reminders of a long-ago monastic age. See chapter 5.

- **Kildrummy Castle** (Aberdeen): Built in the 1200s, this castle was one of northern Scotland's most important strongholds, mingling architectural principles of France with those developed in England and Wales. In 1715, after centuries of playing a decisive role in Scottish history, it was demolished by its enemies and dismantled stone by stone. Thus humbled, it broods as a reminder of former glories. See chapter 9.

- **Elgin Cathedral:** This cathedral was built during the 1100s, and although many other churches were erected in Scotland at the time, Elgin was believed to have been the most beautiful. Burned and rebuilt twice (1290 and 1370), it deteriorated after the Reformation, along with many other Catholic churches, to the point that the belfry collapsed in 1711, shattering most of the roof and some of the walls. Efforts were begun to repair the damage, yet the place remains an evocative ruin. See chapter 9.

- **Skara Brae** (the Orkney Islands): Last occupied around 2500 B.C. and far humbler than the feudal castles you'll find on the Scottish mainland, this cluster of fortified stone buildings is the best-preserved Neolithic village in northwestern Europe. Buried beneath sand for thousands of years, they were uncovered by a storm as recently as 1850. See chapter 12.

## 10 The Best Museums

- **National Gallery of Scotland** (Edinburgh): This museum boasts a small but choice collection whose presence in Edinburgh is firmly entwined with the city's self-image as Scotland's cultural capital (Glaswegians will happily dispute that idea). Highlights include works by Velázquez, Zurbarán, Verrocchio, del Sarto, and Cézanne. See chapter 4.

- **National Museum of Scotland** (Edinburgh): In 1998, the collections of the Royal Museum of Scotland and the National Museum of Antiquities were united into a coherent whole. Here you'll find everything you ever wanted to know about Scotland, from prehistory to the Industrial Age, as represented by the unsparing views of life in the Saltmarket District of Glasgow. It's all here, from a milk bottle once carried by Sean Connery when he was a milkman to a rock that's 2.9 billion years old from the Isle of South Uist. See chapter 4.

- **Burrell Collection** (Glasgow): The contents of this collection were accumulated through the exclusive efforts of Sir William Burrell (1861–1958), an industrialist who devoted the last 50 years of his life to spending his fortune on art. Set in a postmodern building in a suburb of Glasgow, it's one of Scotland's most admired museums, with a strong focus on medieval art, 19th-century French paintings, and Chinese ceramics. See chapter 6.

- **Hunterian Art Gallery** (Glasgow): This museum owns much of the artistic estate of James McNeill Whistler, as well as a re-creation of the home of Scotland's most famous designer, Charles Rennie Mackintosh. Grand oils are on display, including works by Whistler, Reubens, and Rembrandt, as well as one of the country's best collections of 19th-century Scottish paintings. See chapter 6.

- **Glasgow Art Gallery and Museum:** This is Britain's finest municipally funded museum, a source of pride for Glaswegians everywhere. It contains a superb collection of arms and armor, as well as paintings by Whistler and by seemingly everyone else, from Millet to Giorgione, Rembrandt to Dalí. See chapter 6.

- **Aberdeen Art Gallery:** A treasure trove of world art, this prestigious gallery has exhibits ranging from the 1700s to the present, from Hogarth and Reynolds to Picasso. The museum is also home to the most important temporary exhibits in northeast Scotland. See chapter 9.

## 11 The Best Luxury Hotels

- **Howard Hotel** (Edinburgh; ☎ 0131/557-3500): Three adjacent Georgian-style townhouses in an upscale Edinburgh neighborhood have undergone millions of pounds' worth of renovations, creating the most alluring accommodations in a city filled with fine hotels. A restaurant in one of the cellars serves meals inspired by Scotland's traditions and ingredients. See chapter 4.
- **Greywalls Hotel** (East Lothian; ☎ 01620/842-144): Although Sir Edward Lutyens designed dozens of opulent Edwardian homes throughout Britain, this is one of the few that's been converted into a hotel. Built in 1901 in what architects praise as perfect harmony with its setting, Greywalls features walled-in gardens designed by the doyenne of eccentric turn-of-the-century landscape architects, Gertrude Jekyll. This national treasure, representing the Empire's most ostentatious days, is eccentric but eminently comfortable. See chapter 4.
- **Knockinaam Lodge** (Portpatrick; ☎ 01776/810-471): Memories of Winston Churchill's clandestine meetings with General Eisenhower, a beacon of hope during the darkest days of World War II, pervade the Knockinaam. Today the late Victorian country house is as well upholstered and wryly sedate as you'd expect from a top-notch hotel with such a pedigree. Its restaurant is always included in critics' lists of the best of Scotland. See chapter 5.
- **One Devonshire Gardens** (Glasgow; ☎ 0141/339-2001): This is the best-groomed building in a neighborhood filled with similar sandstone-fronted town houses. Ring the doorbell and an Edwardian-costumed maid will answer, curtsy, and usher you inside as if you're an extra in a Merchant/Ivory film. This re-creation of a high-bourgeois, very proper Scottish home from the early 1900s boasts antique furnishings and discreetly concealed modern comforts. See chapter 6.
- **Airds Hotel** (Port Appin; ☎ 01631/730-236): The Airds's stucco-sheathed exterior resembles that of hundreds of other Scottish waterside buildings. Inside, however, this Relais & Châteaux member is unexpectedly luxurious, offering an award-winning cuisine and a tradition of hospitality dating back to 1760. See chapter 7.
- **Rufflets Country House Hotel** (St. Andrews; ☎ 01334/472-594): Set on 10 acres near Scotland's most prestigious golf course, this house has won virtually every hotel award possible and offers predominantly Queen Anne–style furnishings along with lovely gardens. See chapter 8.
- **Auchterarder House** (Auchterarder; ☎ 01764/663-646): Scholars refer to the Auchterarder's design as a perfect example of the Scots Jacobean Revival as interpreted by 1830s builders. Guests refer to it as a supremely comfortable hotel with well-appointed accommodations, a worthy dining room, and a polite, hard-working staff. Afternoon tea, plus a sampling of the bar's inventory of single malts, is part of the experience. See chapter 9.
- **Kinnaird** (Dunkeld; ☎ 01796/482-440): An 18th-century hunting lodge for the duke of Atholl, Kinnaird dominates an enormous estate—9,000 acres of moor, mountain, and forest. You'll find all the accoutrements of a British country house in high-Edwardian style. The supremely comfortable interiors contrast

dramatically with the tempests of the great outdoors, and its dining room is among the finest in the country. See chapter 9.

- **Raemoir House** (Banchory; ☎ 01330/824-884): A perfect retreat from the modern world, this 18th-century mansion is set on a 3,500-acre estate. Tudor four-posters, rich red brocades, paneled walls, and museum-caliber antiques transport you into an elegant past. You sleep well in supreme comfort and enjoy top-quality food, including poached salmon from the River Dee. See chapter 9.
- **Culloden House** (Inverness; ☎ 01463/790-461): If you'd like to sleep where Bonnie Prince Charlie did, head for this Adam-style Georgian mansion on 40 acres of parkland. Scottish tradition appears at every turn, from the grandly pro-portional lounge to the sound of a bagpiper on the grounds. Several rooms have spa baths and antique four-posters. Dinner in the Adam Room is an elegant affair, with French culinary skills applied to the finest Scottish produce. See chapter 10.
- **Carnegie Club at Skibo Castle** (Dornoch; ☎ 01862/894-600): Andrew Carnegie called his glorious Highland castle and estate Heaven on Earth, and so it is. A private residential golf/sporting club, it stands on a 7,500-acre estate in one of Europe's last great wilderness areas. It was owned by the Carnegie family until the early 1980s and is one of the few places left where you can see how the privileged of the Gilded Age lived. See chapter 10.
- **Inverlochy Castle** (near Fort William; ☎ 01397/702-177): This castle was built in 1863 by Lord Abinger in a style that set into stone the most high-blown hopes of Scottish Romantics. Today, lovers can follow in the footsteps of Queen Victoria amid the frescoed walls of this Scottish baronial hideaway. See chapter 10.
- **Dower House** (Muir of Ord; ☎ 01463/870-090): Set on 3 isolated acres of mature garden, this small but choice hotel offers attractive lodgings along with a cuisine known throughout Scotland. Although a midsummer visit is beautiful, Dower House's elegant Scottish-country warmth is especially appealing during blustery squalls and gales off-season. See chapter 10.

## 12  The Best Moderately Priced Hotels

- **The Malmaison** (Leith, outside Edinburgh; ☎ 0131/555-6868): One of Scot-land's best middle-bracket hotels (though it's on the high side of moderate), Mal-maison is at the port of Leith, about a 15-minute taxi ride northeast of Edinburgh's center. Named after Joséphine's mansion outside Paris, it celebrates the Auld Alliance of France and Scotland and was created from a 1900 Victorian building. Malmaison once housed indigent seamen but today is a chic and rea-sonably priced oasis of charm. See chapter 4.
- **Malmaison** (Glasgow; ☎ 0141/572-1000): Linked to a hotel with the same name in Edinburgh (see above), this Malmaison dates from the 1830s, when it was built as a Greek Orthodox church. Now converted into one of the best of Glasgow's moderately priced hotels (though its prices are creeping up into the expensive range), it welcomes visitors with Scottish hospitality and houses them with quite a bit of style. See chapter 6.
- **Inn at Lathones** (St. Andrews; ☎ 01334/840-494): In the golfing capital of Scotland, this was a 2-century-old manor that has been lovingly restored with excellent accommodations. Scottish hospitality and tradition permeate the place, also known for its "Taste of Scotland" menu. See chapter 8.

- **Jays Guest House** (Aberdeen; ☎ 01224/638-295): This is one of the finest guesthouses in the granite city of Aberdeen, with newly renovated bright and airy accommodations. Owner Alice Jennings makes sure the maintenance is high and the welcome genuine. See chapter 9.
- **Polmaily House Hotel** (Drumnadrochit; ☎ 01456/450-343): During your search for Nessie, the Loch Ness Monster, you can find lodgings at this inn. The building dates from the 18th century and offers tasteful Edwardian-style living on an 18-acre farm of mixed gardens and woodland. See chapter 10.
- **Cuillin Hills Hotel** (Portree, Isle of Skye; ☎ 01478/612-003): Built in the 1820s as a hunting lodge for the MacDonald clan, this manor house has been skillfully converted into a small hotel. It attracts nature lovers to its nearby hills of heath and heather and offers lovely rooms and great food using some of the best Highland produce. See chapter 11.

## 13  The Best Upscale Restaurants

- **Pompadour Restaurant** (in the Caledonian Hotel, Edinburgh; ☎ 0131/459-9988): Named after the mistress of Louis XV, this dining room that opened in 1925 was once viewed as the only place in Edinburgh where you could find a decent meal. It's still serving them today—better than ever. Scottish specialties reign supreme at lunch, giving way in the evening to cuisine celebrating the Auld Alliance with France. Go for the multicourse tasting menu. See chapter 4.
- **La Potinière** (Gullane; ☎ 01620/843-214): With a pretty, understated decor, intimate La Potinière brings touches of big-city sophistication to a rural setting. It's one of the region's best dining rooms, run by a husband and wife who infuse the place with their own personalities. See chapter 4.
- **Rogano** (Glasgow; ☎ 0141/248-4055): Generations of Glaswegians have commended Rogano as a symbol of mercantile Scotland between the world wars, with a decor evoking the dining room of one of the great 1930s art-deco ocean liners. The uniformed waiters handle all comers with charm and deft good manners. See chapter 6.
- **Airds Hotel** (Port Appin; ☎ 01631/730-236): Around 1700, these premises were used to feed and house travelers after a ferry transit. Today, Airds is a citadel of Scottish cuisine, elevating dishes like Loch Fyne kippers to something with a cult following. Its haunch of venison with rowanberry jam is also notable. See chapter 7.
- **The Georgian Room** (in the DeVere Cameron House hotel, Balloch; ☎ 01389/755-565): The setting is lavishly Victorian and the food an award-winning blend of Scottish and French. Indulge in a rabbit-and-hare terrine encased in a sheathing of leeks. See chapter 8.
- **Inverlochy Castle** (near Fort William; ☎ 01397/702-177): Cherubs cavort across frescoed ceilings and chandeliers drip with Venetian crystal in a dining room created in the 1870s for a mogul. A Relais & Châteaux member, Inverlochy is likely to draw aristocrats and movie stars with a cuisine focusing on flavorful and natural interpretations of Scottish delicacies. Examples are Loch Fyne oysters with watercress-cream sauce and loin of Scottish venison with roasted pears. See chapter 10.
- **Ostlers Close** (Cupar, Fife; ☎ 01334/655-574): Chef Jimmy Graham is one of the finest in the St. Andrews area, and he's known to pick his own wild mushrooms. Golfers with discriminating palates flock to this modestly appointed

place, which makes the best use of fish and seafood from the Fife coast and ducks from a local free-range supplier. Everything is accurately cooked and delectable. See chapter 8.

- **The Cross** (Kingussie; ☎ **01540/661-166**): Housed in a cleverly converted 19th-century tweed mill, The Cross is a lot more chic than you'd ever have imagined. The menu items are a celebration of Scottish ingredients, prepared with modern international palates in mind. An example is the West Coast seafood salad with ultrafresh monkfish, scallops, prawns, and asparagus. See chapter 9.

## 14  The Best Moderately Priced Restaurants

- **Henderson's Salad Table** (Edinburgh; ☎ **0131/225-2131**): Acclaimed as Scotland's best vegetarian restaurant, Henderson's is good enough to appeal to non-vegetarians as well. An array of fresh, nutritious food is spread out before you every day—even a version of vegetarian haggis. The hot dishes are excellent and the homemade desserts reason enough to visit. See chapter 4.
- **Two Fat Ladies** (Glasgow; ☎ **0141/339-1944**): This amusingly named restaurant (no connection to the show of the same name on the TV Food Network), a local favorite, serves excellent modern British cuisine, with an emphasis on seafood. Not everything on the menu is fattening—in fact, some specialties are very contemporary in taste and flavor, like sea bass teriyaki and pan-fried squid salad with coriander-flavored yogurt sauce. See chapter 6.
- **Braeval Restaurant** (Aberfoyle; ☎ **01877/382-711**): The rustic setting manages to elevate the rough walls and flagstone floor of an old water mill to a high art form. And the food served at Braeval is elegant and intricate, like lobster lasagna and wild Scottish boar fillet with cabbage and juniper berries. See chapter 8.

## 15  The Best Pubs

- **Café Royal Circle Bar** (Edinburgh; ☎ **0131/556-1884**): The Café Royal Circle stands out in a city famous for its pubs. This longtime favorite, boasting lots of atmosphere and Victorian trappings, attracts a sea of drinkers, locals as well as visitors. See chapter 4.
- **Deacon Brodie's Tavern** (Edinburgh; ☎ **0131/225-6531**): This is the best spot for a wee dram or a pint along Edinburgh's Royal Mile. It perpetuates the memory of Deacon Brodie, good citizen by day and robber by night, the prototype for Robert Louis Stevenson's *Dr. Jekyll and Mr. Hyde*. It's been around since 1806 and has a cocktail-lounge bar and a large rowdy tavern. See chapter 4.
- **Globe Inn** (Dumfries; ☎ **01387/252-335**): In the Borders, this was Robert Burns's favorite *howff* (small cozy room). Today, you can imbibe as he did in a pub that's been in business since 1610. He liked the place so much that he had a child with the barmaid. A small museum is devoted to Burns. See chapter 5.
- **Corn Exchange** (Glasgow; ☎ **0141/248-5380**): There was a time when it took a bit of courage or a foolish heart to enter a Glasgow pub. Those bad old days are long forgotten at this reliable pub in the center. In the mid-1800s, the Corn Exchange was here (hence the name), but today it's a watering hole with good drinks and modestly priced bar platters. See chapter 6.
- **Rabbie's Bar** (Ayr; ☎ **01292/262-112**): Robert Burns didn't confine his drinking to Dumfries. Ayr was also one of his hangouts, and this favorite pub is a nostalgic reminder of another era. Bits of pithy verse by Burns adorn the walls, and

the collection of imported beers is the best in the area. There's even entertainment several nights a week. See chapter 6.

- **Dreel Tavern** (Anstruther; ☎ **01333/310-727**): Dreel is a 16th-century wood-and-stone coaching inn that was converted into a pub where old salts from the harbor and other locals gather to unwind on windy nights. Try the Orkney Dark Island on hand pump. Anstruther, 46 miles (74km) northeast of Edinburgh, is a gem of a Scottish seaside town and former fishing port. See chapter 8.
- **Ship Inn** (Elie; ☎ **01333/330-246**): Down at the harbor in this little port town, the Ship Inn is one of the best places for a pint along the east coast. The building dates from 1788, and the pub from 1830. In summer, you can enjoy your pint outside with a view over the water, but on blustery winter days, the blazing fireplace is the attraction. Stick around for dinner—the menu ranges from pheasant to venison to fresh seafood, not your typical pub grub. See chapter 8.
- **Prince of Wales** (Aberdeen; ☎ **01224/640-597**): Furnished with church pews and antiques, the Prince of Wales features the city's longest bar counter. Oilmen from the North Sea join the regulars to ask for tap beers like Courage Directors and sample the chef's Guinness pie. You'll find real flavor and authentic atmosphere; it's a good place to mingle with the locals in a mellow setting. See chapter 9.

# 16  The Best Shopping

- **Celtic Jewelry:** Modern reproductions of Celtic jewelry are one of Scotland's most creative craft forms. Some pieces reflect early Christian themes, like the Gaelic cross so often displayed in Presbyterian churches. Others are pure pagan, and sometimes Nordic, rich with symbols like dragons, intertwined ovals, and geometrics that would gladden the heart of a Celtic lord. You'll find the stuff all over Scotland, displayed proudly as symbols of the national aesthetic. Another common theme commemorates the yearnings for a politically independent country (Luckenbooths, entwined hearts surmounted by a monarch's crown). Clan brooches, ornate kilt pins, and other jewelry are often adorned with the Highland thistle and sometimes rendered in fine gold, silver, or platinum.
- **Sheepskins:** Some of the rocky districts of Scotland contain more sheep than people. Tanned sheepskins are for sale in hundreds of shops and usually accompanied by advice from the sales staff on what to do with them once you return home. *Note:* Black sheepskins are much rarer than white ones.
- **Sweaters, Tartans & Fabrics:** Sweaters come in every style and design, from bulky rough fishermans' pullovers to silky cashmere cardigans. Some factories pride themselves on duplicating the tartans of every Scottish clan; others stick to 50 or so of the more popular designs. A meter of fine tartan fabric sells for around £35 ($59.50). For a more authentic experience, buy your garment directly from whoever sewed or knitted it. You'll find ample opportunities at isolated crofts and crafts shops around the countryside. Another option is the Edinburgh Woolen Mills, with outlets from southern England to the northern tier of Scotland. Walkerburn in the Borders is a particularly good center in which to shop for textiles.
- **Liquor:** One of the most famous liquors in the world is named after the country that produces it: Scotch whisky (spelled without the "e") is distilled and aged throughout the country. Use your trip to Scotland as an opportunity to try new single malts (Laphroig and MacCallan are our favorites) and bring a bottle or two home.

# Planning Your Trip: The Basics

2

This chapter is devoted to the where, when, and how of your trip—the advance planning required to get it together and take it on the road. Because you may not know exactly where in Scotland you want to go or what surrounds the major city you want to see, we begin with a quick rundown on the various regions.

## 1 The Regions in Brief

Scotland is Great Britain's oldest geological formation, divided into three major regions: the **Southern Uplands,** smooth, rolling moorland broken with low crags and threaded with rivers and valleys, between the central plain and the English border; the **Central Lowlands,** where three valleys and the estuaries (firths) of the Clyde, Forth, and Tay rivers make up a fertile belt from the Atlantic Ocean to the North Sea; and the granite **Highlands,** with lochs, glens, and mountains, plus the hundreds of islands to the west and north. Each of these regions is then made up of smaller regions (see below).

*Note:* Consult the map on pp. 2–3 of this guide to visualize the areas described below.

### EDINBURGH & THE LOTHIAN REGION

This area includes not only the country's capital but also West Lothian, most of Midlothian, and East Lothian. Half medieval and half Georgian, **Edinburgh** is at its liveliest every August at the International Arts Festival, but you can visit Edinburgh Castle and Holyroodhouse and walk the Royal Mile year-round. This is one of Europe's most beautiful capitals, and in 3 days you can do it royally, taking in the highlights of the Old Town and the New Town, which include some of the country's major museums. Edinburgh is surrounded by major attractions like the village of **Cramond,** the ancient town of **Linlithgow,** and **Dirleton,** the "prettiest village in Scotland."

### THE BORDERS & GALLOWAY REGIONS

Witness to a turbulent history, the Borders and Galloway regions between England and Scotland are rich in castle ruins and Gothic abbeys.

Home of the cashmere sweater and the tweed suit, **the Borders** proved a rich mine for the fiction of Sir Walter Scott. Highlights are **Kelso,** which Scott found "the most beautiful," and **Melrose,** site of the ruined Melrose Abbey and Scott's former home of Abbotsford. Ancient monuments include Jedburgh Abbey and Dryburg Abbey, Scott's burial place. At Floors Castle, outside Kelso, you can see one of the great mansions designed by William Adam.

Southwestern Scotland is known as **the Galloway region.** It incorporates much of the former stamping ground of Robert Burns and includes centers like **Dumfries, Castle Douglas,** and **Moffat.** Highlights are the artists' colony of **Kidcudbright,** the baronial Threave Garden, Sweetheart Abbey outside Dumfries (the ruins of a Cisterian abbey from 1273), and the Burns Mausoleum at Dumfries.

## GLASGOW & THE STRATHCLYDE REGION

A true renaissance has come to the once-grimy industrial city of Glasgow, and we recommended you spend at least 2 days in "the greatest surviving example of a Victorian city." Of course, part of the fun of going to Glasgow is enjoying meeting Glaswegians and, if only temporarily, becoming part of their life. But there are plenty of museums and galleries, too, notably the Burrell Collection, a wealthy shipowner's gift of more than 8,000 items from the ancient world to the modern; the Hunterian Art Gallery, with its array of masterpieces by everybody from Rembrandt to Whistler; and the Art Gallery and Museum at Kelvingrove, home of Britain's finest civic collection of British and European paintings.

Glasgow is at the doorstep of one of the most historic regions of Scotland. You can explore Robert Burns country in the Strathclyde region, especially the district around Ayr and Prestwick, or visit a string of famous seaside resorts (including Turnberry, which boasts some of the country's greatest golf courses). An especially worthwhile destination in this region is Culzean Castle, overlooking the Firth of Clyde and designed by Robert Adam in the 18th century.

## ARGYLL & THE SOUTHERN HEBRIDES

Once the independent kingdom of Dalriada, the **Argyll Peninsula** of western Scotland is centered at **Oban,** a bustling port town and one of Scotland's leading coastal resorts. Ace attractions here are **Argyll Forest Park,** actually three forests—Benmore, Ardgartan, and Glenbranter—covering some 60,000 acres. You can also visit **Loch Awe,** a natural moat that protected the Campbells of Inveraray from their enemies to the north, and explore some of Scotland's most interesting islands, including the **Isle of Arran,** called "Scotland in miniature." The **Isle of Islay** is the southernmost of the Inner Hebrides, with lonely moors, lochs, tranquil bays, and windswept cliffs. The **Isle of Jura,** the fourth largest of the Inner Hebrides, is known for its red deer, and it was on this remote island that George Orwell wrote his masterpiece *1984*. Finally, you can visit **Kintyre,** the longest peninsula in Scotland, more than 60 miles (97km) of beautiful scenery, sleepy villages, and sandy beaches.

## FIFE & THE CENTRAL HIGHLANDS

The "kingdom" of **Fife** is one of the most history-rich parts of Scotland, evocative of the era of romance and pageantry during the reign of the early Stuart kings. Its most enchanting stretch is a series of villages called **East Neuk.** And **Culross,** renovated by the National Trust, could well be the most beautiful village in Scotland. Opening onto the North Sea, **St. Andrews,** the "Oxford of Scotland," is the capital of golf and boasts many great courses. The area is rich in castles and abbeys, notably Dunfermline Abbey, burial place of 22 royal personages, and Falkland Palace and Gardens, where Mary Queen of Scots came for hunting and hawking. You can also visit **Stirling,** dominated by its castle, where Mary Queen of Scots lived as an infant monarch. **Loch Lomond,** largest of the Scottish lakes, is fabled for its "bonnie bonnie banks," and the **Trossachs** are perhaps the most beautiful area in Scotland, famed for their moors, mountains, and lakes.

## ABERDEEN & THE TAYSIDE & GRAMPIAN REGIONS

Carved from the old counties of Perth and Angus, **Tayside** takes its name from its major river, the Tay, running for 119 miles (192km). One of the loveliest regions, it's known for salmon and trout fishing. Major centers are **Perth,** former capital of Scotland, standing where the Highlands meet the Lowlands; **Dundee,** an old seaport and royal burgh on the north shore of the Firth of Tay; and **Pitlochry,** a popular resort that's an ideal base for touring the Valley of the Tummel. The area abounds in castles and palaces, including Glamis, linked to British royalty for 10 centuries, and Scone, an art-filled palace from 1580. The great city of the north, **Aberdeen** is called Scotland's "granite city" and ranks third in population. It's the best center for touring "castle country." **Braemar** is known for its scenery as well as for being the site of every summer's Royal Highland Gathering, and Balmoral Castle at Ballater was the "beloved paradise" of Queen Victoria and still is home to the royal family. Finally, you can follow the **Whisky Trail** to check out some of Scotland's most famous distilleries, including Glenlivet and Glenfiddich.

## INVERNESS & THE WEST HIGHLANDS

Land of rugged glens and majestic mountain landscapes, the Highlands is one of the great meccas of the United Kingdom. The capital is **Inverness,** one of the oldest inhabited localities in Scotland, and another city of great interest is **Nairn,** old-time royal burgh and seaside resort. Ace attractions are **Loch Ness,** home of the legendary "Nessie," and **Cawdor Castle,** the most romantic in the Highlands, linked with Macbeth. The **Caledonian Canal,** launched in 1803, stretches for 60 miles (97km) of man-made canal, joining the natural lochs. As you proceed to the north you can visit the **Black Isle,** a historic peninsula, before heading for such far northern outposts as **Ullapool,** an 18th-century fishing village on the shores of Loch Broom (and for some, a gateway to the Outer Hebrides), and **John o' Groats,** the most distant point to which you can drive, near the northernmost point of mainland Britain, **Dunnet Head.**

## THE HEBRIDEAN ISLANDS

The chain of the Inner Hebrides lies just off the west coast of the mainland. The major center is the **Isle of Skye,** a mystical island and subject of the Scottish ballad "Over the Sea to Skye." If you have time to visit only one island, make it Skye—it's the most beautiful and intriguing. However, the **Isle of Mull,** third largest of the Inner Hebrides, is also rich in legend and folklore, including ghosts, monsters, and the "wee folk." **Iona,** off the coast of Mull, is known as the "Grave of Kings," with an abbey dating from the 13th century. Those with time remaining can also explore the Outer Hebrides, notably **Lewis,** the largest and most northerly. Along with the island of **Harris,** Lewis stretches for a combined length of some 95 miles (153km). This is relatively treeless land of marshy peat bogs and ancient relics.

# THE ORKNEY & SHETLAND ISLANDS

These northern outposts of British civilization are archipelagos consisting of some 200 islands, about 40 of which are inhabited. With a rich Viking heritage, they reward visitors with scenery and antiquities. Major centers of the Orkneys are **Kirkwall,** established by Norse invaders and the capital of the Orkneys for 9 centuries, and **Stromness,** the main port or the archipelago and once the last port of call before the New World. **Lerwick** is the capital of the Shetlands and has been since the 17th century. All these islands are filled with ancient monuments: The most outstanding are Midhower Broch and Tombs on Rousay, dating from the Iron Age and called the "great ship of death"; Quoyness Chambered Tomb, on Sanday, a spectacular chambered cairn from 2900 B.C.; the Ring of Brodgar between Loch and Stennes, a stone circle of some 36 stones dating from 1560 B.C. and called the "Stonehenge of Scotland," and Skara Brae, a Neolithic village joined by covered passages last occupied about 2500 B.C.

## 2 Visitor Information

Before you go, you can get information from the **British Tourist Authority** in the **United States:** 551 Fifth Ave., Suite 701, New York, NY 10176-0799 (☎ **800/462-2748,** or 212/986-2200 in New York), or 625 North Michigan Ave., 10th floor, in Chicago (same toll-free number as for the New York office). In **Canada:** 111 Avenue Rd., Suite 450, Toronto, ON M5R 3J8 (☎ **888/VISIT-UK** in Canada, or 905/405-1840 in Toronto). In **Australia:** Level 16, Gateway, 1 Macquarie Place, Sydney, NSW 200 (☎ **02/9377-4400**). In **New Zealand:** Suite 305, Dilworth Building, Customs and Queen streets, Auckland 1 (☎ **09/303-1446**).

The Web address for the British Tourist Authority is **www.visitbritain.com.** The e-mail address is **travelinfo@bta.org.uk.**

If you're in London and are contemplating a trip north, you can visit the **Scottish Tourist Board,** 19 Cockspur St., London SW1 Y5BL (☎ **020/ 7930-8661**); it's open Monday to Friday 9:30am to 5:30pm and Saturday noon to 4pm. Once you're in Scotland, you can visit the **Edinburgh and Scotland Information Centre,** Waverley Market, 3 Princes St., Edinburgh EH2 2QP (☎ **0131/473-3800**). July and August, it's open Monday to Saturday 9am to 8pm and Sunday 10am to 8pm. May, June, and September, hours are Monday to Saturday 9am to 7pm and Sunday 10am to 7pm. October to April, hours are Monday to Saturday 9am to 6pm and Sunday 10am to 6pm.

There are more than 170 **tourist centers** in Scotland, all well signposted in their cities or towns; some are closed in winter, however.

## 3 Entry Requirements & Customs

### ENTRY REQUIREMENTS

All Americans, Canadians, Australians, and New Zealanders must have a **passport** with at least 2 months remaining validity. No visa is required. The immigration officer may also want proof of your intention to return home (usually a round-trip ticket). If your passport is lost or stolen while traveling, head to your consulate as soon as possible for a replacement.

If you're planning to fly from the United States or Canada to the United Kingdom and then on to a country that requires a visa (India, for example), you should secure that visa before you arrive in Britain.

Your valid **driver's license** and at least 1 year of driving experience are required to drive personal or rented cars.

## CUSTOMS

**WHAT YOU CAN BRING INTO SCOTLAND**  For visitors, goods fall into two basic categories: purchases made in a non–European Union (EU) country (or bought tax free in the EU) and purchases on which tax was paid in the EU. In the former category, limits on imports by individuals (17 and older) include 200 cigarettes, 50 cigars, or 250 grams (8.8 oz.) of loose tobacco; 2 liters (2.1 qt.) of still table wine, 1 liter of liquor (over 22% alcohol content), or 2 liters of liquor (under 22%); and 2 fluid ounces of perfume. In the latter category, limits are much higher: An individual may import 800 cigarettes, 200 cigars, and 1 kilogram (2.2 lb.) of loose tobacco; 90 liters (23.4 gal.) of wine, 10 liters (2.6 gal.) of alcohol (over 22%), and 110 liters (28.6 gal.) of beer; plus unlimited amounts of perfume. Customs will also allow you to bring in whatever sporting equipment you'll need—within reason, of course. This includes tennis, golfing, fishing, and skiing equipment. Be sure to check with your airline to determine baggage restrictions.

**WHAT YOU CAN BRING HOME**  Returning **U.S. citizens** who have been away for 48 hours or more are allowed to bring back, once every 30 days, $400 worth of merchandise duty free. You'll be charged a flat rate of 10% duty on the next $1,000 worth of purchases. Be sure to have your receipts handy. On gifts, the duty-free limit is $100. You can't bring fresh foodstuffs into the States; tinned foods, however, are allowed. For more info, contact the **U.S. Customs Service,** 1301 Constitution Ave. (P.O. Box 7407), Washington, DC 20044 (☎ **202/927-6724**), and request the free pamphlet *Know Before You Go.* It's also available on the Web at **www.customs.ustreas.gov**.

For a clear summary of **Canadian** rules, visit the comprehensive Web site of the **Canada Customs and Revenue Agency** at **www.ccra-adrc.gc.ca**.

Citizens of **Australia** should request the helpful Australian Customs brochure *Know Before You Go,* available by calling ☎ **1-300/363-263** from within Australia, or 61-2/6275-6666 from abroad. For additional information, go online to **www.dfat.gov.au** and click on "Hints for Australian Travellers."

For **New Zealand** customs information, contact the New Zealand Customs Service at ☎ **09/359-6655,** or go online to **www.customs.govt.nz**.

## 4 Money

### CURRENCY

The currency of Britain is the **pound sterling (£),** made up to 100 **pence (p).** Scotland issues its own pound notes, but English and Scottish money is interchangeable. Pence come in 1p, 2p, 5p, 10p, 20p, 50p, and £1 coins. Notes are issued in £1, £5, £10, £20, and £50 denominations.

For the moment at least, Britain has decided not to join the rest of the European Community in the switch to the euro, the new single European currency; the traditional British pound sterling will remain the coin of the realm.

Although exchange rates are more favorable at the point of arrival, it's always wise to exchange at least some money before going abroad. This way, you avoid delays and the lousy rates at the airport exchange booths. When exchanging money, you're likely to get a better rate for traveler's checks than for cash.

At this writing, the price conversions in this book have been computed at the rate of $1 U.S. equals 55p (or £1 = $1.70). Bear in mind that exchange rates always fluctuate for a variety of reasons, so it's important to check the latest quotes before your trip. Go online at **www.x-rates.com**.

*Time Out* recently did a survey of exchange facilities, and American Express came out on top, with the lowest commission charged on dollar transactions. **American Express** is at 139 Princes St., Edinburgh (☎ **800/221-7282** or 0131/225-7881), and other locations throughout the city. It charges no commission when cashing traveler's checks; however, a flat rate of £2 ($3.40) is charged when exchanging the dollar to the pound. Most other agencies tend to charge a percentage rate commission (usually 2%) with a £2 to £3 ($3.40 to $5.10) minimum charge.

## ATMS

ATMs are linked to a national network that most likely includes your home bank. **Cirrus** (☎ **800/424-7787;** www.mastercard.com/atm) and **Plus** (☎ **800/843-7587;** www.visa.com/atms) are the two most popular networks; check the back of your ATM card to see which network your bank belongs to. Use the toll-free numbers to locate ATMs in your destination.

ATMs are commonly available in all Scottish cities and towns, even in many villages. Of course, for the latter you should always check to be sure.

Make sure the PINs on your bankcards and credit cards will work in Scotland. You'll need a **four-digit code** (six digits won't work), so if you have a six-digit code you'll have to get a new PIN for your trip. If you're unsure about this, contact Cirrus or Plus (see below). Be sure to check the daily withdrawal limit at the same time.

## CREDIT CARDS

Credit cards are invaluable when traveling. They're a safe way to carry money and provide a convenient record of all your expenses. You can also withdraw cash advances from your credit cards at any bank (but you'll start paying hefty interest on the advance the moment you receive the cash and won't get frequent-flyer miles on an airline credit card). At most banks, you don't even need to go to a teller; you can get a cash advance at the ATM if you know your PIN.

## TRAVELER'S CHECKS

You can get traveler's checks at almost any bank. **American Express** offers checks in denominations of $10, $20, $50, $100, $500, and $1,000. You'll pay a service charge ranging from 1% to 4%. You can also get American Express traveler's checks over the phone by calling ☎ **800/221-7282** or 800/721-9768, or you can buy checks online at **www.americanexpress.com**. AmEx gold or platinum cardholders can avoid paying the fee by ordering over the telephone; platinum cardholders can also purchase checks fee-free in person at AmEx Travel Service locations (check the Web site for the office nearest you). American Automobile Association members can get checks fee-free at most AAA offices.

**Visa** offers traveler's checks at Citibank branches and other financial institutions nationwide; call ☎ **800/227-6811** to find the purchase location near you. **MasterCard** also offers traveler's checks through **Thomas Cook Currency Services;** call ☎ **800/223-9920** for a location near you.

If you carry traveler's checks, be sure to keep a record of their serial numbers (separately from the checks, of course), so you're ensured a refund in case they're lost or stolen.

## 5 When to Go

The cheapest time to travel to Scotland is off-season: **November 1 to December 12** and **December 26 to March 14.** In the past few years, airlines have been offering irresistible fares during these periods. And **weekday flights** are cheaper than weekend fares (often by 10% or more).

Rates generally increase **March 14 to June 5** and in **October,** then hit their peak in the high seasons between **June 6 and September 30** and **December 13 and 24.** July and August are when most Britons take their holidays, so besides the higher prices, you'll have to deal with crowds and limited availability of accommodations.

Sure, in winter Scotland may be rainy and cold—but it doesn't shut down when the tourists leave. In fact, the winter season gives visitors a more honest view of Scottish life. Additionally, many hotel prices drop by 20%, and cheaper accommodations offer weekly rates (unheard of during peak travel times). By arriving after the winter holidays, you can take advantage of post-Christmas sales to buy your fill of woolens, china, crystal, silver, fashion, handicrafts, and curios.

In short, spring offers the countryside at its greenest, autumn brings the bright colors of the northern Highlands, and summer's warmth gives rise to the many outdoor music and theater festivals. But winter offers savings across the board and a chance to see Britons going about their everyday lives largely unhindered by tourist invasions.

### WEATHER
Weather is of vital concern in Scotland. It can seriously affect your travel plans. The Lowlands usually have a moderate year-round temperature. In spring, the average temperature is 53°F (11.6°C), rising to about 65°F (18.3°C) in summer. By the time the crisp autumn has arrived, the temperatures have dropped to spring levels. In winter, the average temperature is 43°F (6°C). Temperatures in the north of Scotland are lower, especially in winter, and you should dress accordingly. It rains a lot in Scotland, but perhaps not as much as age-old myths would have it: The rainfall in Edinburgh is exactly the same as that in London. September can be the sunniest month.

### HOLIDAYS
The following holidays are celebrated in Scotland: New Year's (January 1–2), Good Friday and Easter Monday, May Day (May 1), spring bank holiday (last Monday in May), summer bank holiday (first Monday in August), Christmas Day (December 25), and Boxing Day (December 26).

## Scotland Calendar of Events

You can get details of specific events at many of the festivals below from the official Web site **www.go-edinburgh.co.uk**.

### January
- **Burns Night,** Ayr (near his birthplace), Dumfries, and Edinburgh. Naturally, during the celebrations to honor Robert Burns, there's much toasting with scotch and eating of haggis, whose arrival is announced by a

bagpipe. For details, call ☎ **01292/443-700** in Ayr, **0131/473-3800** in Edinburgh, or **01387/253-862** in Dumfries. January 25.

- **Up Helly Aa,** Lerwick, in the Shetland Islands. The most northerly town in Great Britain still clings to tradition by staging an ancient Norse fire festival whose aim is to encourage the return of the sun after the pitch-dark days of winter. Its highlight is the burning of a replica of a Norse longboat. For details, call ☎ **01595/693-434** in Lerwick. Last Tuesday in January.

- **Celtic Connections,** Glasgow. During this celebration of the Celtic roots that combined with other cultures to form modern Scotland, paid concerts are performed in churches, auditoriums, and meeting halls throughout the city. A prime venue is the Old Fruit Market on Albion Street, drawing dance troupes from throughout Scotland, Wales, and Ireland. For tickets and details, call ☎ **0141/287-5511.** Throughout January and February.

### February

- **Aberdeen Angus Cattle Show,** Perth. Staged early in the month, this show draws the finest cattle raised in Scotland. Sales are lively. For details, call ☎ **01738/638-353** in Perth.

### March

- **Whuppity Scourie,** Lanark. Residents of the Strathclyde get so tired of winter they stage this traditional ceremony to chase it away. For details, call ☎ **01555/661-661** in Lanark. March 1.

- **Annual Drama Festival,** Tobermory. This cultural event draws some of Britain's finest theatrical talent to the Isle of Mull. For details, call ☎ **01688/302-182** in Tobermory. Mid- to late March.

### April

- **Hamilton Flat Races,** Hamilton, near Glasgow. The races take place 2 to 3 days every month from March to April. For details, call the Hamilton race course at ☎ **01698/283-806.** March to April.

- **Edinburgh Folk Festival,** at various venues, Edinburgh. For details on this feast of Scottish folk tunes, call ☎ **0131/473-3800.** Generally first of April.

- **Exhibitions at the Royal Scottish Academy,** Edinburgh. Changing exhibits of international interest are offered here annually. For details, call ☎ **0131/473-3800.** Mid-April.

- **Kate Kennedy Procession and Pageant,** St. Andrews. This historic university pageant is staged annually in the university city of St. Andrews, in eastern Scotland. For details, call ☎ **01334/472-021** in St. Andrews. April.

### May

- **Scottish Motorcycle Trials,** Fort William. The trials are run for 6 days at the beginning of the month, drawing aficionados from all over Europe. For details, call ☎ **01397/703-781** in Fort William. Early May.

- **Highland Games and Gatherings,** at various venues throughout the country, including Aberfeldy, Perth, Crieff, Ballater, Oban, and Portree on the Isle of Skye. More details are available from the Edinburgh and Scotland Information Centre (see "Visitor Information" earlier in this chapter). Early May to mid-September.

- **Pitlochry Festival Theatre,** Pitlochry. Scotland's "theater in the hills" launches its season in mid-May. For details, call ☎ **01796/472-215** in Pitlochry. May to October.

## June

- **Promenade Concerts,** Glasgow. These concerts by the Scottish National Orchestra are given at the Glasgow Royal Concert Hall. For details, call ☎ **0141/204-4400** in Glasgow. Throughout June (sometimes into July).
- **Lanimer Day,** Lanark. This week of festivities features a ritual procession around the town's boundaries, the election of a Lanimer Queen and a Cornet King, and a parade with floats, along with Highland dances and bagpipe playing. For details, call ☎ **01555/661-661.** The Thursday between June 6 and 12.
- **Guid Nychtburris (Good Neighbors).** This age-old festival is an event similar to, but less impressive than, the Selkirk Common Riding (see below). For details, call ☎ **01387/253-862** in Dumfries. Mid-June.
- **Royal Highland Show,** at the Ingliston Showground, outskirts of Edinburgh. This show is devoted to agriculture and commerce. For details, call ☎ **0131/473-3800.** Mid- to late June.
- ✪ **Selkirk Common Riding.** This is Scotland's most elaborate display of horsemanship, celebrating Selkirk's losses in the 1560 Battle of Flodden—only one Selkirk soldier returned alive from the battle to warn the town before dropping dead in the marketplace. Some 400 horses and riders parade through the streets, and a young unmarried male is crowned at the sound of the cornet, representing the soldier who sounded the alarm. For details, call ☎ **01750/200-54** in Selkirk. The first Friday following the second Monday in June.
- **Beltane Day,** Peebles. A town "Cornet" rides around to see the boundaries are safe from the "invading" English, a young girl is elected Festival Queen, and her court is filled with courtiers, swordbearers, guards, and attendants. Children of the town dress in costumes for parade floats through the streets. For details, call ☎ **01721/720-138** in Peebles. Mid-June, beginning on a Sunday.
- **Gay Pride,** Edinburgh or Glasgow. Scotland's annual gay pride celebration alternates between Edinburgh and Glasgow. Of course, you'll find a quirky, boisterous parade through the heart of Glasgow or along Princes Street in Edinburgh. As its appeal grows, it might become an annual event for Glasgow, which would be consistent with its role as Scotland's largest and most progressive city. For details, call Glasgow's Gay Switchboard at ☎ **0141/332-8372** or Edinburgh's Gay Switchboard at ☎ **0131/556-4049.** Sometime in June; Edinburgh will play host in 2001.

## July

- **Glasgow International Jazz Festival,** Glasgow. Jazz musicians from all over the world come together to perform at various venues around the city. For details, call ☎ **0141/204-4400** in Glasgow. First week in July.
- **Folk Festival,** Glasgow. Some of the finest Scottish folk music can be heard here at one of the best Scottish folk festivals. For details, call ☎ **0141/204-4400** in Glasgow. Early July.

## August

- **Lammas Fair,** St. Andrews. Although there's a dim medieval origin to this 2-day festival, it's not particularly obvious. Temporary Ferris wheels and whirligigs are hauled in, cotton candy and popcorn are sold, palm readers describe your past and your future, and flashing lights and recorded disco music create something akin to Blackpool-in-the-Highlands. There's even an opportunity for bungee-jumping. For details, call ☎ 01334/472-021 in St. Andrews. Second Monday and Tuesday of August.

- **World Pipe Band Championships,** Glasgow. For this relatively new event (it's only 5 or 6 years old), bagpipe bands from around the world gather on the parklike Glasgow Green in the city's East End. From 11am to about 6pm there's a virtual orgy of bagpiping, as kilted participants strut their stuff in musical and military precision. For details, call ☎ 0141/204-4400 in Glasgow. Mid-August.

✪ **Edinburgh International Festival,** Edinburgh. Scotland's best-known festival is held for 3 weeks (more about this in chapter 4, "Edinburgh & the Lothian Region"). Called an "arts bonanza," it draws major talent from around the world, with more than a thousand shows presented and a million tickets sold. Book, jazz, and film festivals are also staged at this time, but nothing tops the Military Tattoo against the backdrop of spot-lit Edinburgh Castle. For details, contact the Festival Society, 21 Market St., Edinburgh, Scotland EH1 1BW (☎ 0131/473-2001). Three weeks in August.

## September

- **Ben Nevis Mountain Race,** Fort William, in the Highlands. A tradition since 1895, when it was established by a member of the MacFarlane clan, it assembles as many as 500 runners who compete for the coveted Mac-Farlane cup, a gold medal, and a prize of £50 ($85). Runners congregate at the base of Ben Nevis (Britain's highest peak) for registration at 11am and begin running at 2pm in a course that takes them up narrow foot-paths to the summit and back. Bagpipes rise in crescendos at the beginning and end of the experience. For details, call ☎ 01397/704-189 in Fort William. First Saturday in September.

✪ **Highland Games & Gathering in Braemar.** The queen and many members of the royal family often show up for this annual event, with its massed bands, piping and dancing competitions, and performances of great strength by a tribe of gigantic men. For details, contact the tourist office in Braemar, The Mews, Mar Road, Braemar, Aberdeenshire, AB35 5YP (☎ 013397/416-00). First Saturday in September.

- **Ayr Festival,** Ayr. This is the major cultural event on the Ayr calendar, offering an array of film, theater, and music concerts. For details, call ☎ 01292/288-688 in Ayr.

## October

- **Highland Autumn Cattle Show,** Oban, in western Scotland. Since the days of Rob Roy, Oban has been a marketplace for the long-haired tawny cattle whose elongated horns have been associated with the toughness of the Highlands. For this show, buyers and sellers from Britain, as well as such cold-weather climes as Sweden, Norway, and Canada, come to buy cattle (either for stud or for beef purposes). Everything is rather busi-nesslike (but still colorful) in the industrial-looking Caledonian Auction Mart, 3 miles (5km) south of Oban. For details, call ☎ 01631/563-122 in Oban. Mid-October.

**November**

- **Winter Antiques Fair,** Edinburgh. This fair draws dealers and buyers from all over Europe and America. For details, call ☎ **0131/473-3800.** Third week in November.
- **Christmas Shopping Festival,** Aberdeen. For those who want to shop early for Christmas. For details, call ☎ **01224/522-000** in Aberdeen. Third week of November to December.
- **St. Andrews Week,** St. Andrews. This annual festival of exhibits, concerts, sporting events, fireworks displays, and local foods takes place over the week leading up to St. Andrews Day on November 30. For details, call ☎ **01334/472-021.** The week ending November 30.

**December**

- **Flambeaux Procession,** Comrie, Tayside. This torchlight parade takes place on New Year's Eve. For details, call ☎ **01764/652-578** in Crieff. December 31.
- **Hogmanay,** Edinburgh. Hogmanay begins on New Year's Eve and merges into New Year's Day festivities. Events include a torchlight procession, a fire festival along Princes Street, a carnival, and a street theater spectacular. For details, call ☎ **0131/473-3800.** December 31.

## 6 Health & Insurance

### STAYING HEALTHY

You'll encounter few health problems while in Scotland. The tap water is safe to drink, the milk is pasteurized, and health services are good. The mad-cow crisis is over, but caution is always advised. (For example, it's been suggested that it's safer to eat British beef cut from the bone instead of on the bone.)

If you need a doctor, your hotel can recommend one, or you can contact your embassy or consulate. *Note:* U.S. visitors who become ill while in England are eligible only for free emergency care. For other treatment, including follow-up care, you'll be asked to pay.

If you worry about getting sick away from home, you may want to consider **medical travel insurance** (see "Insurance," below). In most cases, however, your existing health plan will provide all the coverage you need. Be sure to carry your identification card in your wallet.

If you suffer from a chronic illness, consult your doctor before your departure. For conditions like epilepsy, diabetes, or heart problems, wear a **Medic Alert Identification Tag** (☎ **800/ID-ALERT;** www.medicalert.org), which will immediately alert doctors to your condition and give them access to your records through Medic Alert's 24-hour hotline.

Pack prescription medications in your carry-on luggage. Carry written prescriptions in generic, not brand-name form, and dispense all prescription medications from their original labeled vials. If you wear contact lenses, pack an extra pair in case you lose one.

Contact the **International Association for Medical Assistance to Travelers (IAMAT;** ☎ **716/754-4883** or 416/652-0137; www.sentex.net/~iamat). This organization offers tips on travel and health concerns in the countries you'll be visiting, and lists many local English-speaking doctors. In Canada, call ☎ **519/836-0102.**

# INSURANCE

There are three kinds of travel insurance: trip-cancellation, medical, and lost-luggage coverage. **Trip-cancellation insurance** is a good idea if you have paid a large portion of your vacation expenses up front (say, by purchasing a package deal). Make sure you buy it from an outside vendor, though, not from your tour operator; you don't want to put all your eggs in one basket.

*Rule number one:* Check your existing policies before you buy any additional coverage you may not need.

Your existing health insurance should cover you if you get sick while on vacation—but if you belong to an HMO, you should check to see whether you are fully covered when away from home. For independent travel health-insurance providers, see below.

Your homeowner's or renter's insurance should cover stolen luggage. The airlines are responsible for only a very limited amount if they lose your luggage on an overseas flight, so if you plan to carry anything really valuable, keep it in your carry-on bag.

The differences between **travel assistance** and insurance are often blurred, but in general, the former offers on-the-spot assistance and 24-hour hotlines (mostly oriented toward medical problems), while the latter reimburses you for travel problems (medical, travel, or otherwise) after you have filed the paperwork. The coverage you should consider depends on how much protection is already in your existing health insurance or other policies. Some credit- and charge-card companies may insure you against travel accidents if you buy plane, train, or bus tickets with their cards. Before purchasing additional insurance, read your policies and agreements over carefully. Call your insurers or credit-card companies if you have any questions.

If you do require additional insurance, try one of the companies listed below, but don't pay for more than you need. If you need only trip-cancellation insurance, don't buy coverage for lost or stolen property, which should be covered by your homeowner's or renter's policy. Trip-cancellation insurance costs approximately 6% to 8% of the total value of your vacation.

Among the reputable issuers of travel insurance are **Access America** (☎ **800/284-8300;** www.accessamerica.com) and **Travel Guard International** (☎ **800/826-1300;** www.travel-guard.com). One company specializing in accident and medical care is **Travel Assistance International** (Worldwide Assistance Services; ☎ **800/821-2828** or 202/828-5894).

Travelers from Australia and New Zealand can receive free medical care as long as they are in possession of their medicare card and photo identification. Canadian travelers are protected by their home province's health insurance plan for up to 90 days after leaving Canada.

## 7 Tips for Travelers with Special Needs

### FOR TRAVELERS WITH DISABILITIES

Many Scottish hotels, museums, restaurants, and sights have wheelchair ramps. Persons with disabilities are often granted special discounts at attractions and, in some cases, nightclubs. These are called "concessions" in Britain. It always pays to ask.

**Moss Rehab ResourceNet (www.mossresourcenet.org)** is a great source for information, tips, and resources relating to accessible travel. You'll find links to a number of travel agents who specialize in planning trips for disabled travelers here and through **Access-Able Travel Source (www.access-able.com),**

another excellent online source. You'll also find relay and voice numbers for hotels, airlines, and car-rental companies on Access-Able's user-friendly site, as well as links to accessible accommodations, attractions, transportation, tours, local medical resources and equipment repairers, and much more.

You can join **The Society for the Advancement of Travelers with Handicaps (SATH),** 347 Fifth Ave., Suite 610, New York, NY 10016 (☎ 212/447-7284; fax 212-725-8253; www.sath.org), to gain access to their vast network of connections in the travel industry. They provide information sheets on destinations and referrals to tour operators that specialize in traveling with disabilities. Their quarterly magazine, *Open World,* is full of good information and resources.

*A World of Options,* a 658-page book of resources for disabled travelers, covers everything from biking trips to scuba outfitters. It costs $35 ($30 for members) and is available from **Mobility International USA** (☎ 541/343-1284, voice and TDD; www.miusa.org). Annual membership for Mobility International is $35, which includes their quarterly newsletter, "Over the Rainbow."

You may also want to join a tour catering to travelers with disabilities. One of the best operators is **Flying Wheels Travel** (☎ 800/535-6790; www.flyingwheels.com), offering various escorted tours and cruises, with an emphasis on sports, as well as private tours in minivans with lifts. Other reputable operators are **Accessible Journeys** (☎ 800/TINGLES or 610/521-0339; www.disabilitytravel.com), for slow walkers and wheelchair travelers; **The Guided Tour** (☎ 215/782-1370); and **Directions Unlimited** (☎ 800/533-5343).

For British travelers, the **Royal Association for Disability and Rehabilitation (RADAR),** Unit 12, City Forum, 250 City Rd., London EC1V 8AF (☎ 020/7250-3222), publishes three holiday "fact packs" for £2 ($3.40) each or £5 ($8.50) for all three. The first provides general info, including planning and booking a holiday, insurance, and finances; the second outlines transportation available when going abroad and equipment for rent; the third deals with specialized accommodations. Another good resource is the **Holiday Care Service,** Imperial Building, 2nd Floor, Victoria Road, Horley, Surrey RH6 7PZ (☎ 01293/774-535; fax 01293/784-647), a national charity advising on accessible accommodations for the elderly and persons with disabilities. Annual membership is £30 ($51).

## FOR GAY & LESBIAN TRAVELERS

Bars, clubs, restaurants, and hotels catering to gays are confined almost exclusively to Edinburgh, Glasgow, and Inverness. Call the **Edinburgh Gay and Lesbian Switchboard** at ☎ 0131/556-4049 or the **Glasgow Gay and Lesbian Switchboard** at ☎ 0141/332-8372 for information about local events.

Scotland doesn't boast much of a gay scene. Gay-bashing happens, especially in the grimy industrial sections of Glasgow, where neo-Nazi skinheads hang out. Although it's a crime, it's rarely punished. Open displays of affection between same-sex couples usually invite scorn in rural Scotland, although there's none of the fanatical homophobia so prevalent among the lunatic fringe in the United States.

The best guide (besides this one) is *Spartacus Britain and Ireland.* Although the first edition of the new *Frommer's Gay & Lesbian Europe* doesn't include Scotland, it does include London, Brighton, and Manchester, in case you're heading to England before or after Scotland. For up-to-the-minute activities in Britain, we recommend *Gay Times* (London). These books and others are available from **Giovanni's Room,** 345 S. 12th St., Philadelphia, PA 19107 (☎ 215/923-2960; giophilp@netaxs.com), or **A Different Light Bookstore,** 151 W. 19th St., New York, NY 10011 (☎ 800/343-4002 or 212/989-4850; www.adlbooks.com).

If you want help planning your trip, **The International Gay & Lesbian Travel Association** (IGLTA; ☎ 800/448-8550 or 954/776-2626; www.iglta.org) can link you up with the appropriate gay-friendly service organization or tour specialist. With around 1,200 members, it offers quarterly newsletters, marketing mailings, and a membership directory that's updated quarterly. Members are kept informed of gay and gay-friendly hoteliers, tour operators, and airline and cruise-line representatives.

*Out and About* (☎ 800/929-2268 or 212/645-6922; www.outandabout. com) has been hailed for its "straight" reporting about gay travel. It offers a monthly newsletter packed with good information on the global gay and lesbian scene. *Out and About*'s guidebooks are available at most major bookstores and through **A Different Light Bookstore,** 151 W. 19th St. (☎ 800/343-4002 or 212/989-4850; www.adlbooks.com), while its Web site features links to gay and lesbian tour operators and other gay-themed travel links.

General U.S. gay and lesbian travel agencies include **Family Abroad** (☎ 800/999-5500 or 212/459-1800) and **Above and Beyond Tours** (☎ 800/397-2681). In the United Kingdom, try **Alternative Holidays** (☎ 020/7701-7040; fax 020/7708-5668; e-mail: info@alternativeholidays.com).

## FOR SENIORS

One of the benefits of age is that travel often costs less. Always bring an ID card, especially if you've kept your youthful glow. Also mention that you're a senior when you first make your travel reservations, since many airlines and hotels offer discount programs for senior travelers.

Seniors over 60 receive special 10% discounts on **British Airways** through its Privileged Traveler program. They also qualify for reduced restrictions on APEX cancellations. Discounts are also granted for BA tours and for intra-Britain air tickets if booked in North America.

Members of the **American Association of Retired Persons** (AARP; ☎ 800/424-3410; www.aarp.org) get discounts on hotels, airfares, and car rentals. The AARP offers members a wide range of special benefits, including *Modern Maturity* magazine and a monthly newsletter. If you're not already a member, do yourself a favor and join.

**SAGA International Holidays,** 222 Berkeley St., Boston, MA 02116 (☎ 800/343-0273), offers inclusive tours and cruises for those 50 and older. SAGA also sponsors the more substantial **"Road Scholar Tours"** (☎ 800/621-2151), which are fun-loving but with an educational bent.

If you want something more than the average vacation or guided tour, try **Elderhostel** (☎ 877/426-8056; www.elderhostel.org) or the University of New Hampshire's **Interhostel** (☎ 800/733-9753), both variations on the same theme: educational travel for senior citizens. On these escorted tours, the days are packed with seminars, lectures, and field trips, and the sightseeing is all led by academic experts. The courses in both programs are ungraded, involve no homework, and often focus on the liberal arts. They're not luxury vacations but are fun and fulfilling.

## FOR FAMILIES

Several books on the market offer tips to help you travel with kids. *Family Travel* (Lanier Publishing International) and *How to Take Great Trips with Your Kids* (The Harvard Common Press) are full of good general advice that can apply to travel anywhere. Another reliable tome, with a worldwide focus, is *Adventuring with Children* (Foghorn Press).

*Family Travel Times* is published six times a year by TWYCH (Travel with Your Children; **888/822-4388** or 212/477-5524), and includes a weekly call-in service for subscribers. Subscriptions are $40 a year for quarterly editions. A free publication list and a sample issue are available by calling or sending a request to the above address.

The University of New Hampshire runs **Familyhostel** (☎ 800/733-9753), an intergenerational alternative to standard guided tours. You live on a European college campus for the 2- or 3-week program, attend lectures and seminars, go on lots of field trips, and do all the sightseeing—guided by a team of experts and academics. It's designed for children 8 to 15, parents, and grandparents.

## FOR STUDENTS

The best resource for students is the **Council on International Educational Exchange (CIEE).** It can set you up with an ID card (see below), and its travel branch, **Council Travel Service** (☎ **800/226-8624;** www.counciltravel. com), is the world's biggest student travel agency operation. It can get you discounts on plane tickets, railpasses, and the like. Ask for a list of CTS offices in major cities so you can keep the discounts flowing (and aid lines open) as you travel.

From CIEE you can get the student traveler's best friend, the $18 **International Student Identity Card (ISIC).** It's the only officially acceptable form of student ID, good for cut rates on railpasses and plane tickets and other discounts. It also provides you with basic health and life insurance and a 24-hour help line. If you're no longer a student but are still under 26 you can get from the same people a **GO 25 card,** which will get you the insurance and some of the discounts (but not student admission prices in museums).

In Canada, **Travel CUTS,** 200 Ronson St., Ste. 320, Toronto, ONT M9W 5Z9 (☎ **800/667-2887** or 416/614-2887; www.travelcuts.com), offers similar services. **USIT Campus,** 52 Grosvenor Gardens, London SW1W 0AG (☎ **020/7730-3402;** www.usitcampus.co.uk), opposite Victoria Station, is Britain's leading specialist in student and youth travel.

### Farmhouse Holidays

One way to understand the agricultural roots of Scotland is overnighting on a Scottish farm. **Scottish Farmhouse Holidays,** Drumtenant, Ladybank, Fife KY15 7UG (☎ **0189/075-1830;** fax 01337/831-301), will find you an appropriate croft. The company was begun in 1982 by Scots-born Jane Buchanan, who describes herself as a farmer's daughter, a farmer's wife, a businesswoman steeped in both agriculture and tourism, and a former exchange student with 4H programs in Michigan and Utah.

Only family-managed working farms are selected for the program, most within easy driving distance of at least a handful of historic sites. Many of the farmhouses are a century or so old and have been in the same family for several generations. Rates for bed-and-breakfast in rooms without a bathroom are £16 to £20 ($27.20 to $34); rates for dinner, bed, and breakfast run £23 to £40 ($39.10 to $68). Rooms with bathrooms are available for an extra £5 ($8.50) per person. Occupants of single rooms usually pay a £5 ($8.50) supplement.

# 8 Getting There

## BY PLANE

The national carrier of Britain, **British Airways** (☎ 800/247-9297 in the U.S. and Canada, 0345/222-111 in England, or 01/610-666 in Ireland; www.british-airways.com), operates the greatest number of flights into all parts of the country, including Scotland. This airline is the only non-U.S. carrier with its own terminal at New York's JFK.

BA serves at least 20 North American cities with nonstop flights at least once a day into London's most convenient airport, Heathrow. From Heathrow, BA offers 22 nonstop flights daily to both Edinburgh and Glasgow. Some Scotland-bound passengers opt for flights into Manchester in England—it's closer than London to Scotland's Highlands and islands. BA offers frequent flights into Manchester, many nonstop, from various parts of the United States.

**American Airlines** (☎ 800/433-7300; www.aa.com) is the U.S. carrier with the most routes into London. May 15 to October 31, American offers a daily nonstop flight to Glasgow from Chicago; the rest of the year, you'll make at least one transfer. In addition, the airline has six daily nonstops from New York to London and one nonstop from Chicago to Manchester, England. Depending on the season, there's also one daily flight from JFK to Manchester via London. American also offers at least one daily nonstop to London from Chicago, Dallas/Fort Worth, Los Angeles, Boston, and Miami.

**United Airlines** (☎ 800/538-2929; www.ual.com) offers daily nonstop service to London from New York, San Francisco, Washington D.C., Los Angeles, and Newark.

**Northwest Airlines** (☎ 800/225-2525; www.nwa.com) operates nonstop flights between Boston and Glasgow daily in summer, somewhat less frequently in winter. It also offers daily nonstops from Minneapolis and Detroit to London. Thanks to Northwest's partnership with Holland's national airline, KLM, it also offers easy connections through Amsterdam to Britain and most of the other countries of Europe.

**Delta** (☎ 800/241-4141; www.delta.com) has daily nonstop flights to London from Atlanta and Cincinnati. **TWA** (☎ 800/892-4141; www.twa.com) offers daily nonstops to London from St. Louis. **Virgin Atlantic Airways** (☎ 800/862-8621; www.flyvirgin.com) flies to London's Gatwick from Boston, Orlando, and Miami and to London's Heathrow from Los Angeles, Newark, and New York. Depending on the point of origin, flights leave four to seven times a week.

For travelers departing from Canada, **Air Canada** (☎ 800/776-3000; www.aircanada.ca) flies daily to London nonstop from Vancouver, Montreal, and Toronto. There are also frequent direct services from Calgary and Ottawa. **Air Canada** also offers daily flights from Toronto to Manchester. An add-on to Glasgow or Edinburgh can be arranged when the initial flight is booked. From Canada, **British Airways** (☎ 800/247-9297; www.british-airways.com) has direct flights to London from Toronto, Montreal, and Vancouver.

For travelers departing from the United Kingdom, **British Airways** (☎ 0345/222-111) flies from Heathrow to both Edinburgh and Glasgow, with frequent daily flights. **KLM UK** (☎ 0990/074-074) flies from Stansted and London City airports to both Edinburgh and Glasgow daily. **Rynair** (☎ 0541/569-569) flies from Stansted outside London to Prestwick on the west coast of Scotland, and **British Midland** (☎ 0345/554-554) flies from Heathrow to both Edinburgh and Glasgow.

For travelers departing from Australia, **British Airways** (☎ 02/8904-8800; www.british-airways.com) has flights to London from Sydney, Melbourne, Perth, and Brisbane. **Qantas** (☎ 008/112-121) offers direct flights with stopovers from Sydney and Melbourne to London. Both airlines have the bonus of a free stopover in Bangkok or Singapore.

For travelers departing from New Zealand, **Air New Zealand** (☎ 0800/737-000) has direct flights to London from Auckland. These flights depart Wednesday, Saturday, and Sunday.

**Aer Lingus** (☎ 800/223-6537 or 01/844-4711 in Ireland; www.aerlingus.ie) flies daily from Dublin to both Glasgow and Edinburgh. Direct flights are also available through **Ryan Air** (☎ 0541/569-569 in England), which flies several times a day from Dublin to Glasgow.

## FLY FOR LESS: TIPS FOR GETTING THE BEST AIRFARES

- **Take advantage of APEX fares.** Advance-purchase booking or APEX fares are often the key to getting the lowest fare. You generally must be willing to make your plans and buy your tickets as far ahead as possible: The **21-day APEX** is seconded only by the **14-day APEX,** with a stay in Scotland of 7 to 30 days. Since the number of seats allocated to APEX fares is sometimes less than 25% of plane capacity, the early bird gets the low-cost seat. There's often a surcharge for flying on a weekend, and cancellation and refund policies can be strict.

- **Watch for sales.** You'll almost never see them during July and August or the Thanksgiving or Christmas seasons, but at other times you can get great deals. In the past couple of years, there have been amazing deals on winter flights to Europe. If you already hold a ticket when a sale breaks, it may even pay to exchange it, which usually incurs a $50 to $75 charge. Note, however, that the lowest-priced fares are often nonrefundable, require advance purchase of 1 to 3 weeks and a certain length of stay, and carry penalties for changing dates of travel. So, when you're quoted a fare, make sure you know exactly what the restrictions are before you commit.

- If your schedule is flexible, ask if you can secure a cheaper fare by **staying an extra day** or by **flying midweek.** (Many airlines won't volunteer this information.)

- **Consolidators,** also known as bucket shops, are a good place to find low fares, often below even the airlines' discounted rates. There's nothing shady about the reliable ones—basically, they're just big travel agents that get discounts for buying in bulk and pass some of the savings on to you. Before you pay, however, ask for a confirmation number from the consolidator and then call the airline itself to confirm your seat. Be prepared to book your ticket with a different consolidator—there are many to choose from—if the airline can't confirm your reservation. Also be aware that consolidator tickets are usually nonrefundable or come with stiff cancellation penalties.

   We've gotten great deals on many occasions from ✪ **Cheap Tickets** (☎ 800/377-1000; www.cheaptickets.com). **Council Travel** (☎ 800/226-8624; www.counciltravel.com) and **STA Travel** (☎ 800/781-4040; www.sta.travel.com) cater especially to young travelers, but their bargain-basement prices are available to people of all ages. Other reliable consolidators include **Lowestfare.com** (☎ 888/278-8830; www.lowestfare.com); **1-800-AIRFARE** (www.1800airfare.com); **Cheap Seats** (☎ 800/451-7200; www.cheapseatstravel.com); and **1-800-FLY-CHEAP** (www.flycheap.com).

- Search the **Internet** for cheap fares—but it's still best to compare your findings with the research of a dedicated travel agent, if you're lucky enough to have one, especially when you're booking more than just a flight. A few of the better-respected virtual travel agents are **Travelocity (www.travelocity.com)** and **Microsoft Expedia (www.expedia.com).**

    **Smarter Living (www.smarterliving.com)** is a great source for great last-minute deals. Take a moment to register, and every week you'll get an e-mail summarizing the discount fares available from your departure city. The site also features concise lists of links to hotel, car rental, and other hot travel deals.

    See **"Planning Your Trip: An Online Directory"** on p. 46 for further discussion on this topic and other recommended sites.

## BY TRAIN

From England, two main rail lines link London to Scotland. The most popular and fastest route is **King's Cross Station** in London to Edinburgh, going by way of Newcastle and Durham. Trains cross from England into Scotland at Berwick-upon-Tweed. Fifteen trains a day leave London for Edinburgh 8am to 6pm; night service is more limited, and you must reserve sleepers. Three of these trains go on to Aberdeen.

If you're going on to the western Highlands and islands, Edinburgh makes a good gateway, with better train connections to those areas than Glasgow.

If you're going via the west coast, trains leave **Euston Station** in London for Glasgow, by way of Rugby, Crewe, Preston, and Carlisle, with nearly a train per hour during the day. Most of these trains take about 5 hours to reach Glasgow. You can also take the *Highland Chieftain,* going direct to Stirling and Aviemore and terminating in Inverness, capital of the Highlands. There's overnight sleeper service from Euston Station to Glasgow, Perth, Stirling, Aviemore, Fort William, and Inverness. It's possible to book a family compartment.

Scotland is served by other trains from England, including regular service from such cities as Birmingham, Liverpool, Manchester, Southampton, and Bristol. If you're in Penzance (Cornwall), you can reach Glasgow or Edinburgh directly by train without having to return to London.

See "Getting Around," below, for information about rail passes.

## BY BUS (COACH)

Long-distance buses, called "motorcoaches" in Britain, are the least expensive means of reaching Scotland from England. Some 20 coach companies run services, mainly from London to Edinburgh or Glasgow. The major operators are **National Express, Scottish Omnibuses, Western SMT, Stagecoach,** and **Eastern Scottish.** It takes 8 to 8½ hours to reach Edinburgh or Glasgow from London.

It's estimated that coach fares are about one-third of the rail charges for comparable trips into Scotland. Most coaches depart from **Victoria Coach Station** in London. If you're visiting June to August, it's wise to make seat reservations at least 3 days in advance (4 or 5 days if possible). For timetables, available from London to Edinburgh, call **National Express** coaches at ☎ **0990/808-080** in London or **Scottish Omnibuses** at ☎ **01847/ 893-123,** or check on all other companies by calling ☎ **08705/505-050.** Travel centers and travel agents also have details. Most travel agents in London sell coach seats and can make reservations for you.

See chapter 3, "The Active Vacation Planner," for tour operators specializing in active outdoor vacations, like walking and biking tours.

# BY CAR

If you're driving north to Scotland from England, it's fastest to take the **M1 motorway** north from London. You can reach M1 by driving to the ring road from any point in the British capital. Southeast of Leeds, you'll need to connect with **A1** (not a motorway), which you take north to Scotch Corner. Here M1 resumes, ending south of Newcastle-upon-Tyne. Then you can take **A696,** which becomes **A68,** for its final run north into Edinburgh.

If you're in the west of England, you can go north along **M5,** which begins at Exeter (Devon). Eventually this will merge with **M6.** Continue north on M6 until you reach a point north of Carlisle. From Carlisle, cross into Scotland near Gretna Green. Continue north along **A74** via Moffat. A74 will eventually connect with **M74** heading toward Glasgow. If your goal is Edinburgh, not Glasgow, various roads will take you east to the Scottish capital, including **M8,** which goes part of the way, as do **A702, A70,** and **A71** (all these routes are well signposted).

# BY PACKAGE TOUR

Another option is booking your flight as part of a travel package like an escorted or a package tour. What you lose in freedom and adventure, you'll gain in time and money saved on accommodations, and even food and entertainment, along with your airline ticket.

The best place to start searching is the travel section of your local Sunday newspaper and the ads in the back of national travel magazines. **Liberty Travel** (www.libertytravel.com) doesn't have a central toll-free number, but check your local directory for one of its many branches. One of the biggest packagers in the Northeast, Liberty usually boasts a full-page ad in Sunday papers. **American Express Vacations** (☎ 800/241-1700; www.americanexpress.com) is another option.

Another good resource is the airlines themselves, which often package their flights together with accommodations. Among the airline packagers, your options include **American Airlines FlyAway Vacations** (☎ 800/321-2121), **Delta Dream Vacations** (☎ 800/872-7786), and **Northwest** (☎ 800/ 225-2525). Some of the airline offerings are escorted tours; others are independent fly/drive packages.

**British Airways** (☎ 800/247-9297; www.british-airways.com) offers a full spectrum of what it calls "designer holidays," constructed for a wide range of people. Offerings range from tightly scheduled motorcoach tours for those who want the greatest amount of guidance to tours designed for independent souls needing no more than discounted car-rental vouchers and reserved rooms at specific types of hotels (ranging from simple inns to fine baronial mansions).

Other companies offering escorted tours include **CIE Tours** (book through any travel agency, not through CIE directly); **Travoca** (☎ 800/992-2003), which offers upscale escorted tours by deluxe motorcoach; and **Trafalgar Tours** (☎ 800/854-0103), which offers affordable packages with lodgings in unpretentious but comfortable hotels.

**A RAIL TOUR  Abercrombie & Kent,** 1520 Kensington Rd., Oak Brook, IL 60521 (☎ **800/323-7308;** fax 630/954-2944; www.abercrombiekent. com), offers the most glamorous rail tours in Europe. A & K is the only U.S. sales agent for an elegant train known as the *Royal Scotsman.* Passengers board the luxury train in Edinburgh and can enjoy either a 4-night Scotland tour, or a new 2-night tour of the east or west coasts of Scotland. The food rivals that served in the finest restaurants, and the package includes bus trips, tours of castles, manor houses, gardens, and historic sites, many of which are not open to the public. The train stops every evening in a quiet place to guarantee passengers a good night's sleep. Two-night tours begin at $2,350 per person for a twin or single cabin. For information on 4-night tours and departure times, please call.

**CRUISES**  No area of Scotland is ever far from a loch, an estuary, or the wide-open sea, a fact that has greatly affected the country's history. One of the best ways to visit its far-flung islands is by ship, offering a luxury and convenience difficult to duplicate any other way.

One company geared for this kind of travel is **Hebridean Island Cruises,** Acorn Park, Skipton, North Yorkshire BD23 2UE (☎ **800/659-2648** in the U.S. and Canada, or 01756/701-338). The company operates the *Hebridean Princess,* a shallow-draft, much-refitted and -retooled remake (1990) of an older vessel. Equipped with 30 staterooms and a crew of 38, it can carry up to 50 passengers in cozy circumstances to some of the most remote and inaccessible regions of Scotland. The ship is equipped with beach landing craft especially useful during explorations of the fragile ecosystems and bird life of the more remote islands.

March to October, the company offers 12 itineraries that focus on nature and ecology or on the castles, gardens, and archaeology of Scotland. Tours usually depart from Oban and cruise through the Inner and Outer Hebrides and the Orkneys, stopping in places like Saint Kilda's, known for its bird life and tundra. The tours and prices vary enormously depending on the date of travel but generally range from 4 to 15 days and cost £1,100 to £16,000 ($1,870 to $27,200). All meals and shore excursions are included, but liquor tabs at the well-stocked bar, wine at dinner, and gratuities are extra.

For more luxurious tours through the islands and lochs of Scotland, contact **Seabourn Cruise Line** (☎ **800/929-9595**), which offers cruises aboard its top-of-the-line yacht *Seaborn Sun,* often as part of longer itineraries around the British Isles.

## 9 Getting Around

### BY PLANE

The **British Airways Europe Airpass** allows travel in a continuous loop to between 3 and 12 cities on BA's European and domestic routes. Passengers must end their journey at the same point they began. If you book such a ticket (say, London to Manchester to Glasgow to Aberdeen to the Shetland Islands, with an eventual return to London), each segment of the itinerary costs about 40% to 50% less than if you'd booked it individually. The pass is available for travel to about a dozen of the most visited cities and regions of Britain, with discounted add-ons available to most of BA's destinations in Europe. It must be booked and paid for at least 7 days before departure from the States, and all sectors of the itinerary must be booked simultaneously. Some changes are permitted in flight dates (but not in the cities visited) after the ticket is issued.

Check with BA (☎ **800/247-9297** or 0345/222-111 in the U.K.; www. british-airways.com) for full details.

Scotland's relatively small scale makes flights between many cities inconvenient and impractical. Although **British Airways** (see above) offers regular flights between Glasgow and Edinburgh, the excellent rail and highway connections usually deter most passengers from flying that route *unless their plane just happens to stop en route to other, more distant, points in Scotland.* Frankly, except for visits to the far-distant Shetlands and Orkneys, we prefer to drive to all but the most inaccessible points. However, British Airways is by far the largest intra-Britain carrier since its recent merger with regional carriers Logan Airways and British Express. Aboard BA from Edinburgh, you can arrange flights to Inverness, Wick, Kirkwall (the Orkneys), and Lerwick (the Shetlands). Aboard **British Midlands** (☎ **0870/607-0555**), you can fly from London to Edinburgh and Glasgow, but it doesn't offer any other routes in Scotland.

## BY TRAIN

The cost of rail travel in Scotland can be quite low. Trains are generally punctual, carrying you across the country or at least to ferry terminals if you're exploring the islands. Timetables are available at all stations, and free timetables covering only certain regions are available at various stations. For £18 ($30.60), a **young person's rail card** (ages 16–25) is sold at major stations. Two passport-size photos are needed. It's estimated this card reduces all fares by one-third for 1 year.

If you plan to travel a great deal on the European railroads, it's worth securing a copy of the ***Thomas Cook European Timetable of European Passenger Railroads.*** It's available from **Forsyth Travel Library,** 226 Westchester Ave., White Plains, NY 10604 (☎ **800/FORSYTH**), for $27.95 plus $4.95 priority airmail postage in the United States or plus $2 (U.S.) for shipments to Canada. You can also find the timetable at major travel bookstores.

For information on rail travel in Scotland, contact **ScotRail,** P.O. Box 49, Cardiff CF1 5YU, Scotland (☎ **0845/755-0033**).

**BRITRAIL PASS** The **BritRail Pass** permits unlimited rail travel in England, Scotland, and Wales on all British Rail routes (it's not valid on ships between the U.K. and the Continent, the Channel Islands, or Ireland). An **8-day pass** costs $400 first-class and $265 standard, a **15-day pass** $600 and $400, a **22-day pass** $760 and $505, and a **1-month pass** $900 and $600. Kids 5 to 15 are charged half fare, and children under 5 travel free.

**Youth passes** (ages 16–25), all standard, are $215 for 8 days, $280 for 15 days, $355 for 22 days, and $420 for 1 month. If you choose to go first class, you pay full adult fare. **Senior citizens** (60 plus) qualify for rates of $340 for 8 days, $510 for 15 days, $645 for 22 days, and $765 for 1 month. All BritRail senior rates are for first-class travel.

*Note:* Prices for BritRail passes are higher for Canadian travelers because of the different conversion rate for Canadian dollars.

BritRail passes can't be obtained in Britain but should be secured before leaving North America either through a travel agent or by contacting **BritRail Travel International,** 500 Mamaroneck Ave., Suite 314, Harrison, NY 10528 (☎ **888/BRITRAIL** or 800/677-8585 in the U.S.; 800/555-2748 in Canada; www.raileurope.com).

**BRITRAIL FLEXIPASS** The **BritRail Flexipass** lets you travel anywhere on British Rail but limits travel to 4, 8, or 15 days within a 30-day period. The

**4-day Flexipass** costs $350 in first class and $235 in standard; seniors pay $300 for a first-class pass, students (ages 16–25) pay $185 for a standard pass. The **8-day pass** is $510 in first class, $340 in standard, $435 seniors, and $240 students. The **15-day Flexipass** (15 days of travel in a 2-month period) is $770 in first class and $515 in standard; seniors pay $655. Students are charged $360 for a 15-day pass, but can spread their travel over a 2-month period.

The Flexipass must also be purchased from your travel agent or from BritRail Travel International in North America (see address above).

**TRAVELPASS FOR SCOTLAND**  If you plan to tour throughout the United Kingdom, one of the above BritRail passes might be appropriate. If you plan to focus intensively on Scotland, however, a BritRail pass might not be adequate. The Scottish Tourist Authorities offer the **Freedom of Scotland Travelpass,** with unlimited transportation on trains and most ferries throughout Scotland and discounts for bus travel. It includes access to obscure bus routes to almost forgotten hamlets and free rides on ferries operated by Caledonian MacBrayne and discounted fares with P&O Scottish Lines. Their ferries connect to the Western Islands, the islands of the Clyde, and the historic Orkneys.

The Travelpass covers all the Scottish rail network and is usable from Carlisle on the western border of England and Scotland and from Berwick-upon-Tweed on the eastern Scottish border. In addition, if you have to fly into London and want to go straight to Scotland from there, a reduced rate is available for a round-trip ticket between London and Edinburgh or Glasgow for Travelpass holders.

The Travelpass is available for 4 days' travel over an 8-day period for $137; 8 days' travel over a 15-day period for $199; and 12 days' travel over a 15-day period for $206. When you validate the pass at the beginning of the journey, you'll get a complete packet of rail, bus, and ferry schedules. For more information, contact **BritRail Travel International,** 500 Mamaroneck Ave., Suite 314, Harrison, NY 10528 (☎ **888/BRITRAIL,** or 800/677-8585 in the U.S., 800/555-2748 in Canada; www.raileurope.com), or the Manager of Public Affairs, British Rail–Scottish Region, **ScotRail,** P.O. Box 49, Cardiff CF1 5YU, Scotland (☎ **0845/755-0033**).

## BY BUS (COACH)

No doubt about it, the cheapest means of transport from London to Scotland is the bus (coach). It's also the least expensive means of travel within Scotland.

All major towns have a **local bus service,** and every tourist office will provide details about half-day or full-day bus excursions to scenic highlights. If you want to explore a particular area, you can often avail yourself of an economical bus pass. If you're planning to travel extensively in Scotland, see the Freedom of Scotland Travelpass, described above.

Many adventurous travelers like to explore the country on one of the **postal buses,** which carry not only mail but a limited number of passengers to rural areas. Ask at any local post office for details. A general timetable is available at the head post office in Edinburgh.

**Eurailpass Warning**

Note that your Eurailpass is *not* valid on trains in Great Britain.

**Scottish CityLink Coaches** are a good bet. They link the major cities (Glasgow and Edinburgh) with the two most popular tourist centers, Inverness and Aviemore. Travel is fast and prices are low. For example, it takes only 3 hours to reach Aviemore from Edinburgh, and Inverness is just 3½ hours from Edinburgh. A direct Scottish CityLink overnight coach makes the run from London to Aviemore and Inverness at reasonable fares.

Coaches offer many other popular runs, including links between Glasgow and Fort William, Inverness and Ullapool, and Glasgow and Oban. For details, contact **Highland Bus and Coach,** Farralane Park, Inverness (☎ 01463/233371), or **Scottish CityLink,** Buchanan Street Bus Station, Glasgow (☎ 0141/332-7133).

## BY CAR

Scotland has many excellent roads, often "dual carriageways" (divided highways), as well as fast trunk roads, linking the Lowlands to the Highlands. In more remote areas, especially the islands of western Scotland, single-lane roads exist. Here caution in driving is most important. Passing places are provided.

However, many of the roads are unfenced, and livestock can be a serious problem when you're driving, either day or night. Drive slowly when you're passing through areas filled with sheep.

**CAR RENTALS**  It's best to shop around, compare prices, and have a clear idea of your needs before you reserve a car. All companies give the best rates to people who reserve at least 2 business days in advance before leaving home and who agree to return the car to its point of origin, and some require drivers be at least 23 years old (in some cases 21). It's also an advantage to keep the car for at least a week, as opposed to 3 or 4 days. Be warned that all car rentals in the United Kingdom are slapped with a whopping 17.5% government tax known as VAT.

To rent a car in Scotland, you must present your passport and own driver's license along with your deposit. No special British or international license is needed.

The three major rental companies are **Avis** (☎ 800/331-2112; www.avis. com), **Budget** (☎ 800/527-0700; www.budgetrentacar.com), and **Hertz** (☎ 800/654-3131; www.hertz.com). We've often found the cheapest rates through Budget, but it's worth noting that frequent flyers on British Airways may be eligible for discounts on Hertz rentals if they make their reservations through the airlines. Good deals are also available through **EuroDollar Rent-a-Car** (☎ 800/800-6000) and **Alamo** (☎ 800/522-9696; www.goalamo.com).

Other companies specializing in European car rentals are **Auto Europe** (☎ 800/223-5555; www.autoeurope.com), **Europe by Car** (☎ 800/ 223-1516, 800/252-9401 in California, or 212/581-3040 in New York; www. europebycar.com), and **Kemwel** (☎ 800/678-0678; www.kemwel.com).

Another bargain option is a car-rental reservations network based in Florida: **I.T.S. of Broward County** (☎ 800/521-0643, 800/227-8990, or 800/248-4350), which represents two of Britain's largest rental companies, Kenning and Town & Country. I.T.S. usually offers prices ranging up to 40% lower than those available at most car-rental kiosks. Prepayment isn't required, but a printed confirmation will be faxed or mailed to anyone who reserves a car in advance. A week's rental of a Rover Mini or Fiat 1.0 costs £75.90 ($129.05) with unlimited mileage and tax; optional collision insurance is around £10.99 ($18.70) per day. Pickup for cars can be arranged at any of the major U.K. airports. Be warned, however, that pickups at certain off-the-beaten-path places might require a phone call on your arrival before an I.T.S. representative arrives. If you're flexible, you might save enough money on the rental to make the inconvenience worthwhile.

In some cases, slight discounts are offered to members of the American Automobile Association (AAA) or the American Association of Retired Persons (AARP). Be sure to ask.

Each company offers a **collision-damage waiver (CDW)** at $15 to $25 per day (depending on the car's value). This extra protection will cover all or part of the repair-related costs if you have an accident. (In some cases, even if you buy the CDW, you'll pay $200 to $300 per accident. Ask questions before you sign.) Check your existing auto insurance and what's available through your credit cards first. (Note that credit cards may cover collision but will usually not cover liability.)

**GASOLINE**   There are plenty of gas ("petrol") stations in the environs of Glasgow and Edinburgh. However, in remote areas they're often few and far between, and many are closed on Sunday. If you're planning a lot of Sunday driving in remote parts, always make sure your tank is full on Saturday.

Note that gasoline costs more in Britain than in North America, and to encourage energy saving the government has imposed a new 25% tax on gas. The price of a liter of gas (about ¼ gallon) is typically 64p ($1.10), including taxes.

**DRIVING RULES & REQUIREMENTS**   In Scotland, you drive on the left and pass on the right. Road signs are clear and the international symbols unmistakable. To drive a car in Scotland, U.S. visitors need a passport and driver's license (no special British license is needed).

*A word of warning:* Pedestrian crossings are marked by striped lines (zebra striping) on the road and flashing orange curbside lights. Drivers must stop and yield the right of way if a pedestrian has stepped into the zebra zone to cross the street. Wearing seat belts is mandatory in the British Isles.

**ROAD MAPS**   The best road map, especially if you're trying to locate some obscure village, is *The Ordnance Survey Motor Atlas of Great Britain,* revised annually and published by Temple Press. It's available at most bookstores in Scotland. If you're in London and plan to head north to Scotland, go to W. & G. Foyle Ltd., 113 and 119 Charing Cross Rd., London WC2 HOEB (☎ 020/7440-3225).

Other excellent maps include the *AAA Road Map of Scotland,* the *Collins Touring Map of Scotland,* and the new *Frommer's Road Atlas: Great Britain.* Before you leave home, you can buy maps at BritRail's **British Travel Shop,** 551 Fifth Ave., 7th Floor, New York, NY 10176 (☎ 212/490-6688; fax 212/490-0219).

**BREAKDOWNS**   Membership in one of the two major auto clubs can be helpful: the **Automobile Association (AA)** at Norfolk House, Priestly Road, Basingstoke, Hampshire RG24 9NY (☎ 0990/500-600), or the **Royal Automobile Club (RAC),** P.O. Box 700, Bristol, Somerset BS99 1RB (☎ 0800/029-029). You can join these clubs through your car-rental agent (members of AAA in the U.S. can enjoy reciprocity overseas). There are roadside emergency telephone boxes about every mile along the motorways. If you don't see one, walk down the road for a bit to the blue-and-white marker with an arrow that points to the nearest box. The 24-hour number to call for the AA is ☎ 0800/887-766; for the RAC, it's ☎ 0800/828-282. In addition, you can call a police traffic unit that will contact either of the auto clubs on your behalf.

## BY FERRY

You can use a variety of special excursion fares to reach Scotland's islands. For the Clyde and Western Isles, contact **Caledonian MacBrayne** (☎ **01475/650-100** or 01475/650-288 for brochures); for the Orkneys and Shetlands, contact **P&O Scottish Ferries** (☎ **01224/57-2615**).

Caledonian MacBrayne, operating 30 ferries in all, sails to 23 Hebridean and all Clyde islands. The fares, times of departure, and even accommodation suggestions are in a special book, *Ferry Guide to 23 Scottish Islands.* There are reasonably priced fares for vehicles and passengers through a "Go As You Please" plan, a kind of island hopscotch program offering a choice of 24 pre-planned routes at a discount off the cost of individual tickets. Tickets are valid for 1 month and can be used in either direction for one trip on each leg of the tour. You choose your own route and can skip from island to island at your own pace. Cyclists can take their bikes aboard free on some routes.

## Fast Facts: Scotland

**American Express**   There's an office at 139 Princes St. in Edinburgh (☎ **0131/718-2506**); hours are Monday to Friday 9am to 5:30pm, and Saturday 9am to 4pm. Another office is at 115 Hope St. in Glasgow (☎ **0141/221-4366**); it's open Monday to Friday 8:30am to 5:30pm, Saturday 9am to noon (9am to 4pm in June and July).

**Auto Clubs**   Call the **Automobile Association** (☎ **800/AAA-HELP**) or the **Royal Automobile Club** (☎ **0141/248-4444**) for details.

**Business Hours**   Most banks are open Monday to Thursday 9:30am to 12:30pm and 1:30 to 3:30pm; Friday hours are often 9:30am to 1:30pm. Basic **bar and pub hours** are Monday to Saturday 11am to 11pm, but this can vary widely; Sunday hours are usually 12:30 to 2:30pm and 6:30 to 11pm, but some pubs are closed Sunday. **Office hours** are Monday to Friday 9am to 5pm; the lunch break lasts an hour, but most places stay open all day. **Post offices** and sub-post offices are centrally situated and open Monday to Friday 9am to 5pm and Saturday 9am to noon. **Stores** are generally open Monday to Saturday 9am to 5:30 or 6pm. Most stores close early on Tuesday or Wednesday afternoon.

**Drug Laws**   Great Britain is becoming increasingly severe in enforcing drug laws. People arrested for possession of even tiny quantities of marijuana have been deported, forced to pay stiff fines, or sentenced to jail for 2 to 7 years. Possession of "white powder" drugs like heroin and cocaine carries even more stringent penalties.

**Drugstores**   In Great Britain they're called "chemist" shops. Every police station in the country has a list of emergency chemists; dial "0" (zero) and ask the operator for the local police. Emergency drugs are normally available at most hospitals, but you'll be examined to see if the drugs you request are really necessary.

**Electricity**   The electricity is 240 volts AC (50Hz). Some international hotels are specially wired to allow North Americans to plug in their appliances, but you usually need a transformer plus an adapter for your electric razor or hair dryer. Ask at the electrical department of a large hardware store for the transformer size you need.

**Embassies & Consulates**   All embassies are in London. There's a **U.S. Consulate** in Edinburgh at 3 Regent Terrace (☎ **0131/556-8315**), open Monday to Friday 1 to 4pm. All other nationals have to use London to conduct their business: The **Canadian High Commission** is at MacDonald House, 1 Grosvenor Sq., W1 (☎ 020/7258-6600), open Monday to Friday 8am to 4pm. The **Australian High Commission** is at the Strand, London WC2B 4LI (☎ 020/7379-4334), open Monday to Friday 9:30am to 3:30pm. The **New Zealand High Commission** is at New Zealand House, 80 Haymarket at Pall Mall, London SW1Y 4TQ (☎ 020/7930-8422), open Monday to Friday 9am to 5pm. The **Irish Embassy** is at 17 Grosvenor Place, London SW1X 7HR (☎ 020/7235-2171), open Monday to Friday 9:30am to 1pm and 2:15 to 5pm.

**Emergencies**  For police, fire, or ambulance, dial ☎ **999.** Give your name, address, phone number, and the nature of the emergency. Misuse of the 999 service will result in a heavy fine (cardiac arrest, yes; dented fender, no).

**Legal Aid**  Your consulate, embassy, or high commission (see above) will give you advice if you run into trouble. They can advise you of your rights and even provide a list of attorneys (for which you'll have to pay if services are used), but they can't interfere on your behalf in the legal processes of Great Britain. For questions about American citizens arrested abroad, including ways of getting money to them, telephone the **Citizens Emergency Center of the Office of Special Consulate Services** in Washington, D.C. (☎ 202/647-5225). Other nationals can go to their nearest consulate or embassy.

**Liquor Laws**  The legal drinking age is 18. Children under 16 aren't allowed in pubs, except in certain rooms, and then only when accompanied by a parent or guardian. Don't drink and drive; the penalties are stiff. Basically, you can get a drink from 11:30am to 11pm, but this can vary widely, depending on the discretion of the local tavern owner. Not all pubs are open on Sunday; those that are generally stay open noon to 3pm and 7 to 10:30 or 11pm. Restaurants are also allowed to serve liquor during these hours, but only to people who are dining on the premises. The law allows 30 minutes for "drinking-up time." A meal, incidentally, is defined as "substantial refreshment." And you have to eat and drink sitting down. In hotels, liquor may be served 11am to 11pm to both guests and nonguests; after 11pm, according to the law, only guests may be served.

**Mail**  Sending an airmail letter to North America costs 44p (75¢) and postcards require a 38p (65¢) stamp. British mailboxes are painted red and carry a royal coat-of-arms as a signature. A letter generally takes about 7 to 10 days to arrive in North America.

**Newspapers & Magazines**  Each major Scottish city publishes its own newspaper. All newsagents (newsstands) carry the major London papers as well. In summer, you can generally pick up a copy of the *International Herald Tribune,* published in Paris, along with the European editions of *USA Today, Time,* and *Newsweek* to bring you up to date on world affairs.

**Pets**  Great Britain has finally eased a 100-year-old mandatory pet quarantine, but rigid requirements are still in place. Now pets need no longer fear a long separation from their Britain-bound families if they pass several tests and can wait long enough. The animal must also be coming from a country that is approved by Britain. All countries in the European

# Getting Your VAT Refund

You can get a VAT refund if you shop at stores that participate in the Retail Export Scheme (signs are posted in the window). When you make a purchase, show your passport and request a Retail Export Scheme form (VAT 407) and a stamped, pre-addressed envelope. Show the VAT form and your sales receipt to British Customs when you leave the country—they may also ask to see the merchandise. After Customs has stamped it, mail the form back to the shop in the envelope provided *before you leave the country.* Your VAT refund will be mailed to you.

Remember: Keep your VAT forms with your passport; pack your purchases in a carry-on bag so you'll have them handy; and allow yourself enough time at your departure point to find a mailbox.

Several readers have reported a VAT refund scam. You must get the refund forms from the retailer on the spot (don't leave the store without one). Some merchants allegedly tell customers they can get a refund form at the airport on their way out of the country. *This isn't true.* The form must be completed by the retailer on the spot or you won't get a refund later.

Union such as Germany, Switzerland, Austria, Spain, Italy, and France are participants in the PETS program, but the United States is not. For information about PETS requirements, check out the Web site at www. maff.gov.uk/animalh/quarantine/index.htm.

**Police**    The best source of help and advice in emergencies is the police (for non–life-threatening situations, dial **"0"** zero and ask for the police, or ☎ **999** for emergencies). If the local police can't assist, they'll have the address of a person who can. Losses, thefts, and other crimes should be reported immediately to the police.

**Rest Rooms**    Public toilets are clean, often have an attendant, and may be used with confidence. Hotels can be used, but they discourage nonguests. Garages (filling stations) don't always have facilities for the use of customers. There's no need to tip, except to a hotel attendant.

**Safety**    Although crime isn't a serious problem for the average visitor, many areas in and around Glasgow are dangerous, with dozens of muggings reported weekly. Caution should always be taken. Never leave your car unlocked and always protect your valuables.

**Taxes**    There's no local sales tax. However, Great Britain imposes a standard **value-added tax (VAT)** of 17.5%. Hotel rates and meals in restaurants are taxed 17.5%; the extra VAT charge will show up on your bill unless otherwise stated. This can be refunded if you shop at stores that participate in the Retail Export Scheme (signs are posted in the window); see the box above.

The departure tax for leaving Britain is £20 ($34) for passengers flying worldwide, including the United States, and £10 ($17) for flights within Britain and the European Union. This tax is accounted for in your ticket.

As part of an energy-saving scheme, the British government has also added a special 25% tax on gasoline ("petrol").

To call Scotland from the United States, dial the **international prefix, 011;** then Scotland's **country code, 44;** then the **city code** (for example, **131** for Edinburgh and **141** for Glasgow—minus the initial zero, which is used only if you're dialing from within the U.K.); then dial the actual **phone number.**

**Telephone & Fax**   Consult "Directory Enquiries" ("Information") to aid you; dial ☎ **153,** give the operator the town where you want the number, the subscriber's name, and then the address.

If you're calling from a **pay phone,** the machine will accept all British coins except 1p. A local call costs 10p (15¢). Phone books contain detailed instructions about how to make a call in the British Isles. You can also dial the operator for assistance. There are special phone booths used only by phonecard holders.

**To call from one U.K. city to another:** Dial the entire city code, including the initial 0 and the 1 that's now an integral part of each British city code. Then dial the local phone number. To **dial direct internationally,** dial 00, then the country code (the United States and Canada 1, Ireland 353, Australia 61, New Zealand 64), the area code, and then the local phone number.

Unless you activate one of the direct-access codes below, try to make international calls from a public pay phone, preferably with a phonecard (see below), since hotels almost invariably charge high markups on international calls. Calls dialed directly from any public phone are usually billed on the basis of the call's duration, not on any supplemental add-on charges. A reduced rate applies to domestic long-distance and international calls placed between 11pm and 8am Monday to Saturday and all day Sunday. Know in advance that direct-dial calls from the United States to anywhere in the United Kingdom are usually much cheaper than equivalent calls placed from Britain to North America; in many cases, it's worthwhile to place a short call to your designated party and then give them a phone number where they can call you back.

If you don't know the phone number of the party you want to call, you can dial **National Directory Enquiries** at ☎ **192;** the call is free. You can access **International Directory Enquiries** at ☎ **192,** but that costs you 25p (45¢) a shot.

Several years ago, British Telecom introduced a series of **phonecards,** available in denominations of £5 ($8.50), £10 ($17), £20 ($34), and £50 ($85). They're sold at thousands of outlets around Britain, including newspaper kiosks, tobacco shops, and cafes. Depending on the phone where you place your call, you either insert your phonecard directly into the phone box or key in the numbers that appear on the face of the card. Phonecards are sold with a one-of-a-kind PIN that's concealed with a painted strip you scratch off after its purchase.

Many travelers find the most convenient way to place international calls is making **collect or calling-card calls** directly from their hotel room or from any public phone in Britain. To do this, if the phone requires it, drop 20p (35¢) into the coin slot. (Don't worry, the call is free, and you'll get your coins refunded before you complete the call.) Then dial the direct access code of any of the U.S.-based long-distance carriers below and you'll be connected to an English-speaking operator who can assist you with the call, regardless of the country you're trying to reach. The following calling-card numbers work all over Britain: To access **AT&T,** dial ☎ **0800/890-0011;** to access **World Phone,** dial ☎ **0800/890-222;** and to access **Sprint,** dial ☎ **0800/890-877.**

To place **collect calls** from Britain to a country beside the United States or Canada, dial ☎ **155,** then tell the operator you intend to make a collect call.

**Time**  Britain is based on Greenwich mean time (GMT), 5 hours ahead of the U.S. East Coast, with British summer time (BST, or GMT plus 1 hour) used roughly from April to October. When it's noon in Edinburgh or Glasgow, it's 7am in New York, 6am in Chicago, 5am in Denver, and 4am in Los Angeles.

**Tipping**  For **cab drivers,** add about 10% to 15% to the fare as shown on the meter. However, if the driver personally unloads or loads your luggage, add 25p (45¢) per bag.

Hotel **porters** get 75p ($1.30) per bag even if you have only one small suitcase. Hall porters are tipped only for special services. **Maids** receive £1 ($1.70) per day. In top-ranking hotels, the **concierge** often submits a separate bill, showing charges for newspapers and the like; if he or she has been particularly helpful, tip extra.

Hotels often add a **service charge** of 10% to 15% to bills. In smaller B&Bs, the tip isn't likely to be included. Therefore, tip for special services, such as the waiter who serves you breakfast. If several people have served you in a B&B, a 10 to 15% will be added to the bill and divided among the staff.

In both **restaurants** and **nightclubs,** a 15% service charge is added to the bill. To that, add another 3 to 5%, depending on the quality of the service. **Waiters** in deluxe restaurants and nightclubs are accustomed to the extra 5%, which means you'll end up tipping 20%. If that seems excessive, you must remember the initial service charge reflected in the fixed price is distributed among all the help. **Sommeliers** (wine stewards) get about £1 ($1.70) per bottle of wine served. Tipping in **pubs** is not common, although in cocktail bars the waiter or barmaid usually gets about £1 ($1.70) per round of drinks.

**Barbers** and **hairdressers** expect 10 to 15%. **Tour guides** expect £2 ($3.40), but it's not mandatory. **Petrol station attendants** are rarely tipped. **Theater ushers** also don't expect tips.

**Water**  Tap water is considered safe to drink throughout Scotland.

# Planning Your Trip:
# An Online Directory

**F**rommer's Online Directory will help you take better advantage of the travel-planning information available online. Part 1 lists general Internet resources that can make any trip easier, such as sites for obtaining the best possible prices on airline tickets. In Part 2, you'll find some top sites specifically for Scotland.

This is not a comprehensive list, but a discriminating selection to get you started. Recognition is given to sites based on their content value and ease of use. Inclusion here is not paid for—unlike some Web-site rankings, which are based on payment. Finally, remember this is a press-time snapshot of leading Web sites; some undoubtedly will have evolved, changed, or moved by the time you read this.

## 1 The Top Travel-Planning Web Sites

*By Lynne Bairstow*

Lynne Bairstow is the co-author of *Frommer's Mexico,* and the editorial director of *e-com* magazine.

### WHY BOOK ONLINE?

Online agencies have come a long way over the past few years, now providing tips for finding the best fare, and giving you suggested dates or times to travel that yield the lowest price if your plans are at all flexible. Other sites even allow you to establish the price you're willing to pay, and they check the airlines' willingness to accept it. However, in some cases, these sites may not always yield the best price. Unlike a travel agent, for example, they may not have access to charter flights offered by wholesalers.

Online booking sites aren't the only places to reserve airline tickets—all major airlines have their own Web sites and often offer incentives (bonus frequent flyer miles or Net-only discounts, for example) when you buy online or buy an e-ticket.

The new trend is toward conglomerated booking sites. By June 2001, a consortium of U.S.- and European-based airlines will launch a site called **Orbitz.com** that will offer fares lower than those available through travel agents. United, Delta, Northwest, American, and Continental have initiated this effort, based on their success at selling airline seats on their own sites.

The best of the travel planning sites are now highly personalized; they store your seating preferences, meal preferences, tentative

# Check Out Frommer's Site

We highly recommend **Arthur Frommer's Budget Travel Online** (**www.frommers.com**) as an excellent travel-planning resource. Of course, we're a little biased, but you'll find indispensable travel tips, reviews, monthly vacation giveaways, and online booking. Among the most popular features of this site are the regular "Ask the Expert" bulletin boards, which feature Frommer's authors answering your questions via online postings.

Subscribe to Arthur Frommer's Daily Newsletter (**www.frommers. com/newsletters**) to receive the latest travel bargains and inside travel secrets in your e-mailbox every day. You'll read daily headlines and articles from the dean of travel himself, highlighting last-minute deals on airfares, accommodations, cruises, and package vacations.

Search our Destinations archive (**www.frommers.com/destinations**) of more than 200 domestic and international destinations for great places to stay and dine and tips on sightseeing. Once you've researched your trip, the online reservation system (**www.frommers.com/booktravelnow**) takes you to Frommer's favorite sites for booking your vacation at affordable prices.

itineraries, and credit-card information, allowing you to quickly plan trips or check agendas.

In many cases, booking your trip online can be better than working with a travel agent. It gives you the widest variety of choices, control, and the 24-hour convenience of planning your trip when you choose. All you need is some time—and often a little patience—and you're likely to find the fun of online travel research will greatly enhance your trip.

## WHO SHOULD BOOK ONLINE?

Online booking is best for travelers who want to know as much as possible about their travel options, for those who have flexibility in their travel dates, and for bargain hunters.

One of the biggest successes in online travel for both passengers and airlines is the offer of last-minute specials, such as American Airlines' weekend deals or other Internet-only fares that must be purchased online. Another advantage is that you can cash in on incentives for booking online, such as rebates or bonus frequent-flyer miles.

Business and other frequent travelers also have found numerous benefits in online booking, as the advances in mobile technology provide them with the ability to check flight status, change plans, or get specific directions from handheld computing devices, mobile phones, and pagers. Some sites will even e-mail or page a passenger if their flight is delayed.

Online booking is increasingly able to accommodate complex itineraries, even for international travel. The pace of evolution on the Net is rapid, so you'll probably find additional features and advancements by the time you visit these sites. The future holds ever-increasing personalization and customization for online travelers.

## TRAVEL-PLANNING & BOOKING SITES

Below are listings for sites for planning and booking travel. The following sites offer domestic and international flight, hotel, and rental-car bookings, plus news, destination information, and deals on cruises and vacation packages. Free (one-time) registration is required for booking.

### Travelocity (incorporates Preview Travel). www.travelocity.com; www.previewtravel.com; www.frommers.travelocity.com

Travelocity is Frommer's online travel-planning and booking partner. Travelocity uses the SABRE system to offer reservations and tickets for more than 400 airlines, plus reservations and purchase capabilities for more than 45,000 hotels and 50 car-rental companies. An exclusive feature of the SABRE system is its **Low Fare Search Engine,** which automatically searches for the three lowest-priced itineraries based on a traveler's criteria. Last-minute deals and consolidator fares are included in the search. If you book with Travelocity, you can select specific seats for your flights with online seat maps, and also view diagrams of the most popular commercial aircraft. Its hotel finder provides street-level location maps and photos of selected hotels. With the **Fare Watcher** e-mail feature, you can select up to five routes and receive e-mail notices when the fare changes by $25 or more.

Travelocity's **Destination Guide** includes updated information on some 260 destinations worldwide—supplied by Frommer's.

*Note to AOL Users:* You can book flights, hotels, rental cars, and cruises on AOL at keyword: Travel. The booking software is provided by Travelocity/ Preview Travel and is similar to the Internet site. Use the AOL "Travelers Advantage" program to earn a 5% rebate on flights, hotel rooms, and car rentals.

### Expedia. http://expedia.com

Expedia is Travelocity's major competitor. It offers several ways of obtaining the best possible fares: **Flight Price Matcher** service allows your preferred airline to match an available fare with a competitor; a comprehensive **Fare Compare** area shows the differences in fare categories and airlines; and **Fare Calendar** helps you plan your trip around the best possible fares. Its main limitation is that like many online databases, Expedia focuses on the major airlines and hotel chains, so don't expect to find too many budget airlines or one-of-a-kind B&Bs here.

### TRIP.com. www.trip.com

TRIP.com began as a site geared toward business travelers, but its innovative features and highly personalized approach have broadened its appeal to leisure travelers as well. It is the leading travel site for those using mobile devices to access Internet travel information.

TRIP.com includes a trip-planning function that provides the average and lowest fare for the route requested, in addition to the current available fare. An on-site "newsstand" features breaking news on airfare sales and other travel

## Staying Secure

More people still look online than book online, partly due to fear of putting their credit-card numbers out on the Net. Secure encryption, and increasing experienced buying online, has removed this fear for most travelers. In some cases, however, it's simply easier to buy from a local travel agent who can deliver your tickets to your door (especially if your travel is last-minute or if you have special requests). You can find a flight online and then book it by calling a toll-free number or contacting your travel agent, although this is somewhat less efficient. To be sure you're in secure mode when you book online, look for a padlock (in Netscape and Internet Explorer) at the bottom of your Web browser.

specials. Among its most popular features are Flight TRACKER and intelliTRIP. **Flight TRACKER** allows users to track any commercial flight en route to its destination anywhere in the United States, while accessing real-time FAA-based flight monitoring data. **intelliTRIP** is a travel search tool that allows users to identify the best airline, hotel, and rental-car rates in less than 90 seconds.

In addition, the site offers e-mail notification of flight delays, plus city resource guides, currency converters, and a weekly e-mail newsletter of fare updates, travel tips, and traveler forums.

**Yahoo! Travel. www.travel.yahoo.com**
Yahoo! is currently the most popular of the Internet information portals, and its travel site is a comprehensive mix of online booking, daily travel news, and destination information. The **Best Fares** area offers what it promises, plus provides feedback on refining your search if you have flexibility in travel dates or times. There is also an active section of Message Boards for discussions on travel in general and specific destinations.

## LAST-MINUTE DEALS & OTHER ONLINE BARGAINS

There's nothing airlines hate more than flying with lots of empty seats. The Net has enabled airlines to offer last-minute bargains to entice travelers to fill those seats. Most of these are announced on Tuesday or Wednesday and are valid for travel the following weekend, but some can be booked weeks or months in advance. You can sign up for weekly e-mail alerts at the airlines' own sites or check sites that compile lists of these bargains, such as **Smarter Living** or **WebFlyer** (see below). To make it easier, visit a site that will round up all the deals and send them in one convenient weekly e-mail.

*Important Note:* See "Getting There" in chapter 2, "Planning Your Trip: The Basics," for the Web addresses of airlines serving Scotland. These sites offer schedules and flight booking, and most have pages where you can sign up for e-mail alerts for weekend deals and other late-breaking bargains.

✪ **1travel.com. www.1travel.com**
Here you'll find deals on domestic and international flights and hotels. 1travel.com's **Saving Alert** compiles last-minute air deals so you don't have to scroll through multiple email alerts. A feature called "Drive a little using low-fare airlines" helps map out strategies for using alternative airports to find lower fares. And **Farebeater** searches a database that includes published fares, consolidator bargains, and special deals exclusive to 1travel.com. *Note:* The travel agencies listed by 1travel.com have paid for placement.

**Bid for Travel. www.bidfortravel.com**
Bid for Travel is another of the travel auction sites, similar to Priceline (see below), which are growing in popularity. In addition to airfares, Internet users can place a bid for vacation packages and hotels.

**Cheap Tickets. www.cheaptickets.com**
Cheap Tickets has exclusive deals that aren't available through more mainstream channels. One caveat about the Cheap Tickets site is that it will offer fare quotes for a route, and later show this fare is not valid for your dates of travel—most other Web sites, such as Expedia, consider your dates of travel before showing what fares are available. Despite its problems, Cheap Tickets can be worth the effort because its fares can be lower than those offered by its competitors.

**LastMinuteTravel.com. www.lastminutetravel.com**
Suppliers with excess inventory come to this online agency to distribute unsold airline seats, hotel rooms, cruises, and vacation packages. It's got great deals, but an excess of advertisements and slow-loading graphics.

# Check Your E-Mail
# While You're on the Road

You don't have to be out of touch just because you don't carry a laptop while you travel. Web browser–based free e-mail programs make it much easier to stay in e-touch.

Just open a freemail account at a browser-based provider, such as **MSN Hotmail (hotmail.com)** or **Yahoo! Mail (mail.yahoo.com)**. AOL users should check out **AOL Netmail**, and **USA.NET (www.usa. net)** comes highly recommended for functionality and security. You can find hints, tips, and a mile-long list of freemail providers at **www. emailaddresses.com**.

Be sure to give your freemail address to the family members, friends, and colleagues with whom you'd like to stay in touch while you're in Scotland. All you'll need to check your freemail account while you're away from home is a Web connection, easily available at Internet cafes, copy shops, and cash- and credit-card Internet-access machines (often available in hotel lobbies or business centers). After logging on, just point the browser to **www.hotmail.com**, **www.yahoo.com**, or the address of any other service you're using. Enter your user name and password, and you'll have access to your mail, both for receiving and sending messages to friends and family back home, for just a few dollars an hour.

The Net Café Guide (**www.netcafeguide.com/mapindex.htm**) will help you locate Internet cafe s at hundreds of locations around the globe. Cybercafes come and go, and are becoming more widespread, so you're likely to find them in more and more towns across Scotland by the time you visit. In Edinburgh, head to the **Cyberia Edinburgh,** 88 Hanover St. (☎ **0131/220-4405;** Bus: 23, 41; e-mail: edinburgh@cybersurf. co.uk). In Glasgow, try the **Internet Café,** 569 Sauchiehall St. (☎ **0141/ 564-1052;** Underground: Buchanan St.; Bus: 57).

**Moment's Notice. www.moments-notice.com**
As the name suggests, Moment's Notice specializes in last-minute vacation deals. You can browse for free, but if you want to purchase a trip you have to join Moment's Notice, which costs $25.

☢ **Priceline.com. http://travel.priceline.com**
Priceline lets you "name your price" for domestic and international airline tickets and hotel rooms. You select a route and dates, guarantee with a credit card, and make a bid for what you're willing to pay. If one of the airlines in Priceline's database has a fare lower than your bid, your credit card will automatically be charged for a ticket.

But you can't say when you want to fly—you have to accept any flight leaving between 6am and 10pm on the dates you selected, and you may have to make a stopover. No frequent-flyer miles are awarded, and tickets are nonrefundable and can't be exchanged for another flight. So if your plans change, you're out of luck. Priceline can be good for travelers who have to take off on short notice (and who are thus unable to qualify for advance purchase discounts). But be sure to shop around first, because if you overbid, you'll be required to purchase the ticket—and Priceline will pocket the difference between what it paid for the ticket and what you bid.

Priceline says that over 35% of all reasonable offers for domestic flights are being filled on the first try, with much higher fill rates on popular routes (New York to San Francisco, for example). They define "reasonable" as not more than 30% below the lowest generally available advance-purchase fare for the same route.

**SkyAuction.com. www.skyauction.com**
An auction site with categories for airfare, travel deals, hotels, and much more.

**Smarter Living. www.smarterliving.com**
Best known for its e-mail dispatch of weekend deals on 20 airlines, Smarter Living also keeps you posted about last-minute bargains.

**Travelzoo.com. www.travelzoo.com**
At this Internet portal, more than 150 travel companies post special deals. It features a Top 20 list of the best deals on the site, selected by its editorial staff each Wednesday night. This list is also available via an e-mailing list, free to those who sign up.

**WebFlyer. www.webflyer.com**
WebFlyer is a comprehensive online resource for frequent flyers and also has an excellent listing of last-minute air deals. Click on "Deal Watch" for a round-up of weekend deals on flights, hotels, and rental cars from domestic and international suppliers.

## ONLINE TRAVELER'S TOOLBOX

**Exchange Rates. www.x-rates.com**
See what your dollar is worth in pounds.

**U.S. Customs Service Traveler Information. www.customs.ustreas.gov/travel/index.htm**

**HM Customs & Excise Passenger Enquiries. www.open.gov.uk**

**Canada Customs and Revenue Agency. www.ccra-adrc.gc.ca**

**Australian Customs. www.dfat.gov.au**

**New Zealand Customs Service. www.customs.govt.nz**
Planning a shopping spree and wondering what you're allowed to bring home? Check the latest regulations at these thorough sites.

**Visa ATM Locator. www.visa.com/pd/atm/**
**MasterCard ATM Locator. www.mastercard.com/atm**
Find ATMs in hundreds of cities around the world. Both include maps for some locations and both list airport ATM locations, some with maps.

**The Weather Channel. www.weather.com**
Weather forecasts for cities around the world.

## 2 The Top Web Sites for Scotland

*Updated by Matthew Garcia*

Also check the Web sites listed for the individual hotel and attractions listings throughout this book.

## GENERAL SCOTLAND SITES

**About.com: UK for Visitors. www.gouk.about.com**
Click on "UK by County" and then on "Scotland" to find lots of links for the country's cities, large and small. Categories include sightseeing, lodging, dining, and pubs.

Online Directory

**Activity Holidays in Scotland. www.active-scotland.co.uk**
If you're looking for some adventure, use this site to learn more about your options (horseback riding, whitewater rafting, and so on) and to find outfitters. Search by region or activity and don't overlook the Travel Tips section.

**Automobile Association–UK. www.theaa.co.uk**
This outstanding guide includes extensive listings and ratings of hotels, bed-and-breakfasts, restaurants, inns and pubs. The hundreds of lodgings, many of which accept online bookings, are ranked by price and quality. You'll also find restaurant reviews and menus.

**Electric Scotland. www.electricscotland.com**
Interested in Scottish history or looking to trace your family name? Electric Scotland includes a history archive of clans and families, with information on crests and tartans. You'll also find regional tourism information—complete with maps—and suggested itineraries for driving through these areas.

**Internet Guide to Scotland. www.scotland-inverness.co.uk/scotland.htm**
This lengthy personal guide compiled by Scotland enthusiast Joanne Mackenzie-Winters includes links to tours, lodging, regional information, and trip reports, as well as the author's observations of this enchanted land.

**National Museums of Scotland. www.nms.ac.uk**
This site includes guides to the Royal Museum, Museum of Flight, Museum of Costume, Museum of Scotland, Museum of Scottish Country Life, and the National War Museum. Each site within a site includes details on current exhibits, events, and advice.

**Scotland Holiday Net. www.aboutscotland.com**
This is a fine place to learn more about lodging, shops, and activities, but be advised that the listings come from the companies themselves—if you see a rave for a golf course or B&B, consider the source. Beyond these listings, Scotland Holiday Net is a terrific resource for learning about castles and tours.

**Scotland Lodgings. www.milford.co.uk/scotland**
This region-by-region guide to lodgings includes everything from standard hotels to quaint inns. Bargains for the slow season are listed as well as some general travel information.

**Scotland Online. www.scotland.net**
This site offers news briefs plus shopping and entertainment information updated daily.

**Scotland Photos. www.scotlandphotos.com**
Enjoy these views of Scotland. From the home page, you can either use the site's search engine or click on any attraction to get thumbnail photos that load quickly. Then click on the photo you like to see the enlarged image.

**Scottish Radiance. www.scottishradiance.com**
This monthly magazine includes features on tall ships and Scottish lighthouses, and a clan map of Scotland. Scroll down to the archives for more. The design is basic, but the stories make this site worth visiting.

**Scottish Tourist Board. www.holiday.scotland.net**
This extensive site offers all the basics, including info on transportation, lodging (searchable by locale, cost, and other criteria), sightseeing, and outdoor activities. You'll also find a listing of upcoming events.

# Tourism Boards Around Scotland

A good way to complement the information in this book is to turn to the Web sites of regional tourism bureaus. These sites include images of attractions, dining and lodging suggestions, and (in some cases) updated events calendars. Below are some of the most important regional tourism bureau sites for Scotland.

- Aberdeen and Grampian Tourist Board: **www.agtb.org**
- Angus and Dundee Tourist Board: **www.angusanddundee.co.uk**
- Argyll and the Southern Hebrides, Loch Lomond, Stirling, and the Trossachs: **www.scottish.heartlands.org**
- Ayrshire and Arran Tourist Bureau: **www.ayrshire-arran.com**
- Dumfries and Galloway Tourist Board: **www.galloway.co.uk**
- Highlands of Scotland Tourist Board: **www.host.co.uk**
- Perth and Perthshire: **www.perth.org.uk**

○ **Travel Scotland. www.travelscotland.co.uk**
Produced in association with the Scottish Tourist Board, this lively site includes restaurant reviews, feature stories (like a piece on visiting a bagpipe maker), sightseeing advice, and upcoming events.

## EDINBURGH SITES

### Edinburgh Dining Guide. www.spidacom.co.uk/edg
Choose by name, cuisine, or price to find restaurants that meet your criteria. The links lead to the restaurants' own sites, where you can see menus, wine lists, and photos.

### ○ Edinburgh Gallery Guide. www.edinburgh-galleries.co.uk
Sample the art at more than two dozen local galleries to help decide which you'd like to visit. Each gallery page includes what's showing, gallery hours, and address and contact information. Also listed are current exhibits at museums.

### Edinburgh and Lothians Tourist Board. www.edinburgh.org
Use this site to find events and festivals, restaurants, tours, lodging, attractions, and even travel tips for transportation to the city.

### Edinburgh Pub Tour. www.electrum.co.uk/pubs
This quirky site is a bit hard to navigate, but if you're into the pub scene, you may find it worthwhile. After clicking on "Start," click on one of the three people in the first image you see: The woman at the left leads you on a tour of pub architecture, the gent in the middle offers a tour of historic pubs, and the guy on the right (who says "Click me and let's party") provides a tour of student hangouts.

### E Info. www.einfo.co.uk
This is a wide-ranging guide to life in Edinburgh for the resident or visitor. Included are listings for businesses, government offices, charities, educational institutions, as well as more tourist-oriented sections on lodgings, restaurants, and pubs.

### Inside Out Edinburgh. www.insideout.co.uk/ed/index2.htm
This directory-style guide has an in-depth section on arts and entertainment plus links to the Web pages of local theaters, galleries, and clubs. It's a good site to check to see what festivals, performances, and shows will be on while you're in Edinburgh.

**Royal Lyceum Theater Company. www.infoser.com/infotheatre/lyceum**
See what performances are coming up at this Edinburgh-based theater company.
Take a virtual tour of the theater and see if any discounts are available through
the Web site. You can even enter an online contest and try to win free tickets
for an upcoming show.

**Time Out Edinburgh. www.timeout.co.uk**
*Time Out*'s Web site lists the latest in everything from sightseeing to night-
clubbing in the Scottish capital.

**Welcome to Edinburgh's Old Town. www.edinburgholdtown.org.uk**
This nicely done tour includes the sights, shops, pubs, cafes, and inns of
Old Town.

**What's on Stage: Edinburgh. www.whatsonstage.com/wos/edinburgh**
Find out what's on in Edinburgh—the listings go beyond theater and include
the annual Edinburgh Festival and other cultural events.

## GLASGOW SITES

**Burrell Collection. www.clyde-valley.com/glasgow/burrell.htm**
This compact site includes basic visitor info, images, and descriptions of the
collection and grounds.

**Daily Record and Sunday Mail. www.record-mail.co.uk/rm**
If you'd like to find out what's going on in Glasgow before you arrive, have a
look at the online edition of this leading newspaper for the latest news, sports,
film, theater, and club reviews.

**Glasgow Life. www.glasgowlife.com**
The nice guide offers recommendations for local dining and entertainment, as
well as exhibits. You'll also find maps, as well as a guest book with suggestions
from other travelers.

**Hunterian Museum and Art Gallery. www.hunterian.gla.ac.uk**
Featuring the work of James McNeill Whistler and Charles Rennie Mackintosh,
the Hunterian is well represented by this extensive Web site. Various sections
of the site cover everything from anatomy to zoology, with the Coin Cabinet
in between. Click on "News" to learn about the latest developments at the
museum.

**Time Out Glasgow. www.timeout.co.uk**
*Time Out*'s Web site lists the latest is everything from sightseeing to night-
clubbing in Scotland's hottest city.

## OTHER SITES OF INTEREST

**Scottish Golf. www.scottishgolf.com**
This site is all about golf in Scotland, with special attention to amateur and
professional competition. It also includes a searchable guide to links around
the country.

**Scottish Golf for All. www.scots4all.com**
Once you get used to this slightly cumbersome site, you'll be able to plan a
golfing holiday at some of the renowned Scottish courses by booking everything from tee times to accommodations.

**Scottish Tartans. www.tartans.scotland.net**
Plaid is always the fashion in Scotland. This site provides a detailed tour
through the world of Highland tartans and explains their clan use and
heraldic purposes.

**Welcome to Burns Country. www.robertburns.org**
The "Songs and Poem Archive" includes more than 500 of Burns's works and access to the authoritative *Burns Encyclopedia*. The site also includes links to newsletters and federations related to the prolific 18th-century poet. And if you think you might be related to him, check the Burns Family Tree.

**✪ WhiskyWeb. www.whiskyweb.com**
If you love Scottish whisky, the site will tempt and inform you. Learn about the proper way to drink the golden elixir or try a sip at the Malt Whisky File, which describes regional variations among scotch whiskies.

## GETTING AROUND

**Rail Europe. www.raileurope.com**
Rail Europe lets you buy Eurail, Europass, and Brit Rail railroad passes online, as well as rail and drive packages and point-to-point travel in 35 European countries. Even if you don't want a railpass, the site offers invaluable first- and second-class fare and schedule information to the most popular European rail routes.

**ScotRail. www.scotrail.co.uk**
Look here for timetables and fares for trips throughout Scotland. You'll find info on the North Highland Line, West Highland Line, and Caledonian Express, as well as online ticket offers.

**Scottish Citylink. www.citylink.co.uk**
Scottish Citylink outlines bus service throughout Scotland and includes connections in England and Northern Ireland. Click on the "Journey Planner" for timetables—you can also check sample fares and discount info on this site. Check "Useful Links" for other valuable transit sites.

**Online Directory**

# 3 The Active Vacation Planner

If you're headed to Scotland to enjoy the outdoors, you can get guidance from the **Scottish Sports Council,** Caledonian House, South Gyle, Edinburgh EH12 9DQ (☎ **0131/317-7200;** fax 0131/ 317-7202), open Monday to Friday 9am to 5pm. It'll supply names of nature areas, playing fields, prices, facilities, and whatever else you need and also send a copy of *Arena,* an info-filled bulletin packed with advice about sporting programs and facilities.

## 1 Teeing Off: Golfing in Scotland

Although golf has become Scotland's pride, don't think the sport was always well received. Monks around St. Andrews weren't applauded when they diverted themselves from a schedule of felling trees and praying to play *gowff,* and James I and James II rather churlishly issued edicts prohibiting its practice. Despite that, however, by the mid-1700s the game was firmly entrenched in Scotland and viewed as a bucolic oddity by Englishmen chasing after the hounds in the milder climes to the south.

Scotland has more than 440 golf courses, many of them municipal courses open to everyone. Some are royal and ancient (such as St. Andrews), others modern and hip. An example of a well-received newcomer is the Loch Lomond course in the Trossachs, established as a private club in 1993. Although they lie as far north as Sutherland, only 6° south of the Arctic Circle, most courses are in the Central Belt, stretching from Stirling down to Edinburgh and Glasgow.

A beginner doesn't need to lug a complete set of golf clubs across the Atlantic, since many courses rent full or half sets. If you're female or plan on playing golf with someone who is, be aware that some courses are restricted to men only, banning women completely or limiting them to designated days. Despite this tradition-bound holdover from another era, women's golf thrives in Scotland, with about 33,000 members in the Scottish Ladies Golfing Association. The Ladies British Open Amateur Championship was first held in 1893 (the U.S. equivalent was first held in 1895). Contact Mrs. L. H. Park, Secretary, **Scottish Ladies Golfing Association** (information about tournaments or finding women golf partners), or Ian Hume, Esq., Secretary, both at the **Scottish National Golf Centre,** Drumoig, Leuchars, St. Andrews, Fife KY16 0DW, Scotland (☎ 01382/ 549-500; fax 01382/549-510). Sharing offices with the Scottish

Ladies Golfing Association is the **Scottish Golf Union,** established in 1920 to foster and maintain a high standard of amateur golf in Scotland.

Any serious golfer who will be in Scotland for a long stay should consider joining a local club. Membership makes it easier to get coveted tee times, and attending or competing in a local club's tournaments can be both fun and sociable. If you won't be staying long, you might not bother, but remember to bring a letter from a golf club in your home country—it can open a lot of doors otherwise closed to the general public.

Access to many private clubs can be dicey, however, particularly those boasting so much tradition that waiting lists for tee-off times can stretch on for up to a year in advance. You can always stay in a hotel (Gleneagles or Turnberry) that has its own course, thereby guaranteeing the availability of tee-off times. Or you can arrange a golf tour (see below).

Abandon forever any hope of balmy tropical weather, azure skies, and lush fairways. Don't anticipate the sprinklers that flood many warm-weather courses in other countries. Scotland's rains and fogs produce an altogether different kind of golf-related aesthetic, one buffeted by coastal winds, sometimes torn by gales and storms, and (in some places) accented only with salt-tolerant tough grasses and wind-blown stunted trees and shrubs like gorse and heather.

Knowing a term or two in advance might help in picking your golf course. The Scots make a strong distinction between their two types of courses: links and upland. **Links courses** nestle into the sandy terrain of coastal regions, and although years of cultivation have rendered their fairways and putting greens emerald colored, there's a vague sense that eons ago the terrain was submerged beneath the water. Links courses are among the famous names in Scotland and include Royal Troon, Turnberry, Prestwick, North Berwick, and Glasgow Gailes. All links courses are on or near the sea. **Upland courses,** by contrast, are based inland and invariably consist of hilly terrain. They're usually drier and less windy than links courses, Nonetheless, it rains a lot in Scotland, so a sweater and rain-gear are recommended for *all* courses. Examples of upland courses, among many others, are Gleneagles, Loch Lomond, and Pitlochry.

## GOLF TOURS

Access for nonmembers to the country's maze of golf courses hasn't always been possible. All that changed in 1988, however, with the establishment of **Golf International,** 275 Madison Ave., New York, NY 10016 (☎ **800/833-1389** or 212/986-9176; www.golfinternational.com), which maintains a branch office in St. Andrews, the ivy-clad *sanctum sanctorum* of the golfing world. The company caters to golfers from moderate to advanced levels and, against hitherto impossible odds, will guarantee its clients starting times at 40 or so of Scotland's most sought-after courses, including St. Andrews, Carnoustie, Royal Troon, Prestwick, and Gullane.

Potential clients, in self-organized groups of 2 to 12, produce a wish list of the courses they'd like to play. Starting times are prearranged (sometimes rigidly) with an ease that an individual traveler or even a travel agent would find impossible. Packages can be arranged for anywhere from 7 to 14 days (the average is about 7 days) and can include as much or as little golf, at as many courses, as you might want. Weekly prices, including hotels, breakfasts, car rentals, greens fees, and the services of a greeter and helpmate at the airport on arrival, range from $2,195 to $4,195 per person. Discounted airfares to Scotland can also be arranged. For details, talk to one of Golf International's agents at the toll-free number above.

Other companies specializing in golf tours are **Adventures in Golf,** 11 Northeastern Blvd., Suite 360, Nashua, NH 03062 (☎ **603/882-8367**); **Classic Golf & Leisure,**

# Scotland's Best Golf Courses

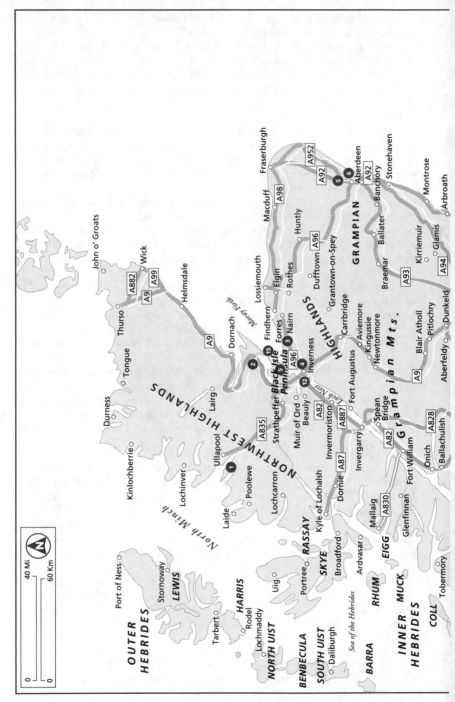

*North Sea*

Note: Nos. 5, 6, 12, and 15 represent multiple sites.

Alexander Park Golf Course **15**
Balnagask Golf Course **5**
Blairgowrie **8**
Bralds Golf Course **12**
Callander Golf Course **11**
Carnoustie Golf Links **7**
Carrick Knowe Course **12**
Craigentinny Golf Course **12**
Gairloch Golf Club **1**
Gleneagles **10**
Hazelhead Golf Course **6**
Knightswood Golf Course **15**
Liberton Golf Course **12**
Machrihansih Golf Club **18**
Murcar Golf Club **5**
Nairn Dunbar Golf Club **3**
Port Royal Golf Course **12**
Portobello Golf Course **12**
Roxburghe Golf Course **14**
Royal Dornoch Golf Club **2**
Royal Troon Golf Club **16**
Silverknowes Golf Course **12**
St. Andrews Courses **9**
Swanston Golf Course **13**
Torhin Hill Golf Course **12**
Torvean Golf Course **4**
Turnberry Hotel Golf Courses **17**
Westhills Golf Course **6**

75706 McLachlin Circle, Palm Desert, CA 92211 (☎ 760/772-2560; www. classic-golf.com); **ITC Golf Tours,** 4134 Atlantic Ave., Suite 205, Long Beach, CA 90807 (☎ 800/257-4981 or 562/595-6905; www.itcgolf.com); **Pery Golf,** 8302 Dunwoody Place, Suite 305, Atlanta, GA 30350 (☎ 800/344-5257 or 770/641-9696; www.perygolf.com); and **Scottish Golf & Travel Service,** 12 Rutland Square, Edinburgh EH1 2BB (☎ 800/847-8064 in U.S. or 0131/221-1500 in Edinburgh).

## THE CLASSIC COURSES

For more details about these fabled golf courses, refer to "The Best Golf" in chapter 1, "The Best of Scotland." In addition to the big names below, many additional courses are listed in the appropriate destination chapters that follow.

The **Carnoustie Golf Links,** Links Parade, Carnoustie, Tayside (☎ 01241/ 853-789; fax 01241/852-720), has a par of 72. This 6,941-yard (6,316m) championship course requires the use of a caddy, costing £30 ($51) for 18 holes. As with most championship courses, electric golf carts aren't allowed, but you can rent a trolley for £3.50 ($5.95) per round. Greens fees are £70 ($119), and club rental, available at Simpson's Golf Shop, 6 Links Parade (☎ 01241/854-477), or David Low's, 7 Links Ave. (☎ 01241/853-439), costs £10 to £15 ($17 to $25.50).

The par-72 **Old Course, St. Andrews,** Golf Place, St. Andrews, Fife (☎ 01334/ 466-666), is a 6,566-yard (5,975m) 18-hole course. Golf was first played here around A.D. 1400, and it's billed as the Home of Golf. This fabled course hosted the 2000 British Open, and witnessed history when Tiger Woods became the youngest golfer in history to complete a grand slam (and only the fifth golfer to ever perform the feat). Greens fees are £75 to £80 ($127.50 to $136), a caddy costs £25 ($42.50) plus tip, and clubs rent for £20 to £30 ($34 to $51) per round. There are no electric carts allowed, and you can rent a trolley on afternoons only between May and September for £3 ($5.10). Reservations must be made in advance.

The 18-hole **Royal Dornoch Golf Club,** Dornoch, Sutherland (☎ 01862/ 810-219), 40 miles (64.5km) north of Inverness, has a par of 70. At this 6,185-yard (5,628m) course, the greens fees are £57 ($96.90) Monday to Friday and £67 ($113.90) Saturday (members only) and Sunday, with a 3-day ticket available for consecutive weekdays only, costing £144 ($244.80). Golf club and trolley rentals are £20 to £30 ($34 to $51) and £3 ($5.10), respectively. Caddy service is available for £20 to £30 ($34 to $51) plus tip.

The par-71 **Royal Troon Golf Club,** Craigend Road, Troon, Ayrshire (☎ 01292/ 311-555; fax 01292/318-204), has one of the largest courses in Scotland, with 7,097 yards (6,458m) of playing area. The greens fee—£125 ($212.50) for a day—includes a buffet lunch and two 18-hole sets. For one round of play, a trolley rents for £4 ($6.80) and a caddy £25 ($42.50); club rental is £20 ($34) per round or £35 ($59.50) per day.

### A Beginner's Warning

Neophytes unfamiliar with the rules of the game just aren't allowed to play any of the country's most legendary golf courses. Many courses will want evidence of your familiarity with the game before you're allowed on the links. Depending on the setting and the season, this could include a letter from your club back home citing your ability and experience or visual proof you've mastered a basically sound swing and an understanding of golf-related etiquette.

The **Turnberry Hotel Golf Courses,** Ayrshire (☎ 01655/331-000; fax 01655/ 331-706), gives priority at its 6,971-yard (6,344m) par-70 course to residents of the hotel. The greens fee of £95 ($161.50) for guests and £120 ($204; Monday to Friday) or £150 ($255; weekends) for nonguests, includes 18 holes on the Ailsa course and an 18-hole round on the less-desirable Arran course. For a round of golf, clubs rent for £35 ($59.50), and caddy service costs £25 ($42.50) plus tip. If you're not staying here, give them a call in the morning to check on any unclaimed tee-off times—but it's a long shot.

## 2 Fishing

Anglers consider Scotland a paradise. Its fast-flowing rivers harbor Atlantic **salmon** (the king of all game fish). The rivers and numerous pristine *lochs* (lakes) allow you to enjoy some of Europe's most beautiful scenery, along with the marvelous hospitality extended by its innkeepers. Permits for fishing (often arranged by your hotel) can be expensive. For one of the grand beats on the River Tay, a week's permit could run into hundreds of pounds. However, there are many lesser-known rivers where a club ticket costs only pounds a day.

The **Tweed** and the **Tay** are just two of the famous Scottish salmon rivers. In Perthshire, the Tay is the broadest and longest river in the country. The Dee, with all its royal associations, is the famous salmon-fishing river of Aberdeenshire. The royal family fishes this river, and the queen herself has been seen casting from these banks. Other anglers prefer to fish the **Spey,** staying at one of the inns along the Malt Whisky Trail. Certain well-heeled fishermans travel every year to Scotland to fish in the lochs and rivers of the **Outer Hebrides.**

In general, Scotland's season for salmon fishing runs from late February until late October, but these dates vary from region to region.

### TYPES OF FISHING

Here's a breakdown of terms you're likely to hear even before you cast your first line into the country's glittering waters.

**COARSE FISHING**    This means going after any species of freshwater fish except salmon and trout. Especially prized trophies, known for putting up a spirited fight, are carp, tench, pike, bream, roach, and perch. Because few lochs actually freeze during winter, the sport can be practiced throughout the year. Local tourist boards all over the country can provide advice.

**GAME FISHING**    Salmon and trout (brown, rainbow, or sea) are the most desired of the game fish and the ones that have inspired the image of a fly fisherman whipping a lure and line in serpentine arcs above a loch. Many vacationers dream of donning bulky rubber waders up to their waists and trying their luck in streams and freshwater lochs. Fly-fishing for salmon and trout is subject to seasonal controls and sometimes requires a permit. For details about game fishing, contact the **Salmon and Trout Association (Scottish Branch),** 10 Great Stuart St., Edinburgh EH3 7TN (☎ and fax **1887/829-239**).

**SEA FISHING**    This simply means fishing from a beach, a rocky shoreline, or a pier. Inshore fishing involves dropping a line into ocean waters within 3 miles (5km) of any Scottish coastline; deep-sea fishing is off a boat more than 3 miles (5km) offshore in a style made popular by cigar-chomping tycoons and Hemingway clones. Offshore waters have produced several species of shark, including porbeagle, thresher, mako, and blue shark. For information about what to expect from deep offshore waters, contact the **Scottish Tourist Board,** 23 Ravelston Terrace, Edinburgh EH14 3TP (☎ 0131/332-2433).

## FISHING CLUBS

Getting permits and information about worthwhile places to fish is easier if you join one of the more than 380 fishing clubs headquartered in Scotland. (The oldest angling club in the world, the Ellem Fishing Club, was founded in Scotland in 1829.) Each of their activities is supervised by the **Scottish Anglers National Association** (☎ 0131/339-8808), which firmly believes that newcomers should learn at the side of the more experienced. Courses and reunions are offered in the fine art of fishing in or around Scotland. For details, contact the Scottish Tourist Board (see above).

# 3  Biking, Walking & Other Active Vacations

## BIKING

Scotland is one of the most gorgeous settings in Europe for a bike trip, but note that bicycles are forbidden on most highways and trunk roads and on what the British call dual carriageways (divided highways). May, June, and September are the best for cycling in spite of the often bad weather. Many of the narrow and scenic roads are likely to be overcrowded with cars in July and August. For the best biking routes, see chapter 1.

The first source of information is the **Scottish Cyclists Union,** which provides an annual handbook and a regular newsletter for members. It's also one of the most potent lobbying groups in Scotland for the inauguration and preservation of cyclists' byways. It distributes maps showing worthwhile bike routes and supports the publication of technical material of interest to cyclists. Contact Jim Riach, Executive Office, Scottish Cyclists Union, The Velodrome, Meadowbrook Stadium, London Road, Edinburgh EH7 6AD (☎ 0131/652-0187; fax 0131/661-0474; www.btinternet.com).

Although based in England, the **Cyclists Tourist Club,** Cotterell House, 69 Meadrow, Godalming, Surrey GU7 3HS (☎ 01483/417-217; fax 01483/426-994; www.ctc.org.uk), offers details on cycling holidays in Scotland. Membership is £25 ($42.50) a year for adults and £15 ($25.50) for those 17 and under. A family with three or more members can get a membership for £40 ($68). This organization will give advice about where to rent or buy a cycle; it also offers free legal advice to members involved in cycle-related accidents and advice about available medical insurance for members.

It's possible to take your bike without restrictions on car and passenger ferries in Scotland. There's almost no case where it's necessary to make arrangements in advance. However, the transport of your bike is likely to cost £1 to £6 ($1.70 to $10.20), plus the cost of your own passage.

The best biking trips in Scotland are offered by **Bespoke Highland Tours,** The Bothy, Camusdarach, Inverness PH39 4NT (☎ 01687/450-272), and **Scottish Border Trails,** Drummore, Venlaw High Road, Peebles EH45 8RL (☎ 01721/720-336; fax 01721/723-004).

U.S.-based **Backroads,** 801 Cedar St. Berkeley, CA 94710-1800 (☎ 800/GO-ACTIVE [462-2848] or 510/527-1555; www.backroads.com), offers a couple of week-long biking tours through Scotland. Accommodations are in charming inns along the way, and fine food, all equipment, and van support are included.

Local rental shops offer a wide range of bicycles, from three-speeds to mountain bikes, and may offer organized trips, ranging from tours of several hours to full-fledged week-long itineraries. We've listed the best local rental shops, with their rates, in the destination chapters that follow.

# BIRD WATCHING

The moors and Highlands of Scotland, partly because of their low population density, attract millions of birds. For reasons not fully understood by ornithologists, the Orkneys shelter absolutely staggering numbers of birds. Bird watchers cite the Orkneys as even richer in native species than the more isolated Shetlands, with species like the hen harrier, short-eared owl, and red-throated diver (a form of Arctic loon) not frequently seen in the Shetlands.

Any general tour of the Orkneys will bring you into contact with thousands of birds, as well as Neolithic burial sites, cromlechs, dolmens, and other items with intriguing backgrounds and histories. A worthy tour operator is **Wild About,** 5 Clouston Corner, Stenness, Orkney KW17 3LD (☎ **01856/851-011**). Minivans will help in spotting birds whose breeding and mating habits will be one of the many other factors discussed on the tours. The per-person cost is £17.50 ($29.75) adult for a full day, and £11.50 ($19.55) adult for a half day. For summer tours, make reservations in advance.

A bird-watching specialist is **Orkney Island Wildlife,** Shapinsay 12, Orkney KW17 2DY (☎ **01856/711-373**). Between May and November, it leads 5-day bird-watching tours that include full board, housing, and exposure to the fields, moors, and wetlands of Shapinsay and Orkney. Tours are conducted from a rustic croft that was upgraded and enlarged into a streamlined modern format in 1990. Your hosts are Paul and Louise Hollinrake, both qualified wardens at the Mill Dam Wetlands Reserve and accredited by the Royal Society for the Protection of Birds. Tours depart every morning around 9am (allowing participants to either sleep late or embark on sunrise expeditions of their own). Lunches are picniclike box-lunch affairs. Touring is by minivan or by inflatable boat, allowing close-up inspection of offshore skerries (small islets without vegetation) and sea caves. No more than six participants are allowed in any tour. All-inclusive prices are £500 to £660 ($850 to $1,122) per person for the 5-day/6-night experience.

During winter and early spring, the entire Solway shoreline, Loch Ryan, Wigtown Bay, and Auchencairn Bay areas are excellent locations for observing wintering wildfowl and waders. Inland, Galloway has a rich and varied range of bird life, including British barn owls, kestrels, tawnies, and merlins. Bird-watching fact sheets are available at tourist offices in Galloway.

# CANOEING

Several canoe clubs offer instruction and advice. Supervising their activities is the **Scottish Canoe Association (SCA),** Caledonia House, South Gyle, Edinburgh EH12 9DH (☎ **0131/317-7314**). It coordinates all competitive canoeing events in Scotland, including slaloms, polo games, and white-water races. It also offers a handbook and a range of other publications, plus promotional material like its own magazine, *Scottish Paddler.* (An equivalent magazine, published in England, is *Canoe Focus.*)

# HIKING & WALKING

Scotland is Valhalla for those who like to walk and hike across mountain and dale, coming to rest on the bonnie, bonnie banks of a loch. For some of the best walks in Scotland, see chapter 1.

In all Scotland, there are no finer long-distance footpaths than the **West Highland Way** and the **Southern Upland Way,** both previewed in chapter 1. One begins north of Glasgow in the town of Milngavie, the other in Portpatrick in Galloway. Information on these paths is provided by the **Scottish Tourist Board,** 23 Ravelston Terrace, Edinburgh EH4 3EU (☎ **0131/332-2433**). Nearly all bookstores in Scotland sell guidebooks documenting these paths.

The Borders (see chapter 4, "Edinburgh & the Lothian Region") is one of the greatest places for walks. All tourist boards in the area provide a free guide, *Walking in the Scottish Borders,* detailing many half-day scenic walks around the various towns. As mentioned, Scotland's longest footpath, the 212-mile (341km) **Southern Upland Way,** also extends through the Borders.

The coastline of **Galloway,** southwest of the Borders, takes in a magnificent coast ideal for walks. Tourist offices also distribute a free guide to 30 walks, *Walking in Dumfries and Galloway.* They also offer free a helpful pamphlet called *Ranger-Led Walks and Events,* outlining scenic hikes through the forests of the southwest.

In central Scotland, the **Cairngorm region** offers the major concentration of ski resorts in the country (such as they are), including Ben Macdui, the second highest peak in Britain at nearly 4,300 feet (1,304m). In the Cairngorm Ski Area, Cairngorm Rangers offer guided walks through the forest to both skilled and beginning hikers. In the area, the **Glenmore Forest Park Visitors Centre** (☎ 1479/861-220) dispenses great information on great walks in the area. It's open daily 9am to 5pm.

The best self-led tours of the Scottish Highlands and islands is offered by **Bespoke Highland Tours,** 14 Belmont Crescent, Glasgow (☎ 0141/334-9017). It has devised a series of treks, lasting from 3 to 12 days, including the **West Highland Way,** that take in the finest scenery in Scotland. Their tours are reasonably priced, ranging from £70 to £395 ($119 to $671.50). **John Fisher,** The Old Inn, Strachur, Argyll (☎ 01369/860-712), specializes in guided walking and hiking holidays. Most of them last 6 days, with 7 nights accommodation at a cost of £375 to £595 ($637.50 to $1,011.50). Groups are small, usually between four and eight. Highlights of these tours include treks across the isles of Mull and Iona. And with **North-West Frontiers,** 18A Braes, Ullapool (☎ 01854/612-628), you can explore remote glens, magnificent mountains and lochs, and isolated islands and beaches. You're likely to see seals, deer, and many species of birds, including divers and golden eagles. Unlike Bespoke (see above), these tours are led by experienced hikers who know the countryside like their backyard.

Some of the most memorable walks in Scotland are along **Loch Lomond** and the **Trossachs.** From tourist information centers and at various bookstores in Scotland, you can purchase a copy of *Walk Loch Lomond and the Trossachs* to guide you on your way.

An organization that can put you in touch with like-minded hikers is the **Ramblers Association (Scotland),** Crusader House, Haig Business Park, Markinch, Fife KY7 6AQ (☎ 01577/861-222). To book a rambling tour before you go to Scotland, contact the **English Lakeland Ramblers** at 18 Stuyvesant Oval, Suite 1A, New York, NY 10009 (☎ 212/505-1020; www.ramblers.com).

## HORSEBACK RIDING & PONY TREKKING

Horseback riding and trekking through the panoramic countryside—from the Lowlands to the Highlands and through all the in-between lands—can be enjoyed by most everyone, from novices to experienced riders.

Although more adventurous riders prefer the hillier terrain of the Highlands, the Borders in the southeast (see chapter 4) is the best for horseback riding—in fact, it's often called Scotland's horse country. Its equivalent in the United States would be Kentucky. On the western coastline, Argyll (see chapter 7, "Argyll & the Southern Hebrides") is another great center for horseback riding, taking in dramatic scenery. The Argyll Forest Park, stretching almost to Loch Fyne, encompasses 60,000 acres and contains some of the lushest scenery in Scotland. It's a favorite for trails leading through forests to sea lochs cut deep into the park, evoking the fjords of Norway.

Pony trekking across moors and dales is reason enough to come to Scotland. Pony trekking originated as a job for Highland ponies that weren't otherwise engaged in toting dead deer off the hills during deer-stalking season. Most treks last from 2½ hours up to a full day, and most centers have ponies suitable for most age groups. You'll find operators in Kirkudbright and on Shetland, plus several in the Hebrides.

## MOUNTAINEERING

Mountain climbing can range from fair-weather treks over heather-clad hilltops to demanding climbs up rock faces in wintry conditions of snow and ice.

The **Southern Uplands,** the **offshore islands,** and the **Highlands** of Scotland contain Britain's best mountaineering sites. Regardless of your abilities, treat the landscape with respect. The weather can turn foul during any season with almost no advance notice and create dangerous conditions. If you're climbing rock faces, you should be familiar with basic techniques and the use of such specialized equipment as carabiners, crampons, ice axes, and ropes. Don't even consider climbing without proper instruction and equipment.

**Ben Nevis** is the highest (but by no means the most remote) peak in Scotland. Despite its loftiness at 4,406 feet (1,336m), it has attracted some daredevils who have driven cars and motorcycles to points near its top; one eccentric even arranged the transport of a dining table with formal dinner service and a grand piano.

If you want to improve your rock-climbing skills, consider joining a club or signing on for a mountaineering course at a climbing center maintained by the Scottish Sports Council. Also contact the **Mountaineering Council of Scotland,** Perth (☎ 01738/638-227; www.mountaineering-scotland.org.uk). Membership allows overnight stays at the club's climbing huts on the island of Skye (in Glen Brittle), in the Cairngorms (at Glen Feshie), and near the high-altitude mountain pass at Glencoe. True rock-climbing aficionados looking to earn certification might contact the **Scottish Mountain Leader Training Board** at Glenmore, Aviemore, Inverness-shire PH22 1QU (☎ 01479/861-248; www.ukmtb.org).

## SAILING & WATERSPORTS

Wherever you travel in Scotland, you're never far from the water. Windsurfing, canoeing, water-skiing, Jet Skiing, and sailing are just some of the sports available at a number of sailing centers and holiday parks. You'll find it easy to rent boats and equipment at any of the major resorts along Scotland's famous lakes.

# 4 Edinburgh & the Lothian Region

Edinburgh (pronounced *Edin*-burra) has been called one of Europe's fairest cities, the Athens of the North, and the gateway to central Scotland. You can use it as a base for excursions to the Borders, the Trossachs (Scotland's Lake District), the silver waters of Loch Lomond, and the Kingdom of Fife on the opposite shore of the Firth of Forth.

Edinburgh is filled with historic and literary association: John Knox, Mary Queen of Scots, Robert Louis Stevenson, Sir Arthur Conan Doyle (creator of Sherlock Holmes and Dr. Watson), Alexander Graham Bell, Sir Walter Scott, and Bonnie Prince Charlie are all part of its past.

In modern times, the city has become famous as the scene of the ever-growing **Edinburgh International Festival,** with its action-packed list of cultural events. But remember the treasures of this ancient seat of Scottish royalty are available all year—in fact, when the festival-hoppers have gone home, the pace is more relaxed, the prices are lower, and the people themselves, under less pressure, return to their traditional hospitable nature.

Built on extinct volcanoes atop an inlet from the North Sea (the Firth of Forth) and enveloped by rolling hills, lakes (*lochs*), and forests, Edinburgh is a city made for walking. Its Old Town and its New Town sport elegant streets, cobbled alleys, lovely squares, and enough circuses and crescents to rival Bath in England; from every hilltop another panoramic view unfolds. Edinburgh's sunsets are spectacularly romantic—Scots call the fading evening light the "gloaming."

Edinburgh was once the cultural capital of the north, but it has lost that position to Glasgow. However, the lively capital is trying its best to regain its old reputation. In fact, if you could visit only two cities in all Great Britain, we'd say make it London first and Edinburgh second. But you may want to budget some time for side trips, too. Notable attractions on the doorstep of Edinburgh are the royal burgh of Linlithgow, where Mary Queen of Scots was born at Linlithgow Palace; the port of North Berwick (today a holiday resort); and lovely Dirleton, with its 13th-century castle ruins.

## 1 Essentials

### ARRIVING

**BY PLANE**   Edinburgh is about an hour's flying time from London, 393 miles (633km) south. **Edinburgh Airport (☎ 0131/333-1000)**

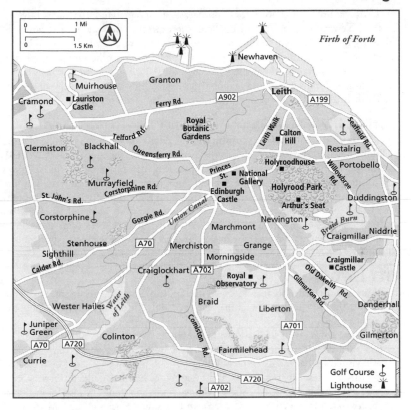

is 6 miles (10km) west of the center, receiving flights from within the British Isles and the rest of Europe. Before heading into town, you might want to stop at the **information and accommodation desk** (☎ 0131/473-3800); it's open daily April to October 6:30am to 10:30pm and November to March 7:30am to 9:30pm. A double-decker Airlink bus makes the trip from the airport to the city center every 10 minutes, letting you off near Waverley Bridge, between the Old Town and the New Town; the fare is £3.30 ($5.60) one way or £5 ($8.50) round-trip, and the trip takes about 25 minutes. A taxi into the city will cost £14 ($23.80) or more, depending on traffic, and the ride will be about 25 minutes.

**BY TRAIN**   InterCity trains link London with Edinburgh and are fast and efficient, providing both restaurant and bar service as well as air-conditioning. Trains from London's Kings Cross Station arrive in Edinburgh at **Waverley Station,** at the east end of Princes Street (☎ 0133/238-7601 in London for rail info). Trains depart London every hour or so, taking about 4½ hours and costing about £53 ($90.10) round-trip. Overnight trains have a sleeper berth, which you can rent for an extra £30 ($51). Taxis and buses are right outside the station in Edinburgh.

**BY BUS**   The least expensive way to go from London to Edinburgh is by bus, but it's an 8-hour journey. Nevertheless, it'll get you there for only about £20 ($34) one way or £30 ($51) round-trip. Scottish CityLink coaches depart from London's Victoria Coach Station, delivering you to Edinburgh's **St. Andrew Square Bus Station,** St. Andrew Square (☎ 0800/23-23-23 for information).

**BY CAR**   Edinburgh is 46 miles (74km) east of Glasgow and 105 miles (169km) north of Newcastle-upon-Tyne in England. No express motorway links London and Edinburgh. The M1 from London takes you part of the way north, but you'll have to come into Edinburgh along secondary roads: A68 or A7 from the southeast, A1 from the east, or A702 from the north. The A71 or A8 comes in from the west, A8 connecting with M8 just west of Edinburgh; A90 comes down from the north over the Forth Road Bridge. Allow 8 hours or more for the drive north from London.

## VISITOR INFORMATION

The **Edinburgh & Scotland Information Centre,** Waverley Shopping Centre, 3 Princes St., at the corner of Princes Street and Waverley Bridge (☎ **0131/ 473-3800;** Bus: 3, 69, 331), can give you sightseeing info and also help find lodgings. The center sells bus tours, theater tickets, and souvenirs of Edinburgh. July and August, hours are Monday to Saturday 9am to 8pm and Sunday 10am to 8pm; May, June, and September, hours are Monday to Saturday 9am to 7pm and Sunday 10am to 7pm; October to April, hours are Monday to Saturday 9am to 6pm and Sunday 10am to 6pm. There's also an **information and accommodation desk** at Edinburgh airport (see above).

## CITY LAYOUT

Edinburgh is divided into an Old Town and a New Town. Chances are, you'll find lodgings in the New Town and visit the Old Town only for dining, drinking, shopping, and sightseeing.

The **New Town,** with its world-famous **Princes Street,** came about in the 18th century in the Golden Age of Edinburgh. Everybody from Robert Burns to James Boswell visited in that era. The first building went up here in 1767, and by the end of the century classical squares, streets, and townhouses had been added. Princes Street runs straight for about a mile; the street is known for its shopping and also for its beauty, as it opens onto the Princes Street Gardens with panoramic views of the Old Town.

North of and running parallel to Princes Street is the New Town's second great street, **George Street.** It begins at Charlotte Square and runs east to St. Andrew Square. Directly north of George Street is another impressive thoroughfare, **Queen Street,** opening onto Queen Street Gardens on its north side. You'll also hear a lot about **Rose Street,** directly north of Princes Street—it boasts more pubs per square block than any other place in Scotland and is filled with shops and restaurants.

Seemingly everyone has heard of the **Royal Mile,** the main thoroughfare of the **Old Town,** beginning at Edinburgh Castle and running all the way to the Palace of Holyroodhouse. This single street bears four names along its length: Castlehill, Lawnmarket, High Street, and Canongate. A famous street to the south of the castle (you have to descend to it) is **Grassmarket,** where once convicted criminals were hung on the dreaded gallows that stood there.

Discovering Edinburgh's many hidden lanes and branching out to some of its interesting satellite communities is one of the pleasures of coming here.

# The Neighborhoods in Brief

**The Old Town**   This area is where Edinburgh began. Its backbone is the **Royal Mile,** a medieval thoroughfare stretching for about a mile from Edinburgh Castle running downhill to the Palace of Holyroodhouse. It's composed of four connected streets: Castlehill, Lawnmarket, High Street, and Canongate (once a separate burgh). "This is perhaps the largest, longest, and finest street for buildings and number of inhabitants in the world," or so wrote English author Daniel Defoe. The same might be said of the street today.

**The New Town**    Lying below the Old Town, the New Town burst into full bloom between 1766 and 1840 and became one of the largest Georgian developments in the world. It takes in most of the northern half of the heart of the city, covering some 790 acres. With about 25,000 citizens living within its boundaries, it's the largest conservation area in all Britain. The New Town is made up of a network of squares, streets, terraces, and circuses, reaching from Haymarket in the west to Abbeyhill in the east. The New Town also goes from Canonmills on the northern perimeter down to Princes Street, its main artery, along the southern tier.

**Marchmont**    About a mile south of High Street, the suburb of Marchmont borders a public park, the Meadows. It was constructed between 1869 and 1914 as a massive building program of new housing for people who could no longer afford to live in the New Town.

**Bruntsfield**    This suburb to the west is named for Bruntsfield Links. Now a residential district of moderate-income families, it was the ground on which James IV gathered the Scottish army he marched to its defeat at Flodden in 1513. Plague victims were once brought here for burial; now suburban gardens have grown over those graves. Many low-cost B&Bs are found in this area.

**Churchill**    Churchill is known as "holy corner" because of the wide array of Scottish churches within its borders at the junctions of Colinton, Chamberlain, and Bruntsfield roads. These churches are primarily for local worshipers and not of artistic interest. Many famous Scots have lived in this district, including Jane Welsh Carlyle and George Meikle Kemp, the architect who created the Scott Monument on Princes Street.

**Leith**    The Port of Leith lies only a few miles north of Princes Street and is the city's major harbor, opening onto the Firth of Forth. The area is currently going through a gentrification process, and many visitors come here for the restaurants and pubs, many of which specialize in seafood. The port isn't what it used to be in terms of maritime might; its glory days were back when stevedores unloaded cargoes by hand. Leith was once a bitter rival of Edinburgh, but now, as one resident put it, "We're just another bloody part of Auld Reekie [local name for Edinburgh]."

## Finding an Address

Edinburgh's streets often follow no pattern whatsoever, and both names and house numbers seem to have been created purposely to confuse. First, the city is checkered with innumerable squares, terraces, circuses, wynds, and closes, which will jut into or cross or overlap or interrupt whatever street you're trying to follow, usually without the slightest warning.

Then the house numbers run in sequences of odds or evens or run clockwise or counterclockwise as the wind blows. That is, when they exist at all. Many establishments don't use street numbers. (This is even truer when you leave Edinburgh and go to a provincial town.) Even though a road might run for a mile, some buildings on the street will be numbered and others will say only "Kings Road" or whatever, giving no number. Before heading out, you should get a detailed map of Edinburgh and ask for a location to be pinpointed; locals are generally glad to assist a bewildered foreigner. If you're looking for an address, try to get the name of the nearest cross street.

**Newhaven**  The fishing village adjacent to Leith, Newhaven was once known as Our Lady's Port of Grace. Founded in the 1400s, this former little fishing harbor with its bustling fishmarket was greatly altered in the 1960s. Many of its "bow-tows" (a nickname for closely knit, clannish residents) were uprooted, like the Leithers, in a major gentrification program. Now many of the old houses of the fisherfolk have been restored, and the fishwife no longer goes from door to door hawking fish from her basket (known as a creel). She'd gut and fillet the fish right on your doorstep if you asked her. Newhaven's harbor is now mostly filled with pleasure craft instead of fishing boats. If your time is limited, you can skip this area, as its attractions are limited.

## 2 Getting Around

Because of its narrow lanes, wynds, and closes, you can explore the Old Town in any depth only on foot. Edinburgh is fairly convenient for the visitor who likes to walk, as most of the attractions are along the Royal Mile or Princes Street or on one of the major streets of the New Town.

### BY BUS

The bus will probably be your chief method of transport. The fare you pay depends on the distance you ride, with the **minimum fare** 50p (85¢) for three stages or less and the **maximum fare** £1.70 ($2.90) for 44 or more stages. (A stage isn't a stop but a distance of about half a mile with a number of stops.) Children 5 to 15 are charged a flat rate of 50p (85¢), but teenagers 13 to 15 must carry a **teen card** (available where bus tickets are sold—see below) as proof of age, and children 4 and under ride free. Exact change is required if you're paying your fare on the bus.

A **family ticket** for two adults and four children goes for £6 ($10.20) a day and another for £1.60 ($2.70) operates 6:30pm onward. The **Edinburgh Freedom Ticket** allows 1 day of unlimited travel on city buses at a cost of £2.40 ($4.10) adults and £1.60 ($2.70) children.

For daily commuters or die-hard Scottish enthusiasts, a **RideCard** season ticket allows unlimited travel on all buses. For adults, the price is £10.50 ($17.85) for 1 week and £30.50 ($51.85) for 4 weeks; tickets for children cost £6.50 ($11.05) for 1 week and £18 ($30.60) for 4 weeks. Travel must begin on Sunday.

You can get these tickets and further information in the city center at the **Waverley Bridge Transport Office,** Waverley Bridge (☎ **0131/554-4494;** Bus: 3, 31), open daily 6:30am to 10:30pm, or at the Hanover Street office (Bus: 3, 31), open daily 9am to 7pm. For details on timetables, call ☎ **0131/555-6363.**

### BY TAXI

You can hail a taxi or pick one up at a taxi stand. Meters begin at £1.80 ($3.05) and increase at 20p (35¢) every 52 seconds. Taxi ranks are at Hanover Street, North St. Andrew Street, Waverley Station, Haymarket Station, and Lauriston Place. Fares are displayed in the front of the taxi and charges posted, including extra charges for night drivers or destinations outside the city limits, and a call-out is charged at 60p ($1).

### Look Both Ways

Remember you're in Great Britain, and cars drive on the left. Always look both ways before stepping off a curb. Lots of new arrivals practically commit suicide crossing the street because they forget which way to look for traffic.

You can also call a taxi: Try **City Cabs** at ☎ **0131/228-1211** or **Central Radio Taxis** at ☎ **0131/229-2468.**

## BY CAR

Don't think about driving in Edinburgh—it's a tricky business, even for natives. However, a car is great for touring the countryside around the city or for heading onward. Most companies will accept your U.S. or Canadian driver's license, provided you've held it for more than a year and are over 21.

**RENTALS**    Many companies grant discounts to people who reserve in advance before leaving home (see "Car Rentals," under "Getting Around" in chapter 2, "Planning Your Trip: The Basics").

Most of the major car-rental companies maintain offices at the Edinburgh airport should you want to rent a car on the spot. Call **Avis** (☎ **0131/333-1866**), **Hertz** (☎ **0131/344-3260**), or **Europcar** (☎ **0131/333-2588**).

**PARKING**    It's expensive and difficult to find. Metered parking is available, but you'll need the right change and have to watch out for traffic wardens who issue tickets. Some zones are marked PERMIT HOLDERS ONLY. Don't park here unless you have a permit as a local resident—your vehicle will be towed if you do. A yellow line along the curb indicates NO PARKING.

Major **parking lots** (car parks) are at Castle Terrace, a large multistory car park convenient for Edinburgh Castle and the west end of Princes Street; at Lothian Road, a surface car park near the west end of Princes Street; at St. John Hill, a surface car park convenient to the Royal Mile, the west end of Princes Street, and Waverley Station; and at St. James Centre (entrance from York Place), a multistory car park close to the east end of Princes Street.

## BY BICYCLE

You can rent bikes by the day or the week from a number of outfits. Nevertheless, bicycling isn't a good idea for most visitors because the city is constructed on a series of high ridges and terraces.

You may, however, want to rent a bike for exploring the flatter countryside around the city. Try **Central Cycle Hire,** 13 Lochrin Place (☎ **0131/228-6333;** Bus: 10), off Home Street in Tollcross, near the Cameo Cinema. Depending on the type of bike, charges range from £10 to £18 ($17 to $30.60) per day. A deposit of £50 to £100 ($85 to $170) is imposed. June to September, the shop is open Monday to Saturday 9:30am to 6pm and Sunday noon to 7pm; October to May, hours are Monday to Saturday 10am to 5:30pm.

**Edinburgh Cycle Hire and Safaris,** 29 Blackfriars St. (☎ **0131/556-5560**), offers day rentals from £15 ($25.50) and weekly rentals from £25 to £70 ($42.50 to $119). It's open daily 10am to 7pm (later in summer) and requires a credit card for a deposit. The **Second Hand Bike Shop,** 25–27 Iona St. (☎ **0131/553-1130**), rents bikes for £10 ($17) per day, requiring a £50 ($85) deposit. It's open Monday to Saturday 9am to 5:30pm.

## Fast Facts: Edinburgh

**American Express**    The office in Edinburgh is at 139 Princes St. (☎ **0131/ 225-7881;** Bus: 3, 39, 69), 5 blocks from Waverley Station. It's open Monday to Friday 9am to 5:30pm and Saturday 9am to 4pm; on Thursday, the office opens at 9:30am.

**Baby-Sitters** The most reliable services are provided by **Guardians Baby Sitting Service,** 13 Eton Terrace (☎ **0131/343-3870**), and **Care Connections,** 45 Barclay Place (☎ **01506/856-106**).

**Business Hours** In Edinburgh, **banks** are usually open Monday to Wednesday 9:30am to 3:45pm and Thursday and Friday 9:30am to 5 or 5:30pm. **Shops** are generally open Monday to Saturday 10am to 5:30 or 6pm; on Thursday stores are open to 8pm. **Offices** are open Monday to Friday 9am to 5pm.

**Currency Exchange** There's a bureau de change of the **Clydesdale Bank** at 5 Waverley Bridge and at Waverley Market.

**Cybercafe** If you're just dying to check your e-mail, head to the **Cyberia Edinburgh,** 88 Hanover St. (☎ **0131/220-4405;** Bus: 23, 41; e-mail: edinburgh@cybersurf.co.uk).

**Dentist** If you have a dental emergency, go to the **Edinburgh Dental Institute,** 39 Lauriston Place (☎ **0131/536-4900;** Bus: 23, 41), open Monday to Friday 9am to 3pm.

**Doctor** You can seek help from the **Edinburgh Royal Infirmary,** 1 Lauriston Place (☎ **0131/536-1000;** Bus: 23, 41). Medical attention is available 24 hours.

**Drugstores** There are no 24-hour drugstores (called chemists or pharmacies) in Edinburgh. The major drugstore is **Boots,** 48 Shandwick Place (☎ **0131/ 225-6757;** Bus: 3, 31), open Monday to Friday 8am to 9pm, Saturday 8am to 7pm, and Sunday 10am to 4pm.

**Embassies & Consulates** See "Fast Facts: Scotland" in chapter 2.

**Emergencies** Call ☎ **999** in an emergency to summon the police, an ambulance, or firefighters.

**Hospital** The most convenient is the **Edinburgh Royal Infirmary,** 1 Lauriston Place (☎ **0131/536-1000;** Bus: 23, 41).

**Laundry/Dry Cleaning** Try **Sundial Launderette,** 7–11 E. London St. (☎ **0131/556-2743;** Bus: 34, 35), open Monday to Friday 8am to 7pm, Saturday 8am to 4pm, and Sunday 10am to 2pm. For your dry-cleaning needs, check out **Johnson's Cleaners,** 23 Frederick St. (☎ **0131/225-8095;** Bus: 23, 41), open Monday to Friday 8am to 5:30pm and Saturday 8am to 4pm.

**Luggage/Storage/Lockers** You can store luggage in lockers at **Waverley Station,** at Waverley Bridge (☎ **0131/550-2333**), open Monday to Saturday 7am to 11pm and Sunday 8am to 11pm.

**Newspapers & Magazines** Published since 1817, *The Scotsman* is a quality daily newspaper. Along with national and international news, it's strong on the arts. Among magazines, the field isn't outstanding, except for the *Edinburgh Review,* published quarterly by the University Press, mainly a cultural journal.

**Police** See "Emergencies," above.

**Post Office** The **Edinburgh Branch Post Office,** St. James's Centre, is open Monday to Friday 9am to 5:30pm and Saturday 9am to noon. For postal information and customer service, call ☎ **0131/550-8232**.

**Rest Rooms** These are found at rail stations, terminals, restaurants, hotels, pubs, and department stores. Don't hesitate to use the system of public toilets, often marked WC, at strategic corners and squares throughout the city. They're perfectly safe and clean but likely to be closed late in the evening.

**Safety**   Edinburgh is generally safer than Glasgow—in fact, it's one of Europe's safest capitals for a visitor to stroll at any time of day or night. But that doesn't mean crimes, especially muggings, don't occur. They do, largely because of Edinburgh's shockingly large drug problem.

**Taxes**   A 17.5% **value-added tax (VAT)** is included in the price of all goods and services in Edinburgh, as elsewhere in Britain. (To find out how to get a VAT refund, see the box in chapter 2.) There are no special city taxes. Quoted hotel prices generally include this tax.

**Weather**   For weather forecasts and road conditions, call ☎ **0891/505-322.** This number also provides data about weather information for Lothian, the Borders, Tayside, and Fife.

# 3  Accommodations

Edinburgh offers a full range of accommodations throughout the year. However, it should come as no surprise that during the 3-week period of the Edinburgh International Festival in August, the hotels fill up; so if you're coming at that time, be sure to reserve far in advance.

The **Edinburgh & Scotland Information Centre,** Waverley Shopping Centre, 3 Princes St., at the corner of Princes Street and Waverley Bridge (☎ **0131/ 473-3800;** fax 0131/473-3881; e-mail: esic@eltb.org; www.edinburgh.org; Bus: 3, 7, 14, 31, 69), compiles a lengthy list of small hotels, guesthouses, and private homes providing a bed-and-breakfast for as little as £15 ($25.50) per person. A £4 ($6.80) booking fee and a 10% deposit are charged. Allow about 4 weeks' notice, especially during summer and during the festival weeks. July and August, hours are Monday to Saturday 9am to 8pm and Sunday 10am to 8pm; May, June, and September, hours are Monday to Saturday 9am to 7pm and Sunday 10am to 7pm; October to April, hours are Monday to Saturday 9am to 6pm and Sunday 10am to 6pm.

There's also an **information and accommodation desk** at Edinburgh Airport (see "Essentials," earlier in the chapter).

If you have an early flight out, you might like to know that one of the hotels most convenient to the airport is the **Swallow Royal Scot,** 111 Glasgow Rd. (☎ **0131/ 334-9191**), off A8 on Edinburgh's western outskirts. It offers standard or executive (more spacious) doubles, each with a good bed and bath, ranging from £125 to £185 ($212.50 to $314.50), breakfast included. The place is large, with 259 rooms, 160 of which are for nonsmokers. Facilities include an indoor pool, a gym, and a sauna/ solarium. The restaurant serves an international cuisine, including some Scottish specialties.

## IN OR NEAR THE CENTER
### VERY EXPENSIVE

✪ **Balmoral Hotel.** Princes St., Edinburgh EH2 2EQ. ☎ **800/225-5843** in the U.S., or 0131/556-2414. Fax 0131/557-3747. 186 units. A/C MINIBAR TV TEL. £215 ($365.50) double; £400 ($680) suite. AE, DC, MC, V. Valet parking £15 ($25.50). Bus: 3, 7, 14, 31, 33, or 69.

This legendary place opened in 1902 as the largest and grandest hotel in the north of Britain and after a $35-million restoration reopened in 1991 under a new name, the Balmoral. Almost directly above the Waverley Rail Station, it features a soaring clock tower many locals consider one of their city's landmarks. Kilted doormen and a bag-piper supply the Scottish presence. Furnished with reproduction pieces, the guest

# Edinburgh Accommodations & Dining

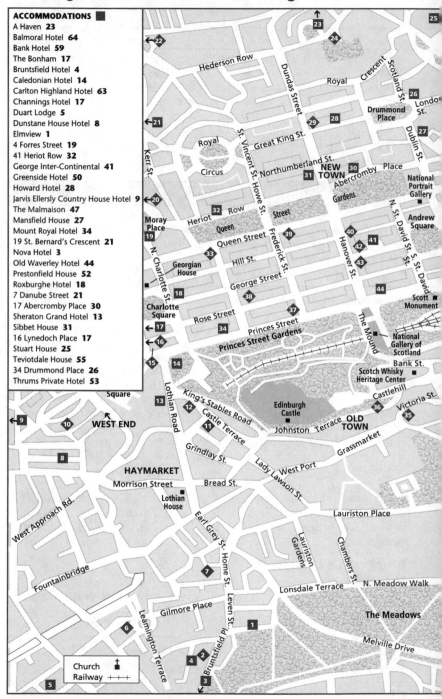

**ACCOMMODATIONS** ■
A Haven **23**
Balmoral Hotel **64**
Bank Hotel **59**
The Bonham **17**
Bruntsfield Hotel **4**
Caledonian Hotel **14**
Carlton Highland Hotel **63**
Channings Hotel **17**
Duart Lodge **5**
Dunstane House Hotel **8**
Elmview **1**
4 Forres Street **19**
41 Heriot Row **32**
George Inter-Continental **41**
Greenside Hotel **50**
Howard Hotel **28**
Jarvis Ellersly Country House Hotel **9**
The Malmaison **47**
Mansfield House **27**
Mount Royal Hotel **34**
19 St. Bernard's Crescent **21**
Nova Hotel **3**
Old Waverley Hotel **44**
Prestonfield House **52**
Roxburghe Hotel **18**
7 Danube Street **21**
17 Abercromby Place **30**
Sheraton Grand Hotel **13**
Sibbet House **31**
16 Lynedoch Place **17**
Stuart House **25**
Teviotdale House **55**
34 Drummond Place **26**
Thrums Private Hotel **53**

Church ✝
Railway +++

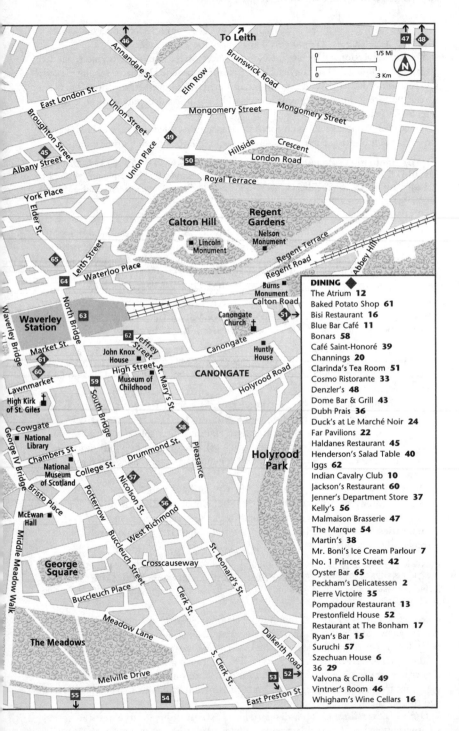

**DINING** ◆

The Atrium **12**
Baked Potato Shop **61**
Bisi Restaurant **16**
Blue Bar Café **11**
Bonars **58**
Café Saint-Honoré **39**
Channings **20**
Clarinda's Tea Room **51**
Cosmo Ristorante **33**
Denzler's **48**
Dome Bar & Grill **43**
Dubh Prais **36**
Duck's at Le Marché Noir **24**
Far Pavilions **22**
Haldanes Restaurant **45**
Henderson's Salad Table **40**
Iggs **62**
Indian Cavalry Club **10**
Jackson's Restaurant **60**
Jenner's Department Store **37**
Kelly's **56**
Malmaison Brasserie **47**
The Marque **54**
Martin's **38**
Mr. Boni's Ice Cream Parlour **7**
No. 1 Princes Street **42**
Oyster Bar **65**
Peckham's Delicatessen **2**
Pierre Victoire **35**
Pompadour Restaurant **13**
Prestonfield House **52**
Restaurant at The Bonham **17**
Ryan's Bar **15**
Suruchi **57**
Szechuan House **6**
36 **29**
Valvona & Crolla **49**
Vintner's Room **46**
Whigham's Wine Cellars **16**

rooms are distinguished and rather large—a graceful reminder of Edwardian sprawl. All contain hair dryers. The hotel is managed by the Forte chain.

**Dining/Diversions:** The elegant No. 1 Princes Street restaurant is recommended later under "Dining." More convivial is the informal brasserie Hadrian's, serving platters, salads, and drinks. Afternoon tea is served in the high-ceilinged Palm Court. There are several bar areas; foremost among these is N.B.'s, a Scottish pub with an entrance directly on Princes Street.

**Amenities:** Concierge; 24-hour room service; laundry/valet; baby-sitting; hairdresser; large health club with Jacuzzi, sauna, exercise equipment, and pool; upscale shops.

✪ **The Bonham.** 35 Drumsheugh Gardens, Edinburgh EH3 7RN. ☎ **0131/226-6050.** Fax 0131/226-6080. www.thebonham.com. E-mail: reserve@thebonham.com. 48 units. A/C MINIBAR TV TEL. £165–£225 ($280.50–$382.50) double; £255–£295 ($433.50–$501.50) suite. AE, DC, MC, V. Bus: 23 or 27.

One of Edinburgh's newest and most stylish hotels occupies three connected townhouses that have functioned since the 19th century as dorms for the local university and as a nursing home. In 1998, all that changed when a team of entrepreneurs poured millions of pounds into its refurbishment, pumped up the style level, and outfitted each high-ceilinged guest room in a hip blend of old and new. Each has an individualized theme, plush upholsteries, and a TV with a keyboard hooked up to a barrage of facilities on the Internet—the first setup of its kind in Europe.

**Dining:** The Restaurant at the Bonham is reviewed under "Dining," below.

**Amenities:** Concierge, 24-hour room service, laundry, baby-sitting.

**Caledonian Hotel.** Princes St., Edinburgh EH1 2AB. ☎ **0131/459-9988.** Fax 0131/225-6632. 249 units. MINIBAR TV TEL. £225–£340 ($382.50–$578) double; from £360 ($612) suite. Children 15 and under stay free in parents' room. AE, DC, MC, V. Parking £7.50 ($12.75). Bus: 33.

Completely renovated in 1991, the hotel remains one of the city's landmarks and offers commanding views over Edinburgh Castle and the Princes Street Gardens. The pastel-colored public rooms are reminiscent of Edwardian splendor, and the guest rooms (many of which are exceptionally spacious) are conservatively but individually styled, with reproduction furniture; they all contain hair dryers. The fifth-floor rooms are the smallest.

**Dining/Diversions:** The hotel contains a traditional pub, Henry J. Beans, and Chisholms Bar. More formal meals are served in Pompadour Restaurant (see "Dining," below). A traditional British tea is featured in the high-ceilinged lounge.

**Amenities:** Concierge, 24-hour room service, baby-sitting, laundry/valet, garden, cashmere shop, health club.

**Carlton Highland Hotel.** 19 North Bridge, Edinburgh EH1 1SD. ☎ **0131/556-7277.** Fax 0131/5562691. 197 units. TV TEL. £193 ($328.10) double; from £300 ($510) suite. Rates include breakfast. Children 14 and under stay free in parents' room. AE, DC, MC, V. Parking £6 ($10.20). Bus: 55.

A century ago, this was one of Edinburgh's leading department stores, with 4 of its 10 stories below sidewalk level. In 1984, this baronial pile was converted into a plush hotel. Its Victorian turrets, Flemish gables, and severe gray stonework rise from a corner on the Royal Mile, near Waverley Station. The interior is a surprisingly bright and airy modern space—each guest room has a kind of Scandinavian simplicity, most with matching tartan drapes and spreads. Amenities include tea/coffeemakers, hair dryers, and trouser presses; the bathrooms tend to be quite small.

**Dining/Diversions:** Quills is designed like a private 19th-century library and offers an international and Scottish regional menu. A buffet is offered at the Eureka.

A pianist entertains in the lounge, and the new coffee bar called Central Perk is based on the cafe in the sitcom "Friends."

**Amenities:** Concierge, 24-hour room service, baby-sitting, laundry/valet, hairdresser, exercise room, pool, solarium, whirlpool, sauna, two squash courts, refurbished gym, aerobics studio.

**George Inter-Continental.** 19–21 George St., Edinburgh EH2 2PB. ☎ **800/327-0200** in the U.S., or 0131/225-1251. Fax 0131/226-5644. www.interconti.com. E-mail: edinburgh@ interconti.com. 195 units. MINIBAR TV TEL. £190–£220 ($323–$374) double; from £475 ($807.50) suite. AE, DC, MC, V. Bus: 41 or 42.

Designed by famed Robert Adam and only yards from St. Andrew Square, the city's financial center, the George opened in 1755, housed the trading room of the Caledonian Insurance Company in 1845, and was enlarged and graced with a new facade in 1881. A new wing was added in 1972, and the place has thrived since as a member of the Inter-Continental Hotel group. The public rooms have retained the style, elegance, and old-fashioned comfort of those in a country house. In various sizes, the guest rooms have undergone frequent refurbishments and offer luxurious beds and hair dryers. The best rooms, opening onto views, are those on the fourth floor and above in the new wing.

**Dining/Diversions:** The Carver's Table, with some of Adam's design still intact, has for almost a century fed diners on prime Scottish beef, lamb, and pork. Le Chambertin is the choice for gourmet French fare. The Gathering of the Clans Bar is decorated with artifacts of the whisky industry and clan mementos. May to October on Sunday to Thursday, Scottish evenings include a show and five-course meal for £39.50 ($67.15).

**Amenities:** Concierge, 24-hour room service, baby-sitting, laundry/valet, nearby gym free for guests.

**✪ Howard Hotel.** 34 Great King St., Edinburgh EH3 6QH. ☎ **0131/557-3500.** Fax 0131/ 557-6515. www.thehoward.com. E-mail: reserve@thehoward.com. 15 units. TV TEL. £245– £275 ($416.50–$467.50) double; £325 ($552.50) suite. Rates include breakfast. AE, DC, MC, V. Bus: 13, 23, 27, or C5.

These three Georgian terrace houses (ca. 1770–1825) have been combined into one of Edinburgh's finest hotels. The decor is a mix of traditional and modern, with antiques and reproductions. The spacious guest rooms have top-notch Georgian-style furnishings and elaborate baths with hair dryers. Hot beverages can be supplied at any time.

**Dining:** The elegant No. 36 restaurant specializes in smoked Scottish salmon and pan-fried Scottish sirloin. Lunches are à la carte and rather light. Drinks are served in the drawing room.

**Amenities:** Concierge, 24-hour room service, baby-sitting, laundry/valet; visits to fitness center outside hotel can be arranged.

**Roxburghe Hotel.** 38 Charlotte Sq. (at the corner of George St.), Edinburgh EH2 4HG. ☎ **0131/240-5500.** Fax 0131/240-5555. www.macdonaldhotels.co.uk. E-mail: info@ roxburghe.macdonald-hotels.co.uk. 201 units. MINIBAR TV TEL. £180 ($306) double; from £230 ($391) suite. Children 13 and under stay free in parents' room. AE, DC, MC, V. Parking £8 ($13.60). Bus: 100.

The heart of the Roxburghe is a stately Robert Adam townhouse of gray stone on a tree-filled square, a short walk from Princes Street. The atmosphere is traditional, reflected in the drawing room with its ornate ceiling and woodwork, antique furnishings, and tall arched windows. In 1998–99, the hotel was enlarged into two neighboring buildings, and £12 million (about $20 million) was spent tripling the original number of guest rooms, which vary in size. The largest are in the original building and maintain features like their imposing fireplaces. The new rooms have more recent furnishings and more up-to-date plumbing. All have clock radios, trouser presses, and tea/coffeemakers, plus sewing kits, hair dryers, and bubble baths.

**Dining:** The traditionally elegant Consort Restaurant serves all meals and is a good place to congregate for drinks. The cheerful Melrose Room Buttery serves light refreshments.

**Amenities:** Concierge; 24-hour room service; dry cleaning/laundry; valet parking; lounge; conference rooms; on-site leisure facilities, including gym, pool, Jacuzzi, beauty therapy room, sauna.

**Sheraton Grand Hotel.** 1 Festival Sq., Edinburgh EH3 9SR. ☎ **800/325-3535** in the U.S. and Canada, or 0131/229-9131. Fax 0131/228-4510. www.sheraton.com. 278 units. A/C MINIBAR TV TEL. June–Sept £230–£245 ($391–$416.50) double, from £350 ($595) suite; off-season £215 ($365.50) double, £300 ($510) suite. Children 16 and under stay free in parents' room. AE, DC, MC, V. Free parking. Bus: 4, 15, or 44.

This former railway siding, a short walk from Princes Street, was developed into a six-story postmodern structure housing a glamorous hotel and an office complex. The hotel is elegant, with soaring public rooms and carpeting in appropriate tones of thistle and mauve. Boasting a central location and a well-chosen staff, this is the most appealing modern hotel in the capital. The spacious, well-furnished guest rooms offer double-glazed windows, plus hair dryers and modem access. Glamorous suites are also available, as are rooms for nonsmokers and rooms equipped for travelers with disabilities. The castle-view rooms on the top three floors are the best.

**Dining/Diversions:** With views over the Festival Square fountain, the main restaurant presents well-prepared main courses and a lavish Sunday buffet. The Terrace, with castle views, is a brasserie-style restaurant where chefs prepare specialties in front of you; the intimate Grill Room provides the best of Scottish produce. The plushly modern cocktail bar is a favorite rendezvous for locals.

**Amenities:** Concierges; 24-hour room service; baby-sitting; laundry/valet; leisure center with indoor pool (too small for lap swimming), whirlpool, sauna, and fully equipped gym; business center.

## EXPENSIVE

**17 Abercromby Place.** 17 Abercromby Place, Edinburgh EH3 6LB. ☎ **0131/557-8036.** Fax 0131/558-3453. www.abercrombyhouse.com. E-mail: eirlyslloyd@virgin.net. 10 units. TV TEL. £100–£120 ($170–$204) double. Rates include breakfast. MC, V. Free parking. Bus: 15 or 100.

Eirlys Lloyd became popular when she ran the highly recommended 28 Northumberland Street nearby. She has since moved into what some guests consider an even better B&B a 5-minute walk north of Princes Street. Although built by a less well-known architect, the gray-stone terrace house was the 1820s home of William Playfair, who designed many of Edinburgh's landmarks, including the Royal Scottish Academy and Surgeon Hall on the campus of the Royal College of Surgeons. While some of the guest rooms are bigger than others, they're all of an acceptable size and are painted in distinct colors and furnished with antiques. The beds vary from king to queen size, and all rooms contain tea/coffeemakers and hair dryers. Two of the rooms in what was once a coach house are connected to the main house. Evening meals can be arranged with prior notice for £25 ($42.50) per person.

**✪ Channings Hotel.** 15 S. Learmonth Gardens, Edinburgh EH4 1EZ. ☎ **0131/315-2226.** Fax 0131/332-9631. www.channings.co.uk. E-mail: reserve@channings.co.uk. 48 units. TV TEL. £125–£170 ($212.50–$289) double; £260 ($442) garden suite. Rates include breakfast. Children 14 and under stay free in parents' room. AE, DC, MC, V. Bus: 41 or 42.

Five Edwardian terrace houses were combined to create a hotel 7 blocks north of Dean Village in a tranquil residential area. Although it's a 5-minute drive from the city center, it maintains the atmosphere of a Scottish country house, with oak paneling, ornate fireplaces, molded ceilings, and antiques. The guest rooms are in a modern style, with trouser presses and hair dryers; the front rooms get the views, but the rear ones get the quiet. The most desirable units are the "Executives," most of which have bay windows and wingback chairs.

**Dining:** Even if you're not a guest consider a meal here, as Channings offers some of the best hotel dining in Edinburgh (see "Dining," below).

**Amenities:** Concierge, room service, laundry.

**Mount Royal Hotel.** 53 Princes St., Edinburgh EH2 2DG. ☎ **0131/225-7161.** Fax 0131/ 220-4671. 158 units. TV TEL. £145–£165 ($246.50–$280.50) double; £170 ($289) triple or family room. AE, DC, MC, V. Bus: 15 or 100.

The Mount Royal, a remake of an 1860s hotel, is right in the middle of Princes Street. A modern world emerges as you climb the spiral staircase or take an elevator to the second floor, with its reception rooms and lounges and floor-to-ceiling windows opening onto views of the Old Town and the castle. There aren't a lot of frills, but the comfort is genuine in the average-sized streamlined guest rooms with a view. All have hair dryers and trouser presses. Be aware this is a tour-group favorite.

**Dining/Diversions:** The main dining room serves reasonably priced lunches and dinners, offering a carving table and à la carte menus. The lounge, with floor-to-ceiling windows and views over the Scott Memorial and Princes Street, provides a wide range of savory and sweet snacks and beverages throughout the day.

**Amenities:** Concierge, room service, laundry/valet.

**Old Waverley Hotel.** 43 Princes St., Edinburgh EH2 2BY. ☎ **0131/556-4648.** Fax 031/ 557-6316. 66 units. TV TEL. £158 ($268.60) double. Rates include breakfast. AE, DC, MC, V. Parking £3 ($5.10) for 12 hrs. Bus: 15 or 100.

Opposite Waverley Station, the Old Waverley dates from 1848, when this seven-floor structure was built to celebrate the then-newfangled railroads. The lounges have been given a contemporary look. The recently refurbished guest rooms have satellite TVs, trouser presses, hair dryers, and direct-dial phones; some look onto Princes Street and the castle.

**Dining:** The hotel has a good carvery-style restaurant serving à la carte and table d'hôte meals; charges depend on how many courses you take but start at £14.50 ($24.65).

**Amenities:** Concierge, 24-hour room service, laundry.

**✪ Prestonfield House.** Priestfield Rd., Edinburgh EH16 5UT. ☎ **0131/668-3346.** Fax 0131/668-3976. www.prestonfieldhouse.com. E-mail: prestonfield_house@compuserve. com. 31 units. TV TEL. £125–£225 ($212.50–$382.50) double; £370 ($629) suite. Rates include breakfast. AE, DC, MC, V. Free parking. Bus: 21 or 33.

The Prestonfield, rising in Jacobean splendor above 14 acres of forest, field, and garden, a 15-minute drive from the center, is more celebrated as a restaurant than as a hotel. It was designed by Sir William Bruce, who also designed Holyroodhouse. Guests appreciate traditional atmosphere and 1689 architecture as well as the peacocks and Highland cattle that strut or stroll across the grounds. The guest rooms are decorated in a Scottish country-house theme, and although varying in size are all spacious enough, with trouser presses and hair dryers. They open onto a view of Arthur's Seat, a golf course, and the recently restored gardens. In 1997, the five rooms in the main house were supplemented by a three-story annex that matches the main house; the rooms here are more up to date, with lots of sun thanks to the large windows.

**Dining/Diversions:** The hotel has one of the city's finest dining rooms (see "Dining," below), plus two bars.

**Amenities:** Concierge, room service, baby-sitting, laundry/dry cleaning, private rooms for meetings or receptions.

## MODERATE

**16 Lynedoch Place.** 16 Lynedoch Place, Edinburgh EH3 7PY. ☎ 0131/225-5507. Fax 0131/236-4185. E-mail: susie.lynedoch@btinternet.com. 5 units. TV. £70–£90 ($119–$153) double. Rates include breakfast. MC, V. Bus: 19.

Aside from the flower-filled front garden (unusual for a house of this type), this stone-fronted Georgian rowhouse is similar to dozens of others. What's unusual about it, however, is that generations of only four families have lived in it since it was built in 1821. "It's the kind of house that makes you want to put down roots," according to Andrew and Susie Hamilton, your affable hosts. You'll find a collection of family antiques, high ceilings with deep cove moldings, a cantilevered staircase illuminated by a glassed-in overhead cupola, pinewood floors, and large windows. The elaborate English/Scottish breakfasts are served in a formal dining room with one oval-shaped end. The midsize guest rooms are cozy, comfortable, and decorated with charm and style. Andrew is Scottish and an expert in planning itineraries through the Highlands, thanks to the time he spent there as a member of the elite Black Watch infantry.

**19 St. Bernard's Crescent.** 19 St. Bernard's Crescent, Edinburgh EH4 1NR. ☎ 0131/332-6162. Fax 0131/225-7739. www.aboutedinburgh.com/stbernards/index.html. E-mail: balfourwm@aol.com. 3 units. £80–£90 ($136–$153) double. Rates include continental or full Scottish breakfast. MC, V. Bus: 24 or 34.

One of the city's most appealing guesthouses occupies the grand home of William Balfour, owner of Edinburgh's Theatre School of Dance and Drama. It was built as an architectural showplace in the early 1800s by the son of Sir Henry Raeburn, one of Scotland's most prominent portraitists. It has grand Doric pillars, a magnificent sandstone staircase that pivots upward around a circular stairwell, and a distinguished collection of 18th- and 19th-century furniture. Guests enjoy access to the salons and sitting rooms (site of a grand piano). The guest rooms are midsize and comfortably appointed, often with four-poster beds. You'll feel as if you're visiting the house of your favorite aunt.

**34 Drummond Place.** 34 Drummond Place, Edinburgh EH3 6PW. ☎ 0131/556-5400. Fax 0131/556-7707. www.aboutedinburgh.com/drummond/index.html. E-mail: popcorn@atlas. co.uk. 3 units. TV. £80–£90 ($136–$153) double; £105 ($178.50) family room for 3. Extra person £25 ($42.50) per night including breakfast. No credit cards. Bus: 13.

A 10-minute walk north of Princes Street, the exterior of this B&B is as severe-looking as John Calvin himself, thanks to a raw granite-fronted 1818 design that's almost identical to that of the townhouses flanking it. The interior, however, is stylish, whimsical, and colorful, incorporating the skillful decorative techniques of owner Kirsty MacGregor and her assistant, Sandra. Your choice of guest rooms includes the large, bright Master Bedroom; the blue-and-cream Star Room; and the floral-patterned Family Room, which in a pinch can host up to three. Views from the front of the house overlook the garden, and views from the back open onto the Firth of Forth.

**4 Forres Street.** 4 Forres St., Edinburgh EH3 6BJ. ☎ 0131/220-5073. www.aboutscotland. co.uk/edin/forres.html. E-mail: forres.street@btinternet.com. 5 units. TV. £80–£100 ($136–$170) double. Rates include breakfast. MC, V. Bus: 82.

Behind a granite facade in the commercial heart of town, this well-managed guest-house is a 2-minute walk from Princes Street. Built in 1825 and later transformed into rather dowdy-looking offices, it was revitalized in the mid-1990s by Jim and Maria Lennon into this cozy B&B. A sweeping staircase leads upstairs to the Yellow, Cream, and Pink Rooms, high-ceilinged and very large. (The Cream Room has the largest bathroom in the house, with its own Jacuzzi.) Less spacious, but still very comfortable, are the Blue and Green Rooms. Unlike many other Edinburgh guesthouses, this one welcomes kids (the Lennons have very young children). No smoking.

○ **41 Heriot Row.** 41 Heriot Row, Edinburgh EH3 6ES. ☎/fax **0131/225-3113.** www. wwwonderful.net. E-mail: erlendc@lineone.net. 2 units, 1 with bathroom. £80 ($136) double without bathroom; £90 ($153) double with bathroom. No credit cards. Bus: 4.

This stone-fronted townhouse was built in 1817 on what was then one of Edinburgh's most prestigious residential streets. Today, it's the home of Scottish-French Erlend and Hélène Clouston, who make an event out of breakfasts and are especially proud of the fenced-in rectangular park across the street (guests can gain access to it); its decorative pond is said to have inspired Robert Louis Stevenson while he was writing *Treasure Island.* A highlight of the house is the impressive wide hallway, at one end of which rises a baronial light-flooded staircase. The furnishings are attractive and upscale, with unusual paintings and prints, exposed flagstone floors, and antique rugs and furnishings. The guest rooms have brass headboards and unusual books, some by writer/journalist Erlend.

○ **7 Danube Street.** 7 Danube St., Edinburgh EH4 1NN. ☎ **0131/332-2755.** Fax 0131/ 343-3648. www.aboutedinburgh.com/danube. E-mail: 7.danubestreet@virgin.net. 5 units. TV TEL. £90 ($153) double. Rates include breakfast. MC, V. Free parking nearby. Bus: 28.

This 1825 B&B, run by Fiona Mitchell-Rose and her husband, Colin, is in Stockbridge, a stylish residential neighborhood a 10-minute walk north of the commercial center. It was designed by noteworthy architect James Milne and was once the home of Scottish painter Horatio McCulloch. The public rooms and spacious guest rooms boast artfully draped chintzes, reflecting Fiona's experience as a decorator in London. The most desirable room has a four-poster bed and direct access down steps to the garden. A small apartment around the corner serves as part of the B&B. All rooms are well stocked with expensive perfumed soaps and shampoos as well as adapters, dental floss, and nail files. You're likely to meet your hosts and other guests in the formal dining room in the morning, where you'll enjoy a lavish breakfast: ample portions of venison sausages, omelets made from free-range eggs, homemade scones, freshly squeezed orange juice, and jams and marmalades put up by Fiona.

**A Haven.** 180 Ferry Rd., Edinburgh, EH6 4NS. ☎ **0131/554-6559.** Fax 0131/554-5252. www.a-haven.co.uk. E-mail: reservations@a-haven.co.uk. 12 units. TV TEL. £60–£98 ($102–$166.60) double. Rates include breakfast. AE, MC, V. Free parking. Bus: 1, 6, 7, 11, 14, 25, C3, 17, 14A, 25A, or 55.

A Haven is a semi-detached gray-stone Victorian house a 15-minute walk or a 5-minute bus ride north of the rail station in an up-and-coming neighborhood. The guest rooms are of various sizes (the biggest on the second floor) and furnished with traditional pieces. The hotel was recently refurbished, and the bathrooms now boast Italian tiles. Some rooms in back overlook the Firth of Forth, and those in the front open onto views of Arthur's Seat. All rooms come with hospitality trays, data ports, and hair dryers. Ronnie Murdock extends a Scottish welcome in this family-type place. He has a licensed bar, but breakfast is the only meal served.

**Bank Hotel.** Royal Mile at 1–3 S. Bridge St., Edinburgh EH1 1LL. ☎ **0131/556-9043.** Fax 0131/558-1362. www.festival-inns.co.uk. 9 units. TV TEL. £60–£150 ($102–$255) double. Rates include breakfast. AE, DC, MC, V. Nearby parking £6 ($10.20). Bus: 4, 15, 31, or 100.

This simple hotel offers better value than many of its competitors in this congested neighborhood beside the Royal Mile. Until around 1990 it was a branch of the Royal Bank of Scotland, and the past is still evident in its bulky no-nonsense design. Today, a restaurant (which demands from its staff more time and attention than the rooms) occupies its first floor. Upstairs, high ceilings, simple furnishings, and king-sized beds provide comfort; all rooms have hair dryers. In the restaurant, you can order freshly made pasta, fish, chicken and vegetarian dishes as well as baguettes, with prices ranging from £1.50 to £4.95 ($2.55 to $8.40). A wooden bar, which was once marble and has now been refurbished with a balcony, stays open 9am to 1am, with a special license to 3am during the festival and at New Year's.

✪ **Sibbet House.** 26 Northumberland St., Edinburgh EH3 6LS. ☎ **0131/556-1078.** Fax 0131/557-9445. www.sibbet-house.co.uk. E-mail: sibbethouse@zetnet.co.uk. 7 units. TV TEL. £90–£110 ($153–$187) double; £130 ($221) suite. Rates include breakfast. MC, V. Free parking. Bus: 13, 23, or 27.

On a residential terrace a 5-minute walk from Princes Street, this sandstone-fronted Georgian house is the cheerful domain of Anita and Danish-born Jens Steffert, who do everything they can to distinguish their home from just another hotel. The small to medium guest rooms are color themed and furnished with antiques (one has a four-poster bed) but also contain hair dryers. Drinks can be served in the drawing room/salon, but breakfast is the only meal served. One reader claimed the stay here was literally like visiting with friends.

**Stuart House.** 12 E. Claremont St., Edinburgh EH7 4JP. ☎ **0131/557-9030.** Fax 0131/557-0563. www.users.globalnet.co.uk/~stuartho. E-mail: june@stuartguesthouse.co.uk. 7 units. TV TEL. £70–£90 ($119–$153) double or twin. AE, DC, MC, V. Closed 1 week at Christmas. Street parking. Bus: 8, 9, or 19.

At the western end of Claremont Street, in one of the many dozens of nearly identical rowhouses, this is a charming B&B run by the Anglo-Scottish team of June and Alex Watson. Convenient for the commercial center, it offers modernized high-ceilinged rooms of an average size that retain many of their original 1830 cove moldings. Each has a tea/coffeemaker and hair dryer. Breakfast is the only meal served. Street parking is available.

### INEXPENSIVE

**Greenside Hotel.** 9 Royal Terrace, Edinburgh EH7 5AB. ☎/fax **0131/557-0022.** www.townhousehotels.co.uk. E-mail: greensidehotel@ednet.co.uk. 15 units. TV TEL. £45–£90 ($76.50–$153) double. Rates include breakfast. AE, DC, MC, V. Bus: 4, 15, or 44.

Behind a chiseled sandstone facade on the back side of Carlton Hill, this four-story Georgian was built in 1786. During a long recent renovation, every effort was made to retain as many Georgian features as possible, including the high ceilings, the original cove moldings, and the elaborate trim. Guests access their rooms via a winding stairs, illuminated by a skylight. The rooms are so large that 10 of them contain a double bed and two singles. (In some cases, these singles are converted from sofas.) The Firth of Forth, the former royal yacht *Britannia,* and the dramatic Forth Road Bridge are visible from the uppermost front floors; a sloping tiered garden, with a patio at the bottom, is visible from the rear windows. Breakfast is served in a formal dining room.

**Mansfield House.** 57 Dublin St., Edinburgh EH3 6NL. ☎ **0131/556-7980.** 9 units, 6 with bathroom. TV. £50 ($85) double without bathroom; £70 ($119) double with bathroom. Rates include continental breakfast. MC, V. Bus: 19 or 39.

Well located in the New Town, this clean and friendly gay guesthouse offers individually decorated rooms of reasonable size, all with tea/coffeemakers. The bathrooms are

---

### ⓘ Family-Friendly Hotels

**Thrums Private Hotel** *(see p. 84)*   This hotel takes its name from J. M. Barrie's fictional name for his hometown of Kirriemuir. Barrie is known to children as the author of *Peter Pan*. Kids are made especially welcome here and are housed in family rooms with their parents.

**Teviotdale House** *(see p. 85)*   Some enthusiastic visitors rate this place the best B&B in Edinburgh. Three rooms are large enough for families with up to four members. A great value.

**Nova Hotel** *(see p. 84)*   This hotel features five spacious family rooms, each designed for total comfort. It's in a quiet, secluded cul-de-sac.

---

clean and fairly well proportioned. The hotel is within walking distance of all the gay bars, clubs, and restaurants. It's always busy, so early booking is advised.

## WEST OF THE CENTER
### EXPENSIVE

**Jarvis Ellersly Country House Hotel.** 4 Ellersly Rd., Edinburgh EH12 6HZ. ☎ **0131/ 337-6888.** Fax 0131/313-2543. 57 units. TV TEL. £139 ($236.30) double; £154 ($261.80) suite. AE, DC, MC, V. Free parking. Bus: 2, 2A, 21, 26, 31, 36, or 36A. Take A8 2½ (4km) miles west of the city center.

Within walled gardens, this three-story Edwardian country house offers privacy in a dignified residential area near the Murrayfield rugby grounds, about a 5-minute ride from the center. The well-equipped guest rooms (with hair dryers), which vary in size, are in the main house or the less desirable annex. After a refurbishment, the Jarvis Ellersly is better than ever and the service first class.

**Dining:** The hotel possesses a well-stocked wine cellar and offers good-tasting Scottish and French meals, with dinner going for £15.95 ($27.10).

**Amenities:** Room service, laundry/valet service.

### MODERATE

**Dunstane House Hotel.** 4 W. Coates, Edinburgh EH12 5JQ. ☎ **0131/337-5320.** Fax 0131/ 337-6169. www.dunstanehousehotel.co.uk. E-mail: reservations@dunstanehousehotel.co.uk. 16 units. TV TEL. £67–£99 ($113.90–$168.30) double. AE, DC, MC, V. Free parking. Bus: 2, 12, 26, 31, or 69.

This stone-sided 1850 house sits behind a pleasant garden, a 10-minute walk from Princes Street in the center of the New Town. The owner maintains the place in well-scrubbed condition, with respectful awareness of the building's architectural importance. Varying from large to medium, the guest rooms have been redecorated recently, and each comes with a radio, trouser press, tea/coffeemaker, and hair dryer. Two have four-poster beds. Antiques or reproductions are used throughout. Homemade soup and sandwiches are available on request for £4.95 ($8.40) until 8pm.

## SOUTH OF THE CENTER
### EXPENSIVE

**Best Western Bruntsfield Hotel.** 69–74 Bruntsfield Place, Edinburgh EH10 4HH. ☎ **800/528-1234** in the U.S. and Canada, or 0131/229-1393. Fax 0131/229-5634. www. thebruntsfield.co.uk. E-mail: bruntdfield@queensferry-hotels.co.uk. 75 units. TV TEL. £115– £155 ($195.50–$263.50) double. AE, DC, MC, V. Free parking. Bus: 11, 15, 16, 17, or 23.

Bruntsfield's neo-Gothic facade overlooks an expanse of park a 15-minute bus ride south of the city heart, opposite what may be the world's oldest golf course, Bruntsfield Links. Like the other 19th-century buildings lining the street, this four-story hotel is built of evenly spaced rows of honey-colored stones. Inside, all is neat and stylish, including French-inspired armchairs and pastel peaches and blues. The nice-sized guest rooms have recently been refurbished, each with a radio, hair dryer, tea/coffeemaker, iron, and voicemail. Some are equipped for travelers with disabilities. The hotel is frequented mainly by businesspeople during the week, giving way to couples and families on weekends.

**Dining:** On the premises is the attractive Potting Shed restaurant, along with The King's Bar.

**Amenities:** Room service, baby-sitting.

## MODERATE

**Elmview.** 15 Glengyle Terrace, Edinburgh EH3 9LN. ☎ **0131/228-1973.** Fax 0131/229-7296. www.elmview.co.uk. 4 units. TV TEL. £75–£95 ($127.50–$161.50) double. MC, V. Bus: 11, 16, 17, 19, or 23.

One of the best things about this stone-fronted rowhouse is the view it provides over the putting greens of Scotland's oldest golf course, Bruntsfield Links. Half a mile (1km) southwest of Princes Street, it was built as a private home in the late 19th century and today functions as a highly personalized small-scale guesthouse. The high-ceilinged rooms are spacious and comfortable, with flower-patterned fabrics and homelike charm. During clement weather, a rear garden provides a pleasant spot for breakfast, prepared and served by Marny and Richard Hill, the resident owners.

**Nova Hotel.** 5 Bruntsfield Crescent, Edinburgh EH10 4EZ. ☎ **0131/447-6437.** Fax 0131/452-8126. www.novahotel.com.uk. E-mail: jamie@scotland-hotels.demon.co.uk. 12 units. TV TEL. £70–£80 ($119–$136) double; £100–£120 ($170–$204) family room for up to 6. MC, V. Bus: 42 or 46.

The Nova, an 1875 Victorian, is on a quiet cul-de-sac a 10-minute ride from the center, with a view over Bruntsfield Links in front and the Pentland Hills in back. It's within walking distance of the Royal Mile and Princes Street. You'll find its guest rooms large and well appointed, with hair dryers, trouser presses, tea/coffeemakers, and central heating. On the ground floor, guests enjoy the lounge that also operates as a cocktail bar. There's street parking.

**Thrums Private Hotel.** 14–15 Minto St., Edinburgh EH9 1RQ. ☎ **0131/667-5545.** Fax 0131/667-8707. 15 units. TV TEL. £70–£90 ($119–$153) double; £90–£120 ($153–$204) family room. Rates include breakfast. MC, V. Free parking. Bus: 3, 7, 8, or 31.

About a mile (1.5km) south of Princes Street, Thrums is a pair of connected antique buildings, one a two-story 1820 Georgian and the other a small circa-1900 inn. The hotel contains recently refurbished high-ceilinged guest rooms with firm mattresses and contemporary (in the inn) or reproduction antique (in the Georgian) furnishings; all come with tea/coffeemakers and hair dryers. The bistro-inspired Thrums restaurant serves £10.50 ($17.85) set-price menus of British food, and there's also a bar and a peaceful garden.

## INEXPENSIVE

**Duart Lodge.** 73 Colinton Rd., Edinburgh EH10 5EF. ☎/fax **0131/447-6036.** 3 units, 2 with private bathroom. £50 ($85) double without bathroom; £60 ($102) double with bathroom. Rates include breakfast. MC, V. Bus: 9, 10, or 45.

Things at Duart Lodge are somewhat strict: Weekday breakfast, for example, is served only during 30 minutes, and the back garden and most of the public rooms are off-limits to guests. However, you may be able to overlook this because of the grand 1902 building by Robert Lorimer, one of Scotland's most famous architects. He designed it for the aristocratic MacLean family, who wanted it to resemble as closely as possible their ancestral home, Duart Castle on the Isle of Mull. You'll find faux crenellations above the russet-colored stone facade, a tile-sheathed inglenook in the front hallway, and a general sense of early-1900s proportions. Michael and Mary Mayer are your hosts, offering generous Scottish breakfasts and comfortable but somewhat spartan-looking guest rooms. The suburban location 2 miles (3km) south of Princes Street is tranquil.

✪ **Teviotdale House.** Grange Loan 53, Edinburgh EH9 2ER. ☎ **0131/667-4376.** Fax 0131/667-4376. www.edinburgh.org. E-mail: teviotdale.house@btinternet.com. 7 units. TV TEL. £56–£90 ($95.20–$153) double. AE, MC, V. Bus: 42.

This three-story 1848 house is Edinburgh's finest B&B, completely nonsmoking and furnished with antiques. Jane E. Coville's attention to detail has earned her an enviable reputation. Each individually decorated guest room has hot and cold running water, a hair dryer, and specialist mattresses; the three largest rooms can act as family accommodations with up to four beds. The home-cooked breakfast may be the highlight of your day's dining and can include smoked salmon, kippers, and home-baked bread and scones. The house is about a 10-minute bus ride from Princes Street, Waverley Station, and Edinburgh Castle, on a main route leading to the heart of the city. There's parking on the street.

## IN LEITH

The satellite neighborhood of Leith was once run-down, but it's now a hip, up-and-coming area.

### EXPENSIVE

✪ **The Malmaison.** 1 Tower Place, Leith, Edinburgh EH6 7DB. ☎ **0131/555-6868.** Fax 0131/468-5002. www.maison.com. E-mail: edinburgh@malmaison.com. 60 units. TV TEL. £110 ($187) double; £165 ($280.50) suite. AE, DC, MC, V. Free parking. Bus: 16 or 22.

This is the most interesting hotel in Edinburgh's dockyard district, a few steps from Leith Water. In the 1990s, it was converted from an 1883 seamen's mission/dorm and is capped by a stately stone clock tower. Its owners have created a hip, unpretentious hotel with a postmodern minimalist decor. The color schemes vary by floor; the purple-and-beige floor has been favored by rock bands who have stayed here during concert tours. Each average-sized room has a CD player, tea/coffeemaker, and hair dryer. The amenities and facilities are sparse, but you'll find the Malmaison Brasserie (see "Dining," below) and a cafe/wine bar favored by locals. In warm weather, tables are set up on the pavement outside, overlooking the harbor.

## CASTLE & COUNTRY-HOUSE HOTELS

To fulfill your fantasy, you might want to spend your first night in Scotland in a real castle or a baronial country house surrounded by gardens and spacious grounds.

### AT BONNYRIGG

**Dalhousie Castle.** Bonnyrigg, Edinburgh, Midlothian EH19 3JB. ☎ **01875/820-153.** Fax 01875/821-936. www.dalhousiecastle.co.uk. E-mail: res@dalhousiecastle.co.uk. 33 units. TV TEL. £160–£200 ($272–$340) double; £255 ($433.50) suite. Rates include breakfast. AE, DC, MC, V. Free parking. Take the A7 Carlisle–Edinburgh road 8 miles (13km) southeast of Edinburgh; it's just outside the village of Bonnyrigg.

Dalhousie dates from 1450 and has entertained such illustrious guests as Edward I, Henry IV, Oliver Cromwell, Sir Walter Scott, Robert Bruce, and Queen Victoria. It overlooks the banks of South Esk, where the red sandstone to build it was quarried. Today, this turreted house with ramparted terraces and battlements is the seat of the Ramsays of Dalhousie, who have converted it into a luxury hotel. The guest rooms (all with hair dryers) have plenty of space for sitting and relaxing, although each varies greatly from its neighbor in size and decor; the suite has a four-poster bed. The castle's dungeon restaurant offers many local Scottish dishes. The hotel can arrange salmon and trout fishing, horseback riding, and shooting.

## AT NORTH MIDDLETON

**Borthwick Castle.** North Middleton, Gorebridge, Midlothian EH23 4QY. ☎ **01875/ 820514.** Fax 01875/821702. 10 units. TEL. £115–£195 ($195.50–$331.50) double. Rates include breakfast. AE, DC, MC, V. Free parking. Take A7 about 12 miles (19km) south of Edinburgh; the castle is ¾ of a mile (1.2km) south of the hamlet of North Middleton.

In a pastoral valley, this is the ancestral home of Lord Borthwick, with a noble twin-towered keep (1430) that's the finest example of its kind in Britain today. It was here the ill-fated Mary Queen of Scots, besieged by both pro-English and pro-Calvinist forces that tried to destroy her, found refuge with her third husband, the earl of Bothwell, in 1567. In 1650, the castle was besieged by Oliver Cromwell's armies, and you can still see the damage inflicted by their cannons. Inside, the centerpiece is the Great Hall, boasting a minstrels' gallery, a hooded fireplace, a 40-foot vaulted Gothic ceiling, a medieval armor collection, and an alcove bar with a full collection of single-malt whiskies. All the guest rooms contain tea/coffeemakers, hair dryers, and excellent comfortable furnishings. Five contain four-poster beds, and each has a scattering of antiques and chintzes. Borthwick Castle is known for its excellent cuisine, personal service, and authentic medieval ambience. A four-course candlelight dinner, £28 ($47.60) per person, is served in the Great Hall; the cuisine is modern British with a heavy use of local produce.

# 4 Dining

Rivaled only by Glasgow, Edinburgh boasts the finest restaurants in Scotland, and the choice is more diverse at the millennium than ever before. Even if you don't care for some of the more exotic regional fare, like haggis (spicy intestines), you'll find an array of top French dining rooms along with other foreign fare, especially Indian. And you'll find more and more restaurants catering to vegetarians. But we advise you go native and sample many of the dishes Edinburgh is known for doing best, especially fresh salmon and seafood, game from Scottish fields, and Aberdeen Angus steaks. What's the rage at lunch? Stuffed potatoes (baked potatoes with a variety of stuffings). Many Scots make a lunch out of just one of these.

Some restaurants have sections reserved for nonsmokers and others don't. If smoking and dining (or nonsmoking and dining) are very important to you, inquire when making your reservation.

*Note:* For the locations of the restaurants below, see the "Edinburgh Accommodations & Dining" map on pp. 74–75.

## IN THE CENTER: THE NEW TOWN
### EXPENSIVE

✪ **The Atrium.** 10 Cambridge St. (beneath Saltire Court). ☎ **0131/228-8882.** Reservations recommended. Fixed-price lunch £14–£18 ($23.80–$30.60); dinner main courses £13.50–£18.50 ($22.95–$31.45). AE, DC, MC, V. Mon–Fri noon–2:30pm; Mon–Sat 6:30– 10:30pm. Closed 1 week at Christmas. MODERN SCOTTISH/INTERNATIONAL.

Frequently written about and frequently copied, the Atrium opened in 1993 in the beautifully designed atrium of an office complex. The designers created a moody environment for 60, with flickering oil lamps, dark colors, junkyard sculpture, tables assembled from railroad ties, and chairs slipcovered in natural canvas. It's a cross between an Argentine hacienda and upscale Beverly Hills bistro. The menu items change with the inspiration of chef Alan Maglieson and his manager, James Sankey, but may include seared salmon with ham and pea stew sauce; sea bass with herbed potatoes, asparagus, baby spinach, oysters, and baby fennel; or lamb with tarragon sauce. The desserts are marvelous, particularly the glazed lemon tart with berry coulis and crème fraîche.

**Bonars.** 56 St. Mary's St. ☎ **0131/556-5888.** Reservations required. Table d'hôte lunch menu £11 ($18.70); main courses £14.85–£17.50 ($25.25–$29.75). MC, V. Daily noon–2pm and 5–10pm. Bus: 1, 6, 34, or 35. MODERN SCOTTISH/FRENCH.

Just off the Royal Mile, between Cowgate and Canongate, Bonars is known for using the finest Scottish ingredients in its classic French cuisine and for offering a carefully chosen wine list and highly polished service. This is a good choice if you need to dine early before the theater. The menu changes regularly but is likely to feature fresh fish, perhaps halibut, often braised and served with scallops and red shellfish bisque. Certain dishes are Italian in origin, and the risotto with wild mushrooms and roasted olives with a carpaccio of hare is particularly good.

**Channings.** In Channings Hotel, 15 S. Learmonth Gardens. ☎ **0131/315-2225.** Reservations recommended. Fixed-price lunch £12 ($20.40) for 2 courses, £15 ($25.50) for 3 courses; fixed-price dinner £19.50 ($33.15) for 2 courses, £24.50 ($41.65) for 3 courses. AE, MC, V. Mon–Sat 12:30–2pm and 6:30–10pm. Closed Dec 26–29. Bus 41 or 42. SCOTTISH/INTERNATIONAL.

This is the main dining room of a previously recommended Edwardian charmer of a hotel, offering traditional decor and elegant service from a well-trained staff. The exemplary cuisine is created by head chef Richard Glennie and his first-class team, letting natural flavors shine through and using superior-quality fresh Scottish ingredients. The chefs know, for example, to go to the "Baines of Tarves" for his free-range Aberdeen chickens or to Iain Mellis for his cheese. The lunch menu provides a varied assortment of choices, including roasted monkfish tail on a white bean and smoked bacon cassoulet, and wild rabbit and artichoke terrine on mustard piccalilli with herb leaf salad. For dinner, you might opt for the terrine of seared tuna, potatoes, and slow-roasted tomatoes, or new season lamb saddle. To finish off a delectable dinner, try the hot banana and butterscotch soufflé with honeycomb ice cream. The restaurant is proud of its extensive wine list, which incorporates the old standards and newer, more exciting choices.

In addition to the formal dining room, there is a less formal brasserie with a log fireplace and a casual, relaxed atmosphere where you can enjoy bar meals, light lunches, and dinners.

**Cosmo Ristorante.** 58A N. Castle St. ☎ **0131/226-6743.** Reservations required. Main courses £13–£20 ($22.10–$34). AE, MC, V. Mon–Fri 12:30–2:15pm; Mon–Sat 7–10:30pm. Bus: 31 or 33. ITALIAN.

Even after more than 30 years in business, Cosmo is still one of the most popular Italian restaurants in town, where courtesy, efficiency, and good cooking draw in the crowds. In season, you can ask for mussels as an appetizer, and the soups and pastas are always reliable (the cost and size of your pasta portion are doubled if you order it as a main course). The kitchen is known for its *saltimbocca* (veal with ham) and Italian-inspired preparations of fish. This isn't the greatest Italian dining in Britain, but you'll certainly have a good filling meal.

**Dome Bar & Grill.** 14 George St. ☎ **0131/624-8624.** Reservations required lunch and dinner. Main courses £7–£13 ($11.90–$22.10) at lunch, £10–£17 ($17–$28.90) at dinner; fixed-price dinner menu £30 ($51). AE, DC, MC, V. Restaurant, Sun–Thurs noon–9:30pm; Fri–Sat noon–10:30pm; bar, Sun–Thurs noon–11:30pm, Fri–Sat noon–1am. Bus: 3, 21, 26, 31, or 85. INTERNATIONAL.

In a restored Georgian building with an elaborate domed ceiling, this bar and grill is part of the Dome entertainment complex. Throughout are elaborate columns, pedimental sculptures, and marble mosaic floors. The menu is ambitious and creative, with dishes like duck liver pâté with Cumberland sauce and oat cakes, venison-and-pheasant terrine, mullet fillet with horseradish mash, Aberdeen Angus fillet, and vegetable risotto with goat-cheese gatin.

**Ducks at Le Marché Noir.** 2–4 Eyre Place. ☎ **0131/558-1608.** Reservations recommended. Main courses £12–£15 ($20.40–$25.50) at lunch, £15–£20 ($25.50–$34) at dinner. AE, DC, MC, V. Sat–Mon 7–9:30pm; Tues–Fri 12:30–2pm and 7–9:30pm. Bus: 23 or 27. SCOTTISH/FRENCH.

Occupying an early-1900s wood-fronted house whose exterior and interior are decorated in shades of dark green, Ducks offers a handful of dishes honoring the traditions of Scotland—like baked haggis in filo pastry on a bed of turnip purée and red-wine sauce. More modern dishes are boudin of chicken and foie gras with wilted spinach and applesauce; seared salmon with leeks, asparagus, zucchini, and a salad of pickled ginger and sesame; roasted rack of lamb with thyme juice and roasted vegetables; and grilled red snapper with wild rice and lime-marinated sweet potato pickles. Owner Malcolm Duck has hired an excellent kitchen staff who take justifiable pride in every dish they turn out.

**Haldanes Restaurant.** 39A Albany St. (in the Albany Hotel building). ☎ **0131/556-8407.** Reservations recommended. Set-price lunch £10.50–£15 ($17.85–$25.50); set-price dinner £22.50–£27.50 ($38.25–$46.75). AE, DC, MC, V. Daily noon–2pm and 6–10pm. Bus: 15. SCOTTISH.

In a pair of cellar dining rooms decorated in royal blue and gold, this restaurant features the cuisine of George Kelso, whose wife, Michelle, directs the waitstaff. You can dine in the verdant garden in nice weather. George is a master in the kitchen and applies a light touch to dishes he cooks with innovation and style. Menu items include a traditional haggis in phyllo pastry with tatties (roasted turnips) and whisky sauce; pan-fried crab cakes with a salsa of tomatoes and spring onions; a panache of West Coast scallops, monkfish, and salmon with saffron-flavored risotto and roasted asparagus; and pavé of lamb with mint-flavored herb crust, wild mushrooms, and zucchini. For dessert, try the caramelized lemon tarte with crème fraîche.

**Martin's.** 70 Rose St., North Lane. ☎ **0131/225-3106.** Reservations required. Main courses £8.50–£12 ($14.45–$20.40) at lunch, £18–£21 ($30.60–$35.70) at dinner. AE, DC, MC, V. Tues–Fri noon–2pm; Tues–Sat 7–10pm. During festival in Aug Mon–Sat 6:30–11pm. Closed Dec 24–Jan 23, 1 week in May/June, and 1 week Sept/Oct. Bus: 2, 4, 15, 21, or 44. SCOTTISH.

Owners Gay and Martin Irons and their trio of top chefs are deeply committed to wild and organically grown foods and include them when they can. Although the setting is unlikely, off Edinburgh's pub street and down an unpromising alley, the restaurant's celadon-green rooms are now a landmark. The menu changes daily to take advantage of the freshest ingredients, and Martin's father provides herbs from his own garden. The best of the country's venison, fish (especially salmon), and West Coast shellfish appear regularly, roasted, baked, poached, or served in a casserole. Wild mushrooms are a particular favorite. You might try breast of guinea fowl with burgundy jus, phyllo

## Oh, Give It a Try!

Haggis, the much-maligned national dish of Scotland, is certainly an acquired taste. But you've come all this way—why not be brave and give it a try? **Macsween of Edinburgh Haggis** is a long-established family business specializing in haggis. Macsween haggis includes lamb, beef, oatmeal, onions, and a special blend of seasonings and spices cooked together. There's also an all-vegetarian version. Both are sold in vacuum-packed plastic bags that require only reheating in a microwave or regular oven. You can find this company's product at food stores and supermarkets throughout Edinburgh. Two central distributors are **Peckham's Delicatessen,** 155–159 Bruntsfield Place (☎ 0131/229-7054), open daily 8am to 8pm, and **Jenner's Department Store,** 2 East Princes St. (☎ 0131/260-2242), open Monday to Saturday 9am to 6pm and Sunday noon to 5pm.

parcels filled with langoustines and organic leeks in basil dressing, or a charcoal-grilled tuna steak with Scottish shiitake mushrooms and avocado-and-tomato compote. Many of the cheeses are unpasteurized farmhouse delights, including a pressed goat cheese from the Orkneys. You can also opt for a delectable fruit tart or a homemade sorbet like basil, lime, and elderflower. No children under 8 are allowed.

**Oyster Bar.** 17 W. Register St. ☎ **0131/556-4124.** Reservations recommended year-round, but essential during the festival. Main courses £13.90–£28.50 ($23.65–$48.45). AE, DC, MC, V. Mon–Sat noon–2pm and 7–10:15pm; Sun 7:30–10:15pm. Bus: 42 or 44. SEAFOOD/GAME.

This restaurant is the most dramatic in Edinburgh, thanks to its richly ornate Victorian bar and soaring windows inset with stained-glass depictions of 19th-century Scotsmen in full Highland dress. An intimate quiet corner in the large busy Café Royal emporium, the Oyster Bar specializes in seafood and game. You might like the salmon with mussels, shrimp with Camembert and white wine, or oak-smoked haddock poached in cream and topped with spinach.

✪ **Pompadour Restaurant.** In the Caledonian Hotel, Princes St. ☎ **0131/459-9988.** Reservations required. Jacket required. Fixed-price lunch menu £15.50–£18.50 ($26.35–$31.45); main courses £20–£25 ($34–$42.50). AE, DC, MC, V. Tues–Fri 12:30–2pm; Tues–Sat 7:30–9:30pm. Bus: 4, 15, or 44. SCOTTISH/FRENCH.

On the mezzanine of the Caledonian Hotel, the Pompadour is one of Edinburgh's best, serving fine Scottish and French cuisine. The restaurant has been refurbished in a Louis XV decor—after all, it bears the name of his mistress. The chef blends cuisine moderne with traditional menus, and his daily menu reflects the best available from the market, with Scottish salmon, venison, and other game often included. The menu also features fresh produce from local and French markets—items like goose liver with wild mushrooms, lamb fillet with spinach and rosemary, and charlotte of marinated salmon filled with seafood. The wine list is lethally expensive, with bottles from the New World strangely absent.

✪ **36.** 36 Great King St. ☎ **0131/556-3636.** Reservations recommended. Set-price lunch £16.50–£19.50 ($28.05–$33.15); dinner main courses £14.95–£18.50 ($25.40–$31.45). AE, DC, MC, V. Sun–Fri noon–2pm; daily 7–10pm. Bus: 23 or 27. SCOTTISH/INTERNATIONAL.

The food here is among the most creative in town, thanks to lots of fresh Scottish produce and chef Malcolm Warham's sophistication. The setting is a stark basement, whose minimalist white walls act as a backdrop for prism-like lighting fixtures. The unusual menu items may include chilled tomato mousse with warm asparagus hollandaise and a salad of baby fennel; terrine of confit of rabbit with cucumber–red onion piccalilli; and Scotch beef fillet with shallot-thyme glaze, dauphinoise potatoes, and Arran Island mustard sauce. Especially noteworthy is a grilled fillet of sea bream with cod brandade and black olive, thyme, and tomato sauce. Roast breast of guinea fowl with black pudding is another house specialty.

## MODERATE

**Bisi Restaurant.** 10 Randolph Place. ☎ **0131/225-6060.** Reservations recommended. Main courses £6.25–£9.95 ($10.65–$16.90). AE, DC, MC, V. Daily noon–10:30pm. Bus: 3, 34, or 35. ITALIAN.

You'll find fresh pasta—lasagna, cannelloni, rigatoni, fusilli, and so on—at great prices here. While the chefs are from central Italy and most of the sauces hail from Sicily to Rome, there are varieties from the northern provinces. The menu changes every few weeks and may include sauces like *matriciana,* with Italian bacon and onions; *piet-montese* with meat ragu, mushrooms, and red wine; and *puttanesca,* with black olives, kippers, anchovies, and tomatoes. The assortment of Italian desserts includes tiramisu and *torta amoretta.*

**Blue Bar Café.** 10 Cambridge St. ☎ **0131/221-1222.** Reservations recommended. Set-price lunch £9–£12 ($15.30–$20.40); main courses £8.50–£15 ($14.45–$25.50). AE, DC, MC, V. Daily noon–3pm and 6–11pm. Bus: 10, 11, 16, or 27. INTERNATIONAL.

In the building containing the Traverse Theatre, this attractive bistro is the less expensive sibling of the Atrium (see above). You'll find a mostly white minimalist decor (with touches of blue) and solid oaken tables and a cheerful staff. The sophisticated menu changes with the seasons and the chef's inspiration but might include delectable crabmeat spring rolls with sweet-and-sour chili dip; warm pigeon salad garnished with a poached egg; succulent breast of duck with a compote of figs and apple *jus;* and a perfect charcoal-grilled tuna with basil-flavored noodles.

**Café Saint-Honoré.** 34 NW Thistle Street Lane. ☎ **0131/226-2211.** Reservations recommended. Main courses £7.50–£12.50 ($12.75–$21.25) at lunch; fixed-price meal £13.50–£18 ($22.95–$30.60) pre-theater, £13.75–£18 ($23.40–$30.60) at dinner. AE, DC, MC, V. Mon–Fri noon–2:15pm; Mon–Fri (pre-theater meal) 5:30–7pm; Mon–Sat 7–10pm and sometimes 11pm. Bus: 3, 16, 17, 23, 27, or 31. FRENCH/SCOTTISH.

This French-inspired bistro is behind a blue-and-gold storefront, a short walk north of Frederick Street. The menu is revised every day, based on what's fresh in the market and

## Tea for Two

If you're looking for a bit of refreshment while sightseeing, try **Clarinda's Tea Room,** 69 Canongate (☎ **0131/557-1888**), for the very British experience of afternoon tea. This cubbyhole of a tearoom is only steps from Holyroodhouse and decorated in the manner you'd expect, with lace tablecloths, bone china, and antique Wedgwood plates on the walls. There are plenty of teas from which to choose, plus a long list of tempting sweets. Homemade soup, lasagna, baked potatoes with cheese, salads, and similar dishes are also offered. It's open Monday to Saturday 9am to 4:45pm and Sunday 10am to 4:45pm.

Another choice is **Ryan's Bar,** 2 Hope St. (☎ **0131/226-6669**), near the northwestern corner of the West Princes Street Gardens. It serves tea daily 10:30am to 10pm. If you want a more formal tea ceremony, try the Palm Court at the **Balmoral Hotel,** Princes Street (☎ **0131/556-2414**), serving tea daily noon to 4:30pm.

what inspires the chef. An upbeat staff serves a cuisine that includes venison with juniper berries and wild mushrooms, local pheasant in garlic wine sauce, and lamb kidneys with broad beans Toulouse style. The fish is usually very fresh. Dinners are candlelit and intimate, and the ambience is relaxed, with soft jazz playing; lunches are popular with workers at nearby offices and so are brisk and breezy.

**The Marque.** 19–21 Causewayside. ☎ **0131/466-6660.** Reservations recommended. Main courses £10–£15 ($17–$25.50); set-price lunch and pre- and post-theatre dinner £10 ($17) for 2 courses. AE, MC, V. Tues–Thurs 11:45am–2pm and 5:45–10pm; Fri 11:45am–2pm and 5:45–11pm; Sat 12:30–2pm and 5:45–11pm; Sun 12:30–2pm and 5:45–10pm. Bus 42. SCOTTISH/INTERNATIONAL.

The Marque is ideally located for the theater and offers reasonably priced pre- and post-theater dinners. Owned and operated by Lara Kearney, John Rutter, and Glyn Stevens, all formerly of the Atrium, this is a fast-growing, popular place. The bold yellow walls and black-and-white chessboard floor give this converted antique shop a unique, contemporary look. The cuisine is ambitious and seductive. The professionals who run this place know flavor and seek out the finest ingredients at the market. Main courses include breast of duck, halibut roasted in olive oil, chargrilled tuna, and chicken and fois gras terrine with onion jam. The rhubarb crumble with tamarind ice cream or white, dark, and milk chocolate terrine with caramel ice cream is a great way to end an enjoyable meal.

**No. 1 Princes Street.** In the Balmoral Hotel, 1 Princes St. ☎ **0131/556-2414.** Reservations recommended. Main courses £7–£12 ($11.90–$20.40); 2-course meal £15–£20 ($25.50–$34). AE, DC, MC, V. Mon–Fri noon–2:30pm; Sat–Thurs 6:30–10:30pm; Fri 7–10:30pm. SCOTTISH/CONTINENTAL.

This is the Balmoral's premier restaurant, a crimson enclave a floor below the reception area, its walls studded with Scottish memorabilia in patterns informal enough to be sporting and still formal enough to be elegant. You'll sit in comfortably upholstered armchairs as the staff pampers you and serves food so good you won't mind paying such high tabs. You can try pan-seared Isle of Skye monkfish with saffron mussel broth; roulade of Dover sole with langoustine, oyster, and scallop garnish; or grilled Scottish beef fillet with bourguignon sauce. Vegetarians can order from a separate menu. The desserts include a variety of sorbets, British cheeses, or exotic choices like mulled wine parfait with cinnamon sauce. The wide-ranging wine list bears celestial prices.

✪ **Restaurant at The Bonham.** In The Bonham Hotel, 35 Drumsheugh Gardens. ☎ **0131/623-9319.** Reservations recommended. Main courses £6.50–£7.50 ($11.05–$12.75) at lunch, £10–£15 ($17–$25.50) at dinner. AE, DC, MC, V. Mon–Sat 12:30–2:30pm; Mon–Fri 6:30–9:30pm, Sat–Sun 6:30–10pm. Bus: 23 or 27. SCOTTISH/CALIFORNIAN.

The setting at one of Edinburgh's most charming restaurants combines the building's 19th-century oak paneling and deep ceiling coves with modern paintings, oversized mirrors, and high-tech lighting. Lunch is a bit simpler than dinner, offering choices like delightful roast duck with apple-flavored mayonnaise and toasted brioche, followed by navarin of lamb in tomato-garlic sauce with mashed potatoes. Dinner is a tour de force, offering a sophisticated blend of Scottish ingredients and California inspiration. Menu items include savory crab-and-coriander cheesecake with gazpacho dressing, jasmine-smoked pork with honeyed parsnip purée and rosemary oil, chicken breast with black-pudding mashed potatoes, and pan-fried ostrich fillet with parsnip mash and red wine jus. The tempting desserts include deep-fried vanilla-fudge ice cream with passion-fruit sauce.

## INEXPENSIVE

**Far Pavilions.** 10 Craigleith Rd., Comely Bank. ☎ **0131/332-3362.** Reservations recommended. 2-course lunch £6.50 ($11.05); 3-course lunch £6.95 ($11.80); main courses £7–£14 ($11.90–$23.80) dinner. AE, DC, MC, V. Mon–Fri noon–2pm; Mon–Sat 5:30–11:30pm. Bus: 19, 39, 55, 81, or X91. INDIAN/INTERNATIONAL.

Since it was opened in 1987 by the father-son Chaudhry team, this Indian restaurant has fine-tuned its cuisine and service. You might appreciate a drink at the cocktail bar near the entrance before confronting the long menu with dishes from the Portuguese colony of Goa and the north Indian province of Punjab. Highly recommended is the house specialty, *murgi massala*—tandoori chicken that falls off the bone, thanks to slow cooking in a garlic-based butter sauce. Menu items include curry dishes influenced by British tastes as well as authentic dishes, plus the garnishes and side dishes that form a worthy Indian meal. Many dishes are vegetarian based, redolent with herbs and sometimes mild yogurt bases.

**◆ Henderson's Salad Table.** 94 Hanover St. ☎ **0131/225-2131.** Main courses £3.50–£4.75 ($5.95–$8.05); fixed-price meal £5.95 ($10.10) at lunch, £10.95 ($18.60) at dinner. AE, MC, V. Mon–Sat 7:30am–10:45pm. Bus: 23 or 27. VEGETARIAN.

Furnished with pinewood tables (often shared) and chairs, this is a self-service Shangri-La for health-food lovers and those who want a nutritious salad. Hot dishes, like vegetarian moussaka or various pasta dishes, are offered as well. A new twist on the national dish of Scotland is vegetarian haggis, neeps (turnips), and tatties (potatoes). Among the homemade desserts, you may choose a fresh-fruit salad or a cake with double-whipped cream and chocolate sauce. The wine cellar provides a choice of 30 wines, most of which may be ordered by the glass. Live music, ranging from classical to jazz to folk, is played every evening. The adjoining Bistro Bar serves meals with table service daily 11am to 5pm; when the restaurant is closed, entry is on a side street around the corner.

**Indian Cavalry Club.** 3 Atholl Place. ☎ **0131/228-3282.** Reservations required. Main courses £7–£14 ($11.90–$23.80); 2-course buffet lunch £6.95 ($11.80); 5-course table d'hôte dinner £19.50 ($33.15). AE, DC, MC, V. Daily noon–2pm and 5:30–11:30pm. Bus: 3, 21, 23, or 26. INDIAN.

The Indian Cavalry Club is more than your average curry place. The elegant atmosphere evokes the British heyday in India, when Queen Victoria was known as Empress of India. You'll find the classic and tandoori Indian food items, plus many dishes based on recipes from Nepal or Burma. Vegetarians flock here, and much of the cuisine is steamed. The restaurant has many areas, including the ground-floor Officer's Mess and the marquee-style Club Tent downstairs.

**Suruchi.** 14A Nicholson St. ☎ **0131/556-6583.** Reservations recommended. Main courses £8–£13 ($13.60–$22.10); fixed-price lunch £4.95–£5.95 ($8.40–$10.10); fixed-price pre-theater dinner £9.95 ($16.90). DC, MC, V. Daily noon–2pm and 5:30–11:30pm. Bus: 30 or 33. INDIAN.

This interesting Indian restaurant occupies a gray-stone early-19th-century storefront opposite the Festival Theater. The three dining rooms are showcases for exclusively Indian furniture, artwork, table linens, embroideries, and artifacts; note the elaborate blue wall tiles and the rows of miniature paintings from the owner's hometown of Jaipur, in Rajastan. Every month, a culinary festival features the artwork, music, and cuisine of a different region of India. The set-price menu changes daily and is always an interesting option. Be sure to call ahead about the pre-theater dinner, as it's not always served. The menu, written in the Edinburgh dialect, divides the country's cuisine regionally to help you understand the complexities and subtleties. Items include grilled kebabs and vegetarian dishes, lamb, seafood, and chicken *tikka massalams* (slow-cooked with herbs and spices in an earthenware casserole). There's also an unusual version of fresh Scottish trout. Light jazz is presented at dinner Wednesday and Friday.

**Szechuan House.** 12–14 Leamington Terrace. ☎ **0131/229-4655.** Reservations recommended. Main courses £6–£8.50 ($10.20–$14.45). AE, MC, V. Tues–Sun 5:30pm–midnight. Bus: 10. SZECHUAN.

You don't come here for elegant trappings but to get zesty chile-hot platters of poultry and fish, especially chicken, duck, and prawns. You might begin with fish-head soup and follow with diced chicken with chiles or fried squid family style. Vegetarians can also dine happily. The cookery is classic and authentic, since the chef, Chao Gang Liu, comes from the Szechuan province and has brought along his bag of spices to tempt the once-tame palates of Scotland.

**Valvona & Crolla.** 19 Elm Row. ☎ **0131/556-6066.** Breakfast £4.95 ($8.40); pizzas, pastas, or platters £3.50–£10 ($5.95–$17). AE, DC, MC, V. Cafe with limited food service Mon–Sat 8am–5pm; full lunch service Mon–Sat noon–3pm. Bus: 7, 10, 11, 12, or 14. INTERNATIONAL.

In 1872, an Italian immigrant opened this restaurant, and it's still going strong, sharing space with a delicatessen and food emporium selling exotic coffees, Parma ham, Italian cheeses, breads, and takeout sandwiches and casseroles. A satellite room, a few steps down from the main shopping area, contains a cafe and luncheon restaurant where the food is very fresh and prices refreshingly low. You can order three kinds of breakfast (continental, Scottish, or vegetarian) for £3.95 ($6.70); platters of pasta, mixed sausages, and cold cuts; or crostini, risottos, and omelets. Also on sale is an inventory of books and gift items. The place caters to a daytime crowd of office workers and harried shoppers who dash in for midday sustenance.

**Whigham's Wine Cellars.** 13 Hope St. ☎ **0131/225-8674.** Reservations recommended. Main courses £5.50–£10.50 ($9.35–$17.85). AE, DC, MC, V. Mon–Thurs noon–midnight; Fri–Sat noon–1am. Bus: 2, 4, or 34. SEAFOOD/VEGETARIAN.

Whigham's Wine Cellars is in the heart of Edinburgh's financial center. Wine was bottled here in the mid–18th century, and Whigham's used to ship it to the American colonies. Walk across the mellowed stone floors until you find an intimate alcove, where you can make your selection from an assortment of appetizers and *plats du jour* or from the chalkboard specials. The smoked fish (not just salmon) and the fresh oysters from Loch Fyne are exceptional; smoked venison occasionally appears on the menu. A range of international wines is offered.

# IN THE CENTER: THE OLD TOWN
## EXPENSIVE

**Dubh Prais.** 123B High St., Royal Mile. ☎ **0131/557-5263.** Reservations recommended. Main courses £6.50 ($11.05) at lunch, £11.90–£16.50 ($20.25–$28.05) at dinner. AE, MC, V. Tues–Fri noon–2pm; Tues–Sat 6–10:30pm. Bus: 11. SCOTTISH.

The Gaelic name of this all-Scottish restaurant along the Royal Mile translates as the Black Pot, reinforcing the image of old-fashioned Scottish recipes bubbling away in a stewpot above a fireplace. In dining rooms adorned with stenciled versions of thistles, you'll be fed well by members of the McWilliams family. Menu items are time-tested and not at all experimental but flavorful nonetheless. Examples are smoked salmon, ragout of wild mushrooms and Ayrshire bacon with garlic sauce, saddle of venison with juniper sauce, and suprême of salmon with grapefruit-flavored butter sauce.

## ⊕ Family-Friendly Restaurants

**Mr. Boni's Ice Cream Parlour**   Mr. Boni's is at 4 Lochrin Bridge (☎ 0131/229-5319). Every kid comes away loving Mr. Boni, who makes the best home-made ice cream in Edinburgh, plus sandwiches, jumbo hot dogs, and beef burgers with French fries.

**Henderson's Salad Table** *(see p. 92)*   Edinburgh's leading vegetarian restaurant has an array of nutritious salads, followed by some of the most delectable home-made desserts in the city.

**Baked Potato Shop** *(see p. 95)*   Children delight in being taken to this worker's favorite place, where they can order flaky baked potatoes with a choice of half a dozen hot fillings along with all sorts of other dishes, including chili and 20 kinds of salads. It's cheap, too.

**Iggs.** 15 Jeffrey St. ☎ **0131/557-8184.** Reservations recommended. Main courses £15.50–£20 ($26.35–$34); fixed-price lunch £12.50 ($21.25) for 2 courses, £15.50 ($26.35) for 3 courses; fixed-price dinner £29.50 ($50.15). AE, MC, V. Mon–Sat noon to 2:30pm and 6–10:30pm. Bus 1 or 35. SPANISH/SCOTTISH.

Just off the Royal Mile in Old Town, this Victorian-style establishment is the domain of a dynamic chef, Andrew McQueen, who is not afraid to experiment but also seems well grounded in the classics. A dinner here is made more charming by the attention from the waitstaff, clad in pink polo shirts. Elegant meals are concocted from the freshest ingredients, often from Scotland. Typical of a dish made from exceptional products with a finely honed technique is the rack of Highland lamb with spring vegetables. If you want to go more exotic, opt for the loin of veal on a truffle and Gruyère risotto given extra flavor by a Madeira sauce. "Hand-dived" scallops come with a cod brandade. After you think you've had every dessert in the world, along comes a honey-roasted butternut squash cheese cake with a caramel sauce.

**Jackson's Restaurant.** 209 High St., Royal Mile. ☎ **0131/225-1793.** Reservations recommended. Main courses £13.50–£18 ($22.95–$30.60); fixed-price dinner £25 ($42.50). AE, DC, MC, V. Daily noon–2:30pm and 6–10:30pm. Bus: 35. SCOTTISH.

Serving a cuisine described as "Scottish with a French flair," this bustling restaurant is in the austere but cozy stone cellar of a 300-year-old building. Choose your cocktail from almost 40 kinds of Highland malts, and then select from a Taste of Scotland menu featuring local ingredients. The charming staff will help you translate such items as "beasties of the glen" (haggis with rosemary-and-garlic sauce); "kilted salmon" pan-fried in green ginger-and-whisky sauce; and noisettes of venison in a blackberry, red currant, and port-wine sauce.

### MODERATE

**Pierre Victoire.** 10–14 Victoria St. ☎ **0131/225-1721.** Reservations necessary. Main courses £7–£12 ($11.90–$20.40); fixed-price lunch £6.90 ($11.75). MC, V. Daily noon–3pm and 6–11pm. Bus: 1, 34, or 35. FRENCH.

This was the model for the chain of Pierre Victoires that have sprouted up in Edinburgh. It's an ideal, if chaotic, stop if you're antique shopping and climbing Victoria Street and is one of the most popular evening gathering places. Wine specials direct from France are posted on the chalkboard. In a bistro setting with crowded tables, you can order grilled mussels in garlic with Pernod butter, salmon with ginger, or roast pheasant with cassis. Vegetarians are welcome.

## INEXPENSIVE

**Baked Potato Shop.** 56 Cockburn St. ☎ **0131/225-7572.** Food items 50p–£2.80 (85¢–$4.75). No credit cards. Daily 9am–9pm (to 10pm in summer). Bus: 5. VEGETARIAN/ WHOLE FOOD.

The least expensive restaurant in a very glamorous neighborhood, this place attracts mobs of office workers. You order at the countertop and your food is then served in recycled cardboard containers. Only free-range eggs and whole foods are used. You'll find more than 20 kinds of salads, large and flaky baked potatoes stuffed with your choice of half a dozen hot fillings, India-inspired curried dumplings known as *bhajias,* mushroom risotto, chili, and cauliflower in cheese sauce. There's even a version of vegetarian haggis. Inside is only a small table for no more than six, but there's lots of seating outdoors in the vicinity of the Royal Mile.

# SOUTH OF THE CENTER
## EXPENSIVE

✪ **Kelly's.** 46 W. Richmond St. ☎ **0131/668-3847.** Reservations recommended. Fixed-price 3-course meal £10 ($17) at lunch, £27 ($45.90) at dinner. DC, MC, V. Mon–Sat noon–2pm and 6–10pm. Bus: 11, 12, or 14. MODERN SCOTTISH/MODERN FRENCH.

Serving a discriminating crowd of barristers, financiers, artists, and employees of the nearby university, the stylish Kelly's is a 20-minute walk south of the center in a residential neighborhood. It offers a setting of flowers, bleached-pine furniture, watercolors, and unusual ceramics. The meals are prepared by Andrew Ramage, who manages the dining room as well. Focusing on fresh ingredients, the menu includes such dishes as asado of lamb in olive-and-herb crust with spicy couscous, roast breast of Barbary duck with black pepper and blueberries, and lobster ravioli with asparagus. The desserts may include caramelized lemon tart.

# IN LEITH

In the northern regions of Edinburgh, the old port town of Leith opens onto the Firth of Forth. It was a city in its own right until it (and its harbor facilities) were slowly absorbed into Edinburgh. After decades of decay, it has become an arty neighborhood with a collection of restaurants, wine bars, and pubs.

## EXPENSIVE

**Vintner's Room.** The Vaults, 87 Giles St., Leith. ☎ **0131/554-6767.** Reservations recommended. Table d'hôte meal £11–£14.50 ($18.70–$24.65) lunch, £15–£19.50 ($25.50–$33.15) dinner. AE, MC, V. Mon–Sat noon–2pm and 7–10pm. Closed 2 weeks at Christmas. Bus: 7 or 10. FRENCH/SCOTTISH.

Many Edinburghers consider a trek to the Vintner's Room well worth the effort. The stone-fronted building (1650) began as a warehouse for the barrels of Bordeaux (claret) and port that came in from Europe's mainland. Near the entrance, beneath a ceiling of venerable oaken beams, a wine bar serves drinks and food platters beside a large stone fireplace. Most people, however, head for the small but elegant dining room, decorated with elaborate Italianate plasterwork and lit with flickering candles. Owners Tim and Sue Cummings, who manage the kitchens and front rooms, respectively, prepare a robust cuisine that may include seafood salad with mango mayonnaise, pigeon-and-duck terrine, pork loin with mustard sauce, and turbot fillet with crabmeat essence. A superb dessert is the two-chocolate mousse with a bitter-chocolate sauce. The wine list is appropriately elaborate.

## MODERATE

**Denzler's.** 121 Constitution St., Leith. ☎ **0131/554-3268.** Reservations recommended. Main courses £7–£12 ($11.90–$20.40); fixed-price meal £9 ($15.30) lunch, £11.50 ($19.55) dinner; table d'hôte menu £19.50 ($33.15). AE, DC, MC, V. Tues–Fri noon–2pm and 6:30–10pm; Sat 6:30–10pm. Bus: 16. SCOTTISH/SWISS.

Just beyond Leith Walk, this restaurant took over the former North of Scotland Bank building. Today many consider it Leith's finest dining choice. Nothing could be more typically Swiss than *Bundnerpattli*, an appetizer of wafer-thin slices of air-dried Swiss beef and ham from the Grisons. The most typical main course is *émincée de veau zurichoise*, slices of veal with mushrooms in a cream sauce served with spaetzle. Of course, it wouldn't be a Swiss restaurant without fondue or without a collection of Swiss wines that include Swiss Fendant and Dole, as well as those from such faraway places as Chile and Argentina.

**Malmaison Brasserie.** In the Malmaison Hotel, 1 Tower Place. ☎ **0131/555-6868.** Reservations recommended for dinner. Fixed-price lunches £9.50–£12.50 ($16.15–$21.25) Mon–Sat, £14.95 ($25.40) Sun; fixed-price dinners £11.50–£14.50 ($19.55–$24.65). Daily noon–2:30pm and 6–10:30pm. Bus: 6, 16, or 22A. FRENCH.

In the previously recommended hotel, this unpretentious brasserie is charming enough to merit a trip out from Edinburgh. The setting is simple, with lots of polished wood and wrought iron. The bistro-inspired menu includes fried steak with pommes frites, sea bass with vinaigrette, sole meunière with rosemary potatoes, and mussel stew with wine roulle. Everyone's favorite dessert is the crème brûlée. Regrettably, the restaurant doesn't have a view of the harbor but faces a side street.

## IN PRESTONFIELD
### EXPENSIVE

**Prestonfield House.** Priestfield Rd., Edinburgh EH16 5UT. ☎ **0131/668-3346.** Reservations preferred. Jacket/tie required. Main courses £13.50–£17.95 ($22.95–$30.50); table d'hôte menu £19 ($32.30) lunch, £26 ($44.20) dinner. AE, DC, MC, V. Daily 12:30–2pm and 7–9:30pm. Bus: 21 or 33. BRITISH.

Hidden amid 23 acres of private parkland and gardens 3 miles (5km) south of Edinburgh's center, this elegant restaurant often hosts locals out to celebrate special occasions. Some kind of manor house has stood here since 1355, but the graceful Dutch-style rooflines of the Jacobean building you see today date from 1687. Highland cattle and peacocks roam the grounds, and inside is an enviable collection of antiques. It's an old-fashioned choice, certainly, but it still offers the same fine quality as always. Menu items include grilled salmon with braised leeks and gazpacho, baked lamb fillet in phyllo with tomatoes and wild mushrooms, marinated smoked pigeon with avocado-and-raspberry salad, and venison-and-oyster pie with spring vegetables.

# 5 Seeing the Sights

## ALONG THE ROYAL MILE

Old Town's **Royal Mile** stretches from Edinburgh Castle all the way to the Palace of Holyroodhouse and bears four names along its length: Castlehill, Lawnmarket, High Street, and Canongate. Walking along, you'll see some of the most interesting old structures in the city, with turrets, gables, and towering chimneys. Take bus no. 1, 6, 23, 27, 30, 34, or 36 to reach it.

✪ **Edinburgh Castle.** Castlehill, at the western end of the Royal Mile. ☎ **0131/ 225-9846.** Admission £7 ($11.90) adults, £6 ($10.20) seniors, £2 ($3.40) age 15 and under. Apr–Sept daily 9:30am–5:15pm; Oct–Mar daily 9:30am–4:15pm.

No place in Scotland is filled with as much history, legend, and lore as Edinburgh Castle, one of the highlights of a visit to this little country. It's believed the ancient city grew up on the seat of a dead volcano, Castle Rock. The early history is vague, but it's known that in the 11th century Malcolm III (Canmore) and his Saxon queen, later venerated as St. Margaret, founded a castle on this spot. The only fragment left of their castle—in fact, the oldest structure in Edinburgh—is **St. Margaret's Chapel,** built in the Norman style, the oblong structure dating principally from the 12th century.

You can visit the **State Apartments,** particularly **Queen Mary's Bedroom,** where Mary Queen of Scots gave birth to James VI of Scotland (later James I of England). Scottish Parliaments used to convene in the **Great Hall.** The highlight is the **Crown Chamber,** housing the Honours of Scotland (Scottish Crown Jewels), used at the coronation of James VI, along with the scepter and sword of state of Scotland. The **French Prisons** were put to use in the 18th century, and these great storerooms housed hundreds of Napoleonic soldiers in the early 19th century. Many of them made wall carvings you can see today. Among the batteries of cannons that protected the castle is **Mons Meg,** a 15th-century cannon weighing more than 5 tons.

✪ **Palace of Holyroodhouse.** Canongate, at the eastern end of the Royal Mile. ☎ **0131/ 556-7371.** Admission £6 ($10.20) adults, £4.50 ($7.65) seniors, £3 ($5.10) ages 15 and under, £13.50 ($22.95) families (up to 2 adults and 2 children). Mon–Sat 9:30am–4:45pm; Sun 10:30am–4:40pm. Closed last 2 weeks in May and 3 weeks in late June and early July (dates vary).

Early in the 16th century, this palace was built by James IV adjacent to an Augustinian abbey David I had established in the 12th century. The nave of the abbey church, now in ruins, still remains, but only the north tower of James's palace is left. Most of what you see was built by Charles II after Scotland and England were united in the 17th century. The palace suffered long periods of neglect, but it basked in glory at the ball thrown by Bonnie Prince Charlie in the mid–18th century, during the peak of his feverish (and doomed) optimism about uniting the Scottish clans in their struggle against the English. Queen Elizabeth II and Prince Philip reside here whenever they visit Edinburgh; when they're not in residence, the palace is open to visitors.

The old wing was the scene of Holyroodhouse's most dramatic incident. Mary Queen of Scots' Italian secretary, David Rizzio, was stabbed 56 times in front of her eyes by her jealous husband, Lord Darnley, and his accomplices. A plaque marks the spot where he died on March 9, 1566. And one of the more curious exhibits is a piece of needlework done by Mary depicting a cat-and-mouse scene (her cousin, Elizabeth I, is the cat).

Highlights of the palace are the oldest surviving section, **King James Tower,** where Mary Queen of Scots lived on the second floor, with Lord Darnley's rooms below. Some of the rich tapestries, paneling, massive fireplaces, and antiques from the 1700s are still in place. The **Throne Room** and other drawing rooms are still used for state occasions. In the rear of the palace is the richly furnished **King's Bedchamber.** The **Picture Gallery** boasts many portraits of Scottish monarchs by Dutch artist Jacob De Witt, who in 1684 signed a contract to turn out one potboiler portrait after another at the rate of one a week for 2 years. However, don't take all the portraits too seriously: Some of these royal figures may have never existed, and the likenesses of some aren't known, so the portraits are from the artist's imagination.

Behind Holyroodhouse begins Edinburgh's largest park, **Holyrood Park.** With rocky crags, a loch, sweeping meadows, and the ruins of a chapel, it's a wee bit of the Scottish countryside in the city. It's a great place for a picnic. If you climb up Holyrood Park you'll come to 823-foot-high **Arthur's Seat,** from which the view is breathtaking. (The name doesn't refer to King Arthur, as many people assume, but perhaps is a reference to Prince Arthur of Strathclyde or a corruption of *Ard Thor,* the Gaelic for "height of Thor." No one knows for sure.) If you visit on a winter morning, you'll think you're in the heart of the Highlands. Arthur's Seat dates from prehistoric times, and with some difficulty you can trace the remains of a quartet of forts, especially in the Dunsapie Loch and Salisbury Crags district. And you can see clusters of cultivated terraces from the Dark Ages, especially on the east flank of the hill, both above and below Queen's Drive.

**Scotch Whisky Heritage Centre.** 354 Castlehill. ☎ **0131/220-0441.** Admission £5.50 ($9.35) adults, £3.85 ($6.55) seniors, £2.75 ($4.70) students with ID, £2.75 ($4.70) ages 5 to 17, £13.50 ($22.95) family ticket. Children 4 and under free. Daily 9:30am–6:30pm.

This center is privately funded by a conglomeration of Scotland's biggest distillers. It highlights the economic effect of whisky on both Scotland and the world and illuminates the centuries-old traditions associated with whisky making, showing the science and art of distilling. You get to see a 7-minute audiovisual show and ride an electric car past 13 sets showing historic moments in the whisky industry. For £10 ($17) extra, you can sample two whiskies during the tour. A tour entitling you to sample four whiskies and take away a miniature bottle is £18 ($30.60) per person.

**Outlook Tower and Camera Obscura.** Castlehill. ☎ **0131/226-3709.** Admission £3.95 ($6.70) adults, £2.50 ($4.25) seniors/children, £11.50 ($19.55) family ticket. Apr–Oct daily 10am–6pm; Nov–Mar daily 10am–5pm.

This 1853 periscope at the top of the Outlook Tower throws a revolving image of nearby streets and buildings onto a circular table. Trained guides point out the landmarks and talk about Edinburgh's fascinating history. In addition, there are several entertaining exhibits, all with an optical theme, plus a well-stocked shop selling books, crafts, and CDs.

**Writers' Museum.** In Lady Stair's House, off Lawnmarket. ☎ **0131/529-4901.** Free admission. Mon–Sat 10am–5pm.

This 1622 house takes its name from a former owner, Elizabeth, the dowager countess of Stair. Today, it's a treasure trove of portraits, relics, and manuscripts relating to three of Scotland's greatest men of letters: Robert Burns (1759–96), Sir Walter Scott (1771–1832), and Robert Louis Stevenson (1850–94). The Burns collection includes his writing desk, rare manuscripts, portraits, and many other items. Also on display are some of Sir Walter Scott's possessions, including his pipe, chess set, and original manuscripts. The museum holds one of the most significant Stevenson collections anywhere, including personal belongings, paintings, photographs, and early editions.

**High Kirk of St. Giles.** High St. ☎ **0131/225-9442.** Free admission, but £1 ($1.70) donation suggested. Easter–Sept Mon–Fri 9am–7pm, Sat 9am–5pm, Sun 1–5pm; October–Easter Mon–Sat 9am–5pm, Sun 1–5pm. Sun services at 8, 10, and 11:30am and 6 and 8pm.

Built in 1120 a short walk downhill from Edinburgh Castle, this church is one of the most important architectural landmarks along the Royal Mile. It combines a dark and brooding stone exterior with surprisingly graceful and delicate flying buttresses. One of its outstanding features is **Thistle Chapel,** housing beautiful stalls and notable

**A Note on Museum Hours**

Be aware that many museums usually closed on Sunday are open on Sunday during the Edinburgh Festival. Some museums open only in summer also are open on public holidays.

---

### ⭐ Frommer's Favorite Edinburgh Experiences

**Contemplating the City and Environs from Arthur's Seat.** At 823 feet (250m) atop Arthur's Seat (which you'll reach by climbing up Holyrood Park), you'll see the Highlands in miniature. The view is magical. Scots congregate here to await the solstice.

**Visiting Dean Village.** About 100 feet (30m) below the level of the rest of the city, Dean Village is an 800-year-old grain-milling town on the Water of Leith. Go here to soak up local color, and enjoy a summertime stroll on the path by the river; it makes for great people-watching.

**Shopping Along Princes Street.** This is the main street of Edinburgh, the local equivalent of New York's Fifth Avenue. Flower-filled gardens stretch along the street's whole south side. When not admiring the flowers, you can window-shop and make selections from the country's finest merchandise, everything from kilts to Scottish crystal.

**Downing a Pint in an Edinburgh Pub.** Sampling a pint of McEwan's real ale or Tennent's lager is a chance to soak up the special atmosphere of Edinburgh. Our favorites are the Abbotsford, Bow Bar, and Kenilworth.

---

heraldic stained-glass windows. A particularly severe period in its history occurred between 1560 and 1572, when John Knox, the ultrastrict leader of the Reformation in Scotland, was its minister. A group of cathedral guides is available at all times to conduct tours.

**Gladstone's Land.** 477B Lawnmarket. ☎ **0131/226-5856.** Admission £3.20 ($5.45) adults, £2.20 ($3.75) children/seniors, £8.60 ($14.60) families. Apr–Oct Mon–Sat 10am–5pm; Sun 2–5pm.

This 17th-century merchant's house is furnished and kept in its original style. On the ground floor is a reconstructed shop booth displaying replicas of goods of the period, and an upstairs four-room apartment is furnished as it might have been in the 17th century. It's worth a visit on your journey along the Royal Mile, if only to get the impression of how confined living conditions were, even for the reasonably well off, before the construction of the New Town.

**John Knox House.** 43–45 High St. ☎ **0131/556-9579.** Admission £2.25 ($3.80) adults, £1.75 ($3) seniors/students, 75p ($1.30) children. Mon–Sat 10am–4:30pm.

Even if you're not interested in the reformer who founded the Scottish Presbyterian church, you may want to visit his late 15th-century house, with its timbered gallery, as it's characteristic of the "lands" that used to flank the Royal Mile. The Oak Room is noteworthy for its frescoed ceiling and for the Knox memorabilia it contains. Born into a prosperous East Lothian peasant family, John Knox is acknowledged as the first Moderator of the Presbyterian Church of Scotland, the tenets of which he established in 1560. He's regarded as the prototype puritan but actually started his professional life as a Catholic priest and was renowned for his sharp wit and sarcasm. Knox lived at a time of great religious and political upheaval, and although he escaped execution, he spent 2 years as a galley slave in France for agitating against papal authority. On his release, he worked tirelessly with the English crown to ensure Protestant victory in Scotland, then closely aligned to Catholic France. Knox was also a writer/historian— his *History of the Reformation* was his greatest literary achievement, but he's better

# Edinburgh Attractions

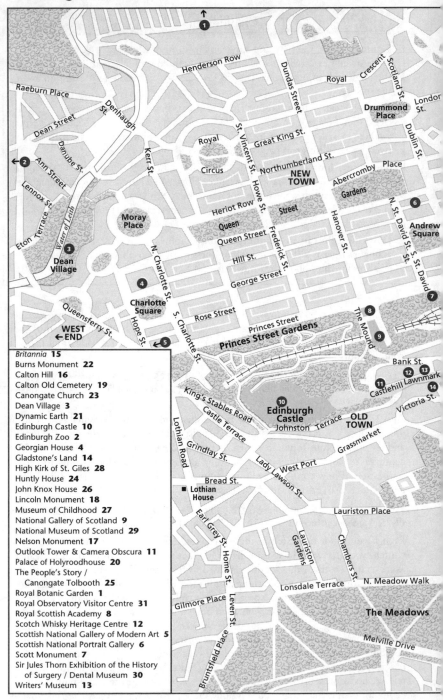

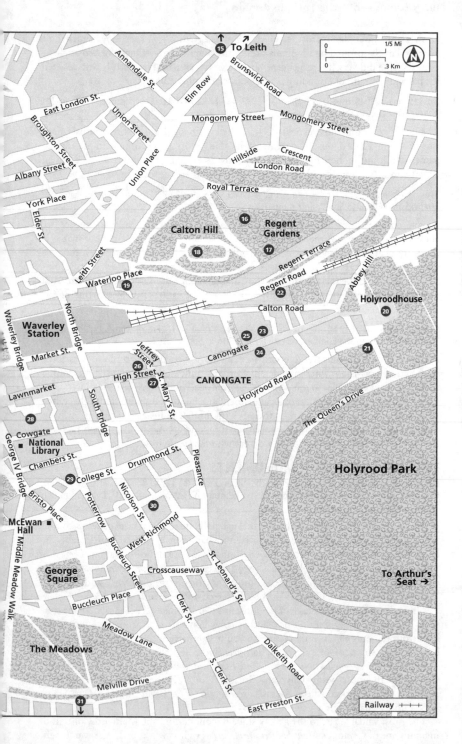

known for the inflammatory treatise *The Monstrous Regiment* [Government] *of Women,* largely inspired by his opposition to the reign of Mary Queen of Scots. However, the title did very little to endear him to Mary's cousin, Elizabeth I, who insisted his particular brand of crusading zeal remain north of the border.

**Museum of Childhood.** 42 High St. ☎ **0131/529-4142.** Free admission. Mon–Sat 10am–5pm; during the Edinburgh Festival, also Sun 2–5pm.

The world's first museum devoted solely to the history of childhood stands just opposite the John Knox House. Contents of its four floors range from antique toys to games to exhibits on health, education, and costumes, plus video presentations and an activity area. Not surprisingly, this is usually the noisiest museum in town.

**The People's Story.** 163 Canongate. ☎ **0131/529-4057.** Free admission. Mon–Sat 10am–5pm (Aug also Sun 2–5pm). Bus 1.

If you continue walking downhill along Canongate toward Holyroodhouse (see above), you'll see one of the handsomest buildings on the Royal Mile: Built in 1591, the Canongate Tolbooth was once the courthouse, prison, and center of municipal affairs for the burgh of Canongate. Now it contains a museum called The People's Story, celebrating the social history of the inhabitants of Edinburgh from the late 18th century to the present, with lots of emphasis on the cultural displacements of the Industrial Revolution.

**Huntly House.** 142 Canongate. ☎ **0131/529-4143.** Free admission. Mon–Sat 10am–5pm; during the Edinburgh Festival, also Sun 2–5pm. Bus: 1.

Across from the Canongate Tolbooth (see above) is this fine example of a restored 16th-century mansion, whose builders preferred a bulky, relatively simple design that suited its role as a secular, rather than an ecclesiastical, building. Today, it functions as Edinburgh's principal museum of local history. The interior contains faithfully crafted reproductions of rooms inspired by the city's traditional industries, including exhibits devoted to glassmaking, pottery, wool processing, and cabinetry, always with a focus on the stamina and struggles of the workers who labored within.

## THE TOP MUSEUMS & MONUMENTS

✪ **National Gallery of Scotland.** 2 The Mound. ☎ **0131/624-6200.** Free admission. Mon–Sat 10am–5pm, Sun 2–5pm; during the Edinburgh Festival, Mon–Sat 10am–6pm, Sun 11am–6pm. Bus: 3, 21, or 26.

In the center of Princes Street Gardens, this gallery is small as national galleries go, but the collection was chosen with great care and has been expanded considerably by bequests, gifts, and loans. A recent major acquisition was Giulio Romano's *Vièrge à la Légende.* Other important Italian paintings are Verrocchio's *Ruskin Madonna,* Andrea del Sarto's *Portrait of a Man,* Domenichino's *Adoration of the Shepherds,* and Tiepolo's *Finding of Moses.* There are also works by El Greco and Velázquez.

The duke of Sutherland has lent the museum two Raphaels, Titian's two Diana canvases and *Venus Rising from the Sea,* and Nicolas Poussin's *The Seven Sacraments.* On loan from the queen is an early Netherlandish masterpiece historically linked to Edinburgh, Hugo van der Goess's *Trinity Altarpiece.* Notable also are Rubens's *The Feast of Herod* and *The Reconciliation of Jacob and Esau* and Rembrandt's *Woman in Bed,* as well as superb landscapes by Cuyp and Ruisdael. In 1982, the gallery made one of its most prized acquisitions, Pieter Saenredam's *Interior of St. Bavo's Church, Haarlem,* his largest and arguably finest painting.

The most valuable gift to the gallery since its foundation, the Maitland Collection, includes one of Cézanne's *Mont St-Victoire* series, as well as works by Degas, van Gogh,

## For Mr. Hyde Fans

Near Gladstone's Land is **Brodie's Close,** a stone-floored alleyway. You can wander into the alley for a view of old stone houses that'll make you think you've stepped into a scene from a BBC production of a Dickens novel. It was named in honor of the notorious Deacon Brodie, a respectable councilor by day and a thief by night (he was the inspiration for Robert Louis Stevenson's *The Strange Case of Dr. Jekyll and Mr. Hyde,* although Stevenson set his story in foggy London town, not in Edinburgh). Brodie was hanged in 1788, and the mechanism used for the hangman's scaffolding had previously been improved by Brodie himself—for use on others, of course. Across the street is the most famous pub along the Royal Mile: **Deacon Brodie's Tavern,** 435 Lawnmarket (☎ **0131/225-6531**).

Renoir, Gauguin, and Seurat, among others. In 1980, two rare works were added: an early Monet, *Shipping Scene—Night Effects,* and a stunning landscape, *Niagara Falls, from the American Side,* by 19th-century American painter Frederic Church. You can also see excellent examples of English painting, and the work of Scottish painters is prominent. In the new wing (opened in 1978), Henry Raeburn is at his best in the whimsical *The Rev. Robert Walker Skating on Duddingston Loch.*

✪ **National Museum of Scotland (NMS).** Chambers St. ☎ **0131/247-4422.** Admission £3 ($5.10) adults, £1.50 ($2.55) seniors/students; £10 ($17) family ticket; free for children under 18. Mon and Wed–Sat 10am–5pm; Tues 10am–8pm; Sun noon–5pm. Walk south from Waverley Station for 10 min. to reach Chambers St. or take bus no. 3, 7, 21, 30, 31, 53, 69, or 80.

After being housed (rather awkwardly) in several locations during the 1990s, the Royal Scottish Museum and the National Museum of Antiquities were united in a single headquarters early in 1998. Their newest incarnation, the National Museum of Scotland, occupies an 1861 building near the Royal Mile that has been radically upgraded and enlarged with a postmodern wing. Displays include Scotland's most impressive collection of decorative arts, ethnography, natural history, geology, archaeology, technology, and science.

✪ **Scottish National Gallery of Modern Art.** Belford Rd. ☎ **0131/556-8921.** Free admission, except for some temporary exhibits. Mon–Sat 10am–5pm; Sun noon–5pm. Bus: 13 stops by the gallery but is infrequent; nos. 18, 20, and 41 pass along Queensferry Rd., a 5-minute walk up Queensferry Terrace and Belford Rd. from the gallery.

Scotland's national collection of 20th-century art occupies a gallery converted from an 1828 school set in 12 acres of grounds a 15-minute walk from the west end of Princes Street. The collection is international in scope and quality despite its modest size. Major sculptures outside include pieces by Henry Moore and Barbara Hepworth. Inside the collection ranges from a fauve Derain and cubist Braque and Picasso to recent works by Paolozzi. English and Scottish art is strongly represented, and you'll find artists from Europe and America, notably Matisse, Miró, Kirchner, Kokoschka, Ernst, Ben Nicholson, Nevelson, Balthus, Lichtenstein, Kitaj, and Hockney. You can study prints and drawings in the Print Room. The licensed cafe sells light refreshments and salads.

**Scottish National Portrait Gallery.** 1 Queen St. ☎ **0131/624-6200.** Free admission, except for some temporary exhibits. Mon–Sat 10am–5pm; Sun noon–5pm. Bus: 18, 20, or 41.

Housed in a red-stone Victorian Gothic building by Rowand Anderson, this portrait gallery gives you a chance to see what the famous people of Scottish history looked

# The Father of Dr. Jekyll & Mr. Hyde

**Robert Louis Stevenson** (1850–94) was a complex, often mysterious character. Some saw him as a poet of intellect and sensitivity like Dr. Jekyll, and others as a debauched scoundrel like Mr. Hyde. Born in Edinburgh, he spent much of his life restlessly roaming the world. He has been alternately hailed as Scotland's greatest writer and dismissed as a writer of tall tales for children with limited brain capacity.

Stevenson was the son of Robert Stevenson, the famed Scottish civil engineer. He was a sickly child and, not surprisingly, a big disappointment to his father. When at age 22 he announced he was an agnostic, his father declared, "My son has rendered my whole life a failure." The meager allowance he received from his father drove the promising author to abandon his parents' respectable upper-class neighborhood and live cheaply among Scotland's lowliest dock areas and bordellos. Determined to roam ("I shall be a nomad"), he traveled to France and wrote early works like *An Inland Voyage* (1878) and *Travels with a Donkey in the Cevennes* (1879).

In 1876, he met a married American, Fanny Osborne, who found him an enticing enigma. Fanny divorced her husband by Christmas 1879 and wed Stevenson the following May. She proved a poor critic of his work: She didn't like *The Sea-Cook* (1881), which became the ever-popular *Treasure Island*. That was followed by *Kidnapped* (1886), which Stevenson set in the moorland and wilderness of western Scotland. But his most famous work was *The Strange Case of Dr. Jekyll and Mr. Hyde* (1886). (By the way, Jekyll should be pronounced *Jee*-kill, according to the author.) Fanny's criticism of the first version of this book caused Stevenson to burn it, but he later felt this version was better than the one he published.

Eventually Stevenson and Fanny settled in Samoa, where he bought 300 acres, hoping to find a climate that would suit his tuberculosis-damaged lungs. The Samoans loved Stevenson—they called him Tusitala ("Teller of Tales")—but not Fanny. (The Samoan servants labeled her the "Witch Woman of the Mountain.") While here, Stevenson worked on his masterpieces, *The Ebb-Tide* (1894) and the unfinished *Weir of Hermiston* (published posthumously in 1896), and translated one of his tales into Samoan. However, his happiness didn't last long, for on December 3, 1894, he suddenly collapsed at only age 43.

More than 200 grieving Samoans dug a road up Mt. Vaea so he could be buried on the mountain he loved. Carved on his grave is his famous requiem:

> *This be the verse you grave for me:*
> *Here he lies where he longed to be;*
> *Home is the sailor, home from the sea,*
> *And the hunter home from the hill.*

like. The portraits, several by Ramsay and Raeburn, include everybody from Mary Queen of Scots to Flora Macdonald to Sean Connery.

**Scott Monument.** In the East Princes St. Gardens. ☎ **0131/529-4068.** Admission £2.50 ($4.25). Mar–May and Oct Mon–Sat 9am–6pm, Sun 10am–6pm; June–Sept Mon–Sat 9am–8pm, Sun 10am–6pm; Nov–Feb Mon–Sat 9am–4pm, Sun 10am–4pm. Bus: 1 or 6.

Looking more like a church spire than a monument to a writer, the Gothic-inspired Scott Monument is Edinburgh's most famous landmark, completed in the mid–19th century. In the center of the 200-plus-foot spire is a large seated statue of Sir Walter Scott and his dog, Maida, with Scott's heroes carved as small figures in the monument. You can climb 287 steps to the top for a spectacular view. From here, you can also see the **Burns Monument,** dedicated to Robert Burns and designed by Thomas Hamilton in 1830, clearly visible along Regent Road.

## MORE SIGHTS

**Dynamic Earth.** Holyrood Rd. ☎ **0131/550-7800.** Admission £5.95 ($10.10) adults, £3.50 ($5.95) children. Apr–Oct daily 10am–6pm; Nov–Mar Wed–Sun 10am–5pm. Bus: 1 or 6.

This former brewery has been converted into a stone amphitheater capped by a futuristic translucent tent. Its interconnected series of galleries celebrate the natural diversity of the physical earth, with emphasis on the seismological and biological processes that led from the Big Bang to the physical world we know today.

The presentation has been called "physical evolution as interpreted by Disney"— audio and video clips; buttons you can push to simulate earthquakes, meteor showers, and views of outer space; replicas of the slimy green primordial soup where life began; time capsules winding their way back through the aeons; and a series of specialized aquariums, some with replicas of primordial life forms, some with actual living sharks, dolphins, and coral. You'll wander through simulated terrains like polar ice caps, tundras, deserts, and grasslands. The most dramatic is a tropical rainforest where skies darken at 15-minute intervals, and torrents of rainfall and creepy-crawlies appear underfoot. The most fun part is the exhibit where you can jump up and down on a monitored platform and your movements are amplified to duplicate an earthquake; seismic instruments record what it would have registered on the Richter scale. Plan to spend at least 90 minutes here. On the premises is a restaurant, a cafe, a children's play area, and a gift shop.

**Georgian House.** 7 Charlotte Sq. ☎ **0131/225-2160.** Admission £5 ($8.50) adults, £3.50 ($5.95) children/students/seniors, £11.70 ($19.90) family ticket; children under 5 free. Apr–Oct Mon–Sat 10am–4:30pm; Sun 2–4:30pm. Bus: 2, 12, 26, or 31.

Architecturally, the most interesting district of New Town is the north side of Charlotte Square, designed by Robert Adam. Together with his brother, James, he developed a symmetrical but airy style with an elegant reworking of Greek and Roman classical motifs. Their influence was widespread, in Britain and America, especially in the U.S. South. Georgian House has been refurbished and opened to the public by Scotland's National Trust. The furniture in this Adam house is mainly Hepplewhite, Chippendale, and Sheraton, all from the 18th century. In a ground-floor bedroom is a sturdy old four-poster with an original 18th-century canopy. The dining-room table is set with fine Wedgwood china and the kitchen stocked with gleaming copper pots and pans.

**Royal Observatory Visitor Centre.** Blackford Hill. ☎ **0131/668-8405.** Admission £3.50 ($5.95) adults, £2.50 ($4.25) ages 5–16/students/seniors; £7 ($11.90) family ticket; free for children 4 and under. Mon–Fri 10am–5pm; Sat–Sun noon–5pm. Bus: 40 or 41.

This center in a public park on Edinburgh's south side exhibits feature images of astronomical objects, Scotland's largest telescope, and antique instruments. An exhibit called "The Universe" uses photographs, videos, computers, and models to take you on a cosmic whirlwind tour from the beginning of time to the farthest depths of space in a couple of hours. The balcony affords a panoramic view of the city, and the astronomy shop is well stocked.

**Sir Jules Thorn Exhibition of the History of Surgery/Dental Museum.** 9 Hill Sq.
☎ **0131/527-1649.** Free admission. Mon–Fri 2–4pm. Bus: 31 or 33.

Edinburgh's rich medical history and associations make the **Exhibition of the History of Surgery** well worth a visit. On the upper floors of a 19th-century townhouse in a tucked-away square, you can chart the development of surgery from 1505 to the 20th century. The exhibits, well presented though sometimes macabre, include such gems as a pocketbook made from the skin of the notorious body snatcher William Burke. The **Dental Museum,** its gleaming glass cases full of every conceivable dentistry tool, is certainly not for the squeamish or those experiencing dental problems!

**Edinburgh Zoo.** 134 Corstorphine Rd. ☎ **0131/334-9171.** Admission £7 ($11.90) adults, £4.50 ($7.65) seniors, £3.80 ($6.45) children, £20–£24.50 ($34–$41.65) families. Apr–Sept daily 9am–6pm; Oct–Mar daily 9am–4:30pm. Parking £1 ($1.65). Bus: 2, 26, 69, 85, or 86.

This zoo is Scotland's largest animal collection, 10 minutes from Edinburgh's city center on 80 acres of hillside parkland offering unrivaled views from the Pentlands to the Firth of Forth. It contains more than 1,500 animals, including many endangered species: snow leopards, white rhinos, pygmy hippos, and many more. The zoo boasts the largest penguin colony in Europe, with four species, plus the world's largest penguin enclosure. April to September, a penguin parade is held daily at 2pm.

## THE MONUMENTS ON CALTON HILL

Calton Hill, rising 350 feet (106m) off Regent Road in the eastern sector, is often credited with giving Edinburgh a look somewhat like that of Athens. It's a hill of monuments; and when some of them were created, they were called "instant ruins" by critics. People visit the hill not only to see its monuments but also to enjoy the panoramic views of the Firth of Forth and the city spread beneath it. The "Parthenon" was reproduced in part on this location in 1824. The intention of the builders was to honor the brave Scottish dead killed in the Napoleonic wars. However, the city fathers ran out of money and the monument (often referred to as "Scotland's shame") was never finished.

The **Nelson Monument** (☎ 0131/556-2716), containing relics of the hero of Trafalgar, dates from 1815 and rises more than 100 feet (30m) above the hill. A time ball at the top falls at 1pm Monday to Saturday. April to September, the monument is open Monday 1 to 6pm and Tuesday to Saturday 10am to 6pm; October to March, hours are Monday to Saturday 10am to 3pm. Admission is £2 ($3.40). Take bus no. 26, 85, or 86.

For Americans, however, the curiosity here is the **Lincoln Monument,** which Edinburghers erected in 1893. It was dedicated to the thousands of American soldiers of Scottish descent who lost their lives in America's Civil War. Below Waterloo Place, on the flatter slope of Calton Hill, you can walk through the **Calton Old Cemetery,** dating from the 1700s. Many famous Scots were buried here, often with elaborate tombs honoring their memory (notably the Robert Adam–designed tomb for philosopher David Hume).

## GARDENS

At the **Royal Botanic Garden,** Inverleith Row (☎ 0131/552-7171), the main areas of interest are the Exhibition Hall, Alpine House, Demonstration Garden, annual and herbaceous borders (summer only), copse, Woodland Garden, Wild Garden, Arboretum, Peat Garden, Rock Garden, Heath Garden, and Pond. Admission is by voluntary donation. It's open daily: April to August 9:30am to 7pm, March and September 9:30am to 6pm, February and October 9:30am to 5pm, and November to January 9:30am to 4pm.

> ### ❓ Did You Know?
>
> - In 1842, the city boasted 200 brothels, with the best on Rose Street. Business peaked annually at the reunion of the General Assembly of the Church of Scotland.
> - Burke and Hare were the original body snatchers, robbing Edinburgh's fresh graves to sell bodies to surgeons for anatomical dissection.
> - William Brodie, the original Dr. Jekyll and Mr. Hyde, ended his days dancing at the end of a hangman's rope suspended from an improved gallows he himself had designed and built.
> - A Scottish mixture of rhubarb, ginger, and magnesia was until quite recently the world's most frequently prescribed medication.
> - In the 18th century, Scotch was drunk as freely as spring water.
> - Edinburgh has the dubious distinction of being the AIDS capital of Europe because of serious heroin abuse in the outer suburbs.

As the New Town grew, the city fathers decided to turn the area below Edinburgh Castle into the **Princes Street Gardens,** now one of the city's main beauty spots. The area was once Nor Loch, a body of water in the city center, but it was drained to make way for a railway line. (When it was still a bog, the great philosopher David Hume fell into it, couldn't remove himself, and called for help from a passing woman. She recognized him, pronounced him an atheist, and wouldn't offer her umbrella to pull him out of the mire until he recited the Lord's Prayer.) The gardens' chief landmark is the Scott Monument, but many find the summer flowers an even bigger attraction.

### DEAN VILLAGE

Beautiful ✪ **Dean Village,** in a valley about 100 feet (30m) below the level of the rest of Edinburgh, is one of the city's most photographed sights. It's a few minutes from the West End, at the end of Bells Brae off Queensferry Street, on the Water of Leith. The settlement dates from the 12th century, and Dean Village's fame grew as a result of its being a grain-milling center.

You can enjoy a celebrated view by looking downstream under the high arches of Dean Bridge (1833), designed by Telford. The village's old buildings have been restored and converted into apartments and houses. You don't come here for any one particular site but to stroll around, people-watch, enjoy the village as a whole. You can also walk for miles along the Water of Leith, one of the most tranquil walks in the greater Edinburgh area.

### ORGANIZED TOURS

For a quick introduction to the principal attractions in and around Edinburgh, consider the tours offered April to late October by **Lothian Region Transport,** 14 Queen St. (☎ **0131/555-6363**). A curtailed winter program is also offered. You can see most of the major sights by double-decker motorcoach, with guided commentary, for £7.50 ($12.75) adults, £6 ($10.20) seniors/students, and £2.50 ($4.25) children. This ticket is valid all day on any LRT Edinburgh Classic Tour bus, allowing you to get on and off at any of the 15 stops. Buses start from the Waverley Bridge near the Scott Monument daily at 9:15am, departing every 15 minutes in summer and about every 30 minutes in winter; if you remain on the bus without getting off, the trip will take about 2 hours.

LRT also operates half-day and full-day motorcoach excursions throughout Scotland. White-sided buses identified by their black trim depart from Waverley Station for "Highland Splendour Tours" to such places as Loch Lomond, Loch Katrine, the Trossachs, St. Andrews, the Isle of Arran, and selected sights in Braemar and Deeside. The prices range from £10 to £25 ($17 to $42.50) per person and sometimes include lunch. Itineraries vary with the day of the week.

You can buy tickets for any of these tours at LRT offices at Waverley Bridge or 27 Hanover St. or at the tourist center in Waverley Market. Advance reservations are a good idea for the half-day and full-day tours. For more information, call ☎ 0131/ 555-6363, 24 hours.

# 6 Special Events

**Hogmanay** begins on New Year's Eve and merges into New Year's Day festivities. It's celebrated throughout Scotland with the ritual kissing of everyone in sight, followed by the time-honored practice of "first footing" with a lump of coal, a bun, and (needless to say) a drop of the hard stuff. But in 1993, the Edinburgh City Council began a 3-day festival that now features street theater; lively processions, illuminated by firebrands; and the burning of a long boat. By 1997, the crush to attend Europe's largest winter festival forced the city to limit numbers; you now have to get tickets to enter the city center after 8pm on New Year's Eve. For details, call ☎ 0131/473-3800.

January 25 is **Burns Night,** *the* night when Scots the world over gather to consume the traditional supper of haggis, neeps (turnips), and tatties (potatoes), accompanied by a wee dram of whisky, while listening to recitals from the works of Scotland's Bard, Robert "Rabbie" Burns, whose birthday is being celebrated. You'll find Burns suppers are held all over town.

By far, the highlight of Edinburgh's year comes in the last weeks of August during the ✪ **Edinburgh International Festival.** Since 1947, the festival has attracted artists and companies of the highest international standard in all fields of the arts, including music, opera, dance, theater, poetry, and prose. During the festival, one of the most exciting spectacles is the **Military Tattoo** on the floodlit esplanade in front of Edinburgh Castle, high on its rock above the city. First performed in 1950, the Tattoo features the precision marching of not only the British Army's Scottish regiments but also performers from some 30 countries, including bands, dancers, drill teams, gymnasts, flag wavers, and motorcyclists, even horses, camels, elephants, and police dogs. The music ranges from ethnic to pop and from military to jazz. Schedules are released each year about 6 months before the festival, but they're subject to change. Tickets range from £8.50 to £24.50 ($14.45 to $41.65), and mail-order bookings are available from the Edinburgh Military Tattoo, Tattoo Office, 32 Market St., Edinburgh EH1 1QB (☎ 0131/225-1188). You can check schedules and buy tickets online at **www.eif. co.uk**.

Less predictable in quality but greater in quantity is the **Edinburgh Festival Fringe,** an opportunity for anybody—professional or nonprofessional, an individual, a group of friends, or a whole company—to put on a show wherever they can find an empty stage or street corner. Late-night revues, outrageous contemporary drama, university theater presentations, even full-length opera—Edinburgh gives them all free rein. As if that weren't enough, Edinburgh has a **Film Festival,** a **Jazz Festival,** a **Television Festival,** and a non-annual **Book Festival** at the same time.

Tickets vary from £5 ($8.50) to about £50 ($85). You can get information from **Edinburgh International Festival,** The Hub, Castle Hill, Edinburgh EH1 7ND (☎ 0131/473-2000; fax 0131/473-2003), open Monday to Friday 9:30am to

# *Britannia:* The People's Yacht

In case Queen Elizabeth II never invited you to sail aboard her 412-foot (125m) yacht, you still have a chance to board this famous vessel since the gangplank has been lowered for the public. The luxury *Britannia* was launched on April 16, 1953, sailed more than a million miles, and was decommissioned on December 11, 1997. Today, the ship rests at anchor in the port of Leith, 2 miles (3km) from Edinburgh's center.

British taxpayers spent £160 million ($264 million) maintaining the royal yacht during most of the 1990s, but by the end of the decade even a major refit would have prolonged the vessel's life for only a few more years. Because of budgetary constraints, it was decided to put it in dry dock. You reach the vessel by going through a visitor center designed by Sir Terence Conran, its centerpiece being the yacht's 41-foot (12.5m) tender floating in a pool. Once on board, you're guided around all five decks by a 90- to 120-minute audio tour. You can walk the decks where Prince Charles and Princess Diana strolled on their honeymoon (we all know how well *that* went), visit the drawing room and the Royal Apartments, and explore the engine room, the galleys, and the captain's cabin.

You must book tickets in advance by calling ☎ **0131/555-5566.** The yacht is open daily except Christmas, with the first tour at 10:30am and the last at 3:50pm. Adults pay £7.50 ($12.75), seniors £5.75 ($9.80), and ages 5 to 17 £3.75 ($6.40). Those 4 and under visit for free; a family ticket, good for two adults and up to two children, costs £20 ($34).

From Waverley Bridge, take either city bus (Lothian Transport) X50 or the Guide Friday tour bus marked on its sides with the word BRITANNIA.

5:30pm. Other info sources are the **Edinburgh Festival Fringe,** 180 High St., Edinburgh EH1 1BW (☎ **0131/226-5257**); **Edinburgh Book Festival,** Scottish Book Centre, 137 Dundee St., Edinburgh EH11 1BG (☎ **0131/228-5444**); **Edinburgh Film Festival,** 88 Lothian Rd., Edinburgh EH3 9BZ (☎ **0131/228-4051**); and **Edinburgh Military Tattoo,** 32 Market St., Edinburgh EHL 1QB (☎ **0131/ 225-1188**).

The most convenient but slightly more expensive way to order tickets for the festival is to purchase them before you leave home from **Global Tickets, Inc.,** 1270 Ave. of the Americas, New York, NY 10020 (☎ **800/223-6108**).

# 7  Sports & Outdoor Pursuits

## SPECTATOR SPORTS

**HORSE RACING**   Place your bets at the **Musselburgh Racecourse,** Musselburgh Park (☎ **0131/665-2859**), about 4 miles (6.5km) east of Edinburgh. In summer, the races are on a flat circular track, but in winter the more elaborate National Hunt format challenges horses and riders to a series of jumps and obstacle courses of great technical difficulty. Admission is £7 ($11.90) to the grand stand or £12 ($20.40) to the club stand.

**RUGBY**   Home of the National Rugby Team of Scotland, **Murrayfield Stadium,** Murrayfield (☎ **0131/346-5000**), is about a mile (1.5km) west of Edinburgh. The sport is played between September and April, usually on Saturday. Some of the most passionate matches are those among teams from the five-nation bloc comprising Scotland, Wales, England, Ireland, and France. These matches are presented only between January and March, when sports enthusiasts in Scotland seem to talk about very little else. Stadium admission ranges from £23 to £35 ($39.10 to $59.50).

**SOCCER**    You might quickly get swept up in the zeal of Edinburghers for their local soccer (referred to as "football") clubs. Both teams, when not battling each other, challenge other teams from throughout Europe. The home of the Edinburgh Hearts (more formally known as the Heart of Midlothian Football Club) is **Tynecastle Park,** Gorgie Road (☎ **0131/337-7004**); the home of the Hibs (short for the Hibernians) is **Easter Road Park,** Easter Road (☎ **0131/661-2159**). The traditional playing times are Saturday afternoons, when games are likely to be televised in pubs throughout Scotland. Tickets range from £10 to £22 ($17 to $37.40).

## ACTIVITIES

**GOLF**    Caddies seem to be a scarce resource—none of the following courses has caddy service.

The par-74 **Silverknowes Golf Course,** Silverknowes Parkway (☎ **0131/336-3843**), is a 6,202-yard (5,644m) course. The greens fee is £9.20 ($15.65) Monday to Friday and £11 ($18.70) Saturday and Sunday for 18 holes, with club and cart rentals costing £10.25 ($17.45) and £1.90 ($3.25), respectively.

Three miles (5km) east of Edinburgh, par-67 **Craigentinny,** Craigentinny Gold, Fillyside Road (☎ **0131/554-7501**), features 5,413 yards (4,926m) of playing area. Clubs rent for £10.75 ($18.25) per round and carts for £1.50 ($2.55). The greens fee is £9.20 ($15.65) Monday to Friday and £11 ($18.70) Saturday and Sunday for 18 holes.

The par-67, 5,306-yard (4,828m) **Liberton Golf Course,** Kingston Grange, 297 Gilmerton Rd. (☎ **0131/664-8580**), requires 2 days' notice if you want to rent clubs, the price of which is included in the greens fees of £20 ($34) Monday to Friday for 18 holes. On weekends, fees are £35 ($59.50). Carts can be rented for £5 ($8.50).

The par-70 **Braids,** Braid House Golf Course, Approach Road (☎ **0131/447-6666**), is 3 miles (5km) south of Edinburgh's city center. The greens fee at this 5,731-yard (5,215m) course is £9.25 ($15.75) Monday to Friday and £11 ($18.70) Saturday and Sunday. Clubs rent for £15.50 to £18.50 ($26.35 to $31.45) including deposit, and carts for £1.50 ($2.55) plus £10 ($17) deposit per 18 holes of play.

Nine miles (14.5km) southwest of Edinburgh, the par-66 **Swanston Golf Course,** Swanston Road (☎ **0131/445-4002**), is an 18-hole, 4,825-yard (4,391m) course. Clubs go for £7 ($11.90) and trolleys for £2 ($3.40); greens fees are £15 ($25.50) per round Monday to Friday and £20 ($34) Saturday and Sunday. The per-day rates are £20 ($34) Monday to Sunday.

The **Portobello,** Stanley Street (☎ **0131/669-4361**), is a 9-hole course with a par of 64. The greens fee at this 2,410-yard (2,193m) course is £4.50 to £9 ($7.65 to $15.30) Monday to Friday and £5 to £10 ($8.50 to $17) Saturday and Sunday. A deposit of £10 ($17) is required for club rental, costing £10.25 ($17.45). Carts go for £1.50 ($2.55) plus £10 ($17) deposit.

The **Carrick Knowe,** Glen Devon Park (☎ **0131/557-5457**), is one of Scotland's larger courses, featuring 6,229 yards (5,668m) of playing area. Five miles (8km) west of Edinburgh, this 18-hole par-71 course was redesigned in 1998 and offers club rentals at £10.65 ($18.10) and trolleys at £1.55 ($2.65). The greens fee is £9.20 ($15.65) Monday to Friday and £11 ($18.70) Saturday and Sunday for 18 holes.

The par-66 **Torphin Hill Golf Course,** Torphin Road (☎ **0131/441-1100**), is a 4,648-yard (4,230m), 18-hole course, offering no caddy services, club rentals, or trolleys.

The greens fee is £14 ($23.80) per round, Monday to Friday and £20 ($34) per day Saturday and Sunday.

**SAILING**    Visit the Firth of Forth firsthand by renting a sailboat and contact the **Port Edgar Sailing Centre,** Port Edgar, South Queensferry (☎ **0131/331-3330**), about 9 miles (14.5km) west of the city center. Between Easter and mid-October, it offers instruction in small-craft sailing, canoeing, and powerboating, as well as half-day rentals. The rate for a dinghy, suitable for four adults, is £24.60 ($41.80) for 2 hours. April to September, the center is open daily 9am to 7:30pm, and boats can be hired to 9pm. In winter, it's open daily 9am to 5pm.

**SWIMMING**    Around Edinburgh are several small Victorian-era pools, but the undisputed leader is the modern Olympic-size **Royal Commonwealth Pool,** 21 Dalkeith Rd. (☎ **0131/667-7211**), on the outskirts of town; take bus no. 3, 7, 21, or 33. Access to the pool is £2.10 ($3.55) before 3pm and £2.60 ($4.40) after. The cost of a sauna is £5.20 to £6.35 ($8.85 to $10.80) or £4.45 to £5.80 ($7.55 to $9.85) with your own towel. The pool is open Monday to Friday 9am to 9pm (Wednesday to 10pm) and Saturday and Sunday 10am to 4pm. Call before you go to avoid arriving during specially scheduled tournaments.

**TENNIS**    Advance reservations are necessary for the tennis courts at the **Craiglock-hart Sports Centre,** 177 Colinton Rd. (☎ **0131/444-1969**). You'll also find badminton courts and a gym. Indoor courts cost £12.45 to £14.45 ($21.15 to $24.55) per hour adults and £7.40 ($12.60) children and are available Monday to Thursday 9am to 9:30pm, Friday 10am to 9:30pm, and Saturday and Sunday 9am to 9pm. The outdoor courts cost £5.70 to £7.20 ($9.70 to $12.25) per hour adults and £2.85 ($4.85) children and are available Saturday to Wednesday 9am until dark and Friday 10am until dark (there's no electric lighting). They're closed when the weather turns cold. Racquet hire costs £1.45 ($2.45). More convenient and sometimes more crowded are a handful of concrete-surfaced **public tennis courts** behind George Square, on the north side of the public park known as the Meadows.

# 8 Shopping

The best buys are in tartans and woolens, along with bone china and Scottish crystal. New Town's **Princes Street** is the main shopping artery. **George Street** and Old Town's **Royal Mile** are also major shopping arteries.

**Shopping hours** are generally Monday to Saturday 9am to 5 or 5:30pm and Sunday 11am to 5pm. Thursdays, many shops remain open to between 7 and 8pm.

## BOOKS
**James Thin, Ltd.** 53 Southbridge. ☎ **0131/556-6743.** Bus: 3, 31.

This is Edinburgh's most respected bookstore. Vast and richly stocked, it's a resource for virtually every academic discipline imaginable yet also stocks a hefty number of counterculture and pop fiction titles, including a section on gay literature.

## BRASS RUBBINGS
✪ **Scottish Stone and Brass Rubbing Centre.** Trinity Apse, Chalmers Close, near the Royal Mile. ☎ **0131/556-4364.** Bus: 1.

You may rub any of the brass or stones on display here to create your own wall hangings, or buy them ready made. Those commemorating Robert the Bruce (king 1306–29) are particularly impressive. The brass you choose is covered in white or black paper, silver wax is used to outline the brass, and then you fill it in with different colors of wax. The cost of equipment ranges from £1.20 to £16 ($2.05 to $27.20).

You can visit the center's collection of replicas molded from ancient Pictish stones, rare Scottish brasses, and medieval church brasses.

## CRYSTAL

✪ **Edinburgh Crystal.** Eastfield, Penicuik (10 miles/16km south of Edinburgh, just off A701 to Peebles). ☎ **01968/675-128.** Bus: 62 (Lowland), 64 or 65 (green), 81 or 87 (red) Waverly bus link. A free minibus from Waverley Station leaves on the hour Mon–Fri 10am–4pm; Sat–Sun 11am–2pm.

Edinburgh Crystal is devoted to handmade crystal glassware. The Visitor Centre (open Monday to Saturday 9am to 4:30pm, Sunday 11am to 4:30pm) contains the factory shop where the world's largest collection of Edinburgh Crystal (plus inexpensive factory seconds) is on sale. Although Waterford is the more prestigious name, Edinburgh Crystal is a serious competitor, its most popular design being the thistle, symbolizing Scotland. It can be traced back to the 17th century, when the glassmaking art was brought here by the Venetians. The center also has a gift shop and a coffee shop specializing in home baking.

Thirty-minute tours of the factory to watch glassmakers at work are given Monday to Friday 9am to 3:30pm; April to September, weekend tours are given 11am to 2:30pm. Tours costs £3 ($5.10) for adults, £2 ($3.40) for children, £7.50 ($12.75) for a family ticket.

## DEPARTMENT STORES & A MALL

**Debenham's.** 109–112 Princes St. ☎ **0131/225-1320.** Bus: 3, 31, 69.

Old reliable Debenham's is still perhaps the best department store in Edinburgh, with a wide array of Scottish and international merchandise displayed in a marble-covered interior.

**Jenner's.** 48 Princes St. ☎ **0131/225-2442.** Bus: 3, 31, 69.

Everyone in Edinburgh has probably been to Jenner's at least once. Its neo-Gothic facade, opposite the Scott Monument, couldn't be more prominent. The store's array of Scottish and international merchandise is astounding. Jenner's often sells much the same merchandise as Debenham's, but it boasts a wider selection of china and glassware, and has a well-known food hall that sells a wide array of homemade products, including heather honey, Dundee marmalade, and a vast selection of Scottish shortbreads and cakes.

**Waverley Market Shopping Centre.** Next to Waverley Station, Princes St. ☎ **0131/557-3759.** Bus: 3, 31, 69.

There's something for everyone at this trilevel mall. You can browse through some 80 shops selling fashions, accessories, gifts, books, jewelry, beauty products, and a wide selection of Scottish arts and crafts. The Food Court has tempting snacks and the Food Hall top-quality produce. Unique handmade items are sold in the craft center.

## DOLLS

**Doll Hospital (Geraldine's of Edinburgh).** 35A Dundas St. ☎ **0131/556-4295.** Bus: 23, 27.

Lined with glass-fronted display cases, this is a basement showroom for Edinburgh's only doll factory, with more than 100 dolls. Each of the heirloom-quality dolls requires about 10 full days' labor to create and has a hand-painted porcelain head and sometimes an elaborate coiffure made from modacrylic fibers. They range from £22.95 to £950 ($39 to $1,615). Also available are fully jointed all-mohair teddy bears that your child will love.

---

## Bring That Passport!

---

Take along your passport when you go shopping in case you make a purchase that entitles you to a **VAT (value-added tax)** refund.

---

# FASHION

**Bill Baber.** 66 Grassmarket. ☎ **0131/225-3249.** Bus: 2, 12.

Near the Royal Mile, 10 to 15 highly creative craftspeople work here, creating artfully modernized adaptations of traditional Scottish patterns designed by Bill and Helen Baber. Everything sells for £65 ($110.50) and up, with the noteworthy exception of whatever's on a sale rack near the entrance. Expect to find traditional Scottish jacquard-patterned knits spiced up with strands of Caribbean-inspired turquoise or aqua; rugged-looking blazers, jackets, and sweaters suitable for treks or bike rides through the moors; and tailored jackets a woman might feel comfortable wearing to a glamorous cocktail party. The clothes are for men and women but not children.

**Corniche.** 2 Jeffrey St. ☎ **0131/556-3707.**

A fashion designer, Nina Grant, operates the most sophisticated boutique in Edinburgh. If it's the latest in Scottish fashion, expect to find it here, even "Anglomania kilts" designed by that controversial lady of fashion herself, Vivienne Westwood. Jackie Burke, a relative newcomer to the design world, has made a splash with her fur-trimmed Harris tweed riding jackets.

**Edinburgh Woollen Mill Shop.** 139 Princes St. ☎ **0131/226-3840.** Bus: 3, 31, 69.

One of about 30 such shops throughout the United Kingdom, the Edinburgh Woollen Mill Shop sells good Scottish woolens, knitwear, skirts, giftware, and travel rugs. Note, however, that most of the merchandise is made in England.

**Schuh.** 6 Frederick St. ☎ **0131/220-0290.**

Schuh has the latest in unique footwear, specializing in the yellow, red, and blue plaid boots made famous by the local rugby team. Expect fierce, funky finds.

✪ **Shetland Connection.** 491 Lawnmarket. ☎ **0131/225-3525.** Bus: 1.

Owner Moira-Ann Leask promotes Shetland Island knitwear, and her shop is packed with sweaters, hats, and gloves in colorful Fair Island designs. She also offers hand-knitted mohair, Aran, and Icelandic sweaters. Items range from fine-ply cobweb shawls to chunky ski sweaters in top-quality wool. A large range of Celtic jewelry and gifts makes this shop a top-priority visit.

# GIFTS

**Ness Scotland.** 367 High St. ☎ **0131/226-5227.**

Along the Royal Mile, Ness Scotland is filled with whimsical accessories searched out by Gordon MacAulay and Adrienne Wells. They have scoured the country from the Orkney Islands to the Borders for that unique item. Displays are hand-loomed cardigans, tasteful scarves, and an array of other items, including charming Dinky bags made during the long winters on the Isle of Lewis.

# JEWELRY

**Alistir Tait.** 116A Rose St. ☎ **0131/225-4105.** Bus: 3, 31, 69.

This is one of the most charming jewelry stores in Edinburgh, with a reputation for selling Scottish minerals like agates; jewelry fashioned from Scottish gold; garnets,

# Tracing Your Ancestral Roots

If you have a name beginning with Mac (which simply means "son of") or one of the other Scottish names, you may have descended from a clan, a group of kinsmen claiming a common ancestry. Clans and clan societies have their own museums throughout Scotland, and local tourist offices will have details about where to locate them. In bookstores throughout Scotland, you can buy clan histories and maps.

Scotland's densest concentration of genealogical records is at the **General Register Office,** New Register House, 3 W. Register St., Edinburgh EH1 3YT (☎ **0131/334-0380;** Bus: 3, 26, 33, 86). Opened in 1863 in a black-brick Victorian headquarters, it contains hundreds of thousands of microfiche and microfilm documents and a computerized system that tells you where to begin looking for whatever records interest you. The strictly self-service system is open Monday to Friday 9am to 4:30pm (it gets crowded in summer). The fee you pay for a full day's access to the records is £17 ($28.05); if you enter after 1pm, you'll pay only £10 ($16.50).

The house has on record details of every birth, marriage, and death in Scotland since 1855. There are also old parish registers, the earliest dating from 1553, listing baptisms, marriages, and burials, but these older records are far from complete. It also has census returns for every decade from 1841 to 1891 and such data records as the foreign marriages of Scots, adopted children's registers, and war registers.

---

sapphires, and freshwater pearls; estate jewelry in every conceivable style; and even modern pieces. If you didn't realize Scotland was so rich in gemstones, think again. Ask to see the artful depictions of Luckenbooths. Fashioned as pendants, usually as two entwined hearts capped by a royal crest, they're associated with the loves and tragedies of Mary Queen of Scots and often accessorized with a baroque pearl. They come in subtle hues of petal, orange, brown, and (most desirable and rare) purple. Prices for Luckenbooths are £28 to £250 ($47.60 to $425)—you can reclaim the tax on them later if you present your passport when making your purchase.

**Hamilton & Inches.** 87 George St. ☎ **0131/225-4898.** Bus: 41, 42.

Since 1866, the prestigious Hamilton & Inches has sold gold and silver jewelry, porcelain and silver, and gift items. You'll find everything you'd want for an upscale wedding present, all sorts of jewelry (including some valuable pieces from estate sales), and two memorable kinds of silver dishes (weighty plates copied from items found in the Spanish Armada wrecks during Elizabeth I's reign and endearingly folkloric quaichs). The *quaichs* originated in the West Highlands as whisky measures crafted from wood or horn and were later gentrified into something like silver porringers or chafing dishes, each with a pair of lugs (ears) fashioned into Celtic or thistle patterns. Also unusual is an exclusive pattern of Hungarian-based Herend china, emblazoned prominently with a Scottish thistle.

**Robert Anthony.** 108B Rose St. ☎ **0131/226-4550.** Bus: 41, 42.

One of Edinburgh's best jewelry stores, Robert Anthony sells new, antique, and second-hand jewelry, as well as gold chains, fine gemstones, and (its specialty) diamonds.

Check out the gold bangles and pendants in 9-karat gold. (If you prefer 18-karat gold, it can be crafted for you in about a week.) Gold replicas of Scottish pipers and/or dancers, thistles, and Edinburgh Castle and its famous Mons Meg cannon make good souvenirs.

## LINENS & BEDS

**Linens Fine.** 30 Dundas St. ☎ **0131/225-6998.** Bus: 23, 27.

The danger of popping into the upscale Linens Fine is you might make a much larger investment than you'd intended when you see the fine-textured sheets and pillowcases. Most feature Italian, Portuguese, and British cotton (not linen), usually in white and cream. (An upscale British brand name is Wendy Woods, Ltd.) There's also a beautiful collection of ornate brass, iron, and wooden beds you can order in several sizes and have shipped anywhere. Beds begin at £550 ($935) and stretch all the way up to £5,000 ($8,500) for something really unusual.

## MUSIC

**Virgin Megastore.** 125 Princes St. ☎ **0131/220-2230.** Bus: 3, 31, 69.

Here you'll find one of the biggest selections of records, CDs, videos, and tapes in Scotland. The shop has a special strength in traditional and Scottish music. The staff is charming and eager to imbue their love of Scottish music to interested visitors.

## TARTANS & KILTS

**Anta.** 32 High St. ☎ **0131/557-8300.**

Some of the most stylish tartans are found at Anta, where "forever plaid" might be the motto. Here Lachian and Anne Stewart, the creative designing team behind Ralph Lauren's home tartan fabrics, present a series of tartans newly invented in unique styles. The woolen blankets with hand-purled fringe are woven on old-style looms.

**Clan Tartan Centre.** 70–74 Bangor Rd., Leith. ☎ **0131/553-5100.** Bus: 7, 10.

This is one of the leading tartan specialists in Edinburgh, regardless of which clan you claim as your own. If you want help in identifying a particular tartan, the staff here will assist you.

✪ **Geoffrey (Tailor) Highland Crafts.** 57–59 High St. ☎ **0131/557-0256.** Bus: 1.

This is the most famous kiltmaker in the Scottish capital. Its customers have included Sean Connery, Charlton Heston, Dr. Ruth Westheimer, members of Scotland's rugby teams, and Mel Gibson (who favors the tartan design Hunting Buchanan and wore his outfit when he received an award from the Scottish government after filming *Braveheart*). Expect a delay of 4 to 8 weeks before your costume can be completed. The company sets up sales outlets at Scottish reunions and Highland Games around the world (there are at least 21 of these in the States every year) and maintains a toll-free number (☎ **800/566-1467**) for anyone who calls from the United States or Canada and wants to be outfitted. Expect to pay from £280 ($476) for a kilt and from £600 ($1,020) for a complete Highland outfit. The company stocks 200 of Scotland's best-known tartan patterns and is revolutionizing the kilt by establishing a subsidiary called 21st Century Kilts, which makes them in fabrics ranging from denim to leather.

Geoffrey is also one of the few kiltmakers to actually weave the object, and you can watch the process at the **Edinburgh Old Town Weaving Company,** 555 Castlehill (☎ **0131/557-0256;** Bus: 1), Monday to Friday 9am to 5pm. Note that the factory doesn't sell kilts directly to visitors.

**James Pringle Woolen Mill.** 70–74 Bangor Rd., Leith. ☎ **0131/553-5161.** Bus: 7, 10.

The mill produces a large variety of top-quality wool items, including a range of Scottish knitwear like cashmere sweaters, tartan and tweed ties, travel rugs, tweed hats, and tam o' shanters. In addition, it boasts one of Scotland's best Clan Tartan Centres, with more than 5,000 tartans accessible. A free audiovisual presentation shows the history and development of the tartan. You can visit free, and there's even a free taxi service to the mill from anywhere in Edinburgh (ask at your hotel).

**John Morrison Ltd.** 461 Lawnmarket. ☎ **0131/225-8149.** Bus 1.

If you can't take your Highland outfit with you, John Morrison Ltd. will mail your order around the world. Women can order a hand-tailored kilt, a semi-kilt, or a kilt skirt, with an evening sash and stole to match. The store specializes in men's kilts, a handwoven worsted in your favorite tartan, with doublets, jackets, and accessories (jabots, cuffs, kilt hose, ties) to match.

**Tartan Gift Shops.** 54 High St. ☎ **0131/558-3187.** Bus 1.

If you've ever suspected you might be Scottish, Tartan Gift Shops has a chart indicating the place of origin (in Scotland) of your family name. You'll then be faced with a bewildering array of hunt and dress tartans for men and women, and the high-quality wool is sold by the yard. There's also a line of lambswool and cashmere sweaters and all the accessories.

## 9  Edinburgh After Dark

Every year in late August, the **Edinburgh International Festival** brings numerous world-class cultural offerings to the city, but year-round there are plenty of choices, whether you prefer theater, opera, ballet, or other diversions. The waterfront district, featuring many jazz clubs and restaurants, is especially lively in summer, and students flock to the pubs and clubs around Grassmarket. Discos are found off High and Princes streets, and in the city's numerous pubs you can often hear traditional Scottish folk music for the price of a pint.

For a thorough list of entertainment options during your stay, pick up a copy of *The List,* a free biweekly entertainment paper available at the tourist office. Before you leave home, you might want to check *Time Out's* latest concert, performance, and nightclub listings on the Web at **www.timeout.co.uk**.

### THE PERFORMING ARTS

**CLASSICAL MUSIC, OPERA & DANCE**   On the eastern edge of Edinburgh, near the old campus of the university, the ✪ **Festival Theatre,** 13–29 Nicolson St. (☎ **0131/662-1112** for administration, 0131/529-6000 for tickets during nonfestival times, 0131/225-5756 for tickets during the festival; Bus: 3, 31, 33), is the showcase of Edinburgh theaters. It has been called Britain's *de facto* Dance House because of its sprung floor, enormous stage (the largest in Britain), and suitability for opera presentations of all kinds. The costs were kept down (it cost a relatively modest £23 million [$39 million]) by partially adapting the Empire Theater that had stood on the site since 1928. The new entity boasts a postmodern facade of concrete and sweeping glass walls, a lobby area dramatically bathed in uplighting and downlighting, and a performance area of 1,900 seats still outfitted in a plush rose-and-cream combination of art deco and neoclassical swirls.

The theater's main role is during the Edinburgh Festival, although its administrators work hard to maintain some of the festival excitement throughout the year. It has become the venue for many dance and theater premieres, partly because of the superb technical facilities, partly as a testing ground before exposing the show to the tough London audiences. Tickets run £5.50 to £45.50 ($9.35 to $77.35), and the box office is open Monday to Saturday 10am to 8pm and Sunday 4 to 8pm.

Edinburgh's second most important theater, the **King's Theatre,** 2 Leven St. (☎ **0131/529-6000;** Bus: 10, 11), presents a wide repertoire of classical entertainment, including ballet and opera. West End productions from London are also presented at this 1,340-seat Victorian theater. Tickets begin at £5 ($8.50), and the box office is open Monday to Saturday 10am to 5pm and Sunday 11am to 6pm.

Edinburgh's largest theater, the 3,100-seat **Playhouse Theatre,** 18–22 Greenside Place (☎ **0870/606-3424;** Bus: 7, 14), was built in 1929 at the height of the vaudeville age. Inspired by London's Palladium, it retains the gold-and-scarlet trappings of its construction and is the home of the **Scottish Ballet** and **Scottish Opera.** The Playhouse also presents rock concerts, operettas, musical comedies, experimental theater, and a wide array of musical acts from North America and Europe. In summer, Edinburgh Festival performances are given here. The box office, which has its own access to Greenside Place, is open Monday to Saturday 10am to 6pm (to 8pm when there's a performance). Tickets run £12 to £30 ($20.40 to $51).

The **Queen's Hall,** Clerk Street (☎ **0131/668-2019;** Bus: 3, 33, 31), is home to the **Scottish Chamber Orchestra** and a major venue for the Edinburgh Festival. It also plays host to a full range of concerts, from classical to rock music, including a Friday-night jazz club. The box office and restaurant are open daily 10am to 5pm. Tickets run £5 to £20 ($8.50 to $34).

**THEATER**   Edinburgh has a lively theater scene. The major venue is the **King's Theatre** (see above), which also presents ballet and opera. The **Netherbow Arts Centre,** 43 High St. (☎ **0131/556-9579;** Bus: 1), offers intriguing and experimental plays; this is new Scottish theater at its best. Ask about lunchtime performances as well. Tickets run £3 to £8 ($5.10 to $13.60), with box office hours Monday to Saturday 10am to 5pm.

The highly respected resident company of the **Royal Lyceum Theatre,** Grindlay Street (☎ **0131/248-4848;** Bus: 11, 15), has a repertoire ranging from Shakespeare to new Scottish playwrights. The theater is a restored 1883 Victorian building, with a restaurant, four bars, and facilities for those with disabilities. The box office is open Monday to Saturday 10am to 7pm, and tickets cost £7 to £13.50 ($11.90 to $22.95) Tuesday to Thursday, rising to £8 to £16 ($13.60 to $27.20) Friday and Saturday.

**Traverse Theatre,** Cambridge Street (☎ **0131/228-1404;** Bus: 11, 15), is one of the few theaters in Britain funded solely to present new plays by new writers and first translations into English of international works. In a modern location, it now offers two theaters under one roof: Traverse 1, seating 250, and Traverse 2, seating 100. On the premises is a bar and cafe, open at 10:30am daily, serving theater patrons throughout the day. Tickets cost £7 to £12 ($11.90 to $20.40). The box office is open Monday to Saturday 10am to 6pm when there's no show; when there is a show, hours are 10am to 8pm, which might include Sundays. During the festival, it's open to 10pm.

## THE CLUB & MUSIC SCENE
### DANCE & ROCK CLUBS
**The Cavendish.** 3 W. Tollcross. ☎ **0131/228-3252.** Cover £6 ($9.90) Fri–Sat. Bus: 11, 15, 23.

This isn't necessarily where you go to hear the next Oasis or Blur, but who knows? A rock legend might be born here every Friday or Saturday, when live bands take the stage. No tennis shoes or jeans. The bar is open Thursday to Saturday 10pm to 3am.

**Club Mercado.** 36–39 Market St. ☎ **0131/226-4224.** Cover £3–£10 ($5.10–$17), depending on what's on. Bus: 1.

The glamorous Club Mercado attracts a crowd from 18 to about 35. Once the headquarters of the Scottish branch of British Rail, it hangs suspended over the rail tracks behind the city's main station. On Friday, the action kicks off with free-admission TFIS, which stands for a somewhat saltier version of "Thank God It's Friday"; it runs 5 to 10pm and caters to youngish workers who indulge in the cut-price drinks while tapping to the kitsch music. Other special nights are alternate-Saturday Viva (a night of eclectic music attracting all sorts from toughs to drag queens) and Eye Candy (basically a rave featuring the latest house music). Sundays are theme nights, and the first Sunday of the month is cabaret night. Open daily 10pm to 3am.

**Po Na Na.** 43B Frederick St. ☎ **0131/226-2224.** Cover £2–£3 ($3.40–$5.10). Bus: 80.

Po Na Na is the Edinburgh branch of the most successful chain of nightclubs in Britain. The theme is a Moroccan casbah, thanks to wall mosaics, brass lanterns, and artifacts shipped in from Marrakech. You'll dance in the cellar of a transformed 19th-century building, beneath a tented ceiling illuminated with strobes. Expect a crowd between 25 and around 40 and a highly danceable mix of house and funk. Po Na Na isn't specifically gay but does draw a strong gay following. Open daily 8pm to 3am.

**Revolution.** 31 Lothian Rd. ☎ **0131/229-7670.** Cover £3–£7 ($5.10–$11.90). Bus: 11, 15.

This is Edinburgh's largest nightclub, popular with an under-25 crowd and with a capacity for 1,500. Mainstream contemporary dance music (plus five bars) attracts the crowds, and there are theme and student nights. Open Wednesday to Saturday 10pm to 3am.

**The Subway.** 69 The Cowgate, off Grassmarket. ☎ **0131/225-6766.** Cover £2 ($3.30) Fri. Bus: 2, 12.

The Subway hosts occasional concerts but is primarily a dance club playing a mix of music from the 1960s to the latest hits. The bar is open Monday to Thursday 5pm to 3am and Friday to Sunday 7pm to 3am.

✪ **The Venue.** 15 Calton Rd. ☎ **0131/557-3073.** Bus 26.

Behind the main Post Office and Waverley Station is the Venue, the principal stage for live music. Some of the biggest bands in the United Kingdom perform here, and other entertainment is by Scottish wannabes. Posters and flyers around town will let you know what's on at any given time.

**Whynot.** 14 George St. ☎ **0131/624-8633.** Cover £3–£7.50 ($5.10–$12.75). Bus: 41, 42.

In the basement of the Dome Bar & Grill (see "Dining," above), Whynot is a hot entertainment complex that opened in the former Bank of Scotland building across from the George Inter-Continental Hotel. It has low ceilings with veil-like curtains above the dance floor and lots of seating coves tucked away for privacy. The club swings Thursday to Sunday 10pm to 3am. On Thursday, there's dancing to the music of the 1960s, 1970s, and 1980s; Friday features mainstream pop; and Saturday features the best in contemporary dance music.

## FOLK MUSIC & *CEILIDHS*

*Ceilidhs* (Scottish hoedowns) are often spontaneous. Many Edinburgh clubs and pubs feature live folk music, but the strolling players tend to be somewhat erratic or irregular in their appearances. It's best to read notices in pubs and talk to the tourist office to see where a ceilidh will be on the night of your visit.

# You Paid What?

**47,000 hotels, 700 airlines, 50 rental car companies. And a few million ways to save money.**

## Travelocity.com

A Sabre Company

Go Virtually Anywhere.

AOL Keyword: Travel

Will you have enough stories to tell your grandchildren?

Yahoo! Travel

Do You YAHOO!?

In addition to pubs that sometimes feature folk music, the **Edinburgh Folk Club** offers Wednesday performances at changing venues from September 16 to June 20. Anyone interested should contact Graham Brotherston at ☎ **077-8896-0732.** The cover is £4 ($6.80) adults and £3 ($5.10) seniors/students, free for children 15 and under.

Some hotels regularly feature traditional Scottish music, and the shows aren't always as touristy as you might think. You can check with the **Carlton Highland Hotel** on North Bridge (☎ **0131/556-7277;** Bus: 3, 31, 33), where a dinner/show costs £39.50 ($67.15) per person, including a full meal of traditional Scottish dishes, unlimited wine, and the performance (the show only is £12/$20.40). Dinner service is daily 7 to 9pm, and the concerts run 9 to 10:15pm. Also call the **George Hotel** on George Street (☎ **0131/225-1251;** Bus: 3, 31, 33) to see if any program is featured at the time of your visit. Performances start at 7:15pm in the Adam's Room, where a ticket sells for £40 ($68), including a full meal and wine. **Jamie's Scottish Evening** is presented at the King James Hotel on Leith Street (☎ **0131/556-0111;** Bus: 7, 14) Sunday to Friday at 7pm, costing £41 ($69.70) for dinner, wine, and a show.

Every night the **Malt Shovel,** 11–15 Cockburn St. (☎ **0131/225-6843;** Bus: 7, 14), dispenses lots of real ales and single-malt whiskies to a neighborhood crowd, but every Tuesday its live bands draw in a bigger-than-average crowd. Live jazz and traditional Scottish music are featured. The club is open Sunday to Thursday 11am to 12:30am and Friday and Saturday 11am to 1am, with no cover. Live music is presented only Tuesday 9 to 11:15pm.

## PUBS & BARS

**The Abbotsford.** 3 Rose St. ☎ **0131/225-5276.** Bus: 3, 31, 33.

Near the eastern end of Rose Street, a short walk from Princes Street, The Abbotsford has served stiff drinks and oceans of beer since 1887. The gaslight era is alive here, thanks to a careful preservation of the original dark paneling, long battered tables, and ornate plaster ceiling. The beers on tap change about once a week, supplementing the roster of single malts. Drinks are served Monday to Saturday 11am to 11pm. Platters of food, £2.50 to £6.60 ($4.25 to $11.20), are dispensed from the bar Monday to Saturday noon to 3pm and 5:30 to 10pm.

**Bow Bar.** 80 West Bow. ☎ **0131/226-7667.** Bus: 2, 12.

Near Edinburgh Castle, the Victorian Bow Bar is arranged around a series of tall beer pulls, antique phonographs, and pendulum clocks. Artfully arranged on shelves are as many as 140 single-malt whiskies from virtually every corner of the country. The only food offerings are simple snacks like steak or minced pie at £1.50 to £2 ($2.55 to $3.40). It's open Monday to Saturday 11am to 11:30pm and Sunday 12:30 to 11pm.

✪ **Café Royal Circle Bar.** 17 W. Register St. ☎ **0131/556-1884.** Bus: 3, 31, 33.

This is Edinburgh's most famous pub. One part is now occupied by the Oyster Bar of the Café Royal, but life in the Circle Bar continues as usual, still with the opulent trappings of the Victorian era. Go up to the serving counter, which stands like an island in a sea of drinkers, and place your order. Hours for the bar are Monday to Wednesday 11am to 11pm, Thursday 11am to midnight, Friday and Saturday 11am to 1am, and Sunday 12:30pm to 11pm. The restaurant is open Sunday to Wednesday noon to 2pm and 7 to 10pm (Thursday to midnight, Friday and Saturday to 1am).

✪ **Deacon Brodie's Tavern.** 435 Lawnmarket. ☎ **0131/225-6531.** Bus: 1.

Opened in 1806, Deacon Brodie's is the neighborhood pub along the Royal Mile. It perpetuates the memory of Deacon Brodie, good citizen by day and robber by night.

The tavern and wine cellars offer a traditional pub setting and lots of atmosphere and contain a cocktail/lounge bar. The tavern is open Sunday to Thursday 10am to midnight and Friday and Saturday 10am to 1am. Light meals beginning at £3.95 ($6.70) are served in the bar 10am to 10pm; in the restaurant upstairs, the food is more substantial and main courses ranging from £4.95 to £12 ($8.40 to $20.40) are served noon to 10pm.

**Drum & Monkey.** 80 Queen St. ☎ **0131/226-9932.** Bus: 80.

A block from Princes Street, the Drum & Monkey opened about a century ago and has functioned as both a Japanese restaurant and the local branch of P. J. Clarke's in New York. After a refurbishment of its Victorian-Gothic decor, it has returned to dispensing pints of lager, stiff drinks, and bar fare. At least eight brands of beer are on tap, and the bar platters, running £3.95 to £6.75 ($6.70 to $11.50), include haggis, bangers and mash, chicken foccacia, Caesar salad, nachos, and burgers. Drinks are served Monday to Friday and Sunday 11:30am to 11pm and Saturday 11:30am to midnight, with food served Monday to Friday 11:30am to 7pm and Saturday 12:30 to 7pm.

**Guildford Arms.** 1–5 W. Register St. ☎ **0131/556-4312.** Bus: 3, 31, 33.

This place got a facelift back to the mauve era of the 1890s, although a pub has stood here for 200 years. This Victorian Italianesque corner pub has seven arched windows with etched glass and an ornate ceiling. It's large, bustling, and at times a bit rough, but is has plenty of character. Upstairs is a fish-and-chips shop run by the same company, where a platter of greasy goodies from the sea begins at £4.50 ($7.65). Place your order at the upstairs bar. At festival time, folk music is presented nightly. It's open Monday to Wednesday 11am to 11pm, Thursday to Saturday 11am to midnight, and Sunday 12:30am to 11pm.

**Kenilworth.** 152–154 Rose St. ☎ **0131/226-4385.** Bus: 3, 31, 33.

The intriguing Kenilworth was named after a Sir Walter Scott novel. Built as a home, it was sold to a brewery in 1904 and turned into a popular pub in the lavish Edwardian style. In 1981, its owners renovated each detail of the elaborately crafted interior. The blue-and-white wall tiles, coupled with the rows of stained-glass windows, a massive wooden bar, and a coal-burning fireplace, make an alluring setting that attracts members of the performing arts. The bar is open Monday to Thursday 10am to 11pm, Friday and Saturday 9am to 1:30am, and Sunday 12:30 to 10:30pm.

## GAY BARS & CLUBS

The heart of the gay community is centered on **Broughton Street** around the Playhouse Theatre (take bus 8, 9, or 19). Be sure to check "The Club & Music Scene" (see above) for the heavily gay crowd at **Po Na Na.**

**C. C. Bloom's.** 23–24 Greenside Place. ☎ **0131/556-9331.**

Named after Bette Midler's character in *Beaches*, C. C. Bloom's is one of Edinburgh's most popular gay spots. The upstairs bar offers drinks and camaraderie; on Thursday and Sunday at 11pm there's karaoke, and Sunday afternoons heat up with a male stripper. The downstairs club offers dancing to a wide range of music, with no cover charge. The bar is open Monday to Saturday 6pm to 3am and Sunday 3pm to 3am.

Next door is **Cafe Habana,** 22 Greenside Place (☎ **0131/556-4349**), drawing a mixed gay crowd daily noon to 1am.

**New Town Bar.** 26B Dublin St. ☎ **0131/538-7775.**

Adjacent to the corner of Queen Street is the New Town Bar, a street-level pub where everyday blokes clad in everything from jeans to business suits gather for a pint or two

# A Wee Dram

It requires a bit of an effort to reach it (take bus no. 10A, 16, or 17 from Princes St. to Leith), but for fans of malt whisky, the **Scotch Malt Whisky Society** has been called the "Top of the Whisky Pyramid" by British distillery industry magazines. It's on the second floor of a 16th-century warehouse at 87 Giles St., Leith (☎ **0131/554-3451;** Bus: 7, 10), designed to store Bordeaux and port wines from France and Portugal. No trendy cocktails here—you won't find anything other than single-malt whiskies selected from a staggering choice from more than 100 distilleries around Scotland, served neat, usually in a dram (unless you want it watered down with branch water).

Beware of the potency of these firewaters: Most single-malt brands contain a mere 40% alcohol, but the alcohol content of the Scotch Malt Whisky Society's special stocks rarely dips below 51% and usually hovers around a head-spinning 60%. Some brands taste gamy, some are peaty, some are fruity, and some are floral. Regardless of what you select, you'll find yourself elbow-to-elbow with fellow drinkers for whom single malts are indeed the water of life. Soups and sandwiches are offered Monday to Saturday noon to 2pm, and the Vintner's Room restaurant (not affiliated with the organization; see "Dining," above) is on the street level.

The place is at its most rollicking and hearty Thursday to Saturday after around 6pm. Mercifully, on those nights shutdown and meltdown is early enough (11pm) to allow everyone to totter off home before any real damage is done. It's open Monday to Wednesday 10am to 5pm, Thursday and Friday 10am to 11pm, and Saturday 10am to 2:30pm and 5 to 11pm.

---

of lager. It's open daily noon to 2am. If you're looking for something a bit less conventional and it happens to be Wednesday to Sunday 10pm to 2am, head into the basement for the Intense Cruise Bar, where the crowd dons its own interpretations of Tom of Finland combat gear, leather, and uniforms. Depending on the crowd, this can be intense, amusing, or both.

**Planet Out.** 6 Baxters Place. ☎ **0131/524-0061.**

This place hosts a mixed crowd but attracts more women than most gay bars. It describes itself as a friendly and unpretentious neighborhood bar where you're likely to run into your favorite gay uncle or aunt and share a bit of family gossip, then meet either the love of your life or a decent building contractor. Drinks are served Monday to Friday 4pm to 1am and Saturday and Sunday 12:30pm to 1am. There's an occasional drag night.

## 10  Side Trips from Edinburgh: The Best of the Lothian Region

Armed with a good map, you can explore the major attractions of the countryside south of the Firth of Forth enveloping Edinburgh in just a day. Most attractions are no more than an hour's drive from Edinburgh. The highlights are **Hopetoun House** of Robert Adam fame and the impressive ruins of **Linlithgow Palace,** birthplace of Mary Queen of Scots in 1542.

One of the best day trips from the Scottish capital is to the city of **Dunfermline,** lying north of Edinburgh. It can easily be visited in a day, which will give you time to see its famous abbey and palace as well as the Andrew Carnegie Birthplace Museum. The ancient town of Dundermline was once the capital of Scotland and is today reached by taking the Forth Road Bridge. See chapter 8, "Fife & the Central Highlands," for more details.

# LINLITHGOW & ITS PALACE

In 1542, Mary Queen of Scots was born in the royal burgh of Linlithgow in West Lothian, 18 miles (29km) west of Edinburgh. You can visit the site of her birth, the roofless Linlithgow Palace. For £2.15 ($3.65) one way and £4.50 ($7.65) round-trip, buses and trains arrive daily from Edinburgh after a 20- to 25-minute ride. If you're driving from central Edinburgh, follow A8 toward Glasgow, and then merge with M9, following the signs to Linlithgow.

✪ **Linlithgow Palace.** On A706, on the south shore of Linlithgow Loch, ½ mile (1km) from Linlithgow Station. ☎ **01506/842-896.** Admission £2.50 ($4.25) adults, £1.90 ($3.25) seniors, £1 ($1.70) children. Daily 9:30am–6:30pm (last admission 6pm).

Birthplace of Mary Queen of Scots, this was once a favorite residence of Scottish kings and is one of the country's most poignant ruins. Although the palace is roofless, its pink-ocher walls climb five floors and are supported on the lower edge by flying buttresses. It's most dramatic and evocative when floodlit at night. Many of the former royal rooms are still remarkably preserved, so you can get a clear idea of how grand it used to be. The queen's suite was in the north quarter but was rebuilt for the homecoming of James VI (James I of Great Britain) in 1620. In one of the many tragic events associated with Scottish sovereignty, the palace burned to the ground in 1746, along with many of the hopes and dreams of Scottish independence. The Great Hall is on the first floor, and a small display shows some of the more interesting architectural relics.

**St. Michael's Parish Church.** Adjacent to Linlithgow Palace. ☎ **01506/842-188.** Free admission. May–Sept daily 10am–4:30pm; Oct–Apr Mon–Fri 10:30am–3pm.

South of the palace stands the medieval kirk of St. Michael the Archangel, site of worship of many a Scottish monarch since its consecration in 1242. Despite being ravaged by the disciples of John Knox (who then chided his followers for their "excesses") and transformed into a stable by Cromwell, this is one of Scotland's best examples of a parish church.

## SEEING THE SIGHTS

✪ **Hopetoun House.** 2 miles (3km) from the Forth Road Bridge near South Queensferry, 10 miles (16km) from Edinburgh off A904. ☎ **0131/331-2451.** Admission £5 ($8.50) adults, £4.50 ($7.65) seniors, £2.70 ($4.60) children, £15 ($25.50) families of up to 6. Easter weekend, May–Sept, and Oct weekends daily 10am–5:30pm (last admission 4:30pm). Closed Oct weekdays and Nov–Apr.

Amid beautifully landscaped grounds laid out along the lines of those at Versailles, Hopetoun is Scotland's greatest Robert Adam mansion and a fine example of 18th-century architecture (note its resemblance to Buckingham Palace). It's the seat of the marquess of Linlithgow, whose grandfather and father were the governor-general of Australia and the viceroy of India, respectively. Seven bays extend across the slightly recessed center, and the classical style includes a complicated tympanum, with hood molds, quoins, and straight-headed windows. A rooftop balustrade with urns completes the ensemble. You can wander through splendid reception rooms filled with 18th-century furniture, paintings, statuary, and other artworks and check out the panoramic view of the Firth of Forth from the roof. After touring the house, you can

# Side Trips from Edinburgh

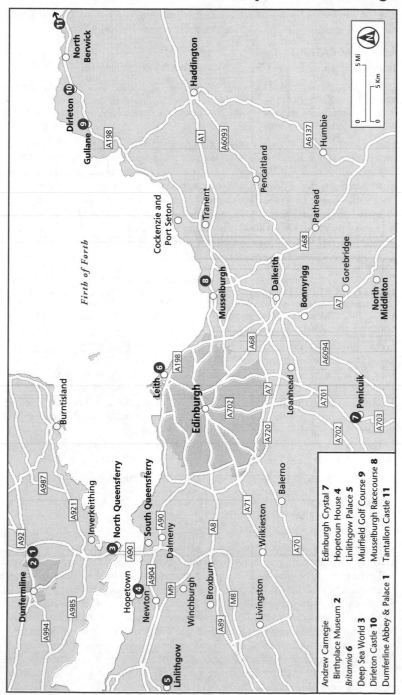

Firth of Forth

Andrew Carnegie
Birthplace Museum **2**
*Britannia* **6**
Deep Sea World **3**
Dirleton Castle **10**
Dumferline Abbey & Palace **1**

Edinburgh Crystal **7**
Hopetoun House **4**
Linlithgow Palace **5**
Muirfield Golf Course **9**
Musselburgh Racecourse **8**
Tantallon Castle **11**

take the nature trail, explore the deer parks, see the Stables Museum, or stroll through the formal gardens. Refreshments are available near the Ballroom Suite.

## ACCOMMODATIONS

You can also rent rooms at **Champany Inn** (see "Dining," below).

**East Bonhard Farm.** Borrowstoun Rd., Linlithgow, W. Lothian EH49 7NT. ☎ **01506/ 825-047.** 2 units. TV. £44 ($74.80) double. Rates include breakfast. No credit cards. From Linlithgow's center, drive north along A803, following the signs to M9, the hamlet of Borrowstoun, and East Bonhard Farm.

This isolated B&B is part of the working farm managed by Margaret Linkston, a horse aficionado and dog and cat lover who rents a pair of rooms in her modern stone-and-masonry farmhouse. About 3 miles (5km) north of Linlithgow, it provides more of a direct contact with the Scot soil and rural earthiness than many other recommendations in this guide. The public areas contain mementos of the family's contacts, thanks to horse breeding and horse shows, with the royal family. The small guest rooms are cozy and functional, each with a tea/coffeemaker. The breakfasts are a showplace for all the bounty of rural Scottish life. No smoking.

## DINING

✪ **Champany Inn.** Champany Corner, Linlithgow, W. Lothian EH49 7LU. ☎ **01506/ 834-532.** Fax 01506/834302. www.champany.com. E-mail: info@champany.com. Reservations required. Main courses £15.50–£30 ($26.35–$51); fixed-price lunch £16.75 ($28.45). AE, DC, MC, V. Mon–Fri 12:30–2pm and 7–10pm. Closed Jan 1–2 and Dec 25. Take M9 until junction 3, then A904 until reaching the restaurant. SCOTTISH.

In this converted farmhouse, you'll find the best steaks in Britain. Owner Clive Davidson is an expert on beef and insists his steaks be 1¼ inches (3cm) thick; his meat is hung for at least 4 weeks, adding greatly to its flavor. He also prepares an assortment of oysters, salmon, and lobsters kept in a pool on the premises. Next door to the main dining room is a chophouse that has less-expensive cuts. You can choose your own cut and watch it being grilled. The wine list has won an award for excellence from *Wine Spectator.* Meals in the chophouse begin at £8.50 ($14.45).

The inn also rents 16 handsomely furnished guest rooms, each with TV, minibar, and phone, costing £135 ($229.50) double, which includes a full breakfast.

**Livingston's.** 52 High St. (opposite the post office). ☎ **01506/846-565.** Reservations recommended. Fixed-price 2-course lunch £12.95 ($22); fixed-price 2-course dinner £23.50 ($39.95), £27.50 ($46.75) 3 courses. MC, V. Tues–Sat noon–2:30pm and 6–9pm. Closed first 2 weeks of Jan. MODERN SCOTTISH/FRENCH.

In converted stables, Chef Julian Wright reigns supreme in this cottage-like restaurant with sandstone walls and Black Watch tartan carpets. A conservatory overlooks a neatly maintained little garden, and the atmosphere is made warm and more romantic by the glow of the candlelight at night. The chef is inventive and uses quality ingredients (usually fresh Scottish produce) imaginatively. To whet your appetite, start with the roast peppers and apples. The saddle of venison is the most requested dish, and rightly so. It comes in a cassis sauce with glazed shallots and a cassoulet of butter beans. Although the menu changes, pigeon pie and brambles often appear, perhaps a risotto of wild mushrooms and truffles made all the more delectable by a shaving of Parmesan. Dessert selections are elegant, such as the chilled soup of strawberries and champagne accompanied by a chocolate mousse. There is an ample wine list, including bottles from California.

# NORTH BERWICK

This royal burgh, created in the 14th century, was once an important Scottish port. In East Lothian, 24 miles (39km) east of Edinburgh, today it's an upmarket holiday resort. Visitors are drawn to its golf courses, beach sands, and harbor life on the Firth of Forth. You can climb the rocky shoreline or enjoy the heated outdoor pool in July and August.

North Berwick is on a direct rail line from Edinburgh (trip time: 30 min.). There's also bus service from Edinburgh, taking 1¼ hours. Both cost £2.25 ($3.80) one way. If you're driving, take A1 in the direction marked THE SOUTH and DUNBAR; then turn onto A198, following the signs to North Berwick.

## SEEING THE SIGHTS

At the **Information Centre,** Quality Street (☎ **01620/892-197**), you can pick up data on how to take boat trips to the offshore islands, including **Bass Rock,** a breeding ground inhabited by about 10,000 gannets. The gannets return from Africa in the spring, usually around April, to nest here until the autumn winds blow too cold and they head south again. It's possible to see the rock from the harbor, but the viewing is even better at **Berwick Law,** a volcanic lookout point.

Some 2 miles (3km) east of North Berwick and 25 miles (40km) east of Edinburgh on A198, stand the ruins of the 14th-century diked and rose-colored **Tantallon Castle** (☎ **01620/892-727**). This was the ancient stronghold of the Douglases from its construction in the 14th century until its defeat by Cromwell's forces in 1650. Overlooking the Firth of Forth, the castle ruins still are formidable, with a square five-story central tower and a dovecote, plus the shell of its east tower, a D-shaped structure with a wall from the central tower. April to September, it's open daily 9:30am to 6:30pm; October to March, hours are Monday to Wednesday and Saturday 9:30am to 4pm, Thursday 9:30am to 4:30pm, and Sunday 2 to 4:30pm. Admission is £2.50 ($4.25) adults, £1.90 ($3.25) seniors, and £1 ($1.70) children.

## ACCOMMODATIONS & DINING

**The Glebe House.** 4 Law Rd., N. Berwick, E. Lothian EH39 4PL. ☎ /fax **01620/892-608.** www.aboutscotland.com/glebe/house.html. E-mail: J.A.Scott@tesco.net. 4 units, 3 with bathroom. £60 ($102) double without bathroom; £70 ($119) double with bathroom. Rates include breakfast. No credit cards.

This dignified 18th-century home belongs to Gwen and Jake Scott, who have worked hard to preserve its original character as the pastor's residence for the nearby Presbyterian Church. Because of the many golf courses nearby, Glebe House is especially favored by golfers and lies a minute's walk south of the town's main street, near the edge of the sea. Each cozy guest room comes with a tea/coffeemaker and boasts part of Mrs. Scott's collection of hand-painted porcelain, artfully arranged on tabletops, in wall niches, and on hanging shelves. (If you ask, she'll point out the various manufacturers, which include Quimper, Rouen, and Staffordshire.) Views from the windows include 4 acres of field, garden, and horse paddock. The breakfasts are served amid the formal furnishings of a high-ceilinged dining room.

**The Marine.** 18 Cromwell Rd., N. Berwick, E. Lothian EH39 4LZ. ☎ **800/225-5843** in the U.S., or 01620/892-406. Fax 01620/894-480. 83 units. TV TEL. £85–£120 ($144.50–$204) double; from £160 ($272) suite. AE, DC, MC, V.

This turreted Victorian commands panoramic views across the West Links Course, some of whose putting greens come close to the hotel's foundations. It's a home for Nicklaus, Trevino, Player, and most of the U.S. Ryder Cup Team during the Open and is in an area with almost 20 golf courses nearby. The hotel has recently undergone refurbishment, and you'll find the aura of an elegant country house. Although the guest rooms vary in size, all have hair dryers, tea/coffeemakers, and trouser presses. The bar is lined with antique golfing photos. Additional facilities are saunas, snooker, a putting green, tennis, gardens, children's playgrounds, and an outdoor heated pool (open May to September). The dining room serves the best food in town: The cuisine is international, with many Scottish specialties, and table d'hôte dinners start at £15.95 ($27.10). Even if you're not a guest, you can dine here.

## GULLANE & THE MUIRFIELD GOLF COURSE

Lying 19 miles (30.5km) east of Edinburgh in East Lothian, Gullane, with a population of around 2,000, is an upscale resort with a fine sandy beach. Not only does it contain one of Scotland's great country hotels, but it's also home to a small restaurant some food critics feel is the best in the country.

There's no rail service into Gullane. Buses from Edinburgh depart from the St. Andrews Square bus station and include nos. 124 and 125. For information, call **0800/23-23-23.** Buses from Edinburgh take from 20 to 25 minutes and cost £2.45 ($4.15) each way or £4.75 ($8.05) round-trip. If you're driving, take A1 in the direction marked THE SOUTH and DUNBAR; then turn onto A198, following the signs to Gullane.

In meager ruins, **St. Andrew's Collegiate Church** fell into disuse when James VI transferred the parish church 2 miles (3km) east to Dirleton. On the western edge of the village, **Gullace Hill** is today a nature reserve and bird sanctuary, with some 200 species of birds spotted here. You can take a small wood footbridge from the car park into the reserve.

What really puts Gullane on the tourist map, other than its fine dining and accommodations, is the 1891 ✪ **Muirfield Golf Course,** ranked 6 among the world's 100 greatest golf courses by the editors of *GolfWeb.* Developed from a boggy piece of low-lying links, Muirfield has hosted 10 open championships and is a par-70, 6,601-yard (6,007m), 18-hole course. A round of golf costs £80 ($136). For more information, call ☎ **01620/842-123.**

### ACCOMMODATIONS

✪ **Greywalls Hotel.** Muirfield, Duncur Rd., Gullane, E. Lothian EH31 2EG. ☎ **01620/842-144.** Fax 01620/842-241. www.greywalls.co.uk. E-mail: hotel@greywalls.co.uk. 23 units. TV TEL. £188–£200 ($319.60–$340) double. Rates include Scottish breakfast. AE, DC, MC, V. Closed Oct 15–Apr 15. Follow the signs from A198 about 5 miles (8km) from N. Berwick.

This Edwardian country house was designed as a private home by the most renowned architect of his day, Sir Edwin Lutyens. It was visited from time to time by Edward VII, who admired the views across the Firth of Forth and south to the Lammermuir Hills. The gardens were laid out by one of England's most respected landscape architects, Gertrude Jekyll, who often worked with Lutyens. In the paneled library, guests relax on comfortable sofas before a blazing log fire (in cool weather). The guest rooms vary in size: Some smaller ones are simply decorated; the more spacious ones are furnished with period pieces.

**Dining:** The food served in the elegant dining room reflects culinary expertise. Light French-style dishes are made almost as appealing to the eye as to the palate. Specialties include fresh seafood. A five-course table d'hôte dinner is served for £35 ($59.50).

**Amenities:** 24-hour room service, laundry, baby-sitting, hard tennis court, croquet lawn, 10 golf courses within 5 miles (8km).

## DINING

✪ **La Potinière.** Main St., Gullane. ☎ **01620/843-214.** Reservations required. Fixed-price 4-course lunch £21.50 ($36.55); fixed-price 5-course dinner £32.50 ($55.25). No credit cards. Sun and Thurs at 1pm; dinner Fri–Sat at 8pm. Closed June 1–8 and Oct. SCOTTISH/FRENCH.

La Potinière is a small but choice restaurant that's beautifully run by David and Hilary Brown. The excellent food produced by Hilary, using local ingredients as much as possible, is complemented by the fine wines in the cellar supervised by David. The first course is usually a subtly flavored soup, which you can follow with a fish dish or one of Hilary's creations. The main courses are all done with flair. They change daily but may include red pepper–and–orange soup, crisp-skinned salmon with virgin olive oil, and breast of corn-fed chicken on savoy cabbage with bacon and garlic and sweet-and-sour sauce. Cheese and dessert wind up the meal. A special dinner is served on Friday and Saturday starting promptly at 8pm; reservations for this five-course gourmet's delight should be made well in advance. No smoking in the dining room.

# DIRLETON: THE PRETTIEST VILLAGE IN SCOTLAND

Another popular day trip, to a point midway between North Berwick and Gullane (see above), is to the lovely little town of Dirleton. The town plan, drafted in the early 16th century, is essentially unchanged today. Dirleton has two greens shaped like triangles, with a pub opposite Dirleton Castle, placed at right angles to a group of cottages. This is a preservation village and subject to careful control of any development. It's on the Edinburgh–North Berwick road (A198). North Berwick (see above) is 5 miles (8km) east and Edinburgh 19 miles (31km) west.

There's no train service to Dirleton. Buses from Edinburgh depart from the St. Andrews Square bus station and include nos. 124 and 125. For information, call ☎ **0800/23-23-23.** Buses from Edinburgh take around 25 minutes and cost £2.95 ($5) one way. If you're driving, take A1 in the direction marked THE SOUTH and DUNBAR; then turn onto A198, following the signs to Dirleton.

## SEEING THE SIGHTS

**Dirleton Castle.** Dirleton, E. Lothian. ☎ **01620/850-330.** Admission £2.50 ($4.25) adults, £1.90 ($3.25) seniors, £1 ($1.70) children. Apr–Sept Mon–Sat 9:30am–6pm, Sun 10am–6pm; Oct–Mar Mon–Sat 9:30am–4pm, Sun 2–4pm.

A rose-tinted 13th-century castle with surrounding gardens, once the seat of the wealthy Anglo-Norman de Vaux family, Dirleton Castle looks like a fairy-tale fortification, with towers, arched entries, and an oak ramp similar to the drawbridge that used to protect it. Reputed to have been fully sacked by Cromwell in 1650, the building was in fact only partially destroyed by him and was further torn down by the Nesbitt family, who, after building nearby Archiefield House, desired a romantic ruin on their land. The prison, bakehouse, and storehouses are carved from bedrock. You can see the ruins of the Great Hall and kitchen, as well as what's left of the lord's chamber where the de Vaux family lived: windows and window seats, a wall with a toilet and drains, and other household features. The 16th-century main gate has a hole through which boiling tar or water could be poured to discourage unwanted visitors.

The castle's country garden and a bowling green are still in use, with masses of flowering plants rioting in the gardens and bowlers sometimes seen on the green. A 17th-century dovecote with 1,100 nests stands at the east end of the garden. A small gate at the west end leads onto one of the village greens.

## ACCOMMODATIONS & DINING

**Castle Inn.** Off A198, Dirleton, E. Lothian EH39 5EP. ☎ **01620/850-221.** 8 units. £56 ($95.20) double. MC, V.

Opposite the village green and the castle and unspoiled by modernization, this is a most satisfactory village inn, with 10 dormer windows and a pair of entrances. The small guest rooms are pleasant and comfortably furnished and contain good beds. The most desirable and spacious rooms are in the main house, with smaller and more modestly furnished rooms in an adjoining modern annex. During the day, you can order light snacks; an evening meal begins at £15 ($25.50) for three courses. Guests are welcome in a lounge with a free-standing stone fireplace, decorated with copper pots, settles and trestle tables against rugged stone walls, and a Victorian mahogany decoration behind the bar.

**Open Arms.** Dirleton, E. Lothian EH39 5EG. ☎ **01620/850-241.** Fax 01620/850-570. E-mail: openarms@clara.co.uk. 10 units. TV TEL. £140–£180 ($238–$306) double. Rates include Scottish breakfast. MC, V. Free parking.

The Open Arms will receive you with you know what. This old stone hostelry has been transformed into a handsome hotel/restaurant, serving the finest food in the area. Off A198 overlooking the castle ruins, the hotel is owned by Mr. and Mrs. Hill. The average-size guest rooms, each with a hair dryer, enjoy room service. Log fires crackle and blaze, and the Open Arms is a golfer's paradise, as it's surrounded by 20 courses within a 20-mile (32km) radius.

The Hills have built a local reputation for serving Scottish dishes, using local produce, plus regional venison, beef, lamb, and freshly caught salmon. The whiskies used in the sauces are of the region too. The restaurant offers a four-course dinner for £29.50 ($50.15). A more reasonably priced brasserie is alongside the restaurant, with main courses at £8 to £12 ($13.60 to $20.40).

## INTO THE DEEP AT DEEP SEA WORLD

Although it's in the Fife region, another popular day trip from Edinburgh is to Deep Sea World. To get there by car from central Edinburgh, drive 12 miles (19km) west, following the signs to Inverkeithing and the Forth Road Bridge. If you're going by train, go to either the Waverley or the Haymarket rail station in Edinburgh and take any train stopping at North Queensferry (departing at 35-minute intervals); from the North Queensferry rail station, follow the prominent signs to Deep Sea World, about a 10-minute walk away. Round-trip fare is £5.25 ($8.90).

**Deep Sea World.** North Queensferry, in Fife. ☎ **01383/411-880.** Admission £6.25 ($10.65) adults, £4.50 ($7.65) students, £3.95 ($6.70) children 3–15, £16.95 ($28.80) family ticket. Children under 3 free. Apr–June and Sept–Oct daily 10am–6pm; July–Aug daily 10am–6:30pm; Nov–Mar Mon–Fri 11am–5pm, Sat–Sun 10am–6pm.

In the early 1990s, a group of entrepreneurs sealed the edges of an abandoned rock quarry with a sheathing of concrete and positioned a 364-foot cement-and-acrylic tunnel on the quarry's bottom. Then they flooded the quarry with a million gallons of seawater, stocked it with a menagerie of watery creatures, and opened as Scotland's most comprehensive aquarium. You can either stand on a moving mechanical sideway or walk on a carpeted surface along the tunnel's length. En route, you pass through underwater microclimates featuring views of a kelp forest; sandy underwater flats that shelter bottom-dwelling schools of stingray, turbot, and sole; murky underwater caves favored by conger eels and small sharks; and a scary underwater trench whose sponge-encrusted bottom careens abruptly away from view. Schools of shark and battalions of as many as 5,000 fish stare back at you. On the premises is a cafe, a gift shop, and an audiovisual show. Allow at least 90 minutes for your visit, and avoid the weekend crowds.

## 5

# The Borders & Galloway Regions

The romantic castle ruins and skeletons of Gothic abbeys in the **Borders** region stand as mute reminders of the battles that once raged between England and the proud Scots. For a long time, the "Border Country" was a no-man's land of plunder and destruction, lying south of the line of the Moorfoot, Pentland, and Lammermuir hill ranges and east of the Annandale Valley and the upper valley of the River Tweed.

The Borders is the land of Sir Walter Scott, master of romantic adventure, who topped the bestseller list in the early 19th century. The remains of the four great mid-12th-century abbeys are here: Dryburgh (where Scott is buried), Melrose, Jedburgh, and Kelso. And because of its abundant sheep-grazing land, the Borders is the home of the cashmere sweater and the tweed suit. Ask at the local tourist office for a "Borders Woollen Trail" brochure, detailing where you can visit woolen mills, shops, and museums and follow the process of weaving from start to finish.

Southwest of the Borders is the often-overlooked **Galloway** region (a.k.a. Dumfries and Galloway), a land of unspoiled countryside, fishing harbors, and romantic ruins. Major centers to visit are the ancient city of Dumfries, perhaps the best base for touring Galloway, and the artists' colony of Kirkcudbright, an ancient burgh filled with color-washed houses. In the far west, Stranraer is a major terminal for those making the 35-mile (56km) ferry crossing into Northern Ireland. Among the major sights are Sweetheart Abbey, outside Dumfries, and the Burns Mausoleum at Dumfries. If time remains, explore beautiful Threave Garden, outside Castle Douglas.

**Edinburgh Airport** is about 40 miles (64.5km) northwest of Selkirk in the Borders and **Glasgow Airport** about 75 miles (121km) north of Dumfries in the Galloway region. Trains from Glasgow run south along the coast, toward Stranraer, intersecting with the rail stations at Ayr and Girvan en route. Another rail line from Glasgow extends due south to Dumfries, depositing and picking up passengers before crossing the English border headed to the English city of Carlisle. In direct contrast, southbound trains from Edinburgh almost always bypass most of the Borders towns en route, making direct, usually nonstop, transits for Berwick, in England. Consequently, to reach most of the Borders towns covered here, you'll probably rely on a rented car or on bus service to Peebles, Selkirk, Melrose, and Kelso, from Edinburgh or Berwick. For train information and schedules, call **National Rail Enquiries** at ☎ 0345/484-950.

If you're coming from England, trains from London's King's Cross Station to Edinburgh's Waverley Station enter Scotland at Berwick-upon-Tweed in 6 hours. From Berwick, a network of local buses runs among the villages and towns. Three rail lines pass through the region from London's Euston Station en route to Glasgow. Dumfries or Stranraer is the best center if you're traveling by rail in the Uplands. **Bus** travel isn't recommended for reaching the regions, but once you get there, you'll find it a reliable means of public transportation, since many smaller towns have no rail connections.

## Driving Through the Regions

**Day 1**   Begin in **Jedburgh,** 325 miles (523km) north of London or 48 miles (77km) southeast of Edinburgh. If you've driven up from England, spend the night in Jedburgh and visit the ruined abbey of Jedburgh and explore Mary Queen of Scots House.

**Day 2**   From Jedburgh, continue northeast on A698 to **Kelso** to see its abbey and Floors Castle, the home of the present duke of Roxburghe. In the environs at Gordon is the historic home of **Mellerstain,** seat of the earls of Haddington. Overnight in Kelso.

**Day 3**   Drive west on A699 toward St. Boswells, but stop first at **Dryburgh Abbey,** where Sir Walter Scott is buried. The Gothic ruins are surrounded by yew trees and cedars of Lebanon. Near Dryburgh, see the famous **"Scott's View"** over the Tweed to the Eildon Hills; from Dryburgh, go north along B6356 (it's signposted). Continue via St. Boswells along A6091 to **Melrose,** where you can visit the ruins of Melrose Abbey and pay an interesting visit to **Abbotsford,** former home of Sir Walter Scott (reached along B6360). Overnight in Melrose.

**Day 4**   Pass through Innerleithen by taking A72 west from Melrose. Stop to look at **Traquair House,** on A72, 16 miles (26km) west of Melrose. From here you can travel to **Peebles** along B7062 for a visit to Neidpath Castle and Dawyck Botanic Garden. Overnight in Peebles.

**Day 5**   Head west along A721, cutting south at A702 to Biggar. When you reach the junction with A701, continue south for **Moffat,** 60 (97km) miles south of Edinburgh. Continue south along A74 via Lockerbie, remembered as the site of the tragic Pan American crash, and A709 west to **Dumfries** for the night.

**Day 6**   Explore around Dumfries in the morning, taking in Threave Castle and Threave Garden. Then get on A75 going southwest into **Castle Douglas,** where you can overnight.

**Day 7**   Take A75 southwest to the junction with A711 leading to **Kirkcudbright,** where you can see the town and enjoy lunch. Then get on A755 going west until you reach the junction of B727, pointing northwest to **Gatehouse-of-Fleet.** After a brief visit, follow the signposts to A75, which will take you south and west across a scenic road opening onto Wigtown Bay until you reach **Newton Stewart** for the night.

**Day 8**   In the morning, continue along A75 west to **Stranraer** for an overnight, visiting **Glenluce Abbey** along the way. If you arrive in Stranraer early enough, pay a late-afternoon visit to **Portpatrick** (follow A77) on the coast. You can find accommodations here or return to Stranraer for the night.

# The Borders & Galloway Regions

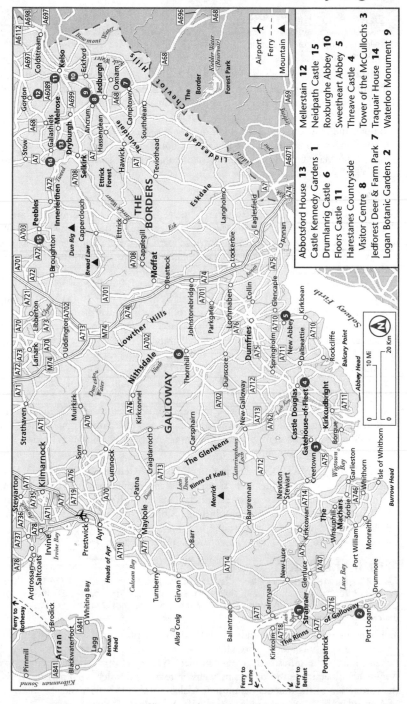

**Legend:**
Airport ✈
Ferry - - -
Mountain ▲

Abbotsford House **13**
Castle Kennedy Gardens **1**
Drumlanrig Castle **6**
Floors Castle **11**
Harestanes Countryside
Visitor Centre **8**
Jedforest Deer & Farm Park **7**
Logan Botanic Gardens **2**

Mellerstain **12**
Neidpath Castle **15**
Roxburghe Abbey **10**
Sweetheart Abbey **5**
Threave Castle **4**
Tower of the McCullochs **3**
Traquair House **14**
Waterloo Monument **9**

## 1 Jedburgh: Gateway to the Borders

48 miles (77km) SE of Edinburgh, 57 miles (92km) N of Newcastle-upon-Tyne, 13 miles (21km) S of Melrose

The little town of Jedburgh, divided by the River Jed, developed around Jedburgh Abbey on a Roman road called Dere Street. Today the market town gives little hint of the turbulence of its early history as home for royalty in the beleaguered Borders area.

If you have limited time to spend in the region, note that Jedburgh is a typical Borders town and makes a good base: It not only boasts some of the most impressive and evocative abbey ruins around but is also the home of a fortified townhouse once inhabited by Mary Queen of Scots. In its environs you can enjoy some of the area's loveliest walks and excursions.

## ESSENTIALS

**GETTING THERE**   There's no direct rail link to Jedburgh. The **nearest rail station** is at Berwick-upon-Tweed (☎ **0345/484-950** for information and tickets), from which you must take two buses (see below). However, depending on the day's schedule, it's sometimes more practical to take a train to Newcastle-upon-Tyne (England) and from there take a bus to Jedburgh (see below).

There are daily **buses** from Edinburgh; a bus leaving Edinburgh at 9:30am arrives in Jedburgh at 11:10am and costs £5.50 ($9.35) one way or £9.25 ($15.75) round-trip. Call ☎ **0990/808-080** for schedules. From England, take the train to Berwick and then the bus (75-minute trip) from Berwick to Kelso. In Kelso, transfer to another bus (six to eight per day) that continues to Jedburgh, after a 25-minute ride. One-way fares are £2.50 ($4.25). For information, call the Jedburgh tourist office (it has all the schedules) or the Kelso bus station (☎ **01573/224-141**). Two buses a day run from Newcastle-upon-Tyne to Jedburgh, taking 90 minutes and charging £8 to £9.50 ($13.60 to $16.15) one way.

If you're **driving,** at Corbridge (in England), continue north into Scotland along A68, using Jedburgh as your gateway into the Borders. From Edinburgh, take A7 and then A68, following the signs to Jedburgh. From the center of Edinburgh, expect driving time of around 75 minutes.

**VISITOR INFORMATION**   The **Jedburgh Visitors' Centre** (☎ 01835/863-435) is at Murray's Green, near the police station, adjacent to the spot where buses pull in, behind the Town Hall, and very close to the famous abbey. It's open in April and May, Monday to Saturday 9:30am to 5pm; in June, Monday to Saturday 9:30am to 6pm; July and August, daily 9am to 8pm; and in September, Monday to Saturday 9:30am to 5pm, and October to March, Monday to Saturday 10am to 4pm.

## SEEING THE SIGHTS

✪ **Jedburgh Abbey.** Abbey Place. ☎ **01835/863-925.** Admission £3 ($5.10) adults, £2.30 ($3.90) seniors, £1 ($1.70) children under 16. Apr–Sept daily 9:30am–6:30pm; Oct–Mar Mon–Sat 9:30am–4:30pm, Sun 2–4:30pm. Last entrance 30 mins. prior to each of the closing hours above.

This famous ruined abbey, founded by David I in 1138, is one of Scotland's finest. Under the Augustinian canons from Beauvais, France, it achieved abbey status in 1152 (when enough of its infrastructure was complete to allow a formal endorsement by the Augustinian hierarchies in Rome), and went on to witness much royal pageantry, like the coronation of the founder's grandson, Malcolm IV (1153–65), and the marriage of Alexander III (1249–86) to his second wife, Yolande de Dreux.

The abbey was sacked in 1544–45 by the English during the frequent wars that ravaged the villages along the Scottish and English borders. Its roof was burned, allowing rains to penetrate and further destroy much of the interior detailing. After 1560, the ascendancy of the straitlaced Church of Scotland acted as a disincentive for rebuilding any grand-scale "papist monuments," so no efforts were made to repair the abbey.

For about 300 years, a small section of it was the town's parish church, but in 1875 other premises were found for day-to-day worship. Then teams of architects set to work restoring the place to its original medieval design. The abbey is still roofless but otherwise fairly complete, with most of its exterior stonework still in place. You can still view the late-12th-century west front; three pedimented gables remain at the doorway, and the solid buttresses and rounded arches in the Norman style are still relatively intact. You can also walk through the nave and the ruins of the former cloister.

In a century-old outbuilding is the **Jedburgh Abbey Visitors' Centre,** Abbey Place (☎ **01835/863-925**), open the same hours as the abbey.

**Mary Queen of Scots House.** Queen St. ☎ **01835/863-331.** Admission £2 ($3.40) adults, £1 ($1.70) seniors/children. Mar–Nov Mon–Sat 10am–4:30pm; Sun noon–4:30pm. Closed Dec–Feb.

Here, in 1566, Mary Stuart spent 6 weeks and almost died of a mysterious ailment after a tiring 40-mile (64.5km) return ride from a visit to her wounded beloved, the earl of Bothwell, at Hermitage Castle (see "Exploring the Countryside," below). In a later lament, commenting on the emotional agonies of the last 20 years of her life, she wrote, "Would that I had died at Jedburgh." The house, in the center of High Street, contains articles dealing with Mary's life, paintings, and engravings. Ancient pear trees still stand on the grounds, a reminder of the days when Jedburgh was famous for its fruit. "Jethard pears" were hawked in the streets of London.

**Castle Gaol.** Castlegate. ☎ **01835/863-254.** Admission £1.25 ($2.15) adults, 75p ($1.30) children/seniors/students. Easter–Sept Mon–Sat 10am–4:45pm, Sun 1–4pm. Closed Oct–Easter.

This museum stands on the site of Jedburgh Castle, a favorite 12th-century royal residence, the scene of many a hunting and hawking party since the ancient Jed Forest once surrounded the area. The castle was torn down in the 15th century to keep it from falling under English control. In the 1820s, a Georgian prison was built in its place and became the most modern in the country. Of passing interest if you have 30 minutes to spare, its three prison blocks are built around the central governor's block. The cells included two windows, a wood bed, and even central heating, a far cry from the typical dungeon prisons of the day. The small museum here shows the life of Jedburgh in the 19th century and many notables once connected to this royal burgh.

## EXPLORING THE COUNTRYSIDE

You can rent a bike in the nearby town of Hawick, at the **Hawick Cycle Centre,** 45 N. Bridge St. (☎ **01450/373-352**), where you'll pay £5 ($8.50) per day and £50 ($85) per week, plus a £50 ($85) deposit. It's open Monday to Thursday 9am to 7pm, Friday 9am to 8pm, Saturday 9am to 5pm, and Sunday noon to 4pm.

**Jedforest Deer and Farm Park.** Camptown, 5 miles (8km) south of Jedburgh along A68. ☎ **01835/840-364.** Admission £3.50 ($5.95) adults, £2.50 ($4.25) ages 3 to 16, £11.50 ($19.55) family ticket; ages 2 and under free. May–Oct daily 10am–5:30pm. Closed Nov–Apr.

You'll find the area's most interesting walks and nature experiences at this deer and farm park. Eighty acres of this 1,000-acre farm are open to the public and dotted with unusual species of pigs, chickens, and especially deer. Owner Marion Armitage prides herself on her herds of red fallow and Asian Sika deer (bred for food), which either nuzzle or flee from visitors. You can buy a bag of special deer food for 30p (50¢) and follow one of the two walking trails along the softly undulating, partially forested terrain. The trail marked with brown signposts requires 30 minutes for the circumference; the trail marked with green signposts requires an hour. Each is peppered with captioned signs and explanations about the flora and fauna you'll see en route.

An unusual side attraction in the park is Diana Durman-Walters and her **Birds of Prey Experience.** Ms. Durman-Walters or a member of her staff exercises their owls, buzzards, eagles, hawks, and falcons at periodic intervals every day, feeding them raw rabbit meat or chicken—but not so much that they lose their incentive to catch rats, rabbit, and field mice during their exercise regimes. If the art of falconry interests you, you can participate in a half-day Hawk Walk at £35 ($59.50) per person or a full-day Hawk Walk at £70 ($119) per person (including a light lunch). Participation requires an advance reservation (call the number above), is limited to no more than six people, and usually includes two birds. Wear sturdy walking shoes and sensible clothing that won't wilt in a rain shower and bring a sense of respect for the ecological balance between hunter and prey in the great Scottish outdoors. If you're willing, you can handle one of these temperamental birds and experience the way it returns to the glove after spotting, catching, and killing a rodent or rabbit.

**Harestanes Countryside Visitor Centre.** At the junction of A68 and B6400, Monteviot. ☎ **01835/830-306.** Free admission. Apr–Oct daily 10am–5pm. Closed Nov–Mar.

For another experience with nature, head north of Jedburgh (it's signposted) to this visitor center. You can follow marked trails or take guided walks through one of the most beautiful spots in the Borders. At the center, the Discovery Room presents displays of wildlife. On site is a gift shop selling local crafts and a tearoom.

**Hermitage Castle.** On an unclassified road (the castle is signposted) between A7 and B6399, 10 miles (16km) south of Hawick in Liddesdale. ☎ **0131/668-8800.** Admission £1.80 ($3.05). Apr–Sept daily 9:30am–6pm. Closed Oct–Mar.

If you want to follow in the footsteps of Mary Queen of Scots, you can drive from Jedburgh to Hermitage Castle. It was to Hermitage that Mary was headed when she made her famous 40-mile (64.5km) ride from Jedburgh to rush to the bedside of her wounded lover, the earl of Bothwell (1535–78), the victim of a raid into Scottish territory by English troops. Still mired in the misty gloom of the Middle Ages, this 1300s castle was restored in the early 1800s. Its original owner, Lord Soulis, was accused of devil worship and boiled alive by the angry townspeople.

## ACCOMMODATIONS

✪ **Ancrum Craig.** Ancrum, Jedburgh, The Borders TD8 6UN. ☎ **01835/830-280.** Fax 01835/830259. www.aboutscotland.com/jed/ancrumcraig.html. E-mail: ancrumcraig@ clara.net. 3 units. TV. £44–£50 ($74.80–$85) double. Rates include breakfast. No credit cards. From Jedburgh, take A68 north for 5 miles (8km), then turn west onto B6400 and follow the signs to Libby's Leaf.

Most of this place dates from the 1830s, when a simple 18th-century farmhouse was massively expanded into a red-sandstone Victorian home. Surrounded by landscaped gardens, with views stretching out over the valley of the Teviot, Ancrum Craig is a fine example of baronial, somewhat chilly, Scottish living. It's owned and run by the Hensen family, but you probably won't have much intimate contact with them. The guest rooms, however, are cozy and homelike. The largest of the three is the Gold Room, with a bay window boasting a sweeping view. The smallest is the Heather

Room, whose window overlooks the original medieval core, long ago made into an outbuilding. In between is the twin-bedded Blue Room, benefiting from a southern exposure. The breakfasts are generous.

**Ferniehirst Mill Lodge.** Hwy. A68, Jedburgh, The Borders TD8 6PQ. ☎ **01835/863-279.** Fax 01835/863-279. http://members.aol.com/ferniemill. E-mail: ferniemill@aol.com. 9 units. TEL. £23 ($39.10) per person. Rates include breakfast; dinner £14 ($23.80). MC, V. Free parking. Take A68 2½ miles (4km) south of Jedburgh.

Built in 1980, this chalet-inspired modern guesthouse is in a quiet neighborhood away from the town center and attracts people (including hunters and anglers) seeking quiet and rural charm. Its pine-paneled guest rooms are functional but comfortable, with tea/coffeemakers. Horseback riding (for experienced riders only) costs about £25 ($42.50) per hour (minimum of 2 hours), and riders must supply their own riding habits. Riding packages are available, but only for equestrians willing to stay for a full week.

**Glenfriar's Hotel.** The Friars, Jedburgh, The Borders TD8 6BN. ☎/fax **01835/862-000.** 6 units. TV. £70–£80 ($119–$136) double. Rates include breakfast. AE, MC, V.

This small private hotel, run by Ms. Jenny Bywater, is in a Georgian house on a quiet corner next to St. John's Church. It features antique wooden furnishings, including four-poster beds in two rooms, and all accommodations have tea/coffeemakers and well-maintained bathrooms with hair dryers. The guest rooms are slightly larger than average. Since Ms. Bywater cooks, cleans, and books rooms single-handedly, she never accepts more than 10 guests at any time.

**The Spinney.** Langley, Jedburgh, The Borders TD8 6PB. ☎ **01835/863-525.** Fax 01835/864-883. www.smoothhounds.co.uk/debra.html. E-mail: thespinney@btinternet.com. 3 units, 2 chalets. TV TEL. £23 ($39.10) per person. Regular double rooms include breakfast, chalet rentals do not. MC, V. Take A68 2 miles (3km) south of Jedburgh.

Run by Mr. and Mrs. Fry, this B&B complex includes a main house plus a modernized cottage with two doubles and two pinewood chalets with bathrooms, sitting rooms, and kitchens. Leather and wood furnishings are found throughout the well-maintained guest rooms, which have hair dryers and beverage makers. The Scottish Tourist Board recently bestowed the guesthouse with a deluxe rating.

## DINING

**Carter's Rest.** Abbey Place. ☎ **01835/863-414.** Main courses £5–£12 ($8.50–$20.40); bar lunches £4.50–£8 ($7.65–$13.60). MC, V. Restaurant daily noon–2:30pm and 6–9pm; pub Mon–Sat 11am–11pm, Sun 11am–10:30pm. SCOTTISH/CONTINENTAL.

This pub, with a downstairs dining room built of old abbey stones, is the favorite gathering place for locals. Owner Mr. Jonentz serves wholesome and hearty food and drink. The simple but tasty menu includes dishes like steaks, scampi, chicken Cordon Bleu, pork or lamb chops, and fresh vegetables in season. The pub also serves eight regional beers on tap.

**Simply Scottish.** 6 High St. ☎ **01835/864-696.** Reservations recommended for dinner. Lunch main courses £4–£7 ($6.80–$11.90); pot of tea with scones, clotted cream, and jam £2 ($3.40); set-price dinner £9.95 ($16.90). MC, V. Daily 10am–9pm. SCOTTISH.

In the heart of town, amid the stripped pinewood floors and heavy pine furniture of what was built around 1900 as a department store, this decent, honest, and well-scrubbed restaurant serves savory meals at lunch and dinner, plus countless pots of tea for all the local shoppers who drop by. Menu items are made entirely from fresh Scottish ingredients and likely to include a salad of smoked chicken and avocado, haggis with white onion sauce, chicken liver pâté with whisky sauce, grilled Borders lamb steak with Arran mustard, casserole of venison with red wine–mushroom sauce, and roasted salmon with herb-flavored butter sauce. A preferred dessert is summer fruit pudding with fruit compote and honey-flavored ice cream. The restaurant is licensed.

## 2 Kelso: Abbey Ruins & Adam Architecture

44 miles (71km) SE of Edinburgh, 12 miles (19km) NE of Jedburgh, 68 miles (109.5km) NW of Newcastle-upon-Tyne, 12 miles (19km) E of Melrose, 23 miles (37km) W of Berwick-upon-Tweed

A typical historic border town like Jedburgh, Kelso lies at the point where the River Teviot meets the River Tweed. Sir Walter Scott called it "the most beautiful, if not the most romantic, village in Scotland." The settlement that grew up here developed into a town around Kelso Abbey.

Kelso today is a flourishing market town, the center of an agricultural district boasting farming and stock raising. But for visitors, the reasons to come here are the ruined abbey and the nearby palatial Floors Castle (by the great architect William Adam) and Mellerstain (begun by William but finished by his son Robert). The town is also one of the best centers for touring the Borders, since it's near Jedburgh, Dryburgh Abbey, and Melrose, among other attractions.

### ESSENTIALS

**GETTING THERE**    The nearest **rail** station connection is Berwick-upon-Tweed, from where you can take a bus to Kelso (see below). For information, call ☎ 0345/484-950.

From Edinburgh, board the **bus** to Galashiels, with connecting service to Kelso; the full trip lasts about 80 minutes and costs £5.50 ($9.35) one way and £10 ($17) round-trip. Phone ☎ 0990/808-080 for more information. From Berwick to Kelso, there are between six and eight buses a day, depending on the day of the week and the season. Transit costs £3.75 ($6.40) each way and takes an hour. Because three bus companies make the run, it's best to call the local tourist office at ☎ 01573/223-464 for the schedules.

If you're **driving** from Jedburgh (see "Jedburgh: Gateway to the Borders," above), follow A698 northeast to Kelso. From Edinburgh, take A7 and follow the signs to Hawick; then change to A68, follow the signs to Jedburgh, and take A6089 to Kelso.

**VISITOR INFORMATION**    The **tourist office** is at Town House, The Square (☎ 01573/223-464). April to June, it's open Monday to Saturday 10am to 5pm and Sunday 10am to 1pm; July and August, hours are Monday to Saturday 9am to 6pm and Sunday 10am to 5pm; September hours are Monday to Saturday 9:30am to 5pm and Sunday 10am to 5pm; and October hours are Monday to Saturday 9:30am to 4:30pm and Sunday 10am to 1pm.

### SEEING THE SIGHTS

**Kelso Abbey.** Bridge St. Free admission. Apr–Dec Mon–Sat 10am–6:30pm, Sun 2–6:30pm; Jan–Mar by arrangement only.

Once a great ecclesiastical center, Kelso Abbey has lain in ruins since the late 16th century, when it suffered its last and most devastating attack by the English, who ripped off its roofs, burned it, and declared it officially defunct. The lands and remaining buildings were given to the earl of Roxburghe. The oldest (1128) and probably largest of the Border abbeys, it was once one of the richest, collecting revenues and rents from granges, fisheries, mills, and manor houses throughout the region. In 1919, the abbey was given to the nation.

Although the remains of this abbey may not be as impressive as those of Jedburgh (see "Jedburgh: Gateway to the Borders," above), Kelso has had its moments in history, including the crowning of the infant James III. At the entrance is part of the south recessed doorway, where some of the sculpture on the arches is still fairly intact. The massive west transept tower still suggests its original massive construction, and a trio of building sections with round-headed openings remain. The west front and tower are still visible, the whole flanked by buttresses crowned with rounded turrets. A partial cloister here dates from 1933, when it was built as the Roxburghe family vault. Sir Walter Scott knew Kelso Abbey well, as he spent time here studying at Waverley Cottage, which you can see from the abbey's parking area; it was once the Kelso Grammar School, where the famous author learned how to read and write.

✪ **Floors Castle.** Hwy. A697, 2 miles (3km) north of Kelso. ☎ **01573/223-333.** Admission £5 ($8.50) adults, £4.50 ($7.65) seniors, £3 ($5.10) ages 6–15; free for ages 5 and under. Apr–Oct daily 10am–4:30pm (last admission 4pm). Closed Nov–Mar. Follow the signs north from Kelso center.

On the banks of the Tweed, the home of the dukes of Roxburghe was designed in 1721 by William Adam and remodeled in the mid–19th century by William Playfair. Part of the castle contains superb French and English furniture, porcelain, tapestries, and paintings by Gainsborough, Reynolds, and Canaletto. You'll also find a licensed restaurant, a coffee shop, and a gift shop, as well as a walled garden and garden center. You might recognize Floors: It was a major location for the Tarzan film *Greystoke*.

✪ **Mellerstain.** Gordon. ☎ **01573/410-225.** Admission £5 ($8.50) adults, £4 ($6.80) seniors, £2 ($3.40) children. May–Sept Sun–Fri 12:30–5pm; Oct–Apr by arrangement only. From Edinburgh, follow A68 to Earlston, then follow the signs to Mellerstain for another 5 miles (8km); from Kelso, head northwest along A6089 until you see the signposted turn to the left.

Seven miles (11km) northwest of Kelso stands Mellerstain, the seat of the earls of Haddington. This is one of the most famous of the mansions designed by Robert Adam, and one of Scotland's greatest Georgian residences. William Adam built two wings on the house in 1725, and the main building was designed by his more famous son, Robert, some 40 years later. (For more details on the Adam family of architectural geniuses, see the box "Robert Adam: Architect to the King," below.)

Mellerstain is associated with Lady Grisell Baillie (born Grisell Hume). In 1689 at 13 years of age, this Scottish heroine showed great courage by hiding her father in the village church's crypt, bringing him food and supplies in the dead of night, and facing down the English. Hounded by the English, she fled to Holland but returned in triumph with William of Orange (later William I of England) and later married into the Baillie family, scions of Mellerstain. You can see the interior, with its decorations and ceilings and impressive library, as well as paintings and antique furniture. The garden terrace offers a panoramic view south to the lake, with the Cheviot Hills in the distance. Afternoon tea is served, and souvenir gifts are on sale.

## ACTIVE PURSUITS

The 18-hole **Roxburghe Golf Course** (☎ 01573/450-331) is the only championship course in the region. This 7,111-yard (6,471m) course was designed by Dave Thomas, one of Britain's leading golf architects. Guests of the hotel (see "Accommodations & Dining," below) can most easily get tee times, but the course is open to non-members as well. Greens fees are £35 ($59.50) for 18 holes, or £50 ($85) for a

---

# Robert Adam: Architect to the King

In the field of architecture, one Scottish name towers over all the rest: **Robert Adam** (1728–92), whose adaptations of the Italian Palladian style have been admired and duplicated in public and private buildings around the world. He has emerged as Britain's most prestigious neoclassical architect in a century that produced dozens of talented competitors. Today, owning an Adam building is an honor akin to being granted a knighthood by the queen but (if you happen to be selling the building) infinitely more profitable.

Adam's genius derived from his synthesis of the decorative traditions of the French and Italian Renaissance with the ancient monuments of Greece and Rome. His designs are particularly notable for their lavish use of color, inspired by Grecian vase paintings and by what was being excavated from archaeological digs in places like Pompeii. Almost as important, Adam seemed to have a well-developed business sense and a knack for decorating the right house at the right time, and his moneyed clients helped propel him into the spotlight.

Throughout much of his career, he collaborated with his capable but less talented younger brother, **James** (1730–94), who handled many of the workaday details of the projects they executed together. And when an English or Scottish lord or lady hired the Adam brothers, they got more than an intensely detailed building—in most cases, the commission included every aspect of the interior decoration and most of the furnishings. The brothers' education in the visual arts began early: Their father, **William Adam** (1689–1748), was the leading Scottish architect of his day and designed dozens of manor houses in what has been called a crude but vigorous Palladian style.

Robert was born in Kirkcaldy, in Fife, but soon emigrated to the source of most of his large commissions, London. He laboriously studied the architecture

---

full day's play Monday to Friday, rising to £40 ($68) for 18 holes on weekends, or £60 ($102) for a full day's play on weekends.

Our favorite spot for drinking in the scenic countryside is the nearby village of **Kirk Yeetholm,** 7 miles (11km) southeast of Kelso on B6352. This is the northern terminus of the **Pennine Way,** a 250-mile (402.5km) hike that begins down in Yorkshire, England. Today Kirk Yeetholm is filled with tired hikers at the end of the trail, but it was once the Gypsy capital of Scotland—until 1883, a Gypsy queen was crowned here. You can see (at least from the outside) the "Gypsy Palace," really a tiny cottage in the center of the village.

Another place for walking and hiking is around **Smailholm Tower** (☎ 0131/668-8800), on a ridge 8 miles (13km) west of Kelso and 2 miles (3km) south of Mellerstain (see listing, above), signposted off B6404. A so-called peel tower (fortified tower) from the 1500s, it has been restored and rises 60 feet (18m) above a loch, providing some of the best views of the Borders. April to September, it's open daily 9:30am to 6pm, charging £2 ($3.40) admission.

## ACCOMMODATIONS & DINING

**Abbey Bank.** The Knowes, Kelso, The Borders TD5 7BH. ☎/fax **01573/226-550.** www.aboutscotland.com/kelso/abbeybank.html. E-mail: diah@abbeybank.freeserve.co.uk. 7 units, 5 with private bathroom. TV. £44 ($74.80) double without bathroom; £52 ($88.40) double with bathroom. Rates include breakfast. MC, V.

of imperial Rome under the supervision of then-famous French antiquarian C. L. Clérisseau, with whom he toured widely in Italy and Dalmatia (later part of Yugoslavia). In 1764, he compiled the information he gathered during these tours in the widely acclaimed *The Ruins of the Palace of the Emperor Diocletian at Spalatro*. In 1761, Robert, along with architect William Chambers, was appointed architect of the king's works, at the time the most prestigious post in Britain. In 1773, an illustrated volume documented his and his brother's vision, *The Works of Robert and James Adam;* they justifiably claimed credit for revolutionizing the principals of English aesthetics.

The Adam style, a richly detailed yet airy interpretation of neoclassicism, was a radical departure from the more ponderous and sometimes ecclesiastical forms that preceded it. Almost immediately, the Adam interpretation of ceiling decorations and mantelpieces was widely copied throughout Britain. And within less than a generation, this vision radically influenced furniture styles throughout Europe and North America, most notably France's Louis XVI style. Looser derivations are the Directoire, Sheraton, and Empire styles.

Adam buildings in Scotland include the **Old Quad** at Edinburgh University and **Mellerstain** in the Borders (described earlier in this chapter). Many more of his works remain in England, especially London, thanks to his careful cultivation of the wealthy English. Examples are **Kenwood House** (1767–69) in London, **Osterly Park** (1761–80) and **Syon House** (1762–69) in Middlesex, and **Luton Hoo** (1768–75) in Bedfordshire. Much more widespread than Adam buildings, however, are examples of their furniture and interior decoration (especially chairs, sideboards, and mantelpieces), which are proudly displayed in museums and private homes across the United Kingdom and North America.

This sophisticated B&B started out as the home of a local doctor in 1815. Today, it's owned by Douglas McAdam and his wife, Diah, both of whom have lived in Indonesia and Korea. The house is filled with a mix of British and Oriental furniture. Each sunny guest room has a tea/coffeemaker and streamlined modern furniture. Because of Diah's familiarity with Indonesian cuisine, you'll be offered *nasi goreng,* the national rice-based dish, as well as a traditional Scottish breakfast of bacon, sausage, eggs, and haggis. A greenhouse contains peach vines and many of the seedlings Douglas nurtures during the coldest months.

**Cross Keys Hotel.** 36 The Square, Kelso, The Borders TD5 7HL. ☎ **01573/223-303.** Fax 01573/225-792. www.cross-keys-hotel.co.uk. E-mail: cross-keys-hotel@easyneet.co.uk. 28 units. TV TEL. £59–£70 ($100.30–$119) double. Rates include breakfast. AE, MC, V.

Facing the cobbled main square of the town, the facade of this hotel was built in a stately Georgian style in 1769. Since then, guests have included Bonnie Prince Charlie and Beatrix Potter. The public areas are comfortable and busy, vaguely inspired by Scottish art nouveau master Charles Rennie MacIntosh. The midsize guest rooms are well upholstered; each has a tea/coffeemaker. The in-house restaurant serves lunch and dinner daily, and the cozy Scottish-style bar, The 36, boasts an impressive collection of single-malt whiskies.

**Ednam House Hotel.** Bridge St., Kelso, The Borders TD5 7HT. ☎ **01573/224-168.** Fax 01573/226-319. www.ednamhouse.com. 32 units. TV TEL. £92–£112 ($156.40–$190.40) double. Rates include breakfast. MC, V.

The Ednam, on the fringe of Kelso, is a conversion of a 1761 Georgian house often referred to as "that lovely place beside the river." In the oldest section is an unusual collection of antiques, and period furnishings are found throughout. The most expensive accommodations, called the "Prince William rooms," are on the third floor and offer a view of the river; less expensive and scenic are those on the first and second floors. The rooms vary in size, but all come with hair dryers and tea/coffeemakers. For those wanting to chance it with the unreliable Scottish sun, there's a terrace.

**Dining:** A fixed-price dinner is available at £20 ($33) per person, and the daily menu includes dishes like braised guinea fowl, rabbit, and lamb cutlets.

**Amenities:** Sauna, arrangements for golf, baby-sitting, guide for nearby walks and biking.

✪ **Roxburghe Hotel and Golf Course.** Hwy. A698, Helton, Kelso, The Borders TD5 8JZ. ☎ **01573/450-331.** Fax 01573/450-611. www.roxburghe.bordernet.co.uk. E-mail: hotel@ roxburghe.net. 22 units. TV TEL. £150–£165 ($255–$280.50) double; £200–£205 ($340–$348.50) double with four-poster bed; £250–£255 ($425–$433.50) suite. Rates include breakfast. AE, DC, MC, V. Take A698 3 miles (5km) southwest of Kelso.

This late 19th-century castle stands on 200 acres of woodland, lawns, and gardens. It was built as the family home of the Roxburghes, who valued its location on the trout-filled Teviot. In 1982, it was converted into a country hotel: The old stable block contains 6 guest rooms; another 16 are in the main house. All are well appointed, with hair dryers. Amid a subdued but elegant decor, the hotel has four log-burning fireplaces going even in summer.

**Dining:** Most guests are away at lunchtime, although you can grab lunch at the bar. A local chef prepares a Scottish and international cuisine in the evening in a dining room that's open to the public. The last dinner order goes in at 9:45pm.

**Amenities:** A glassed-in conservatory offers clusters of wicker chairs for enjoying drinks or tea when the weather is fine; a tennis court and croquet lawn are on the grounds. Many guests come for the shooting and fishing, others for observing the wildlife, especially deer. Most, however, come for the golf, which can be arranged on the hotel's acclaimed 18-hole course, the only championship course in the region.

## A SIDE TRIP TO DRYBURGH ABBEY

Ten miles (16km) west of Kelso and 4 miles (6km) southeast of Melrose (off A68), you'll find the town of **Dryburgh** and its ruined abbey. The adjoining town is **St. Boswells,** an old village on the Selkirk–Kelso road. Near Dryburgh is ✪ **Scott's View** (take B6356 north) over the Tweed to Sir Walter's beloved Eildon Hills; it's the most glorious vista in the region.

✪ **Dryburgh Abbey.** Hwy. A68, Dryburgh, Roxburghshire. ☎ **01835/822-381.** Admission £2.50 ($4.25) adults, £1.90 ($3.25) seniors, £1 ($1.70) ages 5–15; free for ages 4 and under. Apr–Sept daily 9:30am–6:30pm (July–Aug to 7:30pm); Oct–Mar Mon–Sat 9:30am–4:30pm, Sun 2–4:30pm. Drive south from Dryburgh along B6356 (it's signposted); from Edinburgh take A68 to St. Boswells and turn onto B6404 and then left onto B6356.

These Gothic ruins are surrounded by gnarled yew trees and cedars of Lebanon, said to have been planted by knights returning from the Crusades. It's still a lovely ruin, and its setting in a loop of the Tweed is memorable. The cloister buildings are relatively intact, but not much remains of the church itself, except a few foundation stones. You can see enough fragments to realize the architectural style was transitional, between the Romanesque and the pointed Early English style. Sir Walter Scott is buried here in a pillared side chapel.

## ACCOMMODATIONS & DINING

**Dryburgh Abbey Hotel.** Hwy. B6404, outside St. Boswells, The Borders TD6 0RQ. ☎ **01835/822-261.** Fax 01835/823-945. 37 units. £98–£110 ($166.60–$187) double; £118–£130 ($200.60–$221) suite for 2. Rates include full Scottish breakfast. AE, MC, V.

Next to the abbey ruins, this hotel was built in 1845 as the home of Lady Grisell Baillie and remained in her family until 1929. It's said to be haunted by the "gray lady," who had an ill-fated affair with a monk that led to his execution and her suicide by drowning. New owners took over in 1991 and restored the deteriorated property; when it reopened, the hotel was the first in the Borders to be awarded five crowns by the Scottish Tourist Board. The accommodations include both deluxe rooms with half-tester or four-poster beds and standard abbey- or river-view rooms, all with hair dryers, trouser presses, and tea/coffeemakers.

**Dining/Diversions:** The **Tweed Restaurant** offers some of the finest dining in the area. It serves a Sunday lunch 12:15 to 2:15pm and dinner daily 7 to 9:15pm. A four-course table d'hôte menu is £26 ($44.20). There's also a cocktail bar and lounge and a pool.

**Amenities:** Some 14 golf courses are within an easy drive, and arrangements can be made for salmon and trout fishing. Services include room service, laundry, and babysitting.

## 3 Melrose

37 miles (59.5km) SE of Edinburgh, 70 miles (113km) NW of Newcastle-upon-Tyne, 40 miles (64.5km) W of Berwick-upon-Tweed

Rich in sights, Melrose is one of the highlights of the Borders: It offers one of the most beautiful ruined abbeys in the Borders as well as the region's most widely diversified shopping, and Abbotsford House, former home of Sir Walter Scott, is 2 miles (3km) west. And Melrose is close to the Southern Upland Way, which passes to the north of Melrose. Even if you can take only part of this trail (see chapter 1, "The Best of Scotland"), take a day hike on the section along the River Tweed outside Melrose—it's one of the most delightful and scenic walks in Scotland.

## ESSENTIALS

**GETTING THERE**    The nearest **rail** station is in Berwick-upon-Tweed, where you can catch a bus to Melrose. From Berwick, about five buses per day travel to Melrose; travel time is about 90 minutes. Fares are about £5 ($8.50) one-way and £9 ($15.30) round-trip. Call the tourist office in Berwick-upon-Tweed at ☎ **01289/330-733** for bus schedules and ☎ **0345/484-950** for train schedules.

Many visitors prefer to take the **bus** into Melrose directly from Edinburgh. Travel time by bus from Edinburgh is 90 minutes, and buses depart every 1½ hours throughout the day. Phone ☎ **0990/808-080** for more information.

**Driving** from Edinburgh, you can reach Melrose by going southeast along A7 and following the signs to Galashiels. From Kelso, take A699 west to St. Boswells and at the junction with A6091 head northwest.

**VISITOR INFORMATION**    The tourist office is at **Abbey House,** Abbey Street (☎ **01896/822-555**). In April, May, and October, it's open Monday to Saturday 10am to 5pm and Sunday 10am to 1pm. June and September, hours are Monday to Saturday 10am to 5:30pm and Sunday 10am to 2pm. July and August, hours are Monday to Saturday 9:30am to 6:30pm and Sunday 10am to 6pm.

## SEEING THE SIGHTS

✪ **Melrose Abbey.** Abbey St. ☎ **01896/822-562.** Admission £3 ($5.10) adults, £2.30 ($3.90) seniors, £1 ($1.70) children. Apr–Sept daily 9:30am–6pm; Oct–Mar daily 9:30am–4pm.

These lichen-covered ruins, among the most beautiful in Europe, are all that's left of the ecclesiastical community established by Cistercian monks in 1136. The complex's pure Gothic lines were made famous by Sir Walter Scott, who was instrumental in getting the decayed remains repaired and restored in the early 19th century. In *The Lay of the Last Minstrel*, Scott wrote, "If thou would'st view fair Melrose aright, go visit in the pale moonlight." You can still view its red-sandstone shell, built in the Perpendicular style and filled with elongated windows and carved capitals with delicate tracery. The heart of Robert the Bruce is supposed to be interred in the abbey, but the location is unknown. Look for the beautiful carvings and the tombs of other famous Scotsmen buried in the chancel.

✪ **Abbotsford House.** Hwy. B6360, Melrose. ☎ **01896/752-043.** Admission £3.80 ($6.45) adults, £1.90 ($3.25) children. Apr–Oct daily 9:30am–6pm. Closed Nov–Mar. Head just off A7, south of the junction with A72, onto B6360, some 2½ miles (4km) southeast of Galashiels.

This was the home Sir Walter Scott built and lived in from 1812 until he died. Designed in the Scots baronial style and considered, after his literary works, Scott's most enduring monument, it contains many relics, including artifacts and mementos the famous author collected from the Waterloo battlefield. Other exhibits include his clothes and his death mask. Especially interesting is his study, with his writing desk and chair. In 1935, two secret drawers were found in the desk. One of them contained 57 letters, part of the correspondence between Sir Walter and his wife-to-be.

Scott purchased Cartley Hall farmhouse on the banks of the Tweed in 1812. In 1822, he had the old house demolished and replaced it with the building you see today. Scott was one of Britain's earliest souvenir hunters, scouring the land for artifacts associated with the historical characters he rendered into novel form. One of his proudest possessions was a sword given to the duke of Montrose by English king Charles I for his cooperation (some say collaboration) during the struggles between Scotland and England. The sword is proudly displayed near a gun, sword, dagger, and small knife owned by the sworn enemy of the duke, cattle herder Rob Roy, whose exploits were later crafted by Sir Walter Scott into one of his most enduring dramas (you may remember the Liam Neeson film from a few years back). You can see Scott's study, library (with 9,000 rare volumes), drawing room, entrance hall, and armories— even the dining room overlooking the Tweed where he died on September 21, 1832. There are also extensive gardens and grounds to visit, plus the private chapel, added after Scott's death.

✪ **Thirlestane Castle.** Ten miles (16km) north of Melrose, overlooking Leader Water, about half a mile (1km) from Lauder. ☎ **01578/722-430.** Admission £5 ($8.50) adults, £4 ($6.80) children, £12 ($20.40) families (2 adults and children). May 2–late Oct Sun–Fri 11:15am–5pm (last admission at 4:15pm). Closed late Oct–Apr. Take A68 to Lauder in Berwickshire, 10 miles (16km) north of Melrose and 28 miles (45km) south of Edinburgh on A68.

One of Scotland's most imposing country houses, Thirlestane has been owned by the Lauderdale family since 1218. A T-shaped building, the castle has a keep from around the end of the 16th century and was much altered after Queen Victoria took the throne. The interior is known for its ornamental plaster ceilings, the finest in the country from the Restoration period. In the old nurseries is the Historic Toy Collection, and Border Country Life exhibits depict life in the Borders from prehistoric times to the present.

# A Walk Along the Borders

If you're feeling particularly saintly, you can walk in the footsteps of 7th-century St. Cuthbert along the Scotland-England border. The 62½-mile (101km) path stretches from Melrose, 37 miles (59.5km) southwest of Edinburgh, across the border into northeast England to the Holy Island of Lindisfarne on the Northumberland coast. St. Cuthbert began his ministry in Melrose in about A.D. 650 and later was appointed prior at Lindisfarne. The walk passes many places linked to his legend, prehistoric relics, Roman ruins, and historic castles. The high point is Wideopen Hill, 1,430 feet (434m) above sea level. Permission from landowners along the route has been obtained, and the walk is clearly marked. A leaflet suggests distances you can comfortably cover in a day and makes recommendations for overnight stops. Contact Roger Smith, Walking Development Officer, **Scottish Border Enterprise Center,** Bridge Street, Galashiels TB1 ISW (☎ **01896/758-991;** fax 01896/758-625). To stock up on gear and supplies before you set out, you'll have to stop off in the small town of Galashiels, 3 miles (5km) north of Melrose, and head for **Famous Army Stores,** Unit 8, Douglas Bridge (☎ **01896/757-964**).

✪ **Traquair House.** Hwy. A72, 16 miles (26km) west of Melrose. ☎ **01896/830-323.** Admission £5.20 ($8.85) adults, £4.20 ($7.15) seniors, £2.60 ($4.40) students/children, £14 ($23.80) families of 4. Easter–May and Oct daily 12:30–5:30pm; June–Aug daily 10:30am–5:30pm; Oct Fri–Sun 12:30–5pm. Closed Nov–Easter.

Dating from the 10th century, this is perhaps Scotland's oldest and most romantic house, rich in associations with Mary Queen of Scots and the Jacobite uprisings. The great house is still lived in by the Stuarts of Traquair. One of the most poignant exhibits is an ornately carved oak cradle in the King's Room, in which Mary rocked her infant son, who was to become James VI of Scotland and James I of England. Other treasures here are glass, embroideries, silver, manuscripts, and paintings. Of particular interest is a brew house equipped as it was 2 centuries ago and still used regularly. On the grounds are craft workshops as well as a maze and woodland walks.

## EXPLORING THE COUNTRYSIDE

If you're in Melrose on a Thursday afternoon, you can take a 5-mile (8km), 4-hour guided walk east to **Newstead** (call ☎ **01896/822-651** for details), site of Scotland's biggest Roman settlement, from the 1st century A.D. If you don't have the time or stamina for this walk, you can see artifacts from the site at the **Trimontium Exhibition,** on The Square in Melrose (☎ **01896/822-651**). April to October, it's open daily 10:30am to 4:30pm, charging £1.50 ($2.55) admission. Pottery, a scale model of the Roman fort, and various tools and weapons are on display.

Another great walk is to the ✪ **Eildon Hills,** along B6359, favorite of Sir Walter Scott. From the town, follow the signs to Eildon Walk and allow about 1½ to 2½ hours for the full experience, depending on your walking speed and how long you choose to dawdle en route. The site was once an Iron Age hill fortress and later a Roman signal station. The triple-peak hill is a landmark for miles around, rising to 1,325 feet (402m). At the top you'll have the region's greatest view of the Borders. A path leads up to the saddle between two of the summits.

## SHOPPING

Melrose is one of the best destinations for shopping in the Borders. Most of the town's shops and boutiques are open Monday to Saturday 9:30am to 5pm and Sunday noon to around 4pm.

**The Country Kitchen,** Market Square (☎ **01896/822-586**), displays a comprehensive choice of English, French, and Scottish cheeses, along with pâtés and meat products. You can buy them prepackaged or order up gourmet sandwiches and picnic fixings.

Fishing gear and tackle for fresh- or saltwater fishing is sold at **Angler's Choice,** 23 Market Square, near the top of High Street (☎ **01896/823-070**).

Although **Wilson Opticians,** High Street (☎ **01896/823-223**), chiefly dispenses eyeglasses and contact lenses, it sells a wide array of rain gauges, hydrometers, jogging meters, barometers, thermometers, pedometers, binoculars, and telescopes.

For tartan and other fabrics, visit **The Fabric Shop,** High Street (☎ **01896/823-475**), which both high-class couturiers and homegrown dressmakers find appealing. Gift items, especially impractical-but-charming items in porcelain and china, are available at **Butterfly,** High Street (☎ **01896/822-045**). It's fun to browse through the artfully displayed perfumes, cosmetics, and scented soaps at **The Perfume Platform,** High Street (☎ **01896/823-733**).

**Abbey Wines,** Abbey Street (☎ **01896/823-224**), stocks the town's largest wine selection, plus at least 150 malt whiskies, some from the most obscure distilleries in Scotland.

The town's most complete collection of books is for sale at **Talisman Books,** 9 The Square (☎ **01896/822-196**), in an old-fashioned Edwardian shop.

Feeling chilly in the Scottish fog? A meticulously crafted sweater from **Anne Oliver Knitwear,** 1 Scott's Place (☎ **01896/822-975**), might provide the extra warmth you'll need. Most garments are from top-quality wool or cashmere. **Lochcarron of Scotland,** The Square (☎ **01896/823-823**), is larger, but stocks only its own goods. Designers like Calvin Klein, Vivienne Westwood, Ralph Lauren, and Jean-Paul Gaultier have ordered bulk amounts here for relabeling and distribution.

## ACCOMMODATIONS

**Bon Accord.** Market Square, Melrose TD6 9PQ. ☎ **01896/822-645.** Fax 01896/823-474. www.melrose.bordernet.co.uk/traders/bonaccrd. 9 units. TV TEL. £70 ($119) double; £85–£95 ($144.50–$161.50) family room. Rates include breakfast. MC, V. Closed Dec.25. Follow the A68 into Melrose to the center of town. No children 12 and under.

This well-maintained, family-owned hotel is in the heart of Melrose and easily recognizable by the colorful window boxes adorning its facade in summer. Most accommodations are medium in size and rather functionally but comfortably furnished. Amenities include beverage makers, hair dryers, trouser press, and cable TV. The most spacious units comes with a traditional four-poster bed and draperies; honeymooners sometimes stay here and are welcomed in style with a complimentary bottle of champagne, flowers, and chocolates.

The split-level dining room offers tasty, reasonably priced meals ranging from £5.50 to £13 ($9.35 to $22.10). Meals are also served in the bar, which boasts a fine assortment of beers and wines.

**Burt's Hotel.** Market Square, Melrose, The Borders TD6 9PN. ☎ **01896/822-285.** Fax 01896/822-870. www.burtshotel.co.uk. E-mail: burtshotel@aol.com. 20 units. TV TEL. £88 ($149.60) double. Rates include breakfast. AE, DC, MC, V. Free parking.

Within walking distance of the abbey, this family-run inn was built in 1722 in a traditional three-story townhouse design and offers a taste of small-town Scotland. The decor is modern, with an airy and restful feeling. All the guest rooms have radios, hair dryers, and tea/coffeemakers.

**Dining:** In the attractive bar, which sports Windsor chairs and a coal-burning fireplace, tasty bar lunches and suppers begin at £6.95 ($11.80). In the restaurant overlooking the garden, you can take a prix-fixe lunch for £20.75 ($35.30), or dinner for £27.75 ($47.20). You can also order à la carte. If you want to dine at the hotel, a reservation is needed.

**Amenities:** Room service, baby-sitting, laundry. The staff will arrange tee times and fishing excursions nearby.

**King's Arms Hotel.** High St., Melrose, The Borders TD6 9BP. ☎ **01896/822-143.** Fax 01896/823-812. 7 units. TV TEL. £57.50 ($97.75) double; £65 ($110.50) suite for 2. Extra person £5 ($8.50). MC, V.

One of Melrose's oldest commercial buildings still in use is this 17th-century coaching inn whose three-story stone-and-brick facade overlooks the pedestrian traffic of the main street. Inside is a series of cozy but slightly dowdy public rooms and half a dozen simple but comfortably furnished small guest rooms. Of special interest is the suite, on the opposite side of the courtyard, with its own entrance. The restaurant serves a odd mix of international offerings, including Mexican tacos and enchiladas, Indian curries, British steak pies, and giant Yorkshire puddings.

**Traquair Arms Hotel.** Traquair Rd., Innerleithen, The Borders EH44 6PD. ☎ **01896/830-229.** Fax 01896/830-260. E-mail: traquair.arms@scottishborders.com. 10 units. TV TEL. £58–£80 ($98.60–$136) double. Rates include breakfast; dinner £18 ($30.60). AE, DC, MC, V. Take E69 from Melrose for 14 miles (22.5km).

This small hotel was built as a three-story coaching inn around 1780 and has later Victorian additions. Open fires in the bar lounge and fresh flowers in the dining room create a pleasant ambience. The cozy guest rooms come with tea/coffeemakers, comfortable furnishings, and views over the valley. The hotel is known for fine pub food; vegetarians and others with special dietary needs can be accommodated. All dishes are freshly prepared by chefs Hugh Anderson and Sara Currie. The hotel is within a 5-minute walk of the River Tweed; salmon and trout fishing can be arranged.

## DINING

Don't miss the pastries at Melrose's best bakery, **Jackie Lunn, Ltd.,** High Street (☎ **01896/822-888**).

Two of the town's most likable pubs are the one in the **King's Arms,** High Street (☎ **01896/822-143**), where you'll generally find lots of rugby players lifting a pint or two, and the somewhat more sedate one in **Burts Hotel,** The Square (☎ **01896/822-285**).

**Marmion's Brasserie.** 2 Buccleuch St. ☎ **01896/822-245.** Reservations recommended for dinner. Main courses £3–£7.30 ($5.10–$12.40) at lunch; £11.50–£13.75 ($19.55–$23.40) at dinner. AE, MC, V. Mon–Sat noon–2pm and 6:30–10pm. SCOTTISH.

Across from the post office in a 150-year-old building, this tasteful restaurant is a cross between a brasserie and a coffee shop. The kitchen likes to use all-Scottish ingredients. The cheerful staff will offer menu items that frequently change, but might include dishes like salmon in phyllo with ginger-and-lime sauce; breaded chicken with aged northern Italian Talleggio cheese; swordfish with butter beans, bacon, and sweet onions; exotic ostrich steak in red-wine sauce; and charcoal-grilled steaks done to perfection.

**Melrose Station.** Palma Place. ☎ **01896/822-546.** Reservations recommended. Main courses £1.95–£5.50 ($3.30–$9.35) at lunch, £2.50–£30.95 ($4.25–$52.60) at dinner. MC, V. Wed–Sun noon–2pm; Thurs–Sat 6–9pm. MC, V. SCOTTISH/INTERNATIONAL.

In 1850, an impressive rail station was built in the town center, but a while back, British Rail diverted all service to nearby Berwick-upon-Tweed. Today the station contains a conservatively outfitted restaurant. Lunches here are a lot simpler than dinners and may include prawn-and-egg salad with pesto mayonnaise followed by grilled Italian vegetables with Brie. The hearty dinners may begin with smoked chicken, avocado, and peach salad in curried mayonnaise sauce, followed by haggis in pastry with buttered turnips and Drambuie sauce or roasted duckling breast in cranberry, port, and orange sauce. The restaurant is licensed for wine and beer.

## 4 Selkirk: At the Heart of Scott Country

40 miles (64.5km) SE of Edinburgh, 73 miles (117.5km) SE of Glasgow, 7 miles (11km) S of Galashiels

In the heart of Sir Walter Scott country, Selkirk is a great base if you want to explore many of the region's historic homes, including Bowhill (see below) and Traquair House (see "Melrose," above). Jedburgh and Melrose offer more to see and do, but this ancient royal burgh can easily occupy a morning of your time.

Selkirk was the home town of the African explorer Mungo Park (1771–1806), whose exploits could have made a great Harrison Ford movie. Park was a doctor, but won fame for exploring the River Niger; he drowned while escaping in a canoe from hostile natives. A statue of him is at the east end of High Street in Mungo Park.

### ESSENTIALS

**GETTING THERE**   Berwick-upon-Tweed is the nearest **rail** station, where you can get a connecting bus to Selkirk. The bus ride is just under 2 hours, costing £4.80 ($8.15) one way or £8 ($13.60) round-trip. Call the tourist office in Berwick-upon-Tweed at ☎ **01289/330-733** for bus schedules or ☎ **0345/484-950** for rail information. Most visitors arrive by train from Edinburgh (☎ **0990/808-080** for information).

**Buses** running between Newcastle-upon-Tyne and Edinburgh make stops at Selkirk. The trip takes about 2½ hours and costs £7 ($11.90) one way or £12 ($20.40) round-trip.

**Driving** from Edinburgh, head southeast along A7 to Galashiels, then cut southwest along B6360. The trip takes about an hour. To get here from Melrose, take B6360 southwest to Selkirk; it's a 15-minute drive.

**VISITOR INFORMATION**   A **tourist office** is at Halliwell's House Museum (☎ **01750/720-054**). March to June and September, it's open Monday to Saturday 10am to 5pm and Sunday 2 to 4pm; July and August, hours are Monday to Saturday 10am to 6pm and Sunday 2 to 5pm; and October hours are Monday to Saturday 10am to 4pm and Sunday 2 to 4pm.

### EXPLORING THE AREA

In Selkirk, the former royal hunting grounds and forests have given way to textile mills along its river banks, but there are many beautiful spots in the nearby countryside—notably **St. Mary's Loch,** 14 miles (22.5km) southwest. Scottish sailors and fishermen love this bucolic body of water, as did literary greats like Thomas Carlyle and Robert Louis Stevenson. One of the most panoramic stretches of the Southern Upland Way, one of Scotland's great backpacking trails (see chapter 1), skirts the east shore of

# Sir Walter Scott: Master of Romance

Today it's hard to imagine the fame this poet/novelist enjoyed as the bestselling author of his time. His works are no longer so widely read, but in his day, Sir Walter Scott (1771–1832) was considered a master storyteller. He invented a new genre, the romantic adventure in a panoramic setting. He created lively characters and realistic pictures of Scottish life and customs in such works as *The Heart of Midlothian, Rob Roy,* and *Waverley.* Today he's best known as the prolific father of the historical novel, a genre that began with *Ivanhoe* and its romantic Jewish heroine, Rebecca (played by Elizabeth Taylor in the popular film), followed by *Kenilworth, The Pirate,* and many others. He was also a popular poet.

Born into an older Border family at Edinburgh on August 14, 1771, Scott became permanently lame after an attack of fever in infancy. All his life he was troubled by ill health, then later by finances. He spent his latter years writing to clear his enormous debts. Scott made his country and its scenery fashionable with the English, and even persuaded George IV to wear that once-outlawed tartan during the king's visit to Scotland. Although Scott became the most prominent literary figure in Edinburgh, his heart lay in the Border Country. It was here he chose to live and here he built his house in a style that became known as Scottish baronial, reflecting the nostalgia for medieval days his novels had popularized. Starting with a modest farmhouse, he enlarged Abbotsford into a mansion and fulfilled his ambition to become a *laird* (landlord or property owner). In the economic crash of 1826, he offered the estate to his creditors, who turned it down.

Still heavily in debt and suffering from the effect of several strokes, in 1831 Scott set out on a cruise through the Mediterranean but returned to Abbotsford the following year to die. He was buried at Dryburgh Abbey, sited in a loop of the Tweed 2 miles (3km) from the panoramic view of the river and the Eildon Hills he so admired. It's reported the horses pulling the author's hearse stopped at this spot out of habit, so accustomed were they to Scott's pausing to take in the vista.

Scott's name is also linked to the Trossachs, which he used as a setting for his poem "The Lady of the Lake" and his tale of Rob Roy MacGregor, the 18th-century outlaw. In Edinburgh, the Gothic-inspired Scott Monument is one of the most famous statues in Scotland.

**St. Mary's Loch.** You can take a day hike on the 8-mile (13km) stretch from the loch to Traquair House (see "Melrose," above).

**Bowhill.** Hwy. A708, 3 miles (5km) west of Selkirk. ☎ **01750/222-04.** Admission to house £4.50 ($7.65) adults, £4 ($6.80) seniors, £2 ($3.40) children; admission to Country Park £2 ($3.40). House, July daily 1–4:30pm; Country Park, May–Aug daily 1–4:30pm. Closed other months.

This 18th- and 19th-century Border home of the Scotts, the dukes of Buccleuch, contains a rare art collection, French furniture, porcelain, silverware, and mementos of Sir Walter Scott, Queen Victoria, and the duke of Monmouth. Its paintings include works by Canaletto, Claude, Raeburn, Gainsborough, and Reynolds. In the Country Park surrounding the house, you'll find an Adventure Woodland play area, a Victorian kitchen, an audiovisual presentation, a gift shop, and a tearoom/restaurant. Sotheby's "Works of Art" courses are offered at Bowhill.

## ACCOMMODATIONS & DINING

**Heatherlie House Hotel.** Heatherlie Park, Selkirk, The Borders TD7 5AL. ☎ **01750/ 721-200.** Fax 01750/720-005. www.heatherlie.freeserve.co.uk. E-mail: hhh@heatherlie. freeserve.co.uk. 7 units, 6 with private bathroom. TV TEL. £60 ($102) double with bathroom. Rates include breakfast. MC, V.

An imposing stone-and-slate Victorian mansion with steep gables and turrets, this hotel is set in 2 acres of wooded lands and mature gardens, west from the center along the Green and a short walk from Selkirk. The guest rooms are spotlessly maintained and furnished with reproductions of older pieces. The lone single room has no bathroom of its own.

A coal-burning fireplace adds warmth to the lounge, where reasonably priced bar meals are available daily noon to 9:30pm; the high-ceilinged dining room is open for dinners 6 to 9pm, with main courses ranging from £6.50 to £12 ($11.05 to $20.40). Golf, fishing, and shooting packages can be arranged. About half a dozen golf courses are within a reasonable drive.

## 5 Peebles

23 miles (37km) S of Edinburgh, 53 miles (85km) SE of Glasgow, 20 miles (32km) W of Melrose

Peebles, a royal burgh and county town, is a market center in the Tweed Valley, noted for its large woolen mills and fine knitwear shopping. Scottish kings used to come here when they hunted in Ettrick Forest, 22 miles (35km) away. It's one of hundreds of forests scattered throughout the Borders and is very pretty, but no more so than forested patches closer to the town.

Peebles is known as a writer's town. It was home to Sir John Buchan (Baron Tweedsmuir, 1875–1940), a Scottish author who later was appointed governor-general of Canada. He's remembered chiefly for the adventure story *Prester John* and was the author of *The Thirty-Nine Steps,* the first of a highly successful series of secret-service thrillers and later a Hitchcock film. Robert Louis Stevenson lived for a time in Peebles and drew on the surrounding countryside in his novel *Kidnapped* (1886).

### ESSENTIALS

**GETTING THERE**    The nearest **rail station** is in Berwick-upon-Tweed, but bus connections from there into Peebles are quite inconvenient. It's easier to get from Edinburgh to Peebles by a 50-minute **bus** ride. Bus fares from Edinburgh are around £3 ($5.10) one way. Call ☎ **0345/484-950** for rail and bus information.

If you're **driving,** take A703 south from Edinburgh. Continue west along A6091 from Melrose.

**VISITOR INFORMATION**    The **tourist office** is at the Chamber Institute, 23 High St. (☎ **01721/720-138**). July and August, it's open Monday to Friday 9am to 8pm, Saturday 9am to 7pm, and Sunday 10am to 6pm; June and September, hours are Monday to Saturday 9:30am to 5:30pm and Sunday 10am to 4pm; April and May, hours are Monday to Saturday 9:30am to 5pm and Sunday 10am to 2pm; October hours are Monday to Saturday 9:30am to 4:30pm and Sunday 10am to 2pm; and November to March, hours are Monday to Saturday 9:30am to 12:30pm and 1:30 to 4:30pm.

### EXPLORING THE TOWN & THE COUNTRYSIDE

The tourist office (see above) provides pamphlets describing the best walking tours in the region. The £1 ($1.70) pamphlet **"Walks Around Peebles"** describes 20 walks, including one along the Tweed. That walk is so popular that a detailed description is available in a pamphlet devoted exclusively to it, priced at 40p (70¢). The **Tweed Walk** begins in the center of Peebles, and—with the twists and turns described in the pamphlet—takes you downstream along the river, then upstream along the opposite bank for a return to Peebles. You can follow the path for segments of 2½ miles (4km), 4½ miles (7km), or 7½ miles (12km). Regardless of the length of your walk, you'll pass the stalwart walls of Neidpath Castle.

The **Glentress Bicycle Trekking Centre,** Glentress, Peebles (☎ 01721/722-934), is the place to rent a bike. You'll have to leave a refundable deposit of £50 ($85). Daily rates range from £16 to £18 ($27.20 to $30.60), and rentals must be arranged in advance. It's open daily 9:30am to 5pm.

**Neidpath Castle.** Tweeddale, on A72, 1 mile (1.5km) west of Peebles. ☎ 01721/ 720-333. Admission £3 ($5.10) adults, £2.50 ($4.25) seniors, £1 ($1.70) children, £7.50 ($12.75) families. July 1–Sept 10 Mon–Sat 11am–6pm; Sun 1–5pm. Closed mid-Sept to June.

Once linked with two of the greatest families in Scotland (the Frasiers and the Hayes), Niedpath, a summer attraction, hasn't been occupied since 1958. Part of the interest here is the way the castle's medieval shell was transformed during the 1600s into a residence, using then-fashionable architectural conceits. Enormous galleries were divided into smaller, cozier spaces, with the exception of the Great Hall, whose statuesque proportions are still visible. The hall's medieval stonework is decorated with 11 batik panels crafted in the mid-1990s by noted artist Monica Hanisch; they depict the life and accomplishments of Mary Queen of Scots. Other displays are Roman and Celtic archaeological remnants and material commemorating the Frasiers and their links to Scottish national pride (members of their family were executed by the English at the same time as William Wallace). Other parts of the museum are devoted to the role the castle has played in the filming of movies like *The Bruce* (an English film that had the bad luck to be released simultaneously with *Braveheart*), *Merlin, The Quest Begins,* and the courtyard scene in the recent TV miniseries "Joan of Arc," where the heroine was burnt at the stake. Recently filmed here were new British versions of *Hamlet* and *King Lear.*

**Kailzie Gardens.** Kailzie on B7062, 2½ miles (4km) southeast of Peebles. ☎ 01721/ 720-007. Admission £2.50 ($4.25) adults, 75p ($1.30) children; gardens only £1 ($1.70). Easter–Oct daily dawn–dusk; Nov–Easter daily 11am–5:30pm.

These 17 acres of formal walled gardens, dating from 1812, include a rose garden, woodlands, and *burnside* (streamside) walks. Restored during the past 20 years, it provides a stunning array of plants from early spring to late autumn and has a collection of waterfowl and owls. There's also an art gallery, a shop, and a restaurant.

**Dawyck Botanic Garden.** Hwy. B712, 8 miles (13km) southwest of Peebles. ☎ 01721/ 760-254. Admission £3 ($5.10) adults, £2.50 ($4.25) seniors/students, £1 ($1.70) children, £7 ($11.90) families. Mar–Oct daily 9:30am–6pm. Local bus marked BIGGAR.

This botanic garden, run by the Royal Botanic Garden in Edinburgh, has a large variety of conifers, some exceeding 100 feet (30m) in height, as well as many species of flowering shrubs. There's also a fine display of early-spring bulbs, plus woodwalks rich in wildlife interest.

## SHOPPING

Knitwear, crafted from yarn culled from local sheep, is the best buy in Peebles, and easily found as you stroll the High Street. General shopping hours are Monday to Saturday 9am to 5:30pm. On Sunday, but only in July and August, some shops open 10am to 5pm.

**Woolgathering,** 1 Bridge House Terrace (☎ 01721/720-388), offers knitwear and all kinds of sweaters. Three sprawling branches of **Castle Warehouse,** 1 Greenside (☎ 01721/723-636), 7–13 Old Town (☎ 01721/720-348), and 29–31 Northgate (☎ 01721/720-814), sell gift items with a Scottish flavor as well as clothing, like traditional Scottish garb and anything you might need for a fishing trip.

**Caledonian Countrywear, Ltd.,** 74 High St. (☎ 01721/723-055), and **Out & About,** 2 Elcho St. Brae (☎ 01721/723-590), are sporting-goods stores with lots of durable clothing and hiking boots.

For Border handcrafts like pinewood furniture and handcrafted stoneware and porcelain, go to **Peebles Craft Centre,** 9 Newby Court (☎ 01721/722-875), or the **Couchee Righ,** 26 Northgate (☎ 01721/721-890).

Less than 6 miles (10km) from Walkerburn at Galashiels (head east along A72) is the **Peter Anderson Company,** Nether Mill (☎ 01896/752-091). This factory outlet sells more than 750 types of tartan fabrics, all made on the premises on modernized looms. The factory shop is open Monday to Saturday 9am to 5pm and Sunday noon to 5pm. If it doesn't have a tartan for you (which is doubtful), you can pop into any of the dozens of other shops in the nearby textile town of Galashiels.

## ACCOMMODATIONS

You can also rent affordable rooms at the **Horse Shoe Inn** (see "Dining," below).

### VERY EXPENSIVE

✪ **Cringletie House Hotel.** Eddleston, Peebles, The Borders EH45 8PL. ☎ 01721/730-233. Fax 01721/730-244. www.cringletie.com. E-mail: enquiries@cringletie.com. 13 units. TV TEL. £150–£200 ($255–$340) double. Rates include breakfast. AE, MC, V. Take A703 for 2½ miles (4km) north of Peebles.

This imposing 1861 red-sandstone Victorian mansion with towers and turrets is one of the most delightful country-house hotels in the Borders, known for its charming setting and its luxurious rooms. It stands on 28 acres of well-manicured grounds, featuring a superb walled garden that in itself is worth a visit. The tasteful house is immaculately maintained, with public rooms that range from an elegant cocktail lounge to an adjacent conservatory. There's even a small library, plus a large lounge where fellow guests from all over the world meet and chat, and thankfully, there's an elevator. Each of the spacious bedrooms is individually decorated; several units contain their own original fireplaces, and all have tea/coffeemakers. All of the accommodations open onto views of the extensive grounds. The bathrooms, with both tubs and showers, are maintained in state-of-the-art condition, and come with luxurious toiletries and hair dryers.

**Dining:** The elegant restaurant offers a limited but well-selected menu and attentive service. In season, the vegetables come fresh from the garden. A special dish is a delectable smoked haddock mousse. The three-course lunch Monday to Saturday is £14 ($23.80) and up, Sunday lunch is £17 ($28.90), and a four-course dinner (7 to 9pm) is £32.50 ($55.25). You should be punctual because of the short serving hours (the food is freshly cooked), and you'll need a reservation. Afternoon tea is also served.

**Amenities:** Room service, concierge, baby-sitting, croquet lawn, putting green. The staff can arrange fishing expeditions for you.

### EXPENSIVE/MODERATE

**Castle Venlaw Hotel.** Edinburgh Rd., Peebles EH45 8 QG. ☎ 01721/720-384. Fax 01721/724-066. www.venlaw.co.uk. E-mail: enquiries@venlaw.co.uk. 12 units. TV TEL. £106 ($180.20) double; £116 ($197.20) deluxe; £126 ($214.20) suite. Rates include breakfast. Children under age 12 staying in parents' room £12.50 ($21.25); children 13–16 £16 ($27.20). MC, V. Free parking. Take A703 to Peebles.

Originally built in 1782 and enlarged in 1854, Castle Venlaw lies among 4 acres of woodlands and offers lovely views over the surrounding countryside. The hotel's round tower and craw-stepped gables are an evocative example of the Scottish baronial style. In 1997, John and Shirly Sloggie with their partners, Stephen Hayes and Steve Isaacs, purchased the turreted mansion and transformed it In early 1999, the hotel was completely redecorated, and the heating system and all bathrooms were replaced and modernized.

Castle Venlaw has 12 spacious and individually decorated rooms equipped with beverage makers, satellite TV, and a variety of books and magazines. The suite also provides a sitting room in addition to the bedroom. In the tower at the top of the castle is a spacious family room with a children's den containing bunk beds, games, TV, and VCR.

**Dining:** The formal dining room, with its ornate ceilings, original parquet floor, and fireplace, has an elegant yet comfortable ambience. An extensive menu includes dishes such as roast pigeon on a bed of braised red cabbage with sherry meat glaze, pan-fried prawns with a timbale of couscous flavored with tarragon and beetroot dressing, and blue cheese mousse with a purée of peppers and fresh pickled herbs. For dessert, the date and walnut pudding with chocolate sauce or the passion fruit chinchillas with plum purée will satisfy any sweet tooth. In addition to the à la carte menu, there is a set-price, two-course dinner for £21 ($35.70). The Library Bar also serves a wide variety of food, including more affordable fixed-price meals.

**Amenities:** Room service, laundry.

**The Tontine.** 39 High St., Peebles, The Borders EH45 8AJ. ☎ **01721/720-892.** Fax 01721/729-732. 36 units. TV TEL. £58–£86 ($98.60–$146.20) double. Rates include breakfast. Children 14 and under stay free in parents' room. AE, DC, MC, V. Free parking.

The Tontine was built in 1807 as a private club by a group of hunters who sold their friends shares in its ownership. The construction was executed by French prisoners-of-war during the Napoleonic era; later enlargements were made by the Edwardians. Flower boxes adorn its stone lintels, and a stone lion guards the forecourt fountain. The modestly furnished guest rooms are in an angular modern wing built in back of its 19th-century core; they come with radios, hair dryers, and tea/coffeemakers. The most expensive rooms have river views. The Adam-style dining room is one of the town's architectural gems, with tall fan-topped windows and a minstrels' gallery. The Tweeddale Shoot Bar is cozily rustic.

### INEXPENSIVE

**Whitestone House.** Innerleithen Rd., Peebles, The Borders EH45 8BD. ☎/fax **01721/720-337.** www.aboutscotland.com/peebles/whitestone.html. 5 units, none with private bathroom. TV. £35 ($59.50) double. Rates include breakfast. No credit cards.

On the eastern fringe of Peebles, this dignified dark stone house was built in 1892 to house the pastor of a Presbyterian church that has been demolished and is now the genteel domain of Mrs. Margaret Muir. Its windows overlook a pleasant garden and the glacial deposits of Whitestone Park. The high-ceilinged guest rooms are large and comfortable, evoking life in a quiet private home. Mrs. Muir speaks French and German flawlessly, but presides over breakfast with a Scottish brogue.

## DINING

**Horse Shoe Inn.** Eddleston. ☎ **01721/730-225.** Reservations recommended Sat. Main courses £6–£14 ($10.20–$23.80). AE, DC, MC, V. Easter–Oct Wed–Sun noon–3pm and 6–10pm; Nov–Easter Wed–Sat noon–3pm and 6–9pm, Sun noon–11pm. Take A701 4½ miles (7km) north of Peebles. SCOTTISH.

In the center of the nearby village of Eddleston, this country restaurant serves top-quality beef and steaks. Appetizers include everything from the chef's own pâté with oat cakes to smoked Shetland salmon with brown bread. House favorites are steak-and-stout pie, Meldon game pie, and vegetable moussaka. The main focus is the food and drink served in the bar, site of most lunches and dinners. On Friday and Saturday nights and Sunday lunches, the bar is supplemented with a more formal dining room.

The owners, Mr. and Mrs. Hathoway, bought the old school next door and converted it into a guesthouse with eight rooms at £20 to £35 ($34 to $59.50) per person, depending on the season; the rates include breakfast.

## PEEBLES AFTER DARK

The town has many options for drinking and dining, and some of the most appealing are in the hotels on the town's edge, even though they may seem rather staid at first glance. On Innerleithen Road, the **Park Hotel** (☎ 01721/720-451) and the nearby **Hotel Hydro** (☎ 01721/720-602) contain pubs and cocktail lounges.

For an earthier atmosphere, we highly recommend dropping into Peebles' oldest pub, on the ground floor of the **Cross Keys Hotel,** 24 Northgate (☎ 01721/724-222), where you'll find 300-year-old smoke-stained panels, a blazing fireplace, and an evocatively crooked bar. Ask the bartender about the resident ghost. Like the Loch Ness monster, she's taken on an almost mythic identity since her last sighting, but the rumor goes that she's the spirit of Sir Walter Scott's former landlady, Marian Ritchie. No one will be shy about telling you his or her theory, especially if you're buying.

## 6 Moffat

61 miles (98km) S of Edinburgh, 22 miles (35km) NE of Dumfries, 60 miles (97km) SE of Glasgow

A small town at the head of the Annandale Valley, Moffat thrives as a center of a sheep-farming area, symbolized by a statue of a ram on the wide High Street. It's been a holiday resort since the mid–17th century because of the curative properties of its water, and it was here Robert Burns composed the drinking song "O Willie Brewd a Peck o' Maut." Today people visit this town on the banks of the Annan River for its great fishing and golf.

## ESSENTIALS

**GETTING THERE**    The nearest **rail** station is in Lockerbie, 15 miles (24km) south of Moffat. Call ☎ 0345/848-950 for train information. Getting to Lockerbie sometimes requires a change of train in Dumfries, so passengers from Edinburgh or Glasgow often transfer to a **National Express bus** at Dumfries for the 35-minute trip straight to Moffat's High Street, which costs £3 ($5.10) one way. If you are coming from the Lockerbie rail station, though, you can get a National Express bus to Moffat; they run four times a day, and the fare is £4.05 ($6.90) each way. For more bus information, call ☎ 0990/808-080.

If you're **driving** from Dumfries, head northeast along A701. From Edinburgh, head south along A701; from Peebles, drive west, following the signs to Glasgow, then turn south on A702 and merge onto M74, following the signs to Moffat.

**VISITOR INFORMATION**    A **tourist office** is a 5-minute walk south of the town center, at Unit One, Ledyknowe, off Station Road (☎ 01683/220-620). June to September, it's open Monday to Saturday 9:30am to 6pm and Sunday 11am to 5pm; April, May, and October, hours are Monday to Saturday 10am to 5pm.

# WHAT TO SEE & DO

The region's most famous course is the **Moffat Golf Course,** Coates Hill (☎ **01683/ 220-020**), about a mile (1.5km) southwest of the town center. Non-members can play if they call in advance. For £1.50 ($2.55), the tourist office will sell you a brochure called "Golfing in Dumfries & Galloway."

The waters around Moffat team with salmon, trout, and pike. The best info source about fishing is **Mr. John Jack,** owner/manager of the **Ben Mar Esso Garage,** Station Road (☎ **01683/220-010**), on the town's southern perimeter. He sells fishing permits from £9 to £15 ($15.30 to $25.50) per day, depending on where you want to fish. The tourist office sells a brochure called "Fishing in Dumfries & Galloway" for £1.50 ($2.55).

North of Moffat is lots of panoramic hill scenery. Five miles (8km) northwest is a sheer-sided 500-foot-deep (152m), 2-mile-wide (3km) hollow in the hills called the **Devil's Beef Tub,** where cattle thieves (reivers) once hid cattle lifted in their raids. This hollow is of interest to geologists because of the way it portrays Ice Age glacial action, and it makes for a good day hike in the quiet countryside. To reach it, walk north from Moffat along the **Annan Water Valley Road,** a rural route with virtually no vehicular traffic. In 4 miles (6.5km), the road will descend a steep slope whose contours form an unusual bowl shape. No signs mark the site, but you'll know it when you get there.

Northeast along Moffat Water, past 2,696-foot-high (818m) White Coomb, is the **Grey Mare's Tail,** a 200-foot (61m) hanging waterfall formed by the Tail Burn dropping from Loch Skene; it's part of the National Trust for Scotland.

# ACCOMMODATIONS

You can also find accommodations at **Well View** (see "Dining," below).

**Auchen Castle Hotel.** Beattock, Galloway DG10 9SH. ☎ **01683/300-407.** Fax 01683/ 300-667. www.auchen-castle-hotel.co.uk. E-mail: reservations@auchen-castle-hotel.co.uk. 25 units. TV TEL. £94–£110 ($159.80–$187) double in main house, breakfast included; £44 ($74.80) double in Cedar Lodge, breakfast not included. AE, DC, MC, V. Take A74 for 2 miles (3km) north of Moffat.

About a mile (1.5km) north of the village of Beattock, the area's most luxurious accommodations are at the Auchen, a Victorian mock-castle. It's really a charming country house built in 1849 on the site of Auchen Castle, with terraced gardens and a trout-filled loch. Most of the rooms are spacious. Ask for a room in the main house (which is known as the castle); the others are in the Cedar Lodge, a less desirable annex built in the late 1970s.

**Dining:** The dining room overlooks the gardens, and the efficient staff serves simple yet appetizingly prepared dishes like Scottish roast beef. Lunch (bar lunches only) is served daily noon to 2pm and dinner 7 to 9pm; dinner is £17.45 ($29.65) for three courses or £21.20 ($36.05) for four.

**Amenities:** Room service, concierge, laundry, baby-sitting, shoeshine.

**Beechwood House Hotel.** Harthope Place, Moffat, Galloway DG10 9RS. ☎ **01683/ 220-210.** Fax 01683/220-889. www.smoothhounds.co.uk/hotelbeechwoo.html. 7 units. TV TEL. £77 ($130.90) double with breakfast; £118 ($200.60) double with half-board. AE, MC, V. Free parking.

The Beechwood was the 19th-century headquarters of Miss Thompson's Private Adventure Boarding Establishment and School for Young Ladies. Today it's a charming country hotel/restaurant; you'll spot its facade of chiseled stone at the end of a narrow rural lane. A tea lawn, smooth as a putting green, is the site for outdoor refreshments on sunny days. The guest rooms have a certain amount of homespun charm, with hair dryers and tea/coffeemakers; many have been recently renovated.

**Dining:** If you want to stop in just for a meal (phone in advance), lunch is served daily noon to 1:30pm and dinner 7:30 to 9pm, with a fixed-price dinner at £23.50 ($39.95). The menu is limited but often filled with surprises—for example, a recent meal began with smoked rabbit and wild boar sausages, went on to include braised quail with green and black grapes, and concluded with orange soufflé mousse.

**Amenities:** Room service, baby-sitting, laundry. The staff will arrange tennis, golf, fishing, riding, and pony trekking nearby.

**Moffat House Hotel.** High St., Moffat, Galloway DG10 9HL. ☎ **01683/220-039.** Fax 01683/221-288. www.moffathouse.co.uk. E-mail: moffat@talk.com. 20 units. TV TEL. £70–£90 ($119–$153) double. Rates include breakfast. AE, MC, V. Free parking.

The red- and black-stone Moffat House is one of the town's most architecturally noteworthy buildings; it was constructed in 1751 by John Adam. The modernized guest rooms are comfortable and functional, each with a hair dryer and tea/coffeemaker. Some rooms are equipped for travelers with disabilities.

**Dining:** The hotel offers some of the best food in town, especially at night, when the chef prepares an international menu. Bar suppers are served Monday to Saturday 5:45 to 9pm and Sunday 6 to 8:45pm. However, dinner in the regular restaurant is served 7 to 8:45pm only. A four-course meal costs £22 ($37.40) and is likely to feature haunch of venison, mallard duck in cherry sauce, and fresh salmon.

**Amenities:** Room service, special facilities for children.

**Star Hotel.** 44 High St., Moffat, Galloway DG10 9EF. ☎ **01683/220-156.** Fax 01683/221-524. www.famousestarhotel.com. 8 units. TV TEL. £56 ($95.20) double. AE, MC, V.

With a 17th-century brick facade, this place bears the quirky fame of being the narrowest free-standing hotel in the United Kingdom—it's only 20 feet (6m) wide. The guest rooms are small and unpretentious, with contemporary furnishings.

**Dining:** The food here is popular, and moderately priced meals are served daily noon to 2pm and 5:30 to 8:45pm. Menu items are simple and straightforward but savory, like sliced garlic mushrooms; crispy-coated garlic-and-herb king prawns; chicken, ham, and leek pie; and haggis. By far the most popular dish is the famous mixed grill.

**Amenities:** Room service, baby-sitting, pool table. The staff will arrange fishing and golf nearby.

## DINING

You can also dine at the restaurants in the hotels above.

**Well View.** Ballplay Rd., Moffat DG10 9JU. ☎ **01683/220-184.** www.wellview.co.uk. Reservations recommended. Fixed-price 3-course lunch £13 ($22.10); fixed-price 6-course dinner £28 ($47.60). AE, MC, V. Sun–Fri 12:30–1:15pm; daily 7–8:30pm. Closed 2 weeks Jan–Feb. Take A708 ¾ of a mile (1.2km) east of Moffat. BRITISH/CONTINENTAL.

Come here for some of the best food in the region. The setting is mid-Victorian, with Laura Ashley country-cottage charm and views of the kitchen garden. The set-price menus vary almost daily, depending on the season, and may include roasted breast of Perthshire pigeon with red-wine sauce, roasted saddle of venison with gin-and-juniper sauce, or fillet of Aberdeen Angus beef with whole-grain mustard sauce.

Upstairs are five guest rooms and a junior suite, with modern furniture and reproduction antiques, Laura Ashley fabrics, TVs, clock radios, tea/coffeemakers, and hair dryers. Depending on the season, doubles are £68 to £96 ($115.60 to $163.20) and the suite £75 to £96 ($127.50 to $163.20).

# 7 Dumfries: An Ode to Burns

80 miles (129km) SW of Edinburgh, 79 miles (127km) SE of Glasgow, 34 miles (55km) NW of Carlisle

A county town and royal burgh, the Galloway center of Dumfries enjoys associations with national poet Robert Burns and *Peter Pan* author James Barrie. Burns lived in Dumfries from 1791 until his death in 1796 and wrote some of his best-known songs here, including "Auld Lang Syne" and "Ye Banks and Braes of Bonnie Doon." A statue of Burns stands on High Street; you can visit his house, his favorite pub, and his mausoleum. Barrie was a pupil at the Academy here and later wrote he got the idea for Peter Pan from his games in the nearby garden.

The widest esplanade in Dumfries, **Whitesands,** flanks the edge of the river Nith. It was once the scene of horse and hiring fairs and is a fine place to park your car and explore this provincial town. The town center is reserved for pedestrians, and on the opposite bank of the Nith, the public Deer Park offers a small-scale manicured version of the wild majesty of Scotland. Allow a morning to see the city's major sights, but there's even more to see in the surrounding countryside, including Sweetheart Abbey, Ellisland Farm, and Drumlanrig Castle at Thornhill, which is filled with art, including works by Rembrandt and Leonardo.

## ESSENTIALS

**GETTING THERE**    Seven **trains** per day make the run from Glasgow's Central Station, taking 1¾ hours. Tickets cost £9.20 ($15.65) one way but only £10 to £18.20 ($17 to $30.95) round-trip, depending on time of departure. For 24-hour information, call ☎ 0345/484-950.

Stagecoach **buses** depart from Glasgow (from Buchanan Street Station or Anderston Station); the trip is 2 hours and costs £6.30 ($10.70) one way and £8.50 ($14.45) round-trip. Buses also run to Dumfries from Edinburgh's St. Andrew's Square. The prices are the same as from Glasgow, but the trip is 3 hours. For bus information, call ☎ 01387/253-496.

If you're **driving** from Edinburgh, take A701 to Moffat, then continue southwest to Dumfries. From Glasgow, take M74, which becomes A74 before it approaches Moffat. At Moffat, continue southwest along A701.

**VISITOR INFORMATION**    The **tourist office** is at 64 Whitesands (☎ 01387/253-862), a 2-minute walk from High Street and adjacent to the big car parks. September to March, it's open Monday to Saturday 10am to 5:30pm; April to August, hours are Monday to Saturday 10am to 6pm (July and August also Sunday noon to 4pm).

## EXPLORING THE TOWN

The 18th-century **St. Michael's Church,** on St. Michael's Street, is the original parish church of Dumfries. Its foundation is ancient—the site was sacred before the advent of Christianity, and a Christian church has stood here for more than 1,300 years. The earliest written records date from 1165 to 1214. The church and the churchyard are interesting to visit because of all their connections with Scottish history, continuing through World War II. You can still see the Burns family pew inside.

In St. Michael's Churchyard, a burial place for at least 900 years, stands the neo-Grecian **Burns Mausoleum.** Built of local sandstone and dripping with literary and patriotic nostalgia, the dome-capped mausoleum is one of the most important pilgrimage sites for Burns fans. The poet is buried here along with his wife, Jean Armour, and five of their children. Burns died in 1796, but his remains weren't moved to the tomb until 1815.

The **Mid Steeple** on High Street was built in 1707 as municipal buildings, a courthouse, and a prison. The old Scots "ell" measure of 37 inches (almost 1 meter) is carved on the front, and a table of distances includes the mileage to Huntingdon, England, which in the 18th century was the destination for Scottish cattle driven south for the London markets. Today it's used mostly as municipal archives, and all of its interior is for government office functions.

At Whitesands, the street paralleling the Nith's edge, **four bridges** span the river. The earliest was built by Devorgilla Balliol, widow of John Balliol. Their son, John, was made Scotland's "vassal king" by Edward I of England, the "Hammer of the Scots," who established himself as Scotland's overlord. The bridge (originally with nine arches but now with only six) is still in constant use as a footbridge.

The town's best **shopping** is along the High Street, which is lined with turn-of-the-century facades, and nearby Queensberry Street. **Alternatives,** 73 Queensberry St. (☎ **01387/257-467**), is an attractive new-age shop stocking herbal remedies, artful wind chimes, and gift items, especially jewelry inspired by Celtic designs. You'll find men's and women's kilts in dozens of tartan patterns, as well as sweaters, overcoats, hats, and socks, always at realistic prices, at the **Edinburgh Woolen Mill,** 8 Church Place (☎ **01387/267-351**).

**Burns House.** Burns St. ☎ **01387/255-297.** Free admission. Apr–Sept Mon–Sat 10am–5pm, Sun 2–5pm; Oct–Mar Tues–Sat 10am–1pm and 2–5pm.

In 1796, Scotland's national poet died in this unpretentious, terraced stone house off St. Michael's Street. Although he occupied the house during only the last 3 years of his life, it contains personal relics and mementos as well as much of the original furniture used by Burns during his creative years.

**Robert Burns Centre.** Mill Rd. ☎ **01387/264-808.** Exhibition free; audiovisual theater £1.50 ($2.55) adults, 75p ($1.30) children/seniors/students. Apr–Sept Mon–Sat 10am–8pm, Sun 2–5pm; Oct–Mar Tues–Sat 10am–1pm and 2–5pm. From Whitesands, cross the river at Devorgillas Bridge.

You'll find this converted 18th-century water mill on the banks of the River Nith. Facilities at the center include an exhibit on the poet, a restaurant (see Wishart's in "Dining," below), and an audiovisual theater showing films about Burns and the town of Dumfries.

**Dumfries Museum.** Church St. ☎ **01387/253-374.** Museum free; camera obscura £1.50 ($2.55) adults, 75p ($1.30) children/seniors. Museum, Apr–Sept Mon–Sat 10am–5pm, Sun 2–5pm; Oct–Mar Tues–Sat 10am–1pm and 2–5pm. Camera obscura, Apr–Sept Mon–Sat 10am–5pm, Sun 2–5pm. Cross the river at St. Michael's Bridge Rd. and turn right onto Church St.

Southwestern Scotland's largest museum occupies a converted 18th-century windmill atop Corbelly Hill. Visit it only if you have extra time and an interest in the region's early geology, history, and archaeology. The museum is rich in collections ranging from early Christian stones to artifacts of 18th-century country life. Some exhibits suggest the site's role as an astronomical observatory in 1836; note an 8-inch (20cm) telescope used to observe Halley's Comet in July 1836. The camera obscura, on the upper floor, provides panoramic views of the town and surrounding countryside.

**Old Bridge House.** Mill Rd. at the far end of Devorgillas Bridge. ☎ **01387/256-904.** Free admission. Apr–Sept Mon–Sat 10am–5pm, Sun 2–5pm. From Whitesands, cross the river at Devorgillas Bridge.

Associated with the Burns House (see above), this building dates from 1660, when it replaced a structure that had been on the site since 1431. It was occupied as a private house until as late as 1957 and has been restored and furnished in a style typical of the period between 1850 and 1900, with tons of worthy Victoriana. Devorgillas Bridge itself was constructed in the 16th century.

## FARTHER AFIELD

From Dumfries, you can set out hiking, biking, or driving in all directions. If you're looking for natural beauty, leave by A75 and drive for 7½ miles (12km), turning right at the signpost for Shawhead. Once there, turn right again and follow the signs to **Glenkiln,** 10 miles (16km) from Dumfries. In this remote but scenic spot stands a wild landscape so perfect that Henry Moore decided to place his celebrated "King and Queen" sculpture here. He wrote, "Nature, trees, clouds are nothing geometric or harsh."

If you want to explore the area on two wheels, the **Nithsdale Cycle Centre,** 46 Broon's Rd. (☎ **01387/254-870**), is the place to go. You'll have to leave a £15 ($25.50) deposit; rental rates are £9 ($15.30) daily or £30 ($51) weekly. It's open Monday to Saturday 10am to 5pm and Sunday 11pm to 4pm.

✪ **Sweetheart Abbey.** On A710, New Abbey. ☎ **01387/770-244** (regional office of Historic Scotland). Admission £1.50 ($2.55) adults, £1.10 ($1.85) seniors, 50p (85¢) children under 16. Apr–Sept daily 9:30am–6:30pm; Oct–Mar Mon, Wed, Sat 9:30am–4:30pm, Thurs 9:30am–12:30pm, Sun 2–4:30pm. Drive 7 miles (11km) southwest from Dumfries on A710 (follow the signs saying SOLWAY FIRTH HERITAGE).

The village of New Abbey is dominated by Sweetheart Abbey's red-sandstone ruins. The walls are mostly extant, even though the roof is missing. Devorgilla Balliol founded the abbey in 1273. With the death of her husband, John Balliol the Elder, she became one of Europe's richest women—most of Galloway, as well as estates and castles in England and Normandy, belonged to her. Devorgilla founded Balliol College, Oxford, in her husband's memory. She kept his embalmed heart in a silver-and-ivory casket by her side for 21 years until her death in 1289 at age 80, when she and the casket were buried in front of the abbey altar. The abbey gained the name of "Dulce Cor," Latin for *sweet heart,* a term that has become a part of the English language.

✪ **Drumlanrig Castle.** Thornhill, 3 miles (5km) north of Thornhill off A76 and 16 miles (26km) southwest of A74 at Elvanfoot. ☎ **01848/330-248** or 01848/331-555. Admission £6 ($10.20) adults, £4 ($6.80) seniors, £2 ($3.40) children, £14 ($23.80) families. May–Aug Mon–Sat 11am–5pm, Sun 1–5pm. Closed Sept–Apr.

This pink castle, built between 1679 and 1689 in a parkland ringed by wild hills, is the seat of the dukes of Buccleuch and Queensberry and contains some outstanding paintings, including a famous Rembrandt, a Leonardo da Vinci, and a Holbein, plus relics related to Bonnie Prince Charlie. There's a playground with amusements for kids and a working crafts center in the old stable yard, and the gardens are gradually being restored to their 1720 magnificence. Meals are served in the old kitchen, hung with gleaming copper.

**Ellisland Farm.** Six miles (10km) north of Dumfries via A76 (follow the signs to Kilmarnock). ☎ **01387/740-426.** Admission £1.50 ($2.55) adults, 75p ($1.30) children/seniors. Apr–Sept Mon–Fri 10am–5pm, Sun 2–5pm; Oct–Mar Tues–Sat 10am–4pm.

From 1788 to 1791, Robert Burns made his last attempt at farming at Ellisland Farm; it was here that he wrote "Tam o' Shanter." After his marriage to Jean Armour, Burns leased the farm from Patrick Miller under the stipulation that he'd assist in erecting the building that's the centerpiece of the homestead. It's still a working farm for sheep and cattle, with many aspects devoted to a museum/shrine honoring Burns and his literary statements. On a circular quarter-mile (about 400m) trail ("the south trail") adjacent to the banks of the Nith, you can retrace the footsteps of Burns, who walked along it frequently during breaks from his writing.

## HITTING THE LINKS & CASTING A LINE

Nearby are the **Dumfries & County Golf Club,** Nunfield, Edinburgh Road (☎ **01387/253-585**), about a mile (1.5km) north of the town center, and the **Dumfries & Galloway Golf Club,** Laurieston Avenue, Maxwell Town (☎ **01387/ 253-582**), about a mile (1.5km) west of the town center. They're available for play by newcomers, but priority tee-off reservations are granted to members.

Galloway's rivers, estuaries, and lakes are particularly rich in salmon and trout. For £1.50 ($2.55), any tourist office here will sell you a copy of the brochure "Fishing in Dumfries & Galloway," listing dozens of fishing sites and giving information about how to get a permit. Some of the best salmon fishing is in the **River Nith,** which flows right through Dumfries. If you want to fish here, you'll have to swallow hard and buy an expensive permit (£50/$85 per day) from the local tourist office. Permits for fishing in local lochs and reservoirs (where you're likely to get brown trout but few if any salmon) may not be as trendy, but it's a lot less expensive.

# ACCOMMODATIONS
## EXPENSIVE

**Cairndale Hotel and Leisure Club.** 132–136 English St., Dumfries, Galloway DG1 2DF. ☎ **01387/254-111.** Fax 01387/250-555. www.cairndalehotel.co.uk. E-mail: sales@cairndale. fsnet.co.uk. 79 units. TV TEL. £105–£125 ($178.50–$212.50) double; from £145 ($246.50) suite. Rates include breakfast. AE, DC, MC, V. Free parking.

A four-story stone-fronted building from around 1900, the Cairndale is a fine choice with handsome public rooms. It's owned and managed by the Wallace family. Its guest rooms have been carefully modernized; all contain hair dryers and tea/coffeemakers. Executive rooms and suites have queen-size beds, minibars, trouser presses, and whirlpool baths.

**Dining/Diversions:** Moderately priced lunches are served in the Sawney Beans Bar and Grill. Dinner, served 7 to 9:30pm in Sawney Beans or in the main dining room, is quite good and may include roast sirloin of Galloway beef, West Coast scallops, mealed herring with Arran sauce, or Ecclefechan flan with Drambuie cream. The fixed-price menus run £15 to £17.50 ($25.50 to $29.75), with main courses at £9 to £12 ($15.30 to $20.40). The Continental Cafe Bar overlooks the indoor pool, and the Forum is a snack bar offering light snacks and refreshments in season. May to October, regular entertainment includes a Saturday dinner dance and a popular Cairndale *ceilidh* (a Scottish hoe-down) and Taste of Burns Country dinner every Sunday with a piper, accordionist, drummer, soloist, and Highland dancer.

**Amenities:** A leisure center includes a heated indoor pool, sauna, steam room, spa bath, solarium, and gym. Room service, concierge, laundry/valet, baby-sitting.

**Station Hotel.** 49 Lovers Walk, Dumfries, Galloway DG1 1LT. ☎ **01387/254-316.** Fax 01387/250-388. www.stationhotel.co.uk. E-mail: info@stationhotel.co.uk. 32 units. TV TEL. £90 ($153) double. Rates include breakfast. AE, DC, MC, V. Free parking.

The Station is among the most traditional in Dumfries, a few steps from the gingerbread-fringed train station. It was built in 1896 of hewn sandstone, in a design of heavy timbers, polished paneling, and soaring ceilings. The modernized but still somewhat dowdy guest rooms contain tea/coffeemakers, hair dryers, comfortable beds, and electric trouser presses.

**Dining:** The welcome and dinner menu at the Dining Room and Courtyard Bistro are purely Scottish. Before dinner, you can enjoy drinks in the lounge bar.

**Amenities:** Room service, baby-sitting. The staff will arrange tee times nearby.

## MODERATE

**Trigony House Hotel.** On the Dumfries–Ayr trunk road, Thornhill, Dumfries, Galloway DG3 5EZ. ☎ **01848/331-211.** Fax 01848/331-303. www.trigonyhotel.co.uk. E-mail: info@ trigonyhotel.co.uk. 8 units. TV TEL. £75 ($127.50) double. Rates include breakfast. MC, V. From Dumfries, drive 13 miles (21km) north along A76, following the signs to Thornhill. Trigony House is 1 mile (1.5km) south of Thornhill.

This pink-sandstone hotel was built around 1895 as the home of a local family. Its name (*trigony*) derives from the shape of the acreage, which is almost like a perfect isosceles triangle. Today it contains a handful of comfortable but unpretentious high-ceilinged guest rooms, each opening onto countryside views. Robin and Thelma Pollack are your hosts and will tell you all about the building's occupant during the 1930s: Frances Shakerley lived to be 107 within the walls of this house and thus became famous as the oldest woman in Scotland.

The hotel operates a busy pub and a dinner-only restaurant. Drop into the pub for affordable platters of simple food at lunch or dinner. The more formal restaurant charges £19.50 ($33.15) for a set-price meal that may include pâté of smoked trout, haggis with whisky-flavored cream sauce, salmon fillets with lime-and-ginger glaze, and strips of beef with whisky-and-oatmeal sauce.

## DINING

**Bruno's.** 3 Balmoral Rd. ☎ **01387/255-757.** Reservations required Sat–Sun. Main courses £5.50–£14.95 ($9.35–$25.40); fixed-price 3-course dinner £17.50 ($29.75); supper pasta menu £7.95 ($13.50). MC, V. Wed–Mon 5:30–10pm. ITALIAN.

It may seem ironic to recommend an Italian restaurant in the heart of Robert Burns territory, but Bruno's serves some of the best food in town. It's unassuming, but that's part of its charm. The chef's repertoire is familiar—first-rate minestrone, homemade pizza and pasta, veal with ham, and spicy chicken—but everything is done with a certain flair. The pork fillet is particularly tender, and the tomato sauce well spiced and blended. Bruno's special three-course menu is popular.

✪ **Globe Inn.** 56 High St. ☎ **01387/252-335.** Main courses £4.20–£5 ($7.15–$8.50). No credit cards. Mon–Thurs 10am–11pm; Fri–Sat 10am–midnight; Sun noon–11pm. Food served Mon–Sat noon–3pm and 6–11pm. SCOTTISH.

This was Burns's favorite haunt, in business since 1610, and he used an old Scottish expression, *howff* (meaning a small cozy room), to describe his local pub. He was definitely a regular; he had a child with the barmaid, Anna Park. You reach the pub down a narrow flagstone passage off High Street, opposite Marks & Spencer department store. You can go for a meal (perhaps kipper pâté, haggis, mealed herring, or Globe steak pie), or just to have a drink and play a game of dominoes. A little museum is devoted to Burns, and on window panes upstairs you can see verses he scratched with a diamond. Taps include Belhaven, Tennet's Lager, McEwen's 60 and 80 Shilling, Galloway Ale, Stela Lager, and Black Throne Cider.

✪ **Wishart's.** In the Robert Burns Centre, Mill Rd. ☎ **01387/259-679.** Reservations recommended. Main courses £12–£14 ($20.40–$23.80). DC, MC, V. Sun noon–2pm; Tues–Sat 7–9:30pm. SCOTTISH.

This is the most unusual restaurant in Dumfries. It's in a renovated grain mill, which you reach by taking a lovely 10-minute stroll across the Nith from the commercial heart of town. Built around 1780 by prominent engineer, Thomas Sneaton, the mill also shelters a small movie theater and the Robert Burns Centre (see above). The dining room's bare wood floors complement the forest-green painted brick walls, which display a riveting series of modern paintings (some for sale).

The offerings are prepared from Scottish ingredients and change with the seasons; they may include imaginative choices like sashimi of sea bass with wasabi, ginger, and garlic; a superb ragout of West Coast shellfish; a confit of wild salmon from the Nith, served with ratatouille, olive oil, and basil; and braised Highland beef with burgundy sauce, wild mushrooms, and parsley purée. Dessert may be strawberry soup with chantilly cream sauce. Mark Wishart is the hardworking owner/chef.

## DUMFRIES AFTER DARK

The town's most famous pub is the previously recommended **Globe Inn,** 56 High St. (☎ 01387/252-335), where Robert Burns tipped many a dram. An equally historic pub loaded with local color is **The Hole in the Wall,** 156 High St. (☎ 01387/252-770), where live music is usually provided by an accordionist. If you want to go dancing, head for either of the town's two discos, **Chancers Nightclub,** 25 Munches St. (☎ 01387/263-170), or **The Junction,** 36 High St. (☎ 01387/267-262). The crowd and music at these two clubs changes often, depending on the theme for the night, so call ahead to make sure they'll suit you on any given evening.

## 8  Castle Douglas

16 miles (26km) SW of Dumfries, 98 miles (158km) SW of Edinburgh, 49 miles (79km) SE of Ayr

An old cattle- and sheep-market town, Castle Douglas, at the northern tip of Carlingwark Loch, is near such attractions as Threave Castle, Cardoness Castle, Kirkcudbright, and Sweetheart Abbey and just southeast of the Galloway Forest Park. On one of the islets in the loch is an ancient lake dwelling known as a *crannog*.

## ESSENTIALS

**GETTING THERE**    The nearest **rail** station is in Dumfries (see "Dumfries: An Ode to Burns," above); from there, you can take a bus to Castle Douglas. Call ☎ 0345/484-950 for rail information.

The **Great Western Bus Co.** runs buses from Dumfries to Castle Douglas every hour throughout the day and early evening; travel time is about 30 minutes and costs £1.80 ($2.95) one way. Call ☎ 0990/808-080 for bus information.

If you're **driving** from Dumfries, head southwest along A75.

**VISITOR INFORMATION**    A **tourist office** is at the Markethill Car Park (☎ 01556/502-611). April to October, it's open Monday to Saturday 10am to 6pm (July and August, also Sunday 10am to 5pm).

## SEEING THE SIGHTS

Unique in Scotland, **Orchardton Tower,** 5½ miles (9km) southeast of Castle Douglas off A711, is an example of a round tower house (they were usually built in Ireland). It was constructed around 1450 by John Cairns, and later on was purchased by a member of the Maxwell family. The adventures of one family member, Sir Robert Maxwell of Orchardton, a fervent Jacobite captured in the Battle of Culloden, figured in Sir Walter Scott's novel *Guy Mannering*. If you ask the custodian who lives at the cottage next door, he'll let you see inside for free.

The **Mote of Urr,** 5 miles (8km) northeast of Castle Douglas off B794, is a circular mound enclosed by a deep trench. This is an example of the motte-and-bailey type of defense popular in Norman days.

**Threave Castle.** 1½ miles (2.5km) west of Castle Douglas on an islet in the River Dee. Admission (including ferry ride) £2 ($3.40) adults, £1.50 ($2.55) seniors, 75p ($1.30) children under 16. Apr–Sept Mon–Sat 9:30am–6:30pm; Sun 2–6:30pm. Closed Oct–Mar.

Threave Castle is the ruined 14th-century stronghold of the Black Douglases. The seven-story tower was built between 1639 and 1690 by Archibald the Grim, lord of Galloway. In 1455, Threave was the last Douglas stronghold to surrender to James II, who employed some of the most advanced armaments of his day (including a cannon similar to Mons Meg, the massive cannon now displayed in Edinburgh Castle) in its subjection. Over the doorway projects the gallows knob from which the Douglases hanged their enemies. In 1640, the castle was captured by the Covenanters (the rebellious group of Scots who questioned the king's right to make laws) and dismantled.

The site is owned by a public group known as Historic Scotland. To reach it, you must walk half a mile (1km) through farmlands and then take a small boat across the Dee. When you get to the river, you ring a bell signaling the custodian to come and ferry you across. The last sailing is at 6pm. For information, contact Historic Scotland, Longmore House, Salisbury Place, Edinburgh (☎ 01316/688-800).

**Threave Garden.** Off A75 half a mile (1km) west of Castle Douglas. ☎ 01556/502-575. Admission £4.50 ($7.65) adults, £3 ($5.10) children/seniors. Garden, daily 9:30am–sunset; visitor center, Apr–Oct daily 9:30am–5:30pm.

A mile (1.5km) southeast of Threave Castle, these gardens are built around Threave House, a Scottish baronial mansion constructed during the Victorian era. It's run by the National Trust for Scotland, which uses the complex as a school for gardening and a wildfowl refuge. The garden is at its best in April, when the daffodils bloom, and in June, when rhododendrons and the rock garden are in flower. There's a visitor center and a restaurant.

## EXPLORING THE COUNTRYSIDE

Castle Douglas's location near the northern edge of the estuary of Solway Firth offers panoramic views across the water stretching as far as England's Lake District. To best appreciate the beauty of the region, head to the nearby tiny village of **Auchencairn** (pop. 200), 6 miles (10km) south. (If you don't have a rental car, you can take one of about five buses that head there each day from Carlingwark Street in Castle Douglas, for a fare of around 90p/$1.50 one way). At the Balcary Bay Hotel (the only hotel in town), you'll find the start of a loop trail leading along the heather-clad, wind-whipped clifftops above the Solway Firth. Views extend out over Balcary Point and Rasscarel Bay. The walk is clearly marked with brown-and-white signs; allow about 2 hours.

If you want to explore the area by bike, rent one at **Ace Cycles,** Church Street in Castle Douglas (☎ 01556/504-542), open Monday to Saturday 9am to 12:30pm and 1 to 5pm. They rent for £8 to £10 ($13.60 to $17) per day and require a £50 ($85) deposit. Arm yourself with a good map and set out.

## ACCOMMODATIONS

**Douglas Arms.** King St., Castle Douglas, Galloway DG7 1DB. ☎ 01556/502-231. Fax 01556/504-000. E-mail: Doughot@aol.com. 24 units. TV TEL. £68.50 ($116.45) double. Rates include breakfast. AE, MC, V.

The Douglas Arms was a 17th-century coaching inn but has been turned into a modernized hotel behind a rather stark two-story facade. The public rooms are bright and cheerful, giving you a toasty feeling on a cold night. The guest rooms were recently refurbished and include tea/coffeemakers; hair dryers are available on request. Dinner is served daily 6 to 10pm, with an à la carte meal beginning at £7 ($11.90). Trout and salmon are featured on the menu, or you can try the mixed wild mushrooms sautéed in garlic and flambéed in whisky, followed by the roast sirloin of Galloway beef in loose-grain mustard sauce.

**King's Arms.** St. Andrew's St., Castle Douglas, Galloway DG7 1EL. ☎ **01556/502-626.** Fax 01556/502-097. www.gallaway-golf.co.uk. E-mail: david@galloway-golf.co.uk. 10 units, 9 with private bathroom. £56 ($95.20) double with bathroom. Rates include breakfast. MC, V. Free parking.

This inn provides reasonably priced accommodations ranging from single rooms to a family room. The guest rooms are newly redecorated, and nine come with TVs and phones. The helpful staff will direct you to various activities in the area, including a nine-hole golf course a 45-minute drive away.

The sun patio is a great place for tea or coffee or perhaps a sundowner of malt whisky. Guests can enjoy bar snacks (from £4.50/$7.65) during the day and fixed-price or à la carte menus (£5.95/$10.10 and up) in the dining room 6 to 8:45pm. The cuisine is British with a Scottish emphasis; the range is extensive, featuring local produce, Solway salmon, and Galloway beef. A reasonably priced selection of wines is available in the three bars.

**Longacre Manor.** Ernespie Rd., Castle Douglas, Galloway DG7 1LE. ☎ **01556/503-576.** Fax 01556/503-886. www.aboutscotland.co.uk/south/longacre.html. E-mail: ball.longacre@ btinternet.com. 4 units. TV TEL. £70–£90 ($119–$153) double. Rates include breakfast. MC, V. From the center of Castle Douglas, drive half a mile (1km) north, following the signs to Dumfries.

This dignified building on about 1½ acres of forest and garden was constructed in 1927 as the home of a local grain trader. Under the gracious ownership of Elma and Charles Ball, it now offers plushly and conservatively furnished large guest rooms, some with four-poster beds and all with trouser presses, hair dryers, and tea/coffeemakers. The lounge is cozy, and a three-course dinner can be prepared and served in the dining room for £17.50 ($29.75) per person.

**Urr Valley Country House Hotel.** Ernespie Road, Castle Douglas, Galloway DG7 3JG. ☎ **01556/502-188.** Fax 01556/504-055. www.castledouglas.net/urrvalley. 19 units. TV TEL. £65–£75 ($110.50–$127.50) double; £75–£85 ($127.50–$144.50) family room. Rates include breakfast. AE, MC, V. Free parking. Take A75 toward Castle Douglas.

Reached by a long drive, this country hotel in the scenic Urr Valley is privately owned and set in the midst of 14 acres of lush woodlands and gardens, a mile (1.5km) east of the center of Castle Douglas. You're welcomed into a real Scottish macho atmosphere of stag heads and antique rods and reels, along with paneled walls and fireplaces with log fires. Most of the rooms are spacious, and all have comfortable mattresses. Two rooms are set aside for nonsmokers. Extra services include laundry and baby-sitting.

You can have a drink or enjoy a pub meal in the lounge and bar. In the main restaurant, both French and Scottish cuisine are served, with an emphasis on fresh seafood and local produce such as pheasant and Solway salmon. Dare you try the regional specialty, Scottish haggis? A three-course menu costs £16 ($27.20), or you can order à la carte.

## DINING

**Plumed Horse Restaurant.** Main St., Crossmichael (3 miles/5km from Castle Douglas). ☎ **01556/670-333.** Reservations recommended. Main courses £12–£15.95 ($20.40–$27.10). MC, V. Tues–Sun 12:30–1:30pm and 7–9:30pm. Take A713 toward Ayr. SCOTTISH/INTERNATIONAL.

Opened in July 1998, this restaurant combines a high-quality cuisine with a relaxed, village atmosphere; it's set the rest of the local competition on its ear. The white linen tablecloths, crystal, silver, and tableware by Villeroy & Boch lends the Plumed Horse an air of elegance. Chef Tony Borthwick changes the menu regularly, but you might find roast Barbary duck breast, crisp fillet of salmon, scallop ravioli, and roast monkfish among the choices. Desserts such as pistachio and praline parfait and banana brûlée in butterscotch sauce are favorites. Ingredients used in the meals are often luxurious, including wild mushrooms and foie gras. The restaurant also has an extensive wine and champagne list.

# 9  Kirkcudbright: An Artists' Colony

108 miles (174km) SW of Edinburgh, 28 miles (45km) SW of Dumfries, 103 miles (166km) S of Glasgow, 50 miles (80.5km) E of Stranraer, 10 miles (16km) SW of Castle Douglas

The ancient burgh of Kirkcudbright (Kir-*coo*-bree) is at the head of Kirkcudbright Bay on the Dee estuary. Many of this intriguing old town's color-washed houses belong to artists; a lively group of weavers, potters, and painters lives and works in the 18th-century streets and lanes.

What makes Kirkcudbright so enchanting isn't really its sights (although it boasts several) but its artistic life and bohemian flavor. Various festivities take place here July and August; expect to find anything from marching bagpipe bands to exhibitions of Scottish country dancing to torchlight processions. And activities range from raft racing to nearby walks, to a floodlit Tattoo in front of MacLellan's Castle to a puppet festival. Check with the tourist office (see below) about what will be happening when you visit.

## ESSENTIALS

**GETTING THERE**   Kirkcudbright is on the same **bus** route that serves Castle Douglas from Dumfries, with departures during the day about once per hour. The 40-minute ride from Dumfries is about £1.75 ($2.90) one way. For bus information, call ☎ **0990/808-080** or the local tourist office.

If you're **driving** from Castle Douglas, continue along A75 southwest until you come to the junction with A711, which takes you into Kirkcudbright.

**VISITOR INFORMATION**   A **tourist office** is at Harbour Square (☎ **01557/330-494**). July and August, it's open Monday to Saturday 10am to 6pm and Sunday noon to 6pm; September and May, hours are Monday to Saturday 10am to 5pm.

## SEEING THE SIGHTS

In the old town **graveyard** are memorials to Covenanters and to Billy Marshall, the tinker (Gypsy) king who died in 1792 at age 120, reportedly having fathered four children after age 100.

**MacLellan's Castle.** Off High St. ☎ **01557/331-856.** Admission £1.80 ($3.05) adults, £1.30 ($2.20) seniors, 75p ($1.30) children. Apr–Sept Mon–Sat 9:30am–6:30pm, Sun 2–6pm. Closed Oct–Mar.

Dominating the center of town is this castellated castle built in 1582 for the town's provost, Sir Thomas MacLellan. It has been a ruin since 1752, but it's an impressive ruin and worth a visit. A large staircase goes from the cellars on the ground floor to the Banqueting Hall, where a still massive fireplace comes with what was called a "lairds lug" (spy hole). From almost anywhere in town, the jagged fangs of the castle loom overhead.

**Tolbooth Art Centre.** High St. ☎ **01557/331-556.** Admission £1.50 ($2.55) adults, 75p ($1.30) seniors/students/children. Combined ticket with the Stewartry Museum (see below), £2.50 ($4.25) adults, £1.25 ($2.15) concessions. Apr–Oct Mon–Sat 11am–5pm, Sun 2–5pm; Nov–Mar Mon–Sat 11am–4pm.

The large Tolbooth (1629) has functioned as a prison, the town hall, and a court-house. In front of it is a 1610 Mercat Cross and inside a memorial to John Paul Jones (1747–92), the gardener's son from Kirkbean who became a slave trader, a privateer, and eventually the father of the American navy. For a time before his emigration, he was imprisoned for murder here. In 1993, Queen Elizabeth inaugurated the building as a gallery displaying paintings by famous local artists. You'll find works by Jessie M. King, Lena Alexander, Robert Sivell, and S. J. Peploe.

**Broughton House.** 12 High St. ☎ **01557/330-437.** Admission £3.50 ($5.95) adults, £2.50 ($4.25) seniors and children. Apr–Oct Mon–Sat 11am–5:30pm, Sun 1–5pm. Closed Nov–Mar.

Regular exhibits are displayed at this 18th-century mansion that once belonged to artist Edward Atkinson Hornel (1864–1933). His portrait by Bessie McNicol is dis-played in the former dining room. Although largely forgotten today, Hornel was a famous artist in his day, known for the scenes he painted depicting life in his native Galloway. With his bold and colorful style, he became one of the major figures of the Glasgow School of Art. Broughton contains a large reference library with a Burns col-lection, along with pictures by Hornel and other artists, plus antiques and other works of art. At least to us, one of the most appealing aspects of this place is Hornel's small but charming Japanese-style garden, whose plantings and subtle arrangements some-times appeared in his paintings.

**Stewartry Museum.** St. Mary St. ☎ **01557/331-643.** Admission £1.50 ($2.55) adults, 75p ($1.30) seniors/students; free for children under 16. May–Sept Mon–Sat 11am–4pm (June–Sept also Sun 2–5pm). Closed Oct–Apr.

Built by the Victorians in 1892 as a showcase for the region's distinctive culture, this museum contains an unusual collection of antiquities, tools, and artworks depicting the history, culture, and sociology of this part of Galloway.

## ACCOMMODATIONS

**Baytree House.** 110 High St., Kirkcudbright, Galloway DG6 4JQ. ☎/fax **01557/330-824.** www.baytreehouse.com. 3 units. TV. £56–£60 ($95.20–$102) double. No credit cards.

Named after the enormous bay tree in its back garden, this B&B occupies a circa 1780 Georgian-style house whose yellow-painted stone facade faces the main street. The most impressive public room is the drawing salon, a sprawling testimonial to the good life of the 18th century. The midsize guest rooms have been tastefully done in pastels; some contain four-poster beds and/or French windows overlooking the garden. Hard-working owners Robert Watson and Jackie Callander add a touch of style to your breakfast service. If you request it in advance, they'll prepare three-course dinners for £16.50 to £20 ($28.05 to $34) per person.

**Selkirk Arms.** Old High St., Kirkcudbright, Galloway DG6 4JG. ☎ **01557/330-402.** Fax 01557/331-639. www.selikarmshotel.co.uk. 16 units. TV TEL. £90 ($153) double. Rates include breakfast. AE, DC, MC, V. Free parking.

The Selkirk Arms, where Robert Burns stayed when he composed the celebrated "Selkirk Grace," was built in the 1770s in a stone-fronted Georgian design with a slate roof. The guest rooms all have hair dryers, tea/coffeemakers, and standard furniture and garden views. The restaurant/bistro offers a wide range of fresh local produce; bar lunches and suppers are also available. The lounge bar features an array of malt whiskies.

## DINING

**Auld Alliance Restaurant.** 5 Castle St. ☎ **01557/330-569.** Reservations recommended. Main courses £9.50–£15 ($16.15–$25.50). MC, V. Daily 6:30–9:30pm (last booking). Closed Halloween–Easter. SCOTTISH/FRENCH.

One of the most appealing restaurants in the region is this family-owned and -operated place in an interconnected pair of 1880s buildings constructed with stones from the ruins of Kirkcudbright Castle. The restaurant's cooks are almost obsessed with the freshness of the fish they serve, and salmon (likely to have been caught several hours before preparation in the Kirkcudbright estuary and its tributary, the Dee) has all its legendary flavor. A house specialty is queenies (queen-size scallops from deeper waters than the great scallop).

# 10  Gatehouse-of-Fleet

113 miles (182km) SW of Edinburgh, 33 miles (53km) SW of Dumfries, 42 miles (68km) E of Stranraer, 9 miles (14.5km) W of Kirkcudbright, 108 miles (174km) SW of Glasgow

On the Water of Fleet, the sleepy former cotton town of Gatehouse-of-Fleet is really a backwoods kind of place, so don't expect major attractions. But the Scots themselves like to come here; they cherish its setting among dark brooding hills and conifers. Lonely stretches of countryside lie nearby, ideal for walks and picnics in nearly all directions.

Gatehouse-of-Fleet was Kippletringan in Sir Walter Scott's *Guy Mannering*. Burns composed "Scots Wha' Hae wi' Wallace Bled" on the moors nearby and wrote it down in the Murray Arms Hotel here. The town's name probably dates from 1642, when the English government opened the first military road through Galloway to assist the passage of troops to Ireland. In 1661, Richard Murray of Cally was authorized by Parliament to widen the bridge and erect beside it an inn to serve as a tollhouse, with the innkeeper responsible for the maintenance of a 12-mile (19km) stretch of road. This is believed to have been the original house on the "gait" (road) that later became known as the "gait house of Fleet," and by 1790 it was being written in its present form and spelling. This ancient "gait house" is now part of the Murray Arms Hotel, used as a coffee room, and is the oldest building still in existence in the town.

## ESSENTIALS

**GETTING THERE**  Four **buses** a day arrive in Gatehouse-of-Fleet from both Dumfries and Stranraer. Each routing takes 60 to 70 minutes because of frequent stops along the way. A one-way fare into Gatehouse from both Dumfries and Stranraer is around £2.80 ($4.75). For information, call ☎ **0990/808-080.**

To **drive** here from Castle Douglas, continue west along A75.

**VISITOR INFORMATION**  A **tourist office** operates from the Car Park at the southern end of High Street (☎ **01557/814-212**). April, May, June, September, and October, it's open daily 10am to 5pm (to 6pm July and August).

## EXPLORING THE AREA

**Mill on the Fleet.** High St. ☎ **01557/814-099.** Free admission. Easter–Oct daily 10am–5:30pm.

Most people pass through town en route to Cardoness Castle (below), but a worthy stop would be this heritage center installed in a former cotton mill. You might skip the earphone-guided tour about Gatehouse's involvement in the milling industry and concentrate instead on enjoying a light lunch, certainly a spot of tea, and some home-baked items in the tearoom. Look also for the shop selling gifts and local crafts.

**Tower of the McCullochs (aka Cardoness Castle).** ☎ **0131/668-8800.** Half a mile (1km) west of Gatehouse-of-Fleet, on Rte. 75. Admission £2 ($3.40) adults, £1.50 ($2.55) seniors, 75p ($1.30) children under 16. Apr–Sept daily 9:30am–6:30pm; Oct–Mar Sat 9:30am–4:30pm, Sun 2–4:30pm. From the town center, follow the signs to Creetown.

Built in the 15th century on a rocky plateau above the Water of Fleet (River Fleet) and evocative of medieval Scotland at its spookiest, the McCulloch family's semi-ruined castle has a sinister murder hole positioned in the ceiling of its entrance passage. Through this trap door, boiling pitch was poured down onto attackers. The castle may be roofless, but you can still see the 15th-century tower house and even the four floors that rise above a turf mound. The original staircase is still intact, as are the vaulted basement and some fireplaces and stone benches.

One member of the family, Sir Godfrey McCulloch, was the last person in Scotland to be executed by the "Maiden," the Scots version of the guillotine, at Edinburgh in 1697. The other family members didn't fare well either: To celebrate the birth of a new heir, they went skating on a nearby loch, but the ice wasn't firm yet, and all of them went to a watery grave.

## ACCOMMODATIONS & DINING

**Cally Palace Hotel.** Along Hwy. A75, Gatehouse-of-Fleet, Galloway DG7 2DL. ☎ **01557/814-341.** Fax 01557/814-522. 56 units. TV TEL. £104–£200 ($176.80–$340) double; £126 ($214.20) suite. Rates include breakfast. Ask about golf packages. AE, MC, V. Free parking. Take A75 south for 1½ miles (2.5km).

The Cally Palace is a large 1763 mansion on 150 acres of gardens, loch, and wooded parkland. Especially popular with more mature travelers, it's an oasis of peace, a place to relax and enjoy a few days' rest rather than a fleeting overnight. The public lounges are overscale, with some fine period pieces. The guest rooms come in widely varying styles and sizes; some are in a modern annex, others in the historic main building. Some have balconies opening onto the grounds but all have hair dryers and tea/coffeemakers.

**Dining/Diversions:** August to May, a dinner dance is held on Saturday. Every night you can order a four-course table d'hôte dinner for £25 ($42.50). There's also a bar.

**Amenities:** Indoor leisure center, a sauna, table tennis, a pool, and croquet. Tennis, game fishing, and loch boating are available. A par-70, 5,802-yard (5,280m), 18-hole golf course is on-site, with greens fees at £35 ($59.50). Golfing packages are available at a surcharge of £15 ($25.50) per day.

**Murray Arms.** Ann St., Gatehouse-of-Fleet, Galloway DG7 2HY. ☎ **01557/814-207.** Fax 01557/814-370. 13 units. TV TEL. £89 ($151.30) double. Rates include breakfast. AE, DC, MC, V. Free parking.

The Murray Arms is a long white building that functioned as a posting inn in 1760. Its coffeehouse (which sometimes converts into a small-scale art gallery) is even older, dating back to 1642. This is where Burns wrote down his stirring song "Scots Wha' Hae wi' Wallace Bled," an occasion still commemorated by the Burns Room with its Leitch pictures. The inn has been considerably updated now that it's back in the Cally family—and that's as it should be, since it was James Murray of Cally who made it into a coaching inn so long ago. The medium-sized guest rooms overlook the garden or the main street and contain hair dryers and tea/coffeemakers. Some of the rooms are equipped for travelers with disabilities.

**Dining:** You can stop in for a complete dinner in the inn's attractive restaurant opening onto the garden. Specialties include Galloway beef and fresh Solway Firth salmon. There are also three bars.

**Amenities:** Room service, tennis courts, baby-sitting. The staff will arrange golf and horseback riding nearby.

## 11  Stranraer

132 miles (212.5km) SW of Edinburgh, 75 miles (121km) W of Dumfries

The largest town in the area, Stranraer is the terminus of the 35-mile (56km) ferry crossing from Larne, Northern Ireland. An early chapel, built by a member of the Adair family near the 16th-century Castle of St. John, gave the settlement its original name of Chapel, later changed to Chapel of Stranrawer and then shortened to Stranraer. The name is supposed to have referred to the row ("raw") of original houses on the "strand," now largely buried beneath the streets. The Castle of St. John became the town jail and in the late 17th century held Covenanters during the campaigns of religious persecution. The rebellious Covenanters opposed the king's authority to make laws, feeling that should be the task of Parliament.

Frankly, if you're not going on to Ireland, you could skip Stranraer without any great loss to your enjoyment of Scotland. However, the beauty of Castle Kennedy Gardens (see below) is worth the trek, and you'll find lovely places to go for a walk or enjoy a picnic as you explore the countryside.

### ESSENTIALS

**GETTING THERE**   Monday to Saturday, four **trains** per day run from Glasgow to Stranraer, with seven trains on Sunday. The one-way fare is £15.30 ($26), and the trip is 2¾ to 3 hours. Call ☎ **0345/484-950** for rail information.

There are about four **buses** a day into Stranraer from Dumfries, each requiring 2½ hours of transit time and one-way fares of £5 ($8.50). There are also about 10 buses a day from Glasgow, requiring 3¾ hours of transit time and one-way fares of £7 ($11.90). Call ☎ **0990/808-080** for bus schedules.

If you're **driving** from Dumfries, continue west along A75.

**Sealink Ferries** travel between Stranraer and Belfast in Northern Ireland. Seven daily ferries depart Monday to Saturday, with five on Sunday. Trip time is 99 minutes. The one-way fare for travelers without cars is £22 ($37.40) adults and £12 ($20.40) children. A driver with a car pays £135 ($229.50) each way, and a driver with a car and up to four passengers pays £165 ($280.50). Weather conditions can interfere with ferry departures; call ☎ **01776/702-262** in Stranraer for information.

**VISITOR INFORMATION**   A **tourist office** is at Burns House, Harbour Street (☎ **01776/702-595**). November to April, it's open Monday to Saturday 11am to 4pm; in May and June, hours are Monday to Saturday 10am to 5pm, Sunday 11am to 3pm; July to October, hours are Monday to Saturday 9:30am to 5pm, Sunday 10am to 4pm.

## EXPLORING THE AREA

Our favorite drive in the area is the 50-mile (80.5km) excursion around the **Mull of Galloway,** reached via Stranraer by taking A77 south. Land of wild gorse and whin, this is rugged Galloway country (*wild gorse* is a low, thick, and prickly shrub and *whin* is any hard dark-colored rock). Along the way you'll pass sandy beaches (far too cold for those of us from milder climes), rugged cliffs, occasional sheltered bays, as well as sleepy villages and tiny fishing ports. Life here isn't as extreme as it first appears because the Gulf Stream nearby has a warming effect. On a clear day you'll often have a good view of the Irish coastline.

Despite its small size, the town has a great number of **shops.** Most are clustered along Charlotte, George, and Castle streets.

**Rogers Sports,** 26–30 Charlotte St. (☎ **01776/703-996**), can provide all kinds of gear for fair and foul weather and any equipment you might need for hiking on the moors or hitting the links. The **China Shop (Jean Ralstons),** 34 Charlotte St. (☎ **01776/702-697**), carries most of the grand names of British porcelain and crystal, as well as cunning figurines of the animals that trek across the nearby hills.

An art gallery known throughout the region for its evocative landscapes by local artists is the **Waterloo Gallery,** Prince's Street (☎ **01776/702-888**). A short walk from the village of Ardwell, 7 miles (11km) south of Stranraer, at a crossroads known as Clachenmore, the **Clachenmore Art Gallery** (☎ **01776/860-200**) incorporates a coffee shop, a gift shop, and a winning collection of sculptures and paintings by British and Scottish artists. For women, two choice personalized and tasteful clothing shops are **Whispers,** 92 George St. (☎ **01776/706-591**), and **Nowadays,** 35 George St. (☎ **01776/703-938**).

**Castle Kennedy Gardens.** Two miles (3km) east of Stranraer on A75. ☎ **01776/702-024.** Admission £3 ($5.10) adults, £2 ($3.40) seniors, £1 ($1.70) children. Gardens, Easter–Sept daily 10am–5pm (castle not open to the public).

The main attraction here is the ruins of **Castle Kennedy,** a medieval monument whose glory days ended in 1716, when it was sacked and burnt during a border raid by forces of James IV. The ruins are near the White Loch (named because of its clear waters) and the Black Loch (named because of its peat-impregnated dark waters). Surrounding the ruins are gardens containing one of the finest *pinetums* (pine groves) in Scotland. In the early spring, you can wander among blossoming rhododendrons, azaleas, and magnolias. The estate's main building is **Lochinch Castle,** built in the neo-feudal baronial style in 1864 and today the home of Lord Stair (his mother is a cousin of Queen Elizabeth II). You can't go inside Lochinch Castle, except to visit the tearoom.

## ACCOMMODATIONS

**Kildrochet House.** Stranraer, Galloway DG9 9BB. ☎/fax **01776/820-216.** www.kildrochet. co.uk. E-mail: kildrochet@compuserve.com. 3 units. £54 ($91.80) double. Rates include breakfast. MC, V. Drive 3½ miles (6km) south of Stranraer, following A716.

The stone walls of this 1720 house, the dower house for the mother of the lord of the manor, were designed by William Adam, the father of star architect Robert Adam. The guest rooms evoke those in a private home and come with dignified furniture and tea/coffeemakers (but no phones or TVs); hair dryers are available on request. Each has a view over the 3½ acres of gardens and fields surrounding the place. Liz and Peter Witworth are the congenial owners and will prepare an evening meal, served in the family dining room, for any guest who gives advance notice.

✪ **Lighthouse Hotel.** Kirkcolm, Stranraer, Galloway DG9 0QG. ☎ **01776/853-220.** Fax 01776/854-231. www.corsewalllighthousehotel.co.uk. E-mail: corsewall-lighthouse@msn.com. 9 units. TV TEL. £65 ($110.50) per person double; £130 ($221) per person suite. Rates include dinner and breakfast. AE, DC, MC, V. From Stranraer, take A77 for 12 miles (19km) north, following the signs to Kirkcolm and Corsewall Point.

In 1994, the solid stone walls, barns, and outbuildings of a lighthouse-keeper's home were transformed into an upscale inn set beside an 1815 lighthouse. Charming Scots-Canadian emigrés Jim and Mary Neilson welcome guests here. The setting is panoramic, and the place is full of 19th-century charm and romance, which combines the still-functioning lighthouse with the luxuries of a posh little inn and restaurant. Its light still beams at night, warning approaching ships entering the mouth of Loch Ryan. The individually decorated bedrooms are spacious and elegant, filled with amenities such as trouser presses, hair dryers, individually controlled central heating, and beverage makers. Some of the most scenic coastline in the Borders is within and near the 20-acre grounds of the hotel, with fine views that on a clear day can stretch all the way to the coast of Ireland. A wide variety of sea life, seals, birds, and deer can be spotted here.

**Dining:** Dinner is served daily from 7 to 9:30pm. Most ingredients (fresh produce, beef, lamb, salmon, trout, and venison) are local and prepared with skill and finesse. The on-premises pub is open to the public, and passersby are welcome to drop in for drinks and meals. Simple lunch platters at £5 to £6 ($8.50 to $10.20) are served daily noon to 2:30pm.

**Amenities:** Room service, baby-sitting. The staff can arrange outdoor activities from horseback riding, windsurfing, and sailing, to golf and day trips to Ireland.

✪ **West Castle Hotel.** Royal Crescent, Stranraer, Galloway DG9 8EH. ☎ **01776/704-413.** Fax 01776/702-646. www.mcmillanhotels.com. 73 units. TV TEL. £79 ($134.30) double; £99 ($168.30) suite; £109 ($185.30) penthouse. Rates include breakfast. AE, MC, V. Free parking. Walk 3 minutes north from the ferryboat terminal.

This is Stranraer's largest and best hotel, its oldest part built in 1820 by Capt. Sir John Ross, R.N., the Arctic explorer. The owners will give you a brochure relating the exploits of this local hero. The original building has been expanded with a modern flat-roofed addition. The rooms in the older building have more atmosphere and space, but all are comfortably appointed, with good beds and well-maintained bathrooms, plus hair dryers and tea/coffeemakers.

**Dining/Diversions:** The lounges are cozy and the dining room is impressive. Fresh local ingredients are used in the restaurant, where continental fare with Scottish overtones is served; a five-course fixed-price meal, available daily 7 to 9:30pm, costs £21 ($35.70). The bars in the hotel's cellar are well stocked, but we prefer the Ross Lounge, with its views of the harbor. There's dancing to a live band most Saturday nights in winter.

**Amenities:** Garden, a sauna, a solarium, a curling rink (October to April), a games room, and an indoor pool.

# DINING

**L'Apéritif Restaurant.** London Rd. ☎ **01776/702-991.** Reservations recommended. Main courses £7–£20 ($11.90–$34); fixed-price 3-course dinner 5:30–7pm £9.50 ($16.15); pizzas £4–£6 ($6.80–$10.20). AE, MC, V. Mon–Sat noon–2pm and 5:30–9pm. ITALIAN/INTERNATIONAL.

Here you'll find some of the best and most reasonably priced food at the port. Directly east of town, it's operated by Italians who have thrived here for more than 30 years.

One of the two lounges contains a pub popular with locals. Homemade soups, fresh salads, pastas, and hot dishes are offered at lunch for around £6 ($10.20). In the evening you have a choice of continental meals upstairs from an à la carte menu. They also serve pizza.

## STRANRAER AFTER DARK

The town has a few good pubs where you can while away a foggy evening. Small and hospitable but not particularly historic is the **Bridge Pub,** Bridge Street (☎ **01776/704-839**). **The Grapes,** 46 Bridge St. (☎ **01776/703-386**), has a vintage 1940s–1950s decor and has been virtually untouched since it was modernized shortly after World War II. Also worth your tippling and attention is the pub on the ground floor of the **Royal Hotel,** 20–24 Hanover St. (☎ **01776/702-426**), where Thursday to Saturday nights you can enjoy live rock. If you're looking to dance, head for the town's best disco, **The Venue,** Hanover Street (no phone), open Thursday to Saturday.

## 12  Portpatrick: Where the Southern Upland Way Begins

141 miles (227km) SW of Edinburgh, 8 miles (13km) SW of Stranraer, 97 miles (156km) SW of Glasgow, 80 miles (129km) W of Dumfries

Until 1849, steamers sailed the 21 miles (34km) from Donaghdee in Northern Ireland to Portpatrick, which became a "Gretna Green" for the Irish who wanted to marry quickly. Couples would land on Saturday, have the banns called on Sunday, and marry on Monday. When the harbor silted up, Portpatrick was replaced by Stranraer (see above) as a port.

Today you go to Portpatrick not because of its wealth of sights, although the Logan Botanic Gardens is worth the detour from Stranraer. You go instead because it's a major refueling stop for those driving along the Mull of Galloway. Portpatrick captures the flavor of an almost forgotten Scottish fishing port as few others do. It's a land of cliffs and rugged seascapes, with a lighthouse here and there and even a bird reserve.

Hikers come because Portpatrick is the beginning of one of the greatest long-distance footpaths in Scotland, the **Southern Upland Way** (see "The Best Hikes" in chapter 1). Starting here, the 212-mile (341km) jaunt goes all the way to the Cockburnspath on the eastern coast of Scotland. Along the way this path traverses the Galloway Forest Park and other scenic attractions of southern Scotland. Of course, very few will have the time or stamina to take this entire hike. But you can enjoy one of the least challenging stretches, going all the way from Portpatrick to Castle Kennedy (see above), some 7½ miles (12km).

## ESSENTIALS

**GETTING THERE**   Go to Stranraer (see "Stranraer," above) by **train,** then take a bus to Portpatrick, 5 minutes away. For train information, call ☎ **0345/484-950.**

Bus no. 64 from Stranraer makes frequent runs throughout the day to Portpatrick. The 5-minute ride costs around 95p ($1.60) one way. For **bus** information, call ☎ **0990/808-080.**

If you're **driving** from Stranraer, take A77 southwest.

**VISITOR INFORMATION**   The nearest **tourist office** is in Stranraer (see above).

## EXPLORING THE AREA

Commanding a clifftop 1½ miles (2.5km) south of the town center are the ruins of **Dunskey Castle,** a grim keep built in 1510. It's a dramatic site—the original stone walls and the chimney stacks, each rising abruptly from the top of the cliff, are all that remains. To walk or drive there from the town center, follow the clearly marked signs.

Some 10 miles (16km) south of Portpatrick is the little hamlet of Port Logan. In the vicinity is **Logan House** (not open to the public), the seat of the McDougall family, which claimed they could trace their ancestry so far back they were as old as the sun itself. This family laid out the gardens at Logan.

Fourteen miles (22.5km) south of Stranraer off B7065, the **Logan Botanic Garden** (☎ **01776/860-231**), an annex of the Royal Botanic Garden in Edinburgh, contains a wide range of plants from the world's temperate regions. Cordylines, palms, tree ferns, and flowering shrubs grow well in the mild climate of southwestern Scotland. March to October, the garden is open daily 9:30am to 6pm. Admission is £3 ($5.10) adults, £2.50 ($4.25) seniors, £1 ($1.70) children, and £7 ($11.90) families (two adults and up to four children). At the entrance is a pleasant refreshment room.

This fishing port has become something of a magnet for individual artisans who produce charming (and sometimes eccentric) handcrafts. You'll find examples of handcrafted plant pots, slip-cast and glazed figurines, Spanish recycled glass, and Indian coffee tables at the port's largest gift shop, **Lighthouse Pottery,** South Pier (☎ **01776/810-284**). The **Green Gillie Crafts Shop,** High Street (no phone), specializes in woolen jerseys and mittens, throw rugs, and calfskins. At the **Copper Wheel,** High Street (call the local garage at ☎ **01776/810-543** and ask for Ron Farquer), a highly skilled artisan grinds heraldic or freeform designs into wine glasses, beer mugs, and other objects. You can bring your own object or buy one from him. Anglers appreciate his renderings of trout or salmon on a line.

## ACCOMMODATIONS

The **Crown Hotel** (see "Dining," below) also rents rooms.

**Fernhill Hotel.** Heugh Rd., Portpatrick, Galloway DG9 8TD. ☎ **01776/810-220.** Fax 01776/810-596. www.mcmillanhotels.com. 23 units. TV TEL. £85–£110 ($140.25–$181.50) double. Rates include breakfast. AE, MC, V. Free parking. On the approach to Portpatrick, turn right at the War Memorial.

This gray-stone 1872 building stands on its own grounds above the village, looking down at the harbor a 5-minute walk from the first tee of the clifftop Dunskey Golf Course (which is scenic but not challenging). Renovated in 1990, the color-coordinated guest rooms are decorated with flair. The most desirable are the six executive rooms opening onto the sea; three have patio doors leading to private balconies. Many rooms come with tea/coffeemakers, trouser presses, and hair dryers.

**Dining/Diversions:** The cocktail bar with its lounge and the Victorian conservatory have a panoramic view over the town and sea. The excellent cuisine, using Scottish produce whenever available, is one of the reasons for staying here. The house specialty is fresh lobster. Served daily 6:30 to 9:30pm, à la carte meals begin at £10 ($17), with a four-course table d'hôte at £22.50 ($38.25).

**Amenities:** Limited room service and laundry.

✪ **Knockinaam Lodge.** Portpatrick, Galloway DG9 9AD. ☎ **01776/810-471.** Fax 01776/810-435. www.taste-of-scotland.com.knockinaam-lodge.html. 10 units. TV TEL. £230–£320 ($391–$544) double. Rates include breakfast and dinner. AE, DC, MC, V. Free parking. From A77 or A75, follow signs to Portpatrick. It's 2 miles west of Lochans; watch for hotel sign on right.

Built in 1869, Knockinaam Lodge is a three-story, Victorian hunting lodge, surrounded on three sides by towering cliffs. It's a country house of charm and grace in a picturesque coastal setting, boasting some of the finest cuisine served in the south of

Scotland. Since it is west of town, it is far more tranquil than any other hotel in the area. You get a real feel for Scottish manorial living here, especially as you read your paper in the morning room overlooking the sea. This award-winning establishment, owned by Michael Bricker and Pauline Ashworth, also boasts luxurious lawns that lead down to a pristine, private beach. It was here on these 30 acres of private woodland that Sir Winston Churchill met General Eisenhower and their chiefs of staff during the dark days of World War II. The bedrooms are tastefully decorated and filled with thoughtful little extras, each with a modernized bathroom.

**Dining:** In the restaurant, chef Tony Pierce prepares quality dishes made with the finest ingredients. Main courses include ballotine of wild salmon and leek with fromage blanc and caviar, and roast Aberdeen Angus beef with beignet of foie gras and truffle essence. For nonguests, there is a set-price lunch and dinner menu ranging from £29 to £38 ($49.30 to $64.60). The bar offers a wide variety of rare malt whiskies.

**Amenities:** Laundry, baby-sitting, fishing, croquet.

## DINING

The **Knockinaam Lodge** serves the best food in the area (see "Accommodations," above).

**Crown Hotel.** North Crescent, Portpatrick, Galloway DG9 8FX. ☎ **01776/810-261.** Fax 01776/810-551. Reservations recommended. Main courses £10.65–£14.45 ($18.10–$24.55); fixed-price 3-course menu £14.95 ($25.40). MC, V. Daily noon–2:30pm and 6–10pm. SEAFOOD/INTERNATIONAL.

One of the region's most popular restaurants occupies the ground floor of a century-old stone-sided hotel. You might enjoy a drink or two in the pub before heading into the dining room, which opens onto a wide-angled view of the ocean. Meat is available, but the biggest draw is seafood: scampi, monkfish, scallops in wine sauce, mullet, cod, and plaice, salmon, or sole fillets. Some platters, especially one priced at £23 ($39.10), are enormous and can be shared by two.

The Crown maintains 12 simple but clean rooms upstairs, each with bathroom, TV, hair dryer, tea/coffeemaker, and phone. With a hearty Scottish breakfast included, doubles rent for £72 ($122.40).

# Glasgow & the Strathclyde Region

**6**

Glasgow is only 40 miles (64.5km) west of Edinburgh, but there's an amazing contrast between the two cities. Scotland's economic power-house and its largest city (actually Britain's third-largest), up-and-coming Glasgow is now the country's cultural capital and home to half the population. It has long been famous for ironworks and steelworks; the local shipbuilding industry produced the *Queen Mary,* the *Queen Elizabeth,* and other fabled ocean liners.

Once polluted by industry and plagued with some of the worst slums in Europe, Glasgow has been transformed. Urban development and the decision to locate the Scottish Exhibition and Conference Centre here have brought great changes: Industrial grime is being sandblasted away, overcrowding has been reduced, and more open space and less traffic congestion mean cleaner air. Glasgow also boasts a vibrant and even edgy arts scene; it's become one of the cultural capitals of Europe.

The splendor of the city has reemerged. John Betjeman and other critics have hailed Glasgow as "the greatest surviving example of a Victorian city." The planners of the 19th century thought on a grand scale when they designed the terraces and villas west and south of the center.

Glasgow's origins are ancient, making Edinburgh, for all its wealth of history, seem comparatively young. The village that grew up beside a fjord 20 miles (32km) from the mouth of the River Clyde as a medieval ecclesiastical center began its commercial prosperity in the 17th century. As it grew, the city engulfed the smaller medieval towns of Ardrie, Renfrew, Rutherglen, and Paisley.

Glasgow is part of Strathclyde, a powerful and populous district whose origins go back to the Middle Ages. Irish chroniclers wrote of the kingdom of Stratha Cluatha some 1,500 years ago, and Strathclyde was known to the Romans, who called its people Damnonii. The old capital, Dumbarton, on its high rock, provided a natural fortress in the days when locals had to defend themselves against enemy tribes.

The fortunes of Strathclyde changed dramatically in the 18th century, when the Clyde estuary became the gateway to the New World. Glasgow merchants grew rich on tobacco and then on cotton. It was Britain's fastest-growing region during the Industrial Revolution, and Glasgow was known as the Second City of the Empire. In 1736, Greenock was the birthplace of James Watt, inventor of the steam engine. Until 1996, Strathclyde functioned as a government entity that included Glasgow, but it's now broken down into several new divisions: the City of Glasgow; Inverclyde, which includes the important industrial center of Greenock; and several others.

Glasgow is a good gateway for exploring the heart of Burns country, Culzean Castle, and the resorts along the Ayrshire coast, an hour away by frequent train service (see "Side Trips from Glasgow: The Best of the Strathclyde Region," below, for coverage of the best side trips from Glasgow). From Glasgow, you can also tour Loch Lomond, Loch Katrine, and the Trossachs (see chapter 8, "Fife & the Central Highlands"). After a day or so in Glasgow, you can head to Burns country for perhaps another night. Also on Glasgow's doorstep is the scenic estuary of the Firth of Clyde, down which you can cruise on a paddle steamer. The Firth of Clyde, with its long sea lochs—Gareloch, Loch Long, Loch Goil, and Holy Loch—is one of the most scenic waterways in the world.

# 1  Essentials

## ARRIVING

**BY PLANE**    The **Glasgow Airport** is at Abbotsinch (☎ **0141/887-1111**), 10 miles (16km) west of the city via M8. You can use the regular Glasgow CityLink bus service to get to the city center. From bus stop no. 2, take bus no. 900 or 901 to the Buchanan Street Bus Station in the center of town. The ride takes about 20 minutes and costs £2.80 ($4.75). A taxi to the city center costs about £15 ($25.50). You can reach Edinburgh by taking a bus from Glasgow Airport to Queens Station and then changing to a bus for Edinburgh. The entire journey, including the change, should take about 2 hours and costs £6.50 ($11.05) one way or £10 ($17) round-trip.

Monday to Friday, British Airways runs almost hourly shuttle service from London's Heathrow Airport to Glasgow. The first flight departs London at 7:15am and the last at 8:15pm; service is reduced on weekends, depending on volume. For flight schedules and fares, call British Airways in London at ☎ **0181/897-4000.**

From mid-May through October, **American Airlines** (☎ **800/433-7300;** www.aa.com) offers a daily nonstop flight to Glasgow from Chicago; the rest of the year, you'll make at least one transfer. **Northwest Airlines** (☎ **800/225-2525;** www.nwa.com) operates nonstop flights between Boston and Glasgow daily in summer, somewhat less frequently in winter.

**KLM UK** (☎ **0990/074-074**) flies from Stansted and London City airports to Glasgow daily. **British Midland** (☎ **0345/554-554**) flies from Heathrow to Glasgow. **Aer Lingus** (☎ **800/223-6537** or 01/844-4711 in Ireland; www.aerlingus.ie) flies daily from Dublin to Glasgow. Direct flights are also available through **Ryan Air** (☎ **0541/569-569** in England), which flies several times a day from Dublin to Glasgow.

**BY TRAIN**    Headquarters for British Rail is at Glasgow's Central Station and Queen Street Station. For **National Rail Enquiries,** call ☎ **0345/484-950.** For sleeper reservations by credit card, contact Virgin West Coast at ☎ **0345/991-995.** The **Queen Street Station** serves the north and east of Scotland, with trains arriving from Edinburgh every 30 minutes during the day; the one-way trip between the two cities costs £7.30 ($12.40) and takes 50 minutes. You'll also be able to travel to such Highland destinations as Inverness and Fort William from here.

The **Central Station** serves southern Scotland, England, and Wales, with trains arriving from London's Euston and King's Cross Stations (call ☎ **0345/484-950** in London for schedules) frequently throughout the day (trip time is about 5½ hours). The trains leave Euston Monday to Saturday every hour at 35 minutes past the hour until 6:35pm, and then the night train departs at 11:55pm, getting into Glasgow at 6:45am. From Glasgow, trains leave for London every hour 6:15am to 5pm. The night

# Greater Glasgow

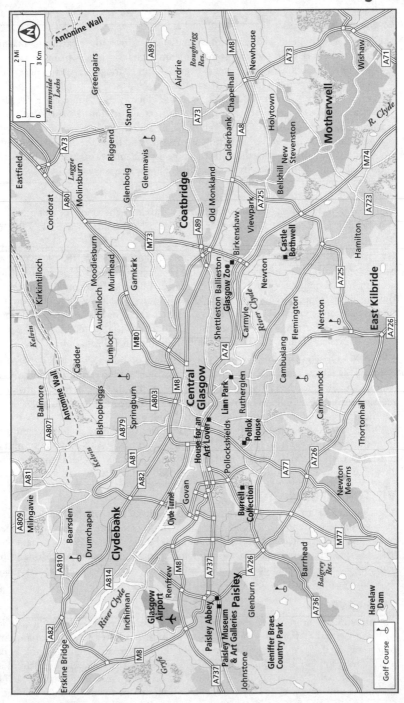

Antonine Wall

2 Mi

3 Km

Fannyside Lochs

Eastfield

A73

Condorat

Balmore

Antonine Wall

Kelvin

A807

A81

A809

Milngavie

Bearsden

Drumchapel

A810

A814

A82

Erskine Bridge

M8

Inchinnan

River Clyde

Gryfe

A82

Kirkintilloch

Cadder

Bishopbriggs

Kelvin

Lumloch

Auchinloch Moodiesburn

Muirhead

Garnkirk

M80

A879

Springburn

A803

M8

A81

A82

Clyde Tunnel

Govan

Renfrew

M8

A737

Glasgow Airport

Paisley Abbey

Paisley Museum & Art Galleries

Johnstone

A737

Glenburn

Paisley

Gleniffer Braes Country Park

Molinsburn

Luggie

A80

Glenboig

Riggend

Stand

Glenmavis

M73

Old Monkland

A89

Shettleston Ballieston

Glasgow Zoo

Central Glasgow

House for an Art Lover

Pollokshields

Pollock House

Burrell Collection

A77

A726

Barrhead

A726

A736

Coatbridge

Greengairs

A89

Airdrie

Roughrigg Res.

Calderbank Chapelhall

A73

A8

Birkenshaw

Viewpark

A725

Carmyle

River Clyde

Newton

Cambuslang

Flemington

Carmunnock

Newton Mearns

Thornliebank

A726

Harelaw Dam

Badgrey Res.

M77

Linn Park

Rutherglen

A74

Newhouse

M8

A73

Motherwell

Holytown

Bellshill New Stevenston

Wishaw

A71

R. Clyde

M74

Castle Bothwell

A725

Hamilton

A723

East Kilbride

Nerston

A726

Thorntonhall

Golf Course

175

Glasgow was built in various sections and districts over the years, and massive sections have been torn down—some for slum clearance, others to make way for new highways. Following a consistent street plan can be tough, as squares or terraces can suddenly interrupt a route you're tracing.

House numbers can run in odds or evens and clockwise or counterclockwise, and sometimes Glaswegians don't even use numbers at all. So don't be surprised to see something like "Blackfriars Street" given as an address without a number. Get a detailed map of Glasgow before setting out. Always find the nearest cross street, then look for your location from there. If it's a hotel or restaurant, the sign for the establishment is likely to be more prominent than the number anyway.

train leaves at 11:55pm. Try to avoid Sunday travel, as the frequency of trains is considerably reduced and the duration of the trip lengthened to at least 7 hours because of more stopovers en route.

**BY BUS**    The **Buchanan Street Bus Station** is 2 blocks north of the Queen Street Station on North Hanover Street (☎ **0141/332-7133**). **National Express** runs daily coaches from London's Victoria Coach Station to Buchanan frequently throughout the day. Buses from London take 7½ to 8½ hours to reach Glasgow, depending on the number of stops en route. Scottish CityLink also has frequent bus service to and from Edinburgh, with a one-way ticket costing £3 to £4.50 ($5.10 to $7.65). Contact National Express Enquiries at ☎ **0990/808-080** for more information.

**BY CAR**    Glasgow is 40 miles (64.5km) west of Edinburgh, 221 miles (356km) north of Manchester, and 388 miles (625km) north of London. From England in the south, Glasgow is reached by M74, a continuation of M8 that goes right into the city, making an S curve. Call your hotel and find out what exit you should take. M8, another express motorway, links Glasgow and Edinburgh.

Other major routes into the city are A77 northeast from Prestwick and Ayr and A8 from the west (this becomes M8 around the port of Glasgow). A82 comes in from the northwest (the Highlands) on the north bank of the Clyde, and A80 also goes into the city. (This route is the southwestern section of M80 and M9 from Stirling.)

## VISITOR INFORMATION

The **Greater Glasgow and Clyde Valley Tourist Board,** 11 George Square (☎ **0141/204-4400;** Underground: Buchanan St.), is the country's most helpful office. October to May, it's open Monday to Saturday 9am to 6pm; June hours are Monday to Saturday 9am to 7pm and Sunday 10am to 6pm; July and August hours are Monday to Saturday 9am to 8pm and Sunday 10am to 6pm; and September hours are Monday to Saturday 9am to 7pm and Sunday 10am to 6pm.

## CITY LAYOUT

The monumental heart of Glasgow—the Victorian City and the Merchant City, along with the Central Station—lies on the north bank of the **River Clyde.** The ancient center has as its core the great Cathedral of St. Kentigern, a perfect example of pre-Reformation Gothic architecture that dates in part to the 12th century. Behind it is the Necropolis, burial ground of many Victorians. Across the square is 1471 Provands Lordship, the city's oldest house. Down **High Street** you'll find the Tolbooth Steeple (1626) at Glasgow Cross, and nearer the River Clyde is **Glasgow Green,** Britain's first public park (1662).

From Ingram Street, South Frederick Street will take you to **George Square,** with its many statues, including one dedicated to Sir Walter Scott. This is the center of modern Glasgow.

The **Merchant City,** a compact area of imposing buildings, is the location of the National Trust for Scotland's shop and visitor center at Hutcheson's Hall. The broad pedestrian thoroughfares of Buchanan Street, Argyle Street, and Sauchiehall Street are the heart of the shopping district.

Glasgow's **West End** is just a short taxi journey from the city center, easily accessible from any part of the city and close to M8 and the Clydeside Expressway. An extensive network of local bus routes serves the West End. The Glasgow Underground operates a circular service; by boarding at any station on the system, you can reach the four stations serving the district: Kelvinbridge, Hillhead (the most central), Kelvin Hall, and Partick.

The West End is Britain's finest example of a great Victorian city, and the terraces of the Park Conservation Area rise to afford excellent views. Across Kelvingrove Park is the Art Gallery and Museum. Nearby, the tower of Glasgow University dominates Gilmorehill. Beyond is the Hunterian Art Gallery, home to a famous collection of Whistlers. Just a few strides away is Byres Road, a street of bars, shops, and restaurants. To the north is the Botanic Gardens.

A little more than 3 miles (5km) southwest of the city center is the **Pollok Country Park** and **Pollok Estate.** An extensive network of bus routes passes close by the park area, which is also served by two suburban rail stations. An electric bus service is in operation from the Country Park gates on Pollokshaws Road to Pollok House and the Burrell Collection Gallery. The Burrell Collection is housed in the heavily wooded Pollok Country Park. This museum is Scotland's top tourist attraction and the focal point of any visit to the South Side. Nearby is the 18th-century Pollok House.

Extensive parklands and greenery characterize the city's southern environs. In addition to the Pollok Country Park and Estate, there's **Haggs Castle Golf Club,** home of the Glasgow Open, and **Bellahouston Park,** scene of the historic papal visit in 1983. En route to the Burrell Collection, you cross by the 148-acre **Queens Park,** honoring Mary Queen of Scots, where panoramic views of the city are possible from the hilltop. Near **Maxwell Park** is the Haggs Castle Museum, housed in a 400-year-old building.

# The Neighborhoods in Brief

See the "Glasgow Attractions" map on pp. 198–199 to see the locations of the following neighborhoods.

**Medieval Glasgow**   This is where St. Mungo arrived in 543 and built his little church in what's now the northeastern part of the city. At the top of High Street stands the Cathedral of St. Kentigern and one of Britain's largest Victorian cemeteries. You enter the Necropolis by crossing over the Bridge of Sighs. Old Glasgow's major terminus is the High Street Station near the former site of the University of Glasgow. Glasgow Green, opening onto the River Clyde, has been a public park since 1662. Today vastly restored medieval Glasgow is the best place for strolls.

**Along the River Clyde**   Once it was said: "The Clyde made Glasgow; Glasgow made the Clyde." Although the city is no longer so dependent on the river, you can still enjoy a stroll along the Clyde Walkway, which stretches from King Albert Bridge, at the western end of Glasgow Green, for 2 miles (3km) downstream to Stohcross, now the site of the Scottish Exhibition and Conference Centre. The river is crossed by several bridges, one named for Queen Victoria and another for her consort, Albert.

This is one of the city's grandest walks; on these waters, Glasgow shipped its manufactured goods around the world. However, if time is limited, you may want to concentrate on the major museums and historic Glasgow instead.

**The Merchant City**    Glasgow spread west of High Street in the 18th century, largely because of profits made from sugar, cotton, and tobacco in trade with the Americas. The Merchant City extends from Trongate and Argyle Street in the south to George Street in the north. Its major terminus is the Queen Street Station and major shopping venue is Argyle Arcade. It's also the site of City Hall and Strathclyde University and boasts some of Britain's most elegant Georgian and Victorian buildings as well as Greek Revival churches. Much of the area was once occupied by tobacco barons, but their buildings have been recycled for other uses.

**Glasgow Center**    Continuing its western progression, the city center of Glasgow is now dominated by the Central Station on Hope Street. This is the major shopping district, including such venues as the Princes Square Shopping Mall. Also here are the Stock Exchange and the Anderston Bus Station (near the Central Station).

**The West End**    Beyond Charing Cross in the west end are the University of Glasgow and several of the city's major galleries and museums, some of which are in Kelvingrove Park. The West End mixes culture, art, and parks, and is dominated by Glasgow University, with the university structures idyllically placed in various parks. The city itself has more green spaces per resident than any other in Europe. Some of the most important of the city's galleries and museums are here, and 40 acres of the West End are taken up by the Botanic Garden.

## 2  Getting Around

The best way to explore Glasgow in on foot. The center is laid out on a grid system, which makes map reading relatively easy. However, many of the major attractions, such as the Burrell Collection, are in the environs, and for those you'll need to rely on public transportation.

*Remember:* Cars drive on the left, so when you cross streets make certain to look both ways.

### BY BUS

Glasgow is serviced by **First Glasgow Bus Company.** The buses are in a variety of colors, the lighter ones (blue and yellow) tending to serve the Kelvin Central and Strathclyde rural areas, with the darker ones covering the urban zones. Service is frequent throughout the day, but after 11pm service is greatly curtailed. The major bus station is the **Buchanan Street Bus Station,** Killermont Street (call ☎ **0141/ 226-4826** for schedules), 2 blocks north of the Queen Station. Fares are £1.20 ($2.05), but you must have exact change. A special round-trip bus ticket for £1.40 ($2.40) operates after 9:30am.

### BY UNDERGROUND

Called the "Clockwork Orange" (from the vivid orange of the trains) by Glaswegians, a 15-stop subway services the city. Most Underground trains operate from these stops every 5 minutes, with longer intervals between trains on Sunday and at night. The fare is 65p ($1.10). Service is Monday to Saturday 6:30am to 10pm and Sunday 11am to 6pm.

The **Travel Centre** at St. Enoch Square (☎ **0141/226-4826**), 2 blocks from the Central Station, is open Monday to Saturday 6:30am to 9:30pm and Sunday 7am to 9:30pm. Here you can buy a £6 ($10.20) **Underground pass,** valid for a week's access to all the Tube lines of Glasgow, as well as access to all the trains serving routes between

Central Station and the southern suburbs, or a £7.50 ($12.75) **daytripper card,** covering one adult and one child for a day. For details, call ☎ **0141/332-7133.**

## BY TAXI

Taxis are the same excellent ones found in Edinburgh or London. You can hail them on the street or call **TOA Taxis** at ☎ **0141/332-7070.** Fares are displayed on a meter next to the driver. When a taxi is available on the street, a taxi sign on the roof is lit a bright yellow. Most taxi trips within the city cost £3.5 to £4 ($5.95 to $6.80). The taxi meter starts at £1.60 ($2.70) and increases by 20p (35¢) every 200 feet (61m), with an extra 10p (15¢) assessed for each additional passenger after the first two. A 60p ($1) surcharge is imposed midnight to 6am. Tip at least 10% of the fare shown on the meter.

## BY CAR

Driving around Glasgow is a tricky business, even for locals. You're better off with public transportation. It's a warren of one-way streets, and parking is expensive and difficult to find. Metered parking is available, but you'll need 20p (35¢) coins, entitling you to only 20 minutes. You must watch out for zealous traffic wardens issuing tickets. Some zones are marked PERMIT HOLDERS ONLY—your vehicle will be towed if you have no permit. A yellow line along the curb indicates no parking. Multistory car parks (parking lots), open 24 hours a day, are found at Anderston Cross and Cambridge, George, Mitchell, Oswald, and Waterloo streets.

If you want to rent a car to explore the countryside, it's best to arrange the rental before leaving home (see chapter 2, "Planning Your Trip: The Basics"). But if you want to rent a car locally, most companies will accept your American or Canadian driver's license. All the major rental agencies are represented at the airport. In addition, **Avis Rent-a-Car** is at 161 North St. (☎ **0141/221-2827;** Bus: 6 or 6A), **Budget Rent-a-Car** at 101 Waterloo St. (☎ **0141/221-9241;** Bus: 38, 45, 48, or 57), and **Europcar** at 38 Anderson Quay (☎ **0141/248-8788;** Bus: 38, 45, 48, or 57).

## BY BICYCLE

Parts of Glasgow are fine for biking, or you might want to rent a bike and explore the surrounding countryside. For what the Scots call cycle hire, go to a well-recommended shop about a half mile (1km) west of the town center, just off Great Western Road: **Gear of Glasgow,** 19 Gibson St., in the Hillhead district (☎ **0141/339-1179;** Underground: Kelvin Bridge or Hillhead). It rents 21-speed trail and mountain bikes that conform well to the hilly terrain of Glasgow and its surroundings. The cost of £12 ($20.40) per day must be accompanied with a cash deposit of £50 ($85) or the imprint of a valid credit card.

# Fast Facts: Glasgow

**American Express**   The office is at 115 Hope St. (☎ **0141/226-3077;** Bus: 38, 45, 48, or 57), open Monday to Friday 8:30am to 5:30pm and Saturday 9am to noon (June and July to 4pm Saturday).

**Business Hours**   Most **offices** are open Monday to Friday 9am to 5 or 5:30pm. Most **banks** are open Monday to Wednesday and Friday 9:30am to 4pm, Thursday 9:30am to 5:30pm, and Saturday 10am to 7pm. Opening times can vary slightly from bank to bank. **Shops** are generally open Monday to Saturday 10am to 5:30 or 6pm. On Thursday, stores remain open until 7pm.

**Currency Exchange**    The tourist office and the American Express office (see above) will exchange most major foreign currencies. City-center banks operate *bureaux de change,* and nearly all will cash traveler's checks if you have the proper ID. **Thomas Cook** at the Glasgow Airport (☎ **0800/1300**) operates a bureau de change service daily 5am to 11pm in summer; off-season hours are Monday to Saturday 8am to 8pm and Sunday 8am to 6pm. It operates a larger branch at 15 Gordon St. (☎ **0141/201-7200;** Underground: Buchanan St.), open Monday to Friday 9am to 5:30pm.

**Dentists**    If you have an emergency, go to the Accident and Emergency Department of **Glasgow Dental Hospital & School NHS Trust,** 378 Sauchiehall St. (☎ **0141/211-9600;** Bus: 57). Its hours are Monday to Friday 9:15am to 3:15pm and Sunday and public holidays 10:30am to noon.

**Doctors**    The major hospital is the **Royal Infirmary,** 82–86 Castle St. (☎ **0141/ 211-4000;** Bus: 2 or 2A).

**Embassies & Consulates**    See "Fast Facts: Scotland" in chapter 2.

**Emergencies**    Call ☎ **999** in an emergency to summon the police, an ambulance, or firefighters.

**Hospitals**    See "Doctors," above.

**Hotlines**    Women in crisis may want to call **Women's Aid** at ☎ **0141/553-2022.** Gays and lesbians can call the **Strathclyde Gay and Lesbian Switchboard** at ☎ **0141/332-8372** daily 7 to 10pm. The **Rape Crisis Centre** is at ☎ **0141/ 331-1990.**

**Internet Access**    At the **Internet Café,** 569 Sauchiehall St. (☎ **0141/564-1052;** Underground: Buchanan St.; Bus: 57), you can send or read e-mail or surf the Web at the rate of £2.50 ($4.25) per 30 minutes. It's open Monday to Thursday 9am to 11pm, Friday 9am to 9pm, Saturday 10am to 9pm, and Sunday 10am to 11pm.

**Laundry/Dry Cleaning**    Try the **Park Laundrette,** 14 Park Rd. (☎ **0141/ 337-1285;** Underground: Kelvin Bridge), open Monday to Friday 8:30am to 7:30pm and Saturday and Sunday 9am to 6:30pm.

**Library**    The **Mitchell Library** is on North Street at Kent Road (☎ **0141/ 287-2999;** Bus: 57). One of the largest libraries in Europe, it's a massive 19th-century pile. Newspapers and books, as well as miles of microfilm, are available. It's open Monday to Thursday 9am to 8pm and Friday and Saturday 9am to 5pm.

**Pharmacies**    The best is **Boots,** 200 Sauchiehall St. (☎ **0141/332-1925;** Bus: 57), open Monday to Wednesday 8:30am to 6pm, Thursday 8:30am to 8pm, Friday and Saturday 8:30am to 6pm, and Sunday 11am to 5pm.

**Newspapers & Magazines**    Published since 1783, the *Herald* is the major newspaper with national, international, and financial news, sports, and cultural listings; the *Evening Times* offers local news.

**Police**    In a real emergency, call ☎ **999.** For other inquiries, contact police headquarters at ☎ **0141/532-2000.**

**Post Office**    The main branch is at 47 St. Vincent's St. (☎ **0141/204-3689;** Underground: Buchanan St.; Bus: 6, 8, or 16). It's open Monday to Friday 8:30am to 5:45pm and Saturday 9am to 5:30pm.

**Rest Rooms**    They can be found at rail stations, bus stations, air terminals, restaurants, hotels, pubs, and department stores. Glasgow also has a system of public toilets, often marked WC. Don't hesitate to use them, but they're likely to be closed late in the evening.

**Safety**   Glasgow is the most dangerous city in Scotland, but it's relatively safe when compared to cities of its size in the United States. Muggings do occur, and often they're related to Glasgow's rather large drug problem. The famed razor gangs of Calton, Bridgeton, and the Gorbals are no longer around to earn the city a reputation for violence, but you still should keep alert.

**Weather**   Call the Glasgow Weather Centre at ☎ **01891/248-7272.**

# 3 Accommodations

It's important to reserve your room well in advance (say, 2 months beforehand), especially in late July and August. Glasgow's hotel rates are generally higher than those in Edinburgh, but many business hotels offer bargains on the weekends.

The airport and the downtown branches of Glasgow's tourist office offer an **Advance Reservations Service**—with 2 weeks' notice, you can book a hotel before your arrival by calling ☎ **0141/221-0049.** The 2-week notification is preferred, but the staff will try its best to reserve rooms for walk-ins, although you're taking a chance that nothing will be available. The cost of any booking is £3 ($5.10).

## CENTRAL GLASGOW
### VERY EXPENSIVE

**Copthorne Hotel.** George Square, Glasgow G2 1DS. ☎ **0141/332-6711.** Fax 0141/332-4264. www.stay-withus.com. E-mail: sales.comodor@millcop.com. 141 units. TV TEL. Mon–Thurs £160 ($272) double, £180 ($306) suite; Fri–Sun £110 ($187) double, £140 ($238) suite. Rates include breakfast Fri–Sun. AE, DC, MC, V. Parking £8 ($13.60). Underground: Buchanan St.

The 1810 Copthorne (with a 1974 addition) is a landmark near the Queen Street Station, where trains depart for the north of Scotland. When the high-ceilinged public rooms were renovated, the designers searched out antiques and glistening marble panels. Each upgraded guest room offers in-house movies, plush carpeting, a trouser press, and a hair dryer. The worst rooms, "Classics," are in the rear with no views; the train station noise can be intolerable. "Connoisseurs" are larger executive rooms. The best rooms, "Antiques," are at the front of the building facing St. George Square and have four-poster or elaborate sleigh beds.

The Copthorne Hotel played a role in world history in 1941: Winston Churchill met in room 21 with FDR's envoy, Harry Hopkins. It was a pivotal meeting, in which Churchill secured Hopkins's support for the Lend-Lease Bill, a commitment that eventually helped usher the United States into World War II.

**Dining/Diversions:** The formal dining room is Windows on the Square, and Le Mirage Cafe and Bar is one of the most alluring spots in Glasgow for a drink or a light meal. The cocktail bar is open to guests only.

**Amenities:** Concierge, 24-hour room service, laundry/valet, baby-sitting, business center, gym.

**Glasgow Hilton International.** 1 William St., Glasgow G3 8HT. ☎ **800/445-8667** in the U.S. and Canada, or 0141/204-5555. Fax 0141/204-5004. www.hilton.com. E-mail: fom-glasgow@hilton.com. 319 units. A/C MINIBAR TV TEL. £180–£215 ($306–$365.50) double; from £390–£520 ($663–$884) suite. Weekend discounts often available. AE, DC, MC, V. Parking £5 ($8.50). Bus: 62.

Glasgow's only five-star hotel occupies Scotland's tallest building (20 floors). Dignified and modern, it rises in the heart of the city's business district, near the northern end

# Glasgow Accommodations & Dining

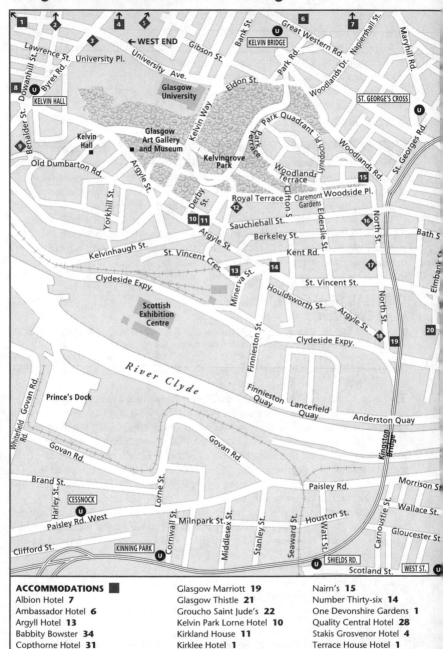

**ACCOMMODATIONS**

Albion Hotel **7**
Ambassador Hotel **6**
Argyll Hotel **13**
Babbity Bowster **34**
Copthorne Hotel **31**
Devonshire Hotel **1**
Glasgow Hilton International **20**

Glasgow Marriott **19**
Glasgow Thistle **21**
Groucho Saint Jude's **22**
Kelvin Park Lorne Hotel **10**
Kirkland House **11**
Kirklee Hotel **1**
Malmaison **25**

Nairn's **15**
Number Thirty-six **14**
One Devonshire Gardens **1**
Quality Central Hotel **28**
Stakis Grosvenor Hotel **4**
Terrace House Hotel **1**
Wickets Hotel **8**

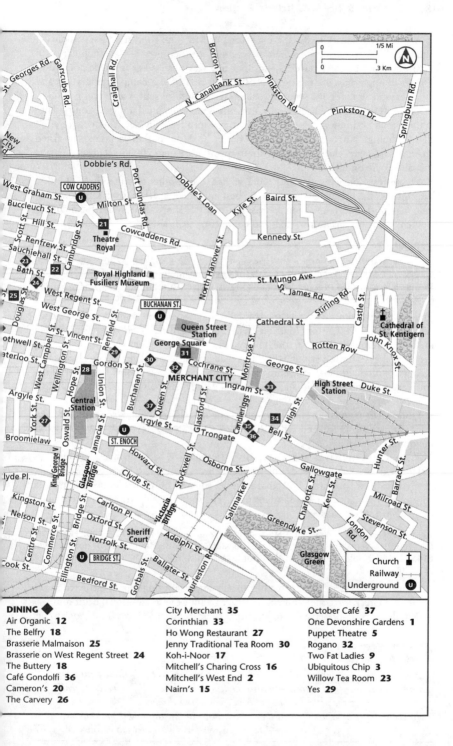

**DINING** ◆
Air Organic **12**
The Belfry **18**
Brasserie Malmaison **25**
Brasserie on West Regent Street **24**
The Buttery **18**
Café Gondolfi **36**
Cameron's **20**
The Carvery **26**
City Merchant **35**
Corinthian **33**
Ho Wong Restaurant **27**
Jenny Traditional Tea Room **30**
Koh-i-Noor **17**
Mitchell's Charing Cross **16**
Mitchell's West End **2**
Nairn's **15**
October Café **37**
One Devonshire Gardens **1**
Puppet Theatre **5**
Rogano **32**
Two Fat Ladies **9**
Ubiquitous Chip **3**
Willow Tea Room **23**
Yes **29**

of Argyle Street and exit 18 (Charing Cross) of M8. The good-sized guest rooms—plush and conservative, with hair dryers and trouser presses—are popular with vacationers and business travelers and offer fine views as far as the Clyde dockyards. The three uppermost are the executive floors, which have a complimentary bar and the enhanced facilities of a semiprivate club. The youthful staff is alert and helpful.

**Dining/Diversions:** The upscale Cameron's is recommended under "Dining," later in this chapter. Almost as appealing is Minskey's, inspired by a New York deli, offering all-day dining. No one ever goes thirsty at the Hilton: Raffles pours two-fisted libations and serves the best gin martini in town; more than 200 kinds of single malts and blends are on offer.

**Amenities:** Concierge; 24-hour room service (even kosher room service!); laundry; baby-sitting; the Leisure Club, one of the best-equipped health clubs in Glasgow, with indoor pool, Jacuzzis, and saunas; massage; two gift shops; hairdresser for men and women; extensive business services and conference facilities.

### EXPENSIVE

**Glasgow Marriott.** 500 Argyle St., Glasgow G3 8RR. ☎ **800/228-9290** in the U.S. and Canada, or 0141/226-5577. Fax 0141/221-7676. www.marriott.com. 300 units. A/C MINIBAR TV TEL. £70–£155 ($119–$263.50) double (rates subject to room availability); £175–£250 ($297.50–$425) suite. AE, DC, MC, V. Free parking. Underground: St. Enoch.

Amid a confusing set of access roads for the highways and commercial boulevards surrounding it, the 13-story Marriott challenges the Hilton as the top business hotel in town. Although we prefer the Hilton, the Marriott is cheaper, and its soaring profile at the Anderston exit of M8 adds a vivid accent to the skyline. The place is big, modern, and chain-hotel efficient. The medium-sized guest rooms have everything you'd expect from an upscale chain, such as king-size beds, hair dryers, coffee/tea trays, irons, voicemail, and data ports.

**Dining/Diversions:** The hotel's four restaurants include a Chinese choice, an Italian restaurant, the Buttery, and Chats bar, where snacks are served all day and locals unwind after work.

**Amenities:** Concierge, 24-hour room service, laundry, baby-sitting, salon, business services, car-rental desk, weekday newspaper delivery. There's an extensive leisure club, newly refurbished in early 2000, that includes squash courts, workout equipment, a whirlpool, a sauna, and a large indoor pool. The staff can help you arrange tee times on five nearby golf courses.

✪ **Malmaison.** 278 W. George St., Glasgow G2 4LL. ☎ **0141/572-1000.** Fax 0141/ 572-1002. www.malmaison.com. 72 units. MINIBAR TV TEL. £105 ($178.50) double; from £145 ($246.50) suite. Rates include VAT but no breakfast. AE, DC, MC, V. Parking nearby £7 ($11.90). Bus: 11.

This hip hotel opened in 1994 in a historically important building constructed in the 1830s as a Greek Orthodox church. In 1997, an annex with additional bedrooms was added, designed to preserve the architectural character of the church's exterior. Inside,

### Impressions

*[Glasgow is] a place which I shall ever hold in contempt as being filled with a set of unmannerly, low-bred, narrow-minded wretches; the place itself, however, is really pretty, and were the present inhabitants taken out and drowned in the ocean, and others with generous souls put in their stead, it would be an honour to Scotland.*
                                                    —David Boswell, in a letter to James Boswell (1767)

few of the original details remain; the decor is sleek and ultramodern. Bedrooms vary in size from smallish to average, but are chic and well-maintained, with extras like CD players, two-line phones, voicemail, data ports, specially commissioned art, top-of-the-line toiletries, and more. There's a small gym on the premises, as well as a brasserie and cafe, both separately recommended under "Dining," later in this chapter. Breakfast is available, but isn't included in the rates.

○ **Nairns.** 13 Woodside Crescent, Glasgow G3 7UP. ☎ **0141/353-0707.** Fax 0141/ 331-1684. www.nairns.co.uk. E-mail: info@nairns.co.uk. 4 units. MINIBAR TV TEL. £110–£160 ($187–$272) double. AE, DC, MC, V. Bus: 44.

Most of the Nairns fame comes from its stylish restaurant (see "Dining," later in this chapter), but its four chic guest rooms are a charming hideaway. Behind an 18th-century brick facade are the Silver Room, graced with a four-poster stainless-steel bed and a bath by über-designer Philippe Starck; the Amber Room, filled with as many tones of honey-brown as possible; the Nantucket Room, a winter retreat filled with leather, nautical accessories, and wood paneling; and the Vermeer Room, whose decor was inspired by the works of the 17th-century Dutch painter.

## MODERATE

**Glasgow Thistle.** 36 Cambridge St., Glasgow G2 3HN. ☎ **0141/332-3311.** Fax 0141/ 332-4050. E-mail: glasgow@thistle.co.uk. 300 units. TV TEL. £80–£150 ($136–$255) double; from £230 ($391) suite. AE, DC, MC, V. Free parking. Underground: Cowcadden.

The lower floors of this recently refurbished hotel have been given a cheerful ambience. It boasts 18 function rooms—especially imposing is the grand ballroom, the largest of its kind in Scotland, seating 1,500. The Scottish-theme guest rooms are a decent size, with trouser presses, tea/coffeemakers, and irons. The Cabin Bar offers snacks and affordable pub lunches; there's also the more upscale Gengis. Services include 24-hour room service and overnight laundry/dry cleaning. Guests also have free use of a gym a 5-minute walk away.

**Groucho Saint Jude's.** 190 Bath St., Glasgow, G2 4HG. ☎ **0141/352-8800.** Fax 0141/ 352-8801. E-mail: info@gruchosaintjudes. 6 units. MINIBAR TV TEL. £85–£95 ($144.50–$161.50) double; £150 ($255) suite. Rates include continental breakfast and newspaper. AE, MC, V. Metered parking. Underground: Cow Caddens.

Opened in July 1999, Groucho Saint Jude's has become one of the hottest spots in Glasgow. Centrally located and 15 minutes from the airport, this two-story townhouse offers clean, comfortable rooms and friendly service. The owner, a one-time member of the popular band Love & Money, attracts a sophisticated, hip young crowd of artists, musicians, writers, and celebs. The Groucho Club, which opened the hotel, remains the most sophisticated and sought-after club in London. But unlike London, which has a members-only policy, the Glasgow entry is open to all who reserve. Groucho Saint Jude is named after the patron saint of sinners, which sets the tone. All rooms have bathrooms (some with showers, some with tubs) and warm, contemporary furnishings. Amenities include room service and laundry service.

The bar, located in the basement, is one of the most popular in Glasgow. The casual, clubby restaurant, serving a combination of modern British and international cuisine, and with prices on the high side of moderate, is also a hot spot, so reserve for dinner here when you book your room.

**Quality Central Hotel.** 99 Gordon St., Glasgow G1 3SF. ☎ **0141/221-9680.** Fax 0141/ 226-3948. www.hotelnet.co.uk/friendly/home.htm. E-mail: admin@gb627.v-net.com. 222 units. TV TEL. Mon–Thurs £88.25–£108 ($150.05–$183.60) double, £120 ($204) suite; Fri–Sun £90 ($153) double or suite with breakfast or £121 ($205.70) with breakfast and

---

### ⓘ Family-Friendly Hotels

**Glasgow Thistle** *(see p. 185)*    This hotel offers spacious guest rooms suitable for tucking in children. Kids like the self-service carvery-style lunch, one of the best dining values in Glasgow.

**Glasgow Hilton International** *(see p. 181)*    Children arriving on the weekend are presented with fun packs, containing drawings, games, bubble bath, and comics. Kids enjoy the Leisure Center and the pool. Cots and highchairs are available. The best dining choice here is Minsky's, which offers kids' meals. Room service is more than happy to provide the likes of sausages or chicken nuggets.

**Devonshire Hotel** *(see p. 187)*    Although this elegant small hotel is full of antiques, it's happy to cater to children of whatever age with toys, cots, and highchairs. There's an interconnecting room that's perfect for families to book. Children are offered appropriate videos, and there are special facilities for heating food and sterilizing bottles. The restaurant is fully prepared to cook meals kids adore, like a simplified pizza or fish fingers.

---

carvery dinner. AE, DC, MC, V. Parking £8.50 ($14.45) or £1.80 ($3.05) overnight 5pm–10am. Underground: Central Station.

When it opened in 1883 by the rail station, the Central was the grandest Glasgow had seen, the landmark of the city's most famous street. Now revamped and restored to at least a glimmer of its former glory, the place may be too old-fashioned and creaky for some, but traditionalists like it. The baronial wooden staircase leading from the lobby to the upper floors has been painstakingly stripped and refinished, and sandblasting the facade revealed elaborate Victorian cornices and pilasters. The guest rooms, with an uninspired decor, are priced according to size and plumbing and include hair dryers and excellent beds. The bar has a good selection of Highland malts, and the Entresol restaurant serves freshly prepared Scottish food à la carte or by a carvery selection. The leisure center offers a pool, a Jacuzzi, a spa, a sauna, and two gyms.

### INEXPENSIVE

**Babbity Bowster.** 16–18 Blackfriars St., Glasgow G1 1PE. ☎ **0141/552-5055.** Fax 0141/552-7774. 6 units. £70 ($119) double. Rates include Scottish breakfast. AE, MC, V. Free parking. Underground: Buchanan St.

In Merchant City, this small but delightful Robert Adam–designed hotel doubles as an art gallery. The guest rooms vary in size but are attractive, with Victorian reproductions and white-lace bedding; the front desk will supply hair dryers on request. The well-regarded restaurant attracts students and faculty from Strathclyde University, and displays the work of Glaswegian artists (most are for sale). In the cafe/bar, you'll find traditional Scottish ales, Murphy's stout, and whisky, and musical events are presented on some Saturday and Sunday evenings. In summer, there's an outdoor barbecue area.

**Kirkland House.** 42 St. Vincent Crescent, Glasgow G3 8NG. ☎ **0141/248-3458.** Fax 0141/221-5174. E-mail: adnin@kirkland.gespnet.com. 5 units. TV. £60 ($102) double. Rates include Scottish breakfast. No credit cards. Free parking. Underground: Exhibition Centre.

On a quiet street about a 10-minute walk from the Glasgow Art Gallery and Museum, the university, and the Scottish Exhibition Centre, the Kirkland is an impeccably maintained 1832 Victorian crescent house. A mix of antiques and reproductions is used in the large guest rooms. Each comes with a tea/coffeemaker, and you can borrow a hair dryer on request. You get a warm welcome from owners Carole and Ewing Divers. Ewing is a keen admirer of American swing music and displays a collection of 78-rpm gramophone records, old photographs, and pictures. You're welcome to listen to recordings of Harry James, Benny Goodman, and many others.

## THE WEST END
### VERY EXPENSIVE

**✪ Devonshire Hotel.** 5 Devonshire Gardens, Glasgow G12 0UX. ☎ **0141/339-7878.** Fax 0141/339-3980. www.grassington.co.uk. E-mail: thedevonshire@aol.com. 14 units. TV TEL. £135–£165 ($229.50–$280.50) double; £165–£195 ($280.50–$331.50) suite. Children 9 and under stay free in parents' room. AE, DC, MC, V. Underground: Hillhead.

This is one of Glasgow's most charming small hotels. An imposing Victorian terrace house with a blond-sandstone facade, it was built in the late 1800s but opened as a hotel in 1989. Its mingling of perfect manners with a low-key attitude has attracted Michael Jackson, Whitney Houston, and Bryan Adams, among other celebs. Rumors have been heard about a benign ghost on the top floor, but that doesn't bother the cheerfully efficient Scottish staff. The plush guest rooms usually have antique furnishings and restored detailing and range from comfortably spacious to very large; all include trouser presses and hair dryers.

**Dining:** The pricey restaurant (advance reservations recommended) serves lunch in an upscale pub setting; dinners are formal affairs with lots of Scottish panache.

**Amenities:** Concierge, 24-hour room service, laundry/dry cleaning.

**✪ One Devonshire Gardens.** 1–3 Devonshire Gardens, Glasgow G12 0UX. ☎ **0141/ 339-2001.** Fax 0141/337-1663. www.one-devonshire-gardens.com. E-mail: onedevonshire@ btconnect.com. 27 units. MINIBAR TV TEL. £135–£230 ($229.50–$391) double; £185–£230 ($314.50–$391) suite. AE, DC, MC, V. Free parking. Underground: Hillhead.

In the Hyndland district just west of the center, the house at no. 1 was built in 1880 as an upper-crust home, but by the early 1980s had degenerated into a seedy rooming house. In 1986, a designer bought it and made it even more elegant than it was in its heyday. At the ring of the doorbell, a pair of Edwardian chambermaids with frilly aprons and dust bonnets appear to welcome you. Each of the eight upstairs guest rooms in this building is furnished in period style and with impeccable taste and lots of luxurious accessories. The success of no. 1 led to the acquisition of nos. 2 and 3, bringing the room count to 27. The newer rooms have the same elegant touches and high price tags; all come with trouser presses, hair dryers, and stereos.

**Dining:** See "Dining," later in this chapter, for details on the hotel restaurant.

**Amenities:** Concierge, 24-hour room service, laundry/valet.

### EXPENSIVE

**Stakis Grosvenor Hotel.** 1–10 Grosvenor Terrace, Great Western Rd., Glasgow G12 0TA. ☎ **0141/339-8811.** Fax 0141/334-0710. E-mail: reservations@glasgros.stakis.co.uk. 96 units. TV TEL. Mon–Thurs £128 ($217.60) double, Fri–Sun £190 ($323) double; £168–£250 ($285.60–$425) suite. Rates include Scottish breakfast Fri–Sun. AE, DC, MC, V. Free parking. Underground: Hillhead.

The most interesting thing about this hotel is the way a team of award-winning engineers saved its early 20th-century neoclassical facade, using a revolutionary technique of impregnating the decaying sandstone with fiberglass and concrete. The Cypriot-owned Stakis company almost completely gutted the interior, reconstructing it in a casino-style sweep of crystal chandeliers and brassy accents. The hotel offers fairly standardized guest rooms of an average size that fill up mainly with business travelers during the week and out-of-towners on the weekend. Look for such amenities as trouser presses, hair dryers, and tea/coffeemakers.

**Dining/Diversions:** The hotel has a piano bar in its West End restaurant; it serves a fixed-price buffet lunch for £9.95 ($16.90), a table d'hôte dinner for £17.95 ($30.50), or a choice of à la carte dishes from £10 to £18 ($17 to $30.60). One floor above the lobby is a sitting room with bar service.

**Amenities:** Concierge, 24-hour room service, laundry/valet. Guests can use a large health club nearby for £5 ($8.50) adults, £2.50 ($4.25) children.

## MODERATE

**Kelvin Park Lorne Hotel.** 923 Sauchiehall St., Glasgow G3 7TE. ☎ **0141/314-9955.** Fax 0141/337-1659. 100 units. TV TEL. £75 ($127.50) double; £105 ($178.50) suite. AE, DC, MC, V. Limited free parking. Underground: Kelvin Hall.

In the heart of the residential West End, this is a discreet hotel whose public rooms are in the style of early-1900s Scottish designer Charles Rennie Mackintosh. Although it was built 40 years ago, after his death, its bar (Newberys, honoring Frances Newbery, Mackintosh's mentor) was designed according to Mackintosh's theories. The hotel consists of an early 19th-century building (four floors) and a later five-story structure. The guest rooms, all with hair dryers and trouser presses, were renovated in 1995, resulting in a kind of neutral contemporary comfort; they vary in size, the older ones being noticeably larger.

Newberys bar offers moderately priced meals; there's also the Mediterranean-style Seasons Brasserie. Additional amenities include concierge, 24-hour room service, laundry, and baby-sitting.

**Wickets Hotel.** 52–54 Fortrose St., Glasgow G11 5LP. ☎ **0141/334-9334.** Fax 0141/334-9334. E-mail: wicketshotel@hotelmail.com. 11 units. TV TEL. £69.95 ($118.90) double; £68–£88 ($115.60–$149.60) family room. Rates include Scottish breakfast. AE, MC, V. Free parking. Underground: Partick.

Better known for its restaurant and bar than for its comfortable guest rooms, this hotel from the 1890s is an undiscovered West End gem, opposite one of the city's largest cricket grounds (the West of Scotland Cricket Club). The double rooms are pleasantly spacious, each with a brightly cheerful decor and coffeemaker; hair dryers are available on request.

The Conservatory Restaurant is the glamour spot, offering moderately priced regional and continental fare amid old photos of local cricket teams. You can also order à la carte. Adjacent to the restaurant is an open-air beer garden, one of the few in Glasgow. Randall's wine bar sells wine by the glass in an art deco setting filled with Erté fashion prints. The bar food is excellent.

## INEXPENSIVE

**Albion Hotel.** 405–407 N. Woodside Rd., Glasgow G20 6NN. ☎ **0141/339-8620.** Fax 0141/334-8159. www.s-h-systems.co.uk/hotels/albionho.html. 16 units. TV TEL. £56 ($95.20) double. AE, DC, MC, V. Underground: Kelvin Bridge.

This unpretentious hotel was formed by connecting two nearly identical beige-sandstone rowhouses. In the heart of Glasgow's West End, it offers high-ceilinged guest rooms with modern furniture. Each has a tea/coffeemaker, trouser press, and hair dryer. If your hotel needs are simple, you're likely to be very happy here.

**Ambassador Hotel.** 7 Kelvin Dr., Glasgow G20 8QJ. ☎ **0141/946-1018.** Fax 0141/945-5377. www.smoothhound.co.uk/hotels/ambassador.html. E-mail: ambassadorhotel@talk21.com. 16 units. TV TEL. £57 ($96.90) double. Rates include Scottish breakfast. AE, DC, MC, V. Free parking. Underground: Hillhead.

Across from the BBC Studios and the Botanic Garden, this small hotel in a circa-1900 Edwardian townhouse is one of the better B&Bs in Glasgow. The good-sized guest rooms are furnished with modern pieces and contain trouser presses, ironing boards and irons, hair dryers, tea/coffeemakers, and radio alarms. The hotel is well situated for exploring the West End, with several art galleries and many good local restaurants or brasseries nearby.

**Argyll Hotel.** 969–973 Sauchiehall St., Glasgow G3 7TQ. ☎ **0141/337-3313.** Fax 0141/337-3283. www.argyllhotelglasgow.co.uk. E-mail: info@argyllhotelglasgow.co.uk. 38 units. TV TEL. £68 ($115.60) double. Rates include Scottish breakfast. AE, MC, V. Parking on nearby streets. Underground: Kelvin Hall. Bus: 9, 16, 42, 57, 62, or 64.

This hotel is small but special, a Georgian building near Glasgow University, the Art Gallery and Museum, the Kelvin Hall International Sports Arena, and the Scottish Exhibition Centre. Although completely modernized, it shows a healthy respect for tradition. The guest rooms are comfortable, each with tea/coffeemakers, hair dryers, and digital radios. A couple are large and the rest are average-sized. Room service and dry cleaning/laundry are available. Sutherland's Restaurant serves international and Scottish specialties at all meals, and a special feature is its garden dining.

**Kirklee Hotel.** 11 Kensington Gate, Glasgow G12 9LG. ☎ **0141/334-5555.** Fax 0141/339-3828. www.kirkleehotel.co.uk. E-mail: kirklee@clara.net. 9 units. TV TEL. £69 ($117.30) double. Rates include Scottish breakfast. AE, DC, MC, V. Parking on nearby streets. Underground: Hillhead.

This red-sandstone Edwardian terraced house is graced with a rose garden that has won several awards. Behind the ornate stained-glass door you'll find high-ceilinged guest rooms of an average size, each with a tea/coffeemaker, trouser press, and hair dryer. Rosemary and Douglas Rogen will serve you breakfast in your room. The Kirklee is near the university, the Botanic Gardens, and the major art galleries.

**Number Thirty-Six.** 36 St. Vincent Crescent, Glasgow G3 8NG. ☎ **0141/248-2086.** Fax 0141/221-1477. www.no36.gispnet.com. E-mail: john@gispnet.com. 6 units. TV. £56 ($95.20) double. No credit cards. Bus: 42, 63, or 64.

In the heart of the West End, this hotel occupies the two lower floors of a four-story sandstone building that was conceived as an apartment house in 1848. Hardworking entrepreneur John MacKay maintains his high-ceilinged pastel guest rooms (each decorated uniquely) in fine working order. Breakfast is the only meal served.

**Terrace House Hotel.** 14 Belhaven Terrace, Glasgow G12 0TG. ☎ **0141/337-3377.** Fax 0141/400-3378. 14 units. TV TEL. £58 ($98.60) double. AE, DC, MC, V. Underground: Hillhead.

Behind a severe symmetrical gray-stone facade, this B&B occupies what began as a private rowhouse in the 1850s and was converted into a hotel about a decade ago. It's the property of the brother-and-sister team of Robert and Ann Black, who meticulously maintain the ornate cove moldings, high ceilings, and mix of new and antique furniture. The pastel guest rooms come with tea/coffeemakers.

## IN THE OUTSKIRTS

**Gleddoch House Hotel.** Langbank, Renfrewshire PA14 6YE. ☎ **01475/540711.** Fax 01475/540201. 38 units. TV TEL. £150 ($255) double; £185 ($314.50) suite. Rates include Scottish breakfast. Children in parents' room £7.50 ($12.75) per day. AE, DC, MC, V. Free parking. Drive west along A8/M8 from Glasgow and the Erskine Bridge toward Greenock and Gourock; turn left at the sign for Langbank on B789, going left again under the railway bridge and then steeply up the hill to the hotel entrance on the right.

About 15 miles (24km) west of Glasgow, this deluxe hotel is set on large grounds that include farmlands, riding stables, an 18-hole/par-74 golf course, and gardens. The guest rooms are of varying size and have good bathrooms, plus radios, hair dryers, trouser presses, and tea/coffeemakers. The paneled hall is bright with a roaring fire, with a cozy bar and a conservatory attached to it. The original antiques are still in place throughout the house.

**Dining:** Breakfast is a leisurely help-yourself affair. At lunch, you can order smoked trout and salmon mousse, Highland game broth, and perhaps a traditional warm pudding. A fixed-price lunch begins at £20 ($34). In the evening, there's an expensive four-course fixed-price dinner for £35 ($59.50). Many guests lunch in the Golf Club House.

**Amenities:** Concierge, 24-hour room service, dry cleaning/laundry, baby-sitting (arrange well in advance), secretarial services, 18-hole golf course, sports shop, sauna, squash, snooker, horseback riding, fishing.

# 4  Dining

The days are long gone when a meal out in Glasgow meant mutton pie and chips. Some of the best Scottish food is offered here (especially lamb from the Highlands, salmon, trout, Aberdeen Angus steaks, and exotic delights like moor grouse), and there's an ever-increasing number of ethnic restaurants. This still being Britain, however, you'll find the usual fish-and-chip joints, burger outlets, fried chicken eateries, and endless pubs. Many restaurants close on Sunday, and most are shut by 2:30pm, reopening again for dinner around 6pm.

*Note:* For the locations of the restaurants below, see the "Glasgow Accommodations & Dining" map on pp. 182–183.

## CENTRAL GLASGOW
### VERY EXPENSIVE

**Cameron's.** In the Glasgow Hilton International, 1 William St. ☎ **0141/204-5555.** Reservations recommended. Main courses £20.50–£23 ($34.85–$39.10); table d'hôte menu £19.90–£24.90 ($33.85–$42.35) at lunch, £45 ($76.50) at dinner. AE, DC, MC, V. Mon–Fri noon–2:30pm and 7–10:15pm; Sat 7–10:15pm. Bus: 6A, 16, or 62. MODERN SCOTTISH.

This is the most glamorous restaurant in Glasgow's best hotel, its four sections outfitted like baronial hunting lodges in the wilds of the Highlands. The chef's conservative menu holds few surprises but is a celebration of market-fresh ingredients deftly prepared. Small slip-ups sometimes mar the effect of a dish or two, but we've been dining here since its opening and have always come away pleased. Your best bet is to stay Scottish when ordering. Go with a choice like whisky-cured Isle of Arran salmon, confit of Highland duck, Firth of Lorne sea scallops—and that's only the appetizers. For a main course, try roast Ayrshire pork filet or rack of Scottish lamb with a crust of whisky-steeped oatmeal and Arran mustard, or Highland game with forest mushrooms.

✪ **Rogano.** 11 Exchange Place. ☎ **0141/248-4055.** Reservations recommended. Main courses £19–£30 ($32.30–$51); fixed-price lunch £16.50 ($28.05). AE, DC, MC, V. Restaurant daily noon–2:30pm and 6:30–10:30pm, Sun noon–2:30pm and 6–10:30pm; cafe Mon–Thurs noon–11pm, Fri–Sat noon–midnight, Sun noon–11pm. Underground: Buchanan St. SEAFOOD.

Rogano boasts a perfectly preserved art deco interior from 1935, when Messrs. Rogers and Anderson combined their talents and names to create a restaurant that has hosted virtually every star of the British film industry. You can enjoy dinner amid lapis lazuli clocks, etched mirrors, ceiling fans, semicircular banquettes, and potted palms. The menu changes every 2 months, but always emphasizes seafood, such as halibut in champagne-and-oyster sauce and lobster grilled or Thermidor. There are at least six varieties of temptingly rich desserts, like coconut-and-pineapple parfait with golden rum syrup.

A less expensive menu is offered down in the Cafe Rogano, where main courses begin at £10.95 ($18.60).

## EXPENSIVE

**The Buttery.** 652 Argyle St. ☎ **0141/221-8188.** Reservations recommended. Main courses £13–£20 ($22.10–$34); table d'hôte lunch £16.85 ($28.65); Oyster Bar lunch main courses £5.95–£8.95 ($10.10–$15.20). AE, DC, MC, V. Mon–Fri noon–2:30pm; Mon–Sat 7–10:30pm. Underground: St. Enoch. SCOTTISH/FRENCH.

This is the perfect hunter's restaurant, with oak panels, racks of wine bottles, and an air of baronial splendor. The anteroom bar used to be the pulpit of a church, and the waitresses wear high-necked costumes of which Queen Victoria would have approved. Menu items include smoked trout, rare roast beef, terrine of Scottish seafood, venison, tuna steak with tarragon and tomato-butter sauce, and sea bass prepared in various ways.

Adjacent to The Buttery is the **Oyster Bar,** outfitted in church-inspired Victoriana; its menu is shorter and a bit less expensive. The less formal **The Belfry** is in the cellar (see below).

✪ **Nairns.** In Nairns hotel, 13 Woodside Crescent. ☎ **0141/353-0707.** Reservations recommended. Set menu £13.50–£17 ($22.95–$28.90) at lunch, £27.50 ($46.75) at dinner. AE, DC, MC, V. Mon–Sat noon–2pm and 6–9:45pm. SCOTTISH/MEDITERRANEAN.

This is one of Glasgow's hottest and hippest restaurants, thanks to Nick Nairn's cuisine and a style that blends cutting-edge London with traditional Glasgow. In an 18th-century Georgian building, it offers two monochromatic dining rooms where fabric textures are more heavily emphasized than bright colors.

Menu items change with the season and the chef's inspiration but are likely to include fettuccine of shellfish with mint and coriander; a parfait of chicken livers with foie gras, a toasted brioche, and Cumberland sauce; and carrot, honey, and ginger soup. Main courses include roasted cod with mashed potatoes, wilted greens, and caviar-flavored butter sauce; tarte tatin of shallots with spicy beetroot oil; and maize-fed chicken breast with leeks and prunes, served with a gratin dauphinois. Favorite desserts are Chivas whisky parfait with Earl Grey syrup and classic lemon tart.

**Yes.** 22 W. Nile St. ☎ **0141/221-8044.** Reservations recommended. Restaurant fixed-price lunches £14.95–£17.95 ($25.40–$30.50), fixed-price dinners £23.95–$28.50 ($40.70–$48.45).

---

### ℹ️ Family-Friendly Restaurants

**Willow Tea Room** *(see p. 194)*   Thousands of locals fondly remember coming here as children to enjoy delectable pastries and ice-cream dishes—and it's still a big treat for any kid.

**Brasserie Malmaison** *(see p. 192)*   Dining here is like taking your kid to church—well, not really. The former Greek Orthodox church has given way to a Scottish and continental cuisine. The chefs serve some of the city's best French fries, salmon cakes, and grilled chicken dishes. Adjacent to the brasserie is a cafe with fresh salads, sandwiches, and pizzas.

**Cafe Gandolfi** *(see p. 194)*   Kids always find something to order here, perhaps a soup-and-salad lunch. Of course, it has to be followed by one of the homemade ice creams, the best in the city.

Cafe/bar lunch platters £2–£6 ($3.40–$10.20), fixed-price lunch £11.95 ($20.30); pre-theater fixed-price dinner £9.95–£12.95 ($16.90–$22). AE, DC, MC, V. Restaurant Mon–Fri noon–2:30pm and 7–11pm; cafe/bar Mon–Sat 10am–10:30pm (last order). Bus: 66. MODERN EUROPEAN.

Occupying a dignified building in one of Glasgow's most congested neighborhoods, the bilevel Yes serves sophisticated cuisine in its cellar restaurant and less expensive simpler fare in its street-level cafe/bar. The cafe/bar's dishes bear a strong Mediterranean slant, mainly taking inspiration from Northern Italy. Although the menu changes often, you'll always find buffet-style antipasti as well as assorted pastas and seafood. The cellar room is a lot more charming, with high windows, a purple-and-red decor, and modern Scottish paintings. A pianist performs Wednesday to Saturday evenings. Lunch menus change weekly and the elaborate dinner menus with the season. Expect dishes like gateau of haggis, prepared in several imaginative ways but garnished with whisky sauce and the traditional neeps and tatties; vodka-cured salmon with caviar and baby baked potatoes with sour cream; grilled West Coast seafood with chile, garlic, and lime butter sauce; roast pepper duckling with corn cakes and rhubarb, ginger, and apple reduction; or baked codfish with stuffed herb crust, smoked salmon strips, and vegetable sauce.

## MODERATE

**The Belfry.** In the basement of The Buttery, 652 Argyle St. ☎ **0141/221-0630.** Reservations recommended. Main courses £6.85–£9.95 ($11.65–$16.90). AE, DC, MC, V. Mon–Fri 12:30–2:30pm; Mon–Sat 5:30–11pm. Underground: St. Enoch. SCOTTISH/FRENCH.

The pews, pulpits, and stained glass that adorn this place came from a church in northern England. It's the only pub in Glasgow that affords you a contemplation of Christ in Majesty while you enjoy a pint of ale. The cramped and partially exposed kitchen produces daily specials like steak pie with roast potatoes; roast rack of lamb with rosemary, thyme, and caramelized shallots; and the Belfry mussel bowl with shallots, which can be a starter or a main course. An example of traditional Scottish cooking with a new twist is the popular haggis, neeps, and tatties with whisky sauce. The cook is well known for making clever use of fresh Scottish produce.

**Brasserie Malmaison.** In the Malmaison hotel, 278 W. George St. ☎ **0141/572-1000.** Reservations recommended for dinner Thurs–Sun. Brasserie main courses £7.50–£15 ($12.75–$25.50); Café Mal salads and platters £2.95–£7 ($5–$11.90). AE, DC, MC, V. Brasserie daily noon–2:30pm and 6–11pm; Café Mal daily noon–10:30pm. Bus: 11. SCOTTISH/CONTINENTAL.

In a hip hotel converted from a Greek Orthodox church (see "Accommodations," above), this restaurant in the crypt, beneath the original vaults, serves well-prepared imaginative food in a masculine dark decor, with a large bar and wooden banquettes affording privacy. Menu items arrive in generous portions and include French-style rumpsteak with garlic butter and pommes frites, salmon fish cakes with spinach, charcoal-grilled liver and bacon with creamed potatoes, grilled chicken with roasted red-pepper salsa, and roasted codfish filets with garlic shrimp.

In contrast, the greenhouse-inspired Café Mal, adjacent to the brasserie, has a menu of salads, sandwiches, pizzas, light platters, and drinks.

**Brasserie on West Regent Street.** 176 W. Regent St. ☎ **0141/248-3801.** Reservations not necessary. Table d'hôte menu £17.95 ($30.50). AE, DC, MC, V. Mon–Sat noon–11pm. Bus: Cowcadden St. SCOTTISH/CONTINENTAL.

This upscale brasserie, in a white-painted stone building that was once a private home, contains a pair of recently renovated dining rooms that evoke an elegant supper club in gold, burgundies, and black, graced with live palm trees. The polite service from the white-aproned staff gives a nod to Rogano (see above), which is owned by the same investors. The set-price menus change every 6 weeks and may include venison, chicken livers with Madeira-cream sauce, Scottish oysters, Angus beef fillet with pepper sauce, suprême of Scottish salmon with peppercorn-laced vinaigrette, and various vegetarian dishes.

**City Merchant.** 97–99 Candlebiggs. ☎ **0141/553-1577.** Reservations recommended. Main courses £7.50–£21.95 ($12.75–$37.30); fixed-price dinner £14.95–£24.50 ($25.40–$41.65). AE, DC, MC, V. Mon–Sat noon–11pm; Sun 5–11pm. Underground: St. Enoch. SCOTTISH/INTERNATIONAL.

In the heart of the city, this restaurant, owned and operated by Tony Matteo, offers friendly service and an extensive menu, and serves throughout the day. The cuisine is more reliable than stunning, but it delivers quite an array of well-prepared fresh food at a good price. One longtime regular told us, "It's a cozy place to eat on a rainy day, and we have a lot of those in Glasgow." Try the roast breast of duck, rack of lamb, or escalope of venison. Also tempting are the fast-seared scallops, a classic smoked haddock, or the filet of salmon, as well as fresh crab and lobster when available. Some of the desserts evoke old-time Scotland, such as a "clootie dumpling," made with flour, spices, and fried fruit and served with home-churned butter.

**Ho Wong Restaurant.** 82 York St. ☎ **0141/221-3550.** Reservations required. Main courses £12–£18 ($20.40–$30.60); fixed-price 2-course lunch £8.50 ($14.45). AE, DC, MC, V. Mon–Sat noon–2pm and 5:30pm–midnight; Sun 6pm–midnight. Underground: Central Station. CANTONESE.

Two blocks from the Central Station, Ho Wong is one of the city's finest Chinese restaurants. Jimmy Ho and David Wong opened this remote outpost of their Hong Kong establishment. You can pause for a drink in the cocktail bar, perusing the menu before being shown to your table. The service is obliging. There are at least eight duck dishes on the menu, along with four types of fresh lobster, as well as some "bird's nest" dishes and sizzling platters.

**Mitchell's Charing Cross.** 157 North St., Charing Cross. ☎ **0141/204-4312.** Reservations recommended. Main courses £6.25–£9.50 ($10.65–$16.15) at lunch, £7.95–£12.50 ($13.50–$21.25) at dinner; fixed-price pre-theater supper (5–7pm) £8.95–£10.95 ($15.20–$18.60). AE, DC, MC, V. Mon–Sat noon–2:30pm and 5–10pm. Bus: 23 or 57. MODERN SCOTTISH.

Named for its location near Glasgow's largest library (the Mitchell), this attractively decorated upscale bistro offers Scottish *cuisine moderne*. In a large room lined with plants and sophisticated paintings (usually by Glaswegian artists), you can order from a menu that changes every 2 months. Choices may include red snapper, grouper, salmon, and smoked haddock netted off the Hebridean coast; scallops of Scottish venison; duck; and haggis with fresh tatties and neeps and chive mayonnaise. Even if you miss mealtime here, consider dropping in for a pint or a whisky in the basement bar.

With almost the same prices, hours, and menus (but a less appealing bar), **Mitchell's West End** is at 31–35 Ashton Lane, near Byres Road and the Hillhead Underground station (☎ **0141/339-2220**).

**October.** The Rooftop, Princes Square, Buchanan St. ☎ **0141/221-0303.** Reservations recommended. Main courses £5–£7 ($8.50–$11.90). AE, MC, V. Mon–Thurs noon–8pm; Fri–Sun noon–5pm. Underground: St. Enoch. INTERNATIONAL.

At the top of the Princes Square shopping district, this bar/restaurant offers a widely diversified cuisine. There are several vegetarian dishes, and one of the best is a type of potato sandwich filled with roasted vegetables. Club sandwiches accompanied by cole slaw or salad are very popular and cost £5.25 ($8.90). Main courses are served from

---

| **Tea for Two** |
|---|

For tea, a light lunch, or a snack, try the famed **Willow Tea Room,** 217 Sauchiehall St. (☎ **0141/332-0521;** Underground: Cowcaddens). When it opened in 1904, the Willow became a sensation because of its Charles Rennie Mackintosh design, and it has been restored to its original condition. On the ground floor is a well-known jeweler, M. M. Henderson Ltd. The "room de luxe" is in the heart of the building, and it's fashionable to drop in for tea at any time of day. Reservations are recommended, and afternoon tea with pastry is £7.75 ($13.15). It's open Monday to Saturday 9:30am to 4:30pm and Sunday noon to 4:15pm.

---

5:30 to 7:30pm on Thursday, and night-bites like potato wedges and nachos are offered until 8pm. There's a wide array of choices—everything from a chicken or shrimp Caesar salad to mussels with white wine, flavored with herbs and garlic. Chicken might be blackened with a mash of spring onions and chives and chili sauce. For dessert, try the strawberry brûlée or lemon tart.

✪ **Two Fat Ladies.** 88 Dumbarton Rd. ☎ **0141/339-1944.** Reservations recommended. Fixed-price lunch £11.95–£15.95 ($20.30–$27.10); fixed-price pre-theater supper (6–7pm) £11.95–£15.95 ($20.30–$27.10); fixed-price dinner £21.95–£25.50 ($37.30–$43.35). MC, V. Fri–Sat noon–2pm; Tues–Sat 6–10pm. Bus: 16, 42, or 57. MODERN BRITISH/SEAFOOD.

This ranks high on the list of everybody's favorite restaurants, especially for irreverent diners who appreciate the unexpected. The "Two Fat Ladies" are its street number—a nickname for the number 88 in Scotland's church-sponsored bingo games (there's no connection to the "Two Fat Ladies" of TV Food Network fame). In honor of the name, owner-chef Calum Matheson displays an impossible-to-miss painting of two voluptuous Venus wannabes near the entrance. The custard-colored decor is minimalist and "post punk." Despite the limited hours (lunch is served only 2 days), the restaurant packs in crowds for specialties like pan-fried squid salad with coriander-flavored yogurt sauce, sea bass teriyaki, grilled chicken filet salad with apple chutney, and charcoal-grilled king scallops with tomato-basil sauce. The best dessert is the Pavlova (a chewy meringue) with summer berries and Drambuie sauce.

## INEXPENSIVE

**Cafe Gandolfi.** 64 Albion St. ☎ **0141/552-6813.** Reservations recommended on weekends. Main courses £8–£14 ($13.60–$23.80). MC, V. Mon–Sat 9am–11:30pm; Sun noon–11pm. Underground: St. Enoch/Cannon St. SCOTTISH/FRENCH.

Many university students as well as young professionals will tell you this popular place in Merchant City is their favorite caff—you may sometimes have to wait for a table. A remake of a Victorian pub, it boasts rustic wooden floors, wood benches, and stools. At lunch you should look for chalkboard specials. Vegetarians will find solace here. If you don't fill up on soups and salads, try smoked venison with gratin dauphinois or smoked pheasant with an onion tartlet in winter.

**The Carvery.** In the Forte Posthouse Hotel, Bothwell St. ☎ **08704/009-032.** Reservations required. Buffet £17.50 ($29.75). AE, DC, MC, V. Sun–Fri 6–10pm; Sat 5:30–10pm. Underground: Buchanan St. BRITISH.

The price of a meal at the Carvery is low considering what you get. In an ambience of brick-lined walls and pinpoint lighting, you can select from one of Glasgow's most amply stocked hot and cold buffets, spread on an altarlike centerpiece. It's augmented with carved roasts and joints produced by uniformed chefs. This is hearty cooking of the type that has delighted Brits for years; it's aimed at filling you up more than following the latest foodie trends.

**Corinthian.** 191 Ingram St. ☎ **0141/552-1101.** Reservations recommended. Main courses £6–£17 ($10.20–$28.90); fixed-price pre-theater dinner (daily 5:30–7pm) £9.75 ($16.60) for 2 courses, £12.50 ($21.25) for 3 courses. AE, MC, V. Mon–Sat 11am–midnight; Sun 12:30pm–midnight. Underground: St. Enoch. INTERNATIONAL.

In Lanarkshire House, this restaurant opened in the spring of 2000 with a 25-foot illuminated glass dome as its stunning centerpiece. Crystal chandeliers and rococo friezes make for a luxurious atmosphere and a refined dining experience. The menu is attractive and classic, based on the freshest products available in any season. You might, for example, feast on tender lamb brochettes from Highland sheep or salmon caught in Scottish waters. The chef does an enticing grilled tuna along with home-made desserts. In addition to the main restaurant are two bars where you can relax on fine Italian leather sofas while listening to music spun by the local DJ.

# THE WEST END
## EXPENSIVE

✪ **One Devonshire Gardens.** 1 Devonshire Gardens. ☎ **0141/339-2001.** Reservations required. Fixed-price lunches £21–£27.50 ($35.70–$46.75); dinner main courses £16.50–£23 ($28.05–$39.10). AE, DC, MC, V. Sun–Fri noon–2pm; daily 7–10pm. Underground: Partick. SCOTTISH/FRENCH.

Thanks to an intricate re-creation of the decor and service of the Edwardian Age, this hotel restaurant is one of Glasgow's most unusual venues. Drinks are served in the elegant drawing room, and you dine amid flowery Victorian-inspired striped wallpaper, with servers dressed in white shirts and black vests. Quality ingredients are handled with care and finesse in the kitchen. Perhaps you'll begin with curried-parsnip soup and follow with grilled sea bass or lemon sole; in spring, you can enjoy the rack of Borders lamb.

✪ **Ubiquitous Chip.** 12 Ashton Lane, off Byres Rd. ☎ **0141/334-5007.** Reservations recommended. Restaurant fixed-price lunch £18.95 ($32.20) for 2 courses, £23.95 ($40.70) for 3 courses; fixed-price dinner £27.95 ($47.50) for 2 courses, £32.95 ($56) for 3 courses; bar meals £8 ($13.60) at lunch, £10–£15 ($17–$25.50) at dinner. AE, DC, MC, V. Restaurant Mon–Sat noon–2:30pm and daily 5:30–11pm; bar daily noon–11pm. Underground: Hillhead. SCOTTISH.

This restaurant is inside the rough-textured stone walls of a former stable; its glass-covered courtyard boasts masses of climbing vines. Upstairs is a pub where simple platters are served with pints of lager and drams of whisky; they may include chicken, leek, and white-wine casserole or finnan haddies with bacon (but no fish and chips, as you might think from the name). The cooking in the restaurant is bistro style; the lunch menu changes weekly and dinner menu every 2 weeks. Lunch might include free-range chicken, shellfish with crispy seaweed snaps, or wild rabbit, and dinner might feature free-range pigeon with wild mushrooms or whisky-marinated salmon. Vegetarians are catered to at both meals.

## MODERATE

**Air Organic.** 36 Kelvingrove St. ☎ **0141/565-5200.** Reservations recommended. Main courses £7–£16 ($11.90–$27.20); fixed-price 2-course dinner £10 ($17) daily until 7pm. AE, MC, V. Sun–Tues 11am–11pm; Fri–Sat 11am–midnight. Underground: Hillhead. ORGANIC FUSION.

In Glasgow's West End, space-age Air Organic is designed like an airport lounge, with its white walls and sky-blue tables. The menu, designed to look like a plane ticket, features both organic and non-organic foods. The Thai seafood broth with coconut, lime, and coriander is exceptional, as is the Thai pumpkin curry. The restaurant also specializes in Japanese cooking, with a variety of bento boxes reasonably priced between £10 and £14 ($17 and $23.80). Chefs rely on high-quality raw ingredients for much of their punch (watch for Loch Fyne oysters). We were especially taken with the char-siu roast pork with sticky mustard apples. For dessert, there is nothing better than the steamed banana and ginger pudding. The friendly service, wide range of food choice, and unique design make this a place worth visiting.

✪ **Puppet Theatre.** 11 Ruthven Lane. ☎ **0141/339-8444.** Reservations recommended. Lunch items £3.95–£7 ($6.70–$11.90); dinner main courses £8.95–£19.50 ($15.20–$33.15). AE, MC, V. Tues–Fri and Sun noon–2:30pm and 7–10:45pm; Sat 7–10:45pm. Underground: Hillhead. SCOTTISH/MEDITERRANEAN.

In a partially residential neighborhood about 1½ miles (2.5km) west of the financial district, this restaurant occupies what was a farmhouse in 1870. In 1994, a pair of new owners added a glass-sided conservatory and divided the interior into three glossy dining rooms. If you're looking for quiet conversation, opt for one of the inner rooms, but if you want a festive crowd, request the conservatory. The stylish menu offers interesting choices, like the cream of mussel and onion soup, Aberdeen Angus fillet, market-fresh fish and seafood, pan-roasted guinea fowl and wood pigeon, and several vegetarian dishes. The desserts are sumptuous—perhaps you'll go for iced mango-and-raspberry parfait or poached figs filled with strawberry ice cream.

### INEXPENSIVE

**Koh-i-Noor.** 235 North St., Charing Cross. ☎ **0141/221-1555.** Reservations recommended. Main courses £7–£12 ($11.90–$20.40); fixed-price business lunch £4.25 ($7.25) for 3 courses, £6.75 ($11.50) for 4 courses; Sun–Thurs buffet £9.95 ($16.90); Fri–Sat buffet £11.95 ($20.30). AE, DC, MC, V. Sun–Thurs noon–midnight; Fri–Sat noon–1am. Underground: St. Georges. PUNJABI INDIAN.

This is one of the city's top Indian restaurants. The family that runs this spacious place comes from the Punjab in Pakistan, and naturally Punjabi specialties like *paratha* and *bhuna* lamb are recommended. The Sunday Indian buffet is one of the great food values of the city; the Indian buffet weekdays is another treat. You can also order a three- or four-course business lunch.

## IN THE OUTSKIRTS

✪ **Fifty-Five B.C.** 128 Drymen Rd., Bearsden. ☎ **0141/942-7272.** Reservations recommended for restaurant. Main courses £9.50–£15 ($16.15–$25.50); bar platters £4.95–£5.50 ($8.40–$9.35). AE, MC, V. Restaurant Mon–Tues noon–11pm, Wed–Sat noon–midnight; bar daily noon–3pm and 5–6:30pm. From Glasgow's center, take the Clydesdale Expressway to Anniesland, and from there follow the signs to Bearsden. SCOTTISH/MODERN FRENCH.

Named in honor of the year the ancient Romans invaded Britain (a date memorized by schoolchildren around the country), this restaurant is boisterous and fun. In the suburb of Bearsden, about a 15-minute drive north of Glasgow, it offers a usually crowded large bar area and a quieter, much smaller restaurant. Bar meals may include a sandwich or soup of the day or a combination of the two, pasta, Cajun chicken, and several salads. Pints of lager and frothy drinks like piña coladas and margaritas keep things humming. The restaurant offers more elaborate fare, like duck breast on a bed of pineapple and pink peppercorns, marinated haggis-stuffed chicken with Japanese spices on a bed of stir-fried vegetables, and blackened saddle of venison.

## 5 Seeing the Sights

### THE TOP ATTRACTIONS

The center of Glasgow is **George Square,** dominated by the **City Chambers** Queen Victoria opened in 1888. Of the statues in the square, the most imposing is that of

## Coming Attractions

Scheduled to be fully operational by the late spring of 2001, the **Glasgow Science Centre,** 50 Pacific Quay (☎ 0141/420-5000; www.gsc.org.uk), is expected to be a blockbuster attraction. On the banks of the River Clyde, it lies in the heart of the city, opposite the Scottish Exhibition and Conference Centre.

In three landmark buildings, the center features the first titanium-clad structures in the U.K., including Scotland's only Space Theatre. Other features include innovative laboratories, multimedia and science theaters, and interactive exhibits. The overall theme is that of documenting the challenges facing Scotland in the 21st century. The center is also a showcase depicting Glasgow's contribution to science and technology, past, present, and future. The complex also contains the only 360-degree rotating tower in the world.

Children will love the hands-on activities: You'll be able to make your own soundtrack and animation, do a 3-D head scan and rearrange your own features, or star in your own digital video. At special shows and workshops, you'll see a glass smashed by sound, "catch" shadows, experience a million volts of indoor lighting, see liquid nitrogen, view bacteria that lurk on you, and build a lie detector.

Call for prices and hours, which were not set at press time. You can take the Glasgow Underground from Buchanan Street Station to Cessnock, from which the science center is a 10-minute walk.

---

Sir Walter Scott, atop an 80-foot (24m) column. Naturally, you'll find Victoria along with her beloved Albert, plus Robert Burns. The **Banqueting Hall,** lavishly decorated, is open to the public on most weekdays.

✪ **Burrell Collection.** Pollok Country Park, 2060 Pollokshaws Rd. ☎ 0141/649-7151. Free admission. Mon–Sat 10am–5pm; Sun 11am–5pm. Closed Jan 1 and Dec 25. Bus: 45, 48, or 57.

This museum houses the mind-boggling treasures left to Glasgow by Sir William Burrell, a wealthy shipowner who had a lifelong passion for art collecting. You can see a vast aggregation of furniture, textiles, ceramics, stained glass, silver, art objects, and pictures (especially 19th-century French art) in the dining room, hall, and drawing room reconstructed from Sir William's home, Hutton Castle at Berwick-upon-Tweed. Ancient artifacts, Asian art, and European decorative arts and paintings are featured. There is a restaurant, and you can roam through the surrounding park, 3 miles (5km) south of Glasgow Bridge.

✪ **Glasgow Art Gallery and Museum.** Kelvingrove. ☎ 0141/287-2699. Free admission. Mon–Sat 10am–5pm; Sun 11am–5pm. Underground: Kelvin Hall.

This is the finest municipal gallery in Britain. It boasts a superb collection of Dutch and Italian old masters, including Giorgione and Rembrandt; French 19th-century paintings by Millet, Derain, and others; and Salvador Dalí's *Christ of St. John of the Cross.* Scottish painting is well represented, from the 17th century to the present. One of the major paintings here is Whistler's *Arrangement in Grey and Black no. 2: Portrait of Thomas Carlyle,* the first Whistler to be hung in a British gallery. The artist took great pride in his Scottish background.

Aside from paintings, the museum has an outstanding collection of European arms and armor, displays from the ethnography collections, and a large section devoted to natural history, with major new exhibits on the natural history of Scotland. There are also regularly changing small displays from the decorative art collections, plus

# Glasgow Attractions

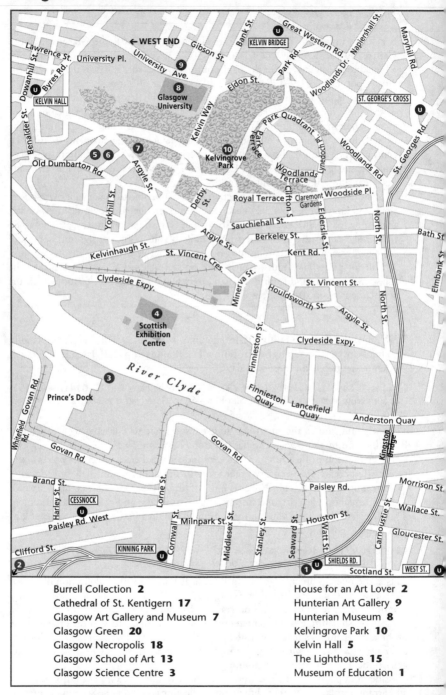

Burrell Collection **2**
Cathedral of St. Kentigern **17**
Glasgow Art Gallery and Museum **7**
Glasgow Green **20**
Glasgow Necropolis **18**
Glasgow School of Art **13**
Glasgow Science Centre **3**

House for an Art Lover **2**
Hunterian Art Gallery **9**
Hunterian Museum **8**
Kelvingrove Park **10**
Kelvin Hall **5**
The Lighthouse **15**
Museum of Education **1**

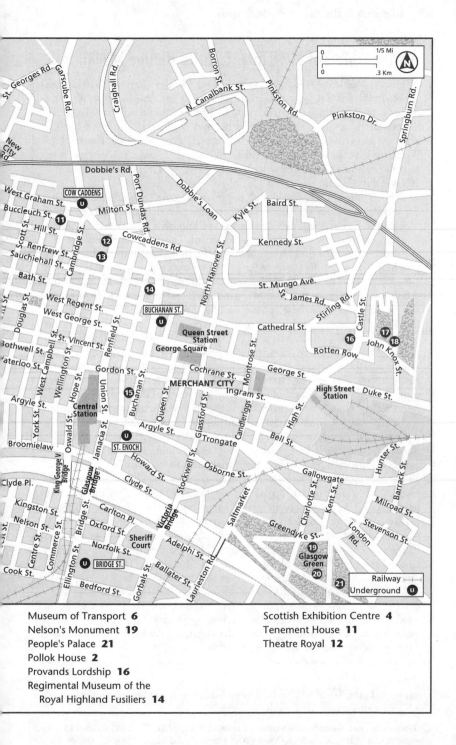

Museum of Transport **6**
Nelson's Monument **19**
People's Palace **21**
Pollok House **2**
Provands Lordship **16**
Regimental Museum of the
  Royal Highland Fusiliers **14**

Scottish Exhibition Centre **4**
Tenement House **11**
Theatre Royal **12**

# A Man Ahead of His Time: Charles Rennie Mackintosh

Although legendary today, tragic genius Charles Rennie Mackintosh (1868–1928) was largely forgotten in Scotland at the time of his death. This brilliant architect, designer, and decorator is a perfect example of the old saw that the prophet is accorded little honor in his own country. His approach, poised between art nouveau and Bauhaus, influenced everyone from Frank Lloyd Wright in Chicago to Josef Hoffmann in Vienna. Mackintosh's ideas, however, were too revolutionary in Glasgow's Victorian age, with its pompous eclecticism and overstuffed fussiness.

Born on June 7, 1868, Mackintosh began his career in 1889 as a draftsman for the architectural firm of Honeyman & Keppie. By the 1880s, Glasgow had become the British Empire's second city, and hundreds of new homes, public buildings, rail stations, and factories were needed. The situation seemed the perfect opportunity for a rising young architect. In 1896, Mackintosh's design for a new headquarters of the Glasgow School of Art won a prestigious competition (actually, he won because his design was the cheapest to build). He had drunk deeply from the creative cauldron of artistic development that swept Europe during the final days of the belle époque, and his theories insisted not that decoration should be constructed but that construction should be decorated. The forms of nature, especially plants, were used in his interiors, which had a simplicity and harmony that were utterly new. Instant applause came from the Vienna secessionists and the arts-and-crafts movement in such faraway places as England and America, but Glasgow wasn't so pleased. Today Mackintosh's design for the headquarters of the **Glasgow School of Art,** 167 Renfrew St. (☎ **0141/0353-4526**), near Charing Cross, is recognized as one of the city's greatest architectural treasures.

Alas, Mackintosh was neither tactful nor diplomatic, and he developed a reputation as a meticulous planner of rigid ideas who refused to compromise with builders or their crews. Later failures to win either commissions or architectural awards led to local ridicule of his avant-garde ideas, a break with his partners, and an eventual move out of Glasgow. He declared Glasgow a Philistine city. Recent research has shown he was actually exiled from his native Scotland in 1914 because of his Austrian/German artistic connections. In London, he continued to have difficulties, and his career there never got off the ground. By 1923, Mackintosh and his wife, English architect Margaret MacDonald, gave up the struggle and moved to the south of France. There he devoted himself to watercolor paintings of botanical specimens and landscapes. The Mackintoshes returned to London in 1927, where the architect died a year later.

Most of the acclaim that made Mackintosh the most famous designer ever to emerge from Scotland came from Europe, England, and the United States. In 1902, Hermann Muthesius, a leading German architect and critic, wrote, "In any enumeration of the creative geniuses of modern architecture, Charles Rennie Mackintosh must be counted among the first."

furniture and other items by Charles Rennie Mackintosh and his contemporaries. Teas and light lunches are available in the museum.

✪ **Hunterian Art Gallery.** University of Glasgow, Hillhead St. ☎ **0141/330-5431.** Free admission. Mon–Sat 9:30am–5pm (Mackintosh House closed 12:30–1:30pm). Underground: Hillhead.

This gallery owns the artistic estate of James McNeill Whistler, with some 60 of his paintings bestowed by his sister-in-law. It also boasts a Charles Rennie Mackintosh collection, including the architect's home (with his own furniture) on three levels, decorated in the original style. The main gallery exhibits 17th- and 18th-century paintings (Rembrandt to Rubens) and 19th- and 20th-century Scottish painters (McTaggart, Scottish Colourists, Gillies, Philipson, and others). Temporary exhibits, selected from Scotland's largest collection of prints, are presented in the print gallery, which also houses a permanent display of print-making techniques. The outdoor courtyard boasts contemporary sculpture.

**Hunterian Museum.** University of Glasgow, Gilmorehill Building. ☎ **0141/330-4221, ext. 4221.** Free admission. Mon–Sat 9:30am–5pm. Closed public holidays. Underground: Hillhead.

Opened in 1807, this is Glasgow's oldest museum, in the main Glasgow University buildings 2 miles (3km) west of the heart of the city. The museum is named after William Hunter, its early benefactor, who donated his private collections to get the museum going. The collection is wide-ranging, from dinosaur fossils to coins to relics of the Roman occupation and plunder by the Vikings. The story of Captain Cook's voyages is pieced together in ethnographic material from the South Seas. The museum has a bookstall and an 18th-century-style coffeehouse.

**The Lighthouse.** 11 Mitchell Lane. ☎ **0141/221-6362.** Free admission to The Lighthouse. Admission to Mackintosh Interpretation Center £2.50 ($4.25) adult, £2 ($3.40) seniors, and £1 ($1.70) children. Mon, Wed, Fri–Sat 10:30am–6pm; Thurs 10:30am–8pm. Underground: Buchanan Station.

Also known as **Scotland's Centre for Architecture, Design and the City,** The Lighthouse opened in July 1999. This building was Charles Rennie Mackintosh's first public commission and housed the *Glasgow Herald* from 1895. Unoccupied for 15 years, the building is now the site of a seven-story, state-of-the-art exhibition center with a unique blue neon-tracked escalator that leads to four galleries, lecture facilities, education suites, and a cafe.

**The Mackintosh Interpretation Centre** is the first facility to provide an overview of Mackintosh's art, design, and architecture. The impressive glass timeline wall illustrates his achievements. There are also interaction stations with models, drawings, and computer and video displays.

Visitors can ride the lift up to the Mackintosh Tower and experience a panorama of the city. In addition to exhibitions, the education program offers tours, lectures, films, and workshops for people of all ages.

The Wee People's City is an interactive play area for children 8 years of age and under. The IT Hotspot features Apple Macintosh computers with printing facilities, video conferencing, and a large selection of software for research, training, and hands-on activities.

**Museum of Transport.** 1 Bunhouse Rd., Kelvin Hall. ☎ **0141/287-2720.** Free admission. Mon–Sat 10am–5pm; Sun 11am–5pm. Closed Jan 1 and Dec 25. Underground: Kelvin Hall.

This museum contains a fascinating collection of all forms of transportation and related technology. Displays include a simulated 1938 Glasgow street with period shopfronts, appropriate vehicles, and a reconstruction of one of the Glasgow Underground stations. An authentic motor-car showroom has a display of mass-produced automobiles. The superb and varied ship models in the Clyde Room reflect the significance of Glasgow and the River Clyde as one of the world's foremost areas of shipbuilding and engineering.

**People's Palace.** Glasgow Green. ☎ **0141/554-0223.** Free admission. Mon–Sat 10am–5pm; Sun 11am–5pm. Closed Jan 1 and Dec 25. Bus: 14, 14A, 18, 18A, 18B, 20, or 62.

The People's Palace (built as a cultural center for the East End between 1895 and 1897) provides a visual record of the rise of Glasgow from its 1175–78 founding. Personal relics of Mary Queen of Scots represent her reign. The bulk of the collections are from Victorian Glasgow, including posters, programs, and props from the music-hall era. Paintings of the city by John Knox and others, portraits of Glaswegians (even St. Mungo), and items relating to trades and industries (such as the Glasgow potteries and stained-glass studios, trade unions, and newspapers) are also featured. There's a tearoom in the Winter Gardens.

The palace is located in **Glasgow Green,** the city's oldest public park. In the park, seek out **Nelson's Monument,** the first of its kind in Britain, and the **Saracen Fountain,** opposite the palace.

**Pollok House.** Pollok Country Park, 2060 Pollokshaws Rd. ☎ **0141/649-7151.** Free admission. Apr–Oct daily 10am–5pm; Nov–Mar daily 11am–4pm. Bus: 57 or 57A.

The ancestral home of the Maxwells, Pollok House was built around 1750, with additions from 1890 to 1908 designed by Robert Rowand Anderson. The house and its 360 acres of parkland were given to the city of Glasgow in 1966. It contains one of the finest collections of Spanish paintings in Britain, with works by El Greco, Goya, and Murillo, among others. There are also displays of silver, ceramics, and glass from the Maxwell family's and the city's collections.

**Tenement House.** 145 Buccleuch St. ☎ **0141/333-0183.** Admission £3 ($5.10) adults, £2 ($3.40) seniors/students/children. Mar–Oct daily 2–5pm. Underground: Cowcaddens.

An 1892 building on Garnethill, not far from the main shopping street, Sauchiehall Street, this house has been called a "Glasgow flat that time passed by." Until her death, Agnes Toward was an inveterate hoarder of domestic trivia. For 54 years she lived in this flat and stuffed it with the artifacts of her era, everything from a porcelain jawbox sink to such household aids as Monkey Brand soap. After her death, the property came into the care of the National Trust for Scotland as a virtual museum of a vanished era.

## MORE ATTRACTIONS

✪ **Cathedral of St. Kentigern.** Cathedral St. ☎ **0141/552-6891.** Free admission. Apr–Sept Mon–Sat 9:30am–6pm, Sun 2–5pm; Oct–Mar Mon–Sat 9:30am–4pm, Sun 2–4pm. Sun services at 11am and 6:30pm. Underground: Queen St. Station.

Also known as St. Mungo's, this cathedral was consecrated in 1136, burned down in 1192, and rebuilt soon after; the **Laigh Kirk (lower church),** whose vaulted crypt is said to be the finest in Europe, remains to this day. Visit the **tomb of St. Mungo** in the crypt, where a light always burns. The edifice is mainland Scotland's only complete medieval cathedral from the 12th and 13th centuries. It was once a place of pilgrimage, but 16th-century zeal purged it of all monuments of idolatry.

Highlights of the interior are the 1400s nave, built later than the choir, with a stone screen (unique in Scotland) showing the seven deadly sins. Both the choir and the lower church are in the mid-1200s First Pointed style. The church, even though a bit austere, is filled with intricate details left by long-ago craftspeople—note the tinctured bosses of the ambulatory vaulting in the back of the main altar. The lower church, reached via a set of steps north of the pulpit, is where Gothic reigns supreme, with an array of pointed arches and piers. Seek out, in particular, the **Chapel of the Virgin,** with its intricate net vaulting and bosses carved with fine detailing. The Blacader Aisle projecting from the south transept was the latest addition to the church, a two-story extension, of which only the lower part was completed in the late Gothic style.

For the best view of the cathedral, cross the Bridge of Sighs into the **Glasgow Necropolis** (☎ 0141/287-3961; Bus: 2 or 27), the graveyard containing almost every type of architecture in the world. Built on a rocky hill and dominated by a statue of John Knox, this fascinating graveyard was opened in 1832. Typical of the mixing of all groups in this tolerant cosmopolitan city, the first person to be buried here was a Jew, Joseph Levi.

**House for an Art Lover.** Bellahouston Park, Dumbreck Rd. ☎ 0141/353-4770. Admission £3.50 ($5.95). Sat–Sun 10am–4pm. Underground: Ibrox. Bus: 9A, 39, 54, 59, or 36.

This house, which opened in 1996, is based on an unrealized and incomplete 1901 competition entry of Charles Rennie Mackintosh. The impressive building, with its elegant interiors, was brought to life by contemporary artists and craftspeople, with architects Graeme Robertson and John Cane expanding the originals and adding missing details. The tour begins in the main hall and leads through the dining room, with its lovely gesso panels, and on to the music room, which shows Mackintosh designs at their most inspirational. Finally, you visit the oval boardroom before entering an audiovisual display. Also here are an art cafe, a design shop, and a striking parkland setting adjacent to Victorian walled gardens.

**Museum of Education.** 225 Scotland St. ☎ 0141/429-1202. Free admission. Mon–Sat 10am–5pm; Sun 2–5pm. Underground: Shiels Rd.

This branch of the Glasgow Museums and Art Galleries organization explores changing lifestyles in Glasgow for the past 4 centuries. In the activities workshop, children can take part in sessions that include weaving, archery, butter making, and sampler sewing.

**Provands Lordship.** Castle St., across from the Cathedral of St. Kentigern. ☎ 0141/552-8819. Free admission. Mon and Wed–Sat 10am–5pm; Sun 11am–5pm. Underground: Queen St. Station.

Built by Bishop Andrew Muirhead as a residence for churchmen, this is Glasgow's oldest house (1471) and the only pre-Reformation building of interest other than the cathedral. Over the years, it has been used as a pastry shop, a soda factory, the abode of Glasgow's city hangman, and a junk shop before it was turned into a museum. The museum houses 17th- and 18th-century furniture, tapestries, and pictures, as well as the key to Leven Castle in Tayside, where Mary Queen of Scots was imprisoned.

**Regimental Museum of the Royal Highland Fusiliers.** 518 Sauchiehall St. ☎ 0141/332-0961. Free admission. Mon–Thurs 9am–4:30pm; Fri 9am–4pm; weekends by appointment only. Tube: Buchanan St.

The collections in this regimental museum include medals, badges, uniforms, pictures, trophies, photographs, records, and memorabilia illustrating the history of the Royal Scots Fusiliers, the Highland Light Infantry, the Royal Highland Fusiliers, and the Glasgow and Ayrshire regiment. Items date back some 300 years. Newer exhibits trace the history of the automobile, ships, trains, motorcycles, and football (soccer).

## ATTRACTIONS IN NEARBY PAISLEY

Paisley, 7 miles (11km) west of Glasgow, became a famous name in the weaving trade during the Industrial Revolution. The Paisley shawl was born here. Actually, the inspiration for the pattern came from India, but no matter—it's forever associated with this industrial town.

---

> ### ✪  Frommer's Favorite Glasgow Experiences
>
> **Touring the Burrell Collection.** The pièce de résistance of Glasgow (some say of Scotland), this gallery is the city's major attraction. See what good taste and an unlimited budget can acquire in a lifetime.
>
> **Following Walkways and Cycle Paths.** Greater Glasgow has an array of trails and bike paths cutting through areas of historic interest and scenic beauty, including the Paisley/Irvine Cycle and Walkway, 17 miles (27km) of unused railway line converted to a trail.
>
> **Riding the World's Last Seagoing Paddle Steamer.** From spring to early fall, the *Waverley* makes day trips to scenic spots on the Firth of Clyde, past docks that once supplied more than half the tonnage of oceangoing ships. Call ☎ **0141/ 221-8152** for details.
>
> **Shopping Paddy's Market.** This daily market by the railway arches on Shipbank Lane gives you the real flavor of the almost-vanished Glaswegian style of street vending.

---

✪  **Paisley Abbey.** Abbey Close. ☎ **0141/889-7654.** Free admission. Mon–Sat 10am–3:30pm; Sun services year-round at 11am and 12:15pm, also at 6:30pm Sept–June. Take the Paisley train from Glasgow's Central Station.

One of the great attractions of Strathclyde, this church grew out of a Cluniac abbey founded in 1163. It was nearly demolished in 1307 on orders of Edward I of England but was subsequently reconstructed. In the mid–16th century, a tower fell in, causing great damage to the transept and choir. New work began around the turn of the 20th century, and by 1928 Paisley Abbey was restored, including a superb stone-vaulted roof. A chapel is dedicated to the monk, St. Mirin, who founded the town. You can also see an 11-foot-high (3.3m) Celtic cross from the 10th century.

**Paisley Museum and Art Galleries.** High St. ☎ **0141/889-3151.** Free admission. Tues–Sat 10am–5pm; Sun 2–5pm; public holidays 9am–5pm. Take the Paisley train from Glasgow's Central Station.

This museum is visited mainly because of its famous collection of Paisley shawls. This teardrop pattern dominated the world of fashion for some 70-odd years, and today the shawls are extremely valuable as collector's items. The museum has amassed these colorful textiles since 1905 and now has more than 700 examples. The museum also has a collection relating to the history of Strathclyde, along with some fine art and natural history displays.

## GARDENS & PARKS

Glasgow's **Botanic Garden,** Great Western Road (☎ **0141/334-2422;** Underground: Hillhead), covers 40 acres; it's an extensive collection of tropical plants and herb gardens. The garden is acclaimed especially for its spectacular orchids and begonias. It's open daily 7am to dusk. Admission is free.

**Linn Park,** on Clarkston Road (Bus: 24 or 36), is 212 acres of pine and woodland, with many scenic walks along the river. Here you'll find a nature trail, pony rides for children, an old snuff mill, and a children's zoo. The park is open daily 8am to dusk. **Gleniffer Braes Country Park** (☎ **0141/884-3794**), Glenfield Road, in Paisley, covers 1,300 acres of woodland and moorland and has picnic areas and an adventure playground. It's open daily dawn to dusk.

## ORGANIZED TOURS

The *Waverley* is the world's last seagoing paddle steamer, and from the last week of June to the end of August (depending on weather conditions), the Paddle Steamer Preservation Society conducts 1-day trips from Anderston Quay in Glasgow to historic and scenic places beyond the Firth of Clyde. As you sail along, you can take in what were once vast shipyards, turning out more than half the earth's tonnage of oceangoing liners. You're allowed to bring your own sandwiches for a picnic aboard, or you can enjoy lunch in the Waverley Restaurant. Boat tours cost £8 to £25 ($13.60 to $42.50). For details, contact **Waverley Excursions,** Waverley Terminal, Anderston Quay, Broomielaw (☎ 0141/221-8152).

There's also regular ferry service run by **Caledonian MacBrayne** (☎ 01475/650-100) in Gourock on the banks of the Clyde. The ferry stands close to the station in Gourock, connected to Glasgow Central Station by trains that leave every hour and take 30 to 45 minutes. The ferry service, which can take cars, runs every hour to the attractive seaside resort of Dunoon at the mouth of the Clyde. The journey takes about 20 minutes, and ferries run every hour from 6:20am to 8:20pm, April to October 16; in winter the service is less frequent and visitors are advised to check beforehand as it's liable to change. The round-trip costs £4.50 ($7.65) adults and £2.25 ($3.80) seniors/children.

The best Glasgow tours are run by **Scotguide Tours,** operated from the Strathclyde Passenger Centre at George Square, opposite the City Chambers (☎ 0141/204-0444; Underground: Buchanan St.). March 27 to October 11, departures are every half hour 9:30am to 4pm. The price is £7 ($11.90) adults, £5.50 ($9.35) students/seniors, and £2.50 ($4.25) children.

## 6  Special & Free Events

The **Glasgow International Jazz Festival** opens in the last days of June and usually runs through the first week of July. This festival has attracted some big names in the past, including the late Miles Davis and also Dizzy Gillespie. Tickets are available from the Ticket Centre, Candleriggs (☎ 0141/287-5511), but some free events are always announced.

On June 10, the **Bearsden** and **Milngavie Highland Games** are held at Burnbray in the small town of Milngavie (pronounced "Mill-guy"), 6 miles (10km) from Glasgow. The games include tug-of-war, wrestling, caber tossing, piping, and Highland dancing and offer a fun day out of the city. Call Cameron Wallace at ☎ 0141/942-5177 for details.

The **Glasgow Fair** (held during most of the month of July) is likely to have carnivals, tea dances, European circuses, Victorian rides, and even a country-and-western stampede. For information, call ☎ 0141/287-2000.

## 7  Sports & Outdoor Pursuits

**BIKING**    The tourist office (see "Visitor Information," in "Essentials," above) provides maps with detailed bicycle paths in the city; there are lots of scenic routes. Bicycle rentals are available from **West End Cycles,** 16–18 Chancellor St. (☎ 0141/357-1344; Underground: Kelvin Hall), charging £12 ($20.40) per day and requiring a deposit of £50 ($85) or two pieces of ID.

**GOLF**    Several courses are near Glasgow, but there's a limited number actually in the city itself. Two nine-hole courses are **Alexander Park,** Alexandra Parade (☎ 0141/556-1294), and **Knightswood,** Lincoln Avenue (☎ 0141/959-6358). Neither offers caddy service or rentals of clubs and carts. Both Alexander, a 2,281-yard (2,076m), par-31 course, and Knightswood, a 2,793-yard (2,542m), par-34 course, charge greens fees of £3.50 ($5.95) per round.

SPORTS COMPLEXES  The **Kelvin Hall International Sports Arena** is on Argyle Street (☎ 0141/357-2525; Underground: Kelvin Hall), near the River Kelvin. It offers volleyball and basketball courts, as well as an indoor track. Daily 9am to 10:30pm, you can use the weight room for £2.60 ($4.40) or the fully equipped gym for £3.85 ($6.55). This is also the country's major venue for national and international sports competitions. Look in the newspapers or check with the tourist office for any events planned at the time of your visit.

The outdoor **Crownpoint Sports Complex,** 183 Crownpoint Rd. (☎ 0141/ 554-8274; Bus 62 or 64), is another major setting for national and international tournaments. It has two artificial turf parks, an athletics park, and a track. Non-members can use the complex Monday to Friday 3 to 10pm and Saturday and Sunday 10am to 5pm. Use of the track costs £1.90 ($3.25), and the weight room goes for £2.60 ($4.40).

The city's newest center (opened 1993) is the **Scotstoun Leisure Centre,** James Drive, Scotstoun (☎ 0141/959-4000; Bus: 9, 44, 62, or 64), about 2 miles (3km) from the center. It's open Monday to Wednesday and Friday 9am to l0pm, Thursday 10am to 10pm, and Saturday and Sunday 9am to 6pm. There's an obligatory induction of £6 ($10.20) for anyone wanting to use the gym and entry thereafter is £3.85 ($6.55).

WATERSPORTS & ICE SKATING  The **Lagoon Leisure Centre,** Mill Street, Paisley (☎ 0141/889-4000), offers indoor facilities with a freeform pool with a wave machine, fountains, and flume. You'll also find sauna suites with sunbeds, Jacuzzis, and a Finnish steam room. The ice rink boasts an international ice pad with six curling lanes and is home to the Paisley Pirates ice hockey team. There are also bar and catering facilities. The center is open for swimming Monday to Friday 10am to 10pm and Saturday and Sunday 9:30am to 5pm. Monday 9 to 10pm it's adults only, and Wednesday 9 to 10pm it's women only. There are frequent trains throughout the day from Glasgow central station to Paisley.

The sauna facilities are open Monday to Friday 10am to 10pm, Saturday 9am to 10pm, and Sunday 9:30am to 5pm. Most days are segregated by gender, so it's important to call beforehand to make sure you're eligible to use the facilities. Ice skating is available Monday to Friday 9:30am to noon and Monday, Wednesday, and Thursday 1:30 to 4pm; Tuesday 12:30 to 3pm and 7:30 to 9:30pm; Friday 2:45 to 5pm and 7:30 to 10pm; Saturday and Sunday 10:45am to 12:45pm and 2:30 to 4:30pm. Admission is £2.35 to £3 ($4 to $5.10) adults and £1.80 to £2.30 ($3.05 to $3.90) children. Skate rental is 85p ($1.45). You can go swimming for £2.30 ($3.90) adults and £1.30 ($2.20) children. A combined ticket for the pool and skating rink goes for £4.10 ($6.95) adults and £3.10 ($5.25) children. Use of the sauna is £3.20 to £4.60 ($5.45 to $7.80).

## 8 Shopping

One of the major hunting grounds is **Sauchiehall Street,** Glasgow's fashion center, where many shops and department stores frequently offer good bargains, particularly in woolen goods. About 3 blocks long, this street has been made into a pedestrian mall. **Argyle Street,** which runs by the Central Station, is another major shopping artery.

All dedicated world shoppers know of **Buchanan Street,** a premier pedestrian thoroughfare. This is the location of the famed Fraser's Department Store (see below). From Buchanan Street you can also enter **Princes Square,** an excellent shopping complex with many specialty stores, restaurants, and cafes.

In the heart of Glasgow is the city's latest and most innovative shopping complex, the **St. Enoch Shopping Centre** (Underground: St. Enoch; Bus: 16, 41, or 44), whose merchandise is less expensive, but a lot less posh, than what you'd find at the Princes Square shopping center. You can shop under the biggest glass roof in Europe. The center is to the east of Central Station on St. Enoch Square.

The **Argyll Arcade** is at 30 Buchanan St. (Underground: Buchanan St.). Even if the year of its construction (1827) weren't set in mosaic tiles above the entrance, you'd still know this is an old collection of shops beneath a curved glass ceiling. The arcade contains what's possibly the largest single concentration of retail **jewelers,** both antique and modern, in Europe, surpassing even Amsterdam. It's considered lucky to purchase a wedding ring here.

Dedicated fashion mavens should take a trip to the **Italian Shopping Centre** (Underground: Buchanan St.), a small complex in The Courtyard, off Ingram Street, where most of the units sell clothes, including Versace, Prada, Gucci, and Armani.

The latest contribution to mall shopping has come in the form of the **Buchanan Galleries** (Underground: Buchanan St.), which connects Sauchiehall, Buchanan, and Argyll streets and was completed in 1999. This plush development includes an enormous **John Lewis department store** and the biggest **Habitat** in Europe—a nirvana for anyone wanting reasonably priced contemporary furniture or accessories.

**The Barras,** held Saturday and Sunday 9am to 5pm, takes place about a quarter of a mile (about .5km) east of Glasgow Cross. This century-old market has some 800 traders selling their wares in stalls and shops. You can not only browse for that special treasure but also become a part of Glasgow life and be amused by the buskers. **Paddy's Market,** by the rail arches on Shipbank Lane, operates daily if you'd like to see an old-fashioned slice of Glaswegian street vending.

General **shopping hours** are Monday to Saturday 9am to 5:30 or 6pm, depending on the merchant. On Thursdays, shops stay open to 8pm.

## ANTIQUES

**Victorian Village.** 53–57 W. Regent St. ☎ **0141/332-0808.** Bus: 23, 38, 45, 48, or 57.

This warren of tiny shops stands in a slightly claustrophobic cluster. Much of the merchandise isn't particularly noteworthy, but there are many exceptional pieces if you're willing to go hunting. Several of the owners stock reasonably priced 19th-century articles; others sell old jewelry and clothing, a helter-skelter of artifacts.

## ART

**Compass Gallery.** 178 W. Regent St. ☎ **0141/221-6370.** Bus: 23, 38, 45, 48, or 57.

This gallery offers refreshingly affordable pieces; you could find something special for as little as £40 ($68), depending on the exhibition. The curators tend to concentrate on local artists, often university students.

### Bring That Passport!

Take along your passport when you go shopping in case you make a purchase that entitles you to a **VAT (value-added tax)** refund.

**Cyril Gerber Fine Art.** 148 W. Regent St. ☎ **0141/221-3095.** Bus: 23, 38, 45, 48, or 57.

One of Glasgow's most respected art galleries veers away from the avant-garde, specializing in British paintings, sculptures, and ceramics crafted between around 1880 and today and Scottish landscapes and cityscapes. Cyril Gerber is a respected art authority with lots of contacts in art circles throughout Britain. Objects begin at around £200 ($340).

## BOOKS
**John Smith & Son.** 57 St. Vincent St. ☎ **0141/221-7472.** Bus: 6, 8, 9A, or 16.

This is a thoroughly Scottish bookshop, part of Scotland's cultural history. It has the best collection of specialized guides to Scotland and maps to the country.

## A DEPARTMENT STORE
**Fraser's Department Store.** Buchanan St. ☎ **0141/221-3880.** Underground: Buchanan St.

Fraser's is Glasgow's version of Harrods. A soaring Victorian-era glass arcade rises four stories, and inside you'll find everything from clothing to oriental rugs, from crystal to handmade local artifacts of all kinds.

## GIFTS & DESIGN
**Catherine Shaw.** 24 Gordon St. ☎ **0141/204-4762.** Underground: Buchanan St.

Named after the long-deceased matriarch of the family that runs the place today, Catherine Shaw is a somewhat cramped gift shop that has cups, mugs, postcards, and gift items based on the designs of Charles Rennie Mackintosh. There's also some highly evocative Celtic mugs called *quaichs* (welcoming cups or whisky measures, depending on who you talk to) and tankards in both pewter and silver. It's a great place for easy-to-pack and somewhat offbeat gifts. Look for another branch at 32 Argyll Arcade (☎ **0141/221-9038**); entrances to the arcade are on both Argyll and Buchanan streets.

**Mackintosh Shop.** In the foyer of the Glasgow School of Art, 167 Renfrew St. ☎ **0141/ 353-4526.** Underground: Buchanan St. or Cowcaddens.

This tiny shop prides itself on its stock of books, cards, stationery, coffee and beer mugs, glassware, and sterling-and-enamel jewelry created from the original designs of Charles Rennie Mackintosh.

Although the shop doesn't sell furniture, the staff will refer you to a craftsman of whose work they approve: **Bruce Hamilton, Furnituremaker,** 4 Woodcroft Ave., Broomhill (☎ **01505/322-550;** Bus: 6, 16, or 44), has been involved in the restoration of many Rennie Mackintosh interiors and has produced a worthy group of chairs, sideboards, and wardrobes authentic to Mackintosh's designs. Expect to pay around £250 ($425), not including upholstery fabric, for a copy of the designer's best-known chair (the Mackintosh-Ingram chair); there'll be a delay of at least a month before your furniture is shipped to your home.

**National Trust for Scotland Shop.** Hutcheson's Hall, 158 Ingram St. ☎ **0141/ 552-8391.** Underground: Buchanan St.

Drop in here for maps, calendars, postcards, pictures, dish towels, bath accessories, and kitchenware. Some of the crockery is in Mackintosh-design styles. The neoclassical building, constructed as a charity and hospice in 1806, is on the site of a larger hospice built in 1641.

## KILTS & TARTANS

✪ **Hector Russell.** 110 Buchanan St. ☎ **0141/221-0217.** Underground: Central Station.

Founded in 1881, Hector Russell is Scotland's oldest kiltmaker. This elegant store might be the most prestigious in Scotland. The welcome of the experienced sales staff is genuinely warm-hearted. Crystal and gift items are sold on street level, but the real heart and soul of the place is on the lower level, where you'll find impeccably crafted and reasonably priced tweed jackets, tartan-patterned accessories, waistcoats, and sweaters of top-quality wool for men and women. Men's, women's, and children's hand-stitched kilts are available.

## MUSIC

**Virgin Retail Music.** Unit 4, Lewis Building, Argyll St. ☎ **0141/221-0103.** Underground: St. Enoch.

The staff here is both knowledgeable and charming, eager to pass on their love of Scottish music. This outlet offers the biggest and best selections of records and tapes in the city, with special strengths and insights in both traditional and contemporary Scottish music.

## PORCELAIN & CRYSTAL

**Stockwell China Bazaar.** 67–77 Glassford St. ☎ **0141/552-5781.** Underground: St. Enoch.

This is Glasgow's largest purveyor of porcelain, its four floors bulging with Royal Doulton, Wedgwood, Noritake, and Royal Worcester, plus crystal stemware by many manufacturers. Anything you buy can be insured and shipped to whatever address you specify.

# 9 Glasgow After Dark

Glasgow, not Edinburgh, is the cultural center of Scotland, and the city is alive with performances. Before you leave home, check *Time Out's* latest round-up of who's playing in the clubs and concert halls; it's on the Web at **www.timeout.co.uk**. After you've arrived, pick up a copy of *Culture City* or *What's On* at the tourist office or your hotel. Both these monthly publications are free and usually contain complete listings of what's happening in Scotland's largest city. In addition, at most newsstands you can get a free copy of *The List,* published every other week. It details arts and other events for Edinburgh as well as Glasgow.

You can buy tickets to most cultural events at the **Ticket Centre,** City Hall, Candleriggs (☎ **0141/227-5511** or 0141/305-7500; Underground: St. Enoch). The box office sells tickets to at least a dozen theaters in the city. You can buy tickets in person Monday to Saturday 9:30am to 6:30pm and Sunday noon to 5pm. Phone reservations are accepted Monday to Saturday 9am to 9pm and Sunday noon to 5pm.

## THE PERFORMING ARTS

**OPERA & CLASSICAL MUSIC** The ✪ **Theatre Royal,** Hope Street and Road (☎ **0141/332-9000;** Underground: Cowcaddens; Bus: 23, 48, or 57), is the home of the **Scottish Opera** as well as of the **Scottish Ballet.** The theater also hosts visiting companies from around the world. Called "the most beautiful opera theatre in the kingdom" by the *Daily Telegraph,* it offers splendid Victorian Italian Renaissance plasterwork, glittering chandeliers, and 1,547 comfortable seats, plus spacious bars and buffets on all four levels. However, it's not the decor but the ambitious repertoire that attracts opera-goers. Ballet tickets run £5 to £32 ($8.50 to $54.40) and opera tickets £5.50 to £45.50 ($9.35 to $77.35). On performance days, the box office is open Monday to Saturday 10am to 7:30pm; on non-performance days, hours are Monday to Saturday 10am to 6pm.

In winter, the **Royal Scottish National Orchestra** offers Saturday-evening concerts at the **Glasgow Royal Concert Hall,** 2 Sauchiehall St. (☎ **0141/332-6633;** Underground: Buchanan St.). The **BBC Scottish Symphony Orchestra** presents Friday-evening concerts at the **BBC Broadcasting House,** Queen Margaret Drive (Underground: St. Enoch), or at **City Halls,** Albion Street (Underground: St. Enoch). In summer, the Scottish National Orchestra has a short Promenade season (dates and venues are announced in the papers). Tickets to all concerts are available at the **Ticket Centre** (see above) and cost £8 to £21 ($13.60 to $35.70).

**THEATER**   Although hardly competition for London's, Glasgow's theater scene is certainly the equal of Edinburgh's. Young Scottish playwrights often make their debuts here, and you're likely to see anything from Steinbeck's *The Grapes of Wrath* to Wilde's *Salome* to *Romeo and Juliet* done in Edwardian dress.

The prime symbol of Glasgow's verve remains the **Citizens Theatre,** Gorbals and Ballater streets (☎ **0141/429-0022;** Bus: 12 or 66), founded after World War II by James Bridie, a famous Glaswegian whose plays are still produced on occasion there. It's home to a repertory company, with tickets at £4 to £10 ($6.80 to $17). The box office hours are under revision, so call ☎ **0141/287-5511** to check. The company is usually closed June to the first week in August.

The **Glasgow Arts Centre,** 12 Washington St. (☎ **0141/221-4526;** Bus: 2, 4, or 21), always seems to be doing something interesting, including children's productions and other theatrical performances. It's open Monday to Friday 9:30am to 5pm and 6:30 to 10pm; in summer, it's closed in the evening. The center is funded by Glasgow Council and performances are free. The **King's Theatre,** 297 Bath St. (☎ **0141/ 248-5153;** Bus: 57), offers a wide range of productions, including straight plays, musicals, and comedies. During winter it's noted for its pantomime presentations. Tickets are £6 to £25 ($10.20 to $42.50), and the box office is open Monday to Saturday 10am to 6pm.

The **Mitchell Theatre,** 6 Granville St. (☎ **0141/287-5511;** Bus: 57), has earned a reputation for small-scale entertainment, ranging from dark drama to dance, as well as conferences and seminars. A small modern theater, it adjoins the well-known Mitchell Library. The theater box office is open when there are performances from 4pm until the show. Ticket prices vary with each production. The **Pavilion Theatre,** 121 Renfield St. (☎ **0141/332-1846;** Bus: 21, 23, or 38), specializes in modern versions of vaudeville (which, as they'll assure you around here, isn't dead). The Pavilion sells its own tickets for £8 to £15 ($13.60 to $25.50); they're not available at City Centre. The box office is open Monday to Saturday 10am to 8pm.

The **Tron Theatre,** 63 Trongate (☎ **0141/552-4267;** Underground: St. Enoch), occupies one of the three oldest buildings in Glasgow, the former Tron Church. The church, with its famous Adam dome and checkered history, has been transformed into a small theater presenting the best of contemporary drama, dance, and music events. The Tron also has a beautifully restored Victorian cafe/bar serving traditional home-cooked meals, including vegetarian dishes and a fine selection of beer and wine. The box office is open Monday to Saturday 10am to 6pm, over the counter and until 9pm by phone. Tickets are £3 to £8 ($5.10 to $13.60) adults and £3 to £4 ($5.10 to $6.80) children.

# THE CLUB SCENE

**The 13th Note.** 50–60 Glassford St. ☎ **0141/553-1638.** Bus: 21, 23, or 38.

This club has moved away from jazz in the past couple of years and now books mainly heavy rock bands on Tuesday, Wednesday, and Thursday nights; country and western on Monday. On Friday, Saturday, and Sunday, the night is dedicated to ambient and alternative music. It's a comfortably funky candlelit club with no cover for entertainment. Open daily noon to midnight.

**Barrowland.** Gallowgate. ☎ **0141/552-4601.** Underground: St. Enoch. Bus: 61 or 62. Cover £8–£20 ($13.60–$34), depending on performer.

This stripped-down hall seats 2,000 and opens only on nights shows are booked, usually 7 to 11pm, but some performances run to 2am. July and August are the quiet months, as most shows are geared toward a student audience that's on vacation then. Cover charges vary widely, and run highest when the hall hosts popular British bands like White Zombie or The Breeders.

**Fury Murry's.** 96 Maxwell St. ☎ **0802/538-550.** Underground: St. Enoch. Cover £2–£6 ($3.40–$10.20).

Most of the crowd here is made up of students looking for nothing more complicated than a good, sometimes rowdy, time listening to disco music that's upbeat but not ultratrendy. It's in a cellar, a 2-minute walk from the very central St. Enoch Shopping Centre. There's a very busy bar, a dance floor, and ample opportunities to meet the best and brightest in Scotland's university system. Jeans and T-shirts are the right garb. It's open Thursday to Sunday 10:30pm to 3:30am. Thursday and Friday features live bands and other nights are strictly for dancing or can be reserved for private parties.

**The Garage.** 490 Sauchiehall St. ☎ **0141/332-1120.** Underground: Buchanan St. Cover £5–£10 ($8.50–$17).

A big student crowd tests the limits of the 800-person capacity here on weekends. In the downstairs area, surrounded by rough stone walls, you get the impression you're in a castle with a Britpop and indie soundtrack. Most regulars, however, gravitate to the huge main dance floor, where lots of shiny metal fixtures stand out in contrast to the stone walls. There are three bars downstairs and two upstairs. Open daily 11pm to 3am.

**Grand Ole Opry.** 2–4 Govan Rd., Paisley Toll Rd. ☎ **0141/429-5396.** Bus: 23 or 23A. Cover £2.50–£10 ($4.15–$16.50).

In a sprawling sandstone building 1½ miles (2.5km) south of Glasgow's center, the Grand Ole Opry is the largest club in Europe devoted to country-western music. There's a bar and dancing arena on both levels and a chuck-wagon eatery serving affordable steaks and other such fare on the upper level. Live music is always performed from a large stage at the front. Performers are usually from the United Kingdom, but a handful of artists from the States turn up. Open Friday to Sunday and occasionally Thursday (if demand warrants it) 6:30pm to 12:30am.

**King Tut's Wah-Wah Hut.** 272 St. Vincent St. ☎ **0141/221-5279.** Bus: 6, 8, 9, or 16. Cover £4–£10 ($6.80–$17).

This sweaty, crowded rock bar has been in business for nearly a decade. It's a good place to check out the Glasgow music and arts crowd, as well as local bands and the occasional international act. Successful Scottish acts My Bloody Valentine and Teenage Fan Club got their start here. Open Monday to Saturday noon to midnight and Sunday 6pm to midnight.

**Nice 'n' Sleazy.** 421 Sauchiehall St. ☎ **0141/333-9637.** Bus: 23 or 48. Cover usually £3 ($5.10); higher if a big name is playing.

This club books live acts Thursday to Sunday. The cover is quite reasonable, but it can get more expensive if you catch a band like the Cranberries, Alice Donut, or Helmet. Holding some 200 patrons, it provides a rare opportunity to catch internationally popular bands in an intimate setting. Upstairs Sunday and Monday nights, DJs spin an eclectic mix of music for dancing, but most people come for the bands. Open daily 11:30am to 11:45pm.

**Renfrew Ferry.** 2 Clyde Place. ☎ **0169/826-5511.** Bus: 21, 23 38 45, 48, or 57. Cover £5.50 ($9.35).

This old car ferry that once provided service on the River Clyde now hosts a Friday-night *ceilidh* (hoe-down) with traditional Scottish music and dancing 9pm to 1am. Other musical acts are booked infrequently during the year.

**Victoria's Nightclub.** 98 Sauchiehall St. ☎ **0141/332-1444.** Underground: Buchanan St. Cover £8 ($13.60) for dance club only, £15.95 ($27.10) for dance club, cabaret, and buffet dinner.

Victoria's prides itself on being the only club in Scotland with cabaret performances. The building is on two floors of high-tech design in the heart of town, with a first-floor dance club and a second-floor cabaret bar/restaurant where singers, comedians, and other artistes amuse and titillate 10pm to 3am on Wednesday, Friday, and Saturday. Dress is smart casual, and the crowd tends to be people over 25, with a bit of money and sophistication. The dance club is open Wednesday to Sunday 10:30pm to 3am and the cabaret Wednesday, Friday, and Saturday 7:30pm to 3am.

## FAVORITE PUBS

**Bon Accord.** 153 North St. ☎ **0141/248-4427.** Bus: 6, 8, or 16.

This amiably battered pub is a longtime favorite. There's an array of hand-pumps—a dozen devoted to real British ales, the rest to beers and stouts from the Czech Republic, Belgium, Germany, Ireland, and Holland. The pub is likely to satisfy your taste in malt whisky as well, and offers affordable bar snacks. Open Monday to Saturday till midnight, Sunday till 11pm.

**Cask and Still.** 154 Hope St. ☎ **0141/333-0980.** Bus: 21, 23, or 38.

Here's the best place for sampling malt whisky. You can taste from a selection of more than 350 single malts, at a variety of strengths (perhaps not on the same night) and maturities (that is, years spent in casks). Many prefer the malt whisky that has been aged in a sherry cask. There's good bar food at lunch, including cold meat salads and sandwiches. Open Monday to Thursday till 11pm, Friday and Saturday till midnight.

✪ **Corn Exchange.** 88 Gordon St. ☎ **0141/248-5380.** Bus: 21, 23, or 38.

Opposite the Central Station, this place was really the Corn Exchange in the mid–19th century but now is one of Glasgow's most popular pubs. Amid dark paneling and high ceilings, you can enjoy a pint of lager till 11pm Sunday to Wednesday, till midnight Thursday to Saturday. Affordable pub grub is served daily noon to 9pm.

**L'Attaché.** 27 Waterloo St. ☎ **0141/221-3210.** Bus: 21, 23, or 48.

One of several traditional Scottish pubs in its neighborhood, L'Attaché is outfitted with stone floors and rows of decorative barrels. At the self-service food counter you can order cheap steak pie, lasagna, and salads; at the bar you can order from an impressive array of single malts. There's a disco on Friday and Saturday nights and a live jazz band on Saturday afternoons. Open Monday to Thursday till 11pm, Friday and Saturday till midnight.

## THE GAY SCENE

There's no strongly visible lesbian bar or nightclub scene in Glasgow. Many lesbians who attend bars frequent those that cater mainly to males.

**Bennet's.** 90 Glassford St. ☎ 0141/552-5761. Underground: St. Enoch. Cover £2–£6 ($3.40–$10.20).

A floor above street level in a building a short walk from the Central Station and George Square, Bennet's is one of the major gay/lesbian nightclubs in town. On certain nights (especially Tuesday) it's the most fun and crowded gay disco in Scotland. The crowd includes men and women 17 to 60, and the music plays on and on, interrupted only by the occasional drag show. Performers are usually imported from London or the States; shows last about 30 minutes and begin after 1am Wednesday and Saturday. Open Wednesday to Sunday 11pm to 3:30am.

**C. D. Frost.** 8–10 W. George St. ☎ 0141/332-8005. Underground: Buchanan St.

Named after the British actress, currently married to actor Jude Law, C. D. Frost is a busy bar catering primarily to a trendy young mixed crowd. It's minimalist chic, with low lighting. Drag acts are occasionally featured, but it's better known for the Wednesday-night quiz, kept in check by resident lesbian Karen Dunbar. Karaoke on Thursday and Sunday offers you the chance to murder a few old faves. Open daily till midnight.

**Court Bar.** 69 Hutcheson St. ☎ 0141/552-2463. Underground: Buchanan St.

This small, cozy pub is a popular meeting place for a gay/lesbian crowd to come together for drinks and talk. The pub gets decidedly more male after 7pm and is a good starting point for a gay evening on the town. Open daily till midnight.

**Waterloo Bar.** 306 Argyle St., near the Central Station. ☎ 0141/221-7359. Underground: Buchanan St.

The friendly bartenders here are a good source of info about what's happening in the gay scene. Attracting a slightly older crowd, Waterloo gets most packed during happy hour (9pm to midnight), when you can make your drink a double for just £2.50 ($4.25). Open daily till midnight.

## 10 Side Trips from Glasgow: The Best of the Strathclyde Region

As Sir Walter Scott dominates the Borders, the presence of Robert Burns is felt in the Strathclyde region around Ayr and Prestwick. A string of famous seaside resorts stretches from Girvan to Largs. Some of Britain's greatest golf courses, including Turnberry, are here, and Prestwick, of course, is the site of one of Scotland's airports.

Glasgow makes a good gateway to Burns Country, as it has excellent bus and rail connections to Ayr, which is your best bet for exploring the area. If you're driving, take A77 southwest from Glasgow to Ayr. Prestwick and Troon link directly north of Ayr along the coastal road.

### AYR: A POPULAR WEST COAST RESORT

The royal burgh of Ayr is the most popular resort on Scotland's west coast. It's 81 miles (130km) southwest of Edinburgh, 35 miles (56km) southwest of Glasgow, and 5 miles

## Backpacking the West Highland Way

One of Scotland's most legendary long-distance footpaths is the **West Highland Way** (see "The Best Hikes" in chapter 1, "The Best of Scotland"), set aside by the government in 1967 to preserve its beauty. It begins north of Glasgow in the town of Milngavie and winds its way for 95 miles (153km) north along Loch Lomond with its bonnie, bonnie banks. The trail continues through Glencoe, site of a famous passage, and goes on to Fort William and eventually to Ben Nevis, Scotland's highest mountain. The most dramatic part of this walk is from the Bridge of Orchy to Glencoe.

Trains run frequently throughout the day from the Queen's Street railway station in Central Glasgow to Milngavie, starting point of the walk. The 15-minute trip costs £2 ($3.40) one way. For more information and a map of this footpath, contact the **Scottish Tourist Board,** 23 Ravelston Terrace, Edinburgh EH4 3EU (☎ **0131/ 332-243;** Underground: Buchanan St.).

---

(8km) south of Prestwick. A busy market town, it offers 2½ miles (4km) of beach (alas, pollution has spoiled them) and is a manufacturing center for fabrics and carpets, so you might want to allow time to browse through its shops. With its steamer cruises, fishing, golf, and racing, Ayr faces the Isle of Arran and the Firth of Clyde.

For centuries, Ayr has been associated with horse racing, and it now boasts the top racecourse in Scotland. One of the main streets of the town is named Racecourse Road for a stretch near the town center.

Trains from Glasgow's Central Station (call ☎ **0345/484-950**) will whisk you to Ayr. The 50-minute trip costs £4.95 ($8.40). From Glasgow, Stagecoach Express buses arrive in Ayr in 1½ hours, costing £4.95 ($8.40) one way. For departure info, call ☎ **01292/613-500.**

The **Ayr Tourist Information Centre** is at Burns House, Burns Statue Square (☎ **01292/288-688**). Easter to August, it's open Monday to Saturday 9:15am to 6pm (July and August also Sunday 10am to 5pm); September to Easter, hours are Monday to Saturday 9:15am to 5pm.

### SEEING THE SIGHTS

Ayr is full of Burns associations. The 13th-century **Auld Brig o' Ayr,** the poet's "poor narrow footpath of a street / Where two wheelbarrows tremble when they meet" was renovated in 1910.

On Blackfriar's Walk on the banks of the River Ayr, the **Auld Kirk of Ayr** dates from 1653–55, when it replaced the 12th-century Church of St. John, which had been seized by Cromwell and dismantled. Its greatest curiosity is a series of "mort safes" in the cemetery dating from 1655—they were grimly used to cover freshly filled graves to discourage body-snatchers. Robert Burns was baptized in the kirk. The church is open Monday to Saturday 8:30am to 7pm and Sunday noon to 7pm.

The **Wallace Tower,** on High Street, is another attraction, rising some 112 feet (34m). Constructed in 1828, it has a statue of William Wallace (remember *Braveheart?*) by local sculptor James Thom. Tradition holds that Wallace was imprisoned here and made a daring escape.

Another architectural curiosity is **Loudoun Hall** (☎ **01292/616-183**), Boat Vennal, at the junction of Hope and High Streets, off Cross Street, in the heart of town. A wealthy merchant had this townhouse constructed in the late 1400s, and it's one of the oldest examples of burgh architecture left in the country. Mid-July to the end of August, it's open Monday to Saturday 11am to 6pm.

# Side Trips from Glasgow

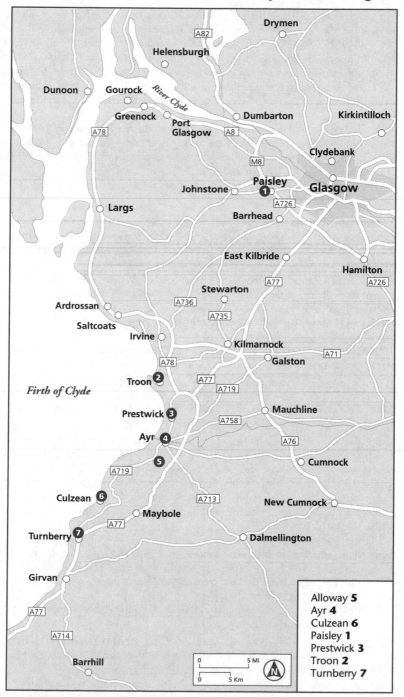

Alloway **5**
Ayr **4**
Culzean **6**
Paisley **1**
Prestwick **3**
Troon **2**
Turnberry **7**

About 1½ miles (2.5km) south of Ayr off the road to the Burns Cottage at Alloway (below), the **Maclaurin Gallery and Rozelle House,** on Monument Road in Rozelle Park (☎ 01292/443-708), are installed in what had been stables and servants' attached to a manor house. A Henry Moore bronze sculpture and a major collection of contemporary art are on display, as well as changing exhibits of sculpture, paintings, and crafts. A nature trail winds through the woodland. You can visit Monday to Saturday 10am to 5pm; April to October, it's also open Sunday 2 to 5pm. Admission is free.

About 1½ miles (2.5km) north of the town center, the **Ayr Racecourse** (☎ 01292/ 264-179) is open year-round. Races are usually held Friday, Saturday, and Monday, generally at 2:15pm. Peak racing season is May to October, with jumping events held every year in November, January, and April.

There are three nearby golf courses; the best is the municipal **Belle Isle Golf Course** (☎ 01292/441-258).

## ACCOMMODATIONS

**Caledonian Hotel.** Dalblair Rd., Ayr, Ayrshire KA7 1UG. ☎ **01292/269-331.** Fax 01292/ 610-722. 118 units. TV TEL. £105 ($178.50) double; £140 ($238) suite. AE, DC, MC, V. Free parking.

The 1970s Caledonian is a few hundred yards from Ayr's seashore and 500 yards (455m) from the rail station. It offers large refurbished guest rooms with radios, hair dryers, and tea/coffeemakers; many have sea views.

**Dining:** Hudson's Bar and Grill is a lively place to meet and eat, with a selection of freshly roasted joints on the captain's table.

**Amenities:** The hotel boasts a fully equipped leisure complex/health club and is near several championship golf courses. Laundry/dry cleaning, 24-hour room service.

✪ **Fairfield House.** 12 Fairfield Rd., Ayr, Ayrshire KA7 2AR. ☎ **01292/267-461.** Fax 01292/261456. E-mail: fairfield-hotel@demon.co.uk. 43 units. TV TEL. £130 ($221) double; £160 ($272) suite. Rates include Scottish breakfast. AE, DC, MC, V. Free parking.

On the seafront near Low Green, this 1912 Edwardian townhouse built for a Glaswegian tea merchant has been restored to its original elegance and converted into Ayr's best hotel. The staff is especially attentive and will help you arrange tee times at nearby golf courses. Noted designer of classic British interiors, Lady Henrietta Spencer-Churchill, created the public and guest rooms in a country-house style. The guest rooms are large, comfortable, and luxurious, often decorated with chintz; they contain amenities like luxury mattresses, trouser presses, and hair dryers, and most of the bathrooms have bidets.

**Dining:** The food at Fairfield has been called an oasis in a culinary desert. In the Conservatory, the best Scottish ingredients—from Highland lamb to Spey salmon— go into the food. Lunch and dinner are served, with main courses at £15 to £20 ($25.50 to $34). The Fleur de Lys serves dinner 7 to 9:30pm, with main courses running £20 to £27 ($34 to $45.90).

**Amenities:** 24-hour room service; laundry/valet; Leisure Club with pool, spa bath, sauna/steam room, solarium, gym.

**Pickwick Hotel.** 19 Racecourse Rd., Ayr, Ayrshire KA7 2TD. ☎ **01292/260-111.** Fax 01292/ 285-348. 15 units. TV TEL. £70 ($119) double. Rates include Scottish breakfast. AE, MC, V. Free parking.

It may seem odd to have a hotel commemorating a character in a Charles Dickens novel in a town noted for its memories of Rabbie Burns, but this late-Victorian hotel, directly east of the Esplanade, does just that. Each routine but clean guest room is of a decent size and bears a Dickensian title; all rooms have radios, hair dryers, trouser presses, and tea/coffeemakers.

In the paneled Pickwick Club, you can soak up the Dickensian atmosphere and enjoy the simple but fresh food. From 5 to 7pm, a fixed-price high tea is served for £7.95 ($13.50), and from 7 to 9pm the à la carte menu offers main courses at £6.50 to £11 ($11.05 to $18.70). Baby-listening devices are installed, dry cleaning/laundry is available, and room service is 24 hours.

**Quality Station Hotel.** Burns Statue Square, Ayr, Ayrshire KA7 3AT. ☎ **01292/263-268.** Fax 01292/262-293. E-mail: admin@gb624.v-net.com. 75 units. TV TEL. £83 ($141.10) double; £105 ($178.50) suite. AE, DC, MC, V. Free parking.

The Station has been an Ayr landmark since 1888. Connected to the town's rail station, it sits behind a red-sandstone exterior, and although it isn't the most modern hotel in town, many visitors consider its high ceilings, elaborate detailing, and old-world charm more than enough reason to check in. Many of the guest rooms are quite spacious but routinely furnished, sometimes with minibars. There's a moderately priced restaurant and a cocktail bar. The hotel's health club offers a gym, solarium, sauna, and Jacuzzi.

**Savoy Park Hotel.** 16 Racecourse Rd., Ayr, Ayrshire KA7 2UT. ☎ **01292/266-112.** Fax 01292/611-488. www.savoypark.com. E-mail: mail@savoypark.com. 15 units. TV TEL. £75–£95 ($127.50–$161.50) double. Rates include breakfast. AE, MC, V. Free parking. Follow A70 for 2 miles, go through Parkhouse St., turn left into Beresford Terrace, and make first right onto Bellvue Rd.

For more than 30 years, the Henderson family has welcomed guests to their classic country hotel, which was designed in the Victorian and Scottish baronial style, with red sandstone walls. The atmosphere is traditional, with paneled walls and ornate ceilings, but modern conveniences have been discreetly added. The more expensive rooms (the superior bedrooms) are large and more charming; the cheaper rooms are smaller and filled with functional pieces. All rooms, however, have soft, warm colors, and include such amenities as hair dryers, beverage makers, and irons.

Evoking a Highland hunting lodge, the Oak Room serves fresh produce and time-tested dishes such as baked lemon sole or medallions of pork fillet with carmelized apple cake. In the Monarch Lounge guests gather to enjoy drinks or bar meals. The Savoy Park is a short drive from 30 first-rate golf courses, and fishing is also possible nearby.

## DINING

**Fouter's Bistro.** 2A Academy St. ☎ **01292/261-391.** Reservations recommended. Main courses £5–£6 ($8.50–$10.20) at lunch, £9–£14.50 ($15.30–$24.65) at dinner; fixed-price lobster lunch (in season only) £14.50 ($24.65). AE, DC, MC, V. Tues–Sat noon–2pm and 6:30–10:30pm. MODERN SCOTTISH.

In the historic heart of Ayr, this restaurant occupies the cellar of what was an 18th-century bank, retaining the original sandstone floor and a vaulted ceiling covered in terra-cotta tiles. Owners Fran and Laurie Black offer you their warm hospitality. The restaurant's name derives from Scottish argot: *foutering about* is a charming way of saying "bumbling about" (although this place is anything but bumbling). The seamless service focus on modern Scottish cuisine with a nod to Thailand. You can sample the likes of venison with rowanberry sauce, local Gresshingham duck with black-cherry sauce, and seafood that includes whatever's fresh, served with saffron cream sauce. One of the most delicious items featured in spring is the organically reared lamb from the neighboring Carrick Hills.

# Robert Burns: National Poet & Penniless Genius

*And, wow! Tam saw an unco sight!*
*Warlocks and witches in a dance:*
*Nae Cotillion, brent new frae France,*
*But hornpipes, jigs, strathspeys, and reels,*
*Put life and mettle in their heels.*

—Robert Burns, *Tam o' Shanter*

Scotland's national poet, Robert Burns (1759–96), or Rabbie, carried the Scottish vernacular to its highest point in his satiric, earthly, and bawdy romantic poems and songs. Born in Alloway in Ayrshire on a wind-tossed night, Burns was the son of an impoverished gardener who encouraged him to read and seek an education. Burns became an unsuccessful farmer and later a taxman, but the world knows him as the "heaven-taught ploughman," author of the narrative masterpiece *Tam o' Shanter* and the humanitarian *A Man's a Man for A' That.*

Rabbie was a great womanizer ("Once heartily in love, never out of it") who fathered at least 15 children, 9 of whom were legitimate. In his short time on earth, he wrote about 370 poems and songs, only to die at age 37, wracked with rheumatic fever and harassed by his debtors for the sum of £5. His pregnant wife, Jean, had to beg a shilling from the poet's brother to feed her children on the day of his funeral.

Every year on his birthday, January 25, the poet is honored all over the world—from Edinburgh to San Francisco, from Bombay to Tokyo—at male-dominated Bachelors' Clubs like the one founded by Burns and his friends. Even Shakespeare doesn't get this kind of attention. At these Burns suppers, guests who are entitled get to wear kilts; non-Scottish admirers of the poet dress formally. After a dram of whisky is drunk as a welcome, the first course, or *Het Hail,* is carried in; it's invariably cock-a-leekie soup, made with chicken and leeks. Next comes *Caller Fish Frae Loch and Sea,* usually fresh salmon. But for the main course, there can be no deviation in the menu: It must be the Great Chieftan o' the Puddin' Race, the dreaded haggis. The chef comes in bearing the haggis on a large platter, preceded by a kilted piper playing "Scotland the Brave." Of course, everyone drinks a whisky to the health of the haggis—after all, a small nip is known as *usquabaugh* ("water of life").

The chairman of the club—again, after a quaff of whisky—takes out a Scottish dirk and recites Burns's "Address to a Haggis" before plunging the blade into the beast. Out gushes the meat, entrails, or whatever the chef decided to stuff into the sheep's stomach. This seasoned mix of minced meat, oatmeal, and onions is enjoyed by all the "bachelors."

The sad truth is that although haggis is consumed at all birthday celebrations for Burns, the poor poet missed out on it himself. He considered haggis "one of the most delicious meals on earth" but rarely could afford it, settling instead for *tatties* (mashed potatoes) or *neeps* (turnips).

---

**Tudor Restaurant.** 8 Beresford Terrace. ☎ **01292/261404.** Main courses from £5 ($8.50); fixed-price meal £4.90 ($8.35) for 2 courses, £5.50 ($9.35) for 3 courses; high tea £5–£8.50 ($8.50–$14.45). MC, V. Mon–Sat 9am–8pm; Sun noon–8pm. SCOTTISH/INTERNATIONAL.

This busy family-oriented restaurant has a real Tudor look with dark half-timbering. Most popular here are the fixed-price lunch and the high tea served 3:15pm to closing. The food items are well prepared and copious and include such rib-sticking specialties as a version of chicken Maryland (breaded and fried breast of chicken with bacon, tomatoes, peaches, and pineapple fritters). The restaurant, in an early-1900s building, is on Burns Statue Square.

## AYR AFTER DARK

The famous ✪ **Rabbie's Bar,** Burns Statue Square (☎ **01292/262-112**), mixes Scottish poetry with electronic music. The exposed stone of the walls is highlighted with the pithy verses of Robert Burns, who used to drop in for a pint of ale and conversation with his friends. A portrait of Rabbie is painted directly onto the wall. However, don't come here expecting poetry readings in a quiet corner. The crowd, while not particularly literary, is talkative and fun and enjoys live music several nights a week. There's a large selection of imported beers, a busy stand-up bar, long rows of crowded banquettes and copper-topped tables, and a large TV screen showing videos. It's open Monday to Saturday 11am to 12:30am and Sunday noon to midnight.

# ALLOWAY: BIRTHPLACE OF RABBIE BURNS

Some 2 miles (3km) south of Ayr, **Alloway** is where Scotland's national poet was born on January 25, 1759, in the gardener's cottage—the "auld clay biggin"—that his father, William Burns, built in 1757.

## SEEING THE SIGHTS

**Auld Brig Over the Ayr,** mentioned in *Tam o' Shanter,* still spans the river, and **Alloway Auld Kirk,** also mentioned in the poem, stands roofless and haunted not far away. The poet's father is buried in the graveyard of the kirk.

**Burns Cottage and Museum.** Alloway. ☎ **01292/441-215.** Admission (also includes admission to Burns Monument and Gardens, below) £2.80 ($4.75) adults, £1.40 ($2.40) children/seniors, £8 ($13.60) families (2 adults and 3 children). Apr–Oct daily 9am–6pm; Nov–Mar Mon–Sat 10am–4pm. Drive 2 miles (3km) south of Ayr on B7024.

The cottage still contains some of its original furniture, including the bed in which the poet was born. Chairs displayed here were said to have been used by Tam o' Shanter and Souter Johnnie. Beside the cottage in which the poet lived is a museum.

**Burns Monument and Gardens.** Alloway. ☎ **01292/441-215.** Admission, see Burns Cottage and Museum, above. Apr–Oct daily 9am–6pm; Nov–Mar Mon–Sat 10am–4pm, Sun noon–4pm. Drive 2 miles (3km) south of Ayr on B7024.

About half a mile (1km) from the Burns Cottage, this monument is a Grecian-style building erected in 1823, containing relics, books, and manuscripts associated with Robert Burns. The gardens, overlooking the River Doon, contain shrubs, some brought back from the Himalayas (especially the rhododendron) that are relatively rare. There's also some well-established topiary. Everything is small-scale but choice.

**Tam o' Shanter Experience.** Murdoch's Lane. ☎ **01292/443-700.** Admission £4.50 ($7.65) adults, £2.20 ($3.75) children/seniors. Daily 9am–6pm. Drive 2 miles (3km) south of Ayr on B7024.

Here, adjacent to the gardens of the Burns Monument, you can watch a multiscreen film on Burns's life, his friends, and his poetry. Information is available from the personnel, and there's a well-stocked gift shop plus a tearoom. The Russians are particularly fond of Burns and his poetry, and many come annually to visit the cottage to pore over his original manuscripts; the museum has been presented with a translation of the poem *Tam o' Shanter* by Russian enthusiasts.

## ACCOMMODATIONS & DINING

**Belleisle House Hotel.** Belleisle Park, Doonfoot Rd., Alloway, Ayr, Ayrshire KA7 4DU. ☎ **01292/442-331.** Fax 01292/445-325. 14 units. TV TEL. £75 ($127.50) double; £80 ($136) bridal suite. Rates include Scottish breakfast. AE, MC, V. Free parking. Drive 2 miles (3km) south of Ayr on A719.

Beside A719, this imposing 1755 country house stands in a public park noted for its two golf courses. It has a stone exterior and interior paneling with ornate carvings depicting some scenes from Burns's *Tam o' Shanter*, with blazing fireplaces adding to the traditional Scottish ambience. The guest rooms range from midsize to spacious, and each has traditional furnishings, including comfortable beds. The place extends a special welcome to children and has a play area set aside for them.

The hotel has two dining rooms: one inspired by the music room of Marie Antoinette at Versailles, the other by her bedroom. The Scottish cooking is excellent, with fixed-price lunches at £10.95 ($18.60) and dinners at £17 ($28.90).

**Brig o' Doon Hotel.** Alloway, Ayr, Ayrshire KA7 4PQ. ☎ **01292/442-466.** Fax 01292/441-999. www.castley-hotels.co.uk. E-mail: brigadoon@castley-hotels.co.uk. 5 units. TV TEL. £100 ($170) double. Rates include Scottish breakfast. AE, MC, V. Free parking. Drive 2 miles (3km) south of Alloway on B7024.

One of Scotland's most famous footbridges, the Brig o' Doon, is a few steps from this newish hotel, on the river's east bank. With 2 acres of gardens (so lovely that they often host weddings), this is the choice place to stay. Everything from the plumbing to the stylish guest rooms (with hair dryers) is state of the art. Reserve early, especially in summer.

## CULZEAN

Some 12 miles (19km) south-southwest of Ayr and 4 miles (6.5km) west of Maybole on A719 is Culzean Castle. Maidens Bus (no. 60) from the Sandgate Bus Station in Ayr runs to Culzean six times per day; a one-day round-trip ticket is £4.05 ($6.90) adults and £2 ($3.40) children.

✪ **Culzean Castle.** Overlooking the Firth of Clyde. ☎ **01655/884-455.** Admission (including entrance to the Country Park below) £7 ($11.90) adults, £5 ($8.50) seniors/children, £18 ($30.60) families (2 adults and 2 children). Apr–Oct daily 10:30am–5:30pm (last admission half an hour before closing). Closed Nov–Mar.

Built by famous Scottish architect Robert Adam at the end of the 18th century, this clifftop creation is a fine example of his castellated style, with a view to the south of Ailsa Craig, a 1,100-foot-high (334m) rounded rock 10 miles (16km) offshore, a nesting ground and sanctuary for seabirds. Culzean (pronounced Cul-*lane*) replaced an earlier Scots tower house as the family seat of the powerful Kennedy clan. In 1945, the castle and grounds were given to the National Trust for Scotland. It's well worth a visit and is of special interest to Americans because of General Eisenhower's connection—in 1946, the National Guest Flat was given to the general for his lifetime in gratitude for his services as supreme commander of Allied Forces in World War II. An exhibit of Eisenhower memorabilia, including his North African campaign desk, is sponsored by Scottish Heritage U.S.A., Inc. Culzean stands near the famous golf courses of Turnberry and Troon, a fact that particularly pleased the golf-loving Eisenhower. The tour also includes the celebrated round drawing room, delicately painted ceilings, and outstanding Adam's oval staircase.

**Culzean Country Park.** On the land surrounding Culzean Castle. ☎ **01655/760-269.** Admission included in admission to Culzean Castle. Daily 9am to dusk.

Part of the land surrounding the castle includes what in 1969 became the first country park in Scotland. The 565-acre grounds include a walled garden, an aviary, a swan pond, a camellia house, an orangery, an adventure playground, a newly restored 19th-century pagoda, as well as a deer park, miles of woodland paths, and beaches. It has gained an international reputation for its Visitor Centre (Adam's home farm) and related visitor and educational services. Up to 200,000 people visit the country park annually.

## TURNBERRY: WORLD-CLASS GOLF

On the Firth of Clyde, the little town of Turnberry, south of the castle, was part of the Culzean Estate, owned by the marquess of Ailsa. It began to flourish early in this century, when the Glasgow and South Western Railway developed rail service, golfing facilities, a recognized golfing center, and a first-class hotel.

From the original two 13-hole golf courses, the complex has developed into the two 18-hole courses, Ailsa and Arran, known worldwide as the ❂ **Turnberry Hotel Golf courses.** The Ailsa, one of the most exacting courses yet devised, has been the scene of numerous championship tournaments and PGA events. Come here for the prestige, but prepare yourself for the kind of weather a lobster fisherman in Maine might find daunting. (Its par is 70, its SSS, 72, and its yardage, 6,976 [6,348m].) Newer, and usually shunted into the role of also-ran, is the Arran Course. Call ☎ **01655/ 331-000** for details. Guests of the hotel get priority on the Ailsa course. The greens fee of £95 ($161.50) for guests, and £120 ($204) (Monday to Friday) or £150 ($255) (weekends) for nonguests, includes 18 holes on the Ailsa course and an 18-hole round on the less-desirable Arran course. Clubs rent for £35 ($59.50), and caddy service costs £25 ($42.50) plus tip. If you're not staying here, give them a call in the morning to check on any unclaimed tee-off times—but it's a long shot.

You might want to take a short drive east of Turnberry to see **Souter Johnnie's Cottage,** Main Road, in Kirkoswald (☎ **01655/760-603**), 4 miles (6.5km) west of Maybole on A77. This was the 18th-century home of the village cobbler, John Davidson (Souter Johnnie), who, with his friend, Douglas Graham of Shanter Farm, was immortalized by Burns in *Tam o' Shanter.* The cottage contains Burnsiana and contemporary cobbler's tools, and in the churchyard are the graves of Tam o' Shanter and Souter Johnnie. Good Friday to September, the cottage is open daily 11:30am to 5pm; October, hours are Saturday and Sunday 11:30am to 5pm. Off-season admittance is sometimes by appointment. Admission is £2 ($3.40) adults and £1.30 ($2.20) seniors/students/children.

A final sight is **Carleton Castle,** along A77 some 14 miles (22.5km) south of Culzean Castle and 3 miles (5km) south, following the coast, from the little seaside town of Girvan. In its heyday it was a watchtower, built to guard the coastline against invaders. A famous ballad grew out of a legend surrounding the castle: It was said to be the headquarters of a baron who married eight times. When this Bluebeard got tired of a wife, he pushed her over the cliff and found himself another. However, he proved no match for his eighth wife, May Cullean. "The Ballad of May Colvin" relates how she's supposed to have tricked and outlived him.

### ACCOMMODATIONS

**Malin Court Hotel.** Turnberry, Ayrshire KA26 9PB. ☎ **01655/331-457.** Fax 01655/ 331-072. www.malincourt.co.uk. E-mail: info@malincourt.co.uk. 18 units. TV TEL. £104–£124 ($176.80–$210.80) double. Rates include breakfast. AE, DC, MC, V. Free parking. Take A74 to Ayr exit, then A719 to Turnberry and Maidens.

On one of the most scenic strips of the Ayrshire coast, this well-run hotel fronts the Firth of Clyde and the Turnberry golf courses. It is not a great country house, but a serviceable, functional, and welcoming retreat with a blend of informality and comfort. Bedrooms, mostly medium in size, have excellent beds, radios, hair dryers, trouser presses, robes, and hospitality trays. The staff can arrange hunting, fishing, riding, sailing, and golf. The hotel's restaurant, Cotters, is one of the best in the area (see "Dining," below).

✪ **Turnberry Hotel, Golf Courses and Spa.** Maidens Rd., Turnberry, Ayrshire KA26 9LT. ☎ **01655/331-000.** Fax 01655/331-706. www.turnberry.co.uk. E-mail: turnberry@ westin.com. 132 units. TV TEL. £297–£318 ($504.90–$540.60) double; £375–£425 ($637.50–$722.50) suite. Rates include Scottish breakfast. AE, DC, MC, V. Free parking.

The 1908 Turnberry, 50 miles (80.5km) south of Glasgow on A77, is a remarkable and opulent Edwardian property. From afar you can see the hotel's white facade, red-tile roof, and dozens of gables. In World War II, it served as a military hospital but is once again one of Britain's grand hotels. The public rooms contain Waterford crystal chandeliers, Ionic columns, molded ceilings, and well-polished oak paneling. Each suite and guest room is furnished in unique early-1900s style and has a marble-sheathed bathroom with hair dryer. The rooms, which vary in size, open onto views of the lawns, forests, and (in some cases) Scottish coastline.

**Dining:** The three dining rooms have differing degrees of formality. Most elegant is the Turnberry Restaurant, serving traditional Scottish and French food, with fixed-price dinners at a whopping £48 ($81.60) for five courses. The Terrace Brasserie is part of the resort's spa facilities and serves light food; the Tappie Toorie Grill is head quarters for the golf facilities.

**Amenities:** Concierge; room service; laundry/valet; 24-hour gym equipment; tennis; Country Club and Spa with leisure center, Turkish bath, sauna, steam rooms, massage, and squash courts. Guests receive priority at the world-class Turnberry Golf Courses.

## DINING

**Cotters Restaurant.** In the Malin Court Hotel, Turnberry. ☎ **01655/331-457.** Reservations recommended. Set-price 2- and 3-course menus £16–£20 ($27.20–$34); lunch items £2–£7 ($3.40–$11.90). AE, DC, MC, V. Daily 12:30–2pm and 7:30–9pm. SCOTTISH.

Exemplary service, a senic location, and good food combine to make a winning combination. Chef Andrea Beach and her team use only the freshest and finest local ingredients. The modern, tasteful decor creates a casual, relaxed atmosphere. The lunch menu offers everything from melon slices to deep-fried haddock in beer batter. For dinner, you might start with melon and peaches glazed with an orange sabayon, or salmon and asparagus terrine with chive butter. For a main course, try the medallions of pork and apple fritter, or the baked Ayrshire lamb and chicken mousseline wrapped in filo pastery. Desserts are tempting and include chocolate and hazelnut tart, warm bread and plum pudding awash in a sea of vanilla sauce, and a fine selection of cheeses.

## PRESTWICK

Prestwick is the oldest recorded baronial burgh in Scotland, but most visitors know it for Prestwick Airport, 2 miles (3km) north of Ayr, 32 miles (51.5km) southwest of Glasgow, and 78 miles (125.5km) southwest of Edinburgh. It was once a big international airport but today is used mainly for charter flights. Prestwick is one of Scotland's most attractive resorts, with its sandy coastlines and golf courses. It opens onto views of Ayr Bay and the Isle of Arran.

Prestwick goes back to at least A.D. 983. The **Mercat Cross** stands outside what used to be the Registry Office and marks the center of the oldest part of Prestwick. Behind St. Ninian's Episcopal Church is **Bruce's Well.** The water from the well is reputed to have cured Robert the Bruce of leprosy.

**Beaches** line the seafront in the heart of Prestwick, but don't expect anything like the Caribbean—it's all very foggy and temperamental, but bracing. The most desirable golf course in Prestwick is the **Nicholas Golf Club,** Grangemuir Road (☎ 01292/ 477-608).

Trains from the Central Station in Glasgow leave hourly from Prestwick; call ☎ 0345/ 484-950 in Glasgow for details. Buses from the Buchanan Street Station in Glasgow leave hourly for Prestwick; call ☎ 0990/808-080. From Glasgow, motorists take A77 southwest. The **tourist office** is at nearby Ayr.

## ACCOMMODATIONS & DINING

**St. Nicholas Hotel.** 41 Ayr Rd., Prestwick, Ayrshire KA9 1SY. ☎ **01292/479-568.** Fax 01292/475-793. 12 units. TV TEL. £54 ($91.80) double. Rates include Scottish breakfast. AE, DC, MC, V. Free parking.

This stone Edwardian, on the main road between Prestwick Airport and the train station, is about a 5-minute walk from tennis courts, a pool, and indoor bowling. The hotel has full central heating and double-glazed windows. The moderately sized standardized guest rooms contain tea/coffeemakers, and hair dryers are available on request. The back rooms opening onto the park are quieter; those in front open onto the main road with its traffic. Good food and service prevail in the dining room, where lunch, high tea, and dinner are available.

## TROON & THE ROYAL TROON GOLF CLUB

The resort town of **Troon,** 7 miles (11km) north of Ayr, 31 miles (50km) southwest of Glasgow, and 77 miles (124km) southwest of Edinburgh, looks out across the Firth of Clyde to the Isle of Arran. It's a 20th-century town, its earlier history having gone unrecorded. Troon takes its name from the curiously shaped promontory jutting out into the Clyde estuary on which the old town and the harbor stand. The promontory was called Trwyn, the Cymric word for "nose," and later this became Trone and then Troon. A massive statue of *Britannia* stands on the seafront as a memorial to the dead of the two world wars.

Troon offers several golf links, including the **Royal Troon Golf Club,** Craigend Road, Troon, Ayrshire KA10 6EP (☎ 01292/311-555). This is a 7,097-yard (6,458m) course (one of the longest in Scotland) with an SSS of 74 and a par of 71. Dignified Georgian and Victorian buildings and the faraway Isle of Arran are visible from fairways, which seem deliberately designed to steer your golf balls into the sea or the dozens of sand traps flanking your shot. The Old Course is the more famous, reserved for men. Non-members may play only on certain days. A newer addition, the 6,289-yard (5,723m), par-71 Portland, is open to both men and women and is by some estimations even more challenging than the Old Course. The British Open has been played here off and on since 1923. The greens fee—£125 ($212.50) for a day— includes a buffet lunch and two 18-hole sets. For one round of play, a trolley rents for £4 ($6.80) and a caddy £25 ($42.50); club rental is £20 ($34) per round or £35 ($59.50) per day.

In summer, visitors find plenty of room on Troon's 2 miles (3km) of **sandy beaches** stretching along both sides of its harbor; the broad sands and shallow waters make it a safe haven. From here you can take steamer trips to Arran and the Kyles of Bute.

Trains from Glasgow's Central Station arrive at the Troon station several times daily (trip time: 40 min.). Call ☎ **0345/484-950** for 24-hour information. Trains also connect Ayr with Troon, a 10-minute ride. Buses and trains from Glasgow cost £3.90 ($6.60) each way. From the Ayr bus station, you can reach Troon and other parts of the area by bus, costing £1.25 ($2.15) each way. Call ☎ **0990/808-080** for details. From Prestwick, motorists head north along B749.

## ACCOMMODATIONS

You might want to stay at **Highgrove House** (see "Dining," below).

✪ **Lochgreen House Hotel.** Monktonhill Rd. Southwood, Troon, Ayrshire KA10 7EN. ☎ **01292/313-343.** Fax 011292/317-661. www.costley-hotels.co.uk. E-mail: Lochgreen@ costley-hotels.co.uk. 15 units. TV TEL. £160 ($272) double. Rates include breakfast. AE, MC, V. Free parking. Take B749 to Troon.

Adjacent to the fairways of the Royal Troon Golf Course, one of Scotland's loveliest country-house hotels is set in 30 lush acres of forest and landscaped gardens. The property, under the guidance of its owners, Bill and Catherine Costley, opens onto views of the Firth of Clyde and Ailsa Craig. The interior evokes a more elgant bygone time, with detailed cornices, antique furnishings, and elegant oak or cherry paneling. Guests meet and mingle in two luxurious sitting rooms with log fires, or take long walks on the well-landscaped grounds. The spacious, tasteful, comfortable, and luxurious bedrooms are well equipped with the finest mattresses, beverage makers, and hair dryers. Some of the bedrooms were converted from a stable block, but they are equally as luxurious as the older units. Antiques fill the house, enhanced by beautiful and well-chosen fabrics.

**Dining:** The cuisine is one of the reasons to stay here, or enough of a reason to call for a reservation for dinner if you're a nonguest. See "Dining," below, for a full review.

**Amenities:** Rooom service, baby-sitting, tennis courts, business facilities. The staff will arrange tee times on the Royal Troon Golf Course.

**Piersland House Hotel.** 15 Craigend Rd., Troon, Ayrshire KA10 6HD. ☎ **01292/314-747.** Fax 01292/315-613. 28 units. TV TEL. £119 ($202.30) double; £135–£165 ($229.50–$280.50) suite. Rates include Scottish breakfast. AE, DC, MC, V. Free parking. Drive 3 minutes south of the town center on B749.

This three-story country Victorian was built a century ago by Sir Alexander Walker of the Johnnie Walker whisky family. The importation of 17,000 tons of topsoil transformed its marshy surface into a lush 4-acre garden. The highest prices are for a superior twin (a four-poster double) or a cottage suite (with a bedroom, sitting room, and bathroom) adjacent to the hotel. The moderately sized guest rooms have traditional Scottish country-house styling and such amenities as hair dryers and radios. Full room service is available on request. The hotel and its public rooms are popular as a place to celebrate large birthday parties and wedding receptions.

**Dining/Diversions:** This place is better known as a social center than as a hotel. At lunch and in the evening, folks flock to the ✪ **Walker Bar** for a drink or buffet lunch. On sunny days, the staff sets up tables at the edge of the formal garden, turning it into an outdoor version of a neighborhood pub. The hotel's food is among the best in the area and is served in the Walker Bar and the brasserie. A fixed-price Saturday dinner is £24.50 ($41.65) and might include local scallops and chicken in white-wine sauce. Monday to Friday, there's an à la carte menu and main courses at £10 to £15 ($17 to $25.50).

**Amenities:** Room service, baby-sitting, croquet. The staff will arrange tee times at the Royal Troon Golf Course.

## DINING

You might want to dine at the **Piersland House Hotel** (see "Accommodations," above).

**Fairways Restaurant/Rizzio's Restaurant.** In the Marine Highland Hotel, 8 Crosbie Rd. ☎ **01292/314-444.** Reservations required. Fairways Restaurant main courses at lunch £8.95–£12.95 ($15.20–$22); fixed-price table d'hôte 4-course dinners £25–£27.50 ($42.50–$46.75). Rizzio's Restaurant main courses £6.95–£13 ($11.80–$22.10); pizza and pasta buffet £4–£6.75 ($6.80–$11.50). AE, DC, MC, V. Fairways daily noon–2pm and 7–9:30pm. Rizzio's daily noon–2:30pm and 5:30–10pm. Buffet daily noon–2:30pm and 5:30–7pm. SCOTTISH/INTERNATIONAL.

This landmark 1890s hotel containing two restaurants stands on the Ayrshire coast overlooking the Royal Troon Golf Course. Either can satisfy your hunger pangs with some degree of style. Rizzio's is a cozy wood-paneled dark-red Italian eatery. The more formal Fairways provides a proper and somewhat reserved setting for panoramic views of the Isle of Arran. Here you can enjoy traditional Scottish and French cuisine like pillows of smoked Scottish salmon, followed by rosettes of fillet of Scottish beef in peppercorn sauce or turbot with langoustines or shrimp.

**Highgrove House.** Old Loan's Rd., Troon, Ayrshire KA10 7HL. ☎ **01292/312-511.** Reservations recommended. Main courses £6–£12 ($10.20–$20.40) at lunch, £12–£14 ($20.40–$23.80) at dinner. AE, MC, V. Daily noon–2:30pm and 6–9:30pm. Drive 2 miles (3km) north of Troon on A78. TRADITIONAL SCOTTISH.

This white-painted, red-roofed brick building is charming, isolated on a hillside known for its scenic view over the sea and the Isle of Arran. Its bustling restaurant moves big crowds in and out quickly. Menu items include several varieties of steamed salmon, accompanied by a changing array of sauces and such garnishes as crayfish or shrimp; médaillons of Angus beef with rondelles of pâté and peppercorn sauce; and médaillons of Scottish venison with rowanberry sauce.

Upstairs are nine average-sized simple but comfortable guest rooms with TVs, phones, and hair dryers; breakfast included, they rent for £85 ($144.50).

✪ **Lochgreen House Hotel Restaurant.** Monktonhill Rd., Southwood. ☎ **01292/313-343.** Reservations required. Set-price menu £20 ($34) for a 3-course lunch; £30 ($51) for a 4-course dinner. AE, MC, V. Daily noon–2pm and 7–9pm. Take B749 to Troon. SCOTTISH/FRENCH.

Chef Andrew Costley and his skilled team aim to please, tempting you with the finest seafood, game, and prime Scottish beef. The setting of the elegant dining room, with its views of woodland and garden, makes the food taste even better somehow. Everything conspires to make this one of the most agreeable culinary stopovers in the region. The service is as flawless as the food. For a main course, and for flair and technique, sample the poached halibut on a mussel and fennel stew with saffron potatoes and chives. Or savor the flavor of the confit leg of duckling wrapped in pancetta and served with rocket and a thyme vinegar essence. The wine list roams the world for inspiration, and the desserts are freshly made, often using the fresh fruit of the season.

# 7

# Argyll & the Southern Hebrides

The old county of Argyll (in Gaelic, *Earraghaidheal*, "coastland of the Gael") on and off the coast of western Scotland is a rewarding journey. Summers along the coast are usually cool and damp and winters relatively mild but wet, with little snow.

The major center of Gaelic culture for the district is **Oban** ("small bay"), a great port for the Western Isles: the gateway to Mull, largest of the Inner Hebrides; to the Isle of Iona, the cradle of Scottish Christianity; and to Staffa, where Fingal's Cave inspired Mendelssohn to write the *Hebrides Overture* (for these islands, see chapter 11, "The Hebridean Islands"). A number of colorful destinations are near the port town of Oban, including **Port Appin** and **Inveraray,** where you can soak up the atmosphere of this region in a more rural setting.

There are several island destinations off the Argyll coast meriting your time. The long **peninsula of Kintyre** separates the islands of the Firth of Clyde, including **Arran,** from the islands of the Inner Hebrides, notably **Mull, Islay,** and **Jura.** (For information on Mull, see chapter 11.)

From the Isle of Islay to the Mull of Kintyre, the climate is mild. The land is rich and lush, especially on Arran. The peat deposits on Islay lend flavor to the making of such fine malt whiskies as Lagavulin, Bruichladdick, and Laproaig. There's a diversity of scenic beauty: hills and glens, fast-rushing streams, and little roads that eventually lead to coastal villages displaying B&B signs in summer. The unspoiled and remote island of Jura is easily reached from Islay.

And the best news for last: These islands, as well as the Kintyre peninsula, are among the best travel bargains in the British Isles.

## Driving Through the Region

The ideal way to tour the Argyll Peninsula is by car. Take A82 north-west from Glasgow to the western Highlands. You can also drive to the Kintyre Peninsula (A816 from Oban, heading south). Destinations around Kintyre can be reached by one of the Caledonian MacBrayne ferries.

**Day 1** From the Scottish mainland at Ardrossan, southwest of Glasgow, head west on a car ferry to **Brodick,** capital of the **Isle of Arran.** Overnight there or pick one of the adjoining villages. See the island's major attraction, Brodick Castle. The ferry arrives in less than an hour. From Brodick, you can head south along A841, which goes around

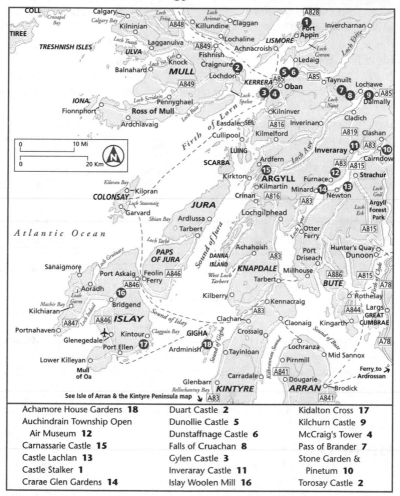

# Argyll & the Southern Hebrides

| | | |
|---|---|---|
| Achamore House Gardens **18** | Duart Castle **2** | Kidalton Cross **17** |
| Auchindrain Township Open Air Museum **12** | Dunollie Castle **5** | Kilchurn Castle **9** |
| Carnasarie Castle **15** | Dunstaffnage Castle **6** | McCraig's Tower **4** |
| Castle Lachlan **13** | Falls of Cruachan **8** | Pass of Brander **7** |
| Castle Stalker **1** | Gylen Castle **3** | Stone Garden & Pinetum **10** |
| Crarae Glen Gardens **14** | Inveraray Castle **11** | Torosay Castle **2** |
| | Islay Woolen Mill **16** | |

the entire island, passing all the attractions of major interest, before bringing you back to Brodick.

**Day 2**   Leave Brodick the next morning and head to the ferry terminal at Lochranza. Here you can cross the Kilbrannan Sound by car ferry from the north of Arran, landing at Claonaig on the **Kintyre Peninsula.** Take B842 south to the capital of **Campbeltown** for the night. After checking into a hotel there, follow B842 south to the fabled **Mull of Kintyre** at the southern tip for an afternoon's exploration.

**Day 3**   In the morning, drive northwest along A83 to Tayinloan, where a 20-minute car ferry crosses the Sound of Gigha to the **Isle of Gigha.** Since there are so few roads here, you may want to leave your car parked and explore the island by bicycle (rentals available near where the ferry docks). After spending most of the day exploring this ancient island and its famous gardens, return to Kintyre for the night and drive north along the western coast (A83) to the fishing port of Tarbert for an overnight stop.

**Day 4**   From Kennacraig on the Kintyre Peninsula, take a 2½-hour trip across the bay to Port Ellen on the **Isle of Islay** (summer only). To see Islay, take A846 north to

Brigend and then northeast to Port Askaig. You can find accommodations there or at several other places on the island.

**Day 5**   Take the short ferry crossing at Port Askaig and spend the day exploring the **Isle of Jura.** You can overnight there in its one hotel or return to Islay.

**Day 6**   From Islay, return to the peninsula of Kintyre and go along A83 north toward Inveraray. You can explore the western coast of **Loch Fyne** before arriving at **Inveraray,** where you can view its castle.

**Day 7**   Head northeast from Inveraray along A819 for an overnight stay at **Dalmally.** Use this day to explore both the eastern and the western shores of scenic **Loch Awe.**

**Day 8**   Take A85 west to **Oban** and arrive before lunch—plenty of time to view its numerous attractions, including some of the highlights in the environs, especially the Crinan Canal and the old capital of Dunadd.

## 1  The Isle of Arran: Scotland in Miniature

Brodick: 74 miles (119km) W of Edinburgh, 29 miles (47km) W of Glasgow

At the mouth of the Firth of Clyde, the Isle of Arran is often described as "Scotland in miniature" because of its wild and varied scenery—the glens, moors, lochs, sandy bays, and rocky coasts that have made the country famous. Once you're on Arran, buses will take you to various villages, each with its own character. A coast road, 60 miles (97km) long, runs around the length of the island.

Arran boasts some splendid mountain scenery, notably the conical peak of **Goatfell** in the north, reaching a height of 2,866 feet (869m), called the "mountain of the winds." Arran is also filled with beautiful glens, especially **Glen Sannox,** in the northeast, and **Glen Rosa,** north of Brodick. Students of geology flock to Arran to study igneous rocks of the Tertiary. Cairns and standing stones at Tormore intrigue archaeologists as well. The island is only 25 miles (40km) long and 10 miles (16km) wide and can be seen in 1 day.

## ESSENTIALS

**GETTING THERE**   High-speed electric trains operate from Glasgow Central direct to Ardrossan Harbour, taking 1 hour and costing £4.20 ($7.15) one way. For 24-hour rail inquiries, call ☎ **0345/484-950.** (If you're driving from Glasgow, head southwest along A737 until you reach Ardrossan.) At Ardrossan, you must make a 30-minute ferry crossing to Arran, arriving in Brodick, Arran's main town, on its east coast.

In summer, a small ferry runs between Lochranza in the north of Arran across to Claonaig in Argyll, providing a gateway to the Highlands and a visit to Kintyre. There are six boats daily, and the fare is £46.30 ($78.70) for a vehicle, plus £8.20 ($13.95) per passenger for a return journey. For information about ferry departures (which change seasonally), check with **Caledonian MacBrayne** (☎ **0990/650-000**) at the ferry terminal in Gourock.

**VISITOR INFORMATION**   The **tourist office** is at The Pier, Brodick (☎ **01770/ 302-140**). June to August, it's open Monday to Saturday 9am to 7:30pm and Sunday 10am to 5pm; September to May, hours are Monday to Saturday 9am to 5pm.

## EXPLORING THE ISLAND

After the ferry docks at Brodick, you may want to head for Arran's major sights, **Brodick Castle** and the **Isle of Arran Heritage Museum** (see below).

# The Isle of Arran & the Kintyre Peninsula

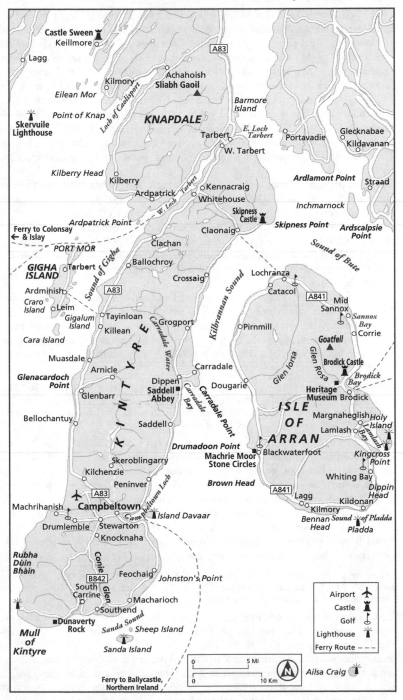

Castle Sween
Keillmore

Lagg

Kilmory

Eilean Mor

Achahoish
Sliabh Gaoil

A83

Barmore
Island

Point of Knap

KNAPDALE

Skervuile
Lighthouse

Loch of Caolisport

Tarbert
W. Tarbert

E. Loch
Tarbert

Portavadie

Glecknabae
Kildavanan

Kilberry Head

Kilberry

Ardpatrick

Kennacraig
Whitehouse

Ardlamont Point

Straad

Skipness
Castle

Inchmarnock

Ferry to Colonsay
& Islay

Ardpatrick Point

W. Loch Tarbert

Claonaig

Skipness Point

Ardscalpsie
Point

PORT MÒR

GIGHA
ISLAND

Tarbert

Clachan

Ballochroy

Crossaig

Sound of Gigha

Sound of Bute

Lochranza
Catacol

A841

Mid
Sannox

Sannox
Bay
Corrie

Ardminish
Craro
Island

Leim

Gigalum
Island

A83

Tayinloan
Killean

Grogport

Carradale Water

Kilbrannan Sound

Pirnmill

Goatfell

Glen Iorsa

Glen Rosa

Brodick Castle

Brodick
Bay

Cara Island

Muasdale

Arnicle

Carradale

Dougarie

Heritage
Museum

Brodick

Glenacardoch
Point

Glenbarr

Dippen
Saddell
Abbey

Carradale Bay

Carradale Point

ISLE
OF
ARRAN

Margnaheglish

Lamlash

Holy
Island

Bellochantuy

K I N T Y R E

Saddell

Drumadoon Point
Machrie Moor
Stone Circles

Brown Head

Blackwaterfoot

Lamlash Bay

Kingcross
Point

Skeroblingarry

Kilchenzie

Peninver

Campbeltown Loch

A841

Whiting Bay

Dippin
Head

Machrihanish

A83

Campbeltown

Drumlemble

Stewarton

Island Davaar

Lagg

Kilmory

Kildonan

Knocknaha

Bennan
Head

Sound of Pladda

Rubha
Dùin
Bhàin

Conie Glen

B842

Feochaig

Johnston's Point

Pladda

South
Carrine

Macharioch

Southend

Dunaverty
Rock

Sanda Sound

Sheep Island

Mull
of
Kintyre

Sanda Island

| | |
|---|---|
| Airport | ✈ |
| Castle | ♜ |
| Golf | ⛳ |
| Lighthouse | 🗼 |
| Ferry Route | - - - |

0          5 Mi

0          10 Km

N

Ferry to Ballycastle,
Northern Ireland

Ailsa Craig

The best way to discover the island's beauty is to stroll around. Right beyond the Isle of Arran Heritage Museum, at the point where String Road divides the island, you can follow the signs to a beauty spot called **Glen Rosa.** This is the island's loveliest glen, and you might want to pick up the makings of a picnic lunch before setting out. Another great walk is to the village of **Corriegills,** which is signposted along A841 south of Brodick. As you stroll, you'll be treated with the finest views of Brodick Bay.

The most intriguing walks on the island are signposted. But if you're really serious about hiking, buy one of two detailed guides at the tourist office—*Seventy Walks in Arran* for £2.50 ($4.25) and *My Walks in Arran* for £2.25 ($3.80). While at the office, ask about any guided walks the Forestry Commission might be conducting. They are scheduled frequently in summer and range from 2 to 5 hours, costing £2 to £4 ($3.40 to $6.80).

If you'd prefer to do your exploring on two wheels, stop by **Mr. Bilsland,** The Gift Shop, Brodick (☎ **01770/302-272**). You'll pay a £10 ($17) deposit; rental rates include a helmet and are £7.50 to £8.50 ($12.75 to $14.45) daily or £25 to £30 ($42.50 to $51) weekly. It's open daily 9am to 6pm. **Brodick Cycles,** Brodick (☎ **01770/302-460**), requires a £5 to £25 ($8.50 to $42.50) deposit, depending on the type of bike. Daily rentals range from £5 to £9.50 ($8.50 to $16.15), with £17 to £36 ($28.90 to $61.20) for a full week. It's open Monday to Saturday 9am to 6pm and Sunday 10am to 6pm.

South from Brodick is the village/resort of **Lamlash,** opening onto Lamlash Bay. From here, a ferry takes you over to Holy Island with its 1,000-foot (303m) peak. A disciple of St. Columba founded a church on this island. In the north, **Lochranza** is a village with unique appeal. It opens onto a bay of pebbles and sand, and in the background lie the ruins of a castle that reputedly was the hunting seat of Robert the Bruce.

✪ **Brodick Castle.** 1½ miles (2.5km) north of the Brodick pierhead. ☎ **01770/302-202.** Admission to both castle and gardens £6 ($10.20) adults, £4 ($6.80) seniors/students. Children 18 and under free. Castle Apr–Oct daily 11am–4:30pm (to 5pm July– Aug); gardens and Country Park daily 11am–sunset. Bus: Any labeled "Brodick Castle."

The historic home of the dukes of Hamilton, this red-sandstone castle dates from the 13th century and contains superb silver, antiques, portraits, and objets d'art. Some castle or other has stood on this site since about the 5th century, when the Dalriad Irish, a Celtic tribe, came here and founded their kingdom. The castle is the property of the National Trust for Scotland and boasts award-winning gardens. Laid out in the 1920s by the duchess of Montrose, they're filled with shrubs, trees, perennials, and herbs from Tasmania, New Zealand, Chile, the Himalayas, and northern Britain. Especially noteworthy are the rhododendrons, which are one of the focal points of the Country Park (semi-domesticated forest) bordering the more formal gardens.

**Isle of Arran Heritage Museum.** Rosaburn, 1½ miles (2.5km) north of the Brodick ferry piers. ☎ **01770/302-636.** Admission £2 ($3.40). Apr–Oct Mon–Sat 10am–5pm, Sun 11am–4pm. Bus: Any labeled "Brodick Castle."

A compound of antique structures once used as outbuildings for the nearby castle, this museum provides the best overview of life on Arran from prehistoric times to the present. The most prominent of the buildings is a stone-sided cottage filled with 19th-century memorabilia, costumes, and artifacts, including a working kitchen. Also on site is a blacksmith's shop and forge, an area containing geological artifacts, and an archive room and small library housing some of the historic records associated with Arran and the castle. Access to the archive room is reserved for bona fide scholars pursuing academic research.

## SHOPPING

Divided into three businesses, the **Duchess Court Shops,** Home Farm, Brodick (☎ 01770/302-831), is made up of the Home Farm Kitchen, selling locally produced chutneys, jams, and marmalades; the Nature Shop, dealing in books, jewelry, wood carvings, puzzles, T-shirts, and other assorted goods; and Something Special, selling natural grooming products. Located 6 miles (10km) north of Brodick in Corrie, **Corriecraft & Antiques,** Hotel Square (☎ 01770/810-661), sells small Arran antiques and pottery.

In Lamlash, **Patterson Arran Ltd.,** The Old Mill (☎ 01770/600-606), offers chutneys, mustards, preserves, and other locally produced condiments. The **Old Byre Showroom,** Auchencar Farm (☎ 01770/840-227), 5 miles (8km) north of Blackwaterfoot along the coastal road in Machrie, sells sheepskin, leather, and tweeds, but its biggest draw is the large selection of locally produced handknit and machine-knitted wool sweaters.

## ACCOMMODATIONS
### IN BRODICK

✪ **Auchrannie Country House Hotel.** Auchrannie Rd., Brodick, Isle of Arran KA27 8BZ. ☎ 01770/302-234. Fax 01770/302-812. www.auchrannie.co.uk. E-mail: Info@auchrannie. co.uk. 28 units. MINIBAR TV TEL. £122 ($207.40) double with breakfast; £162 ($275.40) double with half-board. AE, MC, V.

Acclaimed as the island's finest hotel and restaurant, this Victorian mansion (once the home of the dowager duchess of Hamilton) also features the best resort facilities. In its pristine glory, it stands on 6 acres of landscaped gardens and woods about a mile (1.5km) from the Brodick ferry terminal. The restoration here was done with taste and imagination. The guest rooms in the extended new wing are the most comfortable, but all rooms are furnished with taste, using select fabrics and decorative accessories and offering radios, hair dryers, and tea/coffeemakers.

**Dining/Diversions:** You can enjoy drinks in the cocktail bar or sun lounge before heading for the Garden Restaurant, which offers fixed-price dinners—pricey, but the finest on Arran. The chef is really in his element when preparing West Coast seafood. Nonguests should reserve ahead. You can also enjoy Brambles Bistro, offering a wide range of snacks and tasty food throughout the day and evening.

**Amenities:** Concierge, room service, baby-sitting, laundry, indoor pool, turbo spa, Turkish bath, sauna, solarium, snooker room, salon.

✪ **Kilmichael Country House Hotel.** Brodick, Isle of Arran KA27 8BY. ☎ 01770/302-219. Fax 01770/302-068. 9 units. TV TEL. £120 ($204) double; £150 ($255) suite. Rates include Scottish breakfast. V.

The island's most scenically located house, the Kilmichael was awarded the prestigious "Country House Hotel of the Year" award by A Taste of Scotland in 1998. It's said to be the oldest house on the island, perhaps once a stamping ground for Robert the Bruce, complete with some reports of a resident ghost. A combination of the tasteful new and the antique is used throughout. The guest rooms are beautiful, as are the bathrooms, with luxury beauty products and hair dryers. The aura of gentility is reflected in the log fires and fresh flowers from the garden. Most important, the staff is helpful and welcoming.

**Dining:** The food is also noteworthy, using local produce whenever possible. International dishes are featured, and fine wines and an attention to detail go into the expensive fixed-price menus.

## IN LAMLASH

**Glenisle Hotel.** Shore Rd., Lamlash, Isle of Arran KA27 8LS. ☎ **01770/600-559.** Fax 01770/600-966. 13 units. TV TEL. £34 ($57.80) per person with Scottish breakfast; £94 ($159.80) double with half-board. MC, V. Take the Whiting bus from Brodick.

Across the road from the waterfront, Glenisle could be one of the oldest buildings in the village, but no one knows its age or even the century of its construction. The well-kept gardens of this white-sided B&B, with a view across the bay to the Holy Isle, have flower beds and tall old trees. The reception lounge, water-view dining room, and lounge where drinks are available are cheerfully decorated. Each relatively simple but comfortable guest room has flowered curtains, a radio, electric blankets, and a tea/coffeemaker. Hair dryers are available at reception. A fixed-price three-course dinner here costs £16 ($27.20).

## IN WHITING BAY

**Grange House Hotel.** Whiting Bay, Isle of Arran KA27 8QH. ☎/fax **01770/700-263.** 9 units, 7 with private bathroom. TV. £55 ($93.50) double without bathroom; £70 ($119) double with bathroom. Rates include Scottish breakfast. MC, V.

Opening onto views across the Firth of Clyde, this country-house hotel is operated by Janet and Clive Hughes, who take a personal interest in their guests and have an extensive background in catering. A gabled stone house, standing on landscaped grounds, the Grange offers tastefully furnished traditional guest rooms. Some rooms can be arranged to accommodate a family, and one downstairs room is suitable for travelers with disabilities. Eight rooms open onto views of Holy Isle and the Ayrshire coast. The hotel also has a sauna and a spa bath. They no longer serve an evening meal but are happy to make dinner reservations for you in the village.

**Royal Hotel.** Whiting Bay, Isle of Arran KA27 8PZ. ☎/fax **01770/700-286.** 6 units. TV TEL. £50 ($85) double or suite. Rates include Scottish breakfast. No credit cards. Closed Nov–Mar. Take the Whiting bus from Brodick.

This pleasingly proportioned granite house, whose upper stories have been sheathed in white stucco, was built in 1895 as one of the first hotels on Arran. It's located right in the center of the village beside the coastal road. True to its original function as a temperance hotel, it serves no alcohol, but dinner guests can bring bottles of their own wine or beer into the dining room, which serves moderately priced three-course dinners daily at one sitting. Guests enjoy a vista over the bay and its tidal flats from some of the guest rooms. Although all rooms are the same price, one contains a four-poster bed and lots of chintz and another has a small sitting room adjacent to its sleeping area. All come with tea/coffeemakers and hair dryers.

## IN KILDONAN

**Kildonan Hotel.** Kildonan, Isle of Arran, KA27 8SE. ☎ **01770/820-207.** Fax 01770/820-320. 22 units, 6 with private bathroom. £48 ($81.60) double without bathroom; £56 ($95.20) double with bathroom. Rates include Scottish breakfast. No credit cards.

Built as an inn in 1760, with a section added in 1928, the hotel rises a few steps from the island's best beach. It's in Scottish farmhouse style, with a slate roof, white-painted stone walls, and ample views of seabirds and gray seals basking on the rocks of Pladda Island opposite. The Kildonan is owned by Maurice Deighton, his wife, Audrey, and their sons and daughters-in-law, any of whom you're likely to find cooking, tending one of the two bars, or cleaning the guest rooms. They can arrange diversions like putting, boating, fishing, table tennis, water-skiing, and scuba diving for you. The rooms range from small to midsize and are traditionally furnished, with comfortable beds.

The spacious dining room serves moderately priced dinners; less formal lunches and dinners are served in the bar. A specialty available in either setting is crab or lobster salad made from shellfish caught by one of the Deighton sons. A crowd of locals is likely to compete in a friendly fashion over the dartboard and billiards tables in the pub.

## IN BLACKWATERFOOT

**Kinloch Hotel.** Blackwaterfoot, Isle of Arran KA27 8ET. ☎ **01770/860-444.** Fax 01770/ 860-447. www.kinloch-arran.com. E-mail: kinloch@com.co.uk. 51 units. TV TEL. £64 ($108.80) per person with half-board (Scottish breakfast and dinner); £115 ($195.50) suite. AE, DC, MC, V. Take the Blackwaterfoot bus from Brodick.

This hotel, made from two joined cream-colored Victorian buildings, appears deceptively small from the road. It's actually the largest building in the village of Blackwaterfoot, with a contemporary wing jutting out along the coast. The midsize guest rooms are modestly comfortable and conservative, each with an intercom, excellent mattress, and tea/coffeemaker. Most of the double rooms have sea views, but the singles tend to look out over the back gardens. On the premises are a sauna, solarium, gym, squash court, heated indoor pool, and large dining room.

# DINING
## IN BRODICK

The two hotels reviewed above also have fine restaurants.

**Creelers Seafood Restaurant.** The Home Farm, Brodick. ☎ **01770/302-810.** Reservations recommended. Set-price lunch £8.50–£10.50 ($14.45–$17.85); main courses £7–£13 ($11.90–$22.10) at lunch, £10–£17 ($17–$28.90) at dinner. MC, V. Tues–Sun noon–2:30pm and 6:30–10pm. SCOTTISH.

Several years ago, the 1920s-era dairy farm associated with Brodick Castle, about a mile (1.5km) north of the center of Brodick Village, was transformed into a mini-compound of gift shops and bistros. The most appealing of these is Creelers, a family-run enterprise specializing in seafood. The enterprise includes a "smokery" where salmon, scallops, and duck breast are carefully smoked and served almost immediately. You won't go wrong ordering any of the versions of smoked salmon, presented with capers and horseradish or with mushroom-studded risotto. In a cheerful yellow-and-green dining room, you'll find some of the freshest seafood in Scotland, much of it pulled in from local fishing boats that day. Especially appealing are seared Arran scallops with monkfish and pesto and Scottish lobster with herb-flavored butter sauce.

---

### Seeing the Argyll on Horseback

There's no better way to experience the majestic beauty of the moors, highlands, and headlands in the Argyll area than on horseback. To arrange an outing, contact the **Ardfern Riding Centre,** Croabh Haven, Loch Gilphead, Argyll (☎ **01852/ 500-632**). A 1-hour ride costs £14 ($23.80), a 2-hour ride £24 ($40.80), and a 3-hour ride (with lunch) £35 ($59.50). In addition to maintaining around 16 horses and a working cattle-and-sheep farm between Oban and Loch Gilphead, the center has a cottage that groups of up to eight equestrians can rent at £250 ($425) per week. They cater to British as well as Western riding and have a good supply of boots and hats. The proprietor, Nigel Boase, is a wealth of knowledge and is happy to share ideas and suggestions on possible routes. The center is open all year, but the best time to go is May to the beginning of June and September to October.

## IN LAMLASH

**Carraig Mhor.** Lamlash. ☎ **01770/600-453.** Reservations recommended. Fixed-price menus £18 ($30.60) for 2 courses, £22.50 ($38.25) for 3 courses. MC, V. Mon–Sat 7–9pm. Closed 2 weeks in Jan and first 2 weeks in Feb. Take the Whiting bus from Brodick. CONTINENTAL.

Carraig Mhor, in a modernized pebbledash (a mortar containing a mixture of pebbles) 1700s cottage in the village center overlooking the water, serves imaginative and beautifully presented dinners. You're welcomed by Austrian-born Peter Albrich and his British wife, Penny. The chef, who has had worldwide experience, makes extensive use of local produce, especially seafood and game. All bread and ice creams, among other offerings, are made on the premises. The menu changes seasonally, and there are separate dining rooms for smokers and nonsmokers.

## ARRAN AFTER DARK

Regulars gather in Brodick's pubs to talk, argue, and drink. The **Brodick Bar,** in the center but without a street address (☎ **01770/302-169**), is an old wooden pub open Monday to Saturday 11am to midnight. Drop in for some real Scottish ale and a bar meal of local seafood (meals are served daily noon to 2:30pm and 5:30 to 10pm). Featuring wood-and-leather chairs and walls hung with old photographs and riding gear, **Duncan's Bar,** also in the center but with no street address (☎ **01770/302-531**), keeps the same hours and serves real cask ales and lagers. Meals, available daily noon to 2pm and 5:30 to 8pm, always include a roast and seafood items.

## 2  The Kintyre Peninsula

The longest peninsula in Scotland, Kintyre is more than 60 miles (97km) in length, with scenery galore, sleepy villages, and miles of sandy beaches. It's one of the country's most unspoiled areas, owing perhaps to its isolation. Kintyre was ancient Dalriada, the first kingdom of the Scots.

If you drive all the way to the tip of Kintyre, you'll be only 12 miles (19km) from Ireland. Kintyre is joined to the mainland of Scotland by a narrow neck of land near the old port of Tarbert. The largest town on the peninsula is the port of Campbeltown, on the southeastern coast.

## AREA ESSENTIALS

**GETTING THERE    Loganair** (☎ **0141/889-1111** in Glasgow) makes two scheduled 45-minute flights a day from the Glasgow Airport to Campbeltown, the chief town of Kintyre.

From Glasgow, you can take buses to the peninsula (schedules vary seasonally). The trip takes 4 hours one-way and costs £10.50 ($17.85) each way. Inquire at the **Scottish City Link,** Buchanan Street Bus Station, Glasgow (☎ **0990/505-050**).

Kintyre is virtually an island unto itself, and the most efficient way to travel is by car. From Glasgow, take A82 up to the Loch Lomond side and cut across to Arrochar and go over the "Rest and Be Thankful" route to Inveraray (A83). Then cut down along Loch Fyne to Lochgilphead and continue on A83 south to Tarbert (see below), which can be your gateway to Kintyre. You can take A83 along the western coast or cut east at the junction of B8001 and follow it across the peninsula to B842, which you can take south to Carradale (see below). If your target is Campbeltown, you can reach it by either the western shore (much faster and a better road) or the eastern shore.

# TARBERT

A sheltered harbor protects the fishing port and yachting center of Tarbert, on a narrow neck of land at the northern tip of the Kintyre. It's between West Loch Tarbert and the head of herring-filled Loch Fyne and has been called "the world's prettiest fishing port."

*Tarbert* means "drawboat" in Norse and referred to a place where Vikings dragged their boats across land on rollers from one sea to another. In 1093, King Malcolm of Scotland and King Magnus Barelegs of Norway agreed the Western Isles were to belong to Norway and the mainland to Scotland. An island was defined as anything a Viking ship could sail around, so Magnus proclaimed Kintyre an island by having his dragon ship dragged across the mile (1.5km) of dry land from West Loch Tarbert on the Atlantic to East Loch Tarbert on Loch Fyne. After the Vikings gave way, Kintyre came under the control of the MacDonald lordship of the Isles.

## SEEING THE SIGHTS

The castle at Tarbert dates from the 13th century and was later extended by Robert the Bruce. The castle ruins, **Bruce Castle,** are on a hillock above the village on the south side of the bay. The oldest part still standing is a keep from the 13th century.

One of the major attractions of the peninsula is the remains of **Skipness Castle and Chapel,** at Skipness along B8001, 10 miles (16km) south of Tarbert, opening onto Loch Fyne. The hamlet was once a Norse village. The ruins of the ancient chapel and 13th-century castle look out onto the Sounds of Kilbrannan and Bute. In its heyday it could control shipping along Loch Fyne. A five-story tower remains.

Before striking out to visit the peninsula, consider stopping at the **Tairbeart Heritage Centre** (☎ **01880/820-190**), immediately south of the village. Through various artifacts and exhibits, it traces life on the peninsula that's now largely vanished. Costing £3 ($5.10), it's open daily 10am to 5pm.

## ACCOMMODATIONS

**Stonefield Castle Hotel.** Tarbert PA29 6YJ. ☎ **01880/820-836.** Fax 01880/820-929. 33 units. TV TEL. Sun–Thurs £134–£148 ($227.80–$251.60) double, Fri–Sat £144–£158 ($244.80–$268.60) double; Sun–Thurs £79 ($134.30) minisuite, Fri–Sat £87 ($147.90) minisuite. Rates include half-board. AE, MC, V.

Occupying a commanding position on 66 acres of wooded grounds and luxurious gardens 2 miles (3km) outside Tarbert, the Stonefield, with turrets and a steeply pitched roof, was built in the 19th century by the Campbells. The guest rooms come in a variety of sizes and are well appointed, each with a hair dryer and tea/coffeemaker. The laird collected the rarest plants from every corner of the Empire, and the gardens are one of the world's best repositories for more than 20 species of tree-size Himalayan rhododendrons, which in April are a riot of color. Book well in advance, as Stonefield has a large repeat crowd.

**Dining/Diversions:** The kitchen staff does its own baking, and meals feature produce from the hotel's garden, with dinner starting at a hefty £29.50 ($50.15). There's also a cocktail bar.

**Amenities:** Library, outdoor pool, sauna, yacht anchorage.

**West Loch Hotel.** Tarbert PA29 6YF. ☎ **01880/820-283.** Fax 01880/820-930. 7 units. TV. £57 ($96.90) double. Rates include Scottish breakfast. MC, V.

In a rustic setting beside A83, a mile (1.5km) southwest of town in low-lying flatlands midway between the forest and the loch, this stone inn was built during the 1700s as a staging post for coaches and for farmers driving their cattle to market. Painted white with black trim, it contains two bars and a handful of open fireplaces and wood-burning stoves. The small guest rooms are modestly furnished but comfortable, often with views of the estuary. Each provides a tea/coffeemaker and a hair dryer. The hotel contains a pub and a restaurant specializing in local seafood and game, using only the best local ingredients. The bar, open daily 11am to midnight, serves food at lunch and dinner; the restaurant serves dinner daily.

## DINING

**Anchorage Restaurant.** Harbour St., Quayside. ☎ **01880/820-881.** Reservations recommended. Main courses £9.95–£14.95 ($16.90–$25.40). MC, V. Daily 7–10pm. Closed Jan. SCOTTISH/SEAFOOD.

The Anchorage remains unpretentious despite its many culinary awards. Housed in a stone harborfront building that was once a customs house, it's run by Clare Johnson. Her daily menu includes such seafood dishes as king scallops sautéed with lemon-lime butter and brochette of monkfish with saffron rice. A selection of European wines is available to accompany your fish.

# CARRADALE

On the lusher eastern coast of Kintyre, 14 miles (22.5km) north of Campbeltown, Carradale is a small town opening onto the shores of Kilbrannan Sound. People come here to walk and relax; they can also go pony trekking, windsurfing, or picnicking in several scenic spots that have log tables and benches. **Carradale Beach** is equipped with facilities for watersports, and you can swim if you don't mind the chilly waters. The fishing fleet is anchored in the harbor, and herring boats set out from here each night.

Those interested in historic sites can seek out the ruins of **Saddell Abbey** along B842, 9 miles (14.5km) northwest of Campbeltown. This Cistercian abbey was built in the 12th century by one of the lords of the Isles. The walls of the original building remain, and there are several sculptured grave slabs.

**Wallis Hunter Designs,** The Steading (☎ **01583/431-683**), sells handcrafted gold and silver jewelry inspired by Celtic patterns and the designs of Charles Rennie Mackintosh. Hours are Monday to Friday 8:30am to 5pm and Saturday 9am to 1pm.

## ACCOMMODATIONS & DINING

**Carradale Hotel.** Carradale PA28 6RY. ☎/fax **01583/431-223.** www.carradalehotel.com. E-mail: carradaleh@aol.com. 16 units, 12 with private bathroom. TV. £50 ($85) double without bathroom, £70 ($119) double with bathroom. Rates include breakfast. MC, V.

Built around 1800, the Carradale was the first hotel to open on the eastern side of the peninsula. Set in a garden in the center of this hamlet opposite the War Memorial, it offers a comfortable high-ceilinged dining room, a lounge bar serving pub meals, small pleasantly furnished guest rooms, and squash courts. Fresh local produce, often from the hotel's garden, is used in the kitchen. Affordable bar meals are available at lunch and dinner; more expensive fixed-price menus are available in the restaurant at dinner.

# CAMPBELTOWN

Campbeltown is a fishing port and a resort at the southern tip of the Kintyre Peninsula, 176 miles (283km) northwest of Edinburgh and 135 miles (217km) northwest of Glasgow. Popularly known as the "wee toon," Campbeltown has long been linked with fishing and has a shingle beach. For one of the greatest walks on the peninsula, see Davaar Island, below.

The **tourist office** is at MacKinnon House, The Pier (☎ **01586/552-056**). Late June to mid-September, it's open Monday to Saturday 9am to 6:30pm and Sunday 11am to 5pm; mid-September to late October, hours are Monday to Friday 10am to

5pm and Sunday 10am to 4pm; late October to March, it's open Monday to Friday 10am to 4pm; April hours are Monday to Saturday 10am to 5pm; and May to late June, it's open Monday to Saturday 9am to 5pm and Sunday noon to 5pm.

## EXPLORING THE AREA

**Davaar Island,** in Campbeltown Loch, is accessible at low tide by those willing to cross the Dhorlin, a half-mile (1km) run of shingle-paved causeway; boat trips are also possible (ask at the tourist office). Once on the island, you can visit a **crucifixion cave painting,** the work of local Archibald MacKinnon, painted in 1887. It takes about 1½ hours to walk around this tidal island, with its natural rock gardens.

On the quayside in the heart of town is the 14th-century **Campbeltown Cross.** This Celtic cross is the finest piece of carving from the Middle Ages left in Kintyre.

One of the area's most famous golf courses, the **Machrilhansih Golf Club,** lies nearby (☎ 01586/810-213). It's a 6,228-yard (5,667m) par-70 course. Monday to Friday and Sunday, the greens fees are £25 ($41.25) per round or £40 ($66) per day; on Saturday, the fees are £30 ($49.50) per round or £50 ($82.50) per day. No club rentals are available; trolleys cost £4 ($6.60).

**Oystercatcher Crafts & Gallery,** 10 Hall St. (☎ 01586/553-070), sells Campbeltown pottery, wood carvings, and paintings by local artists. If you'd like to take a scenic drive and go shopping at the same time, head for **Ronachan Silks,** Ronachan Farmhouse at Clachan (☎ 01880/740-242), 25 miles (40km) north of Campbeltown on Route 83. In this unusual location, you can buy high-fashion clothing and accessories, including kimonos, caftans, women's scarves, men's ties, waistcoats, wall hangings, and cushions. Call ahead to confirm opening times.

## ACCOMMODATIONS & DINING

**Argyll Arms Hotel.** Main St., Campbeltown PA28 6AB. ☎ 01586/553-431. Fax 01586/ 553-594. http://membersaol.com/argyllarms/argyllarms.html. E-mail: argyllarms@aol.com. 25 units. TV TEL. £60 ($102) double. Rates include Scottish breakfast. AE, DC, MC, V.

This imposing stone building was once home to the duke of Argyll, who maintained a suite on the second floor even after he sold it as a hotel. The public rooms still possess an aura of Victorian opulence, but the guest rooms are modernized and fairly modest. The rooms come in a variety of sizes, each traditionally furnished. The hotel's two bars (the Farmers Bar and the Wee Toon) are open daily 11am to midnight. The restaurant serves lunch and dinner daily, specializing in moderately priced fish fresh from the quay and other local produce.

**Craigard House.** Low Askomil, Campbeltown PA28 6EP. ☎ 01586/554-242. Fax 01586/551-137. 8 units. £60–£90 ($102–$153) double. Rates include breakfast. MC, V.

The whisky baron who built this house in 1882 was so obsessed that he paid large sums to have all the exterior honey-colored sandstone imported from other parts of Britain. The result is a dignified monastic-looking pile, with a bell tower, perched on the northern edge of the loch about a half mile (1km) from the town center. In the 1940s, the building was badly modernized, but it was brought back nearly to its original splendor by Roger Clark and Pat Winterton. The guest rooms come with contemporary- looking furniture and some vestiges of the original plasterwork, while the public areas are more traditional and Victorian, with original pitch pine floors.

Much of the Wintertons' energy is devoted to their restaurant, where main courses cost £9.25 to £14.95 ($15.75 to $25.40). Menu items change weekly but may include savory fish crêpes with salad garnish, pan-fried duck breast with brandy and pepper-cream sauce, chicken cacciatore, and elaborate desserts. Lunch and dinner are served daily.

## CAMPBELTOWN AFTER DARK

Pubs, not surprisingly, are the nightlife here, including two that host live music. They're easy to find in the center of the village, next door to each other. The **Feathers** Cross Street (☎ 01586/554-604), with stone walls, wooden floors, and hanging lamps, hosts free bands playing a range of musical styles on Thursday night. It's open daily 11am to 12:30am. The **Commercial Cross Street** (☎ 01586/553-703) has a variety of live music on Fridays and alternate Saturdays. A specialty here is real ale. It's open Monday to Saturday 11am to 1am and Sunday 12:30pm to 1am. You'll find a quieter evening at the **Burnside Bar,** Burnside Street (☎ 01586/552-306), open daily 11am to 1am. Conversation and local single malts are the preferred distractions at the old wooden pub "that's always been here."

## SOUTHEND & THE MULL OF KINTYRE

Some 10 miles (16km) south of Campbeltown, the village of Southend stands across from the Mull of Kintyre, and Monday to Saturday three buses a day run here from Campbeltown. It has sandy beaches, a golf course, and views across the sea to the Island of Sanda and to Ireland. Legend has it that footprints on a rock near the ruin of an old chapel mark the spot where St. Columba first set foot on Scottish soil. Other historians suggest the footprints mark the spot where ancient kings were crowned.

You can also go to **Dunaverty Rock,** a jagged hill marking the extreme southern tip of the Kintyre Peninsula. Located 9 miles (14.5km) south of Campbeltown and called "Blood Rock" by the locals, it was once the site of a MacDonald stronghold known as Dunaverty Castle, although nothing remains of it today. And in 1647 it was the scene of a great massacre, where some 300 citizens lost their lives. You can reach it by a local bus (marked SOUTH END) traveling from Campbeltown south about six times a day. Nearby, you'll find a series of isolated, unsupervised **beaches** and the 18-hole **Dunaverty Golf Course** (☎ 01586/830-677).

About 11 miles (18km) from Campbeltown is the **Mull of Kintyre.** From Southend, you can take a narrow road until you reach the "gap," from where you can walk down to the lighthouse, a distance of 1½ miles (2.5km) before you reach the final point. Expect westerly gales as you go along. This is one of the wildest and most remote parts of the peninsula, and it's this desolation that appeals to visitors. The Mull of Kintyre is only 13 miles (21km) from Ireland. When local resident Paul McCartney made it the subject of a song, hundreds of fans flocked to the area.

## 3 The Isle of Gigha & Scotland's Finest Gardens

3 miles (5km) W of Kintyre's western coast

One of the southern Hebrides lying 3 miles (5km) off the Kintyre Peninsula's west coast, the 6-mile-long (10km) Isle of Gigha is often called "sacred" and "legendary." Little changed over the centuries, it boasts Scotland's Garden of Eden.

## ESSENTIALS

**GETTING THERE**    Take a **ferry** to Gigha from Tayinloan, halfway up the west coast of Kintyre. Sailings are daily and take about 20 minutes, depositing you at **Ardminish,** the main hamlet on Gigha. The round-trip fare is £17.45 ($29.65) for an auto plus £4.60 ($7.80) per passenger. For ferry schedules, call ☎ 01880/730-253 in Kennacraig.

**VISITOR INFORMATION**    There's no local tourist office, so ask at Campbeltown on the Kintyre Peninsula (see "The Kintyre Peninsula," above).

**GETTING AROUND**  Since most likely you'll arrive without a car and there's no local bus service, you can either walk or call **McSporran's Taxi** at ☎ **01583/505-251.**

## SEEING THE SIGHTS

Gigha is visited mainly by those wanting to explore its famous gardens, Scotland's finest. Be prepared to spend your entire day walking. The ✪ **Achamore House Gardens,** a mile (1.5km) from the ferry dock at Ardminish, overflow with roses, hydrangeas, camellias, rhododendrons, and azaleas, among other flowering plants and shrubbery. On a 50-acre site, they were the creation of the late Sir James Horlick, one of the world's great gardeners. The house isn't open to the public, but the gardens are open year-round, daily dawn to dusk; admission is £2 ($3.40). For information about the gardens, call the Gigha Hotel (see below).

The island has a rich Viking past (the Vikings stored their loot here after plundering the west coast of Scotland), and cairns and ruins still remain. **Creag Bhan,** the highest hill, rises more than 330 feet (100m). From the top, you can look out onto the islands of Islay and Jura as well as Kintyre; on a clear day, you can also see Ireland. The **Ogham Stone** is one of only two standing stones in the Hebrides that bears an Ogham inscription, a form of script used in the Scottish kingdom of Dalriada. High on a ridge overlooking the village of Ardminish are the ruins of the **Church of Kilchattan,** dating back to the 13th century.

## ACCOMMODATIONS & DINING

✪ **Gigha Hotel.** Ardminish, Isle of Gigha PA41 7AD. ☎/fax **015835/052-54.** Fax 015835/052-44. 13 units, 11 with private bathroom. TV TEL. £112 ($190.40) double without bathroom; £120 ($204) double with bathroom. Rates include half-board. MC, V.

Standing in a lonely windswept location a 5-minute walk from the island's only ferry landing, this white-painted stone hotel was built in the 1700s as a farmhouse. It contains the island's only pub, one of its two restaurants, and its only accommodations except for some cottages. The polite staff rents small but cozy rooms with hair dryers and tea/coffeemakers. Rather expensive fixed-price four-course dinners are served daily to both guests and nonguests; bar lunches are more affordable.

# 4 The Isle of Islay: Queen of the Hebrides

16 miles (26km) W of the Kintyre Peninsula, ¾ mile (1km) SW of Jura

Islay (pronounced "*eye*-lay") is the southernmost island of the Inner Hebrides, separated only by a narrow sound from Jura. At its maximum, Islay is only 20 miles (32km) wide and 25 miles (40km) long. Called the "Queen of the Hebrides," it's a peaceful and unspoiled island of moors, salmon-filled lochs, sandy bays, and wild rocky cliffs—an island of great beauty, ideal for long walks.

## ESSENTIALS

**GETTING THERE**  MacBrayne **steamers** provide daily service to Islay. You leave West Tarbert on the Kintyre Peninsula, arriving in Port Askaig on Islay in about 2 hours. There's also service to Port Ellen. For information about ferry departures, check with Caledonian MacBrayne (☎ **01475/650-100**) at the ferry terminal in Gourock.

**VISITOR INFORMATION**  The tourist office is at **Bowmore,** The Square (☎ **01496/810-254**). May to September, it's open Monday to Saturday 9:30am to 5:30pm and Sunday 2 to 5pm; October to April, hours are Monday to Friday noon to 4pm.

## EXPLORING THE ISLAND

Near **Port Charlotte** are the graves of the U.S. seamen and army troops who lost their lives in 1918 when their carriers, the *Tuscania* and the *Otranto*, were torpedoed off the shores of Islay. There's a memorial tower on the **Mull of Oa,** 8 miles (13km) from Port Ellen. For the greatest **walk** on the island, go along Mull of Oa Road heading toward the signposted solar-powered Carraig Fhada lighthouse, some 1½ miles (2.5km) away. The area is filled with sheer cliffs riddled with caves. Once the Oa peninsula was the haunt of illicit whisky distillers and smugglers.

The island's capital is **Bowmore,** on the coast across from Port Askaig. Here you can see a fascinating Round Church (no corners for the devil to hide in). But the most important town is **Port Ellen** on the south coast, a holiday and golfing resort and Islay's principal port. The 18-hole **Machrie golf course** (☎ **01496/302-310**) is 3 miles (5km) from Port Ellen.

You can see the ancient seat of the lords of the Isles, the ruins of two castles, and several Celtic crosses. The ancient **Kildalton Crosses** are in the Kildalton churchyard, about 7½ miles (12km) northeast of Port Ellen—they're two of the finest Celtic crosses in Scotland. The ruins of the 14th-century fortress, **Dunyvaig Castle,** are just south of Kildalton.

In the southwestern part of Islay in Port Charlotte, the **Museum of Islay Life** (☎ **01496/850-358**) has a wide collection of island artifacts, ranging from unrecorded times to the present. Easter to October, the museum is open Monday to Saturday 10am to 5pm. Admission is £2 ($3.40) adults, £1.20 ($2.05) seniors, and £1 ($1.70) children. The Portnahaven bus from Bowmore stops here.

**Loch Gruinart** cuts into the northern part of Islay, 7 miles (11km) northeast of Port Charlotte and 8 miles (13km) north of Bowmore. As the winter home for wild geese, it has attracted bird watchers for decades. In 1984, the 3,000 acres of moors and farmland around the loch were turned into the **Loch Gruinart Nature Reserve.**

This is another place for great walks. Beaches rise out of the falling tides, but they're too cold and rocky for serious swimming. This is a lonely and bleak coastline, but because of that it has a certain kind of beauty, especially as you make your way north along its eastern shoreline. On a clear day you can see the Hebridean islands of Oronsay and Colonsay in the distance.

## TOURING THE DISTILLERIES

The island is noted for its distilleries, which still produce single-malt Highland whiskies by the antiquated pot-still method. Of these, **Laphroaig Distillery,** less than a mile (1.5km) along the road from Ardbeg to Port Ellen (☎ **01496/302-418**), offers a guided tour in the morning and in the afternoon. Admission is free and includes a sample dram. Call for an appointment. **Lagavoulin,** Port Ellen (☎ **01496/302-400**), offers tours Monday to Friday at 10am, 11:30am, and 2:30pm. Admission is £3 ($5.10) per person and comes with a £3 ($5.10) voucher off the price of a bottle of whisky. A sample is included in the tour. A distillery gift shop is open Monday to Friday 8:30am to noon and 1 to 4:30pm.

**Bowmore Distillery,** School Street, Bowmore (☎ **01496/810-441**), conducts tours Monday to Friday at 10:30am and 2pm. In summer, there are additional tours during the week at 11:30am and 3pm, and Saturday at 10:30am. The admission is £2 ($3.40), which includes a voucher worth £2 ($3.40) off the price of a bottle. Samples are included in the tour. Purchases can be made without taking the tour by stopping at the on-premises gift shop, open Monday to Friday 9am to 4:30pm and Saturday 10am to 12:30pm.

Port Askaig is home to two distilleries, **Bunnahabhain** (☎ **01496/840-646**), which offers tours at no charge by appointment and runs a gift shop on Monday to Friday 9am to 4pm, and **Coal Ila** (☎ **01496/840-207**), which has no tours from October to Easter, but thereafter has four tours (two morning, two afternoon) a day on Monday, Tuesday, Thursday, and Friday and two morning tours on Wednesday. Admission is £3 ($5.10). Its gift shop is open for visitors at the end of each tour.

## SHOPPING

At Bridgend, you can visit the **Islay Woolen Mill** (☎ **01496/810-563**), for more than a century making a wide range of country tweeds and accessories. It made all the tweeds used in Mel Gibson's *Braveheart*. The mill shop, open Monday to Saturday 10am to 5pm, sells a range of items made with the custom-designed Braveheart tweeds, as well as tasteful Shetland wool ties, mufflers, Jacob mufflers and ties, flat caps, travel rugs, and scarves.

Another good place to find souvenirs is **Port Ellen Pottery,** at Port Ellen (☎ **01496/302-345**), which sells brightly colored goblets, jugs, mugs, and other functional wares daily 10am to 5pm. Note that the Pottery is very small and doesn't handle shipping on larger purchases.

## ACCOMMODATIONS

**Bridgend Hotel.** Bridgend, Isle of Islay PA44 7PF. ☎ **01496/810-212.** Fax 01496/810-960. 11 units. TV TEL. £42 ($71.40) per person; £116 ($197.20) per person with dinner. Rates include Scottish breakfast. MC, V.

Victorian spires cap the slate-covered roofs and roses creep up the stone-and-stucco walls of this hotel that's part of a complex including a roadside barn and one of the most beautiful flower and vegetable gardens on Islay. This is one of the oldest hotels on the island, with somber charm and country pleasures. Guests enjoy drinks beside the open fireplaces in the Victorian cocktail lounge and the rustic pub, where locals gather after a day in the fields. Many nonguests opt for a moderately priced dinner in the high-ceilinged dining room. The midsize guest rooms are comfortably and conservatively furnished, each with a hair dryer, trouser press, and tea/coffeemaker.

**Lochside Hotel.** 19 Shore St., Bowmore, Isle of Islay PA43 7LB. ☎ **01496/810-244.** Fax 01496/810-390. www.lochsidehotel.co.uk. E-mail: ask@locksidehotel.co.uk. 8 units. TV TEL. £55–£79 ($93.50–$134.30) double. Rates include breakfast. MC, V. Take ferry from Kennacraig, then the A846 to the village center.

Behind a lackluster facade, this family-run hotel opens onto panoramic views over Loch Indaal in the rear. Alistair and Ann Birse run a fine, welcoming hotel. The medium-sized bedrooms are well maintained, comfortable, and tastefully decorated with such amenities as beverage makers. The hotel bar boasts one of the largest selections of Islay malt whiskies in the world, some 200 in all, and is a favorite hang-out for the locals. The restaurant specializes in moderately priced seafood but offers vegetarian options as well.

**Port Askaig Hotel.** Hwy. A846 at the ferry crossing to Jura, Port Askaig, Isle of Islay PA46 7RD. ☎ **01496/840-245.** Fax 01496/840-295. 8 units. TV. £72 ($122.40) double. Rates include Scottish breakfast. AE, MC, V.

On the Sound of Islay overlooking the pier, this island inn dates from the 18th century but was built on the site of an even older inn. It offers island hospitality and Scottish fare and is a favorite of anglers; the bar is popular with local fisherfolk. Bar meals are available for lunch and dinner; the restaurant serves a fixed-price dinner at £15.75 ($26.80). The guest rooms are a bit small, but each is furnished in a comfortable though not stylish way, with a tea/coffeemaker.

**Port Charlotte Hotel.** Main St., Port Charlotte, Isle of Islay PA48 7TU. ☎ 01496/ 850-360. Fax 01496/850-361. www.milford.co.uk/go/portcharlotte.html. E-mail: carl@ portcharlottehot.demon.co.uk. 10 units. TV TEL. £85 ($144.50) double. Rates include Scottish breakfast. MC, V.

This hotel, built in 1829 as three cottages next to the small sandy beaches of Port Charlotte with views over Loch Indaal, has been refurbished and immediately won a four-crown rating from the Scottish Tourist Board. The guest rooms are beautiful, all with tea/coffeemakers and most with antiques. Features include a large conservatory, a comfortable lounge, and a public bar.

The hotel is also the best place to dine in the area, with main courses at £11 to £16 ($18.70 to $27.20). Typical dishes are sirloin of Islay steak, freshly caught Islay lobster, and grilled fillet of Scottish turbot. For starters, try the Loch Fyne smoked salmon.

## DINING

You can also dine at one of the hotels above.

**The Croft Kitchen.** Port Charlotte, Isle of Islay. ☎ 01496/850-230. Sandwiches £1.50 ($2.55); main courses £4–£7.50 ($6.80–$12.75) at lunch, £7.50–£12.50 ($12.75–$21.25) at dinner. MC, V. Daily 10am–8:30pm (last order). Closed mid-Oct to mid-Mar. BRITISH.

On the main highway running through town, this is a low-slung, homey, and utterly unpretentious diner-bistro with a friendly staff. Holding no more than 40 diners at a time and managed by Douglas and Joy Law, it serves wine, beer, and whisky distilled on Islay, along with generous portions of down-home food. You'll find lots of fresh fish and shellfish, as well as soups, fried scallops, roasted Islay venison with rowanberry jelly, and steamed mussels with garlic mayonnaise.

## ISLAY AFTER DARK

After work, distillery employees gather at the **Harbour Inn,** Main Street in Bowmore (☎ 01496/810-330), an old pub with stone walls, a fireplace, and wooden floors and furnishings. It's open Monday to Saturday 11am to 1am and Sunday noon to 1am. McEwan's beer is served on tap and a wide selection of single malts. Local seafood is served at lunch and dinner. During the summer, reservations are recommended.

## 5  The Isle of Jura: Deer Island

¾ mile (1km) E of Islay

The Isle of Jura is the fourth largest of the Inner Hebrides, 27 miles (43km) long and varying from 2 to 8 miles (3 to 13km) in breadth. It takes its name from the Norse *jura,* meaning "deer island." The red deer on Jura—at 4 feet high (1.2m), the largest wild animals roaming Scotland—outnumber the people by about 20 to 1. The hearty islanders number only about 250, and most of them live along the east coast. Jura is relatively little known or explored, and its mountains, soaring cliffs, snug coves, and moors make it an inviting place.

George Orwell lived on Jura in the bitter postwar winters of 1946 and 1947. Although sick, he was working on his masterpiece *1984,* which was published in 1949. He almost lost his life when he and his adopted son ventured too close to the whirlpool in the Gulf of Corryvreckan. They were saved by local fishermen and he went on to finish his masterwork, only to die in London of tuberculosis in 1950.

## ESSENTIALS

**GETTING THERE**   From Kennacraig (West Loch, Tarbert) you can go to Port Askaig on Islay (see above) taking one of the **Caledonian MacBrayne ferries** (☎ **01880/730-253**). The cost is £36.50 ($62.05) for a car and £6.85 ($11.65) per passenger each way (4-day return tickets are more economical). From Port Askaig, you can take a second ferry to Feolin on Jura; call **Western Ferries** at ☎ **01496/840-681.** Car spaces must be booked in advance. The cost for a vehicle is £6 ($10.20), plus 90p ($1.55) for a passenger one way.

**VISITOR INFORMATION**   The Isle of Islay (see, "The Isle of Islay: Queen of the Hebrides," above) has the nearest tourist information office.

## EXPLORING THE ISLAND

Since most of the island is accessible only by foot, wear sturdy walking shoes and bring raingear. The best place for walks is the **Jura House Garden and Grounds** at the southern tip. These grounds were laid out by the Victorians to take advantage of the natural beauty of the region, and you can visit the gardens with their sheltered walks and panoramic views daily 9am to 5pm. Admission is £2 ($3.40). June to August, it's also the best place on the island to have tea, but only Saturday and Sunday. Call ☎ **01496/820-315** for details.

The capital, **Craighouse,** is hardly more than a hamlet. From Islay, you can take a 5-minute ferry ride to Jura from Port Askaig, docking at the Feolin Ferry berth.

The island's landscape is dominated by the **Paps of Jura** that reach a peak of 2,571 feet (780m) at Beinn-an-Oir. An arm of the sea, **Loch Tarbert** nearly divides the island, cutting into it for nearly 6 miles (10km).

The square tower of **Claig Castle,** now in ruins, was the stronghold of the MacDonalds until they were subdued by the Campbells in the 17th century. The **Jura Distillery,** at Craighouse (☎ **01496/820-240**), is closed in July and August but can be toured any other month for free. A free sample is given away at the end of the tour, which can only be booked by calling ahead for an appointment.

The managers of the island's only hotel conduct special tours by Land Rover to such curiosities as the **Corryvreckan whirlpool,** notorious to west coast sailors. Inquire at the hotel; the cost is about £12 ($20.40). Price and availability are subject to the number wanting to do the tour.

## ACCOMMODATIONS & DINING

**Jura Hotel.** Craighouse, Isle of Jura PA60 7XU. ☎ **01496/820-243.** Fax 01496/820249. 18 units, 12 with private bathroom. £62 ($105.40) double without bathroom, £74 ($125.80) double with bathroom; £95 ($161.50) suite. Rates include Scottish breakfast. AE, DC, MC, V. Closed 2 weeks at Dec–Jan.

The island's only hotel is a sprawling gray-walled building near the center of the hamlet (Craighouse lies east of Feolin along the coast). Sections date from the 1600s, but what you see today was built in 1956. The midsize guest rooms are of high quality, with comfortable mattresses. In this remote outpost, you get a tranquil night's sleep. Kenya-born Fiona Walton and her husband, Steve, are the managing directors. Affordable meals are served daily at lunch and dinner; the dining room's specialty is Jura-bred venison.

# 6 Inveraray

99 miles (159km) NW of Edinburgh, 57 miles (92km) NW of Glasgow, 38 miles (61km) SE of Oban

The small resort and royal burgh of Inveraray occupies a splendid setting on the upper shores of Loch Fyne. It's particularly attractive when you approach from the east on A83. Across a little inlet, you can see the town lying peacefully on a bit of land fronting on the loch.

## ESSENTIALS

**GETTING THERE    By Train**    The nearest rail station is at Dumbarton, 45 miles (72km) southeast, where you can make bus connections to Inveraray (see below). For rail schedules, call ☎ 0345/484-950.

**By Bus**    The National Express operates buses out of Glasgow, heading for Dumbarton, before continuing to Inveraray. Transit time is about 2 hours. Monday to Saturday, four buses make this run (only two on Sunday). A one-way fare is £6 ($10.20) a day, with a round-trip ticket at £10 ($17). For bus schedules, call ☎ 0990/808-080.

**By Car**    From Oban, head east along A85 until you reach the junction with A819, at which point you continue south.

**VISITOR INFORMATION**    The **tourist office** is on Front Street (☎ 01499/ 302-063). June to mid-September, it's open daily 9am to 6pm; mid-September to October, April, and May, hours are Monday to Saturday 9am to 5pm and Sunday noon to 5pm; and November to March, it's open daily noon to 4pm.

## SEEING THE SIGHTS

At one end of the main street of the town is a **Celtic burial cross** from Iona. The parish church is divided by a wall that enables services to be held simultaneously in Gaelic and English.

Since so many of its attractions and those in its environs involve walking, hope for a sunny day. If you like it bright, head for a local beauty spot, the **Ardkinglas Woodland Garden** (☎ 01499/600-263), 4 miles (6.5km) east of Inveraray at the head of Loch Fyne. People drive from all over Britain to see Scotland's greatest collection of conifers and its masses of rhododendrons bursting into bloom in June. Admission is £2 ($3.40), and it's open daily 9am to 5pm.

If you have a car, you can explore this scenic part of Scotland from Cairndow. Head east along A83 until you reach the junction with A815, at which point proceed south along the western shore of Loch Fyne until you come to the famous inn at Creggans (see below), directly north of **Strachur.** Five miles (8km) south from the Creggans Inn along the loch will take you to the old **Castle Lachlan** at Strathiachian, the 13th-century castle of the MacLachlan clan. Now in romantic ruins, it was besieged by the English in 1745. The MacLachlans were fervent Jacobites and played a major role in the uprising.

✪ **Inveraray Castle.** ¾ mile (1km) NE of Inveraray on Loch Fyne. ☎ **01499/302-203.** Admission £4.50 ($7.65) adults, £3.50 ($5.95) seniors, £2.50 ($4.25) children, £12 ($20.40) families. Apr–June and Sept to mid-Oct Sat–Thurs 10am–1pm and 2–5:45pm; July–Aug Mon–Sat 10am–5pm, Sun 1–5:45pm.

The hereditary seat of the dukes of Argyll, Inveraray Castle has been headquarters of the Clan Campbell since the early 15th century. The gray-green stone castle is among the earliest examples of Gothic Revival in Britain and offers a fine collection of pictures and 18th-century French furniture, old English and continental porcelain, and

# Hiking in Argyll Forest Park

Argyll Forest Park, in the southern Highlands, stretches almost to Loch Fyne and is made up of Benmore, Ardgartan, and Glenbranter. The park covers an area of 60,000 acres, contains some of Scotland's most panoramic scenery, and takes in a wide variety of habitats, from lush forests and waterside to bleaker grassy moorlands and mountains. The Clyde sea lochs cut deep into the forested areas, somewhat in the way fjord "fingers" cut into the Norwegian coast; in the northern part are the Arrochar Alps (so called), where Ben Arthur reaches a height of 2,891 feet (877m).

The park attracts those interested in natural history and wildlife as well as rock climbers, hikers, and hill walkers. There are many recreational activities and dozens of forest walks for trail blazers with all degrees of skill. Trails leading through forests to the loftier peaks are strenuous and meant for skilled hikers; others are easier, including paths from the Younger Botanic Garden by Loch Eck leading to Puck's Glen.

There's abundant wildlife in the sea lochs: shark, sea otters, gray seals, sea scorpions, crabs, shrimp, sea lemons, sea anemones, and sea slugs, among other inhabitants. You can rent boats and canoes. One of the park's biggest thrills is exploring the underwater caves of Loch Long.

In the early spring and summer, the park trails are at their most beautiful—woodland birds create choruses of song, and the forest is filled with violets, wood anemones, primroses, and bluebells. Sometimes the wildflowers are so thick they're like carpets. In the rainy climate of the southern Highlands, ferns and mosses also grow abundantly.

To reach the park, take A83 to B828 heading for Loch Goll or follow A815 to Loch Eck and Loch Long. Both Arrochar and Tarbet, stops on the Glasgow–Fort William rail line, are on the periphery of the park's northeast frontier.

The best place for lodging is **Dunoon,** to the south on the Cowal Peninsula, an easy gateway to the park. Dunoon has been a holiday resort since 1790, created for the "merchant princes" of Glasgow. Recreational facilities abound, including an indoor pool, tennis courts, and an 18-hole golf course. To pick up information about the park and a trail map, go to the **Dunoon Tourist Center** at 7 Alexandra Parade (☎ **01369/703-785**). April to late June, September, and October, it's open Monday to Friday 9am to 5:30pm and Saturday and Sunday 10am to 5pm; late June to August, hours are Monday to Saturday 9am to 6pm and Sunday 10am to 5pm; November to March, it's open Monday to Thursday 9am to 5:30pm and Friday 9am to 5pm.

an Armoury Hall, which alone contains 1,300 pieces. On the grounds is a **Combined Operations Museum,** the only one of its kind in the United Kingdom. It displays the role No. 1 Combined Training Centre played at Inveraray in World War II. On exhibit are scale models, newspaper reports of the time, campaign maps, photographs, wartime posters and cartoons, training scenes, and other mementos. A castle shop sells souvenirs and a tearoom serves homemade cakes and scones.

**Auchindran Township Open Air Museum.** About 5 miles (8km) south of Inveraray on A83, just outside the hamlet of Furnace. ☎ **01499/500-235.** Admission £3 ($5.10) adults, £2.50 ($4.25) seniors, £1.50 ($2.55) children, £8 ($13.60) families. Apr–Sept daily 10am–5pm.

Auchindran is an original West Highland common tenancy township, a unique survivor of the long-gone townships once common in the Highlands. More than 20 structures remain, most of them restored to illustrate the lifestyle of Highlanders in bygone days. The Visitor Centre features displays, a shop, and other facilities.

**Crarae Glen Gardens.** 8 miles (13km) southwest of Inveraray along A83, near the hamlet of Minard. ☎ **0154/688-6614.** Admission (Oct–Mar payment is by the honor system—drop your money in the box at the entrance) £2.50 ($4.25) adults, £1.50 ($2.55) children, £7 ($11.90) families. Daily 10am–5pm.

Lying along Loch Fyne, these are among Scotland's most beautiful gardens, some 50 acres of rich plantings along with waterfalls and panoramic vistas of the loch. The gardens are at their best in blooming season. Lots of paths wend their way among the gardens, so you can have a good hike while enjoying the beauty.

## ACCOMMODATIONS & DINING
**Argyll Hotel.** Front St., Inveraray PA32 8XB. ☎ **01499/302-466.** Fax 01499/302-389. 24 units. TV TEL. £62–£74 ($105.40–$125.80) double. Rates include Scottish breakfast. MC, V.

With views of Loch Fyne and Loch Shira, this 1755 inn has been dubbed with several names during its long and varied life, but after a 1998 refurbishment has emerged as the Argyll Hotel. The midsize guest rooms are comfortable and include decors ranging from flowered chintz to modern with no-nonsense functionality, each containing a hair dryer and tea/coffeemaker. There's also a public bar, a residents-only cocktail lounge, and a dignified restaurant where five-course dinners, with a wide choice of food items, cost £23.50 ($39.95).

❂ **Creggans Inn.** Strachur PA27 8BX. ☎ **01369/860-279.** Fax 01369/860-637. www.creggans-inn.co.uk. E-mail: info@creggans-inn.co.uk. 20 units. TV TEL. £98–£130 ($166.60–$221) double; £150–£175 ($255–$297.50) suite. Rates include Scottish breakfast. AE, DC, MC, V.

This inn commemorates the spot where Mary Queen of Scots is said to have disembarked from her ship in 1563 on her way through the Highlands. Painted white with green trim and flanked by gardens, the inn rises across A815 from the sea and is owned by Sir Charles MacLean and his mother, Lady MacLean, author of several best-selling cookbooks, most of which are for sale at the inn. The midsize to spacious guest rooms are elegant and understated, each traditionally furnished and well maintained. You may use the upstairs sitting room and the garden-style lounge.

**Dining:** The restaurant has a charcoal grill that produces succulent versions of Aberdeen Angus steaks and lamb kebabs, but you can also enjoy fresh seafood, venison, and the MacLeans' version of smoked salmon. Lunch and dinner are served daily; reservations are a must. An in-house bar features pub lunches beside an open fire.

**George Hotel.** Main St. East, Inverary PA32 8TT. ☎ **01499/302-111.** Fax 01499/302-098. 12 units. TV. £50–£65 ($85–$110.50) double. Rates include breakfast. MC, V.

One of the most charming hotels in town lies behind a circa-1775 facade. Part of the charm derives from the old-fashioned bar and pub, where the Guinness simply seems to taste better than in less evocative settings. The public areas are marked with flagstone floors, beamed ceilings, and blazing fireplaces. The guest rooms are cozy, done in a conservative style following old-fashioned Scottish models, with tea/coffeemakers. Some have king-size beds (unusual for Scotland) and clawfoot and ball-foot tubs.

**Dining:** The restaurant is among the most popular in town with locals, serving moderately priced lunches and dinners daily. Your choices include smoked salmon pâté, steaks prepared with pepper or mushroom sauce; ham steak, grilled halibut, and grilled Loch Fyne salmon steak with white wine, prawns, and scallops.

## 7  Loch Awe: Scotland's Longest Loch

99 miles (159km) NW of Edinburgh, 24 miles (39km) E of Oban, 68 miles (109km) NW of Glasgow

Only a mile (1.5km) wide in most places and 22 miles (35.5km) long, Loch Awe is the longest loch in Scotland and acted as a natural freshwater moat protecting the Campbells of Inveraray from their enemies to the north. Along its banks are many reminders of its fortified past. In this area the Forestry Commission has vast forests and signposted trails, and a modern road makes it possible to travel around Loch Awe, so more than ever it's a popular angling center and walking center.

### ESSENTIALS

**GETTING THERE**   The nearest train station is in Oban, where you'd have to take a connecting bus. **Scottish CityLink,** 1 Queens Park Place in Oban (call ☎ **01631/ 562-856** for schedules), has service to Glasgow with stopovers at Loch Awe.

If you're driving from Oban, head east along A85.

**VISITOR INFORMATION**   Consult the tourist office in Oban (see, "Oban: Gateway to Mull & the Inner Hebrides," below).

### EXPLORING THE AREA

To the east of the top of Loch Awe, **Dalmally** is small, but because of its strategic position it has witnessed a lot of Scottish history. Its 18th-century church is built in an octagonal shape.

The ruins of **Kilchurn Castle** are at the northern tip of Loch Awe, west of Dalmally, and across from the south bank village of Loch Awe. A stronghold of the Campbells of Glen Orchy in 1440, it's a spectacular ruin with much of the original structure still intact. The ruins have been completely reinforced and balconied so you can now explore it when the weather permits. Access to the ruins is from an unmarked graveled lot. A path leads to the ruin, but you may need a pair of boots if the weather is bad.

A more convenient way to reach it is by taking any of about five boats a day (March to November) departing from the piers in the village of Loch Awe. The ferries are maintained by the **Loch Awe Steam Packet Company,** Loch Awe Piers (☎ **01838/ 200-440**). Per-person transit across the loch (a 10-minute ride each way) costs £6 ($10.20) and includes entrance to the ruins of Kilchurn. This steamship company and the **Hotel Ardanaiseig** (see below) are the only sources of info about the castle, which doesn't maintain an on-site staff.

Once you reach the castle, don't expect a guided tour, as the site is likely to be abandoned except for a patrol of goats and sheep, and there's no guardian to reinforce strict opening hours. Although it's presently owned by a consortium of five local businessmen, its grass is cut and its masonry maintained by Historic Scotland. You can wander at will through the ruins following a self-guided tour marked by signs.

Among other reminders of the days when the Campbells of Inveraray held supreme power in the Loch Awe region, there's a ruined **castle** at Fincharn, at the southern end of the loch, and another on the island of Fraoch Eilean. The Isle of Inishail has an ancient **chapel and burial ground.** The bulk of **Ben Cruachan,** rising to 3,689 feet (1,119m), dominates Loch Awe at its northern end and attracts climbers and hikers. On the Ben is the world's second-largest hydroelectric power station, which pumps water from Loch Awe to a reservoir high up on the mountain.

Below the mountain are the **Falls of Cruachan** and the wild **Pass of Brander,** where Robert the Bruce routed the Clan MacDougall in 1308. The Pass of Brander was the scene of many a fierce battle in bygone times, and something of that bloody past seems to brood over the narrow defile. Through it the waters of the Awe flow on their way to Loch Etive. This winding sea loch is 19 miles (30.5km) long, stretching from Dun Dunstaffnage Bay at Oban to Glen Etive, reaching into the Moor of Rannoch at the foot of the 3,000-foot (910m) **Buachaille Etive** (the Shepherd of Etive), into which Glencoe also reaches.

## ACCOMMODATIONS & DINING

✪ **Hotel Ardanaiseig.** Kilchrenan by Taynuilt PA35 1HE. ☎ **800/548-7790** in the U.S., 800/463-7595 in Canada, or 01866/833-333. Fax 01866/833-222. E-mail: ardaniseig@ clara.net. 16 units. TV TEL. £138–£178 ($234.60–$302.60) double. AE, DC, MC, V. Closed Jan to mid-Feb. Drive 21 miles (34km) south of Oban by following the signs to Taynuilt, then turning onto B845 toward Kilchrenan. Turn left at the Kilchrenan Pub and continue on for 3.9 miles (6km), following signs into Ardanaiseig. No children under 8.

Although this gray-stone manorial seat was built in 1834 by a Campbell patriarch, it's designed along 18th-century lines. Its builder also planted some of the rarest trees in Britain, many of them exotic conifers. Today, clusters of fruit trees stand in a walled garden, and the rhododendrons and azaleas are a joy in May and June. Until recently a private home, the hotel has formal sitting rooms graced with big chintzy chairs, fresh flowers, and polished tables. Upstairs, the guest rooms are uniquely and traditionally furnished. The price of a room depends on its size, ranging from a small room to a master bedroom with a loch view. All contain tea/coffeemakers, hair dryers, and CD players.

**Dining:** The owners have employed an excellent chef who makes skillful use of fresh produce, local salmon, trout, game, and meats. Dinners are opulent and baronial. The dining room serves only sandwiches and soup for lunch daily; a pricey, traditional five-course dinner is served nightly.

**Amenities:** You can rent fishing vessels here, and a golf course is within a 40-minute drive.

## 8  Oban: Gateway to Mull & the Inner Hebrides

85 miles (137km) NW of Glasgow, 50 miles (80.5km) SW of Fort William

One of Scotland's leading coastal resorts, the bustling port of Oban is in a sheltered bay almost landlocked by the island of Kerrera. A busy fishing port in the 18th century, Oban is now heavily dependent on tourism. Since it lacks major attractions of its own, it's often used as a major refueling stop for those exploring the greater west coast of Scotland.

## ESSENTIALS

**GETTING THERE**    From Glasgow, the West Highland lines run directly to Oban, with departures from Glasgow's Queen Street Station (call ☎ **0345/484-950** for 24-hour info). Three trains per day (only two on Sunday) make the 3-hour run to Oban, a one-way fare costing £17.40 ($29.60).

Frequent coaches depart from Buchanan Station in Glasgow, taking about the same time as the train, although a one-way fare is only £10 ($17). Call **Scottish CityLink** at ☎ **01631/332-7133** in Glasgow or ☎ **0163/562-856** in Oban.

If you're driving from Glasgow, head northwest along A82 until reaching Tyndrum, then go west along A85 until you come to Oban.

**VISITOR INFORMATION**    The **tourist office** is on Argyll Square (☎ **01631/ 563-122**). April to mid-June and mid-September to October, it's open Monday to Friday 9am to 5pm and Saturday and Sunday noon to 5pm; mid-June to mid-September, hours are Monday to Saturday 9am to 6:30pm and Sunday 10am to 5pm; and November to March, it's open Monday to Saturday 9:30am to 5pm and Sunday noon to 4pm.

**SPECIAL EVENTS**  The **Oban Highland Games** are held in August, with massed pipe bands marching through the streets. Ask at the tourist office for details. The **Oban Pipe Band** regularly parades on the main street throughout summer.

## EXPLORING THE AREA

To appreciate the coastal scenery of Oban to its fullest, consider renting a bike and cycling around. They're available at **Oban Cycles,** 9 Craigard Rd. (☎ **01631/ 562-444**).

From **Pulpit Hill** in Oban, there's a fine view across the Firth of Lorn and the Sound of Mull. Overlooking the town is an unfinished replica of the Colosseum of Rome, **McCaig's Tower,** built by a banker, John Stuart McCaig, from 1897 to 1900 as a memorial to his family and to create a local work opportunity during an employment slump. Its walls are 2 feet (61cm) thick and 37 to 40 feet (11 to 12m) high. The courtyard within is landscaped, and the tower is floodlit at night. Outsiders have been heard to refer to the tower as "McCaig's Folly," but Obanites are proud of the structure and deplore this term.

Near the little granite **Cathedral of the Isles,** 1 mile (1.5km) north of the end of the bay, is the ruin of the 13th-century **Dunollie Castle,** seat of the lords of Lorn, who once owned a third of Scotland.

On the island of Kerrera stands **Gylen Castle,** home of the MacDougalls, dating back to 1587.

You can visit ✪ **Dunstaffnage Castle** (☎ **01631/562-465**), 3½ miles (5.5km) north, believed to have been the royal seat of the Dalriadic monarchy in the 8th century. It was probably the site of the Scots court until Kenneth MacAlpin's unification of Scotland and the transfer of the seat of government to Scone in the 10th century. The present castle was built about 1263. The castle is open April to October from 9am to 6:30pm (till 8pm July and August), and from November to March from 9:30am to 4:30pm. Admission is £1.80 ($3.05) adults, £1.30 ($2.20) seniors, and 75p ($1.30) children. You can take a bus from the Oban rail station to Dunbeg, but it's still a 1½-mile (2.5km) walk to the castle.

## SHOPPING

**Cathness Glass Oban,** Railway Pier (☎ **01631/563-386**), is the best place for shopping, but you'll find plenty of gift and souvenir shops around town. At this center, locally produced glass items range from functional dinner- and glassware to purely artistic curios. This firm has one of the most prestigious reputations in Scotland.

Many of the craft items produced in local crofts and private homes eventually end up at gift shops in Oban, where they're proudly displayed as among the finest of their kind in the West Country. One of the best outlets is **McCaig's Warehouse,** Argyll Square (☎ **01631/566-335**), where the tartan patterns of virtually every clan in Scotland are for sale, either by the meter or in the form of kilts, jackets, traditional Highland garb, or more modern interpretation of traditional fashions.

Celtic-patterned jewelry, made from gold, silver, or platinum, and sometimes studded with semiprecious gems, is featured at **The Gem Box,** Esplanade (☎ **01631/ 562-180**).

If all other shopping options fail, consider the gift items displayed at the **Oban Tourist Information Office,** Argyll Square (☎ **01631/563-122**). Inventories include tartans, jewelry, woodwork, and glassware, usually crafted into Celtic designs, and books covering the myriad aspects of what to see and do in Scotland.

If you absolutely, positively must have a kilt, a cape, or a full outfit based on your favorite Highland regiment, head for one of the town's two best tailors: **Hector Russell, Kiltmaker,** Argyll Square (☎ **01631/570-240**), and **Geoffrey Tailors,** Argyll Square (☎ **01631/570-557**).

## ACCOMMODATIONS

You may also want to check out the rooms offered at the **Balmoral Hotel** or the **Knipoch Hotel Restaurant** (see "Dining," below).

### EXPENSIVE

**Manor House.** Gallanach Rd., Oban PA34 4LS. ☎ **01631/562-087.** Fax 01631/563-053. www.highlandholidays.net. E-mail: me@managedestates.co.uk. 11 units. TV TEL. £140–£160 ($238–$272) double. Rates include half-board. AE, MC, V. From the south side of Oban, follow the signs for the car ferry but continue past the ferry entrance for about half a mile (1km). No children under 12.

On the outskirts of Oban, opening onto panoramic views of Oban Bay, this 1780 stone house was once owned by the duke of Argyll. Many antiques grace the public rooms. The good-sized guest rooms are filled with tasteful reproductions, and coordinated curtains and bedcovers create a pleasing effect, often in sun-splashed golds and yellows. All have hair dryers and tea/coffeemakers.

**Dining:** The restaurant is one of the most satisfying in the area and reason enough for a visit even if you're not a guest. Covered with elegant cream linen, the tables are lit by candles. The menu emphasizes seafood, but there are vegetarian dishes as well. The fixed-price five-course menu goes for £24.95 ($42.40). Dress is smart casual.

### MODERATE

**Alexandra.** Corran Esplanade, Oban PA34 5AA. ☎ **01631/562-381.** Fax 01631/564-497. 77 units, 2 suites. TV TEL. £75–£95 ($127.50–$161.50) double; £124–£144 ($210.80–$244.80) suite. Rates include Scottish breakfast. AE, MC, V.

On the promenade a mile (1.5km) from the train station, the late-1860s stone Alexandra boasts gables and turreted towers and a Regency front veranda. From its public room you can look out onto Oban Bay, and two sun lounges overlook the seafront. The midsize guest rooms are modestly furnished but pleasing, with hair dryers and tea/coffeemakers. The restaurant, serving good food, also opens onto the panorama. Table d'hôte dinners cost £18.50 ($31.45). Around-the-clock room service is available. The leisure center offers a large indoor pool, steam room, gym, and solarium.

**Caledonian Hotel.** Station Square, Oban PA34 5RT. ☎ **01631/563-133.** Fax 01631/562-998. 70 units. TV TEL. £91–£111 ($154.70–$188.70) double. Rates include Scottish breakfast. AE, DC, MC, V.

The Caledonian, a favorite of coach tours, makes good on its promise of giving you a "taste of the Highlands." A fine example of Scottish 19th-century architecture, it occupies a landmark position, with a good view opening onto the harbor and Oban Bay looking toward the Mull of Kintyre. This convenient location puts you close to the rail, bus, and ferry terminals from which you can book passage to the Isles. The midsize guest rooms have up-to-date amenities and tea/coffeemakers. The front rooms are the most desirable. Good, reasonably priced Scottish fare is served in the dining room.

**Columba Hotel.** The Esplanade, North Pier, Oban PA34 5QD. ☎ **01631/562-183.** Fax 01631/564-683. 50 units. TEL. £75–£95 ($127.50–$161.50) double; £115 ($195.50) suite. Rates include breakfast. AE, MC, V. Free parking. The Scottish Midland Bus Company's Ganavan bus passes by.

One of the most impressive Victorian buildings in Oban, the Columba was built in 1870 by the same McCaig who constructed the hilltop extravaganza known as

McCaig's Tower. The location is among the best in town, and the modernized big-windowed dining room offers views of the port. The small guest rooms are unremarkable but well maintained, each with a tea/coffeemaker. À la carte dinners are served in the restaurant, offering a mix of seafood and local produce. Live folk music is sometimes presented in the informal Harbour Inn Bar.

**Dungallan House Hotel.** Gallanach Rd., Oban PA34 4PD. ☎ **01631/563-799.** Fax 01631/566-711. www.dungallanhotel-oban.co.uk. E-mail: welcome@dungallanhotel-oban. co.uk. 13 units, 11 with private bathroom. TV. £74 ($125.80) double without bathroom; £96 ($163.20) double with bathroom. MC, V. Closed Nov–Feb. From Oban's center, drive half a mile (1km), following the signs to Gallanach.

One of the more upscale inns around Oban is this circa-1870 home built for the Campbells. It was used as a hospital during World War I and as a naval office during World War II, but today is the artfully furnished domain of George and Janice Stewart, who maintain the high-ceilinged proportions and antique furniture with devotion. The guest rooms have been refurbished, each with firm mattresses and quality furnishings. Breakfasts are served in grand style in the formal dining room; dinners can be arranged for £19.50 to £25 ($33.15 to $42.50), and although seating priority is granted to guests, nonguests can usually arrange a meal if they phone ahead. Five acres of forest and gardens surround the house, and views stretch out over the Bay of Oban and its islands.

## INEXPENSIVE

**Foxholes.** Cologin, Lerags, Oban. PA34 4SE. ☎ **01631/564-982.** www.hoteloban.com. 7 units. TV. £55–£59 ($93.50–$100.30) double. Rates include full Scottish breakfast. MC, V. Closed Dec–Mar. Free parking. Take A816 3 miles south of Oban.

Far from a foxhole, this is actually a spacious country house set in a tranquil glen to the south of Oban. Operated by Barry and Shirley Dowson-Park, it's for those seeking seclusion. The cozy, tasteful, and comfortable bedrooms are painted in soft pastels and furnished traditionally. All rooms open onto panoramic views of the countryside and the hotel's well-maintained gardens. Amenities include beverage makers and hair dryers, and all the bathrooms are in excellent condition. In the restaurant, Mrs. Dowson-Park provides traditional, moderately priced Scottish meals.

**Glenburnie.** The Esplanade, Oban PA34 5AQ. ☎/fax **0163/562-089.** E-mail: graeme. strachan@btinternet.com. 14 units. TV. £50–£70 ($85–$119) double. MC, V. Closed Nov–Apr.

One of Oban's genuinely grand houses is on the seafront esplanade a 5-minute walk west of the town center. Built in 1897 of granite blocks, with elegant ecclesiastical-looking bay windows, it was designed as the surgical hospital and home of a prominent doctor. Today, it's a guesthouse operated by Graeme and Allyson Strachan, who have outfitted the rooms with comfy furniture, much of it antique. Each has a tea/coffeemaker.

**Lancaster.** Corran Esplanade, Oban PA34 5AD. ☎/fax **01631/562-587.** 27 units, 24 with private bathroom. TV. £60 ($102) double with bathroom. Rates include Scottish breakfast. MC, V.

Along the seafront on the crescent of the bay, the Lancaster is distinguished by its attractive pseudo-Tudor facade. Its public rooms command views of the islands of Lismore and Kerrera and even the more distant peaks of Mull. The guest rooms are modestly furnished in a somewhat 1960s style, all with hair dryers and tea/coffeemakers. This is only one of the two hotels in Oban featuring a heated indoor pool, a sauna, a whirlpool, and a solarium. Its fully licensed dining room offers moderately priced dinners.

## DINING
### EXPENSIVE

✪ **Knipoch Hotel Restaurant.** Hwy. A816, Kilninver, Knipoch, by Oban PA34 4QT. ☎ **01852/316-251.** Fax 01852/316249. www.knipochhotel.co.uk. Reservations required. Table d'hôte dinner £29.50 ($50.15) for 3 courses, £39.50 ($67.15) for 5 courses. AE, DC, MC, V. Daily 7:30–9pm. Closed mid-Dec to mid-Feb. Drive 6 miles (10km) south of Oban on A816. SCOTTISH.

Oban has a truly fine restaurant 6 miles (10km) south of town on the shores of Loch Feochan. Jenny and Colin Craig, a mother-son team, welcome you to their white-washed Georgian house (the oldest part dates from 1592) and offer a choice of three dining rooms as well as a daily changing menu of five delectable courses. Salmon and halibut are smoked on the premises, and the menu relies heavily on Scottish produce, including fresh fish. Try the cock-a-leekie soup, followed by Sound of Luing scallops. The wine cellar is excellent, especially in its Bordeaux.

The hotel also rents 16 well-furnished rooms, charging £74 to £144 ($125.80 to $244.80) double, Scottish breakfast included.

**The Manor House.** In the Manor House Hotel, Gallanach Rd. ☎ **01631/562-087.** Reservations recommended. Main courses £19 ($32.30); set-price 5-course meal £24.95 ($42.40). AE, MC, V. Tues 6:45–9pm; Wed–Sat noon–2pm and 6:45–9pm. SCOTTISH.

Located in the 1780 house built by the Duke of Argyll, this formal but not stuffy restaurant overlooks Oban Bay and is one of the finest dining choices along the coast. A traditional Scottish cuisine is served—truly fresh and creative cooking—and the chef uses ingredients of the highest quality. Against a backdrop of Georgian paneling, you can peruse the constantly changing menu. Many visitors to the Highlands opt for venison, and here it comes with accompaniments such as black pudding, caramelized root vegetables, and rowanberry glaze. You might also select delicious fresh scallops wrapped in smoked bacon. The waitstaff will also recite some selections for vegetarians. You can order such old-fashioned British desserts as sticky toffee pudding with butterscotch sauce but for something really Scottish, try marinated brambles with whisky custard.

### MODERATE

**Balmoral Hotel.** Craigard Rd., Oban PA34 5AQ. ☎ **01631/562-731.** Reservations recommended in midsummer. Main courses £6.50–£14.50 ($11.05–$24.65); bar meals £2.75–£5.50 ($4.70–$9.35). AE, DC, MC, V. May to mid-Oct daily noon–2pm and 6–10pm; Mar–Apr and mid-Oct to Dec daily noon–2pm and 6–8pm. SCOTTISH/ENGLISH.

At the top of a granite staircase whose corkscrew shape is an architectural marvel, this is one of the most popular restaurants in town. Filled with a 19th-century kind of charm, it contains Windsor chairs and reproduction Georgian tables crafted from darkly stained wood. Specialties include sliced chateaubriand with mushrooms, Isle of Mull rainbow trout, smoked Tobermory trout, Scottish haggis with cream and whisky, venison casserole, and roast pheasant. Less expensive platters are served in the adjacent bar. The hotel stands on the eastern extension of the town's main commercial street (George Street), a 4-minute walk from the center.

The hotel rents 12 well-furnished rooms, with TVs, costing £50 to £66 ($85 to $112.20) double, Scottish breakfast included.

**The Gathering.** Breadalbane St. ☎ **0163/565-421.** Reservations recommended. Bar platters £4.95–£9.95 ($8.40–$16.90); set-price dinners in restaurant £10.95–£15 ($18.60–$25.50). AE, MC, V. June–Sept daily noon–2pm; year-round dinner daily 5–10pm. BRITISH.

Architecturally charming and ringed with verandas, this imposing building opened in 1882 as the site for the annual banquets of a private hunting and social club. Today, its ground floor functions as an Irish pub (open Monday to Saturday 11am to 1am and Sunday noon to 11pm) and its wood-sheathed upper floor as a well-managed restaurant. Dishes are straightforward but nonetheless tasty and well prepared. Menu items include lots of local produce, fish, and game dishes, like pheasant, lobster, and lamb. Especially noteworthy are the Highland venison fillets with port jelly sauce, loin of saddle of venison with herb-and-port sauce, and local crayfish lightly grilled in garlic butter and served with a fresh salad.

**McTavish's Kitchen.** 34 George St. ☎ **01631/563-064.** Main courses £6.95–£12.95 ($11.80–$22); budget 2-course lunch £4.50 ($7.65); fixed-price 3-course dinners £6.25–£15.75 ($10.65–$26.80). MC, V. Self-service restaurant daily 9am–9pm; licensed restaurant daily noon–2pm and 6–10:30pm. SCOTTISH.

Like its cousin in Fort William, this place is dedicated to preserving the local cuisine. Downstairs is a self-service restaurant offering breakfast, lunch, dinner, and teas with shortbread and scones. Upstairs is the Lairds Bar, and on the ground floor is McTavish's Bar, where bar meals are available all day. The licensed second-floor restaurant has a more ambitious Scottish and continental menu with higher prices, but there are also budget lunches. The fixed-price menu includes an appetizer, a main-course choice that features fresh salmon, and a dessert like strawberries or raspberries (in season). The à la carte menu offers haggis, Loch Fyne kippers (oak-smoked herring), prime Scottish steaks, smoked salmon, venison, and local mussels.

## OBAN AFTER DARK

Mid-May to the end of September, entertainment is provided at **MacTavish's Kitchen** (see above), with Scottish music and Highland dancing by local artists nightly 8:30 to 10:30pm. Admission is £3.50 ($5.95) adults and £1.75 ($3) children. Reduced admission for diners is £1.75 ($3) adults and £1 ($1.70) children.

You can while away the evening with the locals at the **Oban Inn,** Stafford Street and the Esplanade (☎ **01631/562-484**), a popular pub with exposed beams and a flag-covered ceiling. Pints include McEwan's Export, Ale, 70 Shilling, and Gillespie's Stout. The pub is open daily noon to 1am.

Another popular hangout is the town's Irish pub, **O'Donnells,** Breadalbane Street (☎ **01631/566-159**), where you can always expect a warm reception. They serve the ever-popular Guinness and a variety of Irish and Scottish malt whisky. Thursday to Saturday, entertainment is either a live band or a DJ. Over the busy summer, something happens almost every night. Hours are daily 11am to 1am.

## SIDE TRIPS FROM OBAN
### THE INNER & OUTER HEBRIDES

Oban is the gateway to **Mull,** largest of the Inner Hebrides, and to the island of **Iona.** See chapter 11 for information about these destinations.

The ferries to the offshore islands run only twice a day until summer; then there are cruises to Iona from early June to late September. For details about ferry services to Mull, Iona, and the Outer Hebrides, get in touch with **Caledonian MacBrayne** in Oban at ☎ **0990/650-000.** It sails to 23 islands, with fares ranging from £40 ($68) for a car and £5.75 ($9.80) per adult passenger for travel to Mull to £107 ($181.90) for a car plus £30.50 ($51.85) per adult passenger for travel to Barra. Book in advance, particularly in summer, as the ferries often sell out.

## PORT APPIN

Some 24 miles (39km) north of Oban lies a scenic lochside district, including Lismore Island. Port Appin is a small village with stone cottages. On an islet near Port Appin, a famous landmark, **Castle Stalker,** was the ancient seat of the Stewarts of Appin, built in the 15th century by Duncan Stewart, son of the first chief of Appin. Dugald, the ninth chief, was forced to sell the estate in 1765, and the castle slowly fell into ruin. It was recently restored and is once again inhabited but no longer open to visitors. In *Monty Python and the Holy Grail,* this was depicted as "Castle Aaaaaaaaaaa." It lies at Portnacroish (where it's signposted), 10 miles (16km) down A828.

### Dining & Accommodations

✪ **Airds Hotel.** Port Appin PA38 4DF. ☎ **01631/730-236.** Fax 01631/730-535. www.airds-hotel.com. E-mail: airds@airds-hotel.com. 16 units. TV TEL. £98–£136 ($166.60–$231.20) double; £149 ($253.30) per person suite. Rates include Scottish breakfast and dinner. MC, V.

The Airds is a former ferry inn dating from 1700 (now a Relais & Châteaux member), in one of the most panoramic spots in the district, midway between Oban and Fort William. It overlooks Loch Linnhe and Lismore island and is an ideal center for touring the area. You can take forest walks; go pony trekking, sea fishing, or trout fishing; or rent boats and arrange for trips to see the seals and visit Lismore. The resident proprietors are the Allen family, who welcome you to their handsomely furnished rooms with excellent beds and beautiful baths. Everything is immaculately maintained in a tranquil setting.

**Dining:** It's the food that makes the Airds so outstanding. Betty Allen, one of Scotland's great cooks, has handed over kitchen duties to her son, Graeme, who's continuing her tradition of creating fine Scottish cuisine from fresh local produce. Daily menus are likely to include cream of red pepper and fennel soup; salad of Loch Linnhe prawns with herb mayonnaise; breast of wood pigeon with foie gras, truffle, chanterelles and Madeira sauce; or wild salmon fillet on a bed of honeyed eggplant with asparagus and hollandaise sauce. Delectable desserts include chocolate ice cream gateau with crème anglaise and plum coulis or poached pear shortcake with caramel-and-lime sauce. A meal will cost £40 ($68). Reservations for dinner, served 7:30 to 8:30pm, are absolutely necessary.

**Amenities:** All-day room service for tea and coffee only, baby-sitting, laundry, garden.

**Pierhouse.** Port Appin PA38 4DF. ☎ **01631/730-302.** Fax 01631/730-400. 12 units. TV TEL. £60–£90 ($102–$153) double. Rates include Scottish breakfast. MC, V.

Although the restaurant associated with this hotel was established by two generations of the McLeod family in 1988, guest rooms are among the newest in Argyll. In 1993, a two-story wing was added containing extra rooms, many with views over the water. All the units, ranging from small to midsize, are comfortably furnished and well maintained. The complex lies in the hamlet's center, adjacent to the pier where ferryboats depart every 2 hours for Lismore Island.

The white-sided restaurant was built as a fisherman's cottage more than 200 years ago. Its location at the edge of the pier allows much of its seafood to remain alive in underwater cages until just before cooking. Venison dishes are available as well. Menu items include several versions of giant prawns, pan-fried scallops with lemon butter or cream-cheese-and-wine sauce, and delectable versions of whatever local fishermens managed to bring in that day. Main courses are £11.50 to £16.95 ($19.55 to $28.80). The restaurant is open daily 12:30 to 2:30pm and 6:30 to 9:30pm. Reservations are recommended.

# Fife & the Central Highlands

## 8

**N**orth of the Firth of Forth from Edinburgh, the County of Fife still likes to call itself a kingdom. Even today, its name suggests the romantic episodes and pageantry during the reign of the early Stuart kings, and some 14 of Scotland's 66 royal burghs lay in this shire. And you can visit many of the former royal palaces and castles, either restored or in colorful ruins.

Legendary **Loch Lomond** is the largest and most beautiful of the Scottish lakes. At Balloch in the south, it's a Lowland landscape of gentle hills and islands. But as it moves north, the loch narrows and takes on a stark, dramatic Highland character, with moody cloud formations and rugged steep hillsides.

The **Trossachs** is the collective name given to that wild Highland area east and northeast of Loch Lomond. Here and along Loch Lomond you find Scotland's finest scenery in moor, mountain, and loch. The area has been famed in history and romance ever since Sir Walter Scott's vivid descriptive passages in "The Lady of the Lake" and *Rob Roy.*

Many sections of the area lie on the doorsteps of Glasgow and Edinburgh; either city can be your gateway to the central Highlands. You can easily reach Dunfermline and St. Andrews by rail from Edinburgh (St. Andrews also has good bus connections with Edinburgh). By car, the main motorway is M9, the express highway that starts on the western outskirts of Edinburgh and is linked to M80 from Glasgow. M9 passes close to Stirling. M90, reached by crossing the Forth Road Bridge, will take you north into the Fife region. Stirling is the region's major rail center, with stops at such places as Dunblane, and much of Loch Lomond has rail connections. The towns and some villages have bus service, but you'll find the connections too limited or infrequent. For bus connections, Stirling is the central point.

However, your best bet for discovering the hidden villages and scenic lochside roads of the Trossachs or the fishing villages of East Neuk is renting a car and driving at your own pace.

## Driving Through the Region

**Day 1** Leave Edinburgh and travel east on A90, following the signs to the Forth Road Bridge. After crossing the bridge, follow the signs into **Dunfermline,** 14 miles (22.5km) northwest of Edinburgh, to visit Dunfermline Abbey and Palace and to see the Andrew Carnegie

Birthplace Museum. Then take A907 6 miles (10km) northwest to **Culross** to explore Culross Abbey and Culross Palace. After lunch, head northeast along the coastal road, beginning southeast of Dunfermline (A92). Follow this route all the way to Elie, going via Kirkcaldy and Buckhaven. At **Elie,** you can explore the villages called the **East Neuk.** Visit **Pittenweem, Anstruther,** and **Crail.** Anstruther or Elie is best for overnighting.

**Day 2**   Continue along the coast, following A917 until you reach **St. Andrews,** capital of golf. It deserves at least an overnight stop; serious golfers, however, will want to stay a lot longer.

**Day 3**   From St. Andrews, take A9 southwest until you see the turnoff for **Falkland,** to the northwest. Make this detour to explore Falkland Palace and Garden. Continue northwest from Falkland until you reach the junction of A91, heading southwest into **Stirling** for the night.

**Day 4**   After exploring Stirling in the morning and having lunch there, follow A9 north to **Dunblane** to see its fabled cathedral. From Dunblane, cut west along A820 to **Doune** to visit its castle, motor museum, and Blair Drummond Safari and Leisure Park. Spend the night in Doune.

**Day 5**   From Doune, head northwest on A84 to **Callander** for the night. Callander is surrounded by some of the finest scenery in the central Highlands, including Leny Park, Leny Falls, Bracklinn, Loch Lubnaig, and even Loch Voil, known to Rob Roy.

**Day 6**   In the morning, leave Callander along A821 on the northern rim of Loch Venachar, which will take you into the **Trossachs.** After driving through the Trossachs, head south to **Aberfoyle** for the night.

**Day 7**   From Aberfoyle, you can head south on A81 and then west along A811 (which becomes B837). This will take you to the eastern shores of **Loch Lomond,** Scotland's largest loch. You can spend an entire day, or a lot more, driving around this loch. Many villages offer cozy accommodations.

## 1 Dunfermline & Its Great Abbey

14 miles (22.5km) NW of Edinburgh, 39 miles (63km) NE of Glasgow, 52 miles (84km) SW of Dundee

The ancient town of Dunfermline was once the capital of Scotland and is easily reached by the Forth Road Bridge, opened by Elizabeth II in 1964. Scots called their former capital the "auld grey town," and it looms large in their history books. The city is still known for its Dunfermline Abbey and former royal palace (now largely gone). When Scotland reunited with England in 1603, the royal court departed to London, leaving Dunfermline to wither with only its memories. In time, however, the town revived as the center of Scottish linen making, specializing in damask. But by World War I, the market had largely disappeared.

Some of the most interesting sights in Fife are within easy reach of Dunfermline, including one of Scotland's most beautiful villages, Culross. Dunfermline also makes the best base for exploring Loch Leven and Loch Leven Castle.

### ESSENTIALS

**GETTING THERE**   Dunfermline is a stop along the main rail route from London via Edinburgh to Dundee, which means it has frequent connections to the Scottish capital. For rail schedules and fares, call ☎ 0345/484-950.

# The Kingdom of Fife

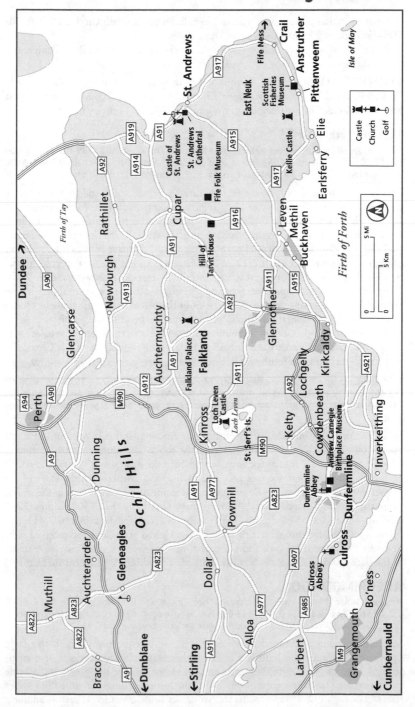

From its station at St. Andrews Square in Edinburgh, Scottish CityLink (☎ **0990/ 505-050**) operates frequent service to Dunfermline.

If you're driving from Edinburgh, take A90 west, cross the Forth Road Bridge, and follow the signs north to the center of Dunfermline.

**VISITOR INFORMATION**    A **tourist booth** is at 13–15 Maygate (☎ **01383/ 720-999**). April to October, it's open Monday to Saturday 10am to 5pm; August hours are Monday to Saturday 10am to 6pm and Sunday 11:30am to 3:30pm.

## SEEING THE SIGHTS

**✪ Dunfermline Abbey and Palace.** St. Margaret's Dr. ☎ **01383/739-026.** Admission £2 ($3.40) adults, £1.50 ($2.55) seniors, 75p ($1.30) children. Apr–Sept daily 9:30am–6pm; Oct–Mar Mon–Wed and Sat 9:30am–4pm, Thurs 9:30am–noon, Sun 2–4pm.

The abbey is on the site of two earlier structures, a Celtic church and an 11th-century house of worship dedicated to the Holy Trinity, under the auspices of Queen Margaret (later St. Margaret). Culdee Church, from the 5th and 6th centuries, was rebuilt in 1072. Traces of both buildings are visible beneath gratings in the floor of the old nave. In 1150, the church was replaced with a large abbey, the nave of which remains, an example of Norman architecture. Later, St. Margaret's shrine, the northwest baptismal porch, the spire on the northwest tower, and the flying buttresses were added. While Dunfermline was the capital of Scotland, 22 royal personages were buried in the abbey. However, the only visible memorial or burial places known are those of Queen Margaret and King Robert the Bruce, whose tomb lies beneath the pulpit.

The once-royal palace of Dunfermline stands adjacent to the abbey. The palace witnessed the birth of Charles I and James I. The last king to reside here was Charles II, in 1651. Today only the southwest wall remains of this once-gargantuan edifice.

**Andrew Carnegie Birthplace Museum.** Moodie St. ☎ **01383/724-302.** Admission £2 ($3.40) adults, £1 ($1.70) seniors; free for ages 15 and under. Apr, May, and Oct Mon–Sat 11am–5pm, Sun 2–5pm; June–Sept Mon–Sat 11am–5pm, Sun 2–5pm; Nov–Mar daily 2–4pm.

In 1835, American industrialist/philanthropist Andrew Carnegie was born at a site about 200 yards (182m) down the hill from the abbey. The museum, at the corner of Moodie Street and Priory Lane, comprises the 18th-century weaver's cottage in which he was born and a memorial hall provided by his wife. Displays tell the story of the weaver's son who emigrated to America to become one of the richest men in the world. From the fortune he made in steel, Carnegie gave away more than $400 million (£244 million) before his 1919 death. Dunfermline received the first of the 2,811 free libraries he provided throughout Britain and the United States and also received public baths and Pittencrieff Park and Glen, rich in history and natural charm. A statue in the park honors Carnegie, who once worked as a bobbin boy in a cotton factory.

## ACCOMMODATIONS

**Davaar House Hotel and Restaurant.** 126 Grieve St., Dunfermline, Fife KY12 8DW. ☎ **01383/721-886.** Fax 01383/623-633. www.taste-of-scotland.com/davaar-house-hotel. html. 10 units. TV TEL. £70 ($119) double. Rate includes breakfast. MC, V.

In a residential neighborhood a 5-minute walk west of the town center, this large Georgian-style house was built late in the 19th century and boasts distinctive architectural features like a sweeping oak staircase, elaborate cove moldings, and marble mantelpieces. The largest guest rooms, with the loftiest ceilings, are one floor above street level; slightly less grand rooms are two floors above street level. Each is uniquely decorated, with strong colors and pastels, in a traditional Scottish style.

The restaurant here is well-recommended; it's open only for dinner Monday to Saturday. Look for moderate prices and home-style cooking from a talented team, with dishes like Scottish salmon with mustard-dill sauce and suprême of chicken and broccoli in phyllo pastry and white-wine sauce. Dessert might be baked raspberry tart with Drambuie-fudge sauce.

**Keavil House Hotel.** Main St., Crossford, Dunfermline, Fife KY12 8QW. ☎ **01383/736-258.** Fax 01383/621-600. www.keavilhouse.co.uk. E-mail: keavil@queensferry-hotels.co.uk. 47 units. TV TEL. £105 ($178.50) double; £125 ($212.50) family suite. AE, DC, MC, V. Closed Dec 31–Jan 1. Free parking. Take A994, 2 miles west of Dunfermline; the hotel is off the main street at the west end of village.

This tranquil country hotel, only a 30-minute drive from Edinburgh, is set on 12 acres of forested land and gardens and offers lots of leisure facilities. The bedrooms are generous in size and well appointed, each with such amenities as a writing desk, hair dryer, trouser press, and beverage maker. Master bedrooms contain four-poster beds.

**Dining:** The hotel offers fine, formal dining in its Conservatory Restaurant (see below) and less formal food in its Armoury Alehouse & Grill.

**Amenities:** The leisure/health club is the finest in the area, with a gym, pool, Jacuzzi, sauna, sunbeds, and a steamroom.

**King Malcolm Thistle Hotel.** Queensferry Rd., Dunfermline, Fife KY11 5DS. ☎ **01383/722-611.** Fax 01383/730865. E-mail: kingmalcolmhotel@hotmail.com. 48 units. TV TEL. £110 ($187) double. Children 13 and under stay free in parents' room. AE, DC, MC, V. Bus: D3 or D4.

The best choice for either a meal or a bed is this modern pastel-colored stylish hotel on a roundabout a mile south of Dunfermline on A823. Named after the medieval king of Fife (and later of Scotland), Malcolm Canmore, it was built in 1972 but thoroughly revamped in 1989. Each well-furnished though rather standardized guest room comes with a trouser press and hair dryer.

**Dining:** Richmond's, a glass-sided bar/restaurant, offers Scottish and continental cuisine at dinner daily; the fixed-price menus are on the high side of moderate. The Canmore Vault's Bar is accessible via a separate entrance.

## DINING

**Conservatory Restaurant.** In the Keavil House Hotel, Main St., Crossford. ☎ **01383/736-258.** Reservations recommended. Main courses £10–£16 ($17–$27.20); set-price 3-course menu £22.50 ($38.25). AE, DC, MC, V. Daily noon–2pm and 7–9pm. Closed Dec 31–Jan 1. MODERN SCOTTISH.

Here you'll enjoy views over extensive gardens. Some of the best of local produce is used deftly here to create true "Taste of Scotland" specialties—and that means the best of Scottish beef, locally caught game, and fish from local rivers. Old-time recipes are given a modern twist here by the chef. The imaginative dishes are served with flair and originality, appealing to both traditionalists and those with more adventurous tastes. Try the scallops on sugar snap peas with lobster sabayon, for example, or a real local specialty, a chanterelle and "tattie" scone pocket with a malt vinegar demi-glaze. You can follow with dessert of caramelized heather honey and apple parfait. There's an extensive and well-chosen wine list.

If you want less formal dining, the hotel also offers the Armoury Alehouse & Grill, with a selection of local beef, fish, and game.

**New Victoria.** 2 Bruce St. ☎ **01383/724-175.** Main courses £3.95–£10.95 ($6.70–$18.60); Scottish high tea £5.45–£12.45 ($9.25–$21.15). AE, MC, V. Mon–Thurs 9am–7pm; Fri–Sat 9am–9pm; Sun 10am–7pm. SCOTTISH.

To reach Dunfermline's oldest restaurant, established in 1923, you must walk up two flights of stairs. Off High Street, in a pedestrian zone in the center overlooking the abbey, the cozy dining room serves generous portions of good old-fashioned cooking based on healthy ingredients. You might begin with a robust soup, then follow with steak-and-kidney pie, grilled fish, roast beef, or any of an array of grilled Aberdeen Angus steaks. It's a good choice if you're in the neighborhood seeking a high tea.

## SIDE TRIPS FROM DUNFERMLINE: CULROSS & LOCH LEVEN

The old royal burgh of **Culross,** 6 miles (10km) west of Dunfermline, has been renovated by the Scottish National Trust and is one of the country's most beautiful. As you walk its cobblestone streets, admiring the whitewashed houses with their crow-stepped gables and red pantiled roofs, you'll feel as if you're taking a stroll back into the 17th century.

Set in tranquil walled gardens in the village center, **Culross Palace** (☎ 01383/ 880-359) was built between 1597 and 1611 for prosperous merchant George Bruce. It contains a most beautiful series of paintings on its wooden walls and ceilings portraying moral scenes with passages in Latin and Scottish, illustrating principles like "Honor your parents" and "The spoken word cannot be retracted." National Trust restoration from 1991 to 1994 involved replacing with Russian pine all the wooden paneling that had rotted, taking care to match the salvaged panels. During the restoration, archaeologists uncovered the remains of a foundation of a long-forgotten building on the east end of the courtyard and the original doorway; there are plans to restore it for use as the public entrance. Easter to September, the palace is open daily 11am to 5pm; October, hours are Saturday and Sunday 11am to 5pm (townhouse and study only); November to Easter, visits are by appointment only. Admission is £5 ($8.50) adults, £3.50 ($5.95) seniors/students, free for 18 and under.

The other important attraction is 6 miles (10km) southwest of Dumferline (take A994, following the signs to Culross): **Culross Abbey,** a Cistercian monastery whose founding father was Malcolm, earl of Fife, in 1217. Parts of the nave are still intact, and the choir serves as the Culross parish church. There's also a central tower. Easter Saturday to the last Saturday in August, the abbey is open daily from 9am to 7pm; at other times, you can visit by prior arrangement with the Church of Scotland (☎ 01383/880-231).

**Loch Leven,** 12 miles (19km) north of Dunfermline and 10 miles (16km) south of Falkland via A911, contains seven islands. On **St. Serf's,** the largest of the islands, are the ruins of the Priory of Loch Leven, built on the site of one of the oldest Culdee establishments in Scotland. If you're interested in seeing the ruins, contact the Kinross tourist office at ☎ 01577/863-680 and they'll put you in touch with one of the fishermen who make boat trips to the island.

In **Kinross,** 25 miles (40km) north of Edinburgh, you can take the ferry over to Castle Island to see the ruins of **Loch Leven Castle** (☎ 07836/313-769). "Those never got luck who came to Loch Leven," and this saying sums up the history of this Douglas fortress dating from the late 14th century. Among its ill-fated prisoners none was more notable than Mary Queen of Scots; inside its forbidding walls she signed her abdication on July 24, 1567, but she escaped from Loch Leven on May 2, 1568. Thomas Percy, seventh earl of Northumberland, supported her cause and "lodged" in the castle for 3 years until he was handed over to the English, who beheaded him at York. Today, you can see a 14th-century tower house and a 16th-century curtain wall, all that remains of a castle that loomed large in Scottish history. April to September, the castle is open daily 9:30am to 6:30pm; October to March, hours are Monday to

Saturday 9:30am to 4:30pm and Sunday 2 to 4:30pm. Admission is £3 ($5.10) adults, £2.30 ($3.90) seniors, and £1 ($1.70) children. The castle admission includes the cost of a round-trip by ferry from Kinross to Castle Island.

## ACCOMMODATIONS & DINING

**Dunclutha Guest House.** 16 Victoria Rd., Leven, Fife KY8 4EX. ☎ **01333/425-515.** Fax 01333/422311. E-mail: pam.leven@dunclutha-accomm.demon.co.uk. 5 units. £52 ($88.40) double. Rate includes breakfast. AE, MC, V.

A 3-minute walk northeast of the town center, this dignified stone house was built around 1890 for the priest at the adjacent Episcopal church. Today, it's the domain of Mrs. Pam McDonald, who infuses lots of personalized hominess into her hotel. The guest rooms are clean and well maintained and (in most cases) sunny thanks to big windows with garden views; they contain comfortable but not particularly dramatic furniture and tea/coffeemakers. Breakfast is the only meal served.

**Nivingston House.** Hwy. 9097, Cleish Hills by B996, Cleish, Perthshire and Kinross KY13 7LS. ☎ **01577/850-216.** Fax 01577/850-238. www.smoothhound.co.uk/nivingstonhouse. E-mail: info@nivingstonhousehotel.co.uk. 17 units. TV TEL. £105 ($178.50) double; £140 ($238) suite. AE, MC, V. Rates include Scottish breakfast. Children 12 and under stay free in parents' room. Closed Jan 1–14. Drive south of Kinross on B9097; it's 2 miles (3km) from exit 5 of M90.

Nivingston, a converted stone farmhouse with parts dating from 1725, is on 12 acres of gardens and offers modernized guest rooms with hair dryers and tea/coffeemakers.

**Dining:** The hotel also serves some of the finest food around, using fresh local produce like Scottish lamb and beef or fresh charcoal-grilled sardines. Typical dishes are venison médaillons pan-fried with red currant, paprika, and marsala sauce; rainbow trout sautéed with almonds, capers, and prawns; and Scottish sirloin steak "Hare and Hounds," with red-wine and Dijon-mustard sauce, glazed with brown sugar. You make your dessert selection from a trolley of luscious treats wheeled to your table. Lunch and dinner are served daily. Make reservations in advance, and expect a high tab.

# 2 East Neuk's Scenic Fishing Villages

Within half an hour's drive south of St. Andrews, on the eastward-facing peninsula incorporating St. Andrews and Anstruther, is the district of East Neuk, dotted with some of eastern Scotland's most scenic and unspoiled fishing villages. You can't reach these villages by rail; the nearest stations are Ladybank, Cupar, and Leuchars, on the main London–Edinburgh–Dundee–Aberdeen line serving northeast Fife. Buses from St. Andrews connect the villages, but you'll really want to have your own car here.

If the weather's right, you can cycle among the villages along some of the most delightful back roads in Fife. Rent a bike at **East Neuk Outdoors,** Cellardyke Park in Anstruther (☎ **01333/311-929**). This same outfitter can also fix you up for a canoe trip.

## PITTENWEEM

If you're at Pittenweem Monday to Saturday morning, try to get caught up in the action at the **fish auction** held under a large shed. The actual time depends on the tides. Afterward, you can go for a walk through the village and admire the sturdy stone homes, some of which have been preserved by Scotland's National Trust.

The *weem* in the name of the town means "cave," a reference to **St. Fillan's Cave** at Cove Wynd (☎ **01333/311-495**) in the vicinity of the harbor. This cave is said to contain the shrine of St. Fillan, a hermit who lived in the 6th century. Hours are

Tuesday to Saturday 10am to 5pm and Sunday noon to 5pm, costing 50p (85¢) admission.

The best way to reach **Anstruther** (see below) is to hike the 1½ miles (2.5km) over to it, since the road isn't paved. If the day is clear, this is one of the loveliest walks in eastern Scotland, as you cross Scottish meadows and say hello to a few lambs. From Pittenweem, follow a signpost directing you to Anstruther. You can also take the walk in reverse, as most visitors do. In Anstruther, the path begins at the bottom of West Brases, a small cul-de-sac off the main road in the village.

### ACCOMMODATIONS

**The Harbour Guest House.** 14 Mid Shore, Pittenweem, Fife KY10 2NL. ☎ **01333/ 311-273.** Fax 01333/310-014. www.pittenweem.com/guesth.htm. 4 units. TV. £46–£50 ($78.20–$85) double. Rates include breakfast. Discounts of £2–£3 ($3.40–$5.10) per person off nightly rate Nov–Mar. AE, DC, MC, V.

Set directly on the harborfront, this charming stone building was erected around 1910 as a private home. The guest rooms contain pinewood furniture and comfortable twin beds, each a cozy, no-frills refuge from the chilly winds and crashing seas. Since it's run by a local company and not by a family, Harbour is a bit more businesslike than a conventional B&B; in fact, it feels like a fishing lodge—the staff will direct you to local entrepreneurs who can take you out for a half-day's fishing or point out spots on the nearby piers and boardwalks where a rod and reel might attract fish.

## ANSTRUTHER

Once an important herring-fishing port, **Anstruther** is now a summer resort, 46 miles (74km) northeast of Edinburgh, 34 miles (55km) east of Dunfermline, 4 miles (6.5km) southwest of Crail, and 23 miles (37km) south of Dundee. The **tourist office** is on High Street (☎ **01333/311-073**); April to September, it's open Monday to Saturday 10am to 5pm and Sunday noon to 5pm (every Tuesday, Wednesday, and Thursday, it closes 1 to 2pm).

You'll enjoy taking a brisk stroll along the beaches here; it's too chilly for swimming, but it's invigorating and scenic nonetheless. The best nearby is **Billow Ness Beach,** a 10-minute walk east of the center.

The **Scottish Fisheries Museum,** St. Ayles, Harbourhead (☎ **01333/310-628;** Bus: 95), is down by the harbor. It was expanded in 1999 to include a neighboring building that was an 18th-century tavern and several re-creations of restored fishing boats. Here you can follow the fisherfolk through every aspect of their industry—from the days of sail to modern times. Associated with the museum but afloat in the harbor is an old herring drifter, *The Reaper,* which you can board to look around. April to October, the museum is open Monday to Saturday 10am to 5:30pm and Sunday 11am to 5pm; November to March, hours are Monday to Saturday 10am to 4:30pm and Sunday 2 to 4:30pm. Admission is £3.50 ($5.95) adults, £2.50 ($4.25) seniors/children, and £10 ($17) families.

From the museum, you can walk to the tiny hamlet of **Cellardyke,** adjoining Anstruther. You'll find many charming stone houses and an ancient harbor where in the year Victoria took the throne (1837), 140 vessels used to put out to sea. You can rent a bike from **East Neuk Outdoors,** Cellardyke Park (☎ **01333/311-929**), where rental rates are £10 ($17) daily and £35 ($59.50) weekly, plus a deposit. It's open daily 9am to 5pm.

The **Isle of May,** a nature reserve in the Firth of Forth, is accessible by boat from Anstruther. It's a bird observatory and a field station and contains the ruins of a 12th-century chapel as well as an early 19th-century lighthouse. **Jon and Lyn Raeper**

(☎ 01333/310-103) maintain a 100-passenger boat departing for the island from the Lifeboat Station in Anstruther Harbour every day May to September, weather permitting. The 5-hour trip, door to door, costs £12.50 ($21.25) adults, £10.50 ($17.85) seniors, and £5.50 ($9.35) children 3 to 14. Between May and July, expect to see hundreds, even thousands, of puffins, who mate on the Isle of May at that time.

## ACCOMMODATIONS

**Craw's Nest Hotel.** Bankwell Rd., Anstruther, Fife KY10 3DA. ☎ **01333/310-691.** Fax 01333/312-216. 50 units. TV TEL. £82 ($139.40) double. Rates include Scottish breakfast. AE, DC, MC, V. Bus: 95.

This black-and-white step-gabled Scottish manse has been converted into a popular hotel, with views over the Firth of Forth and May Island. Many extensions were added under the direction of the owner, Mrs. Edward Clarke, and her son-in-law, Ian Birrell. The midsize guest rooms are handsomely appointed.

The public areas, including a lounge bar as well as a bustling public bar, are simply decorated and cozy. The food is good and the wine priced reasonably in the dining room, where meals are served daily 12:30 to 2pm and 7 to 8:30pm. A three-course lunch runs £12.25 ($20.85) and a three-course dinner £19.75 ($33.55). The bar is open daily 11am to midnight, and meals are served there 12:30 to 2pm and 6 to 9pm.

**Smuggler's Inn.** High St., East Anstruther, Fife KY10 3DQ. ☎ **01333/310-506.** Fax 01333/312-706. 9 units. TV TEL. £59 ($100.30) double. Rates include Scottish breakfast. DC, MC, V. Bus: 95.

An inn has stood on this spot since 1300, and in Queen Anne's day it was a well-known tavern. This warmly inviting inn evokes memories of smuggling days, with low ceilings, uneven floors, and winding stairs. The guest rooms are comfortably furnished. The restaurant serves moderately priced regional cuisine at dinner nightly. Affordable bar lunches are also available.

## DINING

♻ **Dreel Tavern,** 16 High St. (☎ **01333/310-727**), was a 16th-century coaching inn and is now a wood-and-stone pub where locals gather to unwind in the evening. Caledonian 80 Shilling and Orkney Dark Island are available on hand pump, along with two guest beers that change weekly. The pub is open daily 11am to 11pm.

**The Cellar.** 24 East Green, Anstruther. ☎ **01333/310-378.** Reservations recommended. Fixed-price menus £28.50–£32.50 ($48.45–$55.25). AE, DC, MC, V. Wed–Sat 12:30–1:30pm; Mon–Sat 7–9:30pm. Bus: 95. SEAFOOD.

Within the solid stone walls of a cellar that dates from 1875 (but possibly from the 16th century), this seafood restaurant is the best in town. It's lit by candlelight, and in winter, by twin fireplaces at opposite ends of the room. The menu offers fresh fish hauled in from nearby waters and cooked with light-textured sauces. Examples are grilled halibut suprême dredged in bread crumbs and citrus juices and served with hollandaise sauce; lobster, monkfish, and scallops roasted with herb-and-garlic butter and served on sweet pepper risotto; and a limited array of meat dishes.

**Haven.** 1 Shore Rd., Cellardyke, Anstruther. ☎ **01333/310-574.** Reservations recommended. Fixed-price 5-course menu £18.50 ($31.45); bar supper menu £6.95–£11.50 ($11.80–$19.55); high tea £6.95–£7.50 ($11.80–$12.75). MC, V. Daily noon–9:30pm (depending on business, the street-level restaurant, but not the upstairs bar, might close several hours earlier during midwinter). Bus: 95; a James Anderson & Co. bus runs every hour from St. Andrews, 8 miles (13km) south, to the door of the restaurant. SCOTTISH.

This unpretentious harborfront place (two connected 300-year-old fishermen's cottages) serves simple and wholesome food: pan-fried breaded prawns, halibut fillets, Angus steaks, local crabmeat salad, and homemade soups and stews. The upper floor contains one of the town's most popular bars, where the same menu is served. The street level, more formal and sedate, is the site of high teas and evening meals.

# ELIE

With its step-gabled houses and little harbor, Elie, 11 miles (18km) south of Anstruther, is many visitors' favorite village along the coast. Only a 25-minute car ride from Edinburgh, Elie and its close neighbor, Earlsferry, overlook a crescent of gold-sand beach, with more swimming possibilities to be found among sheltered coves. The name Elie is believed to be derived from the *ailie* (island) of Ardross, which now forms part of the harbor and is joined to the mainland by a road. A large stone building, a former granary, at the harbor is a reminder of the days when Elie was a busy trading port. Of all the villages of East Neuk, this one seems more suited for walks and hikes in all directions.

**Earlsferry,** to the west, got its name from an ancient ferry crossing, which Macduff, the thane of Fife, is supposed to have used in his escape from Macbeth.

East of the harbor stands a stone structure known as the **Lady's Tower,** used by Lady Janet Anstruther, a noted 18th-century beauty, as a bathing cabana. Another member of the Anstruther family, Sir John, added the interesting **bell tower** to the parish church that stands in the center of the village.

Beyond the lighthouse, on a point of land to the east of the harbor, lies **Ruby Bay,** so named because you can find garnets here. Farther along the coast is **Fossil Bay,** where you can find a variety of fossils.

## ACCOMMODATIONS

**The Elms.** 14 Park Place, Elie, Fife KY9 1DH. ☎/fax **01333/330-404.** 7 units. £50 ($85) double. Rates include Scottish breakfast. MC, V.

Run by Mr. and Mrs. Terras, this 1880 building is on the wide main street behind a conservative stone facade, with a crescent-shaped rose garden in front. The comfortably furnished but small guest rooms contain washbasins, good beds, hair dryers, and tea/coffeemakers. Home cooking is a specialty of the house, and dishes include Scottish lamb, Pittenweem haddock, haggis, and Arbroath kippers. The house is licensed, and a simple dinner is available to nonguests. In the walled flower garden behind the house is a large conservatory for guests' use.

**Rockview Guest House.** The Toft, Elie, Fife KY9 IDT. ☎ **01333/330-246.** Fax 01333/330-864. E-mail: shipinnelie@aol.com. 6 units. TV. £50 ($85) double. MC, V.

Next to the Ship Inn (see below), the Rockview overlooks fine sandy beaches around Elie Bay. The small guest rooms are nicely furnished, each with a good bed. Maintenance is of a high level, and the welcome is warm. A twin-bedded room has a bunk bed for younger children to share with their parents. Family-run, the guesthouse can accommodate about a dozen people. Of course, food and drink are available at the Ship Inn.

## DINING

✪ **Ship Inn.** The Toft. ☎ **01333/330-246.** Main courses £6–£15 ($10.20–$25.50). MC, V. Mon–Sat 11am–midnight; Sun 12:30–11pm. SCOTTISH.

Even if you're not stopping over in Elie, we suggest you drop in at the Ship (from the center, follow the signs marked HARBOUR) and enjoy a pint of lager or real ale or a whisky from a large selection. The building occupied by this pub with a nautical atmosphere dates from 1778, and a bar has been in business here since 1830. In summer, you can sit outside and look over the water; in colder months, a fireplace burns brightly. On weekends in July and August, a barbecue operates outside. The set menu with daily specials features such items as steak pie, Angus beefsteaks, lasagna, and an abundance of fresh seafood.

## CRAIL

The pearl of the East Neuk of Fife, Crail is 50 miles (80.5km) northeast of Edinburgh, 23 miles (37km) south of Dundee, and 9 miles (14.5km) south of St. Andrews. It's an artists' colony, and many painters live in cottages around its little harbor. Natural bathing facilities are at Roome Bay, and many **beaches** are nearby. The **Balcomie Golf Course** is one of the oldest in the world and is still in good condition.

The old town grew up along the harbor, and you can still see a lot of fishing cottages clustered here. Crab and lobster boats still set out hoping for a big catch. **Upper Crail** overlooks the harbor and also merits exploration. The **tollbooth** dates from 1598 and is crowned by a belfry. **Marketgate** is lined with trees and flanked by two- and three-floor small houses. Follow the walkway to **Castle Walk,** which offers the most panoramic view of Crail.

To understand the villages of East Neuk better, call at the **Crail Museum & Heritage Centre,** 62 Marketgate (☎ **01333/450-869**), which contains artifacts related to fishing and the former trading links of these tiny villages. Admission is free. June to September, the center is open Monday to Saturday 10am to 1pm and 2 to 5pm and Sunday 2 to 5pm.

### ACCOMMODATIONS & DINING

**Croma Hotel.** 33–35 Nethergate, Crail, Fife KY10 3TU. ☎ **01333/450-239.** 6 units. TV TEL. £50 ($85) double. Rates include Scottish breakfast. MC, V. Closed Dec–Jan.

This guesthouse, a block off High Street near the harbor, offers small rooms, very simply furnished but comfortable. One notable feature is the fully licensed Chart Room bar, open 6pm to midnight, where you can drop in for drinks or have a bar meal. The dining room has Windsor chairs in front of the bay window. Many of the artists who live in this little fishing village come here for drinks and dinner.

**Denburn House.** 1 Marketgate, Crail, Fife KY10 3TQ. ☎ **01333/450-253.** www.s-h-systems. co.uk/hotels/denburnhouse.html. E-mail: denburn@fabdial.co.uk. 6 units. £25–£30 ($42.50–$51) double. Rates includes breakfast. No credit cards.

Near the town center, in a historic neighborhood known as Marketgate, this guesthouse occupies a 200-year-old stone-sided building that retains many of its interior architectural features, including the paneling in the lounge and an elaborate staircase. In 1998, most of the interior was tastefully renovated; all the guest rooms were redecorated in a conservative but very pleasing style. In the rear garden is a scattering of lawn furniture and access to the great Scottish outdoors. Everything is very low-key and unpretentious.

## 3 St. Andrews: The Birthplace of Golf

14 miles (22.5km) SE of Dundee, 51 (82km) miles NE of Edinburgh

The medieval royal burgh of St. Andrews was once filled with monasteries and ancient houses that didn't survive the pillages of Henry VIII; regrettably, only a few ruins rising in ghostly dignity remain. Most of the town as you'll see it today was built of local stone during the 18th, 19th, and early 20th centuries. This historic sea town in northeast Fife is also known as the seat where the rules of golf in Britain and the world are codified and arbitrated. Golf was played for the first time in the 1400s, probably on the site of St. Andrews's Old Course, and was enjoyed by Mary Queen of Scots here in 1567. Golfers consider this town to be hallowed ground.

## ESSENTIALS

**GETTING THERE**    BritRail stops 8 miles (13km) away at the town of Leuchars (rhymes with "euchres") on its London–Edinburgh–Dundee–Aberdeen run to the northeast. About 15 trains per day make the trip. Trip time from Edinburgh to Leuchars is about an hour, and a one-way fare is £8.10 ($13.75). For information, call ☎ 0345/484-950.

Once at Leuchars, you can take a bus the rest of the way to St. Andrews. Bus no. 95 departs about every 30 minutes. Fife Scottish bus no. X24 travels from Glasgow to Glenrothes daily, and from there, bus X59 runs to St. Andrews. Buses operate daily 7am to midnight, the trip taking between 2½ and 3 hours. Buses arrive at the St. Andrews Bus Station, Station Road, just off City Road (call ☎ 01334/474-238 for schedules).

By car from Edinburgh, head northwest along A90 and cross the Forth Road Bridge north. Take A921 to the junction with A915 and continue northeast until you reach St. Andrews.

**VISITOR INFORMATION**    The **tourist office** is on 70 Market St. (☎ 01334/472-021). January to March, November, and December, it's open Monday to Saturday 9:30am to 5pm; April hours are Monday to Saturday 9:30am to 5pm and Sunday 11am to 5pm; May, June, September, and October, hours are Monday to Saturday 9:30am to 6pm and Sunday 11am to 5pm; and July and August, hours are Monday to Saturday 9:30am to 7pm and Sunday 10am to 6pm.

## HITTING THE LINKS

All six of the St. Andrews courses are fully owned by the municipality and open to the public on a more-or-less democratic basis—ballots are polled 1 day in advance. This balloting system might be circumvented for players who reserve with the appropriate starters several days or weeks in advance. To play the hallowed Old Course, you must present a current handicap certificate and/or letter of introduction from a bona-fide golf club.

The misty and verdant golf courses are the very symbol of St. Andrews: the famous **Old Course;** the 6,604-yard (6,010m), par-72 **New Course** (opened in 1896); the 6,805-yard (6,192.5m), par-71 **Jubilee Course** (opened in 1897 in honor of Queen Victoria); the 6,112-yard (5,562m), par-70 **Eden** (opened in 1914); the **Balgove** (a nine-hole course for children's golf training, opened in 1972), and the 5,094-yard (4,635.5m), par-67 **Strathtyrum** (the newest and most far-flung, an eight-hole course opened in 1993). Encircled by all of them is the world's most prestigious golf club, the **Royal and Ancient Golf Club** (☎ 01334/472-112), founded in St. Andrews in 1754—it remains more or less rigidly closed as a private-membership men's club. The Royal and Ancient traditionally opens its doors to the public only on St. Andrews Day to view its legendary trophy room. This usually, but not always, falls around November 30.

The **Old Course,** Pilmour Cottage (☎ 01334/466-666), is the world's most legendary temple of golf, one whose difficulty is shaped by nature and the long-ago paths of grazing sheep. Over the centuries, stately buildings have been erected near its start and finish. Aristocrats from virtually everywhere have lent their names and reputations to enhance its glamour, and its nuances have been debated, usually in reverent tones, by golfers in bars and on fairways throughout the world. This fabled par-72 course hosted the 2000 British Open, when golf fans from around the world watched in awe as Tiger Woods became the youngest golfer in history to complete a grand slam (and only the fifth golfer to ever perform the feat). Greens fees are £75 to £80 ($127.50 to $136), a caddy costs £25 ($42.50) plus tip, and clubs rent for £20 to £30 ($34 to $51) per round. There are no electric carts allowed, and you can rent a trolley on afternoons only between May and September for £3 ($5.10).

Facilities for golfers in St. Andrews are legion. Beside the 18th hole of the Old Course, within premises owned/operated by the Rusacks Hotel, are links rooms with lockers, showers, and changing facilities, as well as a dining room and a bar. Virtually every hotel in town maintains some kind of facility to assist golfers.

For more details on golfing in St. Andrews (plus tips on golf associations and golf tours), see "Teeing Off: Golfing in Scotland" in chapter 3, "The Active Vacation Planner."

## SEEING THE SIGHTS

Founded in 1411, the **University of St. Andrews** is the oldest in Scotland and the third oldest in Britain and has been called the "Oxbridge" of Scotland. At term time, you can see packs of students in their characteristic red gowns. The university grounds stretch west of the St. Andrews Castle between North Street and the Scores.

The university's most interesting buildings are the tower and church of St. Salvator's College and the courtyard of St. Mary's College, from 1538. An ancient thorn tree, said to have been planted by Mary Queen of Scots, stands near the college's chapel. St. Leonard's College church is also from medieval days. In 1645, the Scottish Parliament met in what was once the University Library and is now a students' reading room. A modern University Library, containing many rare ancient volumes, was opened in 1976.

**Holy Trinity Church.** Opposite St. Mary's College, off South St. ☎ 01334/474-494. Free admission, but call in advance to make sure someone is in attendance. Apr–Sept daily 10am–noon and 2–4pm.

Called the Town Kirk, this restored medieval church once stood on the grounds of the now-ruined cathedral (see below). The church was moved to its present site in 1410, considerably altered after the Reformation of 1560, and restored in the early 20th century. You'll find much fine stained glass and carvings inside.

**St. Andrews Cathedral and Priory.** Off Pends Rd. ☎ 01334/472-563. Admission £2 ($3.40) adults, £1.50 ($2.55) seniors, 75p ($1.30) children. Apr–Sept daily 9:30am–6pm; Oct–Mar Mon–Sat 9:30am–4pm, Sun 2–4pm.

Near the Celtic settlement of St. Mary of the Rock, by the sea at the east end of town, is the semi-ruin of St. Andrews Cathedral and Priory. It was founded in 1160 and begun in the Romanesque style; however, the cathedral's construction suffered many setbacks. By the time of its consecration in 1318 in the presence of King Robert the Bruce, it had a Gothic overlay. At the time the largest church in Scotland, the cathedral established St. Andrews as the ecclesiastical capital of the country, but today the ruins can only suggest its former beauty and importance. There's a collection of early Christian and medieval monuments, as well as artifacts discovered on the cathedral site.

**Castle of St. Andrews.** The Scores (300 yds. [273m] northwest of the cathedral). ☎ 01334/477-196. Admission £2.50 ($4.25) adults, £1.90 ($3.25) seniors, £1 ($1.70) children. Apr–Sept daily 9:30am–6:30pm; Oct–Mar daily 9:30am–4:30pm.

This ruined 13th-century castle eerily poised at the edge of the sea boasts a bottle dungeon and secret passages. Founded in the early part of the 13th century, it was reconstructed several times and was once a bishop's palace and later a prison for reformers. The bottle dungeon is carved 24 feet (7m) down into the rock, and both prisoners and food were dropped through it. There's said to be no nastier dungeon in all Scotland.

Much of the eeriness here concerns the 1546 arrest of religious reformer George Wishart and the show trial that followed. Convicted by a group of Catholic prelates spearheaded by Cardinal Beaton, Wishart was burned at the stake, reputedly while Beaton and his entourage watched from an upper-floor window. Vowing revenge, a group of reformers waited 3 months before gaining access to the castle while disguised as stonemasons. They overpowered the guards (some they killed, some they threw into the castle's moat) and murdered Beaton—and, rather bizarrely, preserved his corpse in salt so they could eventually give it a proper burial. The reformers retained control of the castle for several months, until the Catholic forces of the earl of Arran laid siege. As part of their efforts, the attackers almost completed a tunnel (they called it "a mine"), dug virtually through rock, beneath the castle walls. The (Protestant) defenders, in response, dug a tunnel ("a countermine") of their own, which intersected the first tunnel at a higher elevation, allowing the defenders to drop rocks, boiling oil, or whatever else on the attackers' heads. The resulting underground battle took on epic proportions during the virtually implacable year-long siege. As part of the tour, you can stumble down the narrow countermine to the place where besieged and besiegers met in this clash.

✪ **Secret Bunker.** Underground Nuclear Command Centre, Crown Buildings (near St. Andrews), Fife. ☎ **01333/310-301.** Admission £6.45 ($10.95) adults, £4.95 ($8.40) seniors, £3.45 ($5.85) ages 5–16, £16.95 ($28.80) families; free for age 4 and under. Apr–Oct daily 10am–5pm. From St. Andrews, follow the signs to Anstruther, driving 7¹/₂ miles (12km) south. At that point, signs show the way to the bunker.

Scotland's best-kept secret for 40 years of cold war, this amazing labyrinth, built 100 feet (30m) below ground and encased in 15 feet (4.5m) of reinforced concrete, is where central government and military commanders would have run the country from if the United Kingdom had been attacked and nuclear war broken out. Built in great secrecy in 1951 to withstand aerial attack, it has a guardhouse entrance designed to look like a traditional Scottish farmhouse. You can visit the BBC studio where emergency broadcasts to Scotland would have been made and the switchboard room set up to handle 2,800 outside lines. The bunker could allow 300 people to live, work, and sleep in safety while coordinating war efforts, like aboveground retaliation. It also contains two cinemas showing authentic cold war films, an audiovisual theater, a cafe, and a gift shop.

You can wander at will through the underground labyrinth, but 30-minute guided tours depart daily at 11am, 1pm, and 3pm. For some amazing reason, the chapel here has been the site of several local weddings since decommissioning in 1993.

## SHOPPING

Specializing in Scottish art, **St. Andrews Fine Arts,** 84A Market St. (☎ **01334/ 474-080**), also sells prints, drawings, and watercolors. Paintings for sale were all produced in the national boundaries of Scotland sometime between 1800 and the present. **Graeme Renton,** 72 South St. (☎ **01334/476-334**), is one of Scotland's leading dealers of oriental carpets, whether you're seeking antique rugs or reasonably priced reproductions. Rugs range from handmade to machine made and come in many sizes, prices, and styles. At **St. Andrews Pottery Shop,** 4 Church Square

(☎ 01334/477-744), an array of decorative stoneware, ceramics, and enameled jewelry—most of it produced locally—is for sale. **Bonkers,** 80 Market St. (☎ **01334/ 473-919**), is a typical tourist shop, hawking T-shirts, regional pottery, and other souvenirs, along with cards and stationery.

## ACCOMMODATIONS
### VERY EXPENSIVE

✪ **Rufflets Country House Hotel.** Strathkinness Low Rd., St. Andrews, Fife KY16 9TX. ☎ **01334/472-594.** Fax 01334/478-703. www.rufflets.co.uk. E-mail: reservations@ rufflets.co.uk. 22 units. TV TEL. £180–£220 ($306–$374) double. Rates include Scottish breakfast. AE, DC, MC, V. Take B939 1¹/₂ miles (2.5km) from St. Andrews.

The garden-and-golf crowd loves this cozy 1924 country house in a 10-acre garden. Each good-sized guest room is furnished in a homelike way (often in Queen Anne style), some with canopied or four-poster beds and all with hair dryers, tea/coffeemakers, and alarm clocks. The most modern rooms are in the new wing, but traditionalists request space in the handsome main building. Reserve well in advance, as Rufflets is very popular with British vacationers.

**Dining:** Even if you aren't staying here, you may want to reserve a table at the garden-style Rufflets Hotel Restaurant, overlooking the award-winning garden. Excellent fresh ingredients are used in the continental and Scottish dishes. Dinner is served daily, with expensive fixed-price menus; reasonably priced bar lunches are also available daily.

**Amenities:** Concierge, room service, laundry/valet.

**Rusacks.** Pilmour Links, St. Andrews, Fife KY16 9JQ. ☎ **800/225-5843** in the U.S., or 01334/ 474-321. Fax 01334/477-896. www.heritage-hotels.com. 68 units. TV TEL. £185 ($314.50) double; £600 ($1,020) suite. AE, DC, MC, V.

A grand Victorian pile built in 1887 by Josef Rusack, a German from Silesia who recognized St. Andrews's potential as a golf capital, Rusacks sits at the edge of the famous 18th hole of Pilmour Links of the Old Course. The hotel's stone walls are capped with neoclassical gables and slate roofs. Inside, chintz picks up the tones from the bouquets of flowers sent in fresh twice a week. Between the panels and Ionic columns of the public rooms, racks of lendable books re-create the atmosphere of a private country-house library. Upstairs, the spacious guest rooms contain some carved antiques and all modern conveniences, but nothing to equal the St. Andrews Old Course Hotel (see below).

**Dining:** Open daily 6am to 5pm, the basement Golf Club has golf-related photos, trompe-l'oeil racks of books, Chesterfield sofas, and vested waiters. Here light meals and snacks are served. The newly opened The Old Course restaurant, overlooking the 18th hole, offers daily specials along with local game, meat, and fish, accompanied by a wine list from a well-stocked cellar; it offers expensive fixed-price menus for dinner nightly.

**Amenities:** Concierge, 24-hour room service, laundry, sauna, solarium.

**St. Andrews Golf Hotel.** 40 The Scores, St. Andrews, Fife KY16 9AS. ☎ **01334/472-611.** Fax 01334/472-188. www.standrews-golf-co.uk. 22 units. TV TEL. £145–£160 ($246.50–$272) double; £185 ($314.50) suite. Rates include Scottish breakfast. AE, DC, MC, V.

A combination of greenery, sea mists, and tradition makes this late-Victorian property extremely popular with golfers, despite the fact that many of them confuse it at first glance with the larger and more prestigious St. Andrews Old Course Hotel (see below). About 200 yards (182m) from the first tee-off of the famous golf course, it was built as a private home and later expanded and transformed into a hotel run by Brian and Maureen Hughes. The comfortable but unstylish midsize guest rooms have such thoughtful extras as coffeemakers, hair dryers, and toiletries. The rooms in the front get the view but also the noise.

**Dining:** Bar lunches are served Monday to Saturday, and table d'hôte dinners are presented nightly in an oak-paneled restaurant with a fireplace. For hotel guests, there's a fixed-price menu of £25 ($42.50); otherwise meals cost £20 to £35 ($34 to $59.50). Informal meals are served in a basement bistro.

**Amenities:** Concierge, room service, laundry/valet, nearby tennis courts.

**✪ St. Andrews Old Course Hotel.** Old Station Rd., St. Andrews, Fife KY16 9SP. ☎ **01334/ 474-371.** Fax 01334/477-668. www.oldcoursehotel.co.uk. 137 units. MINIBAR TV TEL. £344 ($584.80) double; from £395 ($671.50) suite. Rates include Scottish breakfast. Children 11 and under stay free in parents' room. AE, DC, MC, V.

Many dedicated golfers choose the St. Andrews Old Course Hotel, close to A91 on the outskirts of town, where it overlooks the 17th fairway, the Road Hole of the Old Course. (Don't let the name mislead you: The hotel isn't related to the links of the same name, and guests here find access to the course just as difficult as it is elsewhere.) Fortified by finnan haddie and porridge, a real old-fashioned Scottish breakfast, you can face that diabolical stretch of greenery where the Scots have been whacking away since the early 15th century. Some £16 million ($27.2 million) has been spent to transform the place into a world-class hotel (with price tags to match), and the facade was altered to keep it in line with St. Andrews's more traditional buildings; its balconies afford top-view seats at all golf tournaments. The guest rooms and suites have been remodeled and refurbished, offering traditional wooden furniture and state-of-the-art marble bathrooms.

**Dining:** Well-prepared and high-priced international cuisine is served in the Road Hole Grill. In summer, light meals and afternoon tea are served in a casual dining room known as Sands. The Jigger Inn serves real ale and soup and sandwiches at lunch in a traditional pub atmosphere.

**Amenities:** Concierge, 24-hour room service, laundry, baby-sitting; health spa, whirlpool, massage room, steam rooms, beauty/therapy salons, pool, changing and locker rooms, pro shop.

## EXPENSIVE

**Peat Inn.** Cupar, Fife KY15 5LH. ☎ **01334/840-206.** Fax 01334/840-530. www. peatinn.co.uk. E-mail: reception@thepeatinn. 8 units. TV TEL. £145 ($246.50) suite for 2. Rates include Scottish breakfast. AE, DC, MC, V. Closed Sun–Mon. From St. Andrews, drive 7 miles (11km) southwest along A915, then branch onto B940.

About 7 miles from St. Andrews, in the village of Cupar, the Peat is in an inn/post office built in 1760, where beautifully furnished guest rooms and spacious suites are offered and David Wilson prepares exceptional cuisine in the restaurant.

**Dining:** The ingredients are almost all local—even the pigeons come from a St. Andrews farm (they come in a pastry case with wild mushrooms or in Armagnac-and-juniper sauce). For a main course, try the roast monkfish and lobster with asparagus and wild mushrooms. The dessert specialty is a trio of caramel-flavored sweets, including crème caramel, caramel-flavored ice cream, and a caramelized apple pastry, all drizzled with caramel sauce. Prices are high, and lunch and dinner are served Tuesday to Saturday.

## MODERATE

**✪ Inn at Lathones.** By Largoward, St. Andrews, Fife KY9 1JE. ☎ **01334/840-494.** Fax 01334/840-694. www.theinn.co.uk. E-mail: lathones@theinn.co.uk. 14 units. TV TEL. £90–£120

($153–$204) double. Rates include Scottish breakfast. MC, V. Take A915, 5 miles (8km) south-west of the center of St. Andrews.

Once a coaching inn, this 200-year-old manor has been thoughtfully restored and provides a reasonable alternative for golfers who can't afford the grand hotels. All its midsize guest rooms are nicely furnished, with individually controlled heating, tea/coffeemakers, and hair dryers. Two units have log-burning stoves and Jacuzzis. The public rooms reflect Scottish tradition, with open fires and beamed ceilings.

The more formal restaurant is under the guidance of chef Marc Guiburt, who has created a French-inspired continental cuisine using fresh Scottish produce; prices are on the high side of moderate. There's also a more casual grill room, Steak Out.

**Russell Hotel.** 26 The Scores, St. Andrews, Fife KY16 9AS. ☎ **01334/473-447.** Fax 01334/478-279. www.russellhotelstandrews.co.uk. E-mail: russellhotel@talk.21.com. 10 units. TV TEL. £92–£99 ($156.40–$168.30) double. Rates include Scottish breakfast. AE, MC, V. Closed Dec 24–Jan 9.

Once a 19th-century private home, the Russell has an ideal location overlooking St. Andrews Bay, a 2-minute walk from the Old Course's first tee. It's well run by Gordon and Fiona de Vries and offers fully equipped though standard guest rooms with tea/coffeemakers and hair dryers. The cozy Victorian pub serves drinks and bar suppers to a loyal local crowd, and the rather unremarkable restaurant offers moderately priced fixed-price dinners nightly.

### INEXPENSIVE

**Ashleigh House Hotel.** 37 St. Mary St., St. Andrews, Fife KY16 8AZ. ☎ **01334/475-429.** Fax 01334/474383. E-mail: 010764.2770@compuserve.com. 10 units, 9 with private bathroom. TV TEL. £60 ($102) double without bathroom; £80 ($136) double with bathroom. Rates include breakfast. MC, V.

This B&B near the town center was built in 1883 as a fever hospital to quarantine patients afflicted with scarlet fever, diphtheria, and other plagues of the day. After World War I, it was transformed into an orphanage and in the late 1980s was converted to a B&B. The trio of thick-walled stone cottages are connected by means of covered passageways. There's a bar with a wide assortment of single malts and a rough-and-ready kind of charm. The guest rooms are outfitted with good beds and flowered upholsteries, and provide hair dryers and tea/coffeemakers. On the premises is a sauna and solarium.

**Bell Craig Guest House.** 8 Murray Park, St. Andrews, Fife KY16. ☎ **01334/472-962.** www.bellcraig.co.uk. 6 units. TV. £40–£50 ($68–$85) double. Rates include breakfast. MC, V.

Occupying a century-old stone-fronted house in a historic neighborhood, a 3-minute walk from the Old Course, this guesthouse has had long practice at housing the parents of students at the nearby university. Sheila Black, the hardworking owner, operates with decency and pride and makes a point to spruce up each room in a different style at regular intervals. (Our favorite is the one done in tartan.) Each is high-ceilinged, cozy, completely unpretentious, and well scrubbed.

## DINING

**Grange Inn.** Grange Rd., at Grange (on B959). ☎ **01334/472-670.** Reservations recommended. Fixed-price menus £20–£25 ($34–$42.50). AE, DC, MC, V. Daily 12:30–2pm and 7–8:45pm. Drive about 1½ miles (2.5km) from St. Andrews on B959. SCOTTISH/SEAFOOD.

An old-fashioned hospitality prevails in this country cottage with its garden, offering a good choice of dishes made from fresh produce. Local beef and lamb always appear on the menu, as do fish and shellfish from the fishing villages of East Neuk. Fruits and herbs come from Cupar. Typical of the dishes served are beef fillet with port sauce complemented by wild mushrooms or chicken suprême stuffed with julienne of vegetables and coated with almonds, then served on lemon sauce. A classic opener and an old favorite at the inn is a stew of mussels and onions.

✪ **Ostlers Close.** 25 Bonnygate, in the nearby town of Cupar. ☎ **01334/655-574.** Reservations recommended. Main courses £9.50–£12 ($16.15–$20.40) at lunch, £15–£19 ($25.50–$32.30) at dinner. AE, MC, V. Tues and Fri–Sat 12:15–2pm; Tues–Sat 7–9:30pm. Closed 2 weeks mid-May. From St. Andrews, go along A91 for 7 miles (11km) to the southwest until you reach the village of Cupar. BRITISH/INTERNATIONAL.

Sophisticated and intensely concerned with the quality of its cuisine, this charming restaurant occupies a 17th-century building that functioned in the early 20th century as a temperance hotel. Today, in the heart of the hamlet of Cupar, 7 miles (11km) from St. Andrews, it contains a kitchen in what used to be the hotel's stables, with a severely elegant set of dining rooms in the hotel's former public areas. Amanda Graham, co-owner and supervisor of the dining room, is the person you're most likely to meet here, along with a staff serving the cuisine of her husband, Jimmy Graham. Menu items are based on seasonal Scottish produce and likely to include roasted saddle of roe venison with wild mushroom sauce; pan-fried scallops with fresh asparagus and butter sauce; a fresh medley of seafood with champagne-flavored butter sauce; and fillet of Scottish lamb stuffed with skirlie, an old-fashioned but flavorful combination of bacon-flavored oatmeal and herbs. Whenever it's available, opt for the confit of duckling with salted pork and lentils.

## ST. ANDREWS AFTER DARK

The cultural center of St. Andrews is the **Byre Theatre,** Abbey Street (☎ 01334/476-288), which features drama ranging from Shakespeare plays to musical comedies. Being rebuilt from the foundation up, it's expected to be up and running by late 2000 or early 2001. Productions are currently being staged in a variety of venues around town, and tickets cost £8 ($13.60) adults, £5 ($8.50) children. Pick up a weekly version of *What's on in Fife* from the local tourist office to find out what's featured.

   **Victoria,** 1A St. Mary's Place (☎ 01334/476-964), is the place to catch a live band in St. Andrews. This student-filled pub features folk, rock, and blues acts on Thursday and Saturday, as well as karaoke every Friday. Because of the absence of students over the summer, there's no live music. John Smiths, Beamish Stout, McEwans Lager, 78 Shilling, and 80 Shilling are available on tap.

   A pub since 1904, the **Central Bar,** at the corner of Market and College Street (☎ 01334/478-296), is an antiquated room with a jukebox, and it may become rowdy during a football or tennis match. The best brews here are Old Peculiar, Theakstons XB, and McEwans Lager.

   **Chariots,** The Scores (☎ 01334/472-451), in the Scores Hotel, attracts mainly a local crowd, ranging from 30 to 60 years, who gather in the evening for conversation over a pint. Despite a strong regional tradition of beer brewing, two outsiders, Guinness and Millers, are featured on tap.

## 4 Falkland: One of Scotland's Loveliest Villages

21 miles (34km) N of Edinburgh

The royal burgh of Falkland, containing cobblestone streets and crooked houses, lies at the northern base of the hill of East Lomond. Its notable sight is Falkland Palace and Gardens, now owned by the National Trust of Scotland and forever associated with memories of Mary Queen of Scots. In your rush to visit the royal palace, try not to forget to walk around Falkland itself. It's one of the loveliest villages in Scotland.

## ESSENTIALS

**GETTING THERE**    From Edinburgh, take the train to Markinch, the closest rail link to Falkland; the trip is 30 minutes. Call ☎ **0345/484-950** for schedules. From Markinch, bus no. 36 connects with arriving trains and runs to Falkland in 15 minutes.

If you're driving, take A90 northwest of Edinburgh across the Forth Road Bridge, then continue northeast along A921, which leads into A92. At the junction with A912, head northwest to Falkland.

**VISITOR INFORMATION**    The nearest **tourist office** is at 19 Shytes Causeway, Kirkcaldy (☎ **01592/267-775**), 13 miles (21km) south of Falkland. It's open Monday to Saturday 10am to 5pm (to 5:30pm in August).

## SEEING THE PALACE

**✪ Falkland Palace and Gardens.** High St. ☎ **01337/857-397.** Admission to palace and gardens £5 ($8.50) adults, £3.50 ($5.95) seniors/students/children; admission to garden only £2.50 ($4.25) adults, £1.70 ($2.90) seniors/students/children. Apr–Oct Mon–Sat 11am–5:30pm, Sun 1:30–5:30pm. Closed Nov–Mar.

Since the 14th century, Falkland has been connected with Scottish kings and queens. Originally a castle stood on the site of today's palace, but it was replaced in the 16th century. Falkland then became a favorite seat of the Scottish court. James V died here, and Mary Queen of Scots used to come to Falkland for hunting and hawking. It was also here that Francis Stuart, fifth earl of Bothwell, tried to seize his young cousin, James VI, son of Mary Queen of Scots. The gardens have been laid out according to the original royal plans. Falkland also boasts the oldest royal tennis court in the United Kingdom.

## ACCOMMODATIONS

**Covenanter Hotel.** The Square, Falkland, Fife KY15 7BU. ☎ **01337/857-224.** Fax 01337/857-163. www.covenanterhotel.com. 7 units. TV TEL. £48 ($81.60) double or apt. Rates include Scottish breakfast. AE, DC, MC, V.

This has been a popular inn since the early 18th century. The hotel is built of local stone, with high chimneys, wooden shutters, and a Georgian entry and is on a small square opposite the church and palace. With modest modernization, the guest rooms range from small to midsize, each traditionally furnished, with excellent mattresses. For before-dinner drinks, try the Covenanter Cocktail Bar; the old-style dining room serves moderately priced lunch and dinner daily. There's also a moderately priced bistro serving selections like beef-and-ale pie, grilled trout, various steaks, and vegetarian dishes.

## DINING

**Kind Kyttock's Kitchen.** Cross Wynd. ☎ **01337/857-477.** Main courses £3.50–£5.25 ($5.95–$8.90). AE, MC, V. Tues–Sun 10:30am–5:30pm. Closed Dec 24–Jan 5. SCOTTISH.

Near the palace, this restaurant is also an art gallery that displays local crafts and paintings. A specialty is homemade oat cakes with cheese. The bread is also homemade, very fresh tasting. For a tea, we suggest pancakes with fruit and fresh cream. Even better, however, are the tarts with fresh cream. The salads are also good. A cup of scotch broth, served with a slice of whole-meal bread, is a favorite.

## 5  Stirling

37 miles (59.5km) NW of Edinburgh, 28 miles (45km) NE of Glasgow

Stirling is dominated by its impressive castle, perched on a 250-foot (76m) basalt rock formed by the Rivers Forth and Clyde and the relatively small parcel of land between them. The ancient town of Stirling, on the main east-west route across Scotland, grew up around the castle. It lies in the heart of an area so turbulent in Scottish history it was called the "cockpit of Scotland" (here "cockpit" refers to the pit where male chickens would be forced to engage in cockfights). A memorable battle fought here was the Battle of Bannockburn in 1314, when Robert I (the Bruce) defeated the army of Edward II of England and gained Scotland its independence. Another was the Battle of Stirling Bridge in 1297 (see "The True Story of *Braveheart*," below).

Ever since the release of Mel Gibson's *Braveheart,* world attention has focused on the Scottish national hero William Wallace, a freedom fighter who became known as the "hammer and scourge" of the English. However, *Braveheart* was filmed mostly in Ireland, and the Battle of Stirling Bridge in the movie was played out on a plain with not a bridge in sight.

Stirling is the central crossroads of Scotland, giving easy access by rail and road to all its major towns and cities. If you use it as a base, you'll be only a short distance from many attractions, including Loch Lomond, the Trossachs, and the Highlands.

## ESSENTIALS

**GETTING THERE**    Frequent trains run between Glasgow and Stirling (a 45-minute trip) and between Edinburgh and Stirling (a 60-minute trip). A 1-day round-trip ticket from Edinburgh is £5.50 to £8.80 ($9.35 to $14.95) and from Glasgow is £6.20 to £7.70 ($10.55 to $13.10). For schedules, call **National Express Enquiries** at ☎ **0345/484-950.**

Frequent buses run to Stirling from Glasgow (a 45-minute trip). A 1-day round-trip ticket from Glasgow costs £4.20 ($7.15). Check with **Scottish CityLink** (☎ **0990/505-050**) for details.

If you're driving from Glasgow, head northeast along A80 to M80, at which point continue north. From Edinburgh, head northwest along M9.

**VISITOR INFORMATION**    The **tourist office** is at 41 Dumbarton Rd. (☎ **01786/ 475-019**). April to mid-May, it's open Monday to Saturday 9am to 5pm; mid-May to June, hours are Monday to Saturday 9am to 6pm and Sunday 10am to 4pm; July and August, hours are Monday to Saturday 9am to 7pm and Sunday 10am to 5pm; September hours are Monday to Saturday 9am to 6pm and Sunday 10am to 5pm; October hours are Monday to Saturday 9:30am to 5pm; and November to March, it's open Monday to Friday 10am to 5pm and Saturday 10am to 4pm.

## SEEING THE SIGHTS

To get a real feeling for Stirling, stroll the **Back Walk,** beginning near Rob Roy's statue, near the Guildhall in the town center. Following this trail along the outside of the town's once-fortified walls, you'll find good views, see an old watchtower (and a place where prisoners were hanged), and eventually reach Stirling Castle (see below).

✪ **Stirling Castle.** Upper Castle Hill. ☎ **01786/450-000.** Admission to castle £6 ($10.20) adults, £4.50 ($7.65) seniors, £1.50 ($2.55) children; free admission to museum. Castle Apr–Sept daily 9:30am–6pm, Oct–Mar daily 9:30am–5pm; museum, Mon–Sat 10am–5:45pm, Sun 11am–4:45pm.

# Stirling, Loch Lomond & the Trossachs

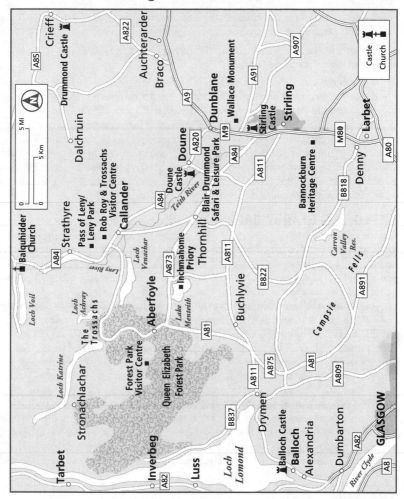

There are traces of a 7th-century royal habitation of the Stirling area, and on the right bank of the Forth, Stirling Castle dates from the Middle Ages, when its location on a dividing line between the Lowlands and the Highlands made it the key to the Highlands. The castle became an important seat of two kings, James IV and James V, both of whom added to it, the latter following classic Renaissance style, then relatively unknown in Britain. Here Mary Queen of Scots lived as an infant monarch for the first 4 years of her life. After its final defeat in 1746, Bonnie Prince Charlie's army stopped here. Later, the castle became an army barracks and headquarters of the Argyll and Sutherland Highlanders, one of Britain's most celebrated regiments. An audio-visual presentation explains what you're about to see.

In the castle is the **Museum of the Argyll and Sutherland Highlanders** (☎ 01786/ 475-165), presenting an excellent exhibit of colors, pipe banners, and regimental silver, along with medals (some of which go back to the Battle of Waterloo) won by Scottish soldiers for valor. Run by Britain's Ministry of Defense, it functions as a showcase for a military unit, some of whose members were at press time in Kosovo and Bosnia as part of the U.N. peacekeeping force.

**Church of the Holy Rude.** St. John St. ☎ **01786/475-275.** Free admission. May–Sept daily 10am–5pm. Closed Oct–Apr.

From the early 15th century, the Church of the Holy Rude is said to be the only church in the country still in use that has witnessed a coronation. It was 1567 when the 13-month-old James VI was crowned here, Mary Queen of Scots' son who was to become James I of England. John Knox preached the sermon. Constructed with the simplest of building tools more than 600 years ago and built as a reminder of the cross (rude) on which Christ was supposedly crucified, the church is memorable for its rough but evocative stonework and its elaborate 19th-century stained glass—particularly on the south side of the choir. Recent restorations have been done in the most tasteful and unobtrusive of styles.

## EXPLORING NEARBY BANNOCKBURN

You can take an interesting detour to Bannockburn, a name that looms large in Scottish history. It was there that Robert the Bruce, his army of 6,000 outnumbered three to one, defeated the forces of Edward II in 1314. Before nightfall on that day, Robert the Bruce had won back the throne of Scotland. The battlefield, which makes for a peaceful walk today, lies off M80, 2 miles (3km) south of Stirling.

At the **Bannockburn Heritage Centre,** Glasgow Road (☎ **01786/812-664**), an audiovisual presentation tells the story of these events, and *The Kingdom of the Scots* exhibit traces the history of Scotland from William Wallace to the Union of Crowns. The queen herself came here in 1964 to unveil an equestrian statue of Bruce. The site is open all year, but the Heritage Centre and shop are open daily 10am to 5:30pm in April to October and daily 11am to 3pm in March, November, and December. The last audiovisual showing is at 5:30pm. Admission is £2.50 ($4.15) adults, £1.70 ($2.90) seniors/children, and £6.70 ($11.40) families.

From the **Borestone,** where Robert the Bruce commanded his forces at the start of his battle for Stirling, you can see Stirling Castle and the Forth Valley. He planted his standards (flags) as inspiration for his troops, and today a flagpole capped with the standards of Scotland still flies proudly from atop this low hill. The location is off M80/M9 at Junction 9.

## SHOPPING

Stirling's town center has some interesting shopping. One good hunting ground is the **Thistle Centre** indoor shopping plaza, home of about 65 shops at the junction of Port Street and Murray Place.

**McCutcheon's,** 51 Baker St. (☎ **01786/461-771**), is a book dealer specializing in antiquarian books. The dealer claims to have everything under the sun—well, the range of books is startlingly vast.

The best woolen gift goods are at **R. R. Henderson,** 6–8 Friar St. (☎ **01786/ 473-681**), a Highland outfitter selling not only woolen goods like sweaters and scarves but also made-to-order kilts and tartans.

Some of the best shopping is not in Stirling itself but in the outlying area. Take A9 to Larbert and at the roundabout follow A18 west until you see the sign for **Barbara Davidson's Pottery Studio,** Muirhall Farm, at Larbert (☎ **01324/554-430**), 9 miles (14.5km) south of Stirling. At this 18th-century farmstead, Barbara Davidson operates a studio and workshop. She's one of Scotland's best-known potters, and a large selection of her functional wares is exhibited and sold here.

# The True Story of *Braveheart*

*Sir Robert the Bruce at Bannockburn*
*Beat the English in every wheel and turn,*
*And made them fly in great dismay*
*From off the field without delay . . .*

—William McGonagall, "The Battle of Bannockburn"

**Robert the Bruce** (1274–1329) was the first of three kings of Scotland named Robert. Although neither Mel Gibson nor Liam Neeson selected this daring man as the subject for a movie, they might well have done so, for Robert the Bruce led a life filled with all the excitement and thrills of a 1930s Errol Flynn adventure flick.

In 1292, Edward I of England gave the Scottish crown to John de Balliol, known as the "vassal king," demanding Scotland pay homage to the English throne. But instead, the Scots formed what was to become known as the Auld Alliance with France in October 1295. Edward viewed this as a declaration of war, and the "Hammer of Scotland" stormed into Scotland, devastating the countryside and capturing and taking home the Stone of Destiny from Scone (the coronation stone of Scottish kings).

William Wallace (1274–1305) defeated the English at the 1297 Battle of Stirling Bridge and was made "Guardian of the Realm." Edward, in turn, defeated Wallace at the Battle of Falkirk the following year. Outlawed for his activities, Wallace hid for 7 years until his capture, at which time he was paraded through the streets of London and hanged and drawn and quartered, with his entrails burned before his eyes as he died. This horrific English method of execution reputedly was devised by Edward especially for Wallace.

Robert the Bruce replaced Wallace as "Guardian of Scotland." In March 1306 Bruce had himself crowned king of Scotland. Edward rushed north and defeated Bruce's forces at Methven and Dalry. Like Wallace, Bruce became an outlaw, forced into hiding, probably on the island of Rathlin off the Irish coast. There he was said to have learned patience, courage, and hope by watching a spider persevere in spinning a web, swinging from one rafter to another on a fragile thread.

In 1307, he returned to Scotland, where he captured Perth in 1313 and Edinburgh in 1314. At Bannockburn, also in 1314, he defeated the forces of Edward's son, Edward II. The pope excommunicated Bruce, and his sovereignty wasn't recognized by the royal houses of Europe.

Upon Edward III's coronation in 1327, the Scots launched a raid into England. The following year, Edward was almost captured when he led a retaliatory army into Scotland. But in 1328 a peace treaty was signed, acknowledging Scotland's independence. David, Bruce's 4-year-old son, was "married" to Joan, Edward III's 7-year-old sister. The Bruce ruled Scotland wisely until his death at Cardross Castle on the Clyde.

East of Stirling, three towns form the **Mill Trail Country:** Alva, Alloa, and Tillicoultry. Many quality textile mills have factory outlets here, offering bargain prices on cotton, woolens, and even cashmere goods. The best selection of sweaters is available in many designs at **Inverallen Handknitters Ltd.,** Alva Industrial Estate, Alva (☎ 01259/762-292). The handknitted traditional sweaters here are particularly appealing. A good selection of clothing for children and infants supplements the selections for men and women at **Glen Alva Ltd.,** Hallpark, Whine Road, Alloa (☎ **01259/723-024**). If you're inspired to knit your own creation, head to **Patons & Baldwins,** Kilcraigo Mill, Alloa (☎ **01259/723-431**), which manufactures quality handknitting and craft yarns.

For more complete details, including any directional information, seasonal closings, or whatever, call or visit the **Mill Trail Visitor Centre,** West Stirling Street at Alva (☎ **01259/769-696**), 9 miles (14.5km) east of the center of Stirling. January to June and October to December, it's open daily 10am to 5pm; July to September, it's open daily 9am to 6pm.

## ACCOMMODATIONS
### EXPENSIVE
**Stirling Highland Hotel.** Spittal St., Stirling, Stirlingshire FK8 1DU. ☎ **01786/272-727.** Fax 01786/272-829. www.paramount-hotels.co.uk. E-mail: stirling@paramount-hotels.co.uk. 94 units. TV TEL. £144 ($244.80) double; £194 ($329.80) suite. AE, DC, MC, V.

Stirling's newest hotel has also become its most important. The stylish Highland was installed, after major renovations, in what was once the Old High School, a Victorian building to which everyone in town has an emotional link. The historic atmosphere was treated with respect, and many of the architectural features were kept. Florals, tartans, and solid wood furnishings dominate the public rooms and the guest rooms; the guest rooms, fairly routine, are in a three-story annex. From its position close to Stirling Castle, the hotel enjoys views over the town and surrounding region.

**Dining/Diversions:** Rather high-priced Scottish cuisine is featured in Scholars Restaurant, while Rizzio's Restaurant serves Italian cuisine. Small but charming, the cocktail bar is usually buzzing in the evening.

**Amenities:** Concierge, room service, baby-sitting, laundry, indoor pool, steam room, squash courts, gym, snooker room, Jacuzzi, solarium.

### MODERATE
**Golden Lion Hotel.** 8–10 King St., Stirling, Stirlingshire FK8 2ND. ☎ **01786/475-351.** Fax 01786/472-755. 67 units. TV TEL. £90 ($153) double. Rates include Scottish breakfast. AE, DC, MC, V.

About a block downhill from Holyrood Church, the Golden Lion was built in 1786 as a coaching inn, but its sandstone shell was greatly enlarged with the addition of modern wings in 1962. It's now one of the oldest and largest hotels in town and has recently improved and modernized most of its guest rooms. The rooms are simple and easy on the eye, with tea/coffeemakers and hair dryers. The cocktail bar is pleasant and popular, and the restaurant serves moderately priced meals daily 11am to 11pm.

✪ **Park Lodge Hotel.** 32 Park Terrace, Stirling, Stirlingshire FK8 2JS. ☎ **01786/474-862.** Fax 01786/449-748. www.stirlinghotel.fsnet.co.uk. E-mail: parklodge@stirlinghotel.fsnet.co.uk. 10 units. TV TEL. £85 ($144.50) double. Rates include Scottish breakfast. MC, V. Bus: 51 or 52.

This stylish hotel occupies a 19th-century Italianate mansion, across from a city park in a residential neighborhood. Built of stone blocks and slates, it has a Doric portico, Tudor-style chimney pots, a Georgian-era core from 1825, and century-old climbing roses and wisteria. Anne and Georges Marquetty house guests in 10 upstairs rooms and suggest they dine at their elegant restaurant, The Heritage (see below), a 10-minute walk away. Each room contains antique furnishings (room no. 6 has a four-poster bed) as well as tea/coffeemakers and hair dryers. You might enjoy tea in a walled garden behind the hotel, with its widely spaced iron benches and terra-cotta statues. On the other side of tall casement windows are a pair of French-inspired salons.

**Terraces Hotel.** 4 Melville Terrace, Stirling, Stirlingshire FK8 2ND. ☎ **01786/472-268.** Fax 01786/450-314. www.hotelnet.co.uk/terraceshotel. E-mail: terraceshotel@compuserve. com. 18 units. TV TEL. £82.50 ($140.25) double. Rates include Scottish breakfast. AE, DC, MC, V.

Built as a fine Georgian house of sandstone, this hotel stands on a raised terrace in a quiet residential neighborhood. It's one of the best values in town. Each midsize guest room is furnished in a country-house motif of flowered curtains and solidly traditional furniture, with a hair dryer and tea/coffeemaker. The half-paneled cocktail bar and velvet-upholstered restaurant are popular settings for local parties and wedding receptions. Melville's Restaurant, serving lunch and dinner daily, offers both a moderately priced Scottish and a continental menu, everything from beef Stroganoff to Wiener schnitzel, from *tagliatelle napolitana* to chicken Kiev.

### INEXPENSIVE

**Allan's Guest House.** 15 Albert Place, Stirling FK8 2RE. ☎ **01786/475-175.** 2 units, none with private bathroom. TV. £40 ($68) double. Rates include breakfast. No credit cards. Closed Nov–Feb.

Private and personal, this rambling 1840s stone house is the domain of Mrs. Allan, who rents two of her five bedrooms to paying guests. The cozy rooms are painted and decorated in shades of pale pink, with good beds and tea/coffeemakers. Within a 10-minute walk north of the town center, this place welcomes families with small children.

✪ **West Plean House.** Denny Rd. (3½ miles [6km] from Stirling on A872), Stirling FK7 8HA. ☎/fax **01786/812-208.** E-mail: westplean@virgin.net. 3 units. £48–£52 ($81.60–$88.40) double. Rates include breakfast. No credit cards. Closed Jan–Feb.

This working farm is a delight. It not only has a lovely walled garden but also is a great base for taking walks into the surrounding woodland. Your hosts are welcoming and helpful, and they offer extremely good value. Their guest rooms are spacious and well furnished, with an eye to comfort and conveniences. Their home-cooked breakfast makes it a winner.

### DINING

✪ **The Heritage.** At the Park Lodge Hotel. 32 Park Terrace, Stirling, Stirlingshire FK8 2QC. ☎ **01786/473-660.** Fax 01786/451-291. Reservations recommended. Main courses £6–£12 ($10.20–$20.40); fixed-price 2-course lunch £12 ($20.40); fixed-price 3-course dinner £17.50 ($29.75). MC, V. Daily noon–2pm and 6:30–9:30pm. Closed Sun in winter. FRENCH/SCOTTISH.

Culinary sophistication and beautiful decor rank this as one of the best restaurants in the district. Near the center of town, a 5-minute walk east of the rail station, it's on a quiet residential street. You enter a gentleman's parlor, with somber walls and enviable antiques, to have a drink before descending to the low-ceilinged basement. Amid a French-inspired decor, you'll taste some of the best cuisine in town, prepared with finesse by Georges Marquetty (owner of the Park Lodge Hotel). In his youth he worked as an executive chef in Paris and later spent 12 years in Cincinnati with his British wife, Anne (where he was voted one of the leading chefs of America). His specialties include scallops, scampi, and prawns in Pernod sauce; fillet of wild venison with port and black-currant sauce; scallops with smoked ham in lemon sauce; and foie gras with truffles.

Upstairs, nine handsomely furnished doubles, each with a bathroom, TV, and phone, rent at £90 ($153), breakfast included.

**Riverway Restaurant.** Kildean, outside Stirling (½ mile [1km] from the center of Stirling, just off M8 beside Junction 10). ☎ **01786/475-734.** Main courses £4.65–£10.50 ($7.90–$17.85); high tea £5.95–£12.50 ($10.10–$21.25). MC, V. Daily 10am–noon (coffee and scones), noon–3pm, and 3–6:30pm (high tea). Closed Mon in summer and Mon–Tues Nov–Easter. SCOTTISH.

This fully licensed restaurant has a local reputation for good food at moderate prices. It has panoramic views of Stirling Castle, the Wallace Monument, and the Ochil Hills. The Riverway offers well-prepared food like honeyed lamb cutlets, deep-fried haddock, and grilled sirloin steaks. At lunch you can order a real Scottish menu, including haggis, neeps, and tatties. The high-tea menu has such rib-sticking fare as fried liver, bacon, and onions. Wine of the house is sold by the glass or the bottle.

## STIRLING AFTER DARK

On the campus of Stirling University, the **Macrobert Arts Centre** (☎ **01786/ 461-081**) offers plays, music, films, and art exhibits. The 497-seat main theater often presents dramas and symphony concerts, while the 140-seat studio theater is used mainly for films. Cinema tickets cost £3.50 ($5.95) adults and £2.50 ($4.25) seniors/children, and theater tickets generally run £7 to £8 ($11.90 to $13.60). Admission to most concerts is £10 to £12 ($17 to $20.40). Call for current listings.

**All that Jazz,** 9 Upper Craigs (☎ **01786/451-130**), is a lively bar popular with students. Music is usually provided via the stereo, but bands also appear infrequently. The bar serves a good range of single malts and pints of Kronenberg, Beamish Red, and McEwans. The adjoining restaurant serves a mix of Cajun and traditional Scottish fare, including the dreaded haggis, between 5 and 10pm every evening. The same menu is available throughout the day in the bar, which is open nightly till midnight or 1am.

**O'Neill's,** 11 Maxwell Place (☎ **01786/459-901**), is a traditional Irish pub popular with Scottish students. Irish and Scottish folk bands play. To find out who's playing, check the flyers posted in the pub. There's never a cover.

**Barnton Bar/Bistro,** 3 Barnton St. (☎ **01786/461-698**), is an art nouveau–style bar with marble-topped tables and high ceilings edged with ornate cornices. It's the center of gay life in Stirling but draws a mixed crowd of students, professionals, and old-timers as well. The Wednesday Quiz Night, where drinkers compete in general-knowledge trivia, is quite popular. There's no cover.

## 6  Dunblane & Its Grand Cathedral

7 miles (11km) N of Stirling, 42 miles (68km) NW of Edinburgh, 29 miles (47km) SW of Perth, 33 miles (53km) NE of Glasgow

A small cathedral city on the banks of the Allan Water, Dunblane takes its name from the Celtic Church of St. Blane, which once stood on the site now occupied by the fine 13th-century Gothic cathedral. The cathedral is the main reason to visit; if that doesn't interest you, you'll find more romantic and lovelier places from which to explore the nearby Trossachs and Loch Lomond (say, Callander or Aberfoyle).

## ESSENTIALS

**GETTING THERE**   Trains run between Glasgow and Dunblane with a stopover at Stirling, a one-way fare costing £4.70 ($8). Rail connections are also possible through Edinburgh via Stirling for £6.40 ($10.90) one way. For 24-hour information, call ☎ **0345/484-950.**

Buses travel from the Goosecroft Bus Station in Stirling to Dunblane, costing £1.65 ($2.70) each way. Call ☎ **01786/446-474** in Stirling for schedules, or contact First Edinburgh Busline at ☎ **01324/613-777.**

If you're driving from Stirling, continue north along M9 to Dunblane.

**VISITOR INFORMATION**   A year-round **tourist office** is on Stirling Road (☎ **01786/824-428**). July and August, it's open Monday to Saturday 10am to 6pm and Sunday noon to 5pm; May, June, and the first 3 weeks of September, hours are Monday to Saturday 10am to 5pm.

## SEEING THE SIGHTS

After you visit the cathedral, you can walk and discover the streets around it. They're narrow and twisting and flanked by mellow old townhouses, many from the 18th century.

✪ **Dunblane Cathedral.** Cathedral Close. ☎ **01786/823-388.** Free admission. Apr–Sept Mon–Sat 9:30am–6:30pm, Sun noon–6:30pm; Oct–Mar Mon–Sat 9:30am–4:30pm, Sun 2–4:30pm.

An excellent example of 13th-century Gothic ecclesiastic architecture, this cathedral was spared the ravages of attackers who destroyed other Scottish worship centers. Altered in the 15th century and restored several times in the 19th and 20th centuries, it may have suffered most from neglect subsequent to the Reformation. A Jesse Tree window is in the west end of the building, and of interest are the stalls, the misericords, the pulpit with carved figures of early ecclesiastical figures, and the wooden barrel-vaulted roof with colorful armorials. A Celtic stone from about A.D. 900 is in the north aisle.

**Cathedral Museum.** On Cathedral Square in the Dean's House. ☎ **01786/823-440.** Free admission. May–Sept Mon–Sat 10:30am–1pm and 2–4:30pm.

In the 1624 Dean's House, the Cathedral Museum contains articles and papers displaying the story of Dunblane and its ancient cathedral; you can also visit an enclosed garden with a very old (restored) well. A 1687 structure on the grounds contains the library of Bishop Robert Leighton, an outstanding 17th-century churchman; if you're a serious scholar, you'll find a great deal of material on the effects of the troubled times in Scotland, most from before the Industrial Revolution. It's open the same hours as the Cathedral Museum.

## ACCOMMODATIONS

✪ **Cromlix House.** Kinbuck, Dunblane FK15 9JT. ☎ **01786/822-125.** Fax 01786/ 825-450. www.cromlixhouse.com. E-mail: reservations@cromlixhouse.com. 14 units. TV TEL. £195–£235 ($331.50–$399.50) double; £225–£310 ($382.50–$527) suite. AE, DC, MC, V. Closed Jan. Take A9 to B8033; the hotel is 3¼ miles (5km) north of Dunblane just beyond the village of Kinbuck.

This manor house, built in 1880 as the seat of a family that has owned the surrounding 3,000 acres for the past 500 years, was transformed into an elegant hotel in 1982. The owners still live on the estate and derive part of their income from organizing hunting and fishing expeditions in the surrounding moors and forests and on the River Allan. Croquet mallets, wellies, and fishing rods in the entrance evoke the atmosphere. Fishing in three private lakes and hunting are available as well as tennis, and you can walk through the surrounding forests and farmland.

The manor has an elegant drawing room with big bow windows, and antiques are among the furnishings of both the public rooms and guest rooms. Bouquets of fresh flowers and open fires in cool weather add to the comfort of the place. The guest rooms (including eight suites with sitting rooms) are carpeted, and most have Queen Anne furnishings.

**Dining:** Guests and nonguests can enjoy lunch or dinner daily, ordering pricey fixed-price menus.

**Kippenross.** Dunblane FK15 0LQ. ☎ **01786/824-048.** Fax 01786/823-124. www. aboutscotland.com/stirling/kippenross.html. 3 units. £72 ($122.40) double. MC, V. From Stirling, drive 5 miles (8km) north, taking A9 toward Perth, then exiting onto B8033 and following the signs to Dunblane.

This country manor has always had the same owners and boasts a richer and more unusual history than many of the region's B&Bs. It was built in 1750 according to the Palladian/neoclassical lines of William Adam, father of Britain's most celebrated neoclassical architect, Robert Adam. Surrounded by 200 acres of parks, lawns, and gardens and artfully landscaped with exotic plantings, it's a perfect example of Scottish country-house living, supervised by the Stirling-Aird family. Two of the guest rooms overlook the sprawling front lawns; the other overlooks the forests at the back. Guests are welcomed into the family's drawing room and to formal breakfasts in the dining room. If any guest wants to stay for dinner and reserves in advance, Susan Stirling-Aird prepares elegant dinners at £22 ($37.40). Guests are invited to bring their own liquor or wine, since the place doesn't have a liquor license. Susan's husband, Patrick, is a devoted ornithologist and bird watcher.

## 7  Doune & Its Medieval Castle

41 miles (66km) NW of Edinburgh, 35 miles (56km) N of Glasgow, 8 miles (13km) NW of Stirling, 5 miles (8km) W of Dunblane

The small market town of Doune is a good center for exploring the Trossachs. The Rivers Teith and Ardoch flow through Doune. Doune is visited today by those wanting to see one of the best preserved medieval castles in Scotland and for those who like to visit the Blair Drummond Safari and Leisure Park. Accommodations and food are found at nearby Dunblane or Stirling.

### ESSENTIALS
**GETTING THERE**    Stirling (see "Stirling," above) is the closest rail link to Doune. Buses from the Stirling bus station on Goosecroft run throughout the day to Doune. Call ☎ **0990/808-080** for more information.

If you're driving from Dunblane (see "Dunblane & Its Grand Cathedral," above), continue west along A820.

**VISITOR INFORMATION**    The nearest **tourist office** is at Dunblane (see "Dunblane & Its Grand Cathedral," above).

### SEEING THE SIGHTS
**Doune Castle.** Hwy. A820, 4 miles (6.5km) west of Dunblane. ☎ **01786/841-742.** Admission £2.50 ($4.25) adults, £1.90 ($3.25) seniors, £1 ($1.70) children; free for children 4 and under. Apr–Sept daily 9:30am–6pm; Oct–Mar Mon–Wed 9:30am–4pm, Thurs 9:30am–noon, Sat 10am–4pm, Sun 2–4pm.

This castle, once a royal palace, stands on the banks of the River Teith. Now owned by the earl of Moray, it was restored in 1883, making it one of the best preserved of Scotland's medieval castles. A keep-gatehouse rises about four floors to a height of almost 100 feet (30m), and to its right are a complex of structures containing the former great halls of the castle. Curtain walls with walks envelop three sides of a large patio. Note an outside staircase rising to the second floor of the lord's grand hall.

**Blair Drummond Safari and Leisure Park.** Blair Drummond. ☎ **01786/841-456.**
Admission £8.50 ($14.45) adults, £4.50 ($7.65) seniors/ages 3–14; free for ages 2 and under.
Easter–early Oct daily 10am–5:30pm. Take exit 10 off M9 onto A84 near Stirling.

South of Doune is the Blair Drummond Safari and Leisure Park. You meet the typical cast of animal-safari characters here, but the park also offers a jungle cruise, a giant
Astroglide, and an amusement arcade, as well as a pet farm and a performing sea lions
show. You can have refreshments at the Watering Hole Bar or in the Ranch Kitchen
( ☎ **01786/841-430**) or use one of the picnic areas.

## 8  Callander & a Trio of Lochs

16 miles (26km) NW of Stirling, 43 miles (69km) N of Glasgow, 52 miles (84km) NW of
Edinburgh, 42 miles (68km) W of Perth

In Gaelic, the Trossachs means the "bristled country," an allusion to its luxuriant
vegetation. The thickly wooded valley contains three lochs: Venachar, Achray, and
Katrine. In summer, the steamer on Loch Katrine offers a fine view of the splendid
wooded scenery.

For many, the small town of Callander makes the best base for exploring the
Trossachs and Loch Katrine, Loch Achray, and Loch Venachar (Aberfoyle is another
excellent choice). For years, motorists—and before them, passengers traveling
by bumpy coach—stopped here to rest up on the once-difficult journey between
Edinburgh and Oban.

Callander stands at the entrance to the Pass of Leny in the shadow of the Callander
Crags. The Rivers Teith and Leny meet to the west of the town.

### ESSENTIALS
**GETTING THERE**   Stirling (see "Stirling," above) is the nearest rail link. Once at
Stirling, continue the rest of the way to Callander on a First Edinburgh Bus from the
Stirling station on Goosecroft Road. Contact the bus station at ☎ **01786/446-474**
or **First Edinburgh Buses** at ☎ **01324/613-777.** A one-way fare is £2.90 ($4.95).

Driving from Stirling, head north along M9, cutting northwest at the junction of
A84 to Callander, bypassing Doune.

**VISITOR INFORMATION**   The **Rob Roy & Trossachs Visitor Centre** is at
Ancaster Square ( ☎ **01877/330-342**). It distributes a map pinpointing all the sights.
January and February, it's open Saturday and Sunday 11am to 4:30pm; March to May
and October to December, hours are daily 10am to 5pm; June hours are daily 9:30am
to 6pm; July and August, hours are daily 9am to 10pm; and September, it's open daily
10am to 6pm. The second floor is home to a permanent **Rob Roy exhibit,** complete
with a video presentation about his life and times. Entrance is £2.75 ($4.70) adults
and £1.45 ($2.45) children.

### EXPLORING THE AREA
In the scenic Leny Hills to the west of Callander beyond the Pass of Leny lie **Leny Park**
and **Leny Falls.** At one time all the lands in Leny Park were part of the Leny estate, home
of the Buchanan clan for more than 1,000 years. In the wild Leny Glen, a naturalist's paradise, you can see deer grazing. Leny Falls is an impressive sight, near the confluence of
the River Leny and the River Teith. In this area you'll see the remains of an abandoned
railway; it's a wonderful footpath or cycling path for exploring this scenic area. Rent a bike
at **Wheels/Trossachs Backpackers,** on Invertrossachs Road in Callander ( ☎ **01877/
331-100;** open daily 10am to 6pm), which charges £12.50 ($21.25) for a full day,

£7.50 ($12.75) for a half-day, and £40 to £50 ($68 to $85) for a week. It also provides bikers with sleeping rooms for £12.50 ($21.25) per night, including continental breakfast, conducts organized walks, and can arrange canoe trips.

Four miles (6.5km) beyond the Pass of Leny lies **Loch Lubnaig** (crooked lake), divided into two reaches by a rock and considered fine fishing waters. Nearby is **Little Leny,** the ancestral burial ground of the Buchanans.

You'll find more falls at **Bracklinn,** 1½ miles (2.5km) northeast of Callander. In a gorge above the town, Bracklinn is one of the most scenic of the local beauty spots.

One of the most interesting sites around Callander is ❂ **Balquhidder Church,** 13 miles (21km) northwest off A84. This is the burial place of Rob Roy MacGregor. The church also has the St. Angus Stone from the 8th century, a 17th-century bell, and some Gaelic Bibles.

A good selection of woolens is at **Callander Woollen Mill,** 12–18 Main St. (☎ **01877/330-273**)—everything from scarves, skirts, and jackets to kilts, trousers, and knitwear. Another outlet for woolen goods, tartans, and woven rugs is the **Trossachs Woollen Mill** (☎ **01877/330-178**), 1 mile (1.5km) north of Callander on A84 in the hamlet of Kilmahog.

The town has an excellent golf course, the wooded and scenic **Callendar Golf Course,** Aveland Road (☎ **01877/330-090**). At this 5,125-yard (4,664m) par-66 course, greens fees are £18 ($29.70) per round or £26 ($42.90) per day on weekdays, £26 ($42.90) per round or £31 ($51.15) per day on Saturdays and Sundays. The trolley charge is included in club rental, which runs from £10 to £15 ($16.50 to $24.75) for 18 holes. No caddy service is available. The hilly fairways offer fine views, and the tricky moorland layout demands accurate tee shots.

## ACCOMMODATIONS

❂ **Arden House.** Bracklinn Rd., Callander FK17 8EQ. ☎ **01877/330-235.** Fax 01877/330-235. www.smoothhound.co.uk/hotels/arden.html. 6 units. TV. £55 ($93.50) double; £60 ($102) suite. Rates include breakfast. MC, V. From Callander, walk for 5 minutes north, following the signs to Bracklinn Falls. No children under 14.

This stone-sided Victorian B&B is instantly recognizable to several generations of British TV viewers because of its 1970s role as the setting for a BBC series, *Dr. Finlay's Casebook.* (Its plot involved two bachelor doctors and their interactions with their attractive housekeeper and the fictional town of Tannochbrae, which was modeled after Callander.) Built in 1870 as a vacation home for Lady Willoughby and still maintained by two attractive bachelors, William Jackson and Ian Mitchell, it offers a soothing rest amid an acre of gardens at the base of a rocky outcropping known as the Callendar Crags. The well-known Bracklinn Falls are within a 5-minute walk. The public areas boast Victorian antiques; the high-ceilinged guest rooms are tasteful and comfortable (the most appealing is the plush Tannochbrae Suite). No smoking.

**Highland House Hotel.** S. Church St. (just off A84, near Ancaster Square), Callander FK17 8BN. ☎ **01877/330-269.** Fax 01877/339-004. www.smoothbound.co.uk/hotels/highland.html. E-mail: highland.house.hotel@lineone.net. 9 units. TV TEL. £40–£50 ($68–$85) double. Rates include Scottish breakfast. MC, V.

Owned and managed by Robert and Lorna Leckie, who took over in 1998, this Georgian stone building stands on a quiet tree-lined street a few yards from the Teith and a short walk from the Visitor Centre. All the charming guest rooms come with radio alarms and tea/coffeemakers. Scottish-style meals are served nightly 6 to 9pm in the dining room or in simpler versions in the bar. Game casserole, with choice pieces of game in a rich red wine and port gravy, is a house specialty. The lounge offers 20 to 25 brands of malt whiskies, some relatively obscure.

## A Side Trip to Loch Voil

This was an area known to Rob Roy MacGregor, who died in 1734 but lives on in legend as the Robin Hood of Scotland and in the Liam Neeson film. If you visit Rob Roy's grave at Balquhidder, you may find this remote part of Scotland so enchanting you'll want to continue to drive west and explore the **Braes o' Balquhidder** and the banks of **Loch Voil,** where you can enjoy some of the loveliest countryside walks in the Trossachs. You can go through the churchyard where the Scottish hero is buried up to Kirkton Glen, continuing along through grasslands to a little lake. This signposted footpath leads to the next valley, called Glen Dochart, before it links up once again with A84, on which Callander lies.

---

✪ **Roman Camp.** Main St., Callander FK17 8BG. ☎ **01877/330-003.** Fax 01877/ 331-533. 17 units. TV TEL. £110–£160 ($187–$272) double; from £180 ($306) suite. Rates include Scottish breakfast. AE, DC, MC, V. As you approach Callander on A84, the entrance to the hotel is signposted between 2 pink cottages on Callander's Main St.

The leading hotel in town, once a 17th-century hunting lodge with pink walls and small gray-roofed towers, was built on the site of a Roman camp. Today you drive up a 200-yard (182m) driveway, with shaggy Highland cattle and sheep grazing on either side. In summer, flower beds are in bloom. Inside you're welcomed to a gracious country house. Seven of the guest rooms are on the ground floor and one is adapted for travelers with disabilities; all have hair dryers and tea/coffeemakers. Some rooms are furnished with bedhead crowns, gilt-framed mirrors, and stenciled furnishings, and others are contemporary with blond-wood pieces.

**Dining:** The dining room was converted in the 1930s from the old kitchen. The ceiling design is based on Scottish painted ceilings of the 16th and 17th centuries. Rather expensive menus, all Scottish country-house fare, are served daily at lunch and dinner. There's a small but cozy cocktail bar. The library, with its ornate plasterwork and richly grained paneling, is an elegant holdover from yesteryear.

## DINING

**Dalgair Hotel.** 113–115 Main St., Callander FK17 8BQ. ☎ **01877/330-283.** Fax 01877/ 331-114. E-mail: nieto@btinternet.com. Reservations recommended in restaurant, not necessary in bar. Table d'hôte 3-course menu £17.50 ($29.75); main courses £10.50–£14 ($17.85–$23.80) in restaurant, £5–£11.95 ($8.50–$20.30) in bar. AE, DC, MC, V. Restaurant daily 6:30–9pm; bar food service daily 11am–9pm. SCOTTISH.

This place is best known for its food and wine cellar. The bar, lined in gray bricks, boasts rustic accessories and flickering candles. The menu choices include halibut and Dover or lemon sole, steaks, and game casseroles. Australian, German, and Austrian wine, sold by the glass, gives the place the aura of a wine bar. More formal meals are served after dark in the restaurant, where menu items might include sliced pork on cucumber noodles with oregano and ginger sauce, chicken fillet in champagne-butter sauce, and preparations of salmon and Angus steaks.

The hotel's eight rooms contain hair dryers, TVs, and phones and rent for £50 to £72 ($85 to $122.40) double, Scottish breakfast included.

**Lade Inn.** Trossachs Rd. at Kilmahog, Callander FK17 8HD. ☎ **01877/330-152.** Main courses £6.85–£14.95 ($11.65–$25.40). MC, V. Mon–Sat noon–2:30pm and 5:30–9pm; Sun 12:30–9pm. Lies 1 mile (1.5km) north of Callander on A84. INTERNATIONAL/SCOTTISH.

Surrounded by fields and within earshot of the Leny River, the Lade was built as a teahouse, then converted after World War II to a pub and restaurant. It attracts residents from the surrounding farmlands as well as visitors from afar to enjoy the Highland scenery (which includes Ben Ledi, one of the region's most prominent peaks) and sample the wide range of cask-conditioned ales and cider. If you're hungry, new owners Angela and Paul Roebuck prepare meals of such Scottish standards as rack of lamb, pigeon, venison, steaks, salmon, and trout.

## CALLANDER AFTER DARK

The **Brigend Hotel Pub,** Bridgend (☎ 01877/330-130), is an old watering hole that has been done up in matching dusky red wood paneling and carpeting. Tennant brews are available on tap. On Friday and Saturday they have karaoke, and Sunday nights enjoy some live Scottish music. Another old-fashioned bar that's a local favorite is the **Crown Hotel Pub,** 13 Main St. (☎ 01877/330-040); it sometimes features live folk music. Otherwise, it's a mellow old place for a pint of lager.

## 9 Aberfoyle: Gateway to the Trossachs

56 miles (90km) NW of Edinburgh, 27 miles (43.5km) N of Glasgow

Looking like an alpine village in the heart of Rob Roy country, the small resort of Aberfoyle, near Loch Ard, is the gateway to the Trossachs, one of the most beautiful and bucolic regions of Scotland. As one poet wrote: "So wondrous and wild, the whole might seem the scenery of a fair dream."

This was the land of Rob Roy (1671–1734), the outlaw and leader of the MacGregors. Sir Walter Scott recounted the outlaw's exploits in *Rob Roy,* first published in 1818. Scott's romantic poem "The Lady of the Lake" greatly increased tourism to the area, eventually luring Queen Victoria, who was enchanted by its beauty. Wordsworth and Coleridge were eventually lured here away from England's Lake District. Wordsworth was so inspired he wrote "To a Highland Girl."

## ESSENTIALS

**GETTING THERE**   It's tough to get here by public transportation; you'll really need to drive. From Stirling, take A84 west until you reach the junction of A873 and continue west to Aberfoyle.

**VISITOR INFORMATION**   The **Trossachs Discovery Centre** is on Main Street (☎ 01877/382-352). April to June, it's open daily 10am to 5pm; July and August hours are daily 9:30am to 7pm; September and October hours are daily 9am to 5pm; and November to March, it's open Saturday and Sunday 11am to 4pm.

## EXPLORING THE AREA

About 4 miles (6.5km) east of Aberfoyle on A81, **Inchmahome Priory** stands on an island in Lake Menteith. From the Port of Menteith, you can take a ferry (£2.80/$4.75 adults, £1.10/$1.85 children) to the island if the weather's right. Once here, you'll find the ruins of a 13th-century Augustinian house where Mary Queen of Scots was sent as a baby in 1547. For information, call ☎ 01877/385-294.

A nature lover's delight, the ✪ **Queen Elizabeth Forest Park** lies between the eastern shore of Loch Lomond and the Trossachs. Some 45,000 acres of moor, woodland, and mountain have been set aside as a preserve for walking and exploring. For walking maps and information, stop at the **Queen Elizabeth Park Visitor Centre** (☎ 01877/382-258), in the David Marshall Lodge, off A821, 1 mile (1.5km) north of Aberfoyle. Mid-March to mid-September, it's open daily 10am to 6pm. Admission is free. From the lodge you'll enjoy views of Ben Lomond, the Menteith Hills, and the Campsie Fells.

Another great walk in the area is the **Highland Boundary Fault Walk,** which goes along the Highland boundary fault edge. Here you can see the most panoramic views of the Highlands to the north and the Lowlands to the south. It begins 6 miles (10km) south of the Trossachs on A821. Detailed information is provided by the Forestry Commission in Abeyfoyle (☎ **01877/382-383**).

North of Aberfoyle, **Dukes Pass** (A821) climbs through Achray Forest past the Queen Elizabeth Forest Park Visitor Centre (see above), where you can stop for snacks and a panoramic view of the Forth Valley. Information on numerous walks, cycling routes, the Achray scenic forest drive, picnic sites, parking areas, and many other activities is available at the center. The road runs to the Trossachs between Lochs Achray and Katrine.

**Loch Katrine,** where Rob Roy MacGregor was born, owes its fame to Sir Walter Scott's poem "The Lady of the Lake." The loch is the principal reservoir of the city of Glasgow. A small steamer, the **S.S.** *Sir Walter Scott,* plies the waters of the loch, which has submerged the romantic poet's Silver Strand. Sailings are twice a day Easter to late October, between Trossachs Pier and Stronachlachar, at a round-trip fare of £5.50 ($9.35) for adults and £3.60 ($6.10) for children/seniors, or £15.20 ($25.85) for families. Prices vary depending on time of day (morning sailings are more expensive). Complete information about sailing schedules is available from the **Strathclyde Water Department,** Lower Clyde Division, 419 Balmore Rd., Glasgow, Lanarkshire G22 6NU (☎ **0141/355-5333**). Light refreshments are available at Trossachs Pier.

If you'd like to explore the countryside on two wheels, head for **Trossachs' Cycle Hire,** Trossachs Holiday Park, Aberfoyle (☎ **01877/382-614**). The daily rental is £13 ($22.10), with weekly rates of £30 ($51). It's open daily 9am to 7pm.

Shoppers will want to check out the **Scottish Wool Centre,** Main Street (☎ **01877/382-850**), which sells a big selection of knitwear and woolens from surrounding mills, including jackets, hats, rugs, sweaters, and cashmere items. It also houses an amphitheater that holds a textile display area, along with live specimens of different breeds of Scottish sheep (but no clones yet). Spinning and weaving demonstrations are also presented, and baby lambs fill a children's petting zoo. Admission to the shop is free, but the exhibition costs £3 ($5.10) adults and £6 ($10.20) families. The whole complex is open daily 9:30am to 6pm, with exhibitions taking place at 11am, noon, 2pm, and 3pm.

## ACCOMMODATIONS

**Covenanters Inn Hotel.** Duchray Rd. (about ½ mile [1km] southwest of Aberfoyle), Aberfoyle FK8 3XD. ☎ **01877/382-347.** Fax 01877/382-785. 50 units. TV TEL. £86–£106 ($146.20–$180.20) double. Rates include half-board. AE, DC, MC, V.

Set on 6 acres overlooking the headwaters of the River Forth, this hotel was built as a home in the early 1800s and gracefully enlarged during the 1960s and 1980s. Its guest rooms are dignified and comfortable, in Scottish country house style. The hotel's name comes from the famous convention held here in 1949, when a group of Scots church and political leaders issued a then-famous Second Covenant promoting the separation of Scotland from England. On Christmas Eve of 1952, the hotel again became famous (or notorious) after the theft from Westminster Abbey of the Stone of Scone. Following appeals from Buckingham Palace, the Stone was recovered after having spent a night here, it's claimed. (A controversy continues as to the authenticity of the recovered artifact.)

Conjecture and speculation about the event still go on, sometimes heatedly, in the bar. The bar serves drinks from a wide selection of single-malt whiskies, as well as affordable bar meals. The more formal restaurant serves moderately priced dinners.

**Creag-Ard House.** Milton, Aberfoyle FK8 3TQ. ☎ **01877/382-297.** www.milford.co.uk/ co/creag-ard.html. 6 units. £50–£60 ($85–$102) double. MC, V. From Aberfoyle, drive a mile (1.5km) west, following B829 toward Kinlochard.

One of the most stately houses in the region is this stone-sided Victorian villa whose steep rooflines and stone-ringed bay windows give it an appealingly quirky, even Gothic-looking allure. Built in 1885 on 3 acres of forested parkland with spectacular stands of azaleas and rhododendrons (blooming in May), it offers cozy, well-upholstered rooms with attractive furniture, lots of sun, and tea/coffeemakers. If advance notice is given, rather pricey dinners can be prepared for guests.

**Loch Achray Hotel.** 9 miles (14.5km) east of Callander on A821, The Trossachs FK17 3HZ. ☎ **01877/376-229.** Fax 01877/376-278. 83 units. TV. £60–£80 ($102–$136) double. Rates include Scottish breakfast. AE, MC, V. Closed 2 weeks in Jan.

This sprawling white-sided hotel is a short walk from Loch Achray on an isolated 45-acre estate between Callander and Aberfoyle. Although parts of its foundation date from Jacobean times, the bulk of what you'll see today was built around the early 1900s as a resort for people interested in the flora and fauna of the Highlands. From the hotel, you can step directly into the Achray Forest, part of the vast Queen Elizabeth National Park. The midsize guest rooms are simple and contemporary, each with a tea kettle, hair dryer, and views over the forest. The dining room serves moderately priced dinners nightly. The hotel bar features live traditional music every night 8:30 to 11pm, including a full-scale ceilidh every Thursday. The hotel is usually heavily booked with visiting tour groups.

## DINING

**✪ Braeval Restaurant.** Callander Rd. (A81). ☎ **01877/382-711.** Reservations required. Main courses £6–£9.50 ($10.20–$16.15); Sat night set menu £30 ($51). MC, V. Tues–Sun 10am–5pm; Sat 7:30–9pm by reservation only. Closed 1 week in Feb, 1 week in June, and 2 weeks in Oct (dates vary). Drive 1 mile (1.5km) east of Aberfoyle on A81 (Callander Rd.). SCOTTISH.

Overlooking a golf course, this restaurant is housed in a former stone mill, and owners Andrew and Pauline Carter kept an antique waterwheel to remind diners of the building's former function. The chefs here have inventiveness and solid technique. We especially like how the kitchen takes full advantage of the region's riches, including game in season. You can come away with a real "taste of Scotland" flavor here. The chef's repertoire embraces both traditional and modern British dishes on a changing fixed-price menu based on the availability of fresh produce. You might begin with game terrine with pear chutney. For main dishes, sample such delights as seared bass bream with salad Niçoise, a lasagna of chicken livers flavored with lemon and thyme, or fillet of salmon with mussel-and-basil butter sauce.

## 10  On the Bonnie, Bonnie Banks of Loch Lomond

The largest of Scotland's lochs, ✪ **Loch Lomond** was the center of the ancient district of Lennox, in the possession of the branch of the Stewart (Stuart) family to which Lord Darnley (second husband of Mary Queen of Scots) belonged. The ruins of Lennox Castle are on Inchmurrin, one of the 30 islands of the loch—one with ecclesiastical ruins, one noted for its yew trees planted by King Robert the Bruce to ensure a suitable supply of wood for the bows of his archers. The loch is fed by at least 10 rivers from west, east, and north and is about 24 miles (39km) long; it stretches 5 miles (8km) at its widest point. On the eastern side is Ben Lomond, which rises to a height of 3,192 feet (968m).

The song "Loch Lomond" is supposed to have been composed by one of Bonnie Prince Charlie's captured followers on the eve of his execution in Carlisle Jail. The "low road" of the song is the path through the underworld that his spirit will follow to his native land after death, more quickly than his friends can travel to Scotland by the ordinary high road.

The easiest way to see the famous loch is not by car but by one of the local ships owned by **Sweeney's Cruisers Ltd.,** and based at Sweeney's Shipyard, 26 Balloch Rd., Balloch G83 8LQ ( ☎ **01389/752-376**). Cruises on various boats last for about an hour and in summer depart every hour 10:30am to 7:30pm (departures in other months are based on demand). At £4.80 ($8.15) per person round-trip, cruises sail from Balloch toward a wooded island, Inchmurrin, year-round home to five families, several vacation chalets, and a summer-only nudist colony. The ship doesn't dock at the island, however.

Of course, you can also see the loch on foot. One of the great marked footpaths of Scotland, the ✪ **West Highland Way** goes along the complete eastern sector of the lovely loch. The footpath actually began at Milngavie outside Glasgow. Serious backpackers often do the entire 95-mile (153km) trail, but you can tackle just sections of it for marvelous day hikes that will allow you to enjoy the scenery along Loch Lomond.

# BALLOCH

At the southern end of Loch Lomond, Balloch is the most touristy of the towns and villages around the lake. It grew up on the River Leven, where the water leaves Loch Lomond and flows south to the Clyde. Today, Balloch is visited chiefly by those wanting to take boat trips on Loch Lomond, which sail in season from Balloch Pier.

## EXPLORING THE AREA

The 200-acre **Balloch Castle Country Park** is on the bonnie banks of Loch Lomond, three-quarters of a mile (1.2km) north of Balloch Station. The present **Balloch Castle** ( ☎ **01389/758-216**), replacing one that dated from 1238, was constructed in 1808 for John Buchanan of Ardoch in the castle-Gothic style. Its visitor center explains the history of the property. The site has a walled garden, and the trees and shrubs, especially the rhododendrons and azaleas, reach the zenith of their beauty in late May and early June. You can also visit a Fairy Glen. The park is open all year, daily 8am to dusk, with no admission. Easter to the end of October, the visitor center is open daily 10am to 6pm.

Dumbarton District's Countryside Ranger Service is based at Balloch Castle and conducts **guided walks** at various locations around Loch Lomond throughout the summer.

## ACCOMMODATIONS & DINING

**Ardoch House.** Gartocharn, near Balloch G83 8ND. ☎ **01389/830-279.** Fax 01389/ 930-623. www.aboutscotland.com/central/ardoch.html. 3 units. TV TEL. £68 ($115.60) double. Rate includes breakfast. MC, V. Closed Nov–Apr. From Balloch, drive along A811 toward Stirling and Gartocharn. Just before Gartocharn, turn left at the 30mph traffic sign.

This impeccably maintained 1830s white farmhouse was extensively renovated by owner/architect David Morgan. Set amid 130 acres of rolling countryside, with spectacular views over the foothills of the Highlands, it provides one of the most charming small-scale accommodations in the region. The guest rooms have large windows, pleasant carpeting and upholsteries, and a sense of intelligent design that gracefully marries newfangled techniques with the building's original core. You're invited into the drawing room, where Lintie Morgan, David's wife, gracefully evokes the region's history and dispenses tips on whatever area of expertise might interest you. Breakfast is the only meal served, but the Morgans will direct you to any of several pubs and restaurants nearby. No smoking.

**Balloch Hotel.** Balloch Rd., Balloch G83 8LQ. ☎ **01389/752-579.** Fax 01389/755-604. 14 units. TV TEL. £63 ($107.10) double. Rates include Scottish breakfast. AE, DC, MC, V. Closed Jan 1 and Dec 25.

Called Balloch's grande dame hotel, this was the first to be built in the town. In 1860 it welcomed the Empress Eugénie, wife of Napoleon III, when she toured Scotland (she slept in the Inchmoan Room). It stands beside the river in the center of the village, offering basic, functionally furnished rooms, each with a hair dryer, trouser press, and tea/coffeemaker.

✪ **DeVere Cameron House.** Alexandria, Loch Lomond, G83 8QZ. ☎ **01389/755-565.** Fax 01389/759-522. www.cameronhouse.co.uk. E-mail: devere.Cameron@airtime.com.uk. 96 units. TV TEL. £225–£265 ($382.50–$450.50) double; £350–£450 ($595–$765) suite. Rates include full Scottish breakfast and membership to the Leisure Club. Children 16 and under stay free in parents' room. AE, DC, MC, V. Take M8 to A82 to Loch Lomand; follow signs to hotel.

Twenty minutes from the Glasgow airport and lying in 108 acres of lush woodland, this ancestral home of novelist Tobias Smollet is a luxurious resort combining elegance, leisure, and adventure. Decorated in soft, warm colors, the good-sized rooms are comfortable and handsomely furnished. The five suites boast sitting rooms with panoramic views. All rooms are equipped with modern bathrooms and amenities such as in-room movies.

**Dining:** The resort has three on-site restaurants, all of which require reservations. For a casual snack or light lunch, visit Breakers. In Smollets, the atmosphere is bright and affords views of the loch while you enjoy meals on the high side of moderate. The Georgian Room, the most formal of the restaurants (jacket and tie required), offers extremely pricey gourmet meals prepared by an award-winning chef. The menu changes regularly, but the quality of the food doesn't.

**Amenities:** Bicycling and jogging trails, nine-hole golf courses, walled garden, tennis courts, children's adventure playground, archery lessons, croquet, steam room, massages, Leisure Club, lagoon pool surrounded by palm trees, gym, squash courts, baby-sitting. In addition, the hotel's cruiser, the *Celtic Warrior,* takes guests on cruises of Loch Lomond, and several boats in a 225-slip marina can be rented for fishing. There are facilities for windsurfing, water-skiing, and sailing.

# LUSS

The village of Luss, 9 miles (14.5km) north of Ballock on A82 on the western side of Loch Lomond, is the traditional home of the Colquhouns. Among its stone cottages, on the water's edge, is a branch of the Highland Arts Studios of Seil. Cruises on the loch and boat rentals may be arranged at a nearby jetty.

If your travels in Scotland inspire you to put on a kilt and blow your own set of bagpipes, stop by **Thistle Bagpipe Works** (☎ **01436/860-250**), in the center of Luss. Here you can not only order custom-made bagpipes but also purchase a clan kilt to go with the instrument. Your neighbors back home will be thrilled.

## ACCOMMODATIONS

**The Lodge on Loch Lomond Hotel.** Luss, Argyll G83 8PA. ☎ **01436/860-201.** Fax 01436/860-203. www.loch-lomond.co.uk. E-mail: lusslomand@aol.com. 29 units. TV TEL. £105–£162 ($178.50–$275.40) double; £165 ($280.50) suite. Rates include full Scottish breakfast. AE, MC, V. Free parking. Take A82 from Glasgow.

Surrounded by mountain, loch, and woodland, you can live in Scottish country house style and take in panoramic views of legendary Loch Lomond. The hotel, in fact, was designed to take in the views. But that's not the only reason to stay here. This hotel, much improved in recent years, offers tasteful bedrooms filled with such amenities as beverage makers, trouser presses, and ironing board. The best rooms are the "executives"; they're set up for wheelchair access, and each contains a two-person sauna. The standard rooms, although smaller, are also comfortable. Recent improvements include a heated swimming pool. The hotel will also arrange local activities, including salmon fishing and private charter cruises along with horseback riding.

**Dining:** The fine restaurant is an excellent reason to stay here, or at least to drop in for an evening (see below).

## DINING

**The Lodge on Loch Lomond Restaurant.** In the Lodge at Loch Lomond Hotel, Luss. ☎ **01436/860-203.** Reservations recommended. Main courses £7.95–£16.45 ($13.50–$27.95). AE, MC, V. Daily noon–2pm and 6–9:30pm. SCOTTISH.

Using only the finest and freshest local ingredients, this restaurant serves individually prepared meals that are among the best in the area. The accommodating staff makes this a relaxed, comfortable place. Although the menu changes, the main courses might include pan-fried venison loin with haggis skirlie, or speared tiger prawns with chili and garlic nut-brown butter. There is a wide selection of Aberdeen Angus beef priced according to weight, and lobster is served in a multitude of ways. For something really Scottish, try roast pheasant with bacon-braised barley and a whisky cream sauce. For those who want a smaller, lighter meal, the menu offers burgers, fish and chips, pasta, and pizza. The quality of the food is excellent, matched by panoramic views of the loch.

## INVERBEG

The village of Inverbeg on the western shore of Loch Lomond stands in a beautiful spot, about 3 miles (5km) north of Luss. (It can be reached in about 40 minutes from Glasgow.) The hamlet is known for its old-time ferry inn (see below), the second-oldest youth hostel in Scotland, and several art galleries. A small fleet of Loch Lomond cruisers can usually be seen in the harbor of Inverbeg Bay, and a ferry to Rowardennan and Ben Lomond plies the route three times a day in summer.

### ACCOMMODATIONS & DINING

**Inverbeg Inn.** Hwy. A82, Luss, Loch Lomond G83 8PD. ☎ **01436/860-678.** Fax 01436/860-686. 20 units. TV TEL. £80–£90 ($136–$153) double. Rates include Scottish breakfast. AE, DC, MC, V.

The site of this inn, 28 miles (45km) north of Glasgow and a 5-minute drive north of Luss, has always been important as the ferry landing servicing the western end of Loch Lomond. In chilly weather, you'll gravitate immediately toward the blazing fireplace in the reception room. About half the routinely furnished guest rooms look out over a rear garden, and each room is comfortable and well maintained.

The pub serves affordable, savory lunches and dinners; there's also a more formal restaurant serving items like breaded prawns, halibut, and T-bone steaks at dinner nightly.

## TARBET

On the western shores of Loch Lomond, Tarbet isn't to be confused with the larger center of Tarbert, headquarters of the Loch Fyne herring industry. Loch Lomond's

Tarbet is merely a village and summer-holiday base with limited accommodations. In the distance you can see the majesty of Ben Lomond. Boats can be launched from the pier, and Tarbet is one of the stops of the steamship *Countess Fiona*.

## ACCOMMODATIONS & DINING

**Tarbet Hotel.** Tarbet, Arrochar G83 7DE. ☎ **01301/702-228.** Fax 01301/702-673. 80 units. TV. £64–£80 ($108.80–$136) double. Rates include half-board. MC, V. Closed Jan.

The Tarbet stands where a simple inn existed more than 400 years ago, at the junction of A82 and A83. A coaching inn was built on the foundation in 1760, and a baronial facade and mock-fortification crenellations were added during the Victorian era. The midsize guest rooms are functional, simply furnished but comfortable. A cozy cocktail lounge looks past a row of very old yew trees onto the lake. Open to guests only, the dining room serves good meals of local produce. The bistro-style snack bar, the Baguetterie, open Thursday to Sunday 10am to 4pm, serves sandwiches.

# Aberdeen & the Tayside & Grampian Regions

**9**

The two historic regions of Tayside and Grampian offer a vast array of sightseeing, even though they're relatively small. Tayside, for example, is about 85 miles (137km) east to west and 60 miles (97km) south to north. The regions share the North Sea coast between the Firth of Tay in the south and the Firth of Moray farther north, and the so-called Highland Line separating the Lowlands in the south from the Highlands in the north crosses both. The Grampians, Scotland's highest mountain range, are to the west of this line.

Carved out of the old counties of Perth and Angus, **Tayside** is named for its major river, the 119-mile-long (192km) Tay. The region is easy to explore, and its waters offer some of Europe's best salmon and trout fishing. Tayside abounds with heather-clad Highland hills, long blue lochs under forested banks, and miles of walking trails. Perth and Dundee are among Scotland's largest cities. Tayside provided the backdrop for many novels by Sir Walter Scott, including *The Fair Maid of Perth, Waverley,* and *The Abbot.* And its golf courses are world famous, ranging from the trio of 18-hole courses at Gleneagles to the open championships links at Carnoustie.

**Grampian** boasts Aberdeen, Scotland's third-largest city, and Braemar, site of the most famous of the Highland gatherings. The queen herself comes here for holidays, to stay at Balmoral Castle, her private residence, a tradition dating back to the days of Queen Victoria and her consort, Prince Albert. The very word *Balmoral* seems to evoke images of tartans and bagpipes. As you journey on the scenic roads of Scotland's northeast, you'll pass moorland and peaty lochs, wood glens and rushing rivers, granite-stone villages and ancient castles, and fishing harbors as well as North Sea beach resorts.

## Driving Through the Region

**Day 1**  From Edinburgh, head west on A90 until you reach the signs for the Forth Road Bridge. After crossing the bridge, take M90 all the way to **Perth,** 44 miles (71km) north of Edinburgh. You'll have time to see some of the sights, such as the Fair Maid's House, before lunch. After lunch, take an excursion to Scone Palace, 2 miles (3km) northeast on the River Tay. Spend the night in Perth.

**Day 2**  From Perth, head 18 miles (29km) west along A85 to **Crieff,** which is on the edge of the Perthshire Highlands. While here, you can visit the Glenturret Distillery and Drummond Castle at Grimsthorpe. Stay overnight in Crieff.

**Day 3** From Crieff, head north on A822 to **Dunkeld,** where you can visit its cathedral and Scottish Horse Museum. Then take A9 northwest to **Pitlochry** for the night.

**Day 4** While still based in Pitlochry, explore some of the major sights in its environs, including the Pass of Killiecrankie, Queens View, and Blair Castle.

**Day 5** Leave Pitlochry in the morning by a different route, A924, which swings northeast and takes you through Glen Brerachan before heading southeast again along A924 and A93 into Rattray. Get on A926 east to **Kirriemuir,** birthplace of Sir James M. Barrie, author of *Peter Pan.* After lunch here, head south on A928 to **Glamis Castle,** which you may remember from *Macbeth.* For lodgings, you can cut south along A928 and A929 to **Dundee.**

**Day 6** The following morning, you'll have a 67-mile (108km) drive north to **Aberdeen,** the Granite City of the northeast. The most scenic route is the coastal road (A92), going via Arbroath, Montrose, and Stonehaven before reaching Aberdeen. Explore some of its attractions in the afternoon and spend the night here.

**Day 7** Leave Aberdeen in the morning, stopping first at **Banchory** with a goal of making Ballater your overnight stopover. Follow A93 west. **Ballater** is 41 miles (66km) west of Aberdeen and is a center for viewing Balmoral Castle, home of the queen, 8 miles (13km) west of Ballater.

**Day 8** In the morning, continue on A93 west to **Braemar** to visit Braemar Castle. Have lunch there. Return to Ballater and take A939 northwest to **Grantown-on-Spey,** a holiday resort that makes a good center for exploring **Speyside,** the valley of the second-largest river in Scotland.

**Day 9** The following morning, leave Grantown-on-Spey and head east along A95 until you come to the junction of B9008. Go south to the **Glenlivet Reception Centre,** which will mark the beginning of the **Whisky Trail.** After Glenlivet you can get on B9009 for a short visit to **Dufftown** before cutting northwest along A941 via the Glen of Rothes toward **Elgin** for the night. Consider a stop in the Speyside town of **Rothes** with its five distilleries.

# 1 Perth: Gateway to the Highlands & Scone Palace

44 miles (71km) N of Edinburgh, 22 miles (35km) SW of Dundee, 64 miles (103km) NE of Glasgow

From its majestic position on the Tay, the ancient city of Perth was the capital of Scotland until the mid–15th century. Here the Highlands meet the Lowlands. Perth makes a good stop if you're heading north to the Highlands. Perth itself has only a few historic buildings, but it does offer some good shopping. The main attraction, Scone Place, lies on the outskirts of Perth, and the surrounding countryside is wonderful for strolling and hiking as you take in the majestic scenery.

## ESSENTIALS

**GETTING THERE** **ScotRail** runs two trains per hour between Edinburgh and Perth, with continuing service to Dundee and Aberdeen. Trip time to Perth is 1½ hours, and the fare is £9.30 ($15.80) each way. Phone ☎ **0345/484950** in Edinburgh for 24-hour information.

Edinburgh and Perth are connected by about 16 buses a day. A one-way fare costs £4.70 ($8). You can even go from London's Victoria Station by bus to Perth, but the

# The Tayside & Grampian Regions

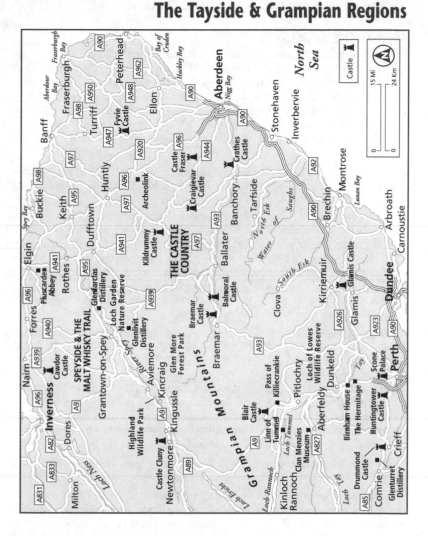

trip takes 12 long hours and costs £24 ($40.80) one way. For bus schedules, check with **CityLink** at ☎ **0990/505-050**.

To drive from Edinburgh, head northwest along A90 and go across the Forth Road Bridge, continuing north along M90.

**VISITOR INFORMATION**   The **tourist office** is at Lower City Mills, West Mill Street (☎ **01738/450-600**). April to June and October, it's open daily 9am to 6pm; July to September, hours are daily 9am to 8pm; and November to March, hours are Monday to Saturday 9am to 5pm.

**SPECIAL EVENTS**   In May, the 10-day **Perth Festival of the Arts** attracts international orchestras and chamber music societies who present a series of mostly musical (rather formal) presentations. There are some dance recitals as well, and a recent trend is a celebration of some aspects of pop culture. Concerts are held in city hall, churches, and auditoriums; some are even held at Scone Palace.

## SEEING THE SIGHTS

For the best view of this scenic part of Scotland, take Bowerswell Road a mile (1.5km) to the east of Perth center to visit **Kinnouill Hill,** rising 792 feet (240m) above Perth. After an easy climb, you can see a bird's-eye view of the geological Highland Line dividing the Highlands from the Lowlands. A marked nature trail beginning at the Braes Road car park leads after a 25-minute walk to the panoramic view from the top. Here you can see a folly, the **Kinnouill Watch Tower,** and its counterpart, a mile (1.5km) to the east, **Binn Hill.** Both structures are imitations of castles along the Rhine.

**Kirk of St. John the Baptist (aka St. John's Kirk).** St. John St. ☎ **01738/633-741.** Free admission. Sun 12:30–3pm; Tues–Fri 10am–noon and 2–4pm; Sun services at 9:30 and 11am.

The main attraction is this pinkish gray sandstone church, with an original foundation believed to be from Pictish times. It has a Gothic-style tower with a pointed spire capped by a golden cockerel. The present choir dates from 1440 and the nave from 1490. In 1559, John Knox preached his famous sermon here, attacking idolatry, which caused a turbulent wave of iconoclasm to sweep across the land. In its wake, religious artifacts, stained glass, and organs were destroyed all over Scotland. The church was restored as a World War I memorial in the mid-1920s and has a fine collection of 20th-century stained-glass windows.

**Branklyn Garden.** 116 Dundee Rd. (A85), Branklyn. ☎ **01738/625-535.** Admission £2.50 ($4.25) adults, £1.70 ($2.90) children/students/seniors, £6.40 ($10.90) families. Mar–Oct daily 9:30am–sunset. Closed Nov–Feb. From the town center, follow the signs to Dundee.

Branklyn Garden has been called the finest 2 acres of private garden in Scotland. Bequeathed to the National Trust for Scotland, it boasts a superb collection of rhododendrons, alpines, and herbaceous and peat-garden plants from all over the world. The garden is especially noteworthy for its collection of Himalayan poppies and extraordinary examples of *acer palmatum* (cut-leaf Japanese maples).

**Perth Art Gallery and Museum.** George St., at the intersection of Tay St. and Perth Bridge. ☎ **01738/632-488.** Free admission. Mon–Sat 10am–5pm.

This museum displays a good collection of paintings illustrating the town's history and people and a selection of archaeological artifacts tracing the early history of the settlement. The growth of the whisky industry and its major role in the area's economy is particularly emphasized. You'll find everything from grandfather clocks to Georgian silver to even an effigy of a 65-pound (29kg) salmon caught by some proud fisherman back in 1922. The most notable artworks are large Scottish landscapes by John Millais (1829–96); the autumnal tints of Tayside are best captured in *Chill October* (1870). Horatio McCulloch (1805–67) was known as a specialist of Highland scenes, and his *Loch Katrine* (1866) is one of his finest works. Some paintings are by foreign masters (not their greatest achievements), as exemplified by Ribera's 17th-century *St. Andrew.*

**Round House and Fergusson Gallery.** Marshall Place. ☎ **01738/441-944.** Free admission. Mon–Sat 10am–5pm.

If you're interested in Scottish art, head for the Round House, home of the Fergusson Gallery, which displays some 6,000 works of Scottish artist J. D. Fergusson (1874–1961). Fergusson is acclaimed as one of the best watercolorists in the country, and his Scottish scenes are widely produced on postcards and calendars. In the paintings *Princess Street Gardens* and *The White Dress,* you can view the muted colors of his early portraits and landscapes. Later, as he was more inspired by Fauvism, his scenes became more vibrant and luminous, as evoked by *Cassis from the West* and *Sails at Royan*. His female nudes, however, always generate the most excitement, especially *Danu Mother of the Gods, The Parasol,* and *Bathers in Green. The Red Dress* from 1950 is very evocative of Glasgow scenes.

**Balhousie Castle.** Hay St., right beyond Rose Terrace on the west side of North Inch. ☎ **0131/310-8530.** Free admission. May–Sept Mon–Sat 10am–4:30pm; Oct–Apr Mon–Fri 10am–3:30pm.

In the 16th century, this was the home of the earls of Kinnoull, but today it houses the Black Watch Regimental Museum, with hundreds of weapons, medals, and documents of the Black Watch regiment from the 18th century on. The museum is filled with curiosities like the back door of Spandau Prison in Berlin, which was rescued from destruction after Rudolf Hess died and the prison was torn down. The regiment was recruited in 1739 by Gen. George Wade to help the government pacify rebellious Highlanders and became famous all over the United Kingdom for its black tartans in contrast to the red of government troops. You can also see pictures, photos, trophies, documents, and uniforms of the Black Watch.

After visiting the castle, you can explore **North Inch,** a 100-acre parkland extending north along the west bank of the Tay. This is the best place to go for a long walk in the Perth area. Today the grounds are given over mainly to sports facilities, especially the domed Bells Sports Centre. North Inch, as depicted in Scott's *The Fair Maid of Perth,* was the site of the great 1396 Clan Combat between 30 champions from the clans Kay and Chattan, attended by Robert III and his queen. There were few survivors.

## SHOPPING

**Cairncross Ltd.,** 18 St. John's St. (☎ 01738/624-367), sells jewelry, both custom-made and from other manufacturers, in gold and silver. The specialty is Scottish freshwater pearls, which they can mount to your liking if you don't see what you want. They also offer Baccarat crystal, clocks, and some antique jewelry. **Timothy Hardie,** 25 St. John's St. (☎ 01738/633-127), deals in antique jewelry and has a large selection of Victorian pieces, including numerous three-stone rings. It also sells antique silver tea service sets. **Whispers of the Past,** 15 George St. (☎ 01738/635-472), offers an odd mix of items: jewelry, both new and antique, ranging from costume baubles to quality gold and silver pieces; china; pine furniture; silk flowers; and some linens.

**C & C Proudfoot,** Unit 104, 104 South St. (☎ 01738/632-483), is an eclectic shop whose merchandise includes leather jackets, handknitted Arran sweaters, Barbour waxed-cotton jackets, sheepskin jackets and rugs, and wool rugs, as well as a range of handbags, briefcases, scarves, and gloves.

**Watson of Perth,** 163–167 High St. (☎ 01738/639-861), has been in business since 1900. It specializes in bone china produced by a number of manufacturers, including Royal Doulton and Wedgwood and also offers cut crystal from Edinburgh, Stuart, Waterford, and other companies. Shipping is a standard part of the business.

**Caithness Glass,** Inveralmond Industrial Estate, on A9 (☎ 01738/637-373), is a glass factory on the edge of Perth. Follow A9, going through the roundabout marked A9 NORTH to Inverness; the factory is in the industrial complex a short way past the roundabout. Its sales outlet sells paperweights, glass vases, and bowls produced at an adjoining site, balanced with a range of Royal Doulton items. While here, you can watch the glassblowers at work.

**Perthshire Shop,** Lower City Mills, Mill Street (☎ **01738/627-958**), is an outlet selling jams, mustards, and oatmeal along with items produced in the neighboring mills. There are wooden bowls, *spirtles* (wooden stirrers often used in making porridge), and Perthshire tartan scarves and ties. They also stock a large selection of cookbooks.

## HITTING THE LINKS NEARBY

North of Perth is one of Scotland's acclaimed golf links, the 18-hole **Blairgowrie,** Golf Course Road, Rosemont, Blairgowrie (☎ **01250/872-622**), which includes 6,229 yards (5,668m) of playing area with a par of 72. The greens fees are £40 to £90 ($68 to $153) for one round, and £60 ($102) for the day, with even higher rates on weekends. There's a pro shop, where you can rent clubs and trolleys; caddy service is £20 ($34) plus tip. This is a challenging course, with a rolling, wild layout of pine, birch, and fir; you might even spot a deer or two grazing on the course, with its wide fairways.

## ACCOMMODATIONS

**Auld Manse Guest House.** Pitcullen Crescent, Perth PH2 7HT. ☎ **01738/629-187.** Fax 01738/629-187. www.s-h-systems.co.uk/hotels/auldman.html. 5 units. TV. £40–£60 ($68–$102) double. MC, V. Bus: 7.

Across the River Tay from the rest of Perth in a quiet residential neighborhood, this stone-sided semidetached house was built in 1887 as the manse (rector's home) for a Presbyterian church that was demolished to make room for an apartment complex in the 1950s. Don't be fooled by the modest proportions you see from the front, as it sprawls back from the road into a generously sized building. Sonia and Alister Rennie are your hosts, offering rather frilly guest rooms, complete with ruffles and pink flourishes. Each has an excellent bed and a tea/coffeemaker. If advance notice is given, dinners can be prepared for around £8 ($13.60) per person. No smoking.

**✪ Dupplin Castle.** Near Aberdalgie, Perth PH2 0PY. ☎ **01738/623-224.** Fax 01738/444-140. www.dupplin.co.uk. E-mail: dupplin@netcomuk.co.uk. 7 units. TEL. £130 ($221) double. Rates include Scottish breakfast. MC, V. From Perth, follow the main highway (M90) to Glasgow, turning left onto B9112 toward Aberdalgie and Forteviot.

This dignified stucco-sheathed mansion with sandstone mullions was built in 1968 by well-known architect Schomber Scott. With 30 acres of grounds and spectacular gardens (some specimens are 250 years old), the site is one of the most beautiful near Perth. All the large guest rooms are decorated in good taste, with antique furniture, hair dryers, and tea/coffeemakers; two rooms can be joined to an extra room to make suites. Many of the rooms overlook the valley of the River Earn. The managers are Derek and Angela Straker, who will serve you a pricey dinner in the style of a casually elegant country house if you reserve 24 hours in advance. You can relax and watch TV in the lounge.

**Hunting Tower.** Crieff Rd. (3½ miles [5.5km] west of Perth on A85), Perth PH1 3JT. ☎ **01738/583-771.** Fax 01738/583-777. 34 units. MINIBAR TV TEL. £99.50–£129.50 ($169.15–$220.15) double; from £99.50 ($169.15) cottage suite. Rates include Scottish breakfast. AE, DC, MC, V.

This late-Victorian country house with a mock Tudor facade is set on 3½ acres of well-manicured gardens. Taste and concern went into the public rooms, with their fine wood paneling, and the guest rooms are also distinguished, ranging from rather large to smaller and more compact. Hair dryers and trouser presses are included; seven have spa bathrooms. The cottage suites, to the right of the hotel, are in a renovated bungalow. Decorated to match the rooms in the main hotel, each has twin beds and a sitting room.

### A History Note

On the grounds of Dupplin Castle is the site of one of Scottish history's most tragic battles: the August 1332 Battle of Dupplin, where the piled bodies of the slain Scots were said to measure a spear's length in depth.

**Dining:** The fine Scottish and continental cuisine is reason enough to stay here. The elegant main restaurant serves nightly table d'hôte dinners costing £15.25 ($25.95) for two courses, £18.75 ($31.90) for three courses, and £19.95 ($33.90) for four courses. The more informal Conservatory serves affordable dinners daily.

**Amenities:** Concierge, room service, baby-sitting.

**✪ Kinfauns Castle.** Kinfauns (3 miles [5km] east of Perth on A90), Perth PH2 7JZ. **☎ 01738/620-777.** Fax 01738/620-778. www.kinfaunscastle.co.uk. 16 units. TV TEL. £180 ($306) double; £260 ($442) junior suite; £300 ($510) suite. Rates include Scottish breakfast. AE, MC, V. Closed 3 weeks in Jan.

This venerable late Victorian sandstone structure offers even more luxurious accommodations than Dupplin Castle. When James Smith, the Scot who ran all of Asia's Hiltons, was told in the 1990s to ship out from his base in Hong Kong, he returned home with some of the Hilton's best furnishings, which he installed in the castle, making for an unusual decorative wedding of Asia and Scotland. You stay here in the lap of luxury on 26 acres of forested lands and gardens close to the Highlands.

The grandeur of the entrance hall sets the tone, holding the six tartans of the families who have inhabited the castle, beginning with James Stuart. The gallery continues the baronial theme, with a ceiling decorated with gold leaf rosettes and an ornately carved fireplace with the family arms. Luxurious and spacious, bedrooms and suites are individually decorated in great style, with all the modern amenities, such as marble bathrooms with phones, beverage makers, hair dryers, and trouser presses. Many of the accommodations have real log fireplaces, and the antique or teak pieces used in the bedrooms are particularly elegant. Of special interest is the Lady Gray lounge, which is unchanged since the castle was built 2 centuries ago; it contains the original white marble fireplace and William Morris machine-printed wallpaper from 1910.

**Dining:** The Library Restaurant (see below) serves the finest food in the area.

**Amenities:** 40 golf courses within a 45-minute radius, plus other sports such as fishing, horseback riding, and hiking. Room service, baby-sitting, concierge, laundry/valet.

**✪ Parklands Hotel & Restaurant.** 2 St. Leonard's Bank, Perth PH2 8EB. **☎ 01738/622-451.** Fax 01738/622-046. E-mail: parklands.perth@virgin.net. 14 units. TV TEL. Mon–Thurs £99–£115 ($168.30–$195.50) double; Fri–Sun £80–£90 ($136–$153) double. Rates include Scottish breakfast. AE, DC, MC, V.

Luxuriously renovated, this hotel near the rail station opened in 1991 and immediately became the most fashionable hotel in Perth. Allen Deeson set out to create a country-house hotel in the middle of the city, and succeeded admirably. The beautifully decorated guest rooms, filled with wood paneling and cornices, overlook the South Inch Park. All are spacious and contain tea/coffeemakers and hair dryers.

**Dining:** Breakfast begins with such classic Scottish dishes as Loch Fyne kippers, deviled kidneys, smoked kedgeree, and scrambled egg with smoked salmon. For dinner you can enjoy sautéed chicken livers with ginger dressing and marinated scallops or oysters in citrus juices flavored with dill and garlic. Sweets include an iced honey-and-whisky mousse on coriander sauce. Fixed-price menus and the à la carte menu are both on the high side of moderate, but affordable light meals and snacks are available for lunch.

**Amenities:** Room service, laundry.

## DINING

**Keracher's Restaurant and Oyster Bar.** 168 South St. (45 min. from Edinburgh on the A90). ☎ **01738/449-777.** Reservations recommended. Main courses £6.90–£15.90 ($11.75–$27.05). MC, V. Mon–Sat noon–2pm and 6–10pm. Closed first 2 weeks in Jan. SCOTTISH/SEAFOOD.

For five generations, the Kerachers have been serving some of the finest seafood in Scotland. Chef Andrew Keracher carries on the family tradition by using the freshest ingredients, which are cooked to order. Dishes are created from the seas and lochs, from the moorlands to the mountains, and from the wild produce from the unspoiled landscapes of Scotland. Food is prepared with imagination and panache, but with a healthy respect for the natural tastes and textures of the produce. Among the main courses on the extensive menu are prime fillet of Pittenweem haddock stuffed with hot kiln salmon in a roast pepper sauce, and fillet of Scottish salmon glazed with honey-mustard and served with a leek and vermouth cream sauce. The excellence doesn't end with the main courses. For dessert, try the steamed ginger pudding with vanilla ice cream and lime Anglais. In addition to the restaurant, there is an Oyster Bar with a retail fish counter where you can grab a quick, tasty full range of Keracher products.

**✪ Let's Eat.** 77–79 Kinnoull St. ☎ **01738/643-377.** Reservations recommended. Main courses £6.50–£11 ($11.05–$18.70) at lunch, £8–£15 ($13.60–$25.50) at dinner. AE, MC, V. Tues–Sat noon–2pm and 6:30–9:45pm. BRITISH/INTERNATIONAL.

Let's Eat is hailed for some of the most creative cuisine in Perth. Linger over a cocktail before the meal while relaxing on one of the sofas near a blazing fireplace. Then in the sprawling terra-cotta-colored setting full of plants, enjoy a selection of seasonal venison and game and fresh fish. Menu items include gratin of goat's cheese studded with roasted peppers and served with rocket salad, new potatoes, and chutney; roasted venison fillet with port-wine sauce (and sometimes juniper berries and herbs); marinated tuna on a bed of couscous; grilled brochettes of monkfish with king prawns, rice, and salad; and chicken breasts in ginger-lime sauce.

**Let's Eat Again.** 33 George St. ☎ **1738/633-771.** Reservations recommended. Main courses £5–£9 ($8.50–$15.30). AE, MC, V. Tues–Sat noon–2pm and 6:30–9:30pm. INTERNATIONAL/ MEDITERRANEAN.

Behind the yellow-and-lime trim of what was built as a home in the 19th century, this upbeat bistro caters to the young-at-heart with well-prepared but relatively inexpensive versions of Mediterranean and international cuisine. Your meal might begin with charcoal-grilled Mediterranean vegetables with mozzarella; smoked haddock and chive-laced risotto; smoked local venison with spicy pears; salmon and codfish cakes with lemon-butter sauce; roasted salmon with sun-dried tomatoes and pesto; or Thai-style chicken curry with noodles. The more upscale Let's Eat (see above) is under the same management but in another neighborhood.

**✪ The Library Restaurant.** In Kinfauns Castle. ☎ **01738/620-777.** Reservations required. Jacket and tie required for men. Set-price 3-course lunch £18.50–£20.50 ($31.45–$34.85); set-price dinner £32 ($54.40) for 3 courses, £35 ($59.50) for 5 courses. AE, MC, V. Daily noon–1:30pm and 7–8:30pm. Closed 3 weeks in Jan. SCOTTISH.

If you'd like to dine in a grand castle with equally grand food and service, head here for one of the showcase hotels and restaurants in Scotland. Using the costliest of

Scottish ingredients, all deftly handled, chef Jeremy Brazelle has established a reputation for excellence. The best of venison, Angus beef, and salmon are offered to you along with one of the finest wine lists in the area. The setting is stately with old paneling and gold-leaf ceilings, along with a display of 13 painted coats-of-arms belonging to Lady Gray, a former resident. Each dish is skillfully and individually prepared with an inventive, carefully honed technique. A sample meal might include pumpkin and leek soup followed by fillet of halibut with buttered noodles, stir-fried vegetables, chili and soy dressing. You might also try roast rump of black-faced lamb with fresh vegetables cooked in the Provençal style with virgin olive oil and garlic.

**Littlejohn's.** 24 St. John's St. ☎ **01738/639-888.** Main courses £4.95–£13.90 ($8.40–$23.65). AE, DC, MC, V. Daily 10am–11pm. INTERNATIONAL.

On one of Perth's busiest commercial streets behind a century-old wood facade, this large dining room has old-fashioned wood paneling, antique signs and prewar memorabilia, and lots of Scottish charm, with jazz playing in the background. Despite the traditional setting, the food is eclectic: pizzas, pastas, Mexican tortillas, burgers, steaks, and an occasional lobster dish. A wide range of sandwiches and vegetarian fare is also offered. There's not much pretentiousness here; you're likely to joke with your waiter as he pours you a beer and slams down your tortillas.

## PERTH AFTER DARK

The Victorian **Perth Repertory Theatre,** 185 High St. (☎ **01738/621-031**), hosts performances of plays and musicals between mid-September and May. From the end of May to early June, it's also a venue for some of the events of the Perth Festival of Arts. Performance nights vary, but shows start at 7:30pm, and the box office is open Monday to Saturday 10am to 7:30pm. Tickets are £6 to £14 ($10.20 to $23.80).

  **Perth City Hall,** King Edward St. (☎ **01738/475-200**), is a year-round venue for musical performances and dances; many local organizations (including the Freemasons, the Royal Geographical Society, churches, and various amateur societies) book events here year after year. Entertainment is usually along the lines of a classical concert or a Highland ball, and ticket prices are at the discretion of the organization sponsoring the event.

## A SIDE TRIP TO SCONE

Old Scone, 2 miles (3km) from Perth on the River Tay, was the ancient capital of the Picts. On a lump of sandstone, the Stone of Destiny, the early Scottish monarchs were enthroned, and for 400 years the British sovereigns were crowned on the stone, which is now in Edinburgh.

### SEEING THE SIGHTS

✪ **Scone Palace.** Along A93, 2 miles (3km) north of Perth. ☎ **01738/552-300.** Admission to house and grounds £5.60 ($9.50) adults, £4.80 ($8.15) seniors, £3.30 ($5.60) children under 16, £16.50 ($28.05) families. Admission to grounds only £2.80 ($4.75) adults, £1.70 ($2.90) children. Good Friday to mid-Oct, palace daily 9:30am–5pm.

The seat of the earls of Mansfield and birthplace of David Douglas (of fir-tree fame), Scone Palace was largely rebuilt in 1802, incorporating the 1580 palace. Inside is an impressive collection of French furniture, china, ivories, and 16th-century needlework, including bed hangings created by Mary Queen of Scots. A fine collection of rare conifers is found on the grounds in the Pinetum. Rhododendrons and azaleas grow profusely in the gardens and woodlands around the palace.

  The mausoleum is about 200 yards (182m) away on Moot Hill, symbolically important as the site where medieval emissaries from most of the clans deposited soil, carried in their boots, from their native regions. The low hillock that resulted, according to legend, was a symbol of the unity of the Scottish nation. And it was here that part of the coronation ceremony for each Scottish king took place. The mausoleum was rebuilt in the early 19th century and in many ways resembles a small country church.

## ACCOMMODATIONS & DINING

✪  **Murrayshall.** New Scone, Perthshire PH2 7PH. ☎ **01738/551-171.** Fax 01738/552-595. 27 units. TV TEL. £120–£130 ($204–$221) double; £150–£160 ($255–$272) suite; £150 ($255) lodge. Rates include Scottish breakfast. AE, DC, MC, V. Take A94 for 1½ miles (2.5km) east of New Scone.

The Murrayshall, an elegant country-house hotel/restaurant on 300 acres of parkland, was completely refurbished in 1987 and reopened as one of the showpieces of Perthshire, with its own championship 18-hole/par-73 golf course. The hotel is traditionally styled in both its public rooms and its guest rooms (whose size and decoration varies). At the end of the main drive is a lodge sleeping up to six. All the accommodations come with hair dryers and trouser presses.

**Dining:** The area's best food is served in the candlelit Old Masters restaurant, which takes its name from the reproductions hanging on the walls. The menu reflects the finest Scottish cuisine; rather expensive fixed-price dinners are served nightly. Main courses might include fillet of Shetland Isles farmed salmon, Scottish beef sirloin, and deep-fried fillet of North Sea haddock. Nonguests are welcome but must reserve.

**Amenities:** 24-hour room service.

## 2  Gleneagles: Hitting the Links

56 miles NE of the Glasgow Airport, 50 miles NW of the Edinburgh Airport

Gleneagles provides a good if pricey base from which to explore central Scotland. This famous golfing center and sports complex is on a moor between Strath Earn and Strath Allan. The center gets its name from the Gaelic *Gleann-an-Eaglias,* meaning "glen of the church." St. Mungo's Chapel, higher up the glen, has monuments of the Haldane family.

Gleneagles has several 18-hole golf courses connected with the hotel: the **King's Course,** the longest one, and the **Queen's Course,** next in length, are among the best in Scotland, and the sports complex is one of the best equipped in Europe.

## ESSENTIALS

**GETTING THERE**  The town is on A9, about halfway between Perth and Stirling, a short distance from the village of Auchterarder. Trains depart from Perth for Gleneagles every 3 to 4 hours; there are also about eight trains a day from Edinburgh. Buses run from Glasgow to Gleneagles every 3 hours.

**VISITOR INFORMATION**  The year-round **tourist office** is at 90 High St., Auchterarder (☎ **01764/663-450**), about 1½ miles (2.5km) east of Gleneagles. November to April, it's open Monday to Friday 10am to 2pm; May to mid-July, hours are Monday to Saturday 9:30am to 5:30pm and Sunday noon to 4pm; mid-July to mid-September, it's open Monday to Saturday 9am to 6pm and Sunday noon to 5pm; and mid-September to October, hours are Monday to Saturday 9:30am to 5:30pm and Sunday noon to 4pm.

## ACCOMMODATIONS & DINING

⭐ **Auchterarder House.** 1 mile (1.5km) from Gleneagles and 1½ miles (2.5km) from Auchterarder (off B8062 between Auchterarder and Crieff), Auchterarder PH3 1DZ. ☎ **01764/663-646.** Fax 01764/662-939. www.wrensgroup.com. 15 units. TV TEL. £200–£350 ($340–$595) double. Rates include Scottish breakfast. AE, DC, MC, V.

Auchterarder House, a fine example of 1830s architecture and construction in the Scots Jacobean style, has been completely restored, its interior refurbished to a high standard of luxury by the St. Christopher Wren Group. The public rooms are as elegant and the guest rooms as comfortable as you'd expect, all with amenities to please a discerning clientele (hair dryers are available on request). The three largest and most desirable rooms are in the main house; the others, a lot smaller, are behind the house or in a turreted wing. You may be content to browse around the 20 acres of grounds, where a fine collection of rare shrubs, trees, and rhododendrons is nurtured.

**Dining:** Afternoon tea is served in the glass conservatory for £10.50 ($17.85). The handsome bar was originally the building's chapel. Lunch and dinner are offered in the Victorian dining room or in the library, where you can choose from two pricey table d'hôte menus.

**Amenities:** 24-hour room service, free courtesy-car service is offered from the Gleneagles station. The staff will help arrange tours of the area as well as sports activities, including coveted tee times.

⭐ **Gleneagles Hotel.** On A824 on A823, Auchterarder PH3 1NF. ☎ **01764/662-231.** Fax 01764/694-387. www.gleneagles.com. E-mail: resort.sales@gleneagles.com. 229 units. MINI-BAR TV TEL. £315–£380 ($535.50–$646) double; from £655 ($1,113.50) suite. Rates include Scottish breakfast. AE, DC, MC, V. Take A9 for 1½ miles (2.5km) southwest of Auchterarder.

Famed for its golf courses, Gleneagles Hotel stands on a 830-acre estate. It was built in isolated grandeur in 1924 and until the early 1990s was the only five-star hotel in Scotland. The service and decor are among the finest in the country, and each luxurious guest room offers views of hills and glens of the surrounding countryside as well as a hair dryer, an ironing board, and a trouser press.

**Dining/Diversions:** You can dine in the Strathearn, which serves elegant and very expensive meals nightly. The chef uses fresh Scottish produce, cooked in a light style but with flair. The emphasis is on regional dishes, and the meals are accompanied by a pianist. Service is impeccable. You can also have pasta and salads at the club, and there's a cocktail bar.

**Amenities:** The hotel maintains legendary **golf courses** sought after throughout the summer and winter. (Diehards have been known to brush away piles of light snow to improve their golfing skills even in January.) The course is open to Gleneagles guests for £80 ($136) per person to play the course's famous 18 holes; nonguests pay £100 ($170).

The hotel's country club, refurbished at a cost of £2,000,000 ($3,400,000) in 1998, is enclosed in a glass dome to provide a year-round tropical climate. It offers members and hotel guests use of two pools, a whirlpool, a Turkish bath, saunas, a plunge pool, and a children's pool. The spa includes rooms for treatments, beauty, and massages. There are also squash courts, a gym, snooker tables, tennis courts, croquet lawns, and a bowling green, not to mention fishing on the River Tay. In addition, there are the Gleneagles Jackie Stewart Shooting School and the Gleneagles Equestrian Centre. For the coddling of golfers, the Dormy House (old name for a clubhouse) beside the 18th greens of the King's and Queen's courses has a restaurant and bar, showers, and changing rooms.

Services include 24-hour room service, laundry/valet, and baby-sitting.

## 3  Crieff & Drummond Castle Gardens

18 miles (29km) W of Perth, 60 miles (97km) NW of Edinburgh, 50 miles (80.5km) NE of Glasgow

At the edge of the Perthshire Highlands, with good fishing and golf, Crieff makes a pleasant stop. This small burgh was the seat of the court of the earls of Strathearn until 1747. The gallows in its marketplace was once used to execute Highland cattle rustlers.

Visitors stop here to see two major attractions: the Glenturret Distillery, the oldest in Scotland, and Drummond Castle Gardens, one of the most formal gardens in Europe.

## ESSENTIALS

**GETTING THERE**   There's no direct rail service. The nearest train stations are 9 miles (14.5km) away at Gleneagles and 18 miles (29km) away at Perth (see "Perth: Gateway to the Highlands & Scone Palace," above). Call ☎ **0345/484-950** for schedules. Once you arrive in Perth, you'll find regular connecting bus service hourly during the day. The one-way bus fare between Perth and Crieff is £2.50 ($4.25). For schedules, call **Stagecoach** at ☎ **01738/629-339.** The bus service from Gleneagles is too poor to recommend.

Driving from Perth, continue west along A85.

**VISITOR INFORMATION**   The **tourist office** is in the Town Hall on High Street (☎ **01764/652-578**). April to mid-July, it's open Monday to Saturday 9:30am to 5:30pm and Sunday 11am to 4pm; mid-July to mid-September, hours are Monday to Saturday 9am to 7pm and Sunday 10am to 6pm; mid-September to October, it's open Monday to Saturday 9am to 7pm and Sunday 10am to 6pm; and November to March, it's open Monday to Friday 9:30am to 5pm and Saturday 10am to 2pm.

## EXPLORING THE AREA

If the day is fair and you're in the mood for hiking, follow the signposts in town to **Knock Hill,** which towers over Crieff. Here you'll be rewarded with some of the most dramatic views of the Highlands. You can also take a day trail into **Strathearn,** the valley of the River Earn, the very center of Scotland. Highland mountains meet gentle Lowland slopes, and moorland mingles with rich green pastures.

For a scenic drive, head out to **Smaa Glen,** a narrow valley shaped like a V to the north of Crieff. Hills rise on either side to 2,000 feet (607m). Here you'll encounter some of the loveliest moorland countryside in the Highlands and will come across **Ossian's Stone,** marking the grave of Ossian, the 3rd-century bard. Leave Crieff by A85, then branch left to take A822. The glen is signposted.

**Stuart Crystal,** Muthill Road (☎ **01764/654-004**), is a factory outlet selling a full line of Stuart crystal. A cutter sets up in the shop and demonstrates his craft on certain days, and there's also a falconry display outside when the weather permits (call ahead to check on both). During demonstrations, one-of-a-kind patterns are cut, and these pieces, available for sale, are very popular as souvenirs. The shop also sells crystal by Wedgwood and Waterford, as well as a line of handcrafted Ortak jewelry, featuring intricate Celtic patterns, Dunoon glazed stoneware mugs, Heritage bronze figurines, and Scottish shortbread. Within the shop is a smaller shop that offers a wide range of Scottish woolens, and you can relax and admire your purchases in the cafe.

The **Crieff Visitors Centre,** on A822, directly south of Crieff (☎ **01764/ 654-014**), is a complex that not only has a restaurant and dispenses information for visitors but also is the site of a paperweight manufacturer. A small pottery factory and an inexpensive restaurant are also here. During the week, you can tour the factory, seeing paperweights being made. The factory also produces hand-painted pottery, often with thistle designs, and millefiore glass. All these items are for sale, of course. Open daily in summer 9am to 6pm, daily in winter 10am to 4pm.

⊙ **Drummond Castle Gardens.** Crieff. ☎ **01764/681-257.** Admission £3 ($5.10) adults, £2 ($3.40) seniors, £1.50 ($2.55) children. Easter–Oct daily 2–6pm. Closed Nov–Easter. Take A822 for 3 miles (5km) south of Crieff.

The gardens of Drummond Castle, first laid out in the early 17th century by John Drummond, second earl of Perth, are among the finest formal gardens in Europe. You can get a panoramic view from the upper terrace, overlooking an example of an early Victorian parterre in the form of St. Andrew's Cross. The multifaceted sundial by John Mylne, master mason to Charles I, has been the centerpiece since 1630. You can visit the castle gardens only, not the castle itself.

**Glenturret Distillery.** Hwy. A85, Glenturret. ☎ **01764/656-565.** Guided tours £3.50 ($5.95) adults, £3 ($5.10) seniors, £2.30 ($3.90) children 12–17; free for ages 11 and under. Mar–Dec Mon–Sat 9:30am–6pm, Sun noon–6pm; Feb Mon–Sat 11:30am–4pm, Sun noon–4pm. Closed Dec 25–26 and Jan. Take A85 toward Comrie; ¾ of a mile (1.2km) from Crieff, turn right at the crossroads; the distillery is ¼ mile (about .5km) up the road.

Scotland's oldest distillery, Glenturret opened in 1775 on the banks of the River Turret. You can see the milling of malt, mashing, fermentation, distillation, and cask filling, followed by a free wee dram dispensed at the end of the tour. Guided tours leave every 10 minutes and take about 25 minutes. The Glenturret Heritage Centre incorporates a 100-seat audiovisual theater and an Exhibition Display Museum. The presentation lasts about 20 minutes. The distillery shop has the full range of the Glenturret Pure Single Highland Malt scotch whisky and the Glenturret malt liqueur, together with an extensive range of souvenirs. At the Smugglers Restaurant and Whisky Tasting Bar, you can taste older Glenturret whiskies.

## ACCOMMODATIONS

**Murraypark Hotel.** Connaught Terrace, Crieff PH7 3DJ. ☎ **01764/653-731.** Fax 01764/655-311. 19 units. TV TEL. £75 ($127.50) double or suite. Rates include Scottish breakfast. AE, DC, MC, V. Approaching from Perth, take the first right after the golf club; the hotel will be on your left.

Built by a sea captain late in the 19th century, this stone-fronted house is in a residential neighborhood about a 10-minute walk from Crieff's center. The older wing's decorative motif is Victorian traditional, evocative of the era in which the hotel was constructed; the newer wing (1993) is more modern and streamlined, although hardly as evocative. All guest rooms feature twin or double beds and offer tea/coffeemakers as well as room service. The rooms vary in size and shape, however. Many open onto views. A golf club is only a 2-minute walk away, and the hotel staff can arrange for you to play on it. The hotel bar is an intimate spot for a pre-dinner cocktail; in the main dining room, the chef specializes in wonderful Scottish, French, and international dishes.

## DINING

⊙ **The Bank.** 32 High St. ☎ **01764/656-575.** Reservations recommended. Main courses £8–£12 ($13.60–$20.40). AE, MC, V. Daily noon–2:30pm and Tues–Sat 7–10pm (Aug, also Sun 7–10pm). MODERN SCOTTISH.

This dignified red-sandstone building was constructed in 1901 as the local branch of the British Linen Bank, now part of the Bank of Scotland. Today, it contains one of the most appealing restaurants in town, thanks to the superb cuisine, a hardworking and talented staff, and a decor of mostly original paneling, an ornate plaster ceiling, and a huge arched window. Menu items change with the seasons and the chef's mood but may include wild mushroom risotto with truffle oil and cheddar cheese from the Isle of Mull; clam chowder garnished with smoked haddock, West Coast mussels, and Ayrshire bacon; prime rib of Scottish beef with potatoes and red-wine sauce; and charcoal-grilled salmon with crayfish, asparagus, and shellfish-studded saffron sauce.

## 4 Aberfeldy

76 miles (122km) NW of Edinburgh, 73 miles (117.5km) NE of Glasgow, 15 miles (24km) SW of Pitlochry, 32 miles (51.5km) NW of Perth

The Birks o' Aberfeldy are among the beauty spots made famous by Robert Burns (his poem refers to the silver birches in the town). Once a Pictish center, Aberfeldy makes a fine base for touring Perthshire's glens and lochs. Loch Tay is 6 miles (10km) west, Glen Lyon 15 miles (24km) west, and Kinloch Rannoch 18 miles (29km) northwest. Of the trio, Glen Lyon is one of central Scotland's most beautiful glens and reason enough to go to sleepy Aberfeldy in the first place. The bridge spanning the Tay was built in 1733 by Gen. George Wade. For a lovely walk, stroll just south of the town center to encounter the thundering **Falls of Moness.**

## ESSENTIALS

**GETTING THERE**   There's no direct rail service into Aberfeldy. You can take a train to either Perth or Pitlochry, then continue the rest of the way by bus. Call ☎ **0345/484-950** for schedules. Connecting buses at either Perth or Pitlochry make the final journey to Aberfeldy. The one-way fare is £3 ($5.10) from Perth or £2 ($3.40) from Pitlochry. The private bus line, **Stagecoach** (☎ **01738/629-339**), handles much of the bus travel to the small towns and villages in the area.

Aberfeldy is about a 1¾-hour drive from Edinburgh and about 2 hours from Glasgow. Take M9 from Stirling, then A9 to Perth, and continue on A9 to Ballinluig, then A827 to Aberfeldy. Or take the scenic route: M9 from Stirling, then A9, turning off at Greenloaning onto A822 to Crieff; continue on A822 to Gilmerton; then after going through Amulree, take A826 to Aberfeldy.

**VISITOR INFORMATION**   A **tourist office** is at The Square (☎ **01887/ 820-276**). April to June, September, and October, it's open Monday to Saturday 9:30am to 8:30pm and Sunday 11am to 4pm; July and August hours are Monday to Saturday 9am to 7pm and Sunday 10am to 6pm; and November to March, it's open Monday to Friday 9:30am to 5pm and Saturday 10am to 2pm.

## EXPLORING THE AREA

On the opposite bank of the Tay, west of the center, is the **Clan Menzies' Museum** (☎ **01887/820-982**), a formerly fortified tower and house from the 1500s now devoted to regional exhibits, including clan relics. April to mid-October, it's open Monday to Saturday 10:30am to 5pm and Sunday 2 to 5pm. Admission is £3 ($5.10).

If from April to October you'd like to go boating on Loch Tay, head for the **Loch Tay Boating Centre,** Carlin and Brett, Pier Road at Kenmore (☎ **01887/830-291**), which rents canoes and cabin cruisers.

Aberfeldy is also a good base for exploring ✪ **Glen Lyon,** one of the most beautiful glens in the central part of the country, with forests, prehistoric sites, and a raging river. It's Scotland's longest glen and the best place for long country walks. Follow A827 to Fearnan, then head north to Fortingall (signposted) if you'd like to see the most attractive part of the glen. A dam is at the head of the loch. A curiosity in the glen is the **Fortingall yew,** which you can see in the churchyard close to the Fortingall Hotel—the tree may be 3,000 years old, and it looks its age. An old Scottish legend claims Pontius Pilate was born next to this weather-beaten old tree; his father, or so the story goes, was once a Roman legionnaire in Scotland.

The town's shops offer good buys in tweeds and tartans, plus other items of Highland dress. The **Highland Gift Shop,** Bridgend (☎ **01887/820-257**), sells only products of Scotland, from Ortak silver jewelry, handknitted sweaters for the whole family, crystal, Scottish books, shortbread, and sweets to anything that can be made of tartan, including soft children's toys and men's and women's clothing. **P & J Haggart,** 32 Dunkeld St. (☎ **01887/820-306**), is a manufacturer of tweeds who turns out an array of men's and women's clothing, all for sale here. Much of what you'll find is outdoor wear. At **Gemini,** 21 Dunkeld St. (☎ **01887/820-625**), you'll find regional ceramic ornaments and pottery, cards, and gift items.

## ACCOMMODATIONS & DINING

✪ **Farleyer House Hotel.** Hwy. B846, Aberfeldy PH15 2JE. ☎ **01887/820-332.** Fax 01887/829-430. www.farleyer.com. E-mail: reservations@farlayer.com. 19 units. TV TEL. £100–£120 ($170–$204) double; £110–£190 ($187–$323) family suite. AE, DC, MC, V. Take B846 for 2 miles (3km) west of Aberfeldy.

A tranquil oasis, this hotel is full of character and stands on 30 acres of grounds in the Tay Valley. It's a former dower house of the Menzies clan, and in the distance you can see Castle Menzies, their 16th-century mansion. The public rooms are beautifully furnished and the large guest rooms well maintained and comfortable. Each has a radio and hair dryer.

**Dining:** The formal dining room offers dinner daily. A typical menu might begin with a salad of wood pigeon and langoustine or a parcel of Aberfeldy cheese and onion confit, followed by Tay salmon or seared loin of Perthshire lamb with chicken-and-tarragon mousse, finishing with mulled summer berries with a natural yogurt sorbet or sticky toffee pudding. This is followed by coffee and truffles. Less formal is the Scottish Bistro, serving lunch and dinner daily.

**Amenities:** Concierge, room service, laundry/valet, baby-sitting; reception will arrange for golf, fishing, sailing, water-skiing, windsurfing, clay shooting, tennis, and swimming.

**Guinach House.** The Birks, Aberfeldy PH15 2ET. ☎ **01887/820-251.** Fax 01887/829-607. 7 units. TV. £91 ($154.70) double with breakfast; £136 ($231.20) double with breakfast and dinner. MC, V.

This hotel's restaurant is one of the most sophisticated in the region, and to overnight here without experiencing it would be unfortunate indeed. The setting is a circa-1900 stone-sided house built by a German-born sea captain who wanted to retire as far inland as possible: The oak tree visible from the windows of many of the rooms has been pinpointed by surveyors as the geographic heart of Scotland, equidistant from each of the outer boundaries. Surrounded by 3 acres of gardens, the Guinach offers nicely decorated high-ceilinged guest rooms, each with tea/coffeemaker.

Menu items are prepared by owner/chef Bert MacKay and served in a dining room supervised by his wife, Marian. On the night of our last visit, two memorable specialties were the parcels of smoked salmon stuffed with smoked salmon mousse on a bed of continental lettuce leaves and served with lime–olive oil dressing and the pheasant breast with a wild mushroom and stuffed game in puff pastry.

## 5  Dunkeld

58 miles (93km) N of Edinburgh, 14 miles (22.5km) N of Perth, 98 miles (158km) SW of Aberdeen

A cathedral town, Dunkeld lies in a thickly wooded valley of the Tay at the edge of the Perthshire Highlands. Once a major ecclesiastical center, it's one of the seats of ancient Scottish history and was an important center of the Celtic church. Dunkeld is a major stop for those doing the cathedral tour, as it's the site of one of Scotland's most famous cathedrals, now a substantial ruin.

But there's much more to Dunkeld than that. It's an attractively restored town that invites exploration on foot. Derelict by the 1950s, most of its 17th-century houses have been restored. Don't miss taking a leisurely stroll to admire the beautiful houses on Cathedral Street.

## ESSENTIALS

**GETTING THERE**    Trains from Perth arrive every 2 hours at unmanned Dunkeld Station, actually in the neighboring town of Birnam. There are 4 trains a day going between Edinburgh and Dunkeld, costing £9.20 ($15.65) for a one-way ticket. Trip time is 1½ hours. For schedules, call ☎ **0345/484-950.**

Pitlochry-bound buses leaving from Perth make a stop in Dunkeld, letting you off at the Dunkeld Car Park. There are five buses in the morning, another five in the afternoon. Trip time is 50 minutes. Contact **Stagecoach** at ☎ **01738/629-339** for schedules.

Driving from Perth, continue north on the Pitlochry road (A9) until you reach Dunkeld.

**VISITOR INFORMATION**    A **tourist office** is at The Cross (☎ **01350/727-688**). April to June, September, and October, it's open Monday to Saturday 9:30am to 5:30pm and Sunday 11am to 4pm; July and August hours are Monday to Saturday 9am to 7pm and Sunday 10am to 6pm.

## EXPLORING THE AREA

The National Trust for Scotland has restored many of the old houses and shops around the marketplace and cathedral that had fallen into decay. The trust owns 20 houses on High Street and Cathedral Street as well. Many of them were constructed in the closing years of the 17th century after the rebuilding of the town following the Battle of Dunkeld. The Trust runs the **Ell Shop,** The Cross (☎ **01350/727-460**), open Easter weekend to December 24, Monday to Saturday 10am to 5:30pm.

Shakespeare fans may want to seek out the oak and sycamore in front of the destroyed **Birnam House,** a mile (1.5km) south. This was believed to be a remnant of the **Birnam Wood** (in Shakespeare's "Scottish play," you may recall, Macbeth could be defeated only when Birnam Wood came to Dunsinane).

The countryside is beautiful around Dunkeld, and you can take great walks and day hikes that stretch out on both sides of the River Tay going from Dunkeld to Birnam. In all, there are 36 miles (58km) of paths and foot tracks that have been joined to create a network of circular routes. Pick up route maps and detailed descriptions from the tourist office and set out on a day's adventure, armed with the makings of a picnic, of course.

**The Hermitage,** lying off A9 about 2 miles (3km) west of Dunkeld, was called a folly when it was built in 1758. Today it makes for one of the most scenic woodland walks in the area. The folly was built above the wooded gorge of the River Braan and restored in 1984. There's no staff here; it's always accessible and free.

Our favorite spot in the area is the **Loch of Lowes Wildlife Reserve** (☎ 01350/ 727-337), 2 miles (3km) from the center of town, along A923 heading northeast. This Wildlife Reserve can be accessed from the south shore, where there's an observation lookout and a visitor center. Filled with rich flora and fauna, the 245-acre reserve takes in the freshwater lake that's home to rare ospreys. Although common in the United States, these large brown-and-white sea-eagles are on the endangered-species list in Britain, and bird watchers from all over the country flock here to observe them. The nesting sites of the birds are fiercely protected.

**Dunkeld Cathedral.** Cathedral St. ☎ **01350/727-688.** Free admission. May–Sept Mon–Sat 9:30am–6:30pm, Sun 2–6:30pm; Oct–Apr Mon–Sat 9:30am–4pm.

Founded in A.D. 815 along the River Tay, this was converted from a church to a cathedral in 1127 by David I. It was built, damaged, and rebuilt in stages between 1452 and 1575. Its greatest destruction occurred in 1560, when the Reformers, who viewed it as a citadel of idolatry, burned the roof. Traces of the 12th-century structure clearly remain today. The choir of the ruined cathedral was renovated in the early part of the 17th century to serve as a parish church. Note the unusual windows at the triforium level. The late Gothic tower was finished in 1501. In 1908, the castle was fully restored to its 1575 version. Surprisingly, it contains an elegant effigy and tomb of the so-called Wolf of Badenoch, known as the slayer of cathedrals and churches in Scotland.

## ACCOMMODATIONS & DINING

**Atholl Arms Hotel.** Bridgehead, Dunkeld PH8 0AQ. ☎/fax **01350/727-219.** www. s-h-systems.co.uk/a05486.html. 14 units. TV TEL. £60–£65 ($102–$110.50) double. AE, MC, V.

At the foot of the Telford Bridge, the Atholl Arms was built in the early 1800s by the duke of Atholl as a coaching inn. Today it has the aura and furnishings of a respectable country home, plus comfortable midsize guest rooms. The pub on site, with a crackling log-burning fireplace, is popular with locals and serves simple, affordable lunches. More elaborate fare is served in the restaurant for dinner nightly.

**Birnam House Hotel.** Perta Rd., Birnam, Dunkeld PH8 0BQ. ☎ **01350/727-462.** Fax 01350/728-979. www.s-h-systems.co.uk/hotels/birnamho.html. 30 units. TV TEL. £88–£110 ($149.60–$187) double. Rates include breakfast. AE, DC, MC, V. From Dunkeld, drive south across the Dunkeld Bridge; then you'll see Perta Road and the hotel.

This mock-medieval building was erected in 1863 in the baronial style as a vacation home for a wealthy industrialist. In the 1960s, the Royal Family of Spain spent part of a vacation here, adding to a roster of royal visitors that has included Empress Eugénie of France. In the 1980s and 1990s, many modernizations were made, stripping the interior of at least some of its ornate detail. What you'll find today is a cozy set of high-ceilinged guest rooms, each uniquely decorated. A bar serves affordable lunches, while formal dinners are served nightly in the restaurant. A 5-minute walk away is the last tree remaining from Birnam Wood, so feared by Macbeth.

**✪ Hilton Dunkeld House Resort Hotel.** Dunkeld PH8 0HX. ☎ **01350/727-771.** Fax 01350/728-924. E-mail: reservations@dunkeld.stakis.co.uk. 97 units. MINIBAR TV TEL. £130 ($221) double; £180–£200 ($306–$340) suite. Rates include Scottish breakfast. AE, DC, MC, V. Drive about a mile (1.5km) northwest of Dunkeld on the road leading to Pitlochry (signposted).

Built in 1903 as the home for the duke and duchess of Atholl, this property was acquired and much enlarged by the Stakis chain. Today it offers the quiet dignity of life in a Scottish country house and is ranked as one of the areas leading leisure and sports hotels. On the banks of the Tay, the 280 acres of grounds are planted with trees and flowering bushes, making a parklike setting. The house is beautifully kept, and the guest rooms come in a wide range of sizes, styles, and furnishings (all include trouser presses and hair dryers). In 1999, a new nine-room wing was added. You can fish for trout and salmon right on the grounds.

**Dining:** The restaurant is one of the finest in the area, paying homage to its Taste of Scotland dishes but also serving an international cuisine; prices are high.

**Amenities:** Room service, laundry/valet, baby-sitting, all-weather tennis courts, indoor pool.

✪ **Kinnaird.** Kinnaird Estate, Kinnaird, Dunkeld PH8 0LB. ☎ **01796/482-440.** Fax 01796/482-289. www.kinnairdestate.com. E-mail: enquiry@kinnairdestate.com. 9 units, 8 estate cottages. TV TEL. £345 ($586.50) double; £440 ($748) suite; £290–£900 ($493–$1,530) estate cottage. Rates include Scottish breakfast and dinner. MC, V. Traveling north on A9 after passing Dunkeld on your right, turn left onto B898 (signposted BALNAGUARD AND DALGUISE); follow this road for 4½ miles (7km) and the main gate of Kinnaird will be on your right. No children under 12.

Opened in 1990 on a 9,000-acre private estate, Kinnaird is a small hotel of great warmth and charm. All the beautifully furnished guest rooms are comfortable and spacious and have king-size beds, hair dryers, and views. Built in 1770 as a hunting lodge for the duke of Atholl, the house was purchased in 1927 by the Ward family. Today its owner, American-born Constance Cluett Ward, has restored the house to its previous grandeur. There are eight cottages on the estate, two of which sleep eight and the others four.

**Dining:** Kinnaird House Restaurant brings a high-caliber (and high-priced) cuisine to the area. Chef Trever Brooks cooks in the post-nouvelle British and continental style with fresh ingredients and has prepared meals for some of the golden palates of Europe. Lobster, Scottish salmon, and the best of local beef, game, and poultry go into his kitchen and turn up like delicate artwork on the plate.

**Amenities:** Concierge, room service, laundry/valet, baby-sitting; sporting facilities include croquet lawn, tennis court, salmon and trout fishing, roe stalking, and shooting for pheasant, grouse, and duck. All equipment is provided, including ghillies, gamekeepers, and kennels for gun dogs.

## 6 Pitlochry: A Taste of the Whisky Trail

71 miles (114km) NW of Edinburgh, 27 miles (43.5km) NW of Perth, 15 miles (24km) N of Dunkeld

A popular resort, Pitlochry is a good base for touring the Valley of the Tummel. Ever since Queen Victoria declared it one of the finest resorts in Europe, it has drawn the hordes. It's also home to the renowned **Pitlochry Festival Theatre,** Scotland's theater in the hills.

Pitlochry doesn't exist just to entertain visitors, although it would appear that way in summer—it also produces scotch whisky. And it's a good overnight stop between Edinburgh and Inverness, 85 miles (137km) north. You can spend a very busy day in town, visiting its famous distilleries, seeing its dam and fish ladder, and budgeting some time for the beauty spots in the environs, especially Loch Rannoch and the Pass of Killiecrankie, both ideal for walks. At Blair Atholl stands one of the most highly visited and intriguing castles in the country, Blair Castle.

## ESSENTIALS

**GETTING THERE**    Five trains per day (☎ **0345/484-950**) arrive from Edinburgh and an additional three per day arrive from Glasgow (trip time from each: 2 hours). A one-way fare is £18.70 ($31.80) from either city.

Buses to Pitlochry arrive hourly from Perth. The one-way fare is £3 ($5.10). Contact **Stagecoach** at ☎ **01738/629-339** for schedules.

Driving from Perth, continue northwest along A9.

**VISITOR INFORMATION**   The **tourist office** is at 22 Atholl Rd. (☎ **01796/472-215**). June to September, it's open daily 9am to 8pm; May and October, hours are daily 9am to 6pm; and November to April, hours are Monday to Friday 9am to 5pm and Saturday 10am to 3pm.

## EXPLORING THE AREA

**Pitlochry Dam** was created because a power station was needed, but in effect the engineers created a new loch. The famous **salmon ladder** here was built to help the struggling salmon upstream. An underwater portion of the ladder (a salmon observation chamber) has been enclosed in glass to give fascinated sightseers a look. An exhibition (☎ **01796/473-152**) is open here Easter to the last Sunday in October, daily 10am to 5:30pm, costing £2 ($3.40) adults, £1.20 ($2.05) seniors, and £1 ($1.70) children.

There are terrific scenic hikes along the **Linn of Tummel,** with several signposted trails going along the river and into the forest directly to the north of the center. Just north of here you come to the stunning ✪ **Pass of Killiecrankie.** If you're driving, follow A9 north. The national trust has established the **Killiecrankie Visitor Centre** here (☎ **01786/473-233**), open April to October daily 10am to 5:30pm. You can learn about a famous battle that occurred here during the 1689 Jacobite rebellion. John Graham of Cleverhouse (1649–89) rallied the mainly Highlander Jacobite army to meet government troops. Graham was killed, and the cause of Scottish independence soon fizzled. You can walk (it's signposted) to Soldier's Leap, where an English soldier is said to have jumped to his death to escape Jacobite pursuers.

B8019 leads to **Loch Rannoch,** almost 10 miles (16km) long and some ¾ mile (1.2km) wide. For many, this is one of the most beautiful lakes in the Highlands. The setting so impressed Robert Louis Stevenson he wrote about it in *Kidnapped* (1886): "Much of it was red with heather, much of the rest broken up with bogs and hags and peaty pools." To see this desolate but awesomely beautiful spot, follow B8019 to the Linn of Tummel north of Pitlochry, venturing onto B846 at the Bridge of Tummel.

Shoppers will want to check out **McNaughtons,** Station Road (☎ **01796/472-722**), which offers a full range of Highland wear, including tweeds, tartans, and the inevitable kilts. There are departments devoted to both men and ladies, and there's also a fabric center, where a wide variety of Scottish fabrics can be purchased by the meter. The shop also carries a good selection of handknitted sweaters.

**Bell's Blairathol Distillery.** Perth Rd., 1½ mile (2.5km) south of town. ☎ **01796/482-003.** Admission £3 ($5.10) adults. Mar–Oct tours every half hour Mon–Sat 9:30am–5pm, Sun noon–5pm; Nov–Feb tours Mon–Sat 10am–4pm, by arrangement.

In 2000, Bell's celebrated 203 years as a popular whisky distillery, and you can take a distillery tour. The fee charged to adults for the tour is redeemable as a voucher off the price of any single-malt purchased in the Visitor Centre, where you'll find Bell's single malt, Bell's blend, and single malts by other regional distilleries.

✪ **Blair Castle.** Blair Atholl. ☎ **01796/481-207.** Admission £6.25 ($10.65). Apr–late Oct daily 10am–6pm. Closed Nov–Mar. From the town center, follow A9 to Blair Atholl, where you'll see signposts.

The major excursion from Pitlochry is to this castle north of the Pass of Killiecrankie. Home of the dukes of Atholl, this is one of the great historic castles of Scotland. Over the years, the castle has seen many alterations and was finally turned into the

Georgian mansion you see today, although it dates from 1269. Allow about 2 hours to tour the palace, with its antiques, 18th-century interiors, and paintings, along with an outstanding arms, armor, and porcelain collection. In the Stewart room, note the portrait of Mary Queen of Scots and her son, James VI. The Picture Staircase is a stunning achievement. On the second floor you can visit a small Georgian drawing room, an elegant dining room with landscape paintings, and the Blue Bedroom once occupied by Victorian beauty Louisa Moncrieffe. None of the six children she bore ever had an heir. On the second floor you can explore the library, the Derby Room with its ducal portraits, and the Tapestry Room with a superb collection of Flemish tapestries. On the ground floor is the 19th-century ballroom. After viewing the castle, you can stroll through the Victorian walled garden and take long walks in the parklands.

**Edradour Distillery.** On A924, Pitlochry. ☎ **01796/472-095.** Free admission. Mar–Oct Mon–Sat 9:30am–5pm, Sun noon–5pm; Nov–Feb Mon–Sat 10am–4pm. Tours every 20 mins.

Take A924 east toward Braemar to find this distillery, Scotland's smallest, 2 miles (3km) outside of town. The Visitor Centre offers distillery tours throughout the day, and the gift shop sells Edradour single malts, as well as various blends that contain the whisky.

## ACCOMMODATIONS

East Haugh House (see "Dining," below) also rents rooms.

**Balrobin.** Higher Oakfield, Pitlochry PH16 5HT. ☎ **01796/472-901.** Fax 01796/474-200. www.milford.co.uk/go/balrobin.html. E-mail: balrobin@globalnet.co.uk. 16 units. TV. £50–£70 ($85–$119) double. Rates include Scottish breakfast. MC, V. Closed Nov–Feb.

A Scottish country house run by the Hohman family since 1980, this traditional hotel opens onto views of the Perthshire hills and the Tummel Valley. The home was a 19th-century cottage used for fishing or shooting holidays. Today a two-star hotel, it offers average-sized guest rooms furnished in simple provincial styling, with hair dryers. Added to the "auld hoose" were a west and east wing in keeping with the stone construction. Affordable dinners are served nightly, and there's a guests-only bar and a country lounge.

**Green Park Hotel.** Clunie Bridge Rd., Pitlochry PH16 5JY. ☎ **01796/473-248.** Fax 01796/ 473-520. 39 units. TV TEL. £66–£128 ($112.20–$217.60) double. Rates include half-board. MC, V.

The Green Park is about half a mile (1km) from the center, at the northwest end of Pitlochry. Against a backdrop of woodland, the white-painted mansion with its carved eaves enjoys a scenic position; its lawn reaches to the shores of Loch Faskally. Visitors who reserve well in advance get one of the half dozen or so rooms in the garden wing, all of which enjoy a loch view. Some rooms have recently been refurbished and all are a reasonably good size and contain hair dryers. Guests order drinks in a lounge overlooking the water (where there's no smoking). Popular during festival season, the dining room serves dinner nightly, with many traditional Scottish dishes.

**Hotel Acarsaid.** 8 Atholl Rd., Pitlochry PH16 5BX. ☎ **01796/472-389.** Fax 01796/ 473-952. E-mail: acarsaid@msn.com. 19 units. TV TEL. £50–£72 ($85–$122.40) double. Rates include breakfast. MC, V.

This graceful but solid-looking stone house was built in 1880 as the home of the countess of Kilbride, who named it the Gaelic word *Acarsaid* for "anchorage." Now Sandy and Ina MacArthur are the no-nonsense owners. Greatly expanded, the hotel contains comfortable and cozy guest rooms, with contemporary furnishings and accessories. The bar area serves snacks at lunch (only for guests), and the more elaborate restaurant offers set-price dinners at £18.50 ($31.45) to the public nightly 5:45 to 8pm. Menu items focus on fresh ingredients, most of them Scottish, with emphasis on preparations of game dishes, salmon, duckling, and beef.

**Killiecrankie Hotel.** A924, Killiecrankie PH16 5LG. ☎ **01796/473-220.** Fax 01796/472-451. www.killiecronkiehotel.co.uk. E-mail: killiecrankie.hotel@btinternet.com. 10 units. TV TEL. £126–£168 ($214.20–$285.60) double. MC, V. Free parking. Signposted from A9 north of Pitlochry.

This typically Scottish country house, built in 1840, is surrounded by 4 acres of lawns and woodlands. The furniture in both the public areas and the guest rooms is made of pine, and the rooms are individually decorated in a variety of subtle colors and contain hair dryers and tea/coffeemakers. The walls are a foot thick, so light sleepers can rest in peace. The restaurant serves expensive dinners to both guests and nonguests, featuring fresh Scottish produce and seasonal meat, fish, and game. The bar is open to guests only daily around lunchtime and in the evening.

**Knockendarroch House.** Higher Oakfield, Pitlochry PH16 5HT. ☎ **01796/473-473.** Fax 01796/474-068. www.knockendarroch.co.uk. E-mail: info@knockendarroch.co.uk. 12 units. TV TEL. £110 ($187) double. Rates include breakfast and dinner. AE, V. Closed Nov–Mar. Turn off A9 going north at PITLOCHRY sign. After rail bridge, take first right, then second left.

Built in 1880, this Victorian mansion opens onto panoramic views of the Tummel Valley. Owned and operated by Tony and Jane Ross, this establishment has won a multitude of awards. Varying in size and style, the bedrooms are comfortable, tastefully furnished, and attractively decorated in soft, cool colors. All rooms include amenities such as beverage-makers, hair dryers, and cable TV. The cozy attic units provide balconies overlooking the rooftops of Pitlochry. Overall, the warmth of the staff and the evocative atmosphere of the mansion make it a place worth visiting.

**Dining:** Before dining, guests are offered a free glass of sherry. In the elegant dining room, you can enjoy delectable meals such as wild venison chops in red wine and juniper berry jus, or the mushroom and nut roast on the chiffonade of cabbage in rich tomato and sherry sauce. The food is of the finest quality and always freshly prepared. Prices are more moderate than you might expect, and reservations are required.

**Amenities:** Room service, laundry, baby-sitting, breakfast trays for early risers.

**Pine Trees Hotel.** Strathview Terrace, Pitlochry PH16 5QR. ☎ **01796/472-121.** Fax 01796/472-460. www.pinetrees-hotel.demon.co.uk. E-mail: info@pinetrees-hotel.demon.co.uk. 20 units. TV TEL. £68–£140 ($115.60–$238) double. Rates include Scottish breakfast. MC, V. Turn right up Larchwood Rd., below the golf course on the north side of Pitlochry.

This country house was built in 1892 on 14 acres of private grounds and is only about a 15-minute walk from the town center and 5 minutes from the golf course, home of the Highland Open Championships. The family-run Pine Trees has spacious public rooms, an atmosphere of warmth and relaxation, and a reputation for good food and wine. The guest rooms are in either the main house or a 1970s annex designed to blend into the period of the central structure; they're constantly being renovated and are furnished with traditional pieces, plus hair dryers. Bar lunches and full luncheon and dinner menus are offered, with fresh and smoked salmon always on the menu. Trout and salmon fishing can usually be arranged.

# DINING

**East Haugh House.** Old Perth Rd., East Haugh, Pitlochry PH16 5JS. ☎ **01796/473-121.** Fax 01796/472-473. www.eastnaugh.co.uk. E-mail: eastnaugh@aol.com. Reservations recommended. Table d'hôte dinner £27.95 ($47.50); bar platters £1.75–£16 ($3–$27.20). MC, V. Restaurant daily 7–9pm; bar daily noon–2:30pm and 6–9pm. Drive a mile (1.5km) south of Pitlochry on A9 toward Inverness; it's across the road from the Tummel River. MODERN BRITISH.

Although it contains 13 comfortable guest rooms, East Haugh House is best known for its well-prepared cuisine. In a Teutonic-looking granite house commissioned in the 1600s by the duke of Atholl for one of his tenant farmers, it offers a menu that relies exclusively on fresh Scottish ingredients and changes every 2 or 3 days. Meals in the cozy bar area may include mixed grills, Scottish lamb, steaks, and haggis. The cuisine in the elegant restaurant is more adventurous, featuring such dishes as zucchini flowers stuffed with wild-mushroom duxelle, grilled and marinated Scottish goat cheese with a mixed leaf and pine-nut salad, terrine of local pigeon with orange salad and *mange tout* (a kind of bean), and many variations of salmon. Desserts might include a dark-chocolate torte with crème fraîche, or a hot thin apple flan with caramel sauce. Scottish-born Neil McGown and his English wife, Lesley, are the hardworking gracious owners.

The spacious guest rooms will make you think you're staying in a country mansion, with hair dryers, phones, and TVs. Depending on the season, with Scottish breakfast included, doubles are £59 to £110 ($100.30 to $187).

## PITLOCHRY AFTER DARK

The town is famous for its **Pitlochry Festival Theatre** (☎ **01796/484-626**). Founded in 1951, the festival theater draws people from all over the world to its repertory of plays (which change daily), its Sunday concerts, and varying art exhibits, presented April 30 to October 9. Performances in the evening begin at 8pm, and on Wednesday and Saturday there's a 2pm matinee. The theater complex opened in 1981 on the banks of the River Tummel near the dam and fish ladder, with a parking area; a restaurant serving coffee, lunch, and dinner; and other facilities for visitors. Tickets for plays and concerts are £13 to £17 ($22.10 to $28.90).

For the area's best pub, head to the **Killiecrankie Hotel,** signposted from A9 north of Pitlochry (☎ **01796/473-220**). In a country hotel set on peaceful grounds, it serves 20 malt whiskies, as well as reasonably priced great food. Try the deep-fried fresh haddock in beer batter or one of the daily specials. Upholstered chairs, wildlife paintings, and plants and flowers make for an inviting atmosphere.

## 7  Dundee & Glamis Castle

63 miles (101.5km) N of Edinburgh, 67 miles (108km) SW of Aberdeen, 22 miles (35.5km) NE of Perth, 83 miles (134km) NE of Glasgow

The old seaport of Dundee, the fourth-largest city in Scotland, is now an industrial city on the north shore of the Firth of Tay. When steamers took over the whaling industry from sailing vessels, Dundee took the lead as home port for the ships from the 1860s until World War I. Long known for its jute and flax operations, Dundee is linked with the production of the rich Dundee fruitcakes and Dundee marmalades and jams. This was also the home of the man who invented stick-on postage stamps, James Chalmers.

Spanning the Firth of Tay is the **Tay Railway Bridge,** opened in 1888. Constructed over the tidal estuary, the bridge is some 2 miles (3km) long, one of the longest in Europe. There's also a road bridge 1¼ miles (2km) long, with four traffic lanes and a walkway in the center.

Dundee has only minor attractions itself, but it's a base for exploring Glamis Castle (one of the most famous in Scotland) and the little town of Kirriemuir, which Sir James M. Barrie, author of *Peter Pan,* disguised in fiction as the Thrums. Dundee also makes a good base for those who want to play at one of Scotland's most famous golf courses, Carnoustie.

## ESSENTIALS

**GETTING THERE**  **ScotRail** offers frequent service among Perth, Dundee, and Aberdeen. A one-way fare from Perth to Dundee is £4.50 ($7.65); from Aberdeen, it's £20.20 ($34.35). There's also frequent rail service between Edinburgh and Dundee, with a round-trip ticket costing £17.40 ($29.60) and trip lasting 1¾ hours. For schedules, call ☎ **0345/484-950.**

**CityLink** buses offer frequent bus service from Edinburgh and Glasgow. Buses leave at the rate of 1 per hour. A one-way fare from Glasgow costs £7 ($11.90); from Edinburgh, £6.50 ($11.05). For schedules, phone ☎ **0990/505-050.**

By car from Edinburgh, take M90 north to Perth, then cut northeast along A85.

**VISITOR INFORMATION**  The **tourist office** is at 21 Castle St. (☎ **01382/527-527**). June to September, it's open Monday to Saturday 9am to 6pm and Sunday noon to 4pm; October to May, hours are Monday to Saturday 9am to 5pm.

## SEEING THE SIGHTS

For a panoramic view of Dundee, the Tay Bridge across to Fife, and the mountains to the north, go to **Dundee Law,** a 572-foot (173.5m) hill a mile (1.5km) north of the city. The hill is an ancient volcanic plug.

**HMS** *Unicorn.* Victoria Dock. ☎ **01382/200-900.** Admission £4 ($6.80) adults, £3 ($5.10) seniors/children, £10 ($17) families. Jan–Mar 25 Mon–Fri 10am–4pm; Mar 26–Oct 31 daily 10am–5pm.

This 46-gun ship of war commissioned in 1824 by the Royal Navy, now the oldest British-built ship afloat, has been restored. You can explore all four decks: the quarter-deck with its 32-pound (14.5kg) carronades, the gundeck with its battery of 18-pound (8kg) cannons and captain's quarters, the berth deck with its officers' cabins and crew's hammocks, and the orlop deck and hold. Various displays portraying life in the sailing navy and the history of the *Unicorn* make this a rewarding visit.

**RRS** *Discovery.* Discovery Quay, Discovery Point. ☎ **01382/201-245.** £5.50 ($9.35) adults, £4.25 ($7.25) seniors, £3.85 ($6.55) children. Apr–Oct Mon–Sat 10am–5pm, Sun 11am–5pm; Nov–Mar Mon–Sat 10am–4pm, Sun 11am–4pm.

This weather-beaten vessel was used by Capt. Robert Scott on polar explorations. An exhibit details Scott's first two expeditions to the Antarctic, and onboard exhibits re-create the rugged life on the ship.

**Verdant Works.** West Henderson's Wind. ☎ **01382/225-282.** Admission £5.50 ($9.35) adults, £4.25 ($7.25) seniors, £3.85 ($6.55) children. Apr–Oct Mon–Sat 10am–5pm, Sun 11am–5pm; Nov–Mar Mon–Sat 10am–4pm, Sun 11am–4pm.

This refurbished ex-mill, known as the Jute House, is dedicated to the history of an industry that sustained Dundee throughout most of the 19th and 20th centuries. The first floor of the museum shows how raw jute from Bangladesh was processed and includes a display on a weaver's loom as well as audiovisual screens and exhibits. On the second floor is a section on the socio-historical aspect of the city and information on how the different social classes lived in 19th-century Dundee. In the courtyard are 18th- and 19th-century street games, such as stilts and whips and tops.

**Broughty Castle.** Castle Green, Broughty Ferry. ☎ **01382/436-916.** Free admission. July–Sept Mon 11am–5pm, Tues–Thurs 10am–1pm and 2–5pm, Sun 2–5pm; Oct–June Mon 11am–5pm, Tues–Thurs 10am–1pm and 2–5pm. Bus: 7S or 76.

This 15th-century estuary fort is 4 miles (6.5km) east of the city center at Broughty Ferry, a fishing village that was the terminus for ferries crossing the Firth of Tay until the bridges were built. Besieged by the English in the 16th century and attacked by

Cromwell's army under General Monk in the 17th, it was restored in 1861 as part of Britain's coastal defenses. The fort's gun battery was dismantled in 1956, and it's now a museum with displays on local history, arms and armor, seashore life, and Dundee's whaling story. The observation area at the top of the castle provides fine views of the Tay estuary and northeast Fife.

## ACCOMMODATIONS

**Craigtay Hotel.** 101 Broughty Ferry Rd, Tayside, Dundee DD4 6JE. ☎ **01382/451-142.** Fax 01382/452-940. www.craigtay.co.uk. 18 units. TV TEL. £51–£70 ($86.70–$119) double. MC, V. From Dundee, drive a mile (1.5km) east of town, following the signs to Broughty Ferry.

Although this hotel was constructed around the core of an 18th-century farm building, few if any hints of its age are visible. In the 1960s, it was Dundee's first disco, before a local entrepreneur transformed it into a tea room. Much enlarged and modernized, it's now a small hotel with functional, modern guest rooms, each with a tea/coffeemaker. The ground floor contains a pub and restaurant, serving moderately priced dinners nightly.

**Hilton Hotel.** Earl Grey Place, Dundee DD1 4DE. ☎ **01382/229-271.** Fax 01382/200-072. E-mail: reservations@dundee.stakis.co.uk. 129 units. TV TEL. £115–£135 ($195.50–$229.50) double; from £250 ($425) suite. AE, DC, MC, V. Free parking. Bus: 1A, 1B, or 20.

This chain hotel helped rejuvenate Dundee's once-seedy waterfront, and is built in a severe modern style. Some of the well-furnished midsized guest rooms overlook the Firth, the river, or the Tay Bridge, and all have hair dryers.

**Dining:** Guests can dine at Juliana's Table Restaurant, featuring buffet-style meals and moderately priced set menus.

**Amenities:** Room service, baby-sitting, laundry/valet, heated indoor pool, exercise equipment, sauna, whirlpool.

**Invercarse Hotel.** 371 Perth Rd., Dundee DD2 1PG. ☎ **01382/669-231.** Fax 01382/644-112. 44 units. TV TEL. £90 ($153) double; £100 ($170) suite. Rates include Scottish breakfast. AE, DC, MC, V. Free parking. From Dundee, drive 3 miles (5km) west on Perth Rd. From the town center, drive along Perth Road, following the signs to the University of Dundee and the Botanic Gardens.

In landscaped gardens overlooking the River Tay, this hotel boasts a tranquil location and Victorian country-house atmosphere. It frequently hosts conferences and local banquets. The guest rooms, in a variety of sizes, open onto views across the Tay to the hills of the Kingdom of Fife and are well furnished, often with pieces crafted from light-grained wood; trouser presses and hair dryers are included. You can enjoy drinks in the bar, furnished in red leather. Moderately priced dinners, featuring a continental or Scottish cuisine, are served nightly.

## DINING

**Jahangir Tandoori.** 1 Sessions St., at the corner of Hawk Hill. ☎ **01382/202-022.** Reservations recommended. Main courses £6.50–£15 ($11.05–$25.50). AE, DC, MC, V. Daily 5pm–midnight. INDIAN.

Built around an indoor fish pond in a dining room draped with the soft folds of an embroidered tent, this is the best Indian restaurant in Dundee and one of the most exotic in the region. Meals are prepared with fresh ingredients and cover the gamut of recipes from both north and south India. The food is sometimes slow-cooked in clay pots and is seasoned to the degree of spiciness you prefer. Both meat and vegetarian dishes are available, and the staff is polite.

## DUNDEE AFTER DARK

Your best choice is the **Dundee Rep Theatre,** Tay Square (☎ **01382/223-530**), which is likely to stage any and everything from *Peter Pan* to a jazz festival or an opera, from plays to Scottish ballet or even flamenco. You can book tickets Monday to Saturday 10am to 7:30pm (to 6pm on performance days). Tickets generally are £5 to £13 ($8.50 to $22.10). On site is the **Het Theatercafe** (☎ **01382/206-699**), open Monday 11am to 7:45pm, Tuesday to Thursday 11am to 9pm, Friday 11am to 10:30pm, and Saturday 10am to 10:30pm. Main courses are £6 to £10 ($10.20 to $17).

## A SIDE TRIP TO GLAMIS CASTLE

The little village of Glamis (pronounced without the *i*) grew up around its famous castle. After Balmoral, visitors to Scotland most want to see Glamis Castle for its architecture and its link with the crown.

✪ **Glamis Castle.** Castle Office, Glamis. ☎ **01307/840-393.** Admission to castle and gardens £6 ($10.20) adults, £4.50 ($7.65) seniors/students, £3 ($5.10) children 5 to 16. Apr–Oct daily 10:30am– 5:30pm (last admission at 4:45pm). Opens at 10am in July–Aug. Admission Nov–Mar is discretionary; you must call ahead. From Dundee, six buses run daily to the village of Glamis, but only three stop directly at the castle (the others require a mile-long walk) at 8:55am, 11:25am, and 12:25pm. The bus trip takes 60 minutes and costs £3.85 ($6.55) round-trip. For bus information, call ☎ 01382/228-054.

For 6 centuries, this castle has been connected to members of the British royal family: Queen Elizabeth, the Queen Mother, was brought up here, and Princess Margaret was born here, making her the first royal princess born in Scotland in 3 centuries. The present owner, the queen's great-nephew, is the 18th earl of Strathmore and Kinghorne and the direct descendant of the first earl. The castle contains Duncan's Hall, where the Victorians claimed Macbeth murdered King Duncan (in the play, the murder takes place at Macbeth's castle near Inverness). In fact, Shakespeare was erroneous as well—he had Macbeth named Thane of Glamis, but Glamis wasn't made a thanedom until years after the play takes place.

The present Glamis Castle dates from the early 15th century, but there are records of a hunting lodge having been here in the 11th century—Malcolm II was carried there mortally wounded in 1034 after having been attacked by his enemies while hunting in a nearby forest.

Glamis Castle has been in the possession of the Lyon family since 1372, when it was given to Sir John Lyon by Robert II. Four years later, Sir John married the king's daughter, Princess Joanna. The castle was altered in the 17th century and restored and enlarged in the 18th and 19th centuries. It contains some fine plaster ceilings, furniture, and paintings. You'll also want to stroll its fine gardens.

A self-service **restaurant** has been installed in the old kitchens, with a chalkboard featuring daily specials and excellent home-cooked and baked dishes. Try the home-made pâté or the salmon and spring onion quiches.

### ACCOMMODATIONS

✪ **Castleton House.** Eassie by Glamis, Forfar DD8 1SJ. ☎ **01307/840-340.** Fax 01307/840-506. www.dundeechamber.co.uk/castleton. E-mail: castleton@fastnet.co.uk. 6 units. TV TEL. £140 ($238) double. Rates include Scottish breakfast and dinner. Children 10 and under stay free in parents' room. MC, V. Drive 3 miles (5km) west of Glamis on A94.

This Victorian hotel has been restored with love and care. In cool weather (often the case around here), you're greeted by welcoming coal fires in the bar and public lounge. The guest rooms of various sizes are furnished with reproduction antiques and come

# In Search of Peter Pan

The little town of **Kirriemuir** is reached by heading north of Glamis Castle for 4 miles (6.5km) or by traveling 16 miles (26km) north of Dundee via A929 and A928. Thousands of visitors yearly come here to pay their respects to Sir James M. Barrie (1860–1937), author of *Peter Pan*. Kirriemuir itself was disguised in fiction as the Thrums of his tales.

The little town of red-sandstone houses and narrow crooked streets, in the heart of Scotland's raspberry country, saw the birth of Barrie in 1860. His father was employed as a hand-loom weaver of linen. **Barrie's birthplace** still stands at 9 Brechin Rd. (☎ **01575/572-646**), now a property of the National Trust for Scotland. The small house contains manuscripts and mementos of the writer. A little wash house outside the four-room cottage was used by Barrie as his first makeshift theater. May to September, the house is open Monday to Saturday 11am to 5pm and Sunday 1:30 to 5pm; October, hours are Saturday 11am to 5pm and Sunday 1:30 to 5pm. Admission is £2.50 ($4.25) adults, £1.70 ($2.90) seniors/students/children.

Barrie first became known for his sometimes-cynical tales of Kirriemuir, disguised as Thrums, in such works as *Auld Licht Idylls* (1888) and *A Window in Thrums* (1889). Barrie turned to the theater and in time became known for bringing supernatural and sentimental ideas to the stage. It's said that talking to a group of children while walking his dog gave him the idea for the stories about Peter Pan, which were first presented to the public in 1904. It wasn't until 1957 that *When Wendy Grew Up: An Afterthought* was published.

He went on to write more dramas, including *Alice Sit-by-the-Fire* (1905), *What Every Woman Knows* (1908), *The Will* (1913), and *Mary Rose* (1920), the latter a very popular play in its day. But who remembers these works today except a Barrie scholar? On the other hand, Peter Pan has become a legendary figure, known by almost every child in the Western world through films, plays, musicals, and the original book.

Although he spent most of his working life in London, Barrie is buried in Kirriemuir Cemetery. To reach **Barrie's grave,** turn left off Brechin Road and follow the cemetery road upward. The path is clearly marked, taking you to the grave pavilion. A camera obscura in the **Barrie Pavilion** on Kirriemuir Hill gives views over Strathmore to Dundee and north to the Highlands.

---

with tea/coffeemakers and hair dryers. You can have meals in the high-ceilinged dining room or the plant-filled conservatory. The chef features a set luncheon and a fixed-price dinner, with a menu that changes daily and is based on the freshest produce. Dishes usually include tender Angus steak, grilled or roasted Highland lamb, and fresh fish, such as North Sea monkfish.

## 8  Carnoustie

12 miles E of Dundee, 59 miles SW of Aberdeen, 68 miles NE of Edinburgh

Carnoustie is the home of the famous ✪ **Carnoustie Golf Links,** Links Parade (☎ **01241/853-789;** fax 01241/852-720). Incorporated in 1880, much of the town of Carnoustie was built because of the stream of golfers who came here to play. Records as early as 1560 refer to *gowff* being played on the surrounding fields, and by the reign of Queen Victoria the course had developed into a factory for training golf instructors and champions who spread word of the game throughout the Empire. The landscape is rugged and, off the fairways, richly clad in gorse with copses of trees. Skilled golfers call the course stimulating; neophytes refer to it as treacherous, particularly the 16th, 17th, and 18th holes, which are among the most difficult in Scotland. In 1999, the British Open was held at this par-72 championship course. This 6,941-yard (6,316m) course requires the use of a caddy, costing £30 ($51) for 18 holes. Electric golf carts aren't allowed, but you can rent a trolley for £3.50 ($5.95) per round. Greens fees are £70 ($119), and club rental, available at **Simpson's Golf Shop,** 6 Links Parade (☎ **01241/854-477**), or **David Low's,** 7 Links Ave. (☎ **01241/853-439**), costs £10 to £15 ($17 to $25.50).

In addition to the championship course above, Carnoustie boasts the **Burnside Course** and the **Buddon Links Course,** opened in the 1970s. To reach Carnoustie from Dundee, go east 10 miles (16km) along A92 or take the coastal road, A930, which is signposted.

## ACCOMMODATIONS

**Hogan House Hotel.** Links Parade, Carnoustie DD7 7JF. ☎ **01241/853-273.** Fax 01241/853-319. www.s-h-systems.co.uk/hotels/glenl.html. E-mail: hoganhousehotel@btinternet.com. 7 units. TV TEL £70–£110 ($119–$187) double. Rates include breakfast. MC, V. Free parking. Off A92, adjoining the golf course.

Sheila and Joe McClory own and operate this three-star hotel overlooking the 18th green of the Carnoustie Golf Links. Golfers and others flock here to enjoy Scottish hospitality in comfortable surroundings. Many rooms open onto panoramic views of the Links, the Tay Estuary, and the countryside. The tastefully decorated bedrooms with attractive color schemes are individually decorated, and four are large enough for families. Amenities include such thoughtful extras as beverage makers, alarm clocks, and hair dryers. Golfers meet at the cocktail lounge and pub, Hogan's Alley, with its extensive collection of golf memorabilia. The hotel restaurant is known for its wholesome food, often made from local produce when available.

## DINING

**11 Park Avenue.** 11 Park Ave. ☎ **01241/853-336.** Reservations recommended. Main courses £11–£16 ($18.70–$27.20). AE, DC, MC, V. Apr–Sept Tues–Sat noon–2pm and 7–10pm; Oct–Dec and Feb–Mar Tues–Sat 7–10pm. Closed Jan. SCOTTISH.

A few steps from High Street, this restaurant is the most prestigious in town. Its dignified gold-and-burgundy premises are a showcase for the cuisine of Stephen Collinson, whose menu items, made with the freshest ingredients, reflect Scottish tradition. Depending on the season, he might tempt you with Scottish mussels in white-wine sauce or lamb fillet with fresh basil and tomato-flavored port-wine sauce. For dessert, nothing is better than the caramelized lemon tart or the selection of Scottish cheeses.

# 9 Aberdeen: The Granite City

130 miles (209km) NE of Edinburgh, 67 miles (108km) N of Dundee

Bordered by fine sandy beaches (delightful if you're a polar bear), Scotland's third city, Aberdeen, is often called the "Granite City," since its buildings are constructed largely of pink or gray granite, hewn from the Rubislaw quarries. The harbor in this seaport is one of the country's largest fishing ports, filled with kipper and deep-sea trawlers, and Aberdeen lies on the banks of the salmon- and trout-filled Don and Dee rivers. Spanning the Don is the **Brig o' Balgownie,** a steep Gothic arch begun in 1285.

Although it hardly compares with Glasgow and Edinburgh, Aberdeen is the center of a vibrant university; it boasts a few marvelous museums and galleries; and it's known for great nightlife and shopping, the best in the northeast. Old Aberdeen is the seat of one of Scotland's major cathedrals, St. Machars. It's also a good base for exploring the greatest castles of Grampian and the towns and villages along the splendid salmon river, Deeside.

## ESSENTIALS

**GETTING THERE**    Aberdeen is served by a number of airlines, including British Airways, British Midland, Easy Jet, and KLM. For flight information, phone the Aberdeen Airport at ☎ **01224/722-331.** The airport is about 7 miles (11km) away from the heart of town and is connected to it by a bus service costing £1.35 ($2.30) one way. Taxis cost about £10 ($17).

Aberdeen has direct rail links to the major cities of Britain. SuperSaver fares, available by avoiding travel on Friday and Saturday, make the price difference between a one-way fare and a round-trip ticket negligible. Another efficient way of saving on fares by another £10 ($17) is by reserving through the booking agency, Apex. For fares in Scotland, call ☎ **0845/755-0033** with at least 48 hours' notice. For fares from London, call ☎ **0845/722-5225** with a minimum of 1 week's notice. The prices here are for tickets bought on the day of departure, excluding Friday, when prices are higher. Nineteen trains per normal weekday arrive from Edinburgh; a regular one-way ticket costs £33.10 ($56.25). Trip time is about 3½ hours. Some 19 trains per day arrive from Glasgow, costing £36.40 ($61.90) one-way or £40.20 ($68.35) round-trip. Some 12 trains per day arrive from London as well, with a one-way fare of £81 ($137.70) and a round-trip fare of only £82 ($139.40). For rail schedules, call ☎ **0345/484-950.**

Several bus companies have express routes serving Aberdeen, and many offer special round-trip fares to passengers avoiding travel on Friday or Saturday. Frequent buses arrive from both Glasgow, costing £18 to £23 ($30.60 to $39.10) round-trip, and from Edinburgh, costing £18 to £23 ($30.60 to $39.10) round-trip. There are also frequent arrivals from Inverness, a round-trip costing £11 ($18.70). For bus schedules in Aberdeen, call ☎ **01224/212-266.**

It's also easy to drive to the northeast. From the south, drive via Edinburgh over the Forth and Tay Road bridges and take the coastal road. From the north and west, approach the area from the much improved A9, which links Perth, Inverness, and Wick.

**VISITOR INFORMATION**    The **Aberdeen Tourist Information Centre** is in St. Nicholas House, Broad Street, Aberdeen, Aberdeenshire AB10 1DE (☎ **01224/ 632-727**). July and August, it's open Monday to Friday 9am to 7pm, Saturday 9am to 5pm, and Sunday 10am to 4pm; April to June and September, hours are Monday to Friday 9am to 5pm and Saturday 10am to 2pm; October to March, it's open Monday to Friday 9am to 5pm and Saturday 10am to 2pm.

## SEEING THE SIGHTS

In old Aberdeen is **Aberdeen University,** a fusion of two colleges. Reached along University Road, **King's College** (☎ **01224/272-137;** Bus: 6, 20) is Great Britain's oldest school of medicine. The college is known for its circa-1500 A.D. chapel with pre-Reformation carved woodwork, the finest of its kind in Scotland; it's open daily 9am to 4:30pm, charging no admission. On Broad Street is **Marischal College** (☎ **01224/273-131**), founded in 1593 by Earl Marischal—it's the world's second

# Aberdeen

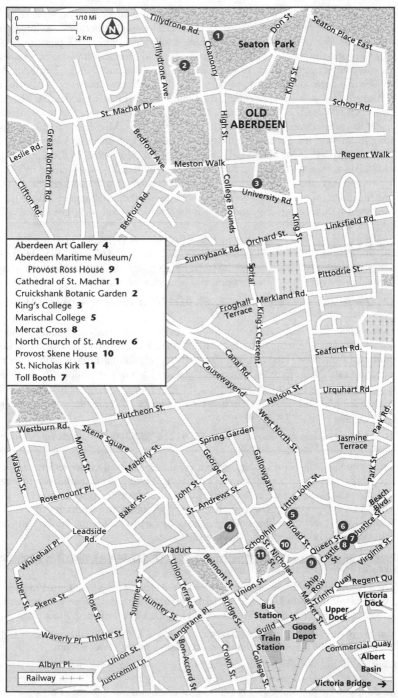

0  1/10 Mi

0  .2 Km

N

Tillydrone Rd.

Don St.

Chanonry ①

Seaton Place East

**Seaton Park**

Tillydrone Ave.

② 

St. Machar Dr.

King St.

School Rd.

**OLD ABERDEEN**

Bedford Ave.

Great Northern Rd.

Leslie Rd.

Clifton Rd.

Bedford Rd.

High St.

Meston Walk

Regent Walk

College Bounds

③ 

University Rd.

King St.

Linksfield Rd.

Orchard St.

Aberdeen Art Gallery **4**
Aberdeen Maritime Museum/
  Provost Ross House **9**
Cathedral of St. Machar **1**
Cruickshank Botanic Garden **2**
King's College **3**
Marischal College **5**
Mercat Cross **8**
North Church of St. Andrew **6**
Provost Skene House **10**
St. Nicholas Kirk **11**
Toll Booth **7**

Sunnybank Rd.

Spital

Pittodrie St.

Froghall Terrace

Merkland Rd.

King's Crescent

Seaforth Rd.

Canal Rd.

Causewayend

Nelson St.

Urquhart Rd.

Park Rd.

Hutcheon St.

West North St.

Jasmine Terrace

Westburn Rd.

Skene Square

Spring Garden

Gallowgate

Mount St.

Maberly St.

George St.

Little John St.

Park St.

Watson St.

Rosemount Pl.

Baker St.

John St.

St. Andrews St.

Beach Blvd.

⑤ 

Broad St.

⑥ 

Justice St.

Leadside Rd.

④ 

Schoolhill

St. Nicholas

⑩ 

Queen St.

⑧ ⑦

Castle St.

Virginia St.

Whitehall Pl.

Viaduct

Belmont St.

⑪ 

Union St.

⑨ 

Ship Row

Regent Qu

Albert St.

Skene St.

Rose St.

Summer St.

Huntley St.

Union Terrace

Bridge St.

Market St.

Trinity Quay

**Victoria Dock**

**Upper Dock**

Waverly Pl.

Thistle St.

Langstane Pl.

Bon-Accord St.

**Bus Station**

Guild St.

**Goods Depot**

**Commercial Quay**

**Albert Basin**

Albyn Pl.

Union St.

Justicemill Ln.

Crown St.

College St.

**Train Station**

Railway ┼┼┼

**Victoria Bridge →**

321

biggest granite structure (El Escorial outside Madrid is much larger). While King's College was Catholic, Marischal was Protestant. The main structure is no longer in use, but on site is the Marischal Museum displaying exhibits and photos of the university and the Scottish culture of the northeast in general; admission is free, and the museum is open Monday to Saturday 10am to 5pm and Sunday 2 to 5pm. In 1860, the colleges joined together to form the nucleus of the University of Aberdeen.

Also at the University of Aberdeen, the **Cruickshank Botanic Garden,** St. Machar Drive (☎ 01224/272-704; Bus: 6, 20), displays alpines, shrubs, and many herbaceous plants, along with rock and water gardens. It's open Monday to Friday 9am to 5pm; in summer, it's also open Saturday and Sunday 2 to 5pm. Admission is free.

The **Cathedral of St. Machar,** Chanonry (☎ 01224/485-988 in the morning or 01224/317-424 in the afternoon; Bus: 1, 2, 3, 4, 5, 6, 7, or 26), was founded in 1131, but the present structure dates from the 15th century. Its splendid heraldic ceiling contains three rows of shields. Be sure to note the magnificent modern stained-glass windows by Douglas Strachan and the pre-Reformation woodwork. The cathedral is open daily 9am to 5pm.

**Alpine Bikes,** 66–70 Holburn St. (☎ 01224/211-455), will rent you a bike so you can go exploring on two wheels. Rates are £12 ($20.40) daily or £24 ($40.80) for weekends, with weekly rates at £60 ($102). It's open Sunday 11am to 5pm, Monday to Wednesday and Friday 9am to 6pm, and Thursday 9am to 8pm.

✪ **Aberdeen Art Gallery.** Schoolhill. ☎ 01224/523-700. Free admission. Mon–Sat 10am–5pm; Sun 2–5pm. Bus: 20.

Built in 1884 in a neoclassical design by A. Marshall MacKenzie, this building houses one of the most important art collections in Great Britain. It contains 18th-century portraits by Raeburn, Hogarth, Ramsay, and Reynolds and acclaimed 20th-century works by Paul Nash, Ben Nicholson, and Francis Bacon. The exhibits also include excellent impressionist pieces by Monet, Pissarro, Sisley, and Bonnard as well as a collection of Scottish domestic silver and examples of other decorative arts. Special exhibits and events are frequently offered.

**Aberdeen Maritime Museum.** Shiprow. ☎ 01224/337-700. Free admission. Mon–Sat noon–3pm; Sun 11am–5pm. Bus: 20.

Using a unique collection of ship models, paintings, artifacts, computer interaction, and exhibits, this museum tells the story of the city's long and fascinating relationship with the sea. A major display on the offshore oil industry features a model of the Murchison oil platform. The complex is on four floors, incorporating the 1593 Provost Ross House linked by a modern glass structure to the granite Trinity Church. Windows open onto panoramic views of the harbor.

**Provost Skene House.** 5 Guestrow, off Broad St. ☎ 01224/641-086. Free admission. Mon–Sat 10am–5pm; Sun 1–4pm. Bus: 20.

The Provost Skene House is named for a rich merchant who was Lord Provost of Aberdeen from 1676 to 1685. Off Broad Street, it's a museum with period rooms and artifacts of domestic life. Provost Skene's kitchen has been converted into a cafe.

**Toll Booth.** Castle St. ☎ 01224/621-167. Admission £2.50 ($4.25) adults, £1.50 ($2.55) seniors/children, £6 ($10.20) families. Mon–Sat 10am–5pm; Sat 12:30–3:30pm.

Constructed in 1629, this building in the city center was converted into a prison during the reign of Charles II, and the cells as well as talking models of famous prisoners are on display today. Alongside this is a history of crime and punishment at the time and (on a slightly lighter note) a permanent exhibit of Charles II's visit to the city as well as

## The Aberdeen Attractions Card

The **Aberdeen Attractions Card** covers admission to the Toll Booth, the Aberdeen Maritime Museum, and the Provost Skene House and costs £5 ($8.50) adults and £3.50 ($5.95) seniors/students/children for unlimited visits over a year. You can buy it at any of the three included sights.

ceremonial costumes. Those interested in municipal development will appreciate the exhibit of maps plotting the growth of Aberdeen from an insignificant village to Scotland's third-largest city.

**Dunnottar Castle.** 2 miles (3km) south of Stonehaven off A92. ☎ **01569/762-173.** Admission £3.50 ($5.95) adults, £1 ($1.70) children. Easter–Oct Mon–Sat 9am–6pm, Sun 2–5pm; Nov–Easter Mon–Fri 9am–3:30pm.

The well-preserved ruins of Dunnottar are on a rocky promontory towering 160 feet (48.5m) above the surging sea, and the best way to get here is by a dramatic 30-minute walk from Stonehaven along the cliffs. "Dunnottar speaks with an audible voice," says an old proverb. "Every cave has a record, every turret a tongue." The ruins include a great square tower and a chapel built in 1392. William Wallace stormed it in 1297 but failed to take it. In 1991, it was the setting for Zeffirelli's film of *Hamlet*, starring Mel Gibson. You can reach Stonehaven from Aberdeen by taking Bluebird Northern bus no. 101, costing £5 ($8.50) round-trip, and then walking for 5 minutes. Trains run about every half an hour from Aberdeen to Stonehaven, costing £4 to £5 ($6.80 to $8.50) round-trip. Departures are every 30 minutes during the day; the trip takes 30 minutes.

## SHOPPING

The main shopping districts center on specialty shops on **Chapel** and **Thistle streets** and well-known chains on **George** and **Union streets.** Of interest to collectors, **Colin Wood,** 25 Rose St. (☎ **01224/643-019**), stocks furniture, wall clocks, and grandfather clocks from the 17th to the early 20th century. Their specialty, however, is maps from the Elizabethan through the Victorian eras, including a good selection of Jacobean maps. The shop also sells 17th- to early 20th-century prints of northern Scotland. You may also want to browse through the eclectic mix of small bric-a-brac antiques at **Elizabeth Watts Studio,** 69 Thistle St. (☎ **01224/647-232**), where items include glass, brass, antique jewelry, china, silver, and a few small furniture pieces. The shop is actually best known for its china and glass restoration studio.

To trace your Scottish ancestry, go to the **Aberdeen Family History Shop,** 164 King St. (☎ **01224/646-323**), where membership to the Aberdeen and North East Family History Society will cost you $12 cash or check. Once you join, you can go through a vast range of publications kept on hand to help members trace their family histories. You'll find a multitude of gifts at **Nova,** 20 Chapel St. (☎ **01224/641-270**), which stocks china, silver jewelry, rugs, clothing, toys, cards, and gift paper.

Other interesting shops are **Grandad's Attic,** 12 Marischal St. (☎ **01224/ 213-699**), selling antiques and collectibles, specializing in art deco ceramics and pine furniture; **Just Scottish,** 4 Upperkirkgate (☎ **01224/621-755**), retailers of quality items—all made in Scotland, including ceramics, knitwear, textiles, silver, and jewelry; and **Alex Scott & Co.,** 43 Schoolhill (☎ **01224/643-924**), the town's finest kiltmakers, which also sells quality Scottish gifts and souvenirs, tartans, and traditional clans and crest.

## HITTING THE LINKS

Aberdeen has a good range of golf courses in and around the city, with several other notable courses within an easy drive. As always, advance reservations are essential at any course. If the two below don't suit you, ask the tourist office for details on your other choices.

Among the top courses is **Balgownie, the Royal Aberdeen Golf Club** (☎ 01224/ 702-221), created in 1780 in classic links style. Its uneven layout, sea breezes, and grassy sand dunes add to the challenge of this 6,204-yard (5,646m), par-70 course. Greens fees are £55 ($93.50) per round, or £75 ($127.50) per day; caddies and carts are available.

Seven miles (11km) west of Aberdeen, the par-69 **West Hills Golf Course,** West Hill Heights, West Hill Skene (☎/fax **01224/740-159**), features 5,921 yards (5,388m) of playing area. There's no caddy service, but you can rent a trolley and clubs. Greens fees are £12 ($20.40) Monday to Friday, £16 ($27.20) Saturday and Sunday.

## ACCOMMODATIONS

Because of increasing numbers of tourists and business visitors to the Granite City, Europe's offshore oil capital, hotels are likely to be heavily booked any time of year. If you haven't booked ahead, it's best to go to the **Aberdeen Tourist Information Centre,** St. Nicholas House on Broad Street (☎ **01224/632-727**). There's a wide range of accommodations, whether you prefer to stay in a family-run B&B, a guesthouse, or a hotel, and the center's staff can usually find just the right kind of lodging.

You can also stay at **Ferryhill House** (see "Dining," below).

### EXPENSIVE

✪ **Ardoe House.** S. Deeside Rd., Blairs, Aberdeen AB12 5YP. ☎ **01224/867-355.** Fax 01224/ 861-283. www.macdonald-hotels.co.uk. E-mail: info@ardoe.macdonald-hotels.co.uk. 69 units. TV TEL. £100 ($170) double; £140 ($238) suite. Children 11 and under stay free in parents' room. AE, DC, MC, V. Free parking. Drive 5 miles (8km) southwest on B9077.

Known for its tranquil setting at the end of a winding drive, this Scottish baronial house, graced with soaring turrets, stands on large grounds on the south bank of the River Dee. It was built in 1878 of silver granite and still retains much of its original design, including its carved oak paneling. You can opt for the traditional guest rooms in the old house or the more modern units in the large extension. All units are a decent size and contain hair dryers.

**Dining/Diversions:** You can relax in the drawing room and cocktail bar before going in to dinner. Naturally, salmon freshly caught in the Dee is the chef's specialty. Dinner, served in the restaurant and Garden Room, is offered nightly. Choose from pricier, more formal meals or affordable bar meals.

**Amenities:** Room service, laundry, pétanque.

**Caledonian Thistle Hotel.** 10–14 Union Terrace (off Union St.), Aberdeen AB10 1WE. ☎ **01224/640-233.** Fax 01224/641-627. E-mail: aberdeen.caledonian@thistle.co.uk. 80 units. MINIBAR TV TEL. £75–£160 ($127.50–$272) double; £130–£210 ($221–$357) suite. Children 11 and under stay free in parents' room. AE, DC, MC, V. Free parking. Bus: 16 or 17.

The Caledonian Thistle occupies a grand stone-fronted Victorian in the center of Aberdeen. Recent restorations have added a veneer of Georgian gloss to one of the most elegant series of public rooms in town. The guest rooms are at the top of a 19th-century stairwell, with Corinthian columns and a freestanding atrium. They vary a good deal in size, but all contain double-glazed windows, tea/coffeemakers, trouser presses, and hair dryers; the front ones can be noisy.

**Dining:** The hotel offers Elrond's (see "Dining," below), plus the more formal Restaurant on the Terrace, serving dinner nightly. Lunch is served Monday to Friday only.
**Amenities:** Concierge, room service, baby-sitting.

**Hilton Aberdeen Treetop.** 161 Springfield Rd., Aberdeen AB15 7AQ. ☎ **01224/ 313-377.** Fax 01224/312-028. www.hilton.com. 112 units. TV TEL. £90–£125 ($153–$212.50) double; £130–£155 ($221–$263.50) suite. AE, DC, MC, V. Free parking. Bus: 11.

A 10-minute drive west of the center of Aberdeen off A93, this comfortable hotel built in the 1960s and renovated in 1991 has a sweeping white facade of traditional design. The windows of its 112 good-size contemporary guest rooms look over landscaped grounds; some rooms have balconies with lake views and half are for nonsmokers.
**Dining/Diversions:** The light modern decor of the main bar with its marbleized walls and comfortable furniture offers a pleasant spot to relax before dining at the elegant Seasons Restaurant or Rocco's Ristorante, the bistro-style Italian restaurant.
**Amenities:** Concierge; room service; laundry; Leisure Club with pool, whirlpool, gym, sauna, jogging machine, sunbeds, two all-weather tennis courts, sports training.

**☼ Marcliffe at Pitfodels.** N. Deeside Rd., Aberdeen AB1 9YA. ☎ **01224/861-000.** Fax 01224/868-860. www.marcliffe.com. E-mail: reservations@marcliffe.com. 42 units. MINI-BAR TV TEL. £115–£165 ($195.50–$280.50) double. AE, DC, MC, V. Free parking. Drive about a mile (1.5km) off A90 at the Aberdeen ring road, A93.

On the city's western edge less than half an hour from the airport, this deluxe hotel is far superior to the Caledonian Thistle and the Ardoe. The traditional three-story manor house was constructed around a courtyard and stands on 6 acres of landscaped grounds. The oriental rugs, placed on stone floors, and the tartan sofas set the decor note in the public rooms; a scattering of antiques add a grace note. The rather spacious guest rooms are furnished in Chippendale and reproduction pieces, with armchairs and desks, plus a host of extras like hair dryers and even fresh milk in the minibar.
**Dining/Diversions:** At breakfast you can sample Aberdeen *rowies*, a local specialty made with butter like a croissant that's been flattened. The conservatory restaurant offers regional dishes like Highland lamb and fresh Scottish salmon, and the more expensive Invery Room is favored by businesspeople entertaining out-of-town guests. In the library lounge, you can choose from more than 130 scotches, 500 wines, and 70 cognacs.
**Amenities:** 24-hour room service, laundry.

**Simpsons.** 59 Queens Rd., Aberdeen AB15 4YP. ☎ **01224/327-777.** Fax 01224/327-700. www.taste-of-scotland.com/simpsons-hotel.html. E-mail: address@simpsonshotel.com. 37 units. TV TEL. £125–£135 ($212.50–$229.50) double; £145 ($246.50) suite. Rates include breakfast. AE, MC, V. Follow signs for A96 North, and turn right at Queens Rd. Roundabout.

Simpsons opened in 1998 and has quickly gained popularity. Two traditional granite townhouses were joined to offer comfortable accommodations. Rooms are decorated with furniture from Spain and painted in rich, bold colors that create a cool, Mediterannean ambience. Amenities include cable TV, air-conditioning, hair dryers, beverage-makers, and complimentary use of the health spa.
**Dining:** The hotel bar and brasserie offers a range of moderately priced Scottish and international dishes, including fresh crab ravioli, and saddle of lamb Wellington with Puy lentils and vegetables. The food is prepared with the finest of local ingredients. Reservations are recommended.
**Amenities:** Room service, laundry, baby-sitting.

## MODERATE

**Craiglynn Hotel.** 36 Fonthill Rd., Aberdeen AB11 6UJ. ☎ **01224/584-050.** Fax 01224/ 212-225. www.craiglynn.co.uk. E-mail: info@craiglynn.co.uk. 9 units, 7 with private bathroom. TV TEL. £78 ($132.60) double with bathroom. Rates include breakfast. AE, DC, MC, V. Bus: 17.

This granite-block Victorian was built in 1901 as a home for a successful fish merchant. Today, it's meticulously managed by Chris and Hazel Mann, who insist on a no-smoking policy and devote lots of time to maintaining a fastidious setting for guests. The high-ceilinged guest rooms are monochromatic, with traditional furniture. If advance notice is given, a moderately priced dinner can be prepared, featuring dishes like fricasée of lamb with local vegetables, several preparations of salmon and turbot, and a house version of sticky toffee pudding with Drambuie-flavored ice cream.

✪ **Jays Guest House.** 422 King St., Aberdeen AB24 3BR. ☎/fax **01224/638-295.** www.jaysguesthouse.co.uk. E-mail: alice@jaysguesthouse.co.uk. 10 units. TV. £56–£80 ($95.20–$136) double. Rates include Scottish breakfast. MC, V. Free parking. Bus: 1, 2, 3, 4, or 7.

This is one of the nicest guesthouses in Aberdeen, mainly because of the high standards of the owner, Mrs. Alice Jennings. It's near the university and the Offshore Survival Centre. Everything runs smoothly, and the guest rooms are bright and airy, each newly renovated, with tea/coffeemakers and central heating.

**Mannofield Hotel.** 447 Great Western Rd., Aberdeen AB10 6NL. ☎ **01224/315-888.** Fax 01224/208-971. www.mannofield.procan.co.uk. 9 units. TV TEL. £69 ($117.30) double. Rates include Scottish breakfast. AE, DC, MC, V. Free parking. Bus: 18 or 24.

Built of silver granite around 1880, this hotel is a Victorian architectural fantasy, with step gables, turrets, spires, and bay windows outside and a sweeping mahogany-and-teakwood staircase inside. Owners Bruce and Dorothy Cryle offer a warm Scottish welcome. The nicely sized guest rooms, refurbished in 1998 with attractive paisley curtains and quilts, offer tea/coffeemakers and hair dryers. Those on the first floor have white walls with a light green decoration, and those upstairs are decorated in a darker green. The hotel, a favorite of business travelers from other parts of Britain, has a good restaurant.

## CASTLE & COUNTRY-HOUSE LIVING NEARBY

**Ardoe Hotel.** S. Deeside Rd. (3 miles [5km] south of Aberdeen on B9077), Blairs, Aberdeen AB12 5YP. ☎ **01224/867-355.** Fax 01224/861-283. www.olstravel.com/hotel/ardoe. E-mail: info@ardoe.macdonald-hotels.co.uk. 112 units. TV TEL. £104 ($176.80) double. MC, V.

This turreted and baronial house from 1878 sits in the midst of lush gardens and manicured grounds, offering panoramic views of the river Dee. Even though it's close to Aberdeen, it's a world apart. Its old-fashioned interior, with wood paneling, carved fireplaces, and stained-glass windows, reflects the best in traditional Victorian style. The mansion was recently expanded, but even so, each room is individually decorated in comfort and style and provided with such amenities as hair dryers, radio alarms, and beverage trays.

In the formal dining room, you can order a blend of traditional and modern Scottish cuisine, using fresh local ingredients that are prepared with French flair. In addition, A Leisure Club offers a swimming pool, a steam room, a sauna, a gym, an aerobics area, and a beauty spa.

✪ **Kildrummy Castle Hotel.** Kildrummy by Alford AB33 8RA. ☎ **019755/71288.** Fax 019755/71345. www.kildrummycastle-hotel.co.uk. E-mail: bookings@kildrummycastle-hotel. co.uk. 16 units. TV TEL. £135–£170 ($229.50–$289) double. Rates include Scottish breakfast. AE, MC, V. Closed Jan. From Aberdeen, take A944 and follow the signs to Alford; then take A97, following the signs to Kildrummy.

This 19th-century gray-stone mansion, on acres of landscaped gardens, overlooks the ruined castle of Kildrummy. Its well-equipped guest rooms vary in size, with hair dryers and tea/coffeemakers. The public rooms have oak-paneled walls and ceilings, mullioned windows, and window seats. The drawing room/bar open onto a flagstone terrace from which you can see the castle gardens.

**Dining:** Traditional, rather expensive Scottish food is served in the handsome dining room, including Cullen skink (smoked haddock soup), fillet of sole stuffed with smoked Scottish salmon, and Aberdeen Angus steaks. Lunch and dinner are served daily.

**Amenities:** Room service, laundry, baby-sitting.

✪ **Pittodrie House Hotel.** Chapel of Garioch, Pitcaple AB5 5HS. ☎ **01467/681-444.** Fax 01467/681-648. 27 units. TV TEL. £140 ($238) double. Rates include Scottish breakfast. AE, DC, MC, V. From Aberdeen, take A96, following the signs to Inverness; remain on A96, bypassing Inverurie, then follow the signs to Chapel of Garioch.

Dating from 1490, the castle here was burned down and then rebuilt in 1675 as a family home—and that changed into a country-house hotel when Royal Deeside became prominent through Queen Victoria's adoption of Balmoral as her holiday retreat. The guest rooms are divided between those in the old house (nicely sized, with good views and antique furniture) and the smaller rooms in the recent extension (decorated in keeping with the style of the house but with less atmosphere). All rooms have hair dryers. The public rooms boast antiques, oil paintings, and open fires.

**Dining:** The elegant restaurant serves venison, grouse, partridge, pheasant, or woodcock and fresh fish. Rather expensive dinners and affordable bar lunches are served daily.

✪ **Thainstone House Hotel & Country Club.** Inverurie AB51 5NT. ☎ **01467/621-643.** Fax 01467/625-084. 48 units. TV TEL. £84–£112 ($142.80–$190.40) double; £180 ($306) suite. Rates include Scottish breakfast. AE, DC, MC, V. From Aberdeen, take A96, following the signs to Inverness; just before Inverurie, turn left and follow the signs to the hotel.

One of northeast Scotland's most elegant country hotels, set on 40 acres, the four-star Thainstone House is a Palladian-style mansion whose adornments give it the air of a country club. It can be a retreat and a center for exploring this historic part of Scotland, including the Malt Whisky Trail. You enter through a grand portal up an elegant stairway. The estate has dim origins in the Dark Ages, and a property that stood here in the 1700s was torched by the Jacobites; James Wilson, the owner, escaped the fire and fled to America, where he later signed the Declaration of Independence. Today's mansion was designed by Archibald Simpson, the famed architect of many of Aberdeen's public buildings. The high ceilings, columns, neoclassical plaster reliefs, and cornices evoke Simpson's trip to Italy. A new section has been added that skillfully blends the old with the new. The guest rooms vary in size and are elegantly furnished, with amenities like direct-dial phone, radios, tea/coffeemakers, hair dryers, and trouser presses. Several rooms have original four-poster beds, and the suite includes a Jacuzzi.

**Dining:** In the Georgian ambience of Simpson's Restaurant, the chef turns out a continental and a "Taste of Scotland" menu with a light, inventive touch. Dining is more informal in Cammie's Grill, where local game is served along with Aberdeen Angus beef, seafood from the coast, and fresh salmon and trout from the Rivers Spey and Don. Lunch and dinner are served daily.

**Amenities:** Room service, laundry, baby-sitting, Jacuzzi and steam room, fully equipped gym, snooker room, pool designed in the style of an ancient Roman bath.

# DINING

**Elrond's Cafe Bar.** In the Caledonian Thistle Hotel, 10–14 Union Terrace. ☎ **01224/ 640-233.** Main courses £8–£10 ($13.60–$17); pot of tea with pastry £2 ($3.40). AE, DC, MC, V. Mon–Sat 10am–midnight; Sun 10am–11pm. Bus: 16 or 17. INTERNATIONAL.

White marble floors, a long oak-capped bar, evening candlelight, and a garden-inspired decor create the ambience here. No one will mind if you show up just for a drink, a pot of tea, a midday salad or snack, or a full-blown feast. Specialties are burgers, steaks, pastas, fresh fish, lemon chicken suprême, chicken Kiev, and vegetarian dishes. This isn't the world's greatest food, but it's a popular venue nevertheless. Although it's in one of Aberdeen's well-known hotels, the restaurant has a separate entrance onto Union Terrace.

**Ferryhill House.** Bon Accord St., Aberdeen AB11 6UA. ☎ **01224/590-867.** Fax 01224/ 586-947. Reservations recommended Sat–Sun. Main courses £6–£12 ($10.20–$20.40). AE, DC, MC, V. Mon–Sat noon–2:30pm and 6–9pm; Sun 12:30–9pm. Free parking. Bus: 16. INTERNATIONAL.

In its own park and garden on the city's southern outskirts, Ferryhill House was built 250 years ago by the region's most successful brick maker and quarry master. It has Georgian detailing, but recent refurbishment has removed many of the original panels and all the ceiling beams. The restaurant boasts one of the region's largest collections of single-malt whiskies—more than 140 brands. There's a fireplace for chilly afternoons and an outdoor beer garden for midsummer, as well as a conservatory. Food items include steak or vegetable tempura, chicken dishes like chicken fajita, fried haddock fillet, pastas, and chili.

Ferryhill House also rents nine standard-sized, modestly furnished guest rooms, all with TVs, phones, and hair dryers. With Scottish breakfast included, the double rate is £79 ($130.35) Sunday to Thursday and £50 ($85) Friday and Saturday.

**Gerard's.** 50 Chapel St. ☎ **01224/639-500.** Reservations recommended. Main courses £9.50–£17 ($16.15–$28.90) at lunch, £9.50–£17 ($16.15–$28.90) at dinner; business lunch £9.95 ($16.90) for 2 courses, £13.50 ($22.95) for 3 courses; fixed-price dinner £18.75 ($31.90) for 2 courses, £23.75 ($40.40) for 3 courses; cafe main courses £5.15–£14.35 ($8.75–$24.40) at lunch, £6–£14.35 ($10.20–$24.40) at dinner. AE, DC, MC, V. Restaurant daily noon–2:30pm and 6–10pm. Cafe daily 10am–midnight; meals noon–2:30pm and 5:30–10pm. FRENCH/INTERNATIONAL.

Restaurateur Gerard Flecher's popular spot is split into the more formal main dining room and the relaxed Cafe Colmar, which has a separate entrance at the rear of the building. Both eateries have a Gallic atmosphere and French-inspired decor, but the cafe features dishes of a far more international nature. In Gerard's, expect fare like pan-fried maigrette of duck and Cumberland sausage with five-bean fricassee on cabernet sauvignon jus or médaillons of Aberdeen Angus fillet on potato crostini with oyster mushrooms, Provençal salsa, and stuffed tomato on an *au poivre* sauce. In the cafe, dishes include roasted Mediterranean vegetables with lemongrass and a spicy Thai sauce in a pastry case on a bed of rice pilaf or chicken breast filled with creamed lemon cheese in leek-cream sauce. The bar stocks a wide range of single malts and ports, along with French wines unavailable elsewhere in the region.

**Martha's Vineyard Bistro/The Courtyard Restaurant.** Alford Lane. ☎ **01224/ 213-795.** Reservations recommended in The Courtyard, not necessary in Martha's Vineyard. Main courses £4–£8 ($6.80–$13.60) in bistro; £10–£16 ($17–$27.20) in restaurant. Mon–Sat noon–2:15pm and Tues–Sat 6:30–9:45pm. AE, DC, MC, V. Bus: 1, 2, 3, or 4.

One of the most appealing restaurant compounds in Aberdeen occupies two floors of what was built around 1900 as an extension of the local hospital. Today, a robust- and rustic-looking bistro (Martha's Vineyard) is on the street level and a more substantial and formal-looking restaurant (The Courtyard) upstairs. The menu in the bistro is more formal than you might have expected and includes smoked salmon and aspara-gus salad and gigot of lamb with a compote of leeks in mustard sauce. Upstairs you'll find dishes like local Brie wrapped in smoked salmon or rosemary-flavored loin of Highland venison with wild mushrooms. Dessert in either place might be warm orange pudding with Grand Marnier sauce served with vanilla-ginger ice cream.

✪ **Silver Darling.** Pocra Quay, Footdee. ☎ **01224/576-229.** Reservations recommended. Main courses £13.90–£19.50 ($23.65–$33.15); fixed-price lunch £19.50 ($33.15). AE, DC, MC, V. Mon–Fri noon–2pm and 7–9:30pm; Sat 7–9:30pm; Sun noon–2:30pm and 6–9pm summer only. Closed Dec 23–Jan 8. Bus: 14 or 15. FRENCH/SEAFOOD.

Silver Darling (a local nickname for herring) is a definite asset to the dining picture in Aberdeen. Occupying a former Customs House at the mouth of the harbor, it spins a culinary fantasy around the freshest catch of the day. You might begin with a savory fish soup, almost Mediterranean in flavor, then go on to one of the barbecued fish dishes. Salmon is the invariable favorite of the more discriminating diners.

## ABERDEEN AFTER DARK

Tickets to events at most venues are available by calling the **Aberdeen Box Office** at ☎ 01224/641-122.

**THE PERFORMING ARTS**   The **Aberdeen Arts Centre,** King Street (☎ **01224/ 635-208**), has a 350-seat theater that is rented to professional and amateur groups host-ing everything from poetry readings and plays to musical concerts in various styles. Ticket prices and performance times vary; call for information. Also on the premises is a 60-seat video projection theater that screens world cinema offerings, and ticket prices vary depending on what is showing but start at £6 ($10.20). A large gallery room holds month-long exhibitions of visual art in many different styles and mediums. A cafe/bar, offering light meals and drinks, is open during performance times.

Near Tarves, about 20 miles (32km) from Aberdeen, you'll find **Haddo House** (☎ **01651/851-440**), which hosts operas, ballets, and plays from Easter to October. An early 20th-century hall built of pitch pine, Haddo House is based on the Canadian town halls that Lord Aberdeen saw in his travels abroad. The hall was built for the people of the surrounding area on Aberdeen family land and the present Lady Aberdeen still lives in a house on this property. Follow B9005, 18 miles (29km) north to Tarves, then follow the National Trust and Haddo House signs 2 miles (3km) east to arrive here. Ticket prices range from £6 to £13 ($10.20 to $22.10). Admittance to the house is £5 ($8.50) for adults and £4.20 ($7.15) for seniors and children. The house is open daily 1:30 to 5pm, the shop 11am to 6pm, and the gardens 9:30am to 6pm. A stylish cafe offers light meals, tea, and other beverages daily, Easter to October, from 11am to 6pm.

The 19th-century **Music Hall,** Union Street (☎ **01224/641-122**), is an ornately gilded 1,282-seat theater that stages concerts by the Scottish National Orchestra, the Scottish Chamber Orchestra, visiting international orchestras, and pop bands, as well as hosting ceilidhs, crafts fairs, and book sales. Tickets for year-round musical perfor-mances average £7.50 to £8.50 ($12.75 to $14.45). The **Aberdeen International Youth Festival** is held annually in this hall in August, and features youth orchestras, choirs, and dance and theater ensembles. Daytime and evening performances are held, and tickets range from £1 to £20 ($1.70 to $34). Contact the Music Hall or the Aberdeen Box Office for more information.

The only theater in the world built entirely of granite, **His Majesty's Theatre,** Rosemount Viaduct (☎ **01224/641-122**), was designed by Frank Matcham in 1906.

The interior is late Victorian, and the 1,445-seat theater stages operas, dance perfor-mances, dramas, classical concerts, musicals, and comedy shows year-round. Tickets range from £7 to £20 ($11.90 to $34).

A mixed venue is the **Lemon Tree,** 5 W. North St. (☎ **01224/642-230**). Its 150-seat theater stages dance recitals, theatrical productions, and stand-up comedy, with tickets generally priced between £3 and £15 ($5.10 and $25.50). On Saturday, there's often a matinee at 2 or 3pm, and evening performances are at 7pm. Downstairs, the 500-seat cafe/theater hosts folk, rock, blues, jazz, and comedy acts, with shows starting between 8 and 10pm. On Wednesday the Folk Club is on stage, and other nights have varied offerings. On Sunday afternoon there's free live jazz.

**DANCE CLUBS**   **DeNiro's,** 120 Union St. (☎ **01224/640-641**), has dancing to house music from 10pm until 2am on Friday and Saturday only. The cover charge is £7 ($11.90), but may vary depending on the guest DJ.

**The Pelican,** housed in the Hotel Metro, 17 Market St. (☎ **01224/583-275**), offers dancing Thursday to Saturday 10pm to 2am. The cover charge on Thursday is £3 to £4 ($5.10 to $6.80) and Friday and Saturday £5 to £8 ($8.50 to $13.60). There's a live band every second Thursday.

The ever-popular **Ministry,** 16 Dee St. (☎ **01224/211-661**), is a sophisticated dance club that features different theme nights throughout the week. On Monday, Moist is a popular student night. On Fridays, guest DJs from England and America take over the sound system, so you might catch New York's hottest DJ of the moment. Cover charges range from £1 to £12 ($1.70 to $20.40) throughout the week, depend-ing on who the DJ is and what's happening.

**A PUB**   The ✪ **Prince of Wales,** 7 St. Nicholas Lane (☎ **01224/640-597**), in the heart of the shopping district, is the best place in the old city center to go for a pint. Furnished with pews in screened booths, it boasts Aberdeen's longest bar counter. At lunch, it's bustling with regulars who devour chicken in cider sauce or Guinness pie. On tap are such beers as Buchan Gold and Courage Directors. Orkney Dark Island is also sold here.

## SIDE TRIPS FROM ABERDEEN: ARCHEOLINK & CASTLE COUNTRY

Aberdeen is the center of "castle country"—40 inhabited castles lie within a 40-mile (64.5km) radius. Below we've described the best of them. But you might also want to visit Archeolink to check out the area's cultural changes over the centuries.

✪ **Archeolink.** Oyne, near Insch. ☎ **01464/851-500.** Admission £3.90 ($6.65) adults, £2.35 ($4) seniors/ages 5–16, £11 ($18.70) families. Apr–Oct daily 10am–5pm. From Aberdeen, drive 23 miles (37km) NW along A96, following the signs to Inverness. Then turn north onto B9002, driving another 1½ miles (2.5km), following the signs.

Although there are more than 4,000 prehistoric sites around Aberdeenshire, this museum offers the most historically accurate, most imaginative, and most ecologically sensitive interpretation. Opened in 1997 and funded by the European Regional Development Fund (ERDF), it occupies 40 big-sky acres whose centerpiece, Berryhill, contains a ruined Iron Age fortress. Lavish landscaping encourages visits by both able-bodied hill climbers and—thanks to a series of ramps—visitors with wheelchairs.

The museum is a celebration of the epic cultural changes that have swept over northeastern Scotland through the previous 70 centuries. The centerpiece is a massive turf-covered concrete dome resembling a small hill. Your tour begins with a 20-minute film showing views of the surrounding landscapes and the equivalent landscapes 7,000 years ago. Dioramas and illustrations provide insights into the region's stone circles and dolmens, and there are gruesome re-creations of Iron Age battles and hunting scenes. Especially intriguing is a gallery devoted to myths and legends. One subdivision of the site, Archeoquest, provides computer-generated personalized details on other prehistoric sites in Aberdeenshire, with directions and access information printed on takeaway maps.

**Castle Fraser.** Sauchen, Inverurie. ☎ **01330/833-463.** Admission £5 ($8.50) adults, £3.50 ($5.95) seniors, children 18 and under free. Apr 21–May and Sept daily 1:30–5:30pm; June–Aug daily 11am–5:30pm; Oct Sat–Sun 1:30–5:30pm. Head 3 miles (5km) south of Kemnay, 16 miles (26km) west of Aberdeen, off A944.

One of the most impressive of the fortresslike castles of Mar, Castle Fraser stands in a 25-acre parkland and woodsy setting and is surrounded by another 350 acres, which you can explore via two trails. The sixth laird, Michael Fraser, began the structure in 1575, and his son finished it in 1636. Its Great Hall is spectacular, and you can wander around the grounds, which include an 18th-century walled garden.

**Kildrummy Castle.** Hwy. A97, Kildrummy. ☎ **019755/71331.** Admission £1.80 ($3.05) adults, £1.30 ($2.20) seniors, 75p ($1.30) children. Easter–Sept daily 9:30am–6:30pm; Oct–Nov daily 9:30am–4pm. Take A97 for 35 miles (56km) west of Aberdeen; it's signposted off A97, 10 miles (16km) west of Alford.

The ruins of the ancient seat of the earls of Mar, this is the most extensive example of a 13th-century castle in Scotland. You can see the four round towers, the hall, and the chapel from the original structure. The great gatehouse and other remains date from the 16th century. The castle played a major role in Scottish history up to 1715, when it was dismantled.

✪ **Fyvie Castle.** Fyrie, Turriff, on the Aberdeen–Banff road (A947). ☎ **01651/891-266.** Admission £6 ($10.20) adults, £4.80 ($8.15) seniors; students 18 and under free. June–Aug daily 11am–4:45pm; May and Sept daily 1:30–4:45pm; Oct Sat–Sun 1:30–4:45pm. Closed Nov–Mar, but admission possible by prior arrangement. In the hamlet of Fyvie, 8 miles (13km) southeast of Turiff and 7 miles (11km) northwest of Old Meldrum. Fyvie is beside the A947, 23 miles (37km) NW of Aberdeen.

The National Trust for Scotland opened this castle to the public in 1986. The oldest part, from the 13th century, has been called the grandest existing example of Scottish baronial architecture. There are five towers, named after Fyvie's five families—the Prestons, Meldrums, Setons, Gordons, and Leiths—who lived here over 5 centuries. *Fyvie* (which means "deer" in Gaelic) was built in a royal hunting forest. The interior, created by the first Lord Leith of Fyvie, a steel magnate, reflects the opulence of the Edwardian era. His collections contain arms and armor, 16th-century tapestries, and important artworks by Raeburn, Gainsborough, and Romney. The castle is rich in ghosts, curses, and legends.

## 10  Banchory: Gateway to Crathes & Craigievar Castles

118 miles (190km) NE of Edinburgh, 17 miles (27km) W of Aberdeen, 55 miles (88.5km) NE of Dundee

In lower Deeside, the pleasant resort of Banchory is rich in woodland and river scenery. Most visitors come to see two of the most popular castles in the Grampian region: Crathes and Craigievar. Once here, they often find themselves enjoying this riverside town itself, the largest community along Deeside.

If you've explored the castles and still have time left, take the South Deeside Road branching to the left and following the signs to Cairn o' Mount along B974. This leads to the village of Fettercairn. Near here is the **Bridge of Feugh** (known as Brig o' Feuch), the local beauty spot spanning the water of Feugh. It makes a great walk, especially in the fall, when you can marvel at the brilliant colors of the trees as salmon demonstrate how to leap. A narrow gorge here opens onto panoramic views of waterfalls.

## ESSENTIALS

**GETTING THERE**    The nearest rail service goes to Aberdeen (for schedules, call ☎ 0345/484-950). From there, a Bluebird bus runs between the bus station on Guild Street in Aberdeen and Braemar, going via Banchory. The one-way fare is £2.55 ($4.35). For more information, call ☎ 01224/212-266 in Aberdeen.

Driving from Aberdeen, head west along A93; or from Braemar, head east along A93.

**VISITOR INFORMATION**    A **tourist office** is on Bridge Street (☎ 01330/ 822-000). March and October, it's open Monday to Saturday 10am to 1pm and 2 to 5pm and Sunday 1 to 5pm; June and September, hours are Monday to Saturday 10am to 1pm and 2 to 6pm and Sunday 1 to 6pm; July and August hours are Monday to Saturday 9:30am to 7pm and Sunday 1 to 7pm.

## SEEING THE SIGHTS

**✪ Crathes Castle and Gardens.** Banchory. ☎ 01330/844-525. Admission £6 ($10.20) adults, £3.40 ($5.80) children/seniors, £13.50 ($22.95) families. Grounds, adventure area, and park daily 9:30am–sunset. Visitor center, shop, and restaurant Good Friday–Oct daily 10am–5:30pm. Castle Good Friday–Oct daily 11am–4:45pm. From Banchory, take A93, following the signs to Aberdeen.

This castle, 2 miles (3km) east of Banchory, has royal historical associations from 1323, when the lands of Leys were granted to the Burnett family by King Robert the Bruce. The Horn of Leys, said to have been given by the Bruce to symbolize the gift, is in the Great Hall. The castle's features include remarkable late 16th-century painted ceilings and a garden that's a composite of eight separate gardens, giving a display all year. The great yew hedges date from 1702. The grounds are ideal for nature study, and there are five trails, including a long-distance layout with ranger service. The complex includes a licensed restaurant, a visitor center with permanent exhibits, a souvenir shop, a plant sales area, a wayfaring course, and picnic areas.

**✪ Craigievar Castle.** Hwy. A980, 6 miles (10km) south of Alford. ☎ 013398/83635. Admission £6 ($10.20) adults, £4 ($6.80) seniors/children. Castle May–Sept daily 1:30–4:45pm; grounds year-round daily 9:30am–sunset.

Structurally unchanged since its completion in 1626, Craigievar Castle is an exceptional tower house where Scottish baronial architecture reached its pinnacle of achievement. It has contemporary plaster ceilings in nearly all its rooms. The castle had been continuously lived in by the descendants of the builder, William Forbes, until it came under the care of the National Trust for Scotland in 1963. The family collection of furnishings is complete.

Some 4 miles (6.5km) south of the castle, clearly signposted on a small road leading off A980, near Lumphanan, is **Macbeth's Cairn,** where the historical Macbeth is supposed to have fought his last battle. Built of timber in a rounded format known by historians as "motte and bailey," it's now nothing more than a steep-sided rounded hillock marked with a sign and a flag.

## ACCOMMODATIONS

**Banchory Lodge.** Dee St., Banchory AB31 5HS. ☎ 01330/822-625. Fax 01330/825-019. E-mail: banchorylodgeht@btconnect.com. 22 units. TV TEL. £130–£145 ($221–$246.50) double. Rates include half-board. AE, DC, MC, V.

On the banks of the Dee, where the Dee joins the Water of the Feugh, Banchory Lodge is an 18th-century country house with much Georgian charm. Some of the well-furnished guest rooms overlook the river; others are in a deluxe annex added in 1994. They range in size from adequate to quite small, and all contain hair dryers. In the dining room, the furnishings and decor are in period style, and specialties include fresh Dee salmon and Aberdeen Angus roast beef, served at lunch and dinner daily. You can fish from the lawn or in one of the hotel's boats by arrangement.

**The Burnett Arms.** 25 High St., Banchory AB31 3HS. ☎ **01330/824-944.** Fax 01330/825-553. E-mail: burnett@msn.com.uk. 16 units. TV TEL. £75 ($127.50) double. AE, DC, MC, V.

Despite frequent renovations, this place still feels like a mid 19th-century coaching inn. It presents to the main street a white-painted facade with black trim, and attracts a busy trade with its bar and cocktail lounge. The guest rooms are outfitted in decorator-inspired colors, in most cases with high ceilings and more space than you'd expect. The best and most dramatic is the Bridal Suite, which is technically not a suite but a large room with a sprawling half-tester bed; it goes for the same rate as the other rooms. Affordable bar platters are available daily at lunch and dinner; high tea is also popular here, and there's a regular, moderately priced dining room.

**⚫ Raemoir House.** Hwy. A980, Banchory AB31 4ED. ☎ **01330/824-884.** Fax 01330/822-171. www.raemoir.com. E-mail: raemoirhse@aol.com. 24 units. TV TEL. £80–£90 ($136–$153) double; from £125 ($212.50) suite. Rates include Scottish breakfast. AE, DC, MC, V. Free parking. Turn off A93 at the eastern end of Banchory onto A980 (Raemoir Rd.); the hotel entrance is at the junction 2 miles (3km) down the road.

Raemoir House is an 18th-century manor standing on 3,500 acres of grounds and offering shooting and fishing. This old-fashioned hotel has a ballroom, fine tapestries, and log fires burning in the colder months. The guest rooms are handsomely decorated; most are quite large and all have trouser presses and hair dryers. Some superior rooms have paneled walls hung with tapestries. The bathrooms here are interesting: Some contain old-world Edwardian tubs in which to soak and others state-of-the-art spa baths. What's so lovely about Scotland is its curious mix: In this case, an 18th-century manor house with its own helipad. The adjoining 16th-century Ha House was once used by Mary Queen of Scots.

**Dining:** Lunch and dinner are served in an attractive Georgian dining room, where rather expensive fixed-price menus feature a standard repertoire of familiar dishes done well. Affordable bar lunches are offered Monday to Saturday.

**Amenities:** Concierge, room service, laundry, baby-sitting, helipad, solarium, sauna; all-weather tennis court, nine-hole/par-3 course.

**Tor-Na-Coille.** Inchmarlo Rd., Banchory AB31 4AB. ☎ **01330/822-242.** Fax 01330/824-012. E-mail: tornacoille@btinternet.com. 23 units. TV TEL. £110 ($187) double. Rates include Scottish breakfast. Children 11 and under stay free in parents' room. AE, DC, MC, V. Closed Dec 25–27. Free parking.

Tor-Na-Coille is an 1873 country-house hotel—really a Victorian ivy-clad mansion—standing on about 8 acres of wooded grounds. The public rooms are suitably spacious and comfortable, and the whisky always tastes good in the modern bar. If you're on your way to see Balmoral or to attend the Highland Gathering at Braemar, you can relax here and enjoy the gracious hospitality, as did Charlie Chaplin and his family, who once used the place as a retreat. The guest rooms, many of which are quite large, have radios, tea/coffeemakers, and hair dryers. The hotel is interesting architecturally, and the room assigned to you may have a lot of character.

**Dining:** Lunches are light meals in the bar, including smoked venison sausage blended with rum and red wine. Dinner is rather expensive, and is accompanied by a pianist on the weekends. This place might be your chance to try real Scottish salmon (the salmon leap at the Falls of Feugh nearby), or the chef's special pheasant, when in season.

**Amenities:** Concierge, 24-hour room service, baby-sitting, laundry, croquet, two squash courts.

## DINING

**Milton Restaurant.** North Deeside Rd., Crathes. ☎ **01330/844-566.** Reservations recommended. Main courses £4–£11.50 ($6.80–$19.55) at lunch, £7–£12.50 ($11.90–$21.25) at dinner. DC, MC, V. Mon–Sat 9:30am–10pm, Sun 9am–7pm. From Banchory, drive 2 miles (3km) east, following the signs to Aberdeen and Crathes. SCOTTISH/INTERNATIONAL.

This restaurant is in a complex of art galleries and gift shops that occupy converted farm buildings east of Banchory in the village of Crathes. Inside, in an artfully rustic setting that includes lots of exposed stone, elaborate iron railings, and potted plants, you'll find a cozy, hip, and friendly environment, where the kitchen is right on top of the latest culinary trends in Glasgow and London. Items are very fresh, with a menu that changes about every 2 weeks. Creative compilations of the mostly Scottish ingredients include fried calamari with sun-dried tomatoes and olive butter; your choice of either a bagel or a bun with rib-eye steak and Stilton cheese; and an excellent version of Thai-style aromatic chicken with Asian greens.

**Raemoir House Restaurant.** In the Raemoir House Hotel, Hwy. A980. ☎ **01330/ 824-884.** Reservations recommended. Fixed-price 2-course dinner £23.50 ($39.95); 3-course dinner £28.50 ($48.45). AE, MC, V. Daily noon–2pm and 7–9pm. MODERN SCOTTISH

On a visit to Scotland, you need to have at least one meal in a Scottish baronial setting. At this previously recommended hotel, set on 3,500 acres of land, you can dine in a Georgian room with views of the garden and distant hills. From a daily changing menu, you can feast on well-prepared local and Scottish produce. The ingredients are always first rate and the preparation imaginative, as evoked by such dishes as seared scallops, served with a Jerusalem artichoke mousse, braised red cabbage, and juniper jus. For a "Taste of Scotland," opt for the roast saddle of venison with quail mousseline. Lighter and less elaborate dishes are also available. Save room for one of the rich, decadent desserts, such as a rich chocolate marquise with coffee bean sauce.

## 11  Ballater & Balmoral Castle

111 miles (179km) N of Edinburgh, 41 miles (66km) W of Aberdeen, 67 miles (108km) NE of Perth, 70 miles (113km) SE of Inverness

On the Dee River, with the Grampian mountains in the background, Ballater is a resort center, but most visitors come here with only one reason in mind—to walk the grounds of Balmoral Castle, the far northern home of the Windsors. The town still centers on its Station Square, where the royal family used to be photographed as they arrived to spend holidays (the railway is now closed). From Ballater you can drive west to view the scenery of Glen Muick and Lochnagar, where you'll see herds of deer. You can also take lovely walks in this area, taking in panoramas of the battlement of cliffs at a mountain called Lochnagar.

Incidentally, the drive between Ballater and Braemar (see "Braemar," below) is very scenic.

## ESSENTIALS

**GETTING THERE**   The nearest rail service gets you to Aberdeen (for schedules, call ☎ 0345/484-950). From there, regular buses run daily from Aberdeen west to

Ballater (a 1¾-hour trip). The bus station in Aberdeen is on Guild Street (call ☎ 01224/212-266), beside the train station. Bus no. 201 from Braemar runs to Ballater (a 30-minute trip). A one-way fare is £3 ($5.10).

Driving from Aberdeen, head west along A93. From Braemar, go east along A93 to reach Ballater.

**VISITOR INFORMATION**    The **tourist office** is at Station Square (☎ 013397/55306). March and October, it's open Monday to Saturday 10am to 1pm and 2 to 5pm and Sunday 1 to 5pm; June and September, hours are Monday to Saturday 10am to 1pm and 2 to 6pm and Sunday 1 to 6pm; July and August hours are Monday to Saturday 9:30am to 7pm and Sunday 1 to 7pm.

## WHAT TO SEE & DO

**Countrywear,** 15 and 35 Bridge St. (☎ 013397/55453), offers country clothing, guns, ammunition, fishing tackle, and other outdoor-related items. At no. 35, a range of women's clothing, including handknits, woolens, and tartans, is sold. **Goodbrand Knitwear,** 1 Braemar Rd. (☎ 013397/55947), mainly sells Scottish machine-made knitwear, with a few handknitted pieces thrown in. Clothing for children, men, and women is available in Shetland wool, lambswool, and cashmere.

**McEwan Gallery,** on A939, 1 mile (1.5km) west of Ballater (☎ 013397/55429), has been selling Scottish paintings, from 17th-century works to contemporary pieces, for a quarter of a century. It also has a large selection of antiquarian books, mainly Scottish and clan histories, as well as books on golf. **Dee Valley Confectioners,** Station Square (☎ 013397/55499), manufactures all its own sweets. Among the delectables sold are hard boilings (hard sugar candies), macaroon bars, toffee, and shortbread.

✪ **Balmoral Castle.** 7 miles (11km) west off A93, Balmoral, Ballater. ☎ 013397/42334. Admission £4 ($6.80) adults, £3 ($5.10) seniors, £1 ($1.70) ages 5–16; free for ages 4 and under. Apr 10–May 30 Mon–Sat 10am–5pm; June 1–Aug 2, daily 10am–5pm. Braemar bus from Aberdeen to Crathie bus station; Balmoral Castle is signposted from there (¼-mile walk [about .5km]).

"This dear paradise" is how Queen Victoria described Balmoral Castle, rebuilt in the Scottish baronial style by her beloved Albert. And Balmoral was the setting for the story of Victoria and her faithful servant, John Brown, as shown in the film *Mrs. Brown.* Today Balmoral is still a private residence of the British sovereign (in fact, you may remember the royals were holidaying here when they received the news about Princess Diana's death). Albert, Victoria's prince consort, leased the property in 1848 and bought it in 1852. As the original castle of the Farquharsons proved too small, the present edifice was built, completed in 1855. Its principal feature is a 100-foot (30m) tower. Of the actual castle, only the ballroom is open to the public; it houses an exhibit of pictures, porcelain, and works of art. On the grounds are many memorials to the royal family. In addition to the gardens, there are country walks, souvenir shops, a refreshment room, and pony trekking for £20 ($34) for a 2-hour ride 10am to noon or 2 to 4pm (available to adults and children over 12).

## ACCOMMODATIONS

You can also stay at the **Green Inn** (see "Dining," below).

**Balgonie Country House.** Braemar Place, Ballater AB35 5NQ. ☎ 013397/55482. www.taste-of-scotland.com/balgonie-country-house.html. E-mail: balgonie@line1.net. 9 units. TV TEL. £115 ($195.50) double. Rates include breakfast. AE, MC, V. Closed Jan. Free parking. Signposted off A93, Ballater–Perth, on the western outskirts.

In the heart of Royal Deeside, to the west of town, this Edwardian country house is set amid 4 acres of gardens, overlooking the Ballater Golf Course and providing panoramic views of Glen Muick. Owners John and Priscilla Finnie welcome you to their well-maintained home, creating a peaceful haven of comfortable bedrooms and fine Scottish food (see below). Bedrooms are named after the fishing pools of the River Dee, and are beautifully furnished and well equipped, with particularly fine beds. The owners can advise on activities in the area, including golfing, salmon fishing, and hiking.

**Craigendarroch Hotel and Country Club.** Braemar Rd., Ballater AB35 5XA. ☎ **013397/ 55858.** Fax 013397/55447. www.hilton.com. E-mail: holidays@stakis.co.uk. 45 units. TV TEL. £141 ($239.70) double; £216 ($367.20) suite. Rates include full Scottish breakfast; £10 ($17) per person supplement for half-board in The Oaks. AE, DC, MC, V. Take A93 a few minutes' drive outside Ballater heading toward Braemar.

The hotel, built in the Scottish baronial style, is set amid old trees on a 28-acre estate. Modern comforts have been added, but the owners have tried to maintain a 19th-century aura. The public areas include a regal oak staircase and a large sitting room. The fair-size guest rooms, opening onto views of the hillside and the River Dee, are furnished uniquely, but all have hair dryers, trouser presses, and small refrigerators (not minibars).

**Dining:** The elegant dining choice is the Oaks Restaurant (see "Dining," below), but you can dine less expensively in the Club House Bistro. A recent addition is the Barbecoa, an outdoor barbecue on the terrace, where you can eat under huge umbrellas that can be heated whenever the weather turns chilly.

**Amenities:** Concierge; 24-hour room service; laundry/dry cleaning; baby-sitting; leisure club with a spa pool, two swimming pools, a sauna, a solarium, various games, and a beauty salon; tennis courts; dry ski slope.

**Darroch Learg Hotel.** Darroch Learg, Braemon Rd. (on A93 at the west end of Ballater), Ballater AB35 5UX. ☎ **013397/55443.** Fax 013397/55252. www.scotlandsheritagehotels. co.uk/hotel/darroch.html. E-mail: darroch.learg@exodus.uk.com. 18 units. TV TEL. £120–£150 ($204–$255) double in main house; £70 ($119) double in Oakhall. Rates include breakfast. AE, DC, MC, V. Closed Christmas and last 3 weeks in Jan. Free parking.

Built in 1888 as an elegant country home, this pink-granite hotel stands in 5 acres of lush woodlands opening onto views of the Dee Valley toward the Grampian Mountains. Constructed at the peak of the golden age of Victorian Royal Deeside, the hotel is imbued with a relaxing charm in its individually styled bedrooms and in its traditional public rooms. The family atmosphere prevails in two drawing rooms, one for smokers, the other for nonsmokers. Bedrooms are good sized and divided between the main house or Oakhall, a baronial mansion on the same grounds. Rooms are decorated with taste and style, some with four-poster beds and private terraces. Modern amenities have been installed, including hair dryers, irons, trouser presses, beverage makers, and radio alarm clocks, and the hotel also offers a laundry service. Some rooms are equipped for guests with disabilities. Activities nearby include golfing, skiing, nature hikes, and tours.

**Dining:** The hotel's main attraction is its Conservatory Restaurant, which is open to nonguests (see "Dining," below). The chef will accommodate special diets by arrangement.

**Amenities:** Room service. The staff will arrange golf, fishing, and horseback riding nearby.

✪ **Deeside Hotel.** 45 Braemar Rd., Ballater AB35 5RQ. ☎ **013397/55420.** Fax 013397/ 55357. www.royaldeeside.org.uk/deeside.htm. E-mail: deesidehotel@talk21.com. 9 units. TV. £44–£52 ($74.80–$88.40) double. Rates include breakfast. MC, V. Closed Jan.

This well-managed guesthouse occupies what was built in 1890 as the retirement home for a tea planter who made his fortune in India. A 3-minute walk west of the town center, its pink-granite exterior is surrounded by about an acre of late-Victorian garden. The small to midsize guest rooms are simple, with white walls and wood furniture. Your hosts, Donald and Alison Brooker, prepare upscale dinners nightly. Recent offerings included grilled oatmeal-dredged herring with Dijon mustard sauce, grilled whole Dover sole served with butter and lemon sauce, and venison fillet with hawthorn jelly.

✪ **Monaltrie Hotel.** 5 Bridge Square, Ballater AB35 5QJ. ☎ **013397/55417.** Fax 013397/ 55180. 24 units. TV TEL. £60–£70 ($102–$119) double. Rates include Scottish breakfast. AE, DC, MC, V. Free parking.

This hotel, built in 1835 of Aberdeen granite, was the first in the region and accommodated the clients of a now-defunct spa that used to be at the opposite end of the Royal Bridge. Today the hotel bustles with a contemporary crowd who comes for the live music played in its pub and for the savory food served in its two restaurants. The more unusual of the two is a Thai restaurant serving dinner Thursday to Tuesday; maintained by Thai-born Laddawan Anderson, it offers fixed-price meals on the high side of moderate. Each of the fair-sized guest rooms has an unobtrusive monochromatic decor and comfortable beds. Hair dryers are available on request. The hotel is a 3-minute walk east of the center of town.

## DINING

**Balgonie Country House Restaurant.** In the Balgonie Country House, Braemar Place. ☎ **013397/55482.** Reservations recommended. Set-price 4-course menu £30 ($51). AE, MC, V. Daily 12:30–2pm and 7–9pm. Closed Jan. SCOTTISH/FRENCH.

For Scottish salmon, local game, Aberdeen Angus beef, or fresh seafood, this restaurant in a previously recommended country hotel is among the finest in the Royal Deeside. John and Priscilla Finnie welcome hotel guests and nonguests to their dining room, where the kitchen makes a major effort to secure some of the finest Scottish products, such as excellent seafood from the east coast and Orkney. John makes use of fresh herbs and tree-ripened fruits grown in the hotel's own gardens. The four-course set menu is changed daily, but you are likely to find tender fillet of beef flambéed in cognac and topped with black peppercorn sauce, or loin of lamb with a red currant jus. While enjoying views of the Glenmuick Hills, you can delight in any number of French-inspired dishes, such as halibut with asparagus and a tomato confit. Special attention is paid to desserts, such as pecan and treacle tart or rice pudding with plum compote.

**The Conservatory Restaurant.** In the Darroch Learg Hotel, Darroch Learg, Braemar Rd. ☎ **013397/55443.** Reservations required. Set-price 3-course menu £33 ($56.10). AE, DC, MC, V. Daily 12:30–2pm and 7–9pm. Closed Christmas and last 3 weeks in Jan. SCOTTISH.

Head here for innovative, imaginative cuisine. This award-winning dining room affords views over the River Dee. Chef David Mutter and his team use only the freshest ingredients, like lamb, venison, and Aberdeen Angus beef. Seafood options include fillet of halibut with basil and olive oil crust combined with fried squid and avocado salsa. You will also find rich, delectable courses, such as ravioli stuffed with foie gras and Parma ham with onion jam, and breast of duck Gressingham with homemade boudin, asparagus, truffle cream, and plum chutney.

**Green Inn.** 9 Victoria Rd., Ballater AB35 5QQ. ☎ and Fax **013397/55701.** Reservations required. Fixed-price menu £24 ($40.80) for 2 courses, £28.50 ($48.45) for 3 courses. AE, DC, MC, V. Mar–Oct daily 7–9pm; Nov–Feb Tues–Sat 7–9pm. SCOTTISH.

In the heart of town, this pink-granite inn was a temperance hotel when it was built in 1840 (that condition has now been rectified). It's one of the finest dining rooms in town, especially for traditional Scottish dishes. The chef emphasizes local produce, including home-grown vegetables when available. In season, loin of venison is served with bramble (blackberry) sauce, and you can always count on fresh salmon and the best of Angus beef.

Three simply furnished but fair-sized guest rooms are rented here, all with TVs; hair dryers are available on request. The half-board rate is £52.50 ($89.25) per person, reduced for a stay of 3 days or more.

**La Mangia Tora.** Bridge Square. ☎ **013397/55999.** Main courses £3.50–£8 ($5.95–$13.60) at lunch, £7–£13 ($11.90–$22.10) at dinner. AE, DC, MC, V. Daily 11am–2pm and 7–9:30pm. INTERNATIONAL.

In a converted early-18th-century stable beside the River Dee in the heart of Ballater, this is one of the most architecturally unusual restaurants in the region. Amid a deliberately rustic decor that includes artfully positioned bales of hay, lots of horsey accessories, and a high wooden ceiling, you can order from a widely varied menu that includes a savory array of barbecue dishes. Examples are chicken, salmon, pastas, meal-sized salads, baguette sandwiches, steaks, and fresh fish, usually prepared as simply as possible as a means of allowing the basic freshness and flavor to come through. Everybody's favorite dessert seems to be sticky toffee pudding.

✪ **Oaks Restaurant.** In the Craigendarroch Hotel and Country Club, Braemar Rd. ☎ **013397/55858.** Reservations recommended. Fixed-price 4-course dinner £28 ($47.60). AE, DC, MC, V. Daily 7–10:30pm. Take A93 for 1 mile (1.5km) west of Ballater. BRITISH.

The region's most glamorous restaurant, the Oaks (Craigendarroch means "Hill of the Oaks" in Gaelic) is in the century-old mansion built by the marmalade kings of Britain, the Keiller family. (Keiller marmalade can still be found in lots of U.K. households.) This is the most upscale of the restaurants in a resort complex that includes hotel rooms, timeshare villas, and access to a nearby golf course. The daily menu includes appetizers like warm salad of queen scallops with bacon, mixed greens, potato, and grapeseed-oil dressing or venison-and-duck terrine with orange and brandy, served with warm black conch vinaigrette. Main courses are more straightforward, like roast rack of lamb, breast of Grampian chicken, loin of venison, or Aberdeen Angus beef fillet.

## BALLATER AFTER DARK

The **Coach House Hotel Pub,** 1 Netherley Place (☎ 013397/55462), is an old pub that has been refurbished as a contemporary bar. Locals gather here during the evening. Every other Sunday, there's karaoke, but the real draw is conversation and on-tap selections of Guinness, Tennant's Lager, 70 Shilling, and 80 Shilling. **Monaltrie Hotel Pub,** 5 Bridge Square (☎ 013397/55417), and its host hotel have been around for 200 years, and the ambience is very old world, with a beamed ceiling and lots of hardwood. On Friday there's a band, usually country-and-western, and a cover charge. On tap, you'll be able to choose from Guinness, Tennant's Lager, Belhaven Best, or Stella.

## 12 Braemar

85 miles (137km) N of Edinburgh, 58 miles (93km) W of Aberdeen, 51 miles (82km) N of Perth

In the heart of some of Grampian's most beautiful scenery, Braemar is known for its romantic castle. It's also a good center for exploring the area that includes Balmoral Castle (see above) and is home to the most famous of the Highland gatherings. This

Highland village is set against a massive backdrop of hills, covered with heather in summer, where Clunie Water joins the River Dee. The massive **Cairn Toul** towers over Braemar, reaching a height of 4,241 feet (1,286.5m).

## ESSENTIALS

**GETTING THERE**    The nearest rail service runs to Aberdeen (for schedules, call ☎ 0345/484-950). From there, six daily buses run west to Braemar. The one-way fare is £6.50 ($11.05), and the trip time is 2 hours and 10 minutes. The bus station in Aberdeen is on Guild Street (call ☎ 01224/212-266), beside the train station.

If you're driving from the south, you can choose from two excellent routes, M6 and A1. Head for Perth and follow the Braemar signs from M90 continuing on A93.

**VISITOR INFORMATION**    The year-round **tourist office** is in The Mews, Mar Road (☎ 013397/41600). April, May, and October to December, it's open Monday to Saturday 10am to 1pm and 2 to 5pm and Sunday noon to 5pm; June and September, it's open daily 10am to 1pm and 2 to 6pm; July and August hours are daily 9am to 7pm.

**SPECIAL EVENTS**    The spectacular ✪ **Royal Highland Gathering** takes place annually in the Princess Royal and Duke of Fife Memorial Park, on the first Saturday of September. The queen herself often attends. These ancient games are thought to have originated with King Malcolm Canmore. That chieftain ruled much of Scotland at the time of the Norman conquest of England, and he selected his hardiest warriors from all the clans for a keen and fair contest. For more information, call the tourist office (see above). Braemar is overrun with visitors during the Gathering, so reserve your hotel room by April if you want to stay anywhere within a 20-mile (32m) radius of Braemar. Call ☎ 01224/288-825 for advance bookings.

## EXPLORING THE AREA

If you're a royal family watcher, you might be able to spot members of the family, even the queen, at **Crathie Church,** 9 miles (14.5km) east of Braemar on A93 (☎ 013397/42208). They attend Sunday services here when they're in residence at Balmoral. Services are at 11:30am; otherwise, the church is open to view April to October, Monday to Saturday 9:30am to 5:30pm and Sunday 2 to 5:30pm.

Nature lovers may want to drive to the **Linn of Dee,** 6 miles (10km) west of Braemar, a narrow chasm on the River Dee that's the best place for scenic walks. Other beautiful spots with good day hiking include **Glen Muick, Loch Muick,** and **Lochnagar.** An unmanned **Glenmuick Wildlife Trust Visitor Centre,** reached by a minor road, is located in Glen Muick, off the South Deeside road. You can pick up leaflets here, but for more information, contact the Memorial Ranger Service at ☎ 013397/55059. An access road joins B976 at a point 16 miles (26km) east of Braemar. The tourist office (see "Essentials," above) will give you a map pinpointing these idyllic places.

Shoppers might check out **Capercaille,** 3 Invercauld Rd. (☎ 013397/41249), which has quality crafts, mostly of Scottish manufacture. Pottery, carved wood, jewelry, and handmade children's toys are representative of the crafts found here, alongside a wide selection of women's handknitted and velvet clothing items. At **Lamont Sporran,** 8 Invercauld Rd. (☎ 013397/41404), you can find complete Highland outfits, including sporran (the small leather or fur pouch used in place of pockets when wearing a kilt), kilts, belts, jackets, stockings, and brogues. **McLeans of Braemar,** 10–12 Invercauld Rd. ☎ 013397/41629), carries a wide range of regional products, from knickknacks to clothing. Among the items are stag-horn and cow-horn crafts, jewelry, china, paperweights, Scottish woolens, tartans and tartan accessories, and men's and women's country clothing.

⭘ **Braemar Castle.** On the Aberdeen–Ballater–Perth road (A93). ☎ **013397/41219.** Admission £3 ($5.10) adults, £2.50 ($4.25) seniors/students, £1 ($1.70) ages 5–15; free for ages 4 and under. Mon after Easter to Oct, Sat–Thurs 10am–6pm. Take A93 for half a mile (1km) northeast of Braemar.

The seat of Capt. A. A. C. Farquharson of Invercauld, this romantic 17th-century castle is a fully furnished residence of architectural grace, scenic charm, and historic interest. Opening onto the Dee River, it was built in 1628 by the earl of Mar, but John Farquharson of Inveraray, the Black Colonel, attacked and burned it in 1689. It was rebuilt in 1748, has barrel-vaulted ceilings and an underground prison, and is known for its remarkable star-shaped defensive-curtain wall. There's a gift shop and a free parking area.

## ACCOMMODATIONS & DINING

**Braemar Lodge Hotel.** 6 Glenshee Rd., Braemar AB35 5YQ. ☎/fax **013397/41627.** 7 units. TV. £50–£72 ($85–$122.40) double; £200–£400 ($340–$680) log cabin. Rates include Scottish breakfast. MC, V. Closed Nov. Free parking.

This hotel, popular with skiers at the nearby Glenshee slopes, was built in 1870 as a hunting lodge on 2 acres at the head of Glen Clunie, half a mile (1km) from the center of Braemar. The fair-sized guest rooms, all with hair dryers, have a strikingly modern decor. On the grounds are also three recently built log cabins with all the modern conveniences; they can sleep up to six. The hotel is on the road to the Glenshee ski slopes, near the cottage where Robert Louis Stevenson wrote *Treasure Island.*

Dinner is served daily, and includes excellent regional dishes; reserve in advance so menus can be planned. The chef's specialties include venison with red wine, bacon, mushroom, and onion sauce; steaks in creamy pepper sauce; and sautéed trout fillet with hollandaise sauce.

**Callater Lodge Hotel.** 9 Glenshee Rd., Braemar AB35 5YQ. ☎ **013397/41275.** Fax 013397/41345. www.maria@callater.demon.co.uk. 7 units, 6 with private bathroom. TV. £46–£50 ($78.20–$85) double without bathroom; £50–£56 ($85–$95.20) double with bathroom. MC, V. Closed Nov–Dec. Free parking.

Full of rural charm and owned by Maria and Michael Franklin, this granite house stands about a quarter-mile (.5km) south of the center of Braemar, off the side of the highway in a 1-acre garden. Built around 1865, with a small-scale enlargement completed during the 1970s, it bristles with both bay and dormer windows and offers a different decor in each of its cozy guest rooms. The restaurant offers moderately priced dinners. The owners will prepare you a picnic for around £5 ($8.25) per person, and offer advice on great scenic places to hike and enjoy your lunch.

**Invercauld Arms Hotel.** Braemar AB35 5YR. ☎ **013397/41605.** Fax 013397/41428. www.peelhotel.com. 68 units. TV TEL. £110 ($187) double. Rates include Scottish breakfast. AE, DC, MC, V. Free parking. Bus: 201 from Aberdeen.

This is an old granite building whose original part dates from the 18th century. In cool weather there's a roaring log fire on the hearth. The guest rooms are comfortably furnished but rather uninspired, varying in size from large to standard; all contain hair dryers. You can go hill walking and see deer, golden eagles, and other wildlife. The hotel can also organize the contacts for fishing and skiing and other pursuits in the nearby area. The upscale Scottish and international fare at dinner can include fresh Dee salmon, Aberdeen Angus beef, venison, and grouse.

## BRAEMAR AFTER DARK

The **Fife Arms Pub,** Mar Road, in the Fife Arms Hotel (☎ 013397/41644), has free live music, usually Scottish dance bands, on 2 weeknights and live rock bands every Saturday night. On tap you'll find McEwan's Lager and 80 Shilling and Foster's Lager. Although the **Invercauld Arms Pub,** in the Invercauld Arms Thistle Hotel (☎ 013397/41605), has retained its wooden beamed ceiling, it has been modernized into a typical bar. This is a popular gathering spot for the locals. On tap you'll find Guinness Export, Foster's Export, Blackthorn Cider, Kronenberg, and McEwan's Lager and 80 Shilling.

# 13  Speyside

The valley of the second-largest river in Scotland, the Spey, is north and south of Aviemore and a land of great natural beauty. A journey north through Speyside will take you toward the Malt Whisky Trail. The Spey is born in the Highlands above Loch Laggan, 40 miles (64.5km) south of Inverness, and runs between the towering Cairngorms on the east and the Monadhliath Mountains on the west. Little more than a creek at its inception, it gains in force, fed by the many "burns" draining water from the hills. It's one of Scotland's great rivers for salmon fishing, and its major center is Grantown-on-Spey.

## NEWTONMORE

The Highland resort of Newtonmore is a good center for the Grampian and Monadhliath mountains and offers excellent fishing, golfing, pony trekking, and hill walking. For a dramatic walk, a track from the village climbs past the Calder River to Loch Dubh and the massive **Carn Ban** (3,087 ft. [936m]), where eagles fly. **Castle Cluny,** ancient seat of the MacPherson chiefs, is 6 miles (10km) west of Newtonmore. There's no local tourist office to go to for information, but if you're staying at one of the little inns or guesthouses in the area, the reception desk will hook you up with any activities in the area.

In Gaelic, "New Town on the Moor" is written *Bail ur ant Sleibh.* Founded in the early 1800s, it's a village of some 1,000 people today, many of whom still understand Gaelic. Newtonmore could easily become your center for touring one of Scotland's most scenic areas, as it is 46 miles (74km) from Fort William on the west coast, 46 miles (74km) from Inverness to the north, and 38 miles (61km) from Pitlochry to the southeast. It's also 113 miles (182km) northwest of Edinburgh. You can even visit the Loch Ness conveniently from Newtonmore.

If you follow A86 southwest of Newtonmore, you'll come to the hamlet of Laggan near the junction with A889, which crosses the River Spey. From here you can follow an unclassified road (signposted) running west up the glen to **Garvamore.** This is an area of great scenic beauty. After 6 miles (10km) the road comes to **Garvamore Bridge,** at the south side of Corrieyairack Pass. Built in 1735 by the English General Wade, this dual-arched bridge was constructed so troops would be able to travel quickly to the Highlands to suppress any possible uprising. Return to A86 and continue west along the western shore of Loch Laggan. The route along this lake offers panoramic views of the Highlands, the kind of scenery Scotland is famous for.

### SEEING THE MUSEUM

**Clan Macpherson House & Museum.** Main St. ☎ **01540/673-332.** Free admission, but donations accepted. Apr–Oct Mon–Sat 10am–5pm, Sun 2:30–5pm. The Edinburgh–Inverness bus stops nearby.

Most motorists zip through on the way to Aviemore, but sightseers may want to stop and visit this museum at the south end of the village. Displayed are clan relics and memorials, including the Black Chanter and Green Banner as well as a charmed sword, and the broken fiddle of the freebooter, James MacPherson, a Scottish Robin Hood. Relics associated with Bonnie Prince Charlie are also here. An annual clan rally is held on the first Saturday of August.

## ACCOMMODATIONS & DINING

**Pines Hotel.** Station Rd., Newtonmore PH20 1AR. ☎ **01540/673-271.** 5 units. TV. £74.50–£77.50 ($126.65–$131.75) double. Rates include Scottish breakfast and dinner. Closed Dec 28–Jan 15. Free parking.

Built in 1903 of somber-looking granite, this house sits on a hill overlooking the Spey Valley a quarter-mile (.5km) west of the hamlet's center. Your hosts are Colin and Pamela Walker, migrants from Brighton. The standard-sized guest rooms are painted in restrained hues and simply decorated with reproduction early-1900s furniture. They have pleasant views of the Highland countryside and come with tea/coffeemakers; hair dryers are available on request. The food offered by Colin is wholesome, straightforward British cuisine, made from fresh ingredients like salmon, lamb, venison, and Aberdeen Angus beef. Pamela is an expert on desserts and is very kind about creating wonders for diabetics and others on low-sugar diets.

## KINGUSSIE

Your next stop along the Spey might be at the little summer resort and winter ski center of **Kingussie** (pronounced King-*you*-see). It's the so-called capital of Badenoch, a district known as the "drowned land" because the Spey can flood the valley when the snows of a severe winter melt in spring. It's a great center for walking and hiking through the beautiful scenery of glen and loch in its environs.

Kingussie practically adjoins Newtonmore (see above), for it lies directly southeast along A86. The location is 117 miles (188km) northwest of Edinburgh, 40 miles (64.5km) south of Inverness, and 12 miles (19km) southwest of Aviemore. There's train service from Edinburgh, with five trains per day, taking 2¾ hours and costing £27.70 ($47.10) one-way. Trains also arrive from Aberdeen at the rate of one per hour (with a change of trains at either Perth or Inverness). The trip takes 4 hours and costs £21.60 ($36.70) one way.

A **tourist center** is on King Street (☎ **01540/661-297**). Hours are Monday to Saturday 10:30am to 5:30pm and Sunday 1 to 5pm year-round.

### EXPLORING THE AREA

Kingussie is in one of Scotland's most scenic areas, and you can set off hiking in many directions. For example, directly south, A9 passes through panoramic scenery set against a backdrop of moor, woodlands, and hills. The highway passes through **Glen Trim** to **Dalwhinnie,** going through the **Pass of Drumochter.** You can also take A86 west from Kingussie to **Glen Roy** and **Spean Bridge,** going through lush glens set off by towering hills. The road dips and climbs beside beautiful **Loch Laggan.** At several points, you might want to get out of your car and go for long walks, past secret lochans and hidden glens. Perhaps you'll even stumble on Brigadoon.

If you'd like to go hiking, the tourist office will help you plan a trip into the **Monadhliath Mountains** (the word in Gaelic means "gray moors"). They loom immediately northward over Kingussie, separating Speyside from the Great Glen. The **Cairngorm Mountains** are far better known, forming the southern flank of Speyside, but the Monadhliaths are equally as beautiful and far less crowded with other hikers and walkers in summer.

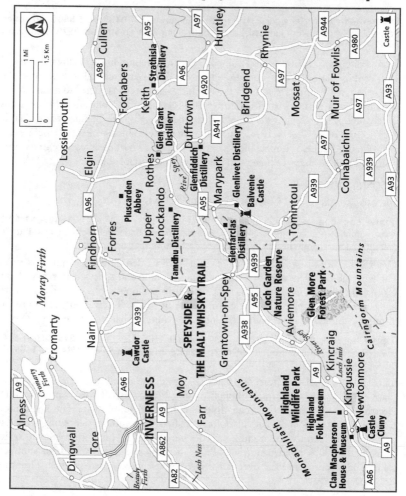

**Insh Marshes,** 2 miles (3km) from Kingussie along B970, after passing by the Ruthven Barracks (see below), is a nature reserve with much more than just birds to see. Along a marked trail, going through meadow and marshland, you can see some of the area's lushest scenery. Six types of wild orchids alone grow here. At two lookout points, high above the marshes, you'll have a good vantage point to spot various birds of prey and hundreds of waterfowl, even wild Scottish deer and others.

**Highland Folk Museum.** Duke St. ☎ **01540/661-307.** Admission £4 ($6.80) adults, £2 ($3.40) children/seniors, £10 ($17) families. Apr–Oct Mon–Fri 10:30am–5:30pm, Sat–Sun 1–5pm.

This was the first folk museum established in Scotland (1934) and remains one of the most important. Its collections are based on the Highlanders' life, and you'll see domestic, agricultural, and industrial items. Open-air exhibits are a *turf kailyard* (kitchen garden), a Lewis Island black house, and old vehicles and carts. Traditional events like spinning, music making, and handcraft fairs are held throughout summer.

**Ruthven Barracks.** Half a mile (1km) south of Kingussie. ☎ **0131/668-8600.** Admission free. Daily 24 hours. From Kingussie, drive south along Ruthven Street to B970, then follow the signs to the barracks.

From a distance, this site evokes a ruined castle on a mound, but it's really the ruins of 18th-century barracks rising out of a hill in the flat River Spey valley floor. After the 1715 Jacobite rising, this was one of four infantry barracks constructed to maintain law and order in the area. But in 1746 Ruthven fell to a second Jacobite attack, when it was largely destroyed except for the ruins you see today. It was here Bonnie Prince Charlie gave his final order, "Let every man seek his own safety." This signaled the absolute end of the doomed cause. The main blocks of the ruin face each other across a central court-yard, and beyond these walls you can see the ruins of a stable block.

## ACCOMMODATIONS

You can also stay at **The Cross** (see "Dining," below).

**Homewood Lodge.** Newtonmore Rd., Kingussie PH21 1HD. ☎ **01540/661-507.** www.bigfoot.com/tildahomewood-lodge. E-mail: homewood-lodge@bigfoot.com. 4 units. £40 ($68) double. Rates include Scottish breakfast. No credit cards.

One of the area's best B&Bs, on half an acre of garden and woodland, this small Highland house offers comfortable large guest rooms and spectacular views of the Cairngorm Mountains. The rooms are pleasantly but simply furnished and come with hair dryers. The sitting room offers an open fire and a TV. Reservations are a must for affordable dinners of good traditional local fare. Summer barbecues are also offered.

**Osprey Hotel.** Ruthven Rd. (at High St.), Kingussie PH21 1EN. ☎/fax **01540/661-510.** www.ospreyhotel.co.uk. E-mail: aiteen@ospreyhotel.co.uk. 8 units. £85–£98 ($144.50–$166.60) double. Rates include half-board. AE, DC, MC, V.

This 1895 Victorian structure, 300 yards (273m) from the rail station, is a convenient place to stay, with comfortable though plain guest rooms, all with central heating, electric blankets, electric fires, hair dryers, and heated towel racks. The hotel has a licensed bar, guest lounge, and TV lounge. Baby-sitting and baby-listening service is provided, and laundry and ironing facilities are available. The place is known for its pure, fresh, 100% homemade food. Prime Scottish meats are served; in summer, salmon and trout from local rivers are offered either fresh or peat-smoked. The wine list is extensive.

## DINING

⊙ **The Cross.** Tweed Mill Brae, off the Ardbroilach road, Kingussie PH21 1TC. ☎ **01540/661-166.** Fax 01540/661-080. www.thecross.co.uk. E-mail: fabulousfood@ thecross.co.uk. Reservations required. Fixed-price 5-course dinner £37.50 ($63.75). MC, V. Mar–Nov Wed–Mon 7–9pm. Closed Dec–Feb. SCOTTISH.

This chic restaurant comes as a surprise: Out of the way in a remote Highland village, it serves superlative meals that involve theater as much as they do fine food. The restaurant stands on 4 acres, with the Gynack Burn running through the grounds. The main building of the complex is an old tweed mill, and the restaurant has an open-beam ceiling and French doors leading onto a terrace over the water's edge, where alfresco dinners are served, depending on the weather. Specialties depend on the availability of produce in the local markets and may include venison Francatelli, wild pigeon with grapes, or Highland lamb with sorrel. A selection from more than 300 wines rounds out any menu. Personal service and attention to detail go into the running of this place, operated by Ruth and Tony Hadley; Ruth's cooking has put it on the gastronomic map of Scotland.

Nine stylish rooms are rented in a new building that's been designed in the old style. Each room is different in size and style—two have canopied beds, and another has a balcony overlooking the mill pond. Doubles, including half-board, go from £190 ($323).

# KINCRAIG

Kincraig enjoys a scenic spot at the northern end of Loch Insh, overlooking the Spey Valley to the west and the Cairngorm Mountains to the east. From Kingussie, continue northeast along A9 (the route north to Aviemore) to reach Kincraig, 37 miles (59.5km) south of Inverness and 119 miles (191.5km) northwest of Edinburgh.

About a mile (1.5km) from Kincraig, 6 miles (10km) south of Aviemore, beside B9152, is the entrance to the **Highland Wildlife Park,** Kincraig (☎ **01540/ 651-270**). Established in 1972 on 260 acres administered by the Royal Zoological Society of Scotland (the folk who operate the Edinburgh Zoo), it incorporates a valley ringed with mountains and terrain that includes peat bogs, birch and pine forests, and tundra. Some of the animals you'll see here are exceedingly rare outside the park—herds of European bison, who enjoy rolling around in the peat bogs in the park's center, red deer, shaggy Highland cattle, wild horses, red foxes, gray wolves, lynx, pine martens (a form of tree weasel), and bears.

Among the protected birds are golden eagles and several species of grouse, including the capercaillie, a large European grouse native to Scotland's pine forests. Roads within the park are designed as drive-throughs allowing maximum exposure to the terrain, thanks to many winding turns. Of the park's 260 acres, 60 are reserved only for trekkers, walkers, and hill climbers. You'll also find a visitor center with a lackluster gift shop, a cafe, and an exhibition center, with ample parking and picnic sites available. The park is open daily at 10am. April to October, the last entrance is at 4pm, except during July and August, when the last entrance is at 5pm. November to March, the last entrance is at 2pm. All people and vehicles are expected to vacate the park within 2 hours of the day's last admission. Admission is £6.50 ($11.05) adults, £5.40 ($9.20) seniors, £4.35 ($7.40) children, £21.80 ($37.05) families.

Adjacent to the park, beside B9152, are a handful of satellite industries, one of the more amusing of which is **Working Sheepdogs,** Leault, Kincraig (☎ **01540/ 651-310**). Here Neil Ross and his family keep eight sheepdogs who corral sheep and perform tricks. There's also a herd of ducks who meander and quack their way through labyrinths. Depending on business, there are between two and four shows daily April to October. Each lasts an hour and is charming for dog lovers despite an undeniable hokeyness. The cost is £3.50 ($5.95) adults and £1.50 ($2.55) children.

## ACCOMMODATIONS

**March House.** Lagganlia, Feshiebridge, Kincraig PH21 1NG. ☎ **01540/651-388.** www.taste-of-scotland.com/march-house.html. 6 units. £44 ($74.80) double. MC, V. From Kincraig, follow B970 east to Feshiebridge. Cross the bridge and drive uphill until you see the red telephone box on right. Turn right and continue driving for half a mile (1km). Total distance from Kincraig is 2 miles (3km).

This house almost looks like a contemporary chalet in Sweden. It was built in 1980 and named after the month it was completed, but it didn't really find itself until it was acquired by Caroline Hayes and her good-natured entourage of friends and staff. Its focal points are an iron wood-burning stove, a pine-sheathed conservatory and library, and sweeping views over a dramatic mountain tableau. Each guest room's decor is based on pinewood trim and a different floral theme, such as poppies. Guests divert themselves with long walks in the surrounding forest.

Make reservations in advance for dinner, which is a good value. Menu items use only fresh produce; since the place is unlicensed, bring your own beer or wine. A recent meal here included crêpes with a creamy leek, ham, and mushroom filling; grilled Scottish lamb with lemon-flavored cabbage and raspberry sauce; and crème brûlée with homemade ice cream.

# GRANTOWN-ON-SPEY

On A939, the resort of Grantown-on-Spey, with its gray-granite buildings, is 34 miles (55km) southeast of Inverness and 24 miles (39km) south of Nairn in a wooded valley commanding views of the Cairngorm Mountains. It's a key center of winter sports in Scotland. Fishermen are also attracted to the salmon fishing in this setting.

Grantown, one of Scotland's many 18th-century planned towns, was founded on a heather-covered moor in 1765 by Sir James Grant of Grant and became the seat of that ancient family. It became famous in the 19th century as a Highland tourist center, enticing visitors with its planned concept, the beauty of surrounding pine forests, the Spey River, and the mountains around it.

From a base here, you can explore the valleys of the Don and Dee, the Cairngorms, and Culloden Moor, scene of the historic 1746 battle.

A **tourist office** is at 54 High St. (☎ **01479/872-773**). April to mid-July and September, it's open Monday to Friday 9am to 5pm and Saturday and Sunday 10am to 4pm; mid-July to August, hours are Monday to Friday 9am to 6pm, Saturday 10am to 5pm, and Sunday 10am to 4pm.

## EXPLORING THE AREA

Grantown-on-Spey is the best center for touring the **Cairngorms** (*Am Monadh Ruadh,* or "red hills," in Gaelic), so called because of the pink granite on their plateaus. Ideal for outdoor activities, this mountain range is excellent for skiing in winter or cycling, golfing, and fishing during warmer months. The local tourist office (see above) can also offer advice about watersports on Loch Morlick and Lock Insh nearby.

The Cairngorm Mountains stretch for 50 miles (80.5km), a huge range that takes in 50 peaks, often rising more than 3,000 feet (910m). Some peaks reach a height of 4,000 feet (1,213m). Much of the plateau of the Cairngorms is a stony desert carved out by the last Ice Age. The road up Glen More past Loch Morlick leads to a chairlift going all the way to the summit. The cost is £6 ($10.20), and it's open daily 9am to 4:30pm, most often later in midsummer. For information, call ☎ **01479/861-261.** This is a very popular lift in the ski season, from December to April. The Ranger Service also operates a program of **walks** in the area, and you can arrange them by calling the **Ranger Base** at ☎ **01479/861-703.** For information about rock and ice climbing, bike tours, and guided walks, call Ron Walker of **Talisman Activities** at ☎ **01479/841-576.**

Eight miles (13km) south of Grantown-on-Spey is the **Loch Garden Nature Reserve,** known for its breeding ospreys. These highly endangered species are zealously protected by the government. Before the 1950s, these birds hadn't been seen in Britain in half a century. A viewing platform here is provided by the Royal Society for the Protection of Birds, and you can visit daily in summer 9am to 5pm; admission is free.

The **Speyside Heather Centre,** Skye of Curr (☎ **01479/851-359**), is a shop that sells nearly 300 varieties of heather and runs a full greenhouse operation. In the gift shop, you'll find small Scottish crafts and gifts, including heather crafts. There's also a restaurant serving simple meals, home baking, and the house specialty, Cloonie dumplings, which resemble Christmas puddings, only less sweet. The restaurant is open Monday to Saturday 9am to 6pm and Sunday 10am to 5:30pm, with main courses costing £2 to £6 ($3.40 to $10.20). The stylish **The Kist,** 74 High St. (☎ 01479/ 873-043), offers regional souvenir items such as Orkney silverware, Border Fine Arts figurines, limited-edition paintings and prints, jewelry, recycled glassware, cards, and Edinburgh, Waterford, and Stuart crystal.

## ACCOMMODATIONS

✪ **The Ardlarig.** Woodlands Terrace, Grantown-on-Spey PH26 3JU. ☎/fax **01479/ 873-245.** www.scottsweb.com/The Ardlarig. E-mail: ardlarig@globalnet.co.uk. 6 units, 4 with private bathroom. £35 ($59.50) double without bathroom; £60 ($102) double with bathroom. Rates include breakfast. AE, DC, MC, V. Closed mid-Feb to mid-Mar.

Reeking of the majesty of the Empire, this granite-sided house was built around 1885 as the home of John Gowdie, retired deputy governor of Nigeria. Several years later, Dr. David Livingstone, African explorer and cartographer, was a house guest. Within a 10-minute walk of the town center, it's the domain of Neil Cairns and his charming fiancée Sally-Anne Harvey, who run the place like a private home and prepare wonderful dinners based on local produce. The guest rooms tend to be green or cream or a combination of both, with high ceilings and most of the original architectural detailing—meticulously crafted from rare pitch pine.

Priority seating in the dining room is given to guests, but nonguests who phone in advance are usually welcomed. Menu items change every day, but past successes have included warm salad of chicken livers and oranges, venison casserole; fillet steak with warm peppercorn sauce, goat's cheese soufflé with cherry tomato salad, and local salmon fillet with sweet ginger sauce.

**Garth Hotel.** The Square, Castle Rd., Grantown-on-Spey PH26 3HN. ☎ **01479/872-836.** Fax 01479/872-116. 17 units. TV TEL. £64–£74 ($108.80–$125.80) double. Rates include Scottish breakfast. MC, V. Free parking.

The elegant Garth was built as a home in the 17th century, standing on 4 acres beside the town square. You'll enjoy the use of a spacious upstairs lounge, whose thick walls, high ceilings, wood-burning stove, and vine-covered veranda make it the perfect place for morning coffee or afternoon tea. The hotel offers spacious handsomely furnished guest rooms with all amenities, including hair dryers. In the dining room, "A Taste of Scotland" dishes are featured, with emphasis on fresh local produce, including seafood, salmon, venison, game, and beef.

✪ **Tulchan Lodge.** Advie, Grantown-on-Spey PH26 3PW. ☎ **01807/510-200.** Fax 01807/510-234. www.tulchan.com. E-mail: estateoffice@tulchan.farce.q.co.uk. 13 units. TEL. £350–£500 ($595–$850) double. Rates include full board. No credit cards. Closed mid-Jan to mid-Apr. Drive 9 miles (14.5km) northeast of Grantown on B9102.

This is the greatest sporting lodge in all Europe, where you're served some of the finest food and wine in Scotland, granted the right to fish and hunt on the sumptuous estate, and offered panoramic views of the Spey Valley. Tulchan Lodge, built in 1906 to serve as the 25,000-acre Tulchan Estate's fishing-and-shooting lodge, is a place for both sports-oriented visitors and travelers who want to experience a place designed with the elegance required by Edward VI, who often came here. Sportspeople are notoriously superstitious and as the number 13 is to be avoided at all times, reception will inform you the hotel has 12 guest rooms plus one. Each room is different in size and furnishings, but all have hair dryers.

**Dining:** In the two elegant dining rooms, Scottish and international dishes are served, with particular attention to Scottish beef, lamb, game, and fresh seafood. The vegetables are grown in the lodge's garden.

**Amenities:** Room service, dry cleaning/laundry service, nightly turndown, baby-sitting with advance notice, secretarial/business services, tennis court, fishing, shooting, nature trails, golf course nearby.

## DINING

**Craggan Mill.** Hwy. A95, ¾ mile (1.2km) south of Grantown-on-Spey. ☎ **01479/ 872-288.** Reservations recommended. Main courses £3.95–£12.50 ($6.70–$21.25). MC, V. May–Sept daily noon–2pm and 6–10pm; Oct–Apr Tues–Sun 7–10pm. Closed the first 2 weeks in Nov. BRITISH/ITALIAN.

This licensed restaurant and lounge bar, a 10-minute walk south of the town center, is housed in a restored ruined granite mill whose waterwheel is still visible. Your appetizer might be smoked trout in deference to Scotland or ravioli inspired by sunny Italy. For a main course, the selection might be breast of chicken with cream or chicken cacciatore, followed by a dessert of either rum-raisin ice cream or peach Melba. You've probably had better versions of all the dishes, but what you get isn't bad and is reasonably priced. A good selection of Italian wines is offered. Cheaper meals are served in the lounge bar.

# 14  West Grampian & the Malt Whisky Trail

Much of the West Grampian region is in the Moray district, on the southern shore of the Moray Firth, a great inlet cutting into the northeastern coast of Scotland, stretching in a triangular shape south from the coast to the wild heart of the Cairngorm Mountains near Aviemore. It's a land steeped in history, as its many castles, battle sites, and ancient monuments testify. It's also very sports oriented, attracting not only fishermen but also golfers.

The major attraction is the 70-mile-long (113km) **Malt Whisky Trail,** running through the glens of Speyside. There are five malt distilleries in the area, known for their production of *uisge beatha* ("water of life"): Glenlivet, Glenfiddich, Glenfarclas, Strathisla, and Tamdhu. Allow about an hour each to visit them. Half the malt distilleries in the country lie along the River Spey and its tributaries, where peat smoke and Highland water are used to turn out single-malt (unblended) whisky.

If you're traveling north on the A9 road from Perth and Pitlochry, your first stop might be **Dalwhinnie,** which has the highest whisky distillery in the world at 1,888 feet (573m). It's not in the Spey Valley but at the northeastern end of Loch Ericht, with views of lochs and forests.

## GLENLIVET & GLENFARCLAS

To reach your first distillery on the Malt Whisky Trail, leave Grantown-on-Spey and head east along A95 until you come to the junction with B9008. Go south along this route and you can't miss it. The location of the **Glenlivet Reception Centre** (☎ **01542/783-220**) is 10 miles (16km) north of the nearest town, Tomintoul. Mid-March to the end of October, it's open Monday to Saturday 10am to 4pm and Sunday 12:30am to 4pm; July and August, hours are Monday to Saturday 10am to 6pm and Sunday 12:30am to 6pm. The £2.50 ($4.25) admission for visitors over 18 includes a £2 ($3.40) voucher off the purchase of a bottle of whisky.

Back on A95, you can visit the **Glenfarclas Distillery** at Ballindalloch (☎ **01807/ 500-245**), one of only two malt-whisky distilleries still independent of the giants. Founded in 1836, Glenfarclas is managed by the fifth generation of the Grant family. It's open Monday to Friday 9am to 5pm (June to September, it's also open Saturday 10am to 4pm and Sunday 12:30 to 4:30pm). The £3.50 ($5.95) admission for visitors over 18 includes a £7 ($11.90) discount on any purchase of £10 ($17) or over. There's a small craft shop, and each visitor is offered a dram of Glenfarclas Malt Whisky.

## ACCOMMODATIONS & DINING

**Minmore House Hotel.** Glenlivet, near Ballindalloch AB37 9DB. ☎ **01807/590-378.** Fax 01807/590-472. www.smoothhound.co.uk/hotels/minmore.html. E-mail: minmorehouse@ ukonline.co.uk. 10 units. TEL. £110–£150 ($187–$255) double, including breakfast, afternoon tea, and 5-course dinner. MC, V. Limited openings in winter—call first.

On 7 acres of grounds next to the Glenlivet Distillery, this house was built around 1850 by George Smith, founder of the distillery. The public rooms, including the drawing room, are elegantly furnished, opening onto views of the Ladder Hills and an outdoor pool. The guest rooms vary from extremely roomy to small, but all are well furnished and have tea/coffeemakers and hair dryers. You can enjoy drinks in the oak-paneled lounge bar, which has an open log fire on chilly nights. The Scottish food is excellent, served in a Regency-style dining room with mahogany tables and matching chairs.

## DUFFTOWN

James Duff, the fourth earl of Fife, founded Dufftown in 1817. The four main streets of town converge at the battlemented **clock tower,** which is also the **tourist office** (☎ **01340/820-501**). April to June, September, and October, the office is open Monday to Saturday 10am to 1pm and 2 to 5:30pm and Sunday 1 to 5pm; July and August hours are Monday to Saturday 10am to 7pm and Sunday 1 to 7pm.

A center of the whisky-distilling industry, Dufftown is surrounded by seven malt distilleries. The family-owned **Glenfiddich Distillery** is on A941, half a mile (1km) north (☎ **01340/820-373**). It's open Monday to Friday 9:30am to 4:30pm (Easter to mid-October, it's also open Saturday 9:30am to 4:30pm and Sunday noon to 4:30pm). Guides in kilts show you around the plant and explain the process of distilling, and you see a film of the history of distilling. At the end of the tour, you're given a dram of malt whisky. There's a souvenir shop. The first whisky was produced on Christmas Day back in 1887.

Other sights include **Balvenie Castle** (☎ **01340/820-121**) along A941, the ruins of a moated stronghold from the 14th century that lie on the south side of the Glenfiddich Distillery. During her northern campaign against the earl of Huntly, Mary Queen of Scots spent 2 nights here. From 1459 to the 17th century, the earls of Atholl retained Balvenie. April to September, it's open daily 9:30am to 6pm. Admission is £1.20 ($2.05) adults, 90p ($1.55) seniors, and 50p (85¢) children.

**Mortlach Parish Church** in Dufftown is one of the oldest places of Christian worship in the country. Its reputed to have been founded in 566 by St. Moluag. A Pictish cross stands in the graveyard. The present church was reconstructed in 1931 and incorporates portions of an older building.

## DINING

✪ **Taste of Speyside.** 10 Balvenie St. ☎ **01340/820-860.** Reservations recommended at dinner. Set menus £8.80 ($14.95) for 2 courses, £10.80 ($18.35) for 3 courses; Speyside platter £10.80 ($18.35). MC, V. Daily 12:30–9pm. Closed Nov–Feb. SCOTTISH.

True to its name, this restaurant in the town center, just off the main square, avidly promotes a Speyside cuisine as well as Speyside malt whiskies, and in the bar you can buy the product of each of Speyside's 46 distilleries. A platter including smoked salmon, smoked venison, sweet-cured herring, malt-whisky pâté, locally made cheese (cow or goat), salads, and homemade oat cakes is offered at noon and at night. Nourishing soup is made fresh daily and served with homemade bread. There's also a choice of meat pies, including venison with red wine and herbs, or rabbit. For dessert, try the heather honey and malt-whisky cheesecake.

## KEITH

Keith, 11 miles (18km) northwest of Huntly, grew up because of its strategic location, where the main road and rail routes between Inverness and Aberdeen cross the River Isla. It has an ancient history, but owes its present look to the town planning of the late 18th and early 19th centuries. Today, it's a major stopover along the Malt Whisky Trail.

The oldest continuously operating distillery in the Scottish Highlands, the **Strathisla Distillery,** Seafield Avenue in Keith (☎ 01542/783-044), was established in 1786 and now operates as a proudly individualistic producer of single malts under the supervision of Chivas & Glenlivet (a division of Seagrams). February to mid-March, it's open Monday to Friday 9:30am to 4pm; mid-March to November 30, hours are Monday to Saturday 9:30am to 4pm and Sunday 12:30 to 4pm. Admission is £4 ($6.80) adults and free for ages 8 to 18; children 7 and under aren't admitted. The admission includes a £2 ($3.40) voucher redeemable in the distillery shop against a 70cl bottle of whisky. Be warned that tours of this distillery are self-guided.

## ROTHES

A Speyside town with five distilleries, Rothes is just to the south of the Glen of Rothes, 49 miles (79km) east of Inverness and 62 miles (100km) northwest of Aberdeen. Founded in 1766, the town is between Ben Aigan and Conerock Hill. A little settlement, the basis of the town today, grew up around **Rothes Castle,** ancient stronghold of the Leslie family, who lived here until 1622. Only a single massive wall of the castle remains.

The region's best distillery tours are offered by the **Glen Grant Distillery** (☎ 01542/783-318). Opened in 1840 by a hardworking and hard-drinking pair of brothers, James and John Grant, and now administered by the Chivas & Glenlivit Group (a division of Seagrams), it's half a mile (1km) north of Rothes, beside the Elgin-Perth (A941) highway and is clearly signposted. June to September, it's open Monday to Saturday 10am to 5pm and Sunday 11:30am to 5pm; mid-March to May 31 and October, hours are Monday to Saturday 10am to 4pm and Sunday 11:30am to 4pm. Admission is £2.50 ($4.25) adults and free for ages 8 to 18; children 7 and under aren't allowed. Visits include a whisky tasting and the opportunity to buy the brands whisky at a discount of £2 ($3.40) per bottle. Although the Grant family's nearby mansion was demolished in the early 1990s, the circa-1896 gardens once associated with the structure were revitalized and restored recently. The waterfall that functions as the centerpiece of the garden's upper region is worth a visit.

## ELGIN

The center of local government in the Moray district, an ancient royal burgh, the cathedral city of **Elgin** is on the Lossie River, 38 miles (61km) east of Inverness and 68 miles (109.5km) northwest of Aberdeen. The city's medieval plan has been retained, with "wynds" and "pends" connecting the main artery with other streets. The castle, as was customary in medieval town layouts, stood at one end of the main thoroughfare, with the cathedral—now a magnificent ruin—at the other. Nothing remains of the castle, but the site is a great place to take a scenic walk. Samuel Johnson and James Boswell came this way on their Highland tour and reported a "vile dinner" at the Red Lion Inn in 1773.

**Lady Hill** stands on High Street, opposite the post office. This is the hilltop location of what was once the royal castle of Elgin. Edward I of England stayed here in 1296 during the Wars of Independence. Only a fragment of the mighty castle now remains. **Birnie Kirk,** at Birnie, 3 miles (5km) south of Elgin and west of A941 to Rothes, was for a time the seat of a bishopric. It dates from about 1140, when it was constructed on the site of a much earlier church founded by St. Brendan. One of the few Norman churches in Scotland still in regular use, it's open daily 10am to 4pm.

On King Street is the ✪ **Elgin Cathedral** (☎ 01343/547-171), off North College Street near A96. Now in substantial ruins, it was once the "lantern of the north." The cathedral was founded in 1224 but destroyed in 1390 by the "wolf of Badenoch," the natural son of Robert II. After its destruction, the citizens of Elgin rebuilt their beloved cathedral and turned it into one of the most attractive and graceful buildings in Scotland; the architect's plan was that of a Jerusalem cross. However, when the central tower collapsed in 1711, the cathedral was allowed to fall into decay. Best preserved is the 13th-century chapter house. Admission is £2 ($3.40) adults, £1.50 ($2.55) seniors, and £1 ($1.70) children. April to September, it's open daily 9:30am to 6:30pm; October to March, hours are Monday to Wednesday and Saturday 9:30am to 4:30pm, Thursday 9:30am to 12:30pm, and Sunday 2 to 4:30pm.

After exploring Elgin, you can drive 6 miles (10km) southwest to **Pluscarden Abbey,** off B9010. This is one of the most beautiful drives in the area, through the bucolic Black Burn Valley where a priory was founded in 1230 by Alexander II. In 1494, the priory had come under Benedictine control. After long centuries of decline, a new order of Benedictines arrived in 1974 and re-established monastic life. You can visit restored transepts, monastic buildings, and the church choir. The admission is free to this active religious community, which is open daily 5am to 8:30pm.

If you're a fan of Scottish ruins, head for **Spynie Palace,** reached along A941 (and signposted). The former 15th-century headquarters of the bishops of Moray was used until 1573, when it was allowed to fall into ruins—for safety reasons, you can view them only from the outside. This is another great place for country walks, and from the top of a tower found here you'll have a magnificent vista over the Laigh of Moray. April to September, it's open daily 9:30am to 6pm; October to March, hours are Saturday 9:30am to 4pm and Sunday 2 to 4:30pm. Admission is £1.80 ($2.95). For more information, call ☎ 01343/546-358.

## ACCOMMODATIONS

**Mansion House Hotel.** The Haugh, Elgin IV30 IAW. ☎ **01343/548-811.** Fax 01343/547-916. 23 units. MINIBAR TV TEL. £120–£150 ($204–$255) double. Rates include Scottish breakfast. AE, DC, MC, V. Follow A96 onto Alexandra Rd. to the turnoff onto Haugh Rd.

The Mansion House is an elegantly appointed hotel, with the baronial proportions of the original design intact. It is at the edge of the River Lossie, about a quarter-mile (about .5km) from the center of Elgin. The guest rooms are standard, each with a radio alarm clock, hair dryer, and tea/coffeemaker; most have four-poster beds. The public rooms include a bistro, a lounge bar, and a dining room. The hotel has a country club with a pool, Jacuzzi, sauna, Turkish bath, and gym.

## DINING

**Abbey Court Restaurant.** 15 Greyfriars St. ☎ **01343/542-849.** Reservations recommended. Main courses £7.95–£16.95 ($13.50–$28.80). AE, DC, MC, V. Mon–Sat noon–2pm; Mon–Thur 6:30–9:30pm; Fri–Sat 6:30–10pm. SCOTTISH/ITALIAN.

Abbey Court, in the center of town behind the County Building, is an excellent restaurant decorated with stone- and earth-colored quarry tile, along with an artificial pergola, a separate bistro corner, and a more formal dining area in the rear with lots of plants. The fresh pasta is homemade and fresh fish delivered daily. Game is also a feature. The cooking is straightforward and unpretentious.

## ELGIN AFTER DARK

Linked historically to the Stewart clan as far back as 1715, **Thunderton House Pub,** Thunderton Place (☎ 01343/554-921), is an 11th-century building best known as the place where Bonnie Prince Charlie stayed for 10 days in 1746 on his way to Culloden. It's reported that his ghost still haunts the room in which he slept. Nowadays, the old pub, with a wood-and-brass bar, is a gathering place for locals who amuse themselves with karaoke on Thursday and Sunday. Occasionally a band is booked as well. The bar keeps Tennant's beers on tap, along with the local brewery Tomintouls real ale.

**Flanagan's,** 4 Shepherd's Close (☎ 01343/549-737), is a small dark bar with brick walls and old floorboards; it's a traditional Irish pub drawing a crowd for Irish and folk bands on weekends. On tap, you can choose from Caffrey's, Guinness, Tenant's Ember and Velvet, three great cask ales, and Scrumpy Jack for cider lovers.

**Cottarhouse,** Thornhill Road (☎ 01343/547-903), is composed of two ancient *cottar*'s (farm workers) cottages and has retained the original wood floors, stone fireplaces, and stone walls. Saturdays you can enjoy live traditional music while drinking the best pint of Guinness in Scotland. Also available are McEwan's 70 Shilling and 80 Shilling.

# FINDHORN

As you travel westward from Elgin to Forres, a turn to the right and then to the left will bring you to Findhorn, a tiny village that used to be a busy commercial fishing port and is today the home of the famous Findhorn Foundation (see below). Findhorn lies at the end of B9011, and a local bus from Forres stops here.

These days, the unique tidal bay at the mouth of the River Findhorn makes the village an ideal center for yacht racing, sailing, and windsurfing. Across the bay from Findhorn is the **Culbin Sands,** under which lies a buried village.

Just before Findhorn Village, you'll see the home of the **Findhorn Foundation,** The Park, Forres IV36 0TZ (☎ 01309/690-311), an international educational community founded in 1962 and based on spiritual principles and organic farming. It owns and runs the **Findhorn Bay Caravan Park** (☎ 01309/690-203) and the macrobiotically conscious **Phoenix Shop** (☎ 01309/690-110), where you can buy health foods, books, and craft items. Tours of the complex are offered in the morning Wednesday to Monday at 10am and every afternoon, April to September, at 2pm. The complex is unpretentious and includes good numbers of aluminum-sided buildings and trailers. But the organization's theories of interdenominational spiritual healing have won it much more fame than its simple setting would suggest. If you're interested in living in the Findhorn community for a while, working and studying, write to the address above or call ☎ 01309/673-655.

## ACCOMMODATIONS

**Crown & Anchor Inn.** Findhorn IV36 3YF. ☎ **01309/690-243.** Fax 01309/690-201. 8 units. TV. £50 ($85) double. Rates include Scottish breakfast. DC, MC, V. Free parking.

The Crown & Anchor dates from 1739, when it was constructed to cater to travelers making the run between Edinburgh and Inverness. On the seafront near the pier, bar snacks and meals are served daily, and fresh fish from both the sea and the local rivers is the house specialty. Locals drop in to enjoy the real ales and malt whiskies served in the bar. The small guest rooms are simply and modestly furnished but clean, each with a good bed.

# Inverness & the West Highlands

## 10

The romantic glens and rugged mountain landscapes of the West Highlands are timeless and pristine. You can see deer grazing only yards from the highway in remote parts and can stop by your own secluded loch to enjoy a picnic or to fish for trout and salmon. The shadow of Macbeth still stalks the land (locals will tell you this 11th-century king was much maligned by Shakespeare). The area's most famous resident, however, is said to live in mysterious Loch Ness: First sighted by St. Columba in the 6th century, "Nessie" has cleverly evaded searchers ever since.

Centuries of invasions, rebellions, and clan feuds are distant memories now. The Highlands aren't as remote as they once were, when many Londoners seriously believed the men of the Highlands had tails.

**Fort William** is a major center for the West Highlands, surrounded by wildly beautiful **Lochaber,** the "land of bens, glens, and heroes." Dominating the area is **Ben Nevis,** Britain's highest mountain. This district is the western end of what is known as the **Glen Mor**—the Great Glen, geologically a fissure dividing the northwest of Scotland from the southeast and containing Loch Lochy, Loch Oich, and Loch Ness. The Caledonian Canal, opened in 1847, linked these lochs, the River Ness, and Moray Firth. It provided sailing boats a safe alternative to the stormy route around the north of Scotland. Larger steamships made the canal out of date commercially, but fishing boats and pleasure steamers still use it. Good roads run the length of the Great Glen, partly following the line of Gen. George Wade's military road. The English general became famous for his road and bridge building in Scotland, which did much to open the Highlands to greater access from the south. From Fort William, you can take steamer trips to Staffa and Iona (see chapter 11, "The Hebridean Islands").

**Aviemore** and the villages and towns of the Spey Valley offer many activities for the visitor. In the Spey Valley you're at the doorway to the **Malt Whisky Trail** (see chapter 9, "Aberdeen & the Tayside & Grampian Regions"). Aviemore is the winter sports capital of Britain, and Aviemore Centre offers a multitude of outdoor pursuits: golfing, angling, skiing, and ice-skating.

**Inverness** and legendary **Loch Ness** are the most popular attractions of the West Highlands and overcrowded in summer, but they're surrounded by villages and towns that also make good centers, especially if you're driving. If you're dependent on public transportation, make Inverness your base, as it has good rail and bus connections to the rest of Scotland and also to England.

Finally, if you have the time to spare, you can extend your stay by visiting the loneliest part of Scotland, the far north. This section of the Highlands, **Sutherland** and **Caithness,** isn't for everyone. Crumbling watchtowers no longer stand guard over anything except the sheep-cropped wilderness. Moss-green glens give way to inland lochs and sea fords. Summer, of course, is the best time to view these deep-blue lochs, towering cliffs, and gentle glens. Many relics of Scotland's turbulent past dot the landscape, with castles left in ruins. Today visitors come to get away from it all and enjoy outdoor pursuits in a wild, pristine, remote setting. Potteries and craft centers have also sprung up, with artisans taking their inspiration from the setting and putting it to work in silversmithing, stone polishing, glassmaking, and most definitely weaving.

## Driving Through the Region

**Day 1**   Using **Fort William** as your gateway to the West Highlands, spend the morning exploring the town, then drive to **Glencoe** after lunch. Lying on the shores of Loch Leven, the glen was the scene of the famous massacre where the Campbells killed the MacDonalds. Return to Fort William for the night.

**Day 2**   Take A830 west to **Mallaig,** 47 miles (76km) northwest of Fort William, one of the most scenic drives in all Scotland. You can either spend the night in this small fishing village or return to Fort William for the night.

**Day 3**   Head for **Aviemore** by following A82 (later A86) northeast, passing through **Newtonmore** and **Kingussie;** either would make a good lunch stop. In the afternoon, view the attractions of this summer/winter resort and spend the night here.

**Day 4**   From Aviemore, retrace your trail along A86 back to the junction at Spean Bridge. Join A82 north here, which will take you along the western shores of **Loch Lochy** and then **Loch Oich.** At Fort Augustus, you can switch over to the left bank and take A82 along the western shores of fabled **Loch Ness** while maintaining a monster watch. At **Urquhart Castle** you'll have one of the best views of the loch, and at **Drumnadrochit** you can see an exhibit devoted to the sea beast. After a stopover, A82 will take you into **Inverness** for the night.

**Day 5**   Spend the morning exploring Inverness. In the afternoon, visit the seaside resort of **Nairn** by heading east along A96. You can also explore the most romantic castle in Scotland, **Cawdor Castle,** of *Macbeth* fame, lying between Inverness and Nairn on B9090. Return to Inverness for the night.

**Day 6**   Devote a day to exploring the **Black Isle,** west of Inverness, reached by A9. Plan an overnight stop in the region, perhaps at **Beauly.**

**Day 7**   Continue north along A9 to **Dornoch,** where you can explore Dunrobin Castle nearby and Dornoch Cathedral. Stay overnight at Dornoch.

**Day 8**   In the morning continue to explore the coastline of northwest Scotland, going all the way to **Wick,** where you can take a break before finishing your drive to **John o' Groats,** the most northerly point of the mainland, where you can spend the night.

**Day 9**   Continue driving west around the coast, taking A836 via **Tongue** (where you can have lunch). Dip south along A838, A894, A837, and A835 to **Ullapool** for 2 nights. On the second day, while based in **Ullapool,** you can take in as many of the scenic excursions in the environs as time will allow.

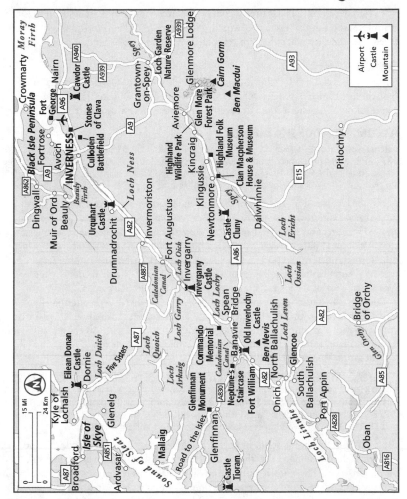

# 1 Around Loch Linnhe & Loch Leven

South of Fort William is one of the most historic sections of Scotland, a group of settlements around Loch Linnhe and Loch Leven (not the also-famous Loch Leven near Dunfermline). The best-known village is **Glencoe,** site of the famous 1692 massacre when the Campbells slaughtered the MacDonalds. Glencoe is the most dramatic glen in Scotland, austere in its beauty. Around both lochs are impressive landscapes and moorland, with flora and fauna unique to the western Highlands. Robert Louis Stevenson captured much of the essence of this moorland and wilderness in his novel *Kidnapped.*

The best all-round outfitter for all kinds of sports in the region near Fort William is **Alfresco Adventure,** Onich (☎ **01855/821-248**). Nick and Angie Scott will rent motorboats, canoes, sailboats, fishing tackle, and more; they're a great source of advice for enjoying the great Highland outdoors. They also offer guided hill walks at £20 ($34) per person for half a day; and guided canoe trips at £40 ($68) per person for a full day.

As for interesting half-day drives, consider an excursion from Fort William to Oban. An interesting full-day excursion would go from Fort William to the Isle of Skye or (even more densely scheduled) from Oban to Mull and on to Iona.

# ONICH

On the shores of Loch Linnhe, the charming little village of Onich lies to the north of Ballachulish Bridge, 9 miles (14.5km) southwest of Fort William. It's a good center if you're taking the western route to Inverness or going to Skye and Fort William.

## ACCOMMODATIONS & DINING

**Allt-nan-Ros Hotel.** Onich, by Fort William PH33 6RY. ☎ **0185/582-1210.** Fax 0185/ 582-1462. www.taste-of-scotland.com/allt-nan-ros-hotel.html. E-mail: allt-nan-ros@zetnet. co.uk. 20 units. TV TEL. £100–£112 ($170–$190.40) double. Rates include breakfast. AE, DC, MC, V. From Fort William, drive 10 miles (16km) south along A82.

Across the highway from the edge of the loch and boasting dozens of elaborate gables and interesting architectural touches, Allt-nan-Ros was built around 1885 as a hunting lodge and weekend getaway for an industrialist. Today, this much enlarged place with relatively recent additions built onto either side offers comfortable guest rooms and a well-managed dining room open to the public. The rooms have dark mahogany furniture and floral-patterned curtains and upholsteries in a style echoing an Edwardian country house, and most offer views of the loch or the stream running through the garden.

**Dining:** The rather expensive meals are a highlight here, with offerings like West Coast lemon sole with herb-flavored risotto and tarragon-flavored sabayon, breast of guinea fowl carved onto a galette of pearl barley and served with sweet lime sauce, and dark-chocolate truffle torte with homemade cinnamon ice cream.

**Amenities:** Room service, baby-sitting.

**Creag Dhu (The Lodge on the Loch).** Creag Dhu, Onich PH33 6RY. ☎ **01855/821-237.** Fax 01855/821463. 18 units, 16 with private bathroom. TV TEL. £91 ($154.70) double without bathroom; £146–£166 ($248.20–$282.20) double with bathroom; £160–£200 ($272–$340) superior double. Rates include half-board. MC, V. Closed Jan 5 to mid-Mar and mid-Nov to Dec 25. Drive 9 miles (14.5km) south to Fort William on A82.

Built in 1860, this house south of Fort William between Ben Nevis and Glencoe, was transformed into a hotel by the Young family. It boasts expansive lochside and mountain views. The midsize guest rooms have hair dryers, trouser presses, excellent mattresses, and tea/coffeemakers. Boating, sailing, water-skiing, and diving are available nearby, along with good sea- and freshwater fishing, pony trekking, riding, golfing, swimming, and tennis.

**Dining:** The kitchen offers traditional Scottish dishes, among other fare. Lunches are affordable bar meals, while dinners are more formal and expensive.

**Amenities:** Rates include complimentary use of the pool, sauna, steam room, gym, and Jacuzzi at the nearby Creag Dhu sibling hotel, Isles of Glencoe. Massage can also be booked there.

**The Lodge on the Loch Hotel.** Onich, by Fort William PH33 6RY. ☎ **0185/582-1237.** Fax 0185/582-1238. www.freedomglen.co.uk. E-mail: reservations@freedomglen.co.uk. 19 units, 17 with private bathroom. TV TEL. £111–£122 ($188.70–$207.40) double. Rates include breakfast. MC, V. Closed Nov–Mar. From Fort William, drive 15 miles (24km) south of town, following A82 and the signs to Glasgow.

Between the edge of the loch and a semi-forested rocky ridge, this granite hotel began late in the 19th century as a home. Today only a handful of the guest rooms (with high ceilings) are in the mansion's core; most are in a bulky-looking extension added in the 1960s but are just as comfortable as the other rooms, with a mix of conservative and traditional furnishings. The most expensive rooms have plush extras like CD players, bathrobes, and Jacuzzi baths. The two singles have no private bathrooms. If the hotel is full, there are two other choices, under the same management, within a short drive. Complimentary tea, coffee, sherry, and homemade shortbread are always out in the lobby.

**Dining:** The restaurant is one of the big draws, serving an expensive set-price dinner that features all-Scottish produce in dishes like Angus beef fillet with red-wine sauce, calf's liver with bacon and onions, and many preparations of salmon, trout, and pheasant. There's also a cocktail bar with a log fire and a fine selection of whiskies.

**Amenities:** Rates include complimentary use of the pool, sauna, steam room, gym, and Jacuzzi at the nearby Creag Dhu sibling hotel, Isles of Glencoe, which is a 5-minute drive away. Massage can also be booked there.

## GLENCOE: SCENERY & SORROW

Near the spot where Loch Leven joins Loch Linnhe, **Ballachulish Bridge** links the villages of North and South Ballachulish at the entrance to Glencoe. The bridge saves a long drive to the head of the loch if you're coming from the north, but the scenic drive to Kinlochleven lets you come on the celebrated wild Glencoe from the east. Glencoe runs from Rannoch Moor to Loch Leven between majestic mountains, including 3,766-foot (1,142m) **Bidean nam Bian.** This is an area of massive splendor, with towering peaks and mysterious glens where you can well imagine the fierce battle among the kilted Highlanders to the skirl of the pipes and the beat of the drums.

Known as the "Glen of Weeping," Glencoe is the place where, on February 11, 1692, the Campbells massacred the MacDonalds—men, women, and children—who'd been their hosts for 12 days. Although mass killings weren't uncommon in those times, this one shocked even the Highlanders because it was a breach of hospitality. The **Monument to the Massacre of Glencoe** at Carnoch was erected by the chief of the MacDonald clan. After the incident, the crime of "murder under trust" was introduced into Scottish law as an aggravated form of murder that carried the same penalty as treason.

The glen, much of which now belongs to the National Trust for Scotland, is full of legend. A tiny lochan is known as the "pool of blood" because by its side some men are said to have quarreled over a piece of cheese and killed each other.

**Glen Orchy,** to the south, is well worth a visit too, for the wild river and photogenic mountain scenery. It was the birthplace of Gaelic bard Duncan Ban MacIntyre, whose masterpiece is the song "In Praise of Ben Doran."

This is great country for hiking and bike rides. In Glencoe village, go to the **Mountain Bike Hire** at the Clachaig Inn (☎ **01855/811-252**), where you can not only rent a bike but also get advice about scenic routes that suit your available time and your ability. The cost is £8.50 ($14.45) per half day or £12.50 ($21.25) per day.

### ACCOMMODATIONS & DINING

You can also choose to base yourself in Fort William (see "Fort William: Gateway to Ben Nevis," below) and explore the Glencoe area on day trips.

✪ **Ballachulish Hotel.** Ballachulish PA39 4JX. ☎ **0185/582-1237.** Fax 01855/821-463. 56 units. TV TEL. £155–£175 ($263.50–$297.50) double. Rates include dinner and breakfast. MC, V. Closed Jan. Drive west of Ballachulish for 2½ miles (4km), following A82 until it intersects with A828. Follow the signs to Ballachulish House.

This elegant country mansion was burned down in the early 1700s because of the association of its owners with the doomed Stuarts. It was rebuilt in 1764 and retains its lime-washed original stone form, even though it was tastefully expanded in 1997. Your hosts are John and Liz Grey and their son, Seumas. The family has spent enormous sums renovating the place since they bought it in 1989, and since then have hosted the occasional celebrity and government official. The good-sized guest rooms have flowered wallpaper and a mix of old and new furniture, and each has a view of the loch or forest. There's a billiard room and ample opportunities for long walks beside the loch (sometimes one or two of the owners' dogs will join you).

**Dining:** Dinner is a treat here, making use of fresh ingredients and careful preparation. Menu items may include prawn cakes with guacamole, spinach and cream cheese crêpes, tomato-mint soup, venison in green-pepper sauce, poached salmon with watercress sauce, and a daily pudding that might be fresh lime tart or apple-flavored sorbet. Nonguests who phone ahead can sometimes visit for dinner. Prices are on the expensive side.

**Amenities:** Room service, pool table, special facilities for children, complimentary membership in leisure club.

**Clachaig Inn.** Glencoe, Ballachulish PA39 4HX. ☎ **01855/811-252.** Fax 01855/811-679. 19 units, 16 with private bathroom. TV TEL. £60–£84 ($102–$142.80) double with bathroom. Rates include Scottish breakfast. MC, V.

After the bleakness of Glencoe, the trees ringing this place make it seem like an oasis. It's the only hotel in the glen (look for the signs on the highway), on the site where the massacre took place, reached by a winding gravel-covered road off the main highway. The Daynes family offers Highland hospitality, good food, and an excellent selection of British ales. They rent some contemporary chalets in the back garden, plus several small to midsize guest rooms in the main house. The furnishings are basic and simple, and some singles are without bathrooms. Live folk music now brings the place alive on Saturday and Wednesday nights.

**King's House Hotel.** Glencoe PA39 4HZ. ☎ **01855/851-259.** Fax 01855/851-216. 22 units, 12 with private bathroom. TEL. £48 ($81.60) double without bathroom; £54 ($91.80) double with bathroom. MC, V. You can arrange to be met at the Bridge of Orchy rail station.

The solid walls of this historic inn were built in the 1600s on a windswept plateau beside A82, 12 miles (19km) southeast of Glencoe village, at the strategic point where Glencoe joins the Glen Etive near a jagged mountain, Buachaille Etive Mor. This is one of Scotland's oldest licensed inns, although modernization has changed its interior. Most of the modestly but comfortably furnished guest rooms offer sweeping views of majestic scenery. Simple meals are served in the bar; the dining room boasts a selection of fine wines and freshly prepared meals. The hotel is near a ski center with a ski lift, a 30-minute walk from its entrance.

## 2 Fort William: Gateway to Ben Nevis

133 miles (214km) NW of Edinburgh, 68 miles (109.5km) S of Inverness, 104 miles (167.5km) N of Glasgow

Fort William, on the shores of Loch Linnhe, is the best place for an overnight stop between here and Inverness in the northeast. It's a good base for exploring **Ben Nevis,** Scotland's highest mountain, and also for a day trip to Glencoe (see above).

Fort William stands on the site of a fort built by General Monk in 1655 to help crush any rebellion Highlanders might have been plotting. After several reconstructions, it was finally torn down in 1864 to make way for the railroad. During the notorious Highland Clearances, many starving and evicted people were shipped from here to America. Today Fort William is a bustling town, thriving very well on the summer tourist trade and filled with shops, hotels, and cafes.

## ESSENTIALS

**GETTING THERE**   Fort William is a major stop on the West Highland rail line that begins at the Queen Street Station in Glasgow and ends at Mallaig on the west coast. Three trains a day run this route at a one-way cost of £15 ($25.50). For schedules, contact the tourist office (see below) or call ☎ **01463/239-026** in Inverness.

Four buses run from Glasgow to Fort William per day, taking 3 hours and costing £10.50 ($17.85) one way. Call the Buchanan Bus Station at ☎ **0141/332-7133** in Glasgow for schedules.

If you're driving from Glasgow, head north along A82.

**VISITOR INFORMATION**   The **tourist office** is at Cameron Centre, Cameron Square (☎ **01397/703-781**). April and May, it's open Monday to Saturday 9am to 5pm and Sunday 10am to 4pm; June to mid-July, hours are Monday to Saturday 9am to 6pm and Sunday 10am to 5pm; mid-July to August, hours are Monday to Saturday 9am to 8:30pm and Sunday 9am to 6pm; September and October, it's open Monday to Saturday 9am to 6pm and Sunday 10am to 5pm; and November to March, hours are Monday to Friday 9am to 5pm and Saturday 10am to 4pm.

## EXPLORING THE AREA

You can reach the ruins of **Old Inverlochy Castle,** scene of a famous battle, by driving 2 miles (3km) north of Fort William on A82. Built in the 13th century, the ruined castle still has round corner towers and a walled courtyard. One of the towers was the keep, the other a water gate. The castle looms in the pages of Scottish history—here in 1645 a small army of Scots defeated government forces, although 1,500 men were lost that day. The former castle was once the stronghold of a clan known as the Comyns, and Inverlochy was the scene of many a battle.

**Neptune's Staircase,** 3 miles (5km) northwest of Fort William off A830 at Banavie, is a series of nine locks that were constructed at the same time as the Caledonian Canal, raising Telford's canal 64 feet (19.5m). This "staircase" is one of Scotland's most prominent engineering triumphs of the mid–19th century, when the eastern seacoast at Inverness was connected, via the canal, to the western seacoast at Fort William. This greatly shortened the distance required for goods moving from the North Sea to the Atlantic Ocean and bypassed the treacherous storms that often rage around Scotland's northern tier.

Since much of Fort William is relatively flat, consider biking. The best rentals are at **Off Beat Bikes,** 117 High St. (☎ **01397/704-008**), costing £8.50 to £10 ($14.45 to $17) for a half day, £12.50 to £15 ($21.25 to $25.50) for a full day. You need only your ID for the deposit. It's open Monday to Saturday 9am to 5:30pm and Sunday 9:30am to 5pm.

In the north end of town, the **Ben Nevis Woolen Mill,** Belford Road (☎ **01397/ 704-244**), is only a shop, not a functioning woolen mill. Here you'll find a large selection of clothing and accessories: wools, tweeds, tartans, and some handknit Arran sweaters. An on-premises restaurant features regional fare.

Shoppers might also want to check out the **Granite House,** High Street (☎ **01397/703-651**), a family-run business that has been around for a quarter of a century. The owners call themselves "giftmongers" and see their shop as a mini-department store. There's a large selection of Scottish jewelry, with silver pieces in both traditional and contemporary designs and numerous watches. Collectibles like Royal

Doulton and Lilliput Lane china and crystal by Edinburgh, Wedgwood, and Border Fine Arts are found here, and the traditional music department offers more than 1,000 Irish and Scottish music CDs and an array of traditional instruments, including penny-whistles and the *bhodrain* (a large drum struck with a single stick using both ends). **Scottish Crafts & Whisky Centre,** 135–139 High St. (☎ **01397/704-406**), is another place with a good mix of the best of all things Scottish: regionally produced jewelry, garden fountains, rugs, and clothing. Whisky connoisseurs will find some limited-edition and very rare bottles stocked, including a 1958 Ben Nevis. Handmade chocolates by Fergusons are also available. **Treasures of the Earth,** Main Street, Corpach (☎ **01397/772-283**), 4 miles (6.5km) west of Fort William along A830, sells crystals, minerals, and polished stones from around the world. They are available loose or set in jewelry, watches, and clocks.

**West Highland Museum.** Cameron Sq. ☎ **01397/702-169.** Admission £2 ($3.40) adults, £1.50 ($2.55) seniors, 50p (85¢) children. June–Sept Mon–Sat 10am–5pm (July–Aug also Sun 2–5pm); Oct–May Mon–Sat 10am–4pm.

The collection in this museum sheds light on all aspects of local history, especially the 1745 Jacobite Rising; it also has sections on tartans and folk life. It is in the center of town next to the tourist office.

**Glenfinnan Monument.** About 14 miles (22.5km) west of Fort William, on A830 toward Mallaig. ☎ **01397/722-250** for visitor center. Admission to visitor center £1.50 ($2.55). Visitor center mid-May to Aug daily 9:30am–6pm; Sept–early May daily 10am–5pm.

At Glenfinnan at the head of Loch Shiel, this monument marks the spot where Bonnie Prince Charlie unfurled his proud red-and-white silk banner on August 19, 1745, in his ill-fated attempt to restore the Stuarts to the British throne. The figure of a kilted Highlander tops the monument. At the visitor center, you can learn of the prince's campaign from Glenfinnan to Derby that ended in his defeat at Culloden.

## ACCOMMODATIONS

There's no shortage of B&Bs in Fort William, most with a good view of Loch Linnhe or Ben Nevis. The tourist office can supply you with a list if the selections below don't suit you or are full.

### VERY EXPENSIVE

✪ **Inverlochy Castle.** Torlundy, Fort William PH33 6SN. ☎ **01397/702-177.** Fax 01397/702-953. 17 units. TV TEL. £290–£380 ($493–$646) double; from £390–£480 ($663–$816) suite. Rates include Scottish breakfast. AE, MC, V. Closed early Jan–late Feb. Free valet parking. Take A82 for 3 miles (5km) northeast of town.

Inverlochy Castle, against the scenic backdrop of Ben Nevis, hosted Queen Victoria in her day. Back then, it was a newly built (1870) Scottish mansion belonging to Baron Abinger. The monarch claimed in her diary, "I never saw a lovelier or more romantic spot." Now a Relais & Châteaux hotel, the Inverlochy has recently undergone a major refurbishment but has retained its charm as well as its large, friendly staff. Luxurious appointments, antiques, artwork, and crystal, plus a profusion of flowers, create a mood of elegance and refinement. The prices certainly reflect this opulence.

**Dining:** The cuisine here is some of the finest in Scotland, with food cooked to order and served on silver platters. Salmon from the Spean, crayfish from Loch Linnhe, and produce from the hotel's own farm garden are part of the fare; partridge and grouse are offered in season. Jackets and ties are required, and no smoking is permitted in the dining room. Nonguests can dine here if there's room, but reservations are mandatory. Lunch and dinner are served daily.

# Climbing Britain's Tallest Mountain

In the Central Highlands, **Ben Nevis,** at 4,406 feet (1,336.5m), is the tallest mountain in Britain. Although it's not exactly ready to challenge the towering Alps, Ben Nevis can still give hikers a good workout. The pony track to the top is often filled with walkers tackling the difficult 8-hour jaunt. The unpredictable Scottish weather adds to the challenge, requiring you to dress in layers and bring along at least a waterproof jacket. The mean monthly temperature of Ben Nevis falls below freezing; snow has been reported at all times of year, even during the hottest months of July and August. Howling winds are frequent.

Hikers head up for the view, but it's not guaranteed because of weather conditions. On a clear day, you can see the Irish foothills some 120 miles (193km) away, the Hebridean Isle of Rhum 92 miles (148km) away, and the Glencoe peaks (Ben Lawers, Torridon, and the Cairngorms). (If you don't want to climb, a cable car can take to a height of 2,300 feet (698m) for viewing.)

The trail is much rougher but even more beautiful if approached from Glen Nevis, one of the country's most scenic glens. Clear rivers and cascading waterfalls add to the drama of the scenery; meadows and moors seem straight out of Austria.

Before going, discuss the climb with the tourist office in Fort William. The staff can give you advice as well as maps of the area, and they'll pinpoint the best starting places. A signpost to the north of Nevis Bridge points to the path up Ben Nevis. Allow 8½ hours total for the under-10-mile (16km) trip. Take along a windbreaker, sturdy footwear, food, and water.

*A word of warning:* Sudden weather changes may pose a safety hazard. And that final 1,000 feet (303m) is really steep terrain, but having gone this far, few can fail the challenge. Some Brits call Ben Nevis the "top of the world." It really isn't. It just feels that way when you finally reach the peak.

---

**Amenities:** Concierge, 24-hour room service, baby-sitting, laundry, tennis, game fishing.

## MODERATE

**Alexandra.** The Parade, Fort William PH33 6AZ. ☎ **01397/702-241.** Fax 01397/705-554. 97 units. TV TEL. £95–£115 ($161.50–$195.50) double. Rates include Scottish breakfast. AE, DC, MC, V.

Across from the rail terminal, the Alexandra boasts the tall gables and formidable granite walls so common in this part of the Highlands. It has been completely modernized, offering pleasant and comfortably furnished guest rooms with tea/coffeemakers. The service and housekeeping standards are good. There are two restaurants and a lounge bar on the premises. The chef makes excellent use of fresh fish, and the wine cellar is amply endowed. The vegetables are simply cooked with enjoyable results. You have free use of all the facilities at the nearby Milton Hotel and Leisure Club.

**The Moorings Hotel.** Banavie, Fort William PH33 7LY. ☎ **01397/772-797.** Fax 01397/ 772-441. 21 units. TV TEL. £68–£92 ($115.60–$156.40) double. Rates include Scottish breakfast. AE, DC, MC, V. Drive 3 miles (5km) north of Fort William to the hamlet of Banavie, beside B8004.

One of the most up-to-date hotels in the region, the Moorings was designed in a traditional style in the mid-1970s, with bay and dormer windows and a black-and-white facade. The interior is richly paneled in the Jacobean style. The guest rooms, most of which have undergone recent redecoration, are attractive and modern. Bar lunches and suppers are served in the Mariner Wine Bar, which offers 40 kinds of wine from around the world. More formal meals are served in the Moorings Restaurant, where an even greater selection of wine (more than 200 vintages) accompanies dishes like smoked venison, Scottish oysters, homemade terrines, cullen skink (traditional smoked-haddock soup), wild salmon in lemon-butter sauce, and halibut in wild-mushroom sauce.

## INEXPENSIVE

**Croit Anna Hotel.** Druimarbin, Fort William PH33 6RR. ☎ **01397/702-268.** Fax 01397/704-099. 92 units, 80 with private bathroom. TV. £32–£36 ($54.40–$61.20) double without bathroom, £60–£93 ($102–$158.10) double with bathroom. Rates include Scottish breakfast. MC, V. Closed Nov–Mar. Take A82 for 2½ miles (4km) south of town.

Overlooking Loch Linnhe, the hotel has fine views of the Ardgour Hills and is owned/managed by the same family who built it on a traditional Highland croft that has been in their possession for more than 250 years. All the midsize guest rooms have tea/coffeemakers, and most have hair dryers. Facilities include a dining room, a games room, a lounge with panoramic views, a gift shop, and a launderette. Entertainment is provided on most evenings in season.

**Lime Tree Studio Gallery.** Achintore Rd., Fort William PH33 6RQ. ☎ **01397/701-806.** www.limetreestudio.co.uk/accom.htm. E-mail: limetree.studio@btinternet.com. 5 units, 3 with private bathroom. TV. £25–£30 ($42.50–$51) double without bathroom; £32–£40 ($54.40–$68) double with bathroom. AE, DC, MC, V.

The premises of this B&B are reputed to be the oldest fully surviving building in Fort William. In the town center, it was built in the early 1800s as the stone manse (pastor's residence) for the nearby Church of Scotland. Today, it's a well-kept B&B, with pastel guest rooms and a portion of its interior devoted to exhibition space for local painters, including well-respected local artist David Wilson, and assorted stained-glass artisans. Dinner can be prepared, if advance notice is given.

**Lochview Guest House.** Heathercroft, Argyll Rd., Fort William PH33 6RE. ☎/fax **01397/703-149.** www.lochaber.com/accommodations/B&B/lochview/lochtariff.htm. E-mail: dkirk@lochaber.almac.co.uk. 8 units. TV TEL. £44–£50 ($74.80–$85) double. Rates include breakfast. MC, V. Closed Nov–Mar.

South from the center of Fort William and about a 15-minute walk uphill is this guesthouse, designed around 1950. The guest rooms are outfitted with comfortable furnishings by Denise and Alan Kirk, who maintain the acre of lawn surrounding their building and protect the view sweeping down over the loch and the rest of the town. Other guesthouses in town might be older, more historic, and with more dignified architecture—but for the price, Lochview represents good value, and the Kirk family are unfailingly generous. No smoking.

## DINING

**Crannog Seafood Restaurant.** Town Pier. ☎ **01397/705-589.** Reservations recommended. Main courses £9.95–£18 ($16.90–$30.60). MC, V. Daily noon–2:30pm and 6–9:30pm. Closed Jan 1–2 and Dec 25–26. SEAFOOD.

Occupying a converted ticket office and bait store in a quayside setting overlooking Loche Linnhe, this restaurant serves seafood so fresh locals claim "it fairly leaps at you." Much of the fish comes from the owners' own fishing vessels or from their own smokehouse, which turns out smoked salmon, mussels, and trout. Bouillabaisse is a chef's specialty, as are Loch Linnhe prawns and langoustines. A vegetarian dish of the day is invariably featured. Look for the daily specials listed on the chalkboard.

**✪ Inverlochy Castle.** Torlundy, Fort William PH33 6SN. ☎ **01397/702-177.** Reservations required. Set-price lunch £28.90 ($49.15); set-price dinner £45 ($76.50). AE, MC, V. Daily 12:30–1:45pm and 7–9:15pm. Closed Jan–Feb. BRITISH.

This is one of the grandest restaurants in Britain (as it should be, at these prices!). The cuisine here has been celebrated ever since Queen Victoria got a sudden attack of the munchies and stopped in "for a good tuck-in." The food, we can only assume, is even better than in her day. You'll dine nowhere better in all of Scotland; your meal will be cooked to order and served on silver platters. The kitchen uses carefully selected local ingredients, including salmon from Spean, crayfish form Loch Linnhe, and produce from the hotel's own farm gardens. Partridge and grouse are offered in season, and roast fillet of Aberdeen angus beef is a classic. The set-price menu has a well-balanced choice, and everything is seasonally adjusted. Some of the finest dishes, served month after month, include a ballotine of foie gras, given added depth and flavor by a lightly smoked apple purée and dried, pungent slices of apple on the side. The chefs also do their own baking, and their specialty, an orange soufflé, may be the best we've ever tasted. Dinner is served in any of three dining rooms, each decorated with period and elaborate furniture presented as gifts to Inverlochy Castle from the king of Norway. The formal service is the finest in the Highlands.

## FORT WILLIAM AFTER DARK

**Ben Nevis Pub,** 103–109 High St. (☎ 01397/702-295), offers free entertainment by rock, blues, jazz, and folk bands on Thursday and Friday. On tap are McEwan's, Foster's, and Kronenberg lagers, McEwan's 70 Shilling, and Guinness and Gillespie's stouts.

   **McTavish's Kitchen,** High Street (☎ 01397/702-406), presents a Scottish show just for tourists. It's fun but corny, featuring tartan-clad dancers, bagpipes, and other traditional instruments every night May to September at 8:30pm. You can see the show with or without dinner. A three-course "Taste of Scotland" meal costs £14.95 ($25.40). On tap is Tennant's Special and Lager, available for £2.35 ($4) per pint. Admission to the show is £1.75 ($3) adults and £1 ($1.70) children if you're eating; the show only is £3.50 ($5.95) adults and £1.75 ($3) children.

   **Grog & Gruel,** 66 High St. (☎ 01397/705-078), serves up regional cask-conditioned ales like Arrol's 80 Shilling. There's an occasional live band on Thursday, ranging from rock and pop to folk and Scottish music.

## 3 Mallaig: Gateway to the Isle of Skye & the Hebrides

179 miles (288km) NW of Edinburgh, 47 miles (76km) NW of Fort William, 96 miles (154.5km) NW of Oban

People visit the small fishing village of Mallaig mainly because it's the departure point for the Isle of Skye (see chapter 11). Most of the fun of Mallaig is getting there, as the road from Fort William to Mallaig is one of the more scenic in Scotland. Steamers call here for the Kyle of Lochalsh, the Isle of Skye, the Outer Hebrides, and the sea lochs of the northwest coast. At the tip of a peninsula, Mallaig is surrounded by moody lochs and hills.

## ESSENTIALS

**GETTING THERE**    Trains from Fort William to Mallaig take you along one of the most panoramic routes in Scotland; the trip is a marvelous experience in and of itself. Four trains per day make the 1½- to 2-hour run; service drops to one train on Sunday over the winter. A one-way ticket costs £7.40 ($12.60). Call ☎ **0345/550-033** for departure times.

Two buses per day run to Mallaig from Fort William (a 90-minute trip); a one-way ticket is £4.80 ($8.15). Call **Sheil Buses** (☎ **01967/431-272**) for departures.

Driving from Fort William, take A830, the scenic road, west to Mallaig.

**VISITOR INFORMATION**    A **tourist office** (☎ 01687/462-170) is in the center of Mallaig, on Main Street; look for the signs. April to June, September, and October, it's open Monday to Saturday 10am to 6:30pm and Sunday 10am to 4pm; July and August hours are Monday to Saturday 9am to 8pm and Sunday 10am to 5pm; November to March, it's open Monday, Wednesday, and Friday 10am to 2pm.

## EXPLORING THE AREA

If you find yourself in Mallaig with time to spare while waiting for a ferry departure, you can visit **Mallaig Marine World,** at the Harbour (☎ 01687/462-292), which has the finest collection of sea creatures from the Sound of Sleat. Some of the exhibits relate to fishing in the area, a long tradition with the locals. It's open daily in May 9:30am to 5:30pm and June to August 9:30am to 9pm. Admission is £2.75 ($4.70).

If you have a lot more time, you can see what the current offerings are at **Bruce Watt Sea Cruises,** Western Isles Guest House (☎ 01687/462-320). This outfitter conducts cruises up the Sound of Sleat, the body of water separating the Isle of Skye from the Scottish mainland. If you go on one of these cruises, you'll also enjoy panoramic vistas of the lochs Hourn and Nevis.

If you're driving, you can take an unmarked road immediately south of Mallaig, going to the remote **Loch Morar,** at some 1,000 feet (303m) known as the deepest lake in the country. This is one of the remotest parts of the Highlands and would make for a lovely walk.

## ACCOMMODATIONS & DINING

**Marine Hotel.** 10 Station Rd., Mallaig PH41 4PY. ☎ **01687/462-217.** Fax 01687/462-821. 19 units. TV. £52–£70 ($88.40–$119) double. Rates include Scottish breakfast. Half-board £44–£48 ($74.80–$81.60) per person. MC, V.

This family-owned business is in the vicinity of the train station. All the comfortably furnished but basic guest rooms are heated and contain firm beds, tea/coffeemakers, and hair dryers. Guests gather in the cocktail bar or TV lounge after enjoying a home-cooked meal, usually locally caught seafood. The Marine stays open all year.

**Springbank Guest House.** East Bay, Mallaig PH41 4QF. ☎/fax **01687/462-459.** 7 units, none with private bathroom. £32 ($54.40) double. Rates include breakfast. MC, V.

On the eastern outskirts of town, across the coastal road from the harbor, this white-painted stone house was built around 1900. Later, a big-windowed wing was added, and it's now site of the comfortable guest lounge. Views from the simple, somewhat spartan, but well-scrubbed guest rooms encompass the coastline of Skye; each has a tea/coffeemaker, and some have a sloping garret-style ceiling. Your hosts are members of the Smith family, who enjoy socializing at breakfast and will prepare a moderately priced dinner on request.

## 4 Invergarry

25 miles (40km) NE of Fort William, 158 (254km) miles NW of Edinburgh

A Highland center for fishing and for exploring Glen Mor and Loch Ness, Invergarry is noted for its fine scenery. At Invergarry the road through the western Highland glens and mountains begins, forming one part of the famous "Road to the Isles" that terminates at Kyle of Lochalsh. If you're rushed for time, you can easily skip this place. Most people stop off here to stay at the Glengarry Castle Hotel, which looks haunted and even has the ruins of a long-abandoned castle on its grounds.

## ESSENTIALS

**GETTING THERE**   The nearest **rail service** runs to Fort William, where you'll have to take a connecting bus to get to Invergarry, a half-hour ride away. Highland Omnibuses offer this service. There's a bus station to go to for information in Fort William, so the tourist office there can provide a list of schedules (see "Fort William: Gateway to Ben Nevis," above).

If you're driving from Fort William, proceed north on the Inverness road (A82) to Invergarry.

**VISITOR INFORMATION**   The nearest **tourist office** is in Fort William (see "Fort William: Gateway to Ben Nevis," above).

## SEEING THE SIGHTS

From Invergarry, drive 3½ miles (5.5km) south, following A82 toward Fort William if you want to visit the 1812 monument **Well of the Heads** (*Tobar nan Ceann* in Gaelic). The only sign indicating the well's position is a grocery store (Well of the Seven Heads Grocery & Convenience Mart). At the store, a staff member will direct you down a short forest path to the well itself. The well was erected by MacDonnell of Glengarry to commemorate the decapitation of seven brothers who had murdered the two sons of a 17th-century chief of Clan Keppoch, a branch of the MacDonnell clan. The seven heads were washed in the well before being presented to the chief of the MacDonnells at Glengarry. An obelisk supports the bronzed heads of the seven victims. A dirk through their hair holds the heads together. The legend of the well, alas, is more exciting than the actual site.

On the grounds of Glengarry Castle Hotel (see below), you can see the meager ruins of **Invergarry Castle,** the stronghold of the MacDonnells of Glengarry. A few grim walls remain. The site of the castle on Raven's Rock, overlooking Loch Oich in the Great Glen, was a strategic one in the days of clan feuds and Jacobite risings. Because the castle ruins aren't safe, you can view them only from outside. From Invergarry, drive 1½ miles (2.5km) south, following A82 toward Fort William, then turn off to follow the signs pointing to the hotel. The ruins lie beside the hotel's very long main driveway, surrounded by trees.

## ACCOMMODATIONS & DINING

**Glengarry Castle Hotel.** Invergarry PH35 4HW. ☎ **01809/501-254.** Fax 01809/501-207. www.glengarry.net. 26 units. TV TEL. £78–£136 ($132.60–$231.20) double. Rates include Scottish breakfast. MC, V. From Invergarry, drive 1½ miles (2.5km) south, following A82 toward Fort William, then turn off to follow the signs pointing to the hotel.

This 1866–69 mansion, with gables and chimneys, is an impressive sight on the River Garry; on the extensive grounds are the ruins of Invergarry Castle (above). Glengarry makes a pleasant base for fishing, tennis, walking, and rowing. The midsize to spacious guest rooms are comfortably old-fashioned, like something from the 1950s. There are two lounges where drinks are served, and the dining room offers good home-cooked but rather basic meals made from local produce. Affordable light lunches are served, but the special Sunday version is more elaborate and expensive. Nightly fixed-price dinners are rather high-priced.

## 5  Aviemore

129 miles (208km) N of Edinburgh, 29 miles (47km) SE of Inverness, 85 miles (137km) N of Perth

A bit tacky for our tastes, Aviemore, a year-round resort on the Spey, was opened in 1966 in the heart of the Highlands, at the foot of the historic rock of **Craigellachie.** The center of Aviemore itself, with ugly concrete structures, has little of the flavor of Scotland. But visitors flock here not for Aviemore itself—they come because of its accessibility to some of the most beautiful scenery in the Highlands, especially the Cairngorm Mountains, known for their skiing in winter or hiking in summer.

### ESSENTIALS

**GETTING THERE**   Aviemore, on the main Inverness–Edinburgh rail line, is the area's major transportation hub. For rail schedules in Aviemore, call ☎ **01479/ 810-221.** Some 12 trains a day from Inverness pass through (trip time: 45 min.), at £9 ($15.30) one way. Twelve trains per day also arrive from Glasgow or Edinburgh. Trip time from each city is 3 hours, and a one-way ticket from either is £28 ($47.60).

Aviemore is on the main Inverness–Edinburgh bus line, with frequent service. The trip from Edinburgh takes about 3 hours (call ☎ **0990/808-080** in Edinburgh for schedules) and costs £4.20 ($7.15). Frequent buses throughout the day also arrive from Inverness (trip time: 40 min.).

If you're driving from Edinburgh, after crossing the Forth Bridge Road, take M90 to Perth, then continue the rest of the way along A9 into Aviemore.

**VISITOR INFORMATION**   The **Highlands of Scotland Tourist Office** (Aviemore branch) is on Grampian Road (☎ **01479/810-363**). June to August, it's open Monday to Friday 9am to 7pm, Saturday 9am to 6pm, and Sunday 10am to 5pm; September to May, hours are Monday to Friday 9am to 5pm and Saturday and Sunday 10am to 5pm.

### EXPLORING THE AREA

North of Aviemore, the **Strathspey Railway,** Dalfaber Road (☎ **01479/810-725;** www.btinternet.com/~strathspey.railway.index.htm), is your best bet in Scotland to learn firsthand what it was like to ride the rails in the 19th century. The railway follows the valley of the River Spey between Boat of Garten and Aviemore, a distance of 5 miles (8km). The train is drawn by a coal-burning steam locomotive. The newest locomotive used was made nearly 4 decades ago, the oldest being of 1899 vintage. The trip is meant to re-create the total experience of travel on a Scottish steam railway that once carried wealthy Victorians toward their hunting lodges in North Britain. The round-trip takes about an hour. The rail station at Boat of Garten, where you can board the train, has also been restored.

Round-trip passage costs £7 ($11.90) first class or £5.40 ($9.20) third class. Schedules change frequently, but from July to the end of August trains make five round-trips daily. From May to June and September, they run daily, and from March to April and October they run Saturday, Sunday, Wednesday, and Thursday. There's no regular service in winter; however, special Christmas season trips are made during which Santa

Claus makes an appearance. To complete the experience, you can wine and dine aboard on Wednesday in July and August, when a single-seating casual lunch is served; the cost for the fare and meal is £17.50 ($29.75). Reservations must be made for the meals. The dining car is a replica of a Pullman parlor car, the Amethyst. For reservations and hours of departure, call ☎ **01479/831-692.**

For the grandest view of the Cairngorm peaks, take the **Cairngorm Chair Lift** (☎ **01479/861-261**), whose lowest section is 10 miles (16km) east of Aviemore. A round-trip passage on the longest chairlift in Scotland costs £6 ($10.20) adults and £3.60 ($6.10) children 17 and under. During summer, the lift runs daily 9am to 5pm (to 5:30pm July and August). In winter, hours are daily 9am to 4pm; the uppermost reaches are closed during periods of high winds. The highest section is 4,084 feet (1,239m) above sea level. In summer, on a clear day you can see Ben Nevis in the west, and the vista of Strathspey from here is spectacular, from Loch Morlich in the Rothiemurchus Forest to the Spey Valley.

Skiers are attracted to the area any time after October, when snow can be expected. You can rent ski equipment and clothing at the Day Lodge at the main Cairngorm parking area. Weather patterns can change quickly in the Cairngorm massif. Call the number above for a report on the latest weather conditions. To reach the area, take A951, branching off from A9 at Aviemore, then head for the parking area at the Day Lodge.

If you'd like to explore the countryside on two wheels, there are several places to rent bikes. **Speyside Sports,** Main Street (☎ **01479/810-656**), rents bikes at £6 ($10.20) for a half day, £10 ($17) for a full day, and £40 ($68) for 6 days. **Bothy Bikes,** 81 Grampian Rd. (☎ **01479/810-111**), charges £10 ($17) for a half day, £14 ($23.80) for a full day. Discounts begin to apply when you rent for 2 days or more.

The tourist office will give you hiking maps and offer advice, especially about weather conditions depending on the season. One of the best trails is reached by following B9760 to the signposted **Glen More Forest Park,** in the vicinity of Loch Morlich.

## ACCOMMODATIONS

**Best Western Aviemore Highlands Hotel.** Aviemore Mountain Resort, Aviemore PH22 1PJ. ☎ **800/528-1234** in the U.S., or 01479/810-771. Fax 01479/811-473. www.aviehighlands. demon.co.uk. E-mail: sales@aviehighlands.demon.co.uk. 103 units. TV TEL. £70–£100 ($119–$170) double. Rates include Scottish breakfast. AE, DC, MC, V.

This resort hotel caters to an outdoorsy clientele. It's a labyrinthine complex of wings, staircases, and long halls, which funnel into public rooms with big windows overlooking the countryside. In summer, doors open to reveal flagstone terraces ringed with viburnum and juniper. You can drink in the Illicit Still Bar, which has an antique whisky still and copper-top tables. Sunday is the ever-popular karaoke night. The main restaurant is capped with a soaring ceiling, trussed with beams. The midsize guest rooms are well furnished, and some family rooms are also available. Room service is provided, and you can use all the leisure and sports facilities at the Red McGregor Hotel.

**Corrour House Hotel.** On B970, Inverdruie by Aviemore PH22 1QH. ☎ **01479/810-220.** Fax 01479/811-500. www.corrourhouse.com. 8 units. TV TEL. £80 ($136) double. Rates include breakfast. AE, MC, V. Closed mid-Nov to Christmas. From Aviemore, drive half a mile (1km) east, following the signs to Glenmore.

This isolated granite house was built around 1880 for the mother of the *laird* (baron) of a much-larger manor house about 2 miles (3km) away. The larger of the houses is privately owned and can't be visited. Set within 4 acres of forest and garden, this guesthouse contains simple but comfortable rooms that are attractively decorated. Your hosts are members of the Catto family, who will prepare you dinner if you arrange it in advance. Many of their dishes have a true taste of Scotland flavor, including smoked trout and horseradish mousse or Ballindalloch pheasant with a sauce made with red wine, oranges, red currants, and fresh herbs.

**Hilton Coylumbridge Resort Hotel.** Rothiemurchus, Aviemore PH22 1QN. ☎ **01479/ 810-661.** Fax 01479/811-309. www.hilton.com. E-mail: reservations@coylumbridge. stakis.co.uk. 175 units. TV TEL. £100 ($170) double; £150 ($255) suite. Half-board rates available for a minimum 2-night stay. AE, DC, MC, V.

On 65 acres of tree-studded grounds, this hotel has extensive sports and leisure facilities. The midsize guest rooms are well appointed, each with movies, a tea/ coffeemaker, fresh fruit, and a daily newspaper. Meals are served in Walker's Restaurant or the Grant Room. In the hotel are two heated pools, a sauna, whirlpool, steam bath, hairdressing salon, gift shop, and games room. There's often evening entertainment, particularly on weekends. In winter, downhill and cross-country skiing equipment and training are available. There's a sports and leisure hall for children called the Fun House.

**Lynwilg House.** Rte. A9, Aviemore PH22 1PZ. ☎ **01479/811-685.** www.lynwilg.co.uk. E-mail: marge@lynwig.co.uk. 4 units. TV. £56–£70 ($95.20–$119) double. Rates include breakfast. MC, V. Follow A9 for 1½ miles (2.5km) south of Aviemore's center, following the signs to Perth.

The Victorian solidity of this house is particularly noteworthy in Aviemore, considering the relative modernity of many others of the resort hotels. It was built by the duke of Richmond in the 1880s overlooking the mountains. Today, under the management of Alan and Marjorie Cleary, it retains 4 acres of its original park and gardens, with high-ceilinged guest rooms containing comfortable furnishings. In front of the house is a croquet lawn, and at the bottom of the well-tended garden is a stream where guests like to relax. Most of the produce used in the dining room here comes from the garden. Moderately priced meals are likely to include roasted duck with red-currant jelly, sea fish and scallop stew with creamy bay sauce, and summer pudding with Drambuie-flavored ice cream.

## DINING

**The Bar/The Restaurant.** In the Dalfaber Golf and Country Club, about a mile (1.5km) north of the center of Aviemore. ☎ **01479/811-244.** Reservations required in the restaurant. Golfer's menu (Thurs only) £10.50 ($17.85); Sun lunch £5.50 ($9.35); bar platters £3.30–£8 ($5.60–$13.60). MC, V. Restaurant Mon–Sat 7:30–9:30pm, Sun noon–9:30pm. Bar daily 11am–11pm. SCOTTISH.

Although the golf course, health club, and leisure facilities of this country club are open only to members, visitors are welcome in the cozy bar and restaurant, which is outfitted in tartan carpets and upholstery, with heavy brocade curtains and views from the big windows. In the bar, where live entertainment is featured nightly, the fare includes venison cutlets or fillets, sandwiches, homemade steak pies, and any of a variety of malt whiskies. The restaurant serves seafood, such as skewered tiger prawns soaked with butter, as well as grilled Angus steaks, main-course salads, and a limited number of vegetarian dishes. Several nights per week, the restaurant hosts theme nights with entertainment: Monday is Indian buffet night and Thursday golfer's night.

## AVIEMORE AFTER DARK

**Crofters,** off Grampian Road at the Aviemore Mountain Resort, a 2-minute walk from the center of Aviemore (☎ **01479/810-771**), has dancing with no cover charge nightly 10pm to 1am, with guest DJs bringing in their own music and setting the mood. The bar serves Tennant's Lager and Guinness on tap. The private drive leading here is well marked from Grampian Road.

## 6 · Along Loch Ness

Sir Peter Scott's *Nessitera rhombopteryx,* one of the world's great mysteries, continues to elude her pursuers. The Loch Ness monster, or "Nessie" as she's more familiarly known, has captured the imagination of the world, drawing thousands of visitors yearly to Loch Ness. Half a century ago, A82 was built alongside the banks of the loch's western shores, and since then many more sightings have been claimed.

All types of high-tech underwater contraptions have gone in after the Loch Ness monster, but no one can find her in spite of the photographs and film footage you might have seen in magazines or on TV. Dr. Robert Rines and his associates at the Academy of Applied Science in Massachusetts maintain an all-year watch with sonar-triggered cameras and strobe lights suspended from a raft in Urquhart Bay. However, some people in Inverness aren't keen on collaring the monster, and you can't blame them: An old prophecy predicts a violent end for Inverness if the monster is ever captured.

The loch is 24 miles (39km) long, 1 mile (1.5km) wide, and some 755 feet (229m) deep. If you'd like to stay along the loch and monster-watch instead of basing yourself at Inverness, we've listed some choices below. Even if the monster doesn't put in an appearance, you'll enjoy the scenery as you walk along the loch. In summer, from both Fort Augustus and Inverness, you can take boat cruises across Loch Ness.

If you're driving, take A82 between Fort Augustus and Inverness running along Loch Ness. Buses from either Fort Augustus or Inverness also traverse A82, taking you to Drumnadrochit.

### DRUMNADROCHIT

The bucolic village of Drumnadrochit is about a mile (1.5km) from Loch Ness at the entrance to Glen Urquhart. It's the nearest village to the part of the loch in which sightings of the monster have been reported most frequently.

Although most visitors arrive at Drumnadrochit to see the Loch Ness monster exhibit (see "Seeing the Sights," below), you can also take an offbeat adventure in the great outdoors at the **Highland Riding Centre,** Borlum Farm, Drumnadrochit (☎ **01456/450-220**). This is an 850-acre sheep farm on moorlands overlooking Loch Ness; follow A82 for about 14 miles (22.5km) west of Inverness and make a reservation in advance. In summer, the stable's 45 horses are booked throughout their working day. Tours depart almost every day, depending on demand; they leave between 9:30am and 5:30pm, last 60 to 120 minutes, and cost £13.50 to £22.50 ($22.95 to $38.25).

**Wilderness Cycles,** The Cottage (☎ **01456/450-223**), will rent you a bike so you can go exploring on your own. Rentals costs £7 ($11.90) for a half day, £12 ($20.40) daily, and £45 ($76.50) weekly. It's open daily 9am to 6pm.

### SEEING THE SIGHTS

**Official Loch Ness Monster Exhibition.** Drumnadrochit. ☎ **01456/450-573.** Admission £5.95 ($10.10) adults, £4.50 ($7.65) students, £3.50 ($5.95) children, £4.50 ($7.65) seniors/ages 7–16, £14.95 ($25.40) families; free for ages 7 and under. Easter–May daily 9:30am–5pm; June and Sept daily 9:30am–6pm; July–Aug daily 9am–8pm; Oct daily 9:30am–5:30pm; Nov–Easter daily 10am–4pm.

This is Drumnadrochit's big attraction, featuring a scale replica of Nessie. It opened in 1980 and has been packing 'em in ever since. You can follow Nessie's story from

# Spotting Nessie

She's affectionately known as Nessie, but her more formal name is *Nessitera rhombopteryx,* and she has the unflattering appellation of the Loch Ness monster. Is she the beast that never was, or the world's most famous living animal? You decide. Real or imagined, she's Scotland's virtual mascot, and even if she doesn't exist, she's one of the major attractions of the country. Who can drive along the dark waters of Loch Ness without staring at the murky depths and expecting a head or a couple of humps to appear above the water's surface at any minute?

Nessie's lineage is ancient. An appearance in A.D. 565 was recorded by respected 7th-century biographer St. Adamnan, not known as a spinner of tall tales. The claim is that St. Columba was en route along Loch Ness to convert Brude, king of the Picts, to Christianity. The saint ordered a monk to swim across the loch and retrieve a boat. However, as he was in midswim, Nessie attacked. The monk's life was saved only when Columba confronted the sea beast with a sign of the cross and a shouted invocation.

Columba's calming effect on Nessie must have lasted over the centuries, because no attacks have been reported since. Of course, there was that accident in the 1500s when a chronicle reported that "a terrible beast issuing out of the water early one morning about midsummer knocked down trees and killed three men with its tail." Again, in 1961, 30 hotel guests reported seeing two humps that rose out of the water just before their craft exploded and sank. Bertram Mill has offered £20,000 to have the monster delivered alive to his circus.

Since Scotland is the land not only of Nessie but also whisky, it might be assumed that some of these sightings were hallucinations brought on by the consumption of far too many "wee drams." However, sightings have come from people of impeccable credentials who were stone sober. Nessie seems to like to show herself to monks, perhaps a tradition dating from St. Columba. Several monks at the Fort Augustus Abbey claim to have seen her. A monk who's an organist at Westminster Cathedral reported a sighting in 1973.

Belief in Nessie's existence is so strong that midget yellow submarines and all types of high-tech underwater contraptions have been used in an attempt to track her down. Many photographs exist—most of them faked—usually from the site of the ruins of Urquhart Castle on the loch's shore. Other photographs haven't been so easily explained.

If Nessie does exist, exactly who is she? A sole survivor from prehistoric times? A gigantic sea snake? It has even been suggested she's a cosmic wanderer through time. Chances are you won't see her on your visit, but you can see a fantasy replica of the sea beast at the Official Loch Ness Monster Exhibition at Drumnadrochit.

A.D. 565 to the present in photographs, audio, and video, and you can climb aboard the sonar research vessel *John Murray.* The Exhibition Centre is the most visited place in the Highlands of Scotland, with more than 200,000 visitors annually.

✪ **Urquhart Castle.** Loch Ness along A82. ☎ **01456/450-551.** Admission £3.80 ($6.45) adults, £2.80 ($4.75) seniors, £1.20 ($2.05) children. Apr–Sept daily 9:30am–6:30pm (to 8:30pm July–Aug); Oct–Mar daily 9:30am–3:45pm. Drive 1½ miles (2.5km) southeast of Drumnadrochit on A82.

This ruined castle, one of Scotland's largest, is on a promontory overlooking Loch Ness. The chief of Clan Grant owned the castle in 1509, and most of the extensive ruins date from that period. In 1692, the castle was blown up by the Grants to prevent it from becoming a Jacobite stronghold. Rising from crumbling walls, the jagged keep still remains. It's at Urquhart Castle that sightings of the Loch Ness monster are most often reported. There's free off-road parking where you can stand and view the ruins from afar.

## ACCOMMODATIONS & DINING

✪ **Polmaily House Hotel.** Drumnadrochit IV3 6XT. ☎ **01456/450-343.** Fax 01456/450-813. E-mail: polmaily@btinternet.com. 14 units. TV TEL. £98–£136 ($166.60–$231.20) double. Rates include Scottish breakfast. MC, V. Drive 2 miles (3km) west of Drumnadrochit on A831.

In 1994, John and Sonia Whittington-Davis, third-generation hoteliers, bought this Edwardian inn that re-creates manorial country-house living. The house, on an 18-acre estate with mixed gardens and woodland, is believed to have been built in 1776. The spacious and elegant guest rooms tastefully filled with antiques have high ceilings, leaded-glass windows, and flowered wallpaper. The hotel has a tennis court and a croquet lawn as well as a heated indoor pool, a sauna, and a gym. The restaurant attracts locals as well as hotel guests with dishes like Aberdeen beef and fresh salmon; fixed-price dinners are rather expensive.

# INVERMORISTON

The village of Invermoriston, 168 miles (270.5km) northwest of Edinburgh and 29 miles (47km) south of Inverness, is one of the most beautiful spots along Loch Ness. **Glenmoriston** is one of the loveliest glens in the Highlands. You can take long walks along the riverbanks, with views of Loch Ness. The area is at the junction of the Loch Ness Highway (A82) and the road to the Isle of Skye (A887).

## ACCOMMODATIONS & DINING

**Glenmoriston Arms Hotel.** At the junction of A82 and A887, Invermoriston IV3 6YA. ☎ **01320/351-206.** Fax 01320/351-308. 8 units. TV TEL. £100–£110 ($170–$187) double. Rates include Scottish breakfast. MC, V.

This has been a roadside inn for 2 centuries. It's a lot like a woodsy hunting lodge, with antique weapons, old trophies, well-polished paneling, and more than 160 varieties of single-malt whisky. The guest rooms are clean and modest and contain radios, hair dryers, and tea/coffeemakers. Rather pricey dinners are served nightly.

# FORT AUGUSTUS

Fort Augustus, 36 miles (58km) south of Inverness along A82 and 166 miles (267km) northwest of Edinburgh, stands at the head (the southernmost end) of Loch Ness. Originally called Kilcumein, the town became fortified after the 1715 Jacobite rising. Gen. George Wade, of road- and bridge-building fame, headquartered here in 1724, and in 1729 the government constructed a fort along the banks of the loch, naming it Augustus after William Augustus, duke of Cumberland, son of George II. Jacobites seized the fort in 1745 and controlled it until the Scottish defeat at Culloden. Now gone, Wade's fort was turned into the Fort Augustus Abbey at the south end of Loch Ness. A Benedictine order was installed in 1867, and the monks today run a Catholic secondary school on the site.

Fort Augustus is mainly a refueling stop for those who want to stay on Loch Ness itself—perhaps in hopes of seeing the monster—instead of anchoring into a larger town like Fort William to the south or Inverness to the north. The only other reason to stop by is that it's the most panoramic place to see the locks of the Caledonian Canal in action.

Bisecting the actual village of Fort Augustus is the **Caledonian Canal,** and the locks are a popular attraction when boats are passing through. Running across the loftiest sections of Scotland, the canal was constructed between 1803 and 1822. Almost in a straight line, it makes its way from Inverness in the north to Corpach in the vicinity of Fort William. The canal is 60 miles (97km) long: 22 man-made miles (35.5km), and the rest are natural lochs. In summer you can take several pleasure craft along this canal, leaving from Fort Augustus.

**Caley Cruisers,** Canal Road, Inverness (☎ **01463/236-328;** fax 01463/714-879; www.caleycruisers.co.uk), maintains a fleet of 50 diesel-powered, 60-horsepower cruisers (with skippers) that a group of two to six people can rent from March to October— even if their marine experience is relatively limited. Rentals last for 1 week, long enough to negotiate the 60 miles (97km) of the Caledonian Canal in both directions between Inverness and Fort William. (There are about 15 locks en route; tolls are included in the rental fee.) Depending on the craft's size and the season, a week's rental ranges from £413 to £1,779 ($702.10 to $3,024.30); the cost of fuel and taxes for a week is £60 to £80 ($102 to $136), plus another £40 ($68) weekly for a reasonably priced insurance policy. Except for the waters of Loch Ness, which can be rough, the canal is calm enough and doesn't pose the dangers of cruising on the open sea.

## ACCOMMODATIONS & DINING

**Inchnacardoch Lodge.** Hwy. A82, Fort Augustus PH32 4BL. ☎ **01320/366-258.** Fax 10320/ 366-248. E-mail: lochness97@aol.com. 15 units. TV TEL. £70–£86 ($119–$146.20) double. Rates include Scottish breakfast. AE, DC, MC, V.

Inchnacardoch Lodge is a family-run hotel in a panoramic setting overlooking Loch Ness, a half-mile (1km) north of the town center. Once a country residence of the Fraser clan's chief, Lord Lovat, the hotel offers comfortable midsize guest rooms with hair dryers and tea/coffeemakers. The common areas have recently been refurbished, but the traditional ambience remains. You can relax in the lounge bar while watching the waters for the mysterious monster; a wee dram of malt too much and you may just find her. If you can tear yourself away from the view of the water, the hotel restaurant offers moderately priced main courses. No smoking.

# 7  Inverness: Capital of the Highlands

156 miles (251km) NW of Edinburgh, 134 miles (216km) NW of Dundee, 134 miles (216km) W of Aberdeen

The capital of the Highlands, Inverness is a royal burgh and seaport at the north end of Great Glen on both sides of the Ness River. For such a historic town, the sights are rather meager, but Inverness is a good center for touring. If your time is limited, confine your visits to Culloden Battlefield, where Bonnie Prince Charlie and his Jacobite army were defeated in 1746; Cawdor Castle of *Macbeth* fame (see "Nairn & Cawdor Castle," below), and Black Isle (see "The Black Isle Peninsula," below), the most enchanting and scenic peninsula in Scotland. All these attractions would fill one busy day even if you don't have time to walk about the center of Inverness itself.

## ESSENTIALS

**GETTING THERE**    Domestic flights from various parts of Britain arrive at the Inverness Airport. Flight time from London's Heathrow to the Inverness/Dalcross Airport is 1¾ hours. Call ☎ **01463/232-471** in Inverness for flight information.

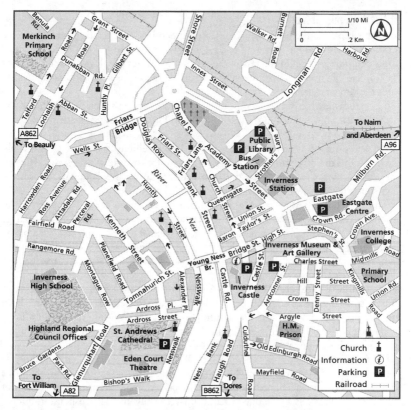

Some five to seven trains per day arrive from Glasgow and Edinburgh (on Sunday, two or three trains). The train takes 3½ hours from either city, and a one-way fare from either is £29.90 ($50.85). Trains pull into Station Square, off Academy Street in Inverness (☎ **0345/484-950** for schedules).

**Scottish CityLink** coaches provide service for the area (☎ **0990/505-050** for schedules). Frequent service through the day is possible from either Edinburgh or Glasgow (a 4-hour trip each way), at a one-way fare of £12.50 ($21.25) or £12 ($20.40), respectively. The bus station is at Farraline Park, off Academy Street (☎ **01463/233-371**).

Driving from Edinburgh, take M9 north to Perth, then follow along the Great North Road (A9) until you reach Inverness.

**VISITOR INFORMATION**   The Inverness branch of the **Highlands of Scotland Tourist Board** is at Castle Wynd, off Bridge Street (☎ **01463/234-353**). October to mid-April, it's open Monday to Friday 9am to 5pm and Saturday 10am to 4pm; mid-April to May, hours are Monday to Friday 9am to 5pm, Saturday 9:30am to 5pm, and Sunday 9:30am to 4pm; June hours are Monday to Friday 9am to 6pm, Saturday 9am to 5pm, and Sunday 9:30am to 5pm; July and August, it's open Monday to Saturday 9am to 6pm and Sunday 9:30am to 5pm; September hours are Monday to Saturday 9am to 6pm and Sunday 9:30am to 5pm.

**SPECIAL EVENTS**   At the **Highland Games** in July, with their sporting competitions and festive balls, the season in Inverness reaches its social peak. For more information and exact dates, consult the tourist office (see above).

## SEEING THE SIGHTS

Inverness is one of the oldest inhabited sites in Scotland. On **Craig Phadrig** are the remains of a vitrified fort, believed to date from the 4th century B.C. One of the most important prehistoric monuments in the north, the **Stones of Clava** are about 6 miles (10km) east of Inverness on the road to Nairn. These cairns and standing stones are from the Bronze Age.

The old castle of Inverness stood to the east of the present street Castlehill, and the site still retains the name "Auld Castlehill." David I built the first stone castle in Inverness around 1141, and the **Clock Tower** is all that remains of a fort erected by Cromwell's army between 1652 and 1657. The rebellious Scots blew up the old castle in 1746 to keep it from falling to government troops, and the **present castle** was constructed by the Victorians in the 19th century. Today this landmark houses the laws courts of Inverness and local government offices.

The 16th-century **Abertarff House,** Church Street, is now the headquarters of An Comunn Gaidhealach, the Highland association that preserves the Gaelic language and culture. Opposite the town hall is the **Old Mercat Cross,** with its Stone of the Tubs, said to be the stone on which women rested their washtubs as they ascended from the river. Known as "Clachnacudainn," the lozenge-shaped stone was the spot where local early kings were crowned.

**St. Andrew's Cathedral** (1866–69), Ardross Street, is the northernmost diocese of the Scottish Episcopal church and a fine example of Victorian architecture, both imposing and richly decorated. Be sure to check out the icons given to Bishop Eden by the tsar of Russia. The cathedral is open daily 8:30am to 6pm. For information, get in touch with the Provost, 15 Ardross St. (☎ **01463/233-535**).

West of the river rises the wooded hill of **Tomnahurich,** known as the "hill of the fairies." It's now a cemetery from which the views are panoramic. This is the best place to go for a country walk. The boat-shaped hillock is immediately to the southwest of the center. In the Ness are wooded islands, linked to Inverness by suspension bridges and turned into parks.

If you're interested in bus tours of the Highlands and cruises on Loch Ness, go to **Inverness Traction,** 6 Burnett Rd. (☎ **01463/239-292**). In summer, there are also cruises along the Caledonian Canal from Inverness into Loch Ness.

Shoppers might want to check out a family-owned shrine to Scottish kiltmaking, **Duncan Chisholm & Sons,** 47–53 Castle St. (☎ **01463/234-599**). The tartans of at least 50 of Scotland's largest clans are available in the form of kilts and kilt jackets for men and women. If your heart is set on something more esoteric, the staff can acquire whatever fabric your ancestors would have worn to make up your garment. A section is devoted to Scottish gifts (ties, scarves, yard goods, kilt pins in thistle patterns) and memorabilia. You can visit the on-premises workshop. If you don't find what you're hankering for, take a short walk down the street to Chisholm's most important competitor, **Hector Russell, Kiltmaker,** 4–9 Huntly St. (☎ **01463/ 222-781**), where an equivalent collection of garments is available. The town's best jewelry store, with an unusual collection of bangles and bracelets inspired by the decorative traditions of Celtic Scotland, is **D&H Norval,** 88 Church St. (☎ **01463/ 232-739**). At **Celtic Spirit,** 14 Church St. (☎ **01463/714-796**), the focus is on New Age books and an unusual collection of wind chimes.

Golfers can head about 40 miles (64.5km) north to hit the links at the renowned **Royal Dornoch Golf Club;** see "Sutherland: The Gem of Scotland," below, for details. Closer at hand, the 5,451-yard (4,960m) **Torvean Golf Course,** Glen Q Road (☎ **01463/711-434**), offers an 18-hole, par-68 course with greens fees of £12.50 ($21.25) Monday to Thursday, and £14.40 ($24.50) Friday to Sunday.

**Inverness Museum and Art Gallery.** Castle Wynd, off Bridge St. ☎ **01463/237-114.** Free admission. Mon–Sat 9am–5pm.

This museum in the town center is a top attraction, its displays representing the social and natural history, archaeology, art, and culture of the Scottish Highlands, with special emphasis on the Inverness district. Don't miss the important collection of Highland silver, with a reconstructed silversmith's workshop, displays on the life of the clans, a reconstruction of a local taxidermist's workshop, a reconstructed Inverness kitchen of the 1920s, and an art gallery. There's also a permanent exhibit on the story of the Inverness district, from local geology and archaeology to the present. Other facilities are a souvenir shop, a coffee shop, and an information service.

**Culloden Battlefield.** Culloden Moor, 6 miles (10km) southeast of Inverness. ☎ **01463/ 790-607** for visitor center. Admission to visitor center £3.50 ($5.95) adults, £2.50 ($4.25) seniors/children, £8.90 ($15.15) families. Visitor center Feb–Mar and Nov–Dec daily 10am–4pm; Apr–Oct daily 9am–6pm.

At Culloden Battlefield, Bonnie Prince Charlie and the Jacobite army were finally crushed on April 16, 1746. Leanach Cottage, around which the battle took place, still stands and was inhabited until 1912. A path leads from the **visitor center** through the Field of the English, where 52 men of the duke of Cumberland's forces who died during the battle are said to be buried. Features of interest include the **Graves of the Clans,** communal burial places with simple stones bearing individual clan names; the great **memorial cairn,** erected in 1881; the **Well of the Dead;** and the huge **Cumberland Stone,** from which the victorious "Butcher" Cumberland is said to have reviewed the scene. The battle lasted only 40 minutes; the prince's army lost some 1,200 men out of 5,000, and the king's army 300 of 9,000. In the visitor center is an audiovisual presentation on the background and history of the famous battle. Also on the premises are a restaurant and book shop.

**Fort George/Queen's Own Highlanders Regimental Museum.** On Moray Firth by the village of Ardersier, 11 miles (18km) northeast of Inverness, 8 miles (13km) northwest of Cawdor along B9006. ☎ **01667/462-777.** Admission £4 ($6.80) adults, £3 ($5.10) seniors, £1.50 ($2.55) ages 5 to 15; free for age 4 and under. Apr–Sept daily 9:30am–5:45pm; Oct–Mar Mon–Sat 9:30am–4:30pm, Sun 2–4:30pm.

Fort George was called the "most considerable fortress and best situated in Great Britain" in 1748 by Lt. Col. James Wolfe, who went on to fame as Wolfe of Quebec. Built after the Battle of Culloden, the fort was occupied by the Hanoverian army of George II and is still an active army barracks. The rampart, almost a mile (1.5km) around, encloses some 42 acres. Dr. Samuel Johnson and James Boswell visited here in 1773 on their Highland trek. The fort contains the admission-free **Queen's Own Highlanders Regimental Museum,** with regimental exhibits from 1778 to today, representing a number of Highland regiments as well as its namesake.

## ACCOMMODATIONS
### VERY EXPENSIVE

✪ **Culloden House.** Culloden, Inverness IV1 7BZ. ☎ **01463/790-461.** Fax 01463/ 792-181. www.culodenhouse.co.uk. E-mail: user@culodenhouse.co.uk. 28 units. TV TEL. £190 ($323) double; £250 ($425) suite. Rates include Scottish breakfast. AE, DC, MC, V. Drive 3 miles (5km) east of Inverness on A96.

Culloden House, a Georgian mansion with a much-photographed Adam facade, includes part of the Renaissance castle in which Bonnie Prince Charlie slept the night before Culloden, the last great battle on British soil. Superbly isolated, with extensive gardens and parkland, it's perfect for a relaxed Highland holiday. At the iron gates to the broad front lawn, a piper in full Highland garb often plays at sundown, the skirl of the bagpipe accompanied by the barking of house dogs. The prince of Wales and the crown prince of Japan have stayed here, perfectly at home among the exquisite furnishings and handsome plaster friezes. The cozy yet spacious guest rooms have sylvan views and a history-laden atmosphere. The hotel maintains traditional ideas of personal service.

**Dining:** In the elegant Adam Dining Room, chef Michael Simpson presents beautifully prepared (if expensive) traditional Scottish cuisine. Fresh produce and in-season game are used, along with high-quality locally raised cattle. Lunch and dinner are served daily.

**Amenities:** Concierge, 24-hour room service, laundry, tennis, sauna, solarium.

## EXPENSIVE

**Bunchrew House Hotel and Restaurant.** Bunchrew, Inverness, Inverness-shire IV3 6TA. ☎ **01463/234-917.** Fax 01463/710-620. www.bunchrew-inverness.co.uk. E-mail: welcome@bunchrew-inverness.co.uk. 11 units. MINIBAR TV TEL. £130–£160 ($221–$272) suite for 2. Rates include Scottish breakfast. AE, MC, V. Drive 3 miles (5km) west of Inverness on A862.

This fine Scottish mansion on the shores of Beauly Firth is the ancestral home of both the Fraser and the McKenzie clans. The house, built by Simon Fraser, eighth Lord Lovat, dates to 1621 and is set in 15 acres of landscaped gardens. You get a glimpse of a bygone era when relaxing in the paneled drawing room with roaring log fires in winter. The good-sized guest rooms are individually designed and decorated; the Lovat Suite has a canopied four-poster bed, and the Wyvis Suite boasts a half-tester bed.

**Dining:** You can dine in the candlelit restaurant on prime Scottish beef, fresh lobster and crayfish, local game and venison, and fresh vegetables. Lunch and dinner are served daily; prices are rather high.

**Amenities:** Room service, laundry, baby-sitting, free fishing on the estate.

✪ **Dunain Park Hotel.** Dunain Park, Inverness IV3 8JN. ☎ **01463/230-512.** Fax 01463/224-532. www.Dunainparkhotel.co.uk. E-mail: Dunainparkhotel@btinternet.com. 13 units. TV TEL. £138–£158 ($234.60–$268.60) double or cottage; from £198 ($336.60) suite. Rates include Scottish breakfast. AE, DC, MC, V. Drive 2 miles (3km) southwest of Inverness on A82.

The Dunain Park stands in 6 acres of garden and woods, between Loch Ness and Inverness. This 18th-century house was opened as a hotel in 1974 and is furnished with fine antiques, china, and clocks, allowing it to retain its atmosphere of a private country house. Although Dunain Park has won its fame mainly as a restaurant, it does offer guest rooms with a host of thoughtful details and pretty, soft furnishings, each with a radio, a hair dryer, and a trouser press.

**Dining:** The breakfast served here is exceptional, but it's at dinner the chef really delivers (see "Dining," below).

**Amenities:** Concierge, room service, laundry, indoor heated pool, sauna.

**Kingsmill's Hotel.** Culcabock Rd., Inverness IV2 3LP. ☎ **01463/237-166.** Fax 01463/225-208. www.swallowhotels.com. 82 units. TV TEL. £165 ($280.50) double; £195 ($331.50) suite. Rates include Scottish breakfast. Children 13 and under stay free in parents' room. AE, DC, MC, V. Take Kingsmill Rd. 1 mile (1.5km) east of the center of Inverness.

Once a private mansion, this hotel is an 18th-century country house of much charm on 4 acres of woodland garden adjacent to an 18-hole golf course. The owner maintains the country-house atmosphere with an informal and hospitable Highland staff. The furnishings throughout are of a high quality, and all the guest rooms are attractively furnished, each with a tea/coffeemaker and hair dryer. A dozen rooms are reserved for nonsmokers.

**Dining:** The fish dishes are exceptional at dinner. Bar lunches and snack meals offer a wide choice, including Scottish fare. A notice in the lobby tells you Robert Burns dined here in 1787 and the "Charles" who signed the guest register in 1982 was (you guessed it) the prince of Wales. His sister, Princess Anne, has also stayed here.

**Amenities:** Concierge, 24-hour room service, laundry/valet, baby-sitting, indoor pool and health spa (with sauna, steam room, spa bath, fitness room, sunbed), salon, children's playground, three-hole minigolf course.

## MODERATE

**Glen Mhor Hotel.** 9–12 Ness Bank, Inverness IV2 4SG. ☎ **01463/234-308.** Fax 01463/713-170. www.glenmhor.co.uk. E-mail: user@glenmhor.co.uk. 45 units. TV TEL. £84–£94 ($142.80–$159.80) double; from £123 ($209.10) junior suite. Rates include Scottish breakfast. AE, DC, MC, V.

On the River Ness, this house of gables and bay windows is a hospitable family-run hotel. From many of the individually styled guest rooms you have views of the river, castle, and cathedral; some are suitable for families. Amenities in the rooms include trouser presses, hair dryers, and baby-listening service. Ten rooms are in an annex called The Cottage. Two of the ground-floor rooms are suitable for travelers with disabilities. In the Riverview Restaurant overlooking the river and specializing in seafood and Scottish dishes, you can enjoy such fine food as salmon caught in the river outside. The wine list is one of the best in the country. There's also a European bistro bar called Nico's.

**Glenmoriston Town House Hotel.** 20 Ness Bank, Inverness IV2 4SF. ☎ **01463/223-777.** Fax 01463/712-378. www.glenmoriston.com. E-mail: glenmoriston@cali.co.uk. 15 units. TV TEL. £70–£125 ($119–$212.50) double. Rates include full Scottish breakfast. AE, MC, V. Free parking.

A four-star selection, this hotel is on the River Ness, a short walk from the town center, and is the finest townhouse hotel in town. Rooms have been stylish refurbished, are well maintained and individually designed, and come with spacious private bathrooms. Some accommodations have four-poster beds, and others are suitable for use as family units. In addition to the standard amenities of hair dryers and beverage makers, each room is equipped with a fax machine and modem data ports. On site is a sauna and gym, and guests can enjoy temporary membership at a nearby Squash and Tennis Club. Of the two hotel restaurants, La Terrazza is open daily for lunch, whereas La Riviera is more formal, specializing in a fine Italian cuisine, with many Tuscan dishes.

**The Royal Highland Hotel.** 18 Academy St., Inverness IV1 1LG. ☎ **01463/231-926.** Fax 01463/710-705. www.royalhighlandhotel.co.uk. E-mail: info@royalhighlandhotel.co.uk. 65 units. TV TEL. £99 ($168.30) double. Rates include breakfast. AE, DC, MC, V.

Constructed of somber gray stone in 1859 across from the rail station, this hotel was built to celebrate the arrival of rail lines connecting the Highlands, through Inverness, to the rest of Britain. Today, it's an antique-strewn, slightly faded hotel, despite gradual modernizations and the contemporary decors in about half its guest rooms. You register in a massive lobby, at one end of which is the showiest staircase in Inverness. The rooms, depending on how recently they were remodeled, are either charmingly dowdy or more modern, but always with Scottish traditionalism. Each has a hair dryer and tea/coffeemaker. The dining room, open only for dinner, retains the elaborate high ceiling of its initial construction and a sense of the Victorian age; fixed-price menus are moderate. Affordable lunch platters are served in the bar. Seafood and West Coast shellfish, including a medley of fresh oysters, are house specialties.

## INEXPENSIVE

**Ballifeary House Hotel.** 10 Ballifeary Rd., Inverness IV3 5PJ. ☎ **01463/235-572.** Fax 01463/717-583. www.ballifearyhousehotel.co.uk. E-mail: info@ballifearyhousehotel.co.uk. 5 units. £70–£76 ($119–$129.20) double. Rates include Scottish breakfast. MC, V. Closed mid-Oct to Easter.

This well-maintained 1876 Victorian stone villa, with a pleasant garden, is one of the area's better B&Bs. Mr. and Mrs. Luscombe, the owners, offer their guests individual attention. The guest rooms, although a bit small, are comfortably furnished, with hair dryers, clock radios, and tea/coffeemakers. This no-smoking hotel discourages families with small children.

**Ivybank Guest House.** 28 Old Edinburgh Rd., Inverness IV2 3HJ. ☎/fax **01463/232-796.** www.host-co.uk. E-mail: ivybank@talk21.com. 5 units, 3 with private bathroom. TV. £45–£50 ($76.50–$85) double without bathroom; £50–£55 ($85–$93.50) double with bathroom. Rates include Scottish breakfast. AE, MC, V.

Ivybank, off Castle Road about a 10-minute walk north of the town center, was built in 1836 and retains its original fireplaces and an oak-paneled and beamed hall with a rosewood staircase. It has a walled and landscaped garden and comfortably furnished guest rooms, each with hot and cold running water, a hair dryer, and a tea/coffeemaker. Mrs. Catherine Cameron is the gracious hostess, making guests feel at ease and welcome. There's ample parking in the walled garden. Breakfast is the only meal served.

**Trafford Bank.** 96 Fairfield Rd., Inverness IV3 5LL. ☎ **01463/241-414.** E-mail: traff@pop.cali.co.uk. 5 units. TV. £60 ($102) double. Rates include breakfast. AE, DC, MC, V. Bus: 19. From the town center, cross the Ness Bridge and turn right at the first traffic light.

In a residential neighborhood about half a mile (1km) west of Invernesss center, this dignified sandstone house was built in 1873 as the manse for the Episcopal bishop of the Inverness cathedral. In 1994, when the bishop retired in a huff because of the ordination of women, the manse became available and was bought by Peter and Caroline McKenzie. Today, it's a B&B with five comfortable, dignified guest rooms and a social life revolving around copious Scottish breakfasts. The rooms come with hair dryers, tea/coffeemakers, and fresh fruit and flowers on arrival. The McKenzies work hard to make your stay pleasant and have built up a loyal North American and British following; they provide complimentary pickup from the bus and train stations as well as the airport. Dinner can be arranged with advance notice.

## DINING

**Cafe 1.** 75 Castle St. ☎ **01463/716-363.** Reservations recommended. Main courses £5–£6.50 ($8.50–$11.05) at lunch, £7–£12.50 ($11.90–$21.25) at dinner. MC, V. Mon–Sat noon–2pm and 6–9:30pm. INTERNATIONAL/SCOTTISH FUSION.

One of the most pleasant restaurants in town is in a century-old stone-fronted building on a street dotted with shops. Inside, you'll find varnished paneling, wooden tables, verdant potted plants, and a soothing New Age atmosphere. The portions are generous, redolent with herbs, and include venison steak with bean sprouts, beetroot, and red caramelized port jus; oven-baked salmon on sweet potatoes with lime-cream sauce; and vegetarian tart studded with caramelized onions and zucchini, served with stewed tomatoes and onions. For dessert, perhaps try the dark-chocolate tart with white-chocolate shavings.

**Dickens International Restaurant.** 77–79 Church St. ☎ **01463/713-111.** Reservations required on weekends. Main courses £7–£13 ($11.90–$22.10). AE, DC, MC, V. Daily noon–2pm and 5:30–11pm. INTERNATIONAL.

On a downtown street next to the oldest house in Inverness, Aberton House, between Bank and Academy streets, this restaurant boasts a decor that has been revamped and updated with furnishings in the style created by Charlie Rennie Mackintosh (1868–1928), Scotland's most famous designer. A wide selection of European, Chinese, and international dishes is offered, including seafood and vegetarian dishes. On the menu are Dickens's own steak, aromatic duck, fresh local salmon, and chateaubriand. The widest choice of side dishes in Inverness is found here, including fried rice, bean sprouts, and cauliflower with cheese.

✪ **Dunain Park Restaurant.** In the Dunain Park Hotel, Dunain Park. ☎ **01463/230-512.** Reservations recommended. Main courses £15.95–£17.95 ($27.10–$30.50). AE, DC, MC, V. Daily 7–9pm. SCOTTISH.

Ann Nicoll presides over the kitchen here, offering Scottish fare with French flair, using fresh local ingredients. A game terrine of chicken and guinea fowl is layered with venison and pigeon, and meats are wrapped in bacon and served with a delicious onion confit. Other dishes that may appear on the changing menu are hare-and-pigeon casserole with roasted shallots and wild mushrooms and Shetland salmon baked in sea salt, served with a white port, lime, and ginger sauce. The restaurant also specializes in Aberdeen Angus steaks. Try one of the desserts from the buffet: crème brûlée, chocolate roulade, or marshmallow pudding.

**Kong's Restaurant.** 64–66 Academy St. ☎ **01463/237-755.** Reservations recommended. Main courses £6.90–£8.65 ($11.75–$14.70); fixed-price menus £12.95–£21 ($22–$35.70) per person. MC, V. Mon–Sat noon–2pm and daily 5:30–11pm. CHINESE/THAI.

Spicy and reasonably priced food await you here. Especially noteworthy is the large array of appetizers, including some dishes from Vietnam. Try the Thai chicken wings or the Szechuan squid before moving on to a wide array of seafood and poultry dishes, along with a selection of pork and beef. The Thai green and red curry dishes are especially flavorful, and the chef's specialties include Peking roast duck and a steam filet of sole flavored with ginger and spring onions. Vegetarians are well catered to here.

**Restaurant Riviera.** In the Glenmoriston Hotel, 20 Ness Bank. ☎ **01463/223-777.** Reservations recommended. Main courses £14.80–£17 ($25.15–$28.90); 3-course fixed-price menu £24.95 ($42.40). AE, DC, MC, V. Daily noon–2pm and 6:30–9:30pm. BRITISH/ITALIAN.

Often hosting local family celebrations, this rather staid restaurant occupies the ground floor of an early-1900s stone-sided hotel on the riverbank near the center of Inverness. At least five chefs labor away in the kitchen. Meals here are part of an entire evening's entertainment, so plan on spending an entire leisurely evening here. Menu items include involtini of smoked salmon stuffed with seafood mousseline, presented with saffron- and dill-flavored dressing; slices of warm breast of duckling scented with heather-flavored honey and dressed with walnut oil; Scottish beef fillet with wild-mushroom polenta, shallots, and Parmesan crackling; and grilled king prawns with roasted tomatoes and pea purée.

**Riva.** 4–6 Ness Walk. ☎ **01463/237-377.** Reservations required. Main courses £5.95–£12 ($9.80–$19.80) in restaurant; sandwiches £3.95 ($6.70) in cafe. MC, V. Restaurant Mon–Sat noon–2pm and 6–9:30pm (last order), Sun 6–9:30pm. Cafe Mon–Sat 10am–9:30pm, except during above-mentioned meal hours. ITALIAN/INTERNATIONAL.

One of Inverness's newest restaurants occupies a site on the opposite *riva* (riverbank) from the rest of the town. Deliberately unpretentious, it has only 18 tables; many of the staff members are family. At least a dozen kinds of pastas can be either starters or main courses. Main courses include tagliatelle with crumbly meatballs, monkfish in red-pepper sauce, and chicken with crispy Parma ham and risotto. Between mealtimes, the place functions as a simple cafe serving sandwiches.

## INVERNESS AFTER DARK

It may be the capital of the Highlands, but Inverness is a sprawling small town without much nightlife. You can spend an evening in the town's pubs sampling single-malt whiskies or beers on tap. Although the pubs here may not have the authentic charm of the isolated pubs in more rural areas, you'll still find a lot of Highlander flavor. Try the pub in the **Loch Ness House Hotel,** Glenurquhart Road (☎ **01463/231-248**), on the western periphery of town; **Gellions Pub,** 8–14 Bridge St. (☎ **01463/ 233-648**); **Gunsmith's Pub,** 30 Union St. (☎ **01463/710-519**); and **MacCallum's,** 40 Union St. (☎ **01463/234-805**). For punk rock and heavy metal, head for either of the town's discos: **Blue,** Rose Street (☎ **01463/222-712**), or **Gs,** 9–21 Castle St. (☎ **01463/233-322**).

## SIDE TRIPS FROM INVERNESS
### MUIR OF ORD

This small town, 10 miles (16km) west of Inverness, makes a good touring center for a history-rich part of Scotland. If you stay at the hotel recommended below, you can take day trips around Black Isle, which boasts beautiful scenery (see "The Black Isle Peninsula," below, for details). Outdoorsy types are drawn here for fishing, golf, and shooting.

### Accommodations & Dining

✪ **Dower House.** Highfield, Muir of Ord IV6 7XN. ☎ **01463/870-090.** Fax 01463/ 870-090. www.thedowerhouse.co.uk. E-mail: info@thedowerhouse.co.uk. 5 units. TV TEL. £110–£120 ($187–$204) double; £130 ($221) suite or cottage; £150 ($255) suite. MC, V. Rates include Scottish breakfast. Drive 1 mile (1.5km) north of A862.

This charming guesthouse is a perfect base for exploring the area. The main house has four good-sized doubles and one suite, decorated in the fine tradition of a Scottish country house, with hair dryers, tea/coffeemakers, and flowers cut from the garden. A small three-bedroom guest cottage is available and perfect for families. Be sure to make reservations for the Dower House well in advance; the comfortable atmosphere is very much in demand.

**Dining:** Even if you don't stay here, call for a dinner reservation. After a cocktail in the lounge, you proceed to the dining room for a four-course meal. Robyn Aitchison is an inspired chef who prepares modern British cuisine using produce grown on the grounds; expensive fixed-price menus are served nightly.

**Amenities:** Room service, baby-sitting.

### BEAULY

The French monks who settled here in the 13th century named it literally "beautiful place"—and it still is. You'll see the **Highland Craftpoint** on your left as you come from Inverness. In summer, there's an interesting exhibit of Scottish handcrafts. Beauly is 12 miles (19km) west of Inverness on A862, and Inverness Traction, a local bus company, has hourly bus service from Inverness.

Dating from 1230, the **Beauly Priory** (☎ **01463/782-309**), now a roofless shell, is the only remaining one of three priories built for the Valliscaulian order, an austere body drawing its main components from the Cistercians and the Carthusians. Some notable windows and window arcading are still left among the ruins. Hugh Fraser of Lovat erected the Chapel of the Holy Cross on the nave's north side in the early 15th century. You can tour the priory at any time; if it's locked, ask for a key from the Priory Hotel across the way.

If you're interested in tweeds, don't miss **Campbells of Beauly,** Highland Tweed House (☎ **01463/782-239**), operated by the same family since 1858. An excellent selection of fine tweeds and tartans is offered, and you can have your material tailored. Blankets, travel rugs, tweed hats (deerstalkers and fishing hats), and kilts are sold, as well as cashmere and lambswool sweaters and Shetland knits. It's on the main street at the south end of the village square, next to the Royal Bank of Scotland.

### Accommodations & Dining

**Priory Hotel.** The Square, Beauly IV4 7BX. ☎ **01463/782-309.** Fax 01463/782-531. www.priory-hotel.com. E-mail: reservations@priory-hotel.com. 36 units. TV TEL. £79 ($134.30) double. Rates include Scottish breakfast. AE, DC, MC, V.

The Priory Hotel is on the historic main square of town, a short walk from the ruins of the priory. The hotel has recently expanded into an adjacent building, adding four rooms to its well-furnished offerings. All rooms are equipped with tea/coffeemakers and ironing boards. A frequently changing dinner menu features a variety of fish and local game as well as a good selection of steaks; bar meals are similar dishes served in smaller portions. In addition, high tea is served daily.

## 8  Nairn & Cawdor Castle

172 miles (277km) N of Edinburgh, 91 miles (146.5km) NW of Aberdeen, 16 miles (26km) E of Inverness

A favorite family seaside resort on the sheltered Moray Firth, Nairn (from the Gaelic for "Water of Alders") is a royal burgh at the mouth of the Nairn River. Its fishing harbor was constructed in 1820, and golf has been played here since 1672—as it still is today.

### ESSENTIALS

**GETTING THERE**    Nairn can be reached by train from the south, with a change at either Aberdeen or Inverness. The service between Inverness and Nairn is frequent; this is the most popular route. For information, check with the Inverness train station at Station Square (☎ **0345/484-950**).

From Inverness, Inverness Traction runs daily buses to Nairn. Call ☎ **0990/ 808-080** for schedules.

If you're driving from Inverness, take A96 east to Nairn.

**VISITOR INFORMATION**    The **tourist office** is at 62 King St. (☎ **01667/ 452-753**). April to mid-May, it's open Monday to Saturday 10am to 5pm; mid-May to June, hours are Monday to Saturday 10am to 5pm and Sunday 11am to 4pm; July and August, hours are Monday to Saturday 9am to 6pm and Sunday from 10am to 5pm; and September and October, hours are Monday to Saturday 10am to 5pm.

### EXPLORING THE AREA

A large uncrowded beach draws crowds in summer. Anglers also find the area is a good spot. Nairn is great walking country, and the tourist office will give you a map and details about the various possibilities, including hikes along the banks of the River Nairn. The best walks are five signposted nature trails, called the **Cawdor Castle Nature Trails.** They're signposted from Cawdor Castle (see below), taking you along some of the loveliest and most varied forests and wooded areas in the Highlands.

**Brodie Country,** on A96, 3 miles (5km) east of Nairn in Brodie (☎ **01309/ 641-555**), is a family-owned shopping complex with shops carrying a variety of merchandise. Of greatest interest are the regionally produced knitwear, gift items, and foodstuff; the latter includes smoked meats, jams, mustards, and other condiments. Also on the premises is a fully licensed restaurant serving Scottish cuisine daily 9:30am to 5:30pm (to 7pm Thursday), with main courses averaging about £6 ($10.20).

**Nairn Antiques,** St. Ninian Place (☎ 01667/453-303), carries a broad range of antiques and a section of upscale crafts and reproductions. Of particular interest are the collections of Scottish pottery, silver, and fine porcelains, but there's also furniture and bric-a-brac from around the world. This is the only shop in the entire north country to stock high-quality Lalique crystal from France.

**A Taste of Moray,** on the Nairn-Inverness Road, 6 miles (10km) north of Nairn (☎ 01667/462-340), is all about the pleasures of preparing and consuming Scottish cuisine, with products ranging from quality cookware to regional domestic stoneware. The food hall offers an array of Scottish condiments and smoked meats, and if shopping here makes you hungry, you can step into the adjacent restaurant, serving seafood dishes and steaks, with main courses averaging £10 ($17). Food service is daily 10am to 9pm.

The 18-hole **Nairn Dunbar Golf Club,** Loch Loy Road (☎ 01667/452-741), consists of 6,700 yards (6,097m) of playing area with a par of 72. Greens fees are £28 ($47.60) per round or £35 ($59.50) per day Monday to Friday, or £33 ($56.10) per round or £45 ($76.50) per day Saturday and Sunday.

✪ **Cawdor Castle.** Between Inverness and Nairn on B9090 off A96, Cawdor. ☎ 01667/404-615. Admission £5.90 ($10.05) adults, £4.90 ($8.35) seniors, £3 ($5.10) children 5–15; under 5 free. May–2nd Sun in Oct daily 10am–5pm.

To the south of Nairn, you'll encounter 600 years of Highland history at Cawdor Castle, since the early 14th century the home of the thanes of Cawdor. Although the castle was constructed 2 centuries after his time, it has nevertheless been romantically linked to Shakespeare's *Macbeth,* once the thane of Cawdor. The castle has all the architectural ingredients you'd associate with the Middle Ages: a drawbridge, an ancient tower (this one built around a tree), and fortified walls. Its severity is softened by the handsome gardens, flowers, trees, and rolling lawns. On the grounds are five nature trails through beautiful woodland, a nine-hole golf course, a putting green, a snack bar, a picnic area, shops, and a licensed restaurant serving hot meals, teas, coffees, and fresh-baked goods all day.

## ACCOMMODATIONS

✪ **The Boath House.** On A96, 2 miles east of Nairn, Auldearn, Nairn IV12 5TE. ☎ 01667/454-896. Fax 01667/455-469. www.boath-house.demon.co.uk. E-mail: wendy@boath-house.demon.co.uk. 7 units. TV TEL. £110–£175 ($187–$297.50) double. Rates include breakfast. AE, DC, MC, V. Free parking.

The Boath House, owned and operated by Don and Wendy Matheson, is a Georgian mansion set amid 20 acres of lush greenery. Built in 1825, the house has been restored to its original style and elegance. Bedrooms are splendidly decorated with antiques and period furniture, and amenities include beverage makers, hair dryers, and cable TV. In spite of its classic look, the atmosphere here is relaxed, casual, and informal. There are two lounges and a library where you can enjoy a dram of whisky. There's an on-site salon, open to both guests and nonguests and offering everything from aromatherapy to galvanic slimming treatments. The salon uses only products with natural ingredients from pure plant and flower essences. The hotel is also home to an award-winning restaurant (see "Dining," below).

**Clifton House.** 1–3 Viewfield St., Nairn, Nairnshire IV12 4HW. ☎ 01667/453-119. Fax 01667/452-836. www.macintyre.clara.net. E-mail: mackintyre@clara.net. 12 units. £100–£107 ($170–$181.90) double. Rates include Scottish breakfast. AE, DC, MC, V. Turn east of the town roundabout on A96.

Clifton House reflects the dynamic personality of J. Gordon Macintyre, owner of this vine-covered honey-sandstone Victorian mansion. It has been his home for over 60 years. Fully licensed, it stands on the seafront, 3 minutes from the beach and equidistant to both golf links. Mr. Macintyre has spent a great deal of time and care in decorating, refurbishing, and preserving the house. Most of the furniture is antique; the collection of paintings, prints, etchings, engravings, and drawings is unusual and extensive. Each guest room is pleasantly appointed, with a hair dryer; however, phones and TVs are purposely not included. Mr. Macintyre organizes a series of concerts, chamber operas, plays, and recitals to entertain his guests. The hotel is a licensed theater, and performances are presented September to March.

**Dining:** The Clifton has the most extensive wine list in the north of Scotland and also serves the best food in Nairn, using only basic fresh raw ingredients cooked with classic techniques. For instance, guinea fowl in Bordeaux wine and bacon, double-stuffed chicken, lamb in mustard, mallard duck, wild salmon, brill, turbot, and sole are among the offerings. Lunch and dinner are served daily. Reservations are necessary. Breakfast is very old-fashioned Scottish (no packaged cereals)—juice is squeezed while you wait, and homemade oat cakes and marmalade and local honey are served 8am to lunchtime.

**Amenities:** Concierge, room service, laundry, baby-sitting.

**Greenlawns Private Hotel.** 13 Seafield St., Nairn IV12 4HG. ☎ **01667/452-738.** Fax 01667/452-738. www.greenlawns.uk.com. E-mail: greenlawns@cali.co.uk. 8 units, 7 with bathroom. TV. £35 ($59.50) double without bathroom; £40–£56 ($68–$95.20) double with bathroom. Rates include Scottish breakfast. AE, MC, V. Turn down Albert St. from A96.

This Victorian house within easy reach of the beaches and golf courses is a pleasant base for touring the Loch Ness region. The new owners, David and Sheila Southwell, have completely refurbished the house while retaining its traditional charm. All the good-sized guest rooms come with tea/coffeemakers as well as electric blankets; two have been upgraded to demi-suites with small sitting areas. The dinner menu changes but might include navarin of Scottish lamb, chicken korma with basamati rice, or the seafood selection of the day. Vegetarian choices are also available. Mrs. Southwell, a certified genealogist, offers help to those who are interested in exploring their Scottish family ties.

# DINING

✪ **The Boath House Restaurant.** In the Boath House, Auldearn. ☎ **01667/454-896.** Reservations recommended. Set-price 4-course menu £29.50 ($50.15). AE, DC, MC, V. Daily noon–2pm and 7–9pm. Closed Mon–Tues for non-residents. On A96, 2 miles east of Nairn. SCOTTISH/CONTINENTAL.

Located in a Georgian mansion, this restaurant is a multiple award winner, including AA "Rosettes" and commendations from the Scottish Chefs Association. Here traditional fare is given a continental twist to create a well-balanced menu that changes daily. The atmosphere is romantic with antique decor, and in the evening, the room is totally bathed in candlelight. Featuring local Scottish fare, menu items might include seared fillet of sea bass on a citrus couscous, tapenade, and a basil-infused oil, or roasted gray-legged partridge with a ragout of red cabbage and onion, plus a port wine and rosemary jus. For a true taste of Scotland, try the roasted saddle of venison with a sweet potato purée. The dessert menu offers some deliciously decadent options, and there is also a good selection of wines.

**Cawdor Tavern.** The Lane, Cawdor. ☎ **01667/404-777.** Reservations recommended for dinner. Main courses £8–£10 ($13.60–$17) at lunch, £8–£12 ($13.60–$20.40) at dinner; set-price menus £16.95–£24.50 ($28.80–$41.65). AE, MC, V. Daily noon–2:30pm and 5:30–9pm. SCOTTISH.

This atmospheric restaurant occupies what was built as a stone-sided carpenter shop for Cawdor Castle, less than 500 feet (152m) away. Inside you'll find a recently installed postmodern sheathing of mahogany and maple and a set of century-old panels donated by the owner of the nearby castle and skillfully resized and reconfigured into their new setting. Many visitors opt just for a drink, choosing any of the single-malt whiskies that adorn the back of the bar. Others come for the food, served in generous portions. Each focuses on local produce, regional fish, and meats. Examples are duck in white-wine sauce, seafood platters, crabmeat-and-salmon cakes with chive-cream sauce, pork fillets with red-wine sauce, and an unusual preparation of chicken stuffed with haggis (nationalistically labeled "chicken Culloden").

**The Longhouse.** 8 Harbour St. ☎ **01667/455-532.** Reservations recommended. Main courses £2.25–£5.95 ($3.80–$10.10) at lunch, £5.95–£15 ($10.10–$25.50) at dinner; high tea £6.45 ($10.95). AE, MC, V. Daily lunch 10am–4:30pm; high tea 4–6:30pm; dinner 5–10pm. Closed Mon in Oct–Mar and 2 weeks in Oct. SCOTTISH.

Opened in 1997, the domain of the Rennie family focuses on traditional Scottish cuisine. In a cream-colored stone house in the center of town, the restaurant is named after the early-1900s building's long and narrow design. Cozy and candlelit, it seats only 33 diners at a time. Menu items are less ambitious at lunch, when platters are likely to include lasagna, fried fillets of fresh fish, and roasted pork with wine sauce. High tea, which includes a platter of food, tea, and homemade pastries, is favored by locals inclined to retire early. At dinner the cuisine shines. Its tradition is strongly Scottish; expect sauces laced with whisky and dishes like black pudding with whisky-mustard sauce; rack of lamb with wine-rosemary sauce and mint-infused poached pears; mussels in white wine, onion, and dill sauce; salmon fillet with white wine, lemon, and prawn sauce; and breaded Aberdeen haddock with a salad garnish. Desserts usually include a slice of shortbread with fresh cream and fresh raspberries. The restaurant is licensed only for alcohol served with a meal.

## NAIRN AFTER DARK

At the comfortable **Claymore House Hotel Bar,** Seabank Road (☎ **01667/ 453-731**), locals gather to drink and talk in a room with a padded bench running all the way around the wall, sofas, and several tables with chairs. During cold weather, an open fireplace takes the chill out of the air, as does the bar's selection of malt whiskies. On tap you'll find the ever-present Guinness alongside guest pumps that feature a real ale, two lagers, and a dark beer. **Clifton House,** 1–3 Viewfield St. (☎ **01667/ 453-119**), offers classical concerts by solo artists and small ensembles about once every 3 weeks September through May. It also stages two plays a year, in November and February or March, with an admission of £9 to £14 ($15.30 to $23.80). An optional Scottish buffet dinner is available for an additional £18 ($30.60) per person.

The old **Millford Hotel Pub,** Mill Road (☎ **01667/453-941**), features live music every Saturday for free, mainly middle-of-the-road country, pop, blues, or folk bands. Once a month, on Sunday, there's a country-and-western night with dancing. On tap you can choose from Tartan Special, McEwan's 60 Shilling, Raeburn's, or Murphy's Stout.

## 9 The Black Isle Peninsula

Cromarty: 23 miles (37km) NW of Inverness (via Kessock Bridge)

The Black Isle is one of Scotland's most enchanting peninsulas, a land rich in history, beauty, and mystery. Part of Ross and Cromarty County, it's northwest of Inverness, a 20-minute drive or bus ride away. A car tour would be about 37 miles (59.5km), but allow plenty of time for stopovers and country walks along the way.

There's much confusion about the name of the peninsula, since it's neither black nor an island. In summer, the land is green and fertile, with tropical plants flourishing. It has forests, fields of broom and whin, and scattered coastal villages. The peninsula has been inhabited for 7,000 years, as 60-odd prehistoric sites testify. Pictish kings, whose thrones passed down through the female line, once ruled this land. Then the Vikings held sway, and the evidence of many Gallows Hills testifies that their justice was harsh.

## ESSENTIALS

**GETTING THERE**    The nearest rail service goes to Inverness. From there, the Highland Bus and Coach Company from Inverness serves the peninsula (nos. 26, 26A, and 126), making stops at North Kessock, Munlochy, Avoch, Fortrose, Rosemarkie, and Cromarty. Buses depart from Farraline Park in Inverness (☎ 01463/ 233-371 for schedules).

If you're driving, and will head to Fortrose as your first stop (see below), take A9 north from Inverness (follow the signs toward Wick). Follow A9 for 4 miles (6.5km) until you see the Kessock Bridge. Go over the bridge and take the second road to the right, toward Munlocky. (Fortrose is 8 miles/13km from this turnoff.) Follow A832 through the village of Munlochy and at the junction take the road right, signposted Fortrose. Continue straight on through Avoch to Fortrose.

**VISITOR INFORMATION**    Ask at the **Inverness tourist office** (see "Inverness: Capital of the Highlands," above) for details on Black Isle, since the peninsula is often included on a day tour from that city.

## FORTROSE & ROSEMARKIE

Fortrose is a good place to start. Along the way you'll pass a celebrated wishing well, or **clootie well,** festooned with rags. Dedicated to St. Boniface, the well has a long tradition, dating back to pagan times. It's said that anyone removing a rag will inherit the misfortunes of the person who placed it there.

The ruins of **Fortrose Cathedral** stand in this sleepy village. Founded in the 13th century, the cathedral was dedicated to St. Peter and St. Boniface. You can still see fine detailing from the 14th century throughout the structure. If you notice that the stones scattered about don't seem to be enough to fill in the gaps, it's because Cromwell's men removed many of them to help build a fort in Inverness. There's no formal tour of the ruins; you can wander through at any time.

Fortrose adjoins **Rosemarkie,** up the road. The site has been inhabited since the Bronze Age. A center of Pictish culture, the town saw the arrival of the first Christian missionaries. It's reported that St. Moluag founded a monastery here in the 6th century. Rosemarkie became a royal burgh in 1216. The twin hamlets share a golf course today, and they're the site of the Chanonry Sailing Club, whose annual regatta brings entries from all over Scotland. Right beyond Rosemarkie is the mysterious **Fairy Glen,** signposted at the end of the village. It's one of the loveliest places in the Black Isle for a long walk.

## ACCOMMODATIONS & DINING

**Royal Hotel.** At the corner of Union and High sts., Fortrose IV10 8SU. ☎ **01381/620-236.** www.royalhotelfortrose.co.uk. E-mail: royalfortrose@cali.co.uk. 17 units, 11 with private bathroom. £50 ($85) double without bathroom; £56 ($95.20) double with bathroom. Rates include half-board. MC, V.

Built in 1865 as a coaching lodging, the Royal overlooks the ancient monument of Fortrose Cathedral. The traditional Victorian house has recently undergone extensive renovations, with guest room upgrades. Proprietor Graham Law has left the common areas mostly untouched, preferring to retain the mix of modern and traditional decor. The hotel has two bars and a lounge where pub meals are served. The restaurant serves traditional Scottish fare made from locally produced ingredients.

## CROMARTY

Cromarty stands at the tip of the peninsula, where the North and South Sutors guard the entrance to the Cromarty Firth, the second-deepest inland waterway estuary in Europe, always of strategic importance to the Royal Navy.

Much of the Black Isle invites country walks, but in Cromarty you may want to stay in the village itself, walking around and exploring each street with its rows of terraced cottages seemingly hunched against the prevailing north winds. The town has been handsomely restored, and the old merchant's houses are superb examples of domestic architecture of the 18th century.

Once a flourishing port and a former royal burgh, the town gave the world a famous son: Hugh Miller. Born here in 1802, Miller was a stonemason as a young man, but in time he became a recognized expert in the field of geology, as well as a powerful man of letters in Scotland. His thatched cottage was built in 1698. **Hugh Miller's Cottage,** Church Street (☎ **01381/600-245**), is on view to the public, containing many of his personal belongings and collections of geological specimens. May 1 to September 30, it's open Monday to Saturday 11am to 1pm and 2 to 5pm, and Sunday 2 to 5pm. Admission is £2 ($3.40) adults and £1.30 ($2.20) students/seniors, and £5.30 ($9) families (two adults and up to six children).

### ACCOMMODATIONS & DINING

**Royal Hotel.** Marine Terrace, Cromarty IV11 8YN. ☎ **01381/600-217.** www.cali. co.uk/highexp/cromvr/. 10 units. TV. £59–£80 ($100.30–$136) double. Rates include Scottish breakfast. AE, DC, MC, V. Bus: 26, 26A, or 126 from Inverness.

The only hotel in town sits on an embankment near one of the deepest estuaries in Europe. Around 1940, the British navy combined a series of waterfront buildings into living quarters for sailors. Today the hotel is a cozy enclave with wood-burning stoves and open fireplaces. The guest rooms are small to medium, each traditionally furnished. There's a comfortable lounge bar, a public bar, and a dining room that spills onto a glassed-in extension opening onto the harbor. The dining room features specialties like steaks and stroganoff. You can also enjoy a good bar menu, with a tempting list of burgers, crêpes, and salads.

## 10 Sutherland: The Gem of Scotland

Sutherland has more sheep than people (a 20-to-1 ratio). It's genuinely off the beaten track, but if you have time to travel this far, you'll find it's perhaps the most beautiful county in Scotland. Adding to the scenic sweep of haunting beauty are lochs and rivers, heather-covered moors and mountains—in all, 2,000 square miles (5,200sq km) of territory. The duke of Sutherland used to own most of it. It may not offer many "attractions," but it's a wonderful setting for outdoor pursuits like golf and fishing.

To the northwest of Inverness, Sutherland has three coastlines—on the north and west, the Atlantic, and on the east, the North Sea. Most villages have populations of only 100 or so hearty souls. Sutherland was the scene of the notorious Highland Clearances, when many residents were driven out from their ancestral crofts. Many made their way to the New World, where they went on to prosperity. The sheep, known as the "white plague," took over after their departure. This dislocation of the

Airport
Castle
Mountain
Golf

Penland Firth

Island of Stroma
Dunnet Head
Duncansby Head
John o' Groats
Nybster
Noss Head
Castles Sinclair & Girnigoe
Wick
Castle of Old Wick
Lybster

A99
A836
A882
A98
A95
A96

Scrabster
Thurso
Grey Cairns of Camster
Bunbeath

Buckie
Banderburgh
Lossiemouth
A96
A941

Melvich
Helmsdale
Lothmore
Elgin
Kinloss
A940
A939

C A I T H N E S S

Strathy Point
Strathy
Halladale River
A897

Dunrobin Castle
Golspie
Tarbat Ness
Dornoch Firth
Moray Firth
Nairn
Cawdor Castle
Stones of Clava
Fort George

Whiten Head
Tongue
Castle Varrich

S U T H E R L A N D

Creag Mhor
A839
Bonar Bridge
Dornoch
Balintore
Cromarty
Black Isle Peninsula
Fortrose
A832
A9

Ben Hope
A838
Ben Kilbreck
Lairg
Invergordon
Dingwall

E A S T E R   R O S S

Durness
Laxford Bridge
A838
Kinloch
Loch Shin
A839
Ardgay
Ben Wyvis
Strathpeffer
Muir of Ord
Beauly
Inverness
A835

Skiage Bridge
Ben More
Ledmore
Invercassley
A837
Beauly Priory

Scourie
A894
A837
A835
Inverpolly National Nature Reserve
Ullapool
Corrieshalloch Gorge
A835
A832

Lochinver
A832
Dundonnell
Tourhaig & Inverewe Gardens
Sgurr Mor
A832
A890

Summer Isles
Priest Island
Gruinard Bay

W E S T E R   R O S S

10 Mi
16 Km

387

people of Sutherland in the 19th century has been termed "an orgy of ruthless social engineering." In many a deserted glen, you can still see traces of former crofting villages.

# DORNOCH

The ancient cathedral city of Dornoch, 63 miles (101.5km) northwest of Inverness and 219 miles (352.5km) northwest of Edinburgh, is Sutherland's major town and the area's most interesting stop. The major sightseeing attraction nearby is **Dornoch Cathedral** (see below). Dornoch is also known for its sandy beaches, but we find they're best left for polar bears if you want to go swimming. However, they make for lovely walks.

A **tourist office** is at The Square (☎ 01862/810-400). July and August, it's open Monday to Friday 9am to 6pm, Saturday 9am to 5:30pm, and Sunday 11am to 5pm; April and September hours are Monday to Friday 9am to 5pm and Saturday 9am to 4pm; October to March, hours are Monday to Friday 9am to 5pm. From the Inverness bus station at Farraline Park, off Academy Street (call ☎ 01463/233-371 for schedules), three local companies run daily buses to Dornoch: Stagecoach, Caledonian Express, and Scottish CityLink. The trip is between 60 and 90 minutes and costs £7.50 ($12.75) one-way.

## EXPLORING THE AREA

The village of Dornoch has long been known for its golf club on the sheltered shores of Dornoch Firth, the northernmost first-class course in the world. The turf of the ✪ **Royal Dornoch Golf Club,** Golf Road (☎ 01862/810-219), is considered sacred by aficionados. Golf was first played here by monks in 1614. Nearby hills divert up to 75% of the rain that falls on adjacent districts, and a curious meander of the Gulf Stream as it bypasses northern Scotland keeps the climate balmier than you'd expect. None of this is lost on sports enthusiasts. The club itself was founded in 1877, and a royal charter was granted by Edward VII in 1906, when he adopted it as one of his favorite causes. Prince Andrew and the duchess of Sutherland are both members today. Its SSS is 73; its par is 70 for an 18-hole yardage of 6,185 (5,628m). Greens fees are £57 ($96.90) Monday to Friday and £67 ($113.90) Saturday (members only) and Sunday, with a 3-day ticket available for consecutive weekdays only, costing £144 ($244.80). Golf club and trolley rentals are £20 to £30 ($34 to $51) and £3 ($5.10), respectively. Caddy service is available for £20 to £30 ($34 to $51) plus tip.

**Dornoch Cathedral,** Castle Street, was built in the 13th century and partially destroyed by fire in 1570. It has had many restorations, including one in 1924, but you can still see its fine 13th-century stonework. The cathedral is famous for its modern stained-glass windows—three are in memory of Andrew Carnegie, the American steel king. The seat covers in the choir stall depicting local flora and fauna were made by locals. The cathedral is open daily 9am to dusk. The **Plaiden Ell,** found in the cathedral's cemetery where a marketplace used to be, was a medieval method for measuring cloth (an *ell* was a unit of measure equaling about 38 inches [96.5cm]). The Ell is carved in stone in a flat shape similar to a tombstone's, but with two pieces of metal rising, each about 2 inches (5cm) above the level of the stone. The distance between those two pieces of metal is an ell. In one of the gardens is the 1722 **witch's stone** marking the spot where the last burning of a so-called witch took place in Scotland. Diagonally opposite is the aptly named **Witches pool.** The local Pipe Band plays in the square on Saturday evenings in summer.

If the weather is fair, Dornoch is great for hiking and country strolls, as the town is flanked by miles of clean sand opening onto chilly waters. You can often see migrant birds on these beaches. At **Embo,** some 3 miles (5km) north of the beaches of Dornoch, you'll come across the remains of two funereal vaults believed to date from around 2000 B.C.

You can drive another 2 miles (3km) north of Embo to the shores of lovely **Loch Fleet,** where there's a meager ruin of **Skelbo Castle.** It's now on a lonely grassy mound, but in the 14th century Skelbo was a powerful fortification and once loomed in the pages of Scottish history. Representatives from the court of Edward I waited here to honor Princess Margaret, Maid of Norway. A marriage between her and Edward's son, or so it was hoped, would have solved the problem of sovereignty in the country. But it wasn't to be. The young girl died following an illness on the voyage. This eventually led to the wars for Scottish independence, with Edward's armies pushing into Scotland to crush the rebellion.

Shoppers should check out the **Dornoch Craft Centre,** Town Jail, Castlestreet (☎ **01862/810-555**), in the center of town opposite the cathedral; it occupies what was the town jail in 1844. You can wander through the selection of Scottish crafts, jewelry, and pottery, then visit the Textile Hall and browse through the range of knitwear, tartans, mohair goods, and tweeds.

## ACCOMMODATIONS & DINING

**Carnegie Club at Skibo Castle.** Skibo Castle, Dornoch IV25 3RQ. ☎ **01862/894-600.** Fax 01862/894-601. www.carnegie.co.uk. E-mail: carnegie/skibo@cali.co.uk. 46 units. TV TEL. £550 ($935) double members; £750 ($1,275) double nonmembers. Rates include meals, drinks, and sporting activities (including greens fees at the resort's golf course). Membership costs £3,000 ($5,100) per year per family. AE, DC, MC, V. The club will send a car to Dornoch or anywhere in Inverness to meet new arrivals.

Skibo Castle is as massive a baronial house as you're likely to find in Scotland, an Edwardian pile created from a unique combination of Scottish heritage and one of the most potent fortunes of the Industrial Revolution. Steel magnate Andrew Carnegie, who emigrated from Scotland's woolen mills to America in the mid–19th century, yearned for a return to the land of his birth after he acquired his fortune. When the Scottish castle of his dreams (Cluny, seat of the McPherson clan) wasn't available at any price, Carnegie settled on the historic but dilapidated Skibo, 5 miles (8km) east of Dornoch. After he bought it in 1898 (for the relatively reasonable price of £85,000/$144,500), Carnegie and his second wife, Louise, massively enlarged the place, pouring £2 million ($3.4 million) into its refurbishment. There they welcomed a stream of distinguished visitors, including Edward VII, during the months every year they spent in Scotland in their final years. Descendants of Carnegie remained on site until 1983.

In 1990, Peter de Savary, the force behind posh semiprivate clubs in London and Antigua, acquired the property and its 7,000 acres, installed an 18-hole golf course designed by Donald Steel following the approximate layout of one used by Carnegie, and created a resort that's a combination golfing mecca and semiprivate club for the celebs, CEOs, and aristocrats who can afford the sky-high rates. About half the elegant guest rooms are within the mansion; others, equally fine, are scattered in the lodges and cottages where the staff of gardeners, ghillies, and caretakers once lived. Meals are served in the style of an Edwardian house party at a long table. Evenings of Scottish dance are featured every Saturday; other nights, there are dinner performances of Scottish flute, Celtic harp, or piano. Sports opportunities (part of the price) include trap and skeet shooting, falconry, trout and salmon fishing, and golf (on the resort's course or at the nearby Royal Dornoch Course).

**Dornoch Castle Hotel.** Castle St., Dornoch IV25 3SD. ☎ **01862/810-216.** Fax 01862/
810-981. 17 units. TV TEL. £70–£82 ($119–$139.40) double. Rates include Scottish breakfast.
AE, MC, V.

This unusual hotel, close to the Royal Dornoch Golf Course, occupies what was once
the residence of the bishops of Caithness, built of local stone in the center of town in
the late 15th or early 16th century. Today its winding stairs, labyrinthine corridors,
and impenetrable cellars have been converted into a well-directed hotel and restaurant.
Six guest rooms are in the original building; the rest are in an extension overlooking
the garden. They all tend to be dowdy, however. Menu specialties in the restaurant
include leg of Sutherland lamb with onion marmalade and Highland Estate venison
with black currants. Reservations are suggested.

**Fourpenny Cottage.** Embo Rd., Dornoch IV25 3HR. ☎/fax **01862/810-727.**
http://homepages.tesco.net~fourpenny. E-mail: fourpenny@tesco.net. 4 units. TV. £30 ($51)
per person double. Rates include Scottish breakfast. No credit cards. Closed Dec–Mar. From
Dornoch center, drive 3 miles (5km) south on the Embo–Golspie road.

This pleasant cottage, 1½ miles (2.5km) north of the famous Royal Dornoch course,
is a favorite of golfers. To cater to all the golfers, they've recently installed a warm-up
green, where golfers can practice before heading onto the formal course. The guest
rooms are divided among the main house, a reconstruction and enlargement of an
antique crofter's cottage, and a modern brick-sided annex. Sheila Board and her family prepare hearty breakfasts and maintain the cozy rooms. The ambience is informal,
akin to that in a private home. According to legend, this was the last parcel of land
sold for four pence in Scottish history—hence its name.

## GOLSPIE

Today, a family resort with a golf course, **Golspie** was once part of the vast holdings
of the earls and dukes of Sutherland. The town, on A9, looks out across the water to
the Dornoch Firth, with a crescent of sandy beach. Golspie, 228 miles (367km) northwest of Edinburgh and 72 miles (116km) northwest of Inverness, is visited chiefly
because of its towering Dunrobin Castle.

### SEEING THE CASTLE

✪ **Dunrobin Castle.** Half a mile (1km) northeast of Golspie on A9. ☎ **01408/633-177.**
Admission £5.50 ($9.35) adults, £4.50 ($7.65) students, £4 ($6.80) seniors/children 5–16,
£16 ($27.20) families (2 adults and 2 children). Apr, May, and Oct Mon–Sat
10:30am–4:30pm, Sun noon–4pm; June–Sept daily 10:30am–5pm. Last entrance 30 minutes
before closing.

Home of the earls and dukes of Sutherland, Dunrobin is the most northerly of the
great houses of Scotland and also the biggest in the northern Highlands, dating in part
from the early 13th century. Its formal gardens are laid out in the manner of Versailles.
On the grounds is a museum containing many relics from the Sutherland family;
trophies and regimental colors of the 93rd Sutherland Highlanders are on view. Some
of the castle's 180 rooms are open to the public—the ornately furnished dining room,
a billiard room-cum-family museum, and the room and gilded four-poster bed where
Queen Victoria slept when she visited in 1872. The countess of Sutherland has apartments here, but many rooms are empty.

### ACCOMMODATIONS & DINING

**Golf Links Hotel.** Church St., Golspie KW10 6TT. ☎ **01408/633-408.** Fax 01408/
634-184. www.home.btconnect.com/golf-links-hotel. E-mail: golflinkshotel@btconnect.com.
9 units. TV. £50 ($85) double; £150–£200 ($255–$340) per week self-service apt. Rates
include Scottish breakfast. MC, V.

From the early 1900s, this was built as the stone rectory for the local minister and was converted to a hotel in 1955. Much of the clientele is golfers drawn to the nearby Golspie, Royal Dornoch, and Brora courses. The rooms in the main building are well furnished and have tea/coffeemakers. The self-service units, rented by the week, are in an annex; all have kitchens and two to four bedrooms. A first-class chef prepares Scottish and continental cuisine served in a dining room opening onto a view of Ben Bhraggie. The contemporary lounge bar looks through big plate-glass windows onto Dornoch Firth, and offers bar lunches. There's also a salon.

## TONGUE

Heading north along A836, you cross high moors and brooding peaks to Tongue, 257 miles (414km) northwest of Edinburgh and 101 miles (163km) northwest of Inverness. For the nature lover and hiker, there's a lot to see, from the mighty cliffs of **Clo Mor,** near Cape Wrath (known for its large colonies of puffins), to waterfalls like **Eas-Coul-Aulin** (the highest in Britain) and the **Falls of Shin,** where you can see salmon leap. Masses of land suddenly rise from a barren landscape, including **Ben Loyal,** known as the queen of Scottish mountains. Any of the district's tourist offices, including the one in Dornoch, can provide you with a map of the local hills, valleys, and walking trails. The one closest to the above-mentioned trekking sites is the office on Main Street in Bettyhill ( ☎ **01641/521-342**), a small village on the coast about 15 miles (24km) from the village of Tongue. July and August, it's open Monday to Saturday 10am to 6pm and Sunday noon to 6pm; September to June, hours are Monday to Saturday noon to 5pm. You can also contact the local police station in Bettyhill at ☎ **01641/521-222** for information about climbing and safety conditions.

West of Tongue on a promontory stand the ruins of **Castle Varrich,** said to have been built by the Vikings. Possibly dating from the 14th century, this castle was the Mackay stronghold. Mackays from North America visit Tongue annually, seeking lore about their ancestral roots. This is a great place for a walk.

**Tongue House,** from 1678, was a home base for the chief of the Mackays, but it now belongs to the estate of the duke of Sutherland. On the shores of the Kyle of Tongue, it has a walled garden and is open to the public only one Sunday in August (check at the tourist office for the day).

A rather dramatic walk from the center is to the **Kyle of Tongue,** crossed by a narrow causeway. Protected from the wild and raging sea nearby, this is a long, shallow inlet. At low tide, wearing a pair of boots, you can walk out to Rabbit Island, a little isle lying at the mouth of Kyle of Tongue. You'll pass towering cliffs, sandy bays, odd rock formations, and deserted rocky islets that time seemingly has forgotten.

### ACCOMMODATIONS & DINING

**Ben Loyal Hotel.** Main St., Tongue IV27 4XE. ☎ **01847/611-216.** Fax 01847/611-212. www.benloyal.co.uk. E-mail: thebenloyalhotel@bt.internet.com. 11 units. TV. £70–£80 ($119–$136) double. Rates include breakfast. MC, V.

This is a good choice, with everything under the careful attention of Paul and Elaine Lewis. The guest rooms are a bit plain but comfortably furnished in the traditional style, with hot- and cold-water basins, electric blankets, and tea/coffeemakers. Several superior rooms have four-poster beds and views over the castle ruins and loch. An à la carte menu is offered in the dining room, where the meals are home-cooked and feature locally reared beef and produce grown on the grounds of the hotel. There is also a five-course fixed-price meal; prices are rather high. A fine wine list and an assortment of malt whiskies complement the cuisine. The Ben Loyal incorporates 19th-century stables, a former post office, a shop, and a village bakery.

**Tongue Hotel.** Tongue, Sutherland IV27 4XD. ☎ **01847/611-206.** Fax 01847/611-345. E-mail: thetonguehotel@aol.com. 15 units. TV TEL. £70–£90 ($119–$153) double. Rates include Scottish breakfast. V.

Since Queen Victoria's day, the best place to stay in town has been the Tongue Hotel, a mile (1.5km) north of the village center beside the road leading to Durness. Built of gray stone in the baronial style in 1850, it began as a hunting lodge for the duke of Sutherland. To identify its builder, an *S* is carved into the stonework high above one of the doorways. The hotel opens onto the Kyle of Tongue and still possesses much of its initial character and antiques. Both the public rooms and the guest rooms are decorated in Victorian style, with flowered curtains and well-upholstered furniture, plus hair dryers and tea/coffeemakers.

The quality of the food served here is famous: A hearty, moderately priced three-course dinner usually includes a choice of game or fresh fish caught in the region. Accessible through a separate entrance is a popular pub with its own open fireplace and impressive collection of whiskies. There's also a more sedate cocktail lounge. In the bar and lounge, you can enjoy affordable pub meals. Offerings often include mussels, oysters, and garlic-sautéed mushrooms, as well as more substantial meals.

# 11  Caithness: Unspoiled Country

It doesn't look like the Highlands at all, but Caithness is the northernmost county of mainland Scotland, where the ancient landscape is gentle and rolling. Within its 700 square miles (1,820sq km) you'll find signs of the Stone Age—the enigmatic Grey Cairns of Camster date from 4000 B.C. The county is filled with cairns, mysterious stone rows and circles, and standing stones. The Vikings once occupied this place with its rock stacks, old harbors, craggy cliffs, and quiet coves, and many place names are in Old Norse. It has churches from the Middle Ages, as well as towering castles on cliff tops. The Queen Mother's home, the Castle of Mey, dating from 1570, is between John o' Groats and Thurso.

Rich in bird and animal life, Caithness is unspoiled country. Fishing draws people to the area: The wild brown trout are found in some 100 lochs, along with salmon in the Thurso and the Wick rivers. Most people head for Caithness with John o' Groats as their final destination. John o' Groats, with its many souvenir shops, is popularly called the extreme northern tip of the British mainland. Actually, Dunnet Head is farther north by a few miles.

Scrabster, a ferry harbor, is the main car-and-passenger service that operates all year to the Orkney Islands (see chapter 12, "The Orkney & Shetland Islands"). There are day trips in summer.

## WICK

The famous old herring port of Wick on the eastern coastline of Caithness is a popular stop for those heading north to explore what's often called the John o' Groats Peninsula. Wick has some claim as a holiday resort as well. Robert Louis Stevenson spent part of his boyhood in Wick when his father worked here on an engineering project. Today a sleepy nostalgia hangs over the town.

Wick lies 287 miles (462km) northwest of Edinburgh and 126 miles (203km) northwest of Inverness. There's daily bus and rail service from Inverness, from which train connections are possible via Edinburgh, Glasgow, or Stirling.

### SEEING THE SIGHTS

At **Caithness Glass,** Airport Industrial Estates (☎ **01955/602-286**), you can watch the glassblowing and tour the factory Monday to Friday 9am to 5pm. The shop and restaurant are open Monday to Friday 9am to 5pm and Saturday 9am to 1pm (to 5pm on Saturday in June to September). The **Wick Heritage Centre,** 20 Bank Row (☎ 01955/605-393), has many exhibits pertaining to the herring-fishing industry in Wick in days of yore. You can also see farm implements from Caithness. May to October, it's open Monday to Saturday 10am to 5pm; last admission is 3:45pm. Admission is £2 ($3.40) adults and 50p (85¢) ages 5 to 16; free for ages 4 and under.

The most important site in the area is the two megalithic **Grey Cairns of Camster,** 6 miles (10km) north of Lybster on the Watten Road off A9. The ruins of the **Castle of Old Wick** are also worth exploring, and they're always accessible. The location is off A9, 1½ miles (2.5km) south of Wick. Once known as Castle Olipant, the ruined structure dates back to the 14th century. You can still see three floors of the old castle, known as Auld Man o' Wick, rising on a rocky promontory. Since the castle didn't have a water source, it couldn't withstand long sieges, and by the 1500s the Scots abandoned it.

You may also want to seek out **castles Sinclair** and **Girnigoe,** 3 miles (5km) north of Wick (follow the airport road in the direction of the Noss Head Lighthouse). These adjacent castles were built on the edge of a cliff overlooking the Bay of Sinclair. At one time they were the stronghold of the Sinclairs, the earls of Caithness. The older structure, Girnigoe, dates from the latter 1400s; Sinclair was constructed in the early years of the 17th century. By 1679 both castles had been deserted and allowed to fall into the meager, lonely ruins you see today.

## ACCOMMODATIONS & DINING

**Breadalbane House Hotel.** 20 Breadalbane Crescent, Wick KW1 5AQ. ☎ **01955/ 603-911.** Fax 01955/603-911. 10 units, 8 with private bathroom. TV. £53 ($90.10) double with bathroom. Rates include Scottish breakfast. AE, MC, V.

This 1891 building on the southern outskirts of town, a 5-minute walk from the center, was once the home of a furniture maker who's thought to have built the interior woodwork, including the door and window frames and the staircase. It's now an unpretentious guesthouse with traditionally furnished rooms (two singles have no private bathroom). You can dine in the restaurant or in the cozy bar. Food offerings vary from curries and steaks to a traditional roast dinner served on weekends.

**Greenvoe.** 8 George St., Wick KW1 4DE. ☎ **01955/603-942.** 3 units, none with private bathroom. £34 ($57.80) double. Rates include Scottish breakfast and light evening snack. No credit cards. Closed 2 weeks at Christmas.

Your hosts here are Dorothy and Jimmy Johnston, whose circa-1983 home occupies a 1½-acre garden near the heart of town. Panoramas from the windows encompass lots of greenery and views over the estuary known as the Wick River. The small guest rooms are color coordinated, functional, and comfortable. A generous Scottish breakfast, as well as an 8:30pm light snack consisting of sandwiches and tea, is included in the rate.

**Mackay's.** Union St., Wick KW1 5ED. ☎ **01955/602-323.** Fax 01955/605-930. www. mckayshotel.co.uk. E-mail: mckays.hotel@caithness.mm.co.uk. TV TEL. £80 ($136) double; £90 ($153) family room. Rates include breakfast. AE, MC, V. Closed Jan 1–2. Opposite Caithness General Hospital.

For more than 40 years, the Lamont family has operated this recently refurbished hotel on the south shore of River Wick. All bedrooms are tastefully decorated and provide a good range of amenities, including cable/satellite TV. In the heart of Wick, the hotel is a short walk to the Heritage Center and the swimming pool/leisure center. The hotel's restaurant, specializing in traditional Scottish fare, offers fixed-price five-course meals on the high side of moderate. There are also two bars, including Ebenezer's, which serve excellent food at reasonable prices.

# JOHN O' GROATS

John o' Groats, 17 miles (27km) north of Wick, is the northern equivalent of Land's End at the tip of the Cornish peninsula in England. The southern tip of England is 878 miles (1,413.5km) south of John o' Groats. Visitors are fond of having their pictures taken at the Last House, standing at the end of A9. From John o' Groats there are views north to the Orkney Islands and the Pentland Firth.

John o' Groats is named after a Dutch ferryman, Jan de Groot. His tombstone can still be seen at Cabisbay Church. The town abounds in souvenir shops, some selling Groatie buckies or small Arctic cowrie shells once used as decoration by the first settlers in Caithness. You can take interesting walks along the coast to **Duncansby Head,** 2 miles (3km) east—one of the most dramatic coastlines in this part of Scotland. Many species of sea birds, especially puffins, live among the jagged cliffs. You can follow a road leading out to a lighthouse suspended on the cliffs. From here you get a panoramic view over Pentland Firth. These turbulent waters over the years have been a nightmare to mariners, with some 400 wrecks reported in the past century and a half. Ever since the days of the Vikings, these waters have been killing seafarers.

In summer, there's a daily passenger-only ferry service to Orkney. Bus tours of the island are included. The Orkney Islands are just a 45-minute sail from John o' Groats across the Pentland Firth (see chapter 12).

## ACCOMMODATIONS & DINING

**Seaview Hotel.** John o' Groats KW1 4YR. ☎/fax **01955/611-220.** 9 units, 5 with private bathroom. TV. £29–£32 ($49.30–$54.40) double without bathroom; £36–£40 ($61.20–$68) double with bathroom. Rates include Scottish breakfast. MC, V.

The Seaview is a family-run hotel whose severe and streamlined sides rise abruptly from a flat windswept landscape beside the town's only highway. Built in the 1950s and enlarged in 1991, it's covered with a roughly textured white stucco locals refer to as pebble dash. Each guest room is a fair size and rather austere but still comfortable, with a tea/coffeemaker and an electric blanket. There's a pub on the premises, where bar lunches and dinners draw an appreciative crowd. Main courses in the formal restaurant are moderately priced.

## JOHN O' GROATS AFTER DARK

In an old converted country school, the **Lythe Arts Centre** (☎ **01955/641-270**) stages performances of innovative and experimental works by small touring companies. The program is year-round and includes drama, dance, jazz, folk, world, and new music. There's also a permanent collection of art related to northern Scotland, and July and August bring touring exhibits of contemporary art, photography, and some crafts. Exhibits are open daily 10am to 6pm; admission is £1.50 ($2.55) adults, £1 ($1.70) seniors, and 50p (85¢) students/children. Performances usually start at 8pm. Advanced booking is necessary for all shows, so call first for scheduling and ticket information. Tickets cost £9 ($15.30) adults, £6 ($10.20) seniors, and £4 ($6.80) students/children. Coffee, tea, and light snacks are available on performance evenings. The arts center is signposted, 4 miles (6.5km) off A99 between Wick and John o' Groats.

# THURSO

Many visitors drive through the northern port of Thurso when they're heading for Scrabster, where year-round ferries leave for the Orkney Islands (see chapter 12). The town is of only mild interest, used mainly as a refueling stop for those who have made it this far north in Scotland. On the River Thurso, it remains a big, bustling holiday resort with a still-active fishing fleet. In the center, many restored townhouses of brown sandstone date from the 1700s. Once allowed to decay, they look prosperous and restored today.

Once an important and major Viking stronghold, Thurso—meaning "river of the God Thor"—knew its greatest power and prestige in the 11th century, when it was ruled by Thorfinn, who had defeated King Duncan's nephew in 1040. In medieval times, Thurso became the major trading town between Scotland and the Norse countries.

To the west are the **cliffs** of Holborn Head and Dunnet Head, which boasts a lighthouse. Many visitors walk out here to the most northern point of mainland Britain for its panoramic views of the southern tier of the Orkneys. A nuclear energy establishment was installed to the west at Dounreay. The town is 133 miles (214km) northwest of Inverness, 21 miles (34km) northwest of Wick, and 20 miles (32km) west of John o Groats.

If you'd like to explore on your own by bike, head for the **Bike Shop,** 35 High St. (☎ **01847/896-124**), where rental rates are £10 ($17) daily or £56 ($95.20) weekly. The deposit is £25 ($42.50), and it's open Monday to Saturday 10am to 5pm.

For information on Thurso, visit the summer-only **tourist office** at Riverside (☎ **01847/892-371**).

## ACCOMMODATIONS & DINING

**Park Hotel.** Located on the right-hand side of the A9 on approach to the Thurso town center, Thurso KW14 8RE. ☎ **01847/893-251.** Fax 01847/893-252. E-mail: parkthurso@ yahoo.co.uk. 11 units. TV TEL. £70 ($119) double. Rates include full Scottish breakfast. AE, DC, MC, V. Closed Jan 1–3.

With an almost Scandinavian style, this hotel offers an ideal location for exploring the northern coast of Scotland. The midsized rooms are comfortable and adequately furnished with double beds. Eight units are large enough for use by families. Amenities include tea/coffeemakers, hair dryers, and complimentary toiletries. Guests receive a warm reception and friendly service. There is a swimming pool, golf course, and bowling alley nearby. Both the on-site lounge and restaurant offer reasonably priced, satisfying meals accompanied by a fine selection of wines, beers, and malt whiskies. High tea is served, too.

# ULLAPOOL

Ullapool is an interesting village, the largest in Wester Ross, 59 miles (95km) northwest of Inverness and 238 miles (383km) north of Glasgow. It was built by the British Fishery Society in 1788 as a port for herring fishers and is still a busy harbor. The original town plan hasn't been changed, and many of the buildings look much as they did at the time of their construction, although mellower and more weather-beaten. Ullapool has long been an embarkation point for travelers crossing the Minch, a section of the North Atlantic separating Scotland from the Outer Hebrides.

A short drive south to Gairloch takes you into the heart of Wester Ross, with its scenery, mountains, and Atlantic seascape.

## EXPLORING THE AREA

One of our favorite towns in this region of Scotland, Ullapool was founded in 1788 on the lovely shores of the salt lake, **Loch Broom.** The site of the ferry docks for the island of Lewis, Ullapool is still a busy, bustling fishing station in the north. Ullapool is also the best embarkation point for trips to the Summer Isles (see below).

One of the most **dramatic and scenic views** in the north of Scotland is possible from Ullapool, a 40-mile (64.5km) run north following the signposts to the village of

Lochiner with its backdrop of mountains. Take A835 north from Ullapool, enjoying the lochside views of Loch Broom as you go along. Along the way you'll pass the hamlet of Armair on Loch Kanaird, until you come to the **Inverpolly National Nature Reserve** of some 27,000 acres, including lochs and lochans, along with the mountain peaks of Cul Mor at 2,786 feet (845m), Cul Beag at 2,523 feet (765m), and Stac Pollaidth at 2,010 feet (610m).

At **Knockan,** 15 miles (24km) north of Ullapool, a signposted nature trail along the cliff offers the most dramatic views in the area and is the best place to observe the flora, fauna, and geology of the area.

At the Ledmore junction, take A837 to the left, passing along **Loch Awe,** with the mountain peaks of Canisp at 2,779 feet (843m) and Ben More Assynt at 3,230 feet (980m) forming a backdrop. You'll reach the 6-mile-long (10km) **Loch Assynt,** which is scenically lovely. The road along this lake-dotted landscape eventually carries you here to **Lochiner,** a hamlet with less than 300 souls. It's known for its scenery, sandy coves, and crofting communities. It still has a busy fishing fleet, although pleasure craft anchor here in summer as well. For tourist information, call ☎ **01854/612-135.**

There are a number of day trips you can take from Ullapool, including a trip to the **Corrieshalloch Gorge,** 12 miles (19km) southeast, a national nature reserve along A835 at Braemore. From this point, the Falls of Measach plunge 150 feet (45.5m) into a mile-long wooded gorge. A bridge over the chasm and a viewing platform offer a panoramic way to enjoy this spectacular scenery.

Another interesting excursion is to the **Inverewe Gardens** (☎ **01445/781-200**). Osgood MacKenzie created these gardens a century and a quarter ago, when he planted species from many countries. An exotic mixture of plants from the South Pacific, the Himalayas, and South America allows the gardens to have color year-round. The gardens can be reached along A832, 6 miles (10km) northeast of Gairloch. They're open Monday to Saturday 9:30am to sunset and Sunday noon to sunset. Admission is £5 ($8.50) adults, £3.50 ($5.95) seniors/children, and £13.50 ($22.95) families (two adults and up to six children).

From either Ullapool or Achiltibuie, you can take excursions in season to the ✪ **Summer Isles,** a beautiful group of almost uninhabited islands off the coast. The islands get their name because sheep are transported here in summer for grazing. The largest is Tanera More. The islands are a mecca for bird watchers. Boat schedules can vary, depending on weather conditions. Information about how to reach the islands is available from the **tourist office** on Argyle Street (☎ **01854/612-135**). April to July and September, it's open Monday to Friday 9am to 5:30pm and Saturday and Sunday 10am to 5pm; August hours are Monday to Saturday 9am to 6pm and Sunday noon to 6pm; October hours are Monday to Friday 10am to 5pm and Saturday noon to 4pm; November to March, it's open Monday to Friday 11am to 4pm.

## ACCOMMODATIONS

✪ **Altanaharrie Inn.** Loch Broom, Ullapool IV26 2SS. ☎ **01854/633-230.** 8 units. £165–£205 ($280.50–$348.50) per person. Rates include half-board. AE, MC, V. Closed Nov–Easter. Transportation is by private ferry.

This is one of those places you feel you shouldn't tell anyone about, for fear they won't have room for you when you get here. The Altanaharrie was once a 17th-century drover's inn on the banks of Loch Broom. There's no access by road, so you're brought over the loch by a private launch. Once you've landed, you're greeted with a warm log fire in a lounge and a dram before dinner. The cooking is among the best in north-west Scotland, using locally caught seafood. Shellfish is kept in creels in the loch until ready for consumption. There's no choice on the five-course menu, but you're asked your likes and dislikes or allergies beforehand. The guest rooms are uncomplicated but exceedingly inviting, housed either in the main building or in small cottages on the grounds. There are no TVs, no room phones, nothing to distract. At night the generator is switched off, and candles and torches provide needed illumination. In the morning, it's a delight to find a breakfast that might include homemade jams, buttery croissants, and perhaps even venison sausages.

**Dromnan House.** Garve Rd., Ullapool IV26 2SX. ☎ **01854/612-333.** Fax 01854/613-364. 7 units. TV. £36–£48 ($61.20–$81.60) double. Rates include breakfast. AE, MC, V.

Mrs. MacDonald is your hostess at this guesthouse occupying a ⅓ of an acre plot on the southern outskirts of town within a 10-minute walk from the center. Built of white-painted stone in the 1970s and later enlarged, it was named after a nearby rise (Dromnan Hill) where one of the MacDonald family's ancestors was born and reared. The place is very well maintained, and the guest rooms are described by the kindly owner as being decorated in a combination of Marks & Spencer department store goods and Shand-Kydd coordinated wallpapers and fabrics designed by the mother of the late Princess Diana. They come with hair dryers and tea/coffeemakers.

**Royal Hotel.** Garve Rd., Ullapool IV26 2SY. ☎ **01854/612-181** or 01942/824-824 for reservations. Fax 01854/612-951. 50 units. TV TEL. £60–£70 ($102–$119) double. Reservations are for a 2-night minimum stay. Rates include Scottish breakfast. MC, V. Closed Nov–early Mar.

The Royal sits on a knoll on the Inverness side of town, overlooking the harborfront. Graced with curved walls and large sheets of glass, it was reconstructed in 1961 from an older building, with an added east wing. It offers well-furnished guest rooms, 21 of which have balconies opening onto views over Loch Broom. Live entertainment in season is offered. Locally produced Scottish fare is served in the dining area. Later, guests sit around a log fire in the well-appointed lounge.

## DINING

**Mariner's Restaurant.** North Rd. ☎ **01854/612-161.** Reservations recommended. Main courses £7–£22 ($11.90–$37.40). DC, MC, V. Daily noon–2pm and 6:30–9:30pm. SCOTTISH/INTERNATIONAL.

Within the simple confines of a somewhat battered motel, this restaurant serves food that's upscale and elegant. Its circa-'70s design might remind you of a roadside motel, if not for the wild and verdant scenery around you. Lunches are rather deceptively promoted as bar snacks, even though they include full-fledged waitress service and elaborate dishes that feature lobster, oak-roasted smoked salmon, and elaborate versions of haggis with black pudding dressed up with hot onion marmalade. Dinners are in the same price range as lunch, but served in a separate dining room, with emphasis on grilled darne of salmon with fennel and Spanish onion slaw garnished with red caviar. Ask about the giant platter of cold West Coast seafood.

On the premises are 10 motel rooms, none particularly distinctive but each clean and unassuming. Costing £50 ($85) double, each has a TV and phone.

# 11 The Hebridean Islands

**O**nce the Hebridean islands were visited only by geologists, bird watchers, and the occasional fisher or mountain climber. Today the chain of islands just off the Scottish mainland that makes up the Inner Hebrides is becoming more and more accessible to the general visitor. But what about the Outer Hebrides? One of the lesser-known parts of Western Europe, these are a splintered sweep of windswept islands stretching for some 130 miles (209km) from the Butt of Lewis in the north all the way to Barra Head in the south. With rugged cliffs, clean beaches, archaeological treasures, and tiny bays, the Outer Hebrides lure more and more visitors every year.

From Gourock, the ferry terminal near Glasgow, **Caledonian MacBrayne** (☎ **01475/650-100** for information, ☎ 0990/650-000 for reservations) sails to 23 Scottish islands in the Firth of Clyde and the Western Isles, including Skye and Mull, as well as the Outer Hebrides. The company also offers inclusive tours ideal for visiting places well away from the beaten track.

If you're driving from the mainland, you can take the "Road to the Isles," heading for the Kyle of Lochalsh if your destination is Skye. For Mull and Iona, Oban is your port. These islands are part of the Inner Hebrides and enjoy fairly good connections with the mainland. The more remote Outer Hebrides are linked by car ferries from mainland ports like Ullapool (call ☎ **01851/702-361** in Stornoway for schedules). The main islands to visit here are Lewis and Harris. Glasgow has air service to the airport at Stornoway on Lewis; call British Airways (☎ **0345/222-111** in Glasgow).

## EXPLORING THE INNER HEBRIDES

If you travel to the Inner Hebrides, the chain of islands just off the west coast of the Scottish mainland, you'll be following in the footsteps of Samuel Johnson and his faithful Boswell. The **Isle of Skye** is the largest. **Mull** has wild scenery and golf courses, and just off its shores is the important **Iona,** the isle that played a major part not only in the spread of Christianity in Britain but also in the preservation of the culture and learning of the ancient world when it was being forgotten all over Europe. Adventurous travelers will also seek out **Coll** and **Tyree** as well as the **Isle of Colonsay** and **Rhum (Rum), Eigg,** or the tiny island of **Raasay,** off Skye.

If your time is limited, we suggest you concentrate on Skye. It offers your best chance for getting the flavor of the Hebrides in a nutshell,

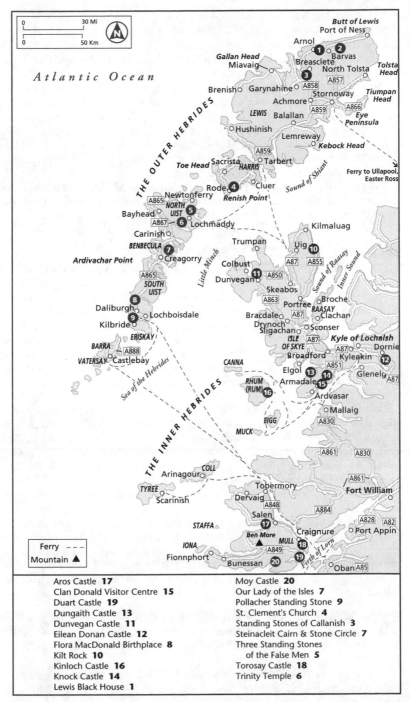

# The Hebrides

0 ___ 30 Mi
0 ___ 50 Km

**Atlantic Ocean**

*Butt of Lewis*
Port of Ness
Arnol ❶
*Gallan Head* Breasclete Barvas ❷
Miavaig North Tolsta *Tolsta Head*
❸ A858 A857
Brenish Garynahine Stornoway *Tiumpan Head*
Achmore A866
A859 *Eye Peninsula*
**LEWIS** Balallan
Hushinish Lemreway
*Kebock Head*
A859
*Toe Head* Sacrista Tarbert
**HARRIS** *Sound of Shiant*
Rode ❹ Cluer
*Renish Point*
Newtonferry Kilmaluag
A865 **NORTH** ❺
Bayhead **UIST** Uig ❿
A867 ❻ Lochmaddy A87 A855
Carinish Trumpan
**BENBECULA** ❼ Colbust *Sound of Raasay*
*Ardivachar Point* Creagorry Dunvegan ⓫ A850 *Inner Sound*
*Little Minch* Skeabos
A865 A863 Broche
**SOUTH** Portree **RAASAY**
**UIST** Bracdale Clachan
Daliburgh ❽ Drynoch Sconser
Kilbride ❾ Lochboisdale Sligachan A87
**ERISKAY** *Kyle of Lochalsh*
**ISLE**
**BARRA** A888 **OF SKYE** Broadford Dornie
**VATERSAY** Castlebay Elgol ⓭ Kyleakin ⓬
Armadale ⓮ Glenelg A87
*Sea of the Hebrides* CANNA ⓯
*RHUM* Ardvasar
*(RUM)* ⓰
**THE INNER HEBRIDES** Mallaig
*EIGG* A830
MUCK
A861 A830
COLL
Arinagour A861
*TYREE* Tobermory **Fort William**
Scarinish Dervaig A848 A884
Salen A828 A82
**STAFFA** ⓱ Craignure Port Appin
*IONA* *Ben More* MULL ⓲
Fionnphort ▲ A849 ⓳
Bunessan ⓴ *Firth of Lorn* Oban A85

Ferry to Ullapool,
Easter Ross

Ferry - - -
Mountain ▲

| | |
|---|---|
| Aros Castle **17** | Moy Castle **20** |
| Clan Donald Visitor Centre **15** | Our Lady of the Isles **7** |
| Duart Castle **19** | Pollacher Standing Stone **9** |
| Dungaith Castle **13** | St. Clement's Church **4** |
| Dunvegan Castle **11** | Standing Stones of Callanish **3** |
| Eilean Donan Castle **12** | Steinacleit Cairn & Stone Circle **7** |
| Flora MacDonald Birthplace **8** | Three Standing Stones |
| Kilt Rock **10** | of the False Men **5** |
| Kinloch Castle **16** | Torosay Castle **18** |
| Knock Castle **14** | Trinity Temple **6** |
| Lewis Black House **1** | |

399

all in a 2-day trip. The island's natural beauty ranges from the rugged Trotternish Peninsula to the jagged peaks of the Cuillin Hills. The Cuillins are called both Black Cuillins (the hills encircling the glacial trough of Loch Coruisk) and Red Cuillins (based on the pink granite found in the hills). A favorite of hill climbers, these often harsh mountains make for some of the grandest walks in Skye.

Our **favorite drive** in all the Hebrides is to the Trotternish Peninsula and northeast Skye, which you can easily tour in a day from Portree, allowing adequate time for many leisurely stops and walks. This is only a 20-mile (32km) peninsula but is so fascinating you can easily spend a day enjoying it. The highlight of the drive is 8 miles (13km) north of Portree: the **Old Man of Storr,** a stone pinnacle standing 160 feet (48.5m) high. Signs indicate a footpath through the forest to reach it. Once at the top you'll be rewarded with great views of the island.

If you have time for one more Hebridean island, make it **Mull.** From Mull, you can also spend an afternoon visiting the ancient ecclesiastical center off the coast at **Iona.** Spend the morning exploring parts of Mull, including a visit to Torosay Castle and Gardens. Have lunch on Mull, then hop over to the little island of Iona.

## EXPLORING THE OUTER HEBRIDES

At first, you may feel you've come to a lunar landscape where there's a sense of infinite time. The character of the **Outer Hebrides** is quite different from that of the Inner Hebrides. This string of islands, stretching for 130 miles (209km), is about 40 miles (64.5km) off the northwest coast of Scotland, and the main islands to visit are **Lewis** and **Harris** (parts of the same island despite the different names), **North Uist, Benbecula, South Uist,** and **Barra.** The archipelago also takes in some minor offshore islands. Gaelic is spoken here; its gentle cadence is said to have been the language spoken in the Garden of Eden. Presbyterianism is still very strong (in one B&B watching TV on Sunday is forbidden). Before you go, you might read Compton Mackenzie's novel *Whisky Galore.*

The islands knew 2 centuries of Viking invasions, but today they are the retreat of many a disenchanted artist from the mainland. They come here, take over old crofter's cottages, and devote their days to such pursuits as pottery making and weaving. Bird watchers flock here to see the habitats of the red-necked phalarope, corncrake, golden eagle, Arctic skua, and grayleg goose. Golfers come here to play on these far-northern courses, including one at Stornoway (Lewis) and another at Askernish (South Uist). Anglers also come here to fish for salmon, brown trout, and sea trout among the fishing lochs.

You can see much of the dim past on these islands, including a version of Stonehenge. A good time to visit is June and July, when adult's and children's choirs compete for honors. You can attend these festivals celebrating Gaelic music and poetry. Each of the main islands has accommodations, and reservations are important. Most are small family-run guesthouses and hotels, and many are crofter's cottages that take in B&B guests, mainly in summer.

## 1 Kyle of Lochalsh: Gateway to the Isle of Skye

204 miles (329km) NW of Edinburgh, 82 (132km) miles SW of Inverness, 125 miles (201km) N of Oban

The popular Kyle of Lochalsh is the gateway to the island of Skye (now reached by toll bridge). You can drive the length of Skye in a day, returning to the mainland by night if you want to.

## ESSENTIALS

**GETTING THERE**   Four **trains** per day (two on Sunday) arrive from Inverness, taking about 2½ hours and costing £14.70 ($25) each way. Call ☎ **0345/484-950** for schedules.

Both **Scottish CityLink** and **Skye-Ways** coaches arrive daily from Glasgow at the Kyle of Lochalsh (trip time: 5 hours), costing £15 ($25.50) each way. Skye-Ways also operates three buses a day from Inverness (trip time: 2 hours), costing £9 ($15.30) one way. Call ☎ **0990/808-080** for schedules.

**Driving** from Fort William, head north along A82 to Invergarry, where you cut west onto A87 to the Kyle of Lochalsh.

**VISITOR INFORMATION**   A **tourist office** is at the Kyle of Lochalsh Car Park (☎ **01599/534-276**). April to June, it's open Monday to Saturday 9am to 5:30pm; July and August hours are Monday to Saturday 9am to 7pm and Sunday 10am to 4pm; September and October hours are Monday to Saturday 9am to 5:30pm.

## A NEARBY ATTRACTION

**Eilean Donan Castle.** Dornie. ☎ **01599/555-202.** Admission £3.75 ($6.40) adults, £3 ($5.10) seniors/students/children, £9 ($15.30) families (2 adults and up to 3 children). Apr–Oct daily 10am–5:30pm; Mar and Nov daily 10am–3pm. Drive 8 miles (13km) east of the Kyle of Lochalsh on A87.

This romantic castle was built in 1214 as a defense against the Danes. In ruins for 200 years, it was restored by Colonel MacRae of Clan MacRae in 1932 and is now a clan war memorial and museum, containing Jacobite relics, mostly with clan connections. A shop here sells kilts, woolens, and souvenirs.

## ACCOMMODATIONS

The lodgings here are limited, just barely adequate to meet the demand for rooms.

**Kyle Hotel.** Main St., Kyle of Lochalsh IV40 8AB. ☎ **01599/534-204.** Fax 01599/534-932. www.btinternet.com/thekylehotel. 31 units. TV TEL. £70–£85 ($119–$144.50) double. Rates include Scottish breakfast. AE, MC, V.

This modernized stone hotel in the center of town, a 5-minute walk from the train station, is your best all-around bet in the moderate category. The midsize guest rooms are furnished in a functional modern style, with hair dryers and tea/coffeemakers. The hotel serves reasonably priced dinners in the lounge nightly.

**Lochalsh Hotel.** Ferry Rd., Kyle of Lochalsh IV40 8AF. ☎ **01599/534-202.** Fax 01599/534-881. www.lockhalsh-hotel.demon.co.uk. E-mail: ndmacrae@lochalsh. 38 units. TV TEL. £60–£95 ($102–$161.50) double. Rates include Scottish breakfast. AE, MC, V.

This landmark hotel was built as a luxury oasis when the British Railway finally extended its tracks in this direction. Today, in memory of the period when it was the headquarters of a Royal Navy mining operation in World War II, a large (defused) mine sits near the flagpole on the seaside lawn. Its crafted small-paned windows with hardwood and brass fittings will remind you of those on an oceangoing yacht. The comfortable guest rooms have been stylishly overhauled. Upscale dinners in the hotel restaurant include the best Scottish cuisine and ingredients. The ground-floor bar stocks a variety of malt whiskies, and the dining room has a panoramic view.

## DINING

**The Seafood Restaurant.** In the Railway Station. ☎ **01599/534-813.** Main courses £6–£9 ($10.20–$15.30) at lunch, £9–£13 ($15.30–$22.10) at dinner. MC, V. Mon–Fri 10am–3pm; daily 6–9pm. Closed Oct–Easter.

This blue-and-white clapboard building (1880) was originally a waiting room for rail passengers en route to other destinations, but now it's one of the most frequented restaurants in town. The menu items are flavorful but unfussy, prepared with attention to detail and lots of natural flavors. Examples are Lochalsh langoustines in herb-flavored butter sauce and local queen scallops in white-wine sauce. The most elaborate seafood platter in town contains hot and cold preparations of mussels, squid, salmon, trout, and shellfish—a meal in itself.

## 2  The Isle of Skye: Star of the Hebrides

83 miles (134km) W of Inverness, 176 miles (283km) NW of Edinburgh, 146 miles (235km) NW of Glasgow

Off the northwest coast of Scotland, the mystical Isle of Skye, largest of the Inner Hebrides, is 48 miles (77km) long and varies between 3 and 25 miles (5km and 40km) wide. It's separated from the mainland by the Sound of Sleat (pronounced Slate). At Kyleakin, on the eastern end, the channel is only a quarter of a mile (about .5km) wide.

Dominating the land of summer seas, streams, woodland glens, mountain passes, cliffs, and waterfalls are the **Cuillin Hills,** a range of jagged black mountains that are a mecca for rock climbers. The Sleat Peninsula, the island's southernmost arm, is known as the "Garden of Skye." There are many stories as to the origin of the name *Skye.* Some believe it's from the Norse *ski,* meaning "cloud," and others say it's from the Gaelic word for "winged." There are Norse names on the island, however, as the Norsemen held sway for 4 centuries before 1263. Overlooking the Kyle is the ruined **Castle Moal,** once the home of a Norwegian princess.

On the island you can explore castle ruins, *duns* (hill forts), and *brochs* (prehistoric round stone towers). For the Scots, the island will forever evoke images of Flora Mac-Donald, who conducted the disguised Bonnie Prince Charlie to Skye after the Culloden defeat.

## ESSENTIALS

**GETTING THERE**    From the Kyle of Lochalsh, **drive** west along the newly constructed toll bridge over the strait to Kyleakin, paying £5.40 ($9.20) to cross one way.

**VISITOR INFORMATION**    There's a **tourist office** at Bayfield House in Portree (☎ 01478/612-137). April to June, it's open Monday to Saturday 9am to 5:30pm; July to mid-August, hours are Monday to Saturday 9am to 8pm and Sunday 10am to 4pm; mid-August to October, it's open Monday to Saturday 9am to 5:30pm; and November to March, it's open Monday to Friday 9am to 5pm and Saturday 10am to 4pm.

## FUN IN THE OUTDOORS AROUND THE ISLAND

**BIKING**    Gently undulating hills, coupled with the good roads and a relative lack of traffic, make the Isle of Skye appealing to cyclists. The island's premier rental outfits are **Island Cycles,** The Green, in the coastal city of Portree (☎ 01478/613-121), and **Fairwinds Bicycle Hire,** Elgol Road, Broadford (☎ 01471/822-270), farther inland, near the center of the island. Both are open daily 9am to 6pm and charge £8 to £10 ($13.60 to $17) a day, depending on the model. Their staff members can point you toward good routes around the island that suit your ability level.

At the **Ferry Filling Station,** Ardvasar, Skye (☎ 01471/844-249), a deposit of £10 ($17) is required. Rentals cost £5 ($8.50) per day and £25 ($42.50) per week. It's open Monday to Saturday. **Island Cycles,** The Green, Portee (☎ 01478/613-121),

charges £12 ($20.40) daily or £48 ($81.60) weekly. It's open Monday to Saturday 9:30am to 5pm.

**BOATING** The coast of Skye is the most ruggedly beautiful this side of the Norwegian fjords, and several entrepreneurs offer boat trips letting you drink in the scenery. Foremost is **Bella Jane Boat Trips,** The Harbourfront, Elgol (☎ **0800/ 731-3089** in Britain or 01471/866-244). From the piers in the village of Elgol, you'll board a sturdy vessel that sails (if there's enough business) daily between Easter and October into the rock-ringed borders of Loch Coruisk, at the foot of the Cuillin Hills. (The hills are rich in bird life, and their microclimates and botany have been compared to some sections of the Swiss Alps.) Most visitors opt for the standard return trip; you're carried to the base of the hills, deposited for 90 minutes of wandering along the nearby beaches and fens, and then returned over water to Elgol. It lasts 3 to 3½ hours and costs £12 ($20.40) per person. If you're hardy and really interested in hiking, you can extend this experience to a full day.

**GOLF** Golfing on Skye means an almost total lack of supervision, weather that can rain out or dry out a game on almost no notice, and often a lack of players. Whether you find this charming depends on your expectations, but overall, the island's best course is the 9-hole **Isle of Skye Golf Club** (☎ 01478/650-414), adjacent to the hamlet of Sconser, on the southeast coast. Maintained by the local municipality, it has a simple snack bar and bar and an on-again/off-again employee who's concerned with cutting the grass whenever necessary. It's not the elaborate experience you'll find on the famous courses elsewhere in Scotland. Less desirable but still prized for its convenience to residents of the **Skeabost House Hotel** (see below) is the 9-hole course associated with the hotel. Although priority tee-offs are granted to hotel guests, nonguests can play if they phone ahead for a reservation. Greens fees at both courses are £14 ($23.80) for a full day's play.

**HIKING**   Any branch of Skye's tourist office will offer advice on the many hikes available through the heather and glens of the island. But for a walking adventure advised only for the stout-hearted and the fit, consider extending a boat trip on the Bella Jane (see above) with an additional 14-mile (22.5km) overland hike from the Cuillin Hills back to more heavily populated regions of the island. To do this, take the boat trip (one-way only) from Elgol to the Cuillin Hills, paying £9 ($15.30). From here, brown-and-white signs direct you across an undulating rock-strewn landscape to the Sligachan Hotel (see below), the premier hotel for hill climbers and trekkers. You can overnight at the hotel or take a bus or taxi the remaining 7 miles (11km) back to Portree.

# KYLEAKIN

The seaport community of Kyleakin is the site of the old ferry terminal where the boats from the Scottish mainland used to arrive before Skye became linked by a bridge. Many visitors still prefer to stay here because of its convenience rather than on more remote parts of the island.

Kyleakin opens onto a small bay and is dominated by a ruin, **Castle Maol,** on a jagged knoll. For a lovely walk, go from the town center up to this ruin from the 12th century, when it was a fortified stronghold of the Mackinnon clan.

## ACCOMMODATIONS

**Dunringell Hotel.** Kyleakin, Isle of Skye IV41 8PR. ☎ **01599/534-180.** Fax 01599/534-460. www.dunringell-hotel.deltapi.uk.com. 18 units, 10 with private bathroom. TV TEL. £36–£44 ($61.20–$74.80) double without bathroom; £48–£68 ($81.60–$115.60) double with bathroom. Rates include Scottish breakfast. MC, V.

Rhododendrons, azaleas, and other flowering shrubs on this hotel's 4½ acres provide a riot of color March to July. At the Dunringell, built in 1912, many of the modestly furnished guest rooms open onto scenic views; all have hair dryers and tea/coffeemakers. There are both smoking and nonsmoking lounges. For those who wish to participate, the proprietors, Mr. and Mrs. MacPherson, hold a short worship service in one of the lounges each evening. No alcoholic beverages are permitted in dining room or lounges.

**White Heather Hotel.** Kyleakin, Isle of Skye IV41 8PL. ☎ **01599/534-577.** Fax 01599/534-427. www2.prestel.co.uk/whiteheather. E-mail: ian@whiteheather.prestel.co.uk. 10 units. TV. £44–£54 ($74.80–$91.80) double. Rates include Scottish breakfast. MC, V. Closed Oct–Feb.

These two connected buildings provide basic accommodations with up-to-date amenities. The small guest rooms are simple but well maintained and equipped with tea/coffeemakers. Moderately priced dinners are served nightly in the dining room; several selections are offered for each course. The hotel lounge, licensed only to serve guests, has a pleasant view of the Castle Maol. The White Heather is convenient to both the ferry dock and the bus terminals.

# SLIGACHAN

The village of Sligachan sits at the head of a sea loch in a setting of scenic beauty with views of the Cuillin Hills (pronounced *Coo*-lin). It's one of the best bases for exploring Skye because of its central location. Visitors enjoy sea-trout fishing, with an occasional

# Crafts on Skye

**Edinbane Pottery,** on A850, 8 miles (13km) east of Dunvegan (☎ **01470/ 582-234**), celebrates its 28th anniversary in 2000. The three artists working in this studio produce wood-fired stoneware and salt-glazed pottery, and they're capable of producing almost anything you might request and can fill custom orders in a wide range of finishes.

Artist Tom Mackenzie's etchings, prints, aquatints, and greeting cards are all inspired by the scenery and day-to-day life of the island. You can find his work at **Skye Original Prints at Portree,** 1 Wentworth St. (☎ **01478/612-544**).

Since 1974, Stewart John Wilson has been designing and producing silver and gold jewelry, ceramic tiles, cheese boards, platters, and clocks, all featuring intricate Celtic patterns. You can see his work at **Skye Silver,** in the Old School, on the Glendale Road (B884), 7 miles (11km) west of Dunvegan (☎ **01470/ 511-263**). The selection of tiles is especially vast, and Stewart's wife, Elizabeth, who tends the shop, is friendly and knowledgeable.

**Craft Encounters,** in the Post Office building in Broadford (☎ **01471/ 822-754**), showcases many of Skye's talented artists. You'll find pewter jewelry, stained-glass light catchers, salt-dough bric-a-brac, folk and landscape paintings, silk scarves, tartan silk ties and potpourri bags, rubber stamps, and handmade *jumpers* (sweaters). Celtic patterns show up on glassware, tableware, linens, and pieces of marquetry. The island's musical talent is represented in a selection of traditional Scottish island music CDs.

**Skye Batik,** 220 yards (200m) from the ferry landing in Armadale (☎ **01471/844-396**), has been voted the best crafts shop in Scotland for 2 years running. Skye Batik sells wall hangings and cotton, tweed, wool, and linen clothing handprinted with Celtic designs from the 6th to the 8th centuries. It's recently opened a new outlet at **The Green,** Portree (☎ **01478/613-331**).

In **Harlequin Knitwear,** next to the Duisdale Hotel on Sleat (☎ **01471/ 833-321**), local knitter Chryssy Gibbs designs men's and women's machine-knit Shetland wool sweaters. Her work is bright and colorful. Despite the fact that she does all the knitting and runs the shop alone, there are numerous sweaters to choose from.

For more knitwear, go to **Ragamuffin,** on the pier in Armadale (☎ **01471/ 844-217**), featuring quality Scottish, Irish, and British handknits for the whole family as well as accessories like hats, gloves, and scarves.

---

salmon caught on the Sligachan River. It's also possible to rent a boat from the hotel below to explore the Storr Lochs, 15 miles (24km) from Sligachan and known for their good brown-trout fishing May to September.

## ACCOMMODATIONS & DINING

**Sligachan Hotel.** Sligachan, Isle of Skye IV47 8SW. ☎ **01478/650-204.** Fax 01478/650-207. www.sligachan.demon.co.uk. E-mail: reservations@sligachan.demon.co.uk. 22 units. TV. £70–£80 ($119–$136) double. Rates include Scottish breakfast. MC, V.

The Sligachan nestles at the foot of the Cuillins on the main road between Portree and Kyleakin and is an ideal center from which to explore Skye. This family-run hotel is one of Skye's oldest coaching inns, built sometime in the 19th century. The guest rooms are old and a bit outdated but still reasonably comfortable. And the food is good, with the restaurant serving freshly caught seafood, as well as at least one vegetarian selection, in moderately priced dinners nightly. The bar also serves simple meals along with a fine selection of malt whiskies, in front of an open fireplace.

## PORTREE

Skye's capital, Portree, is the port for steamers making trips around the island and linking Skye with the 15-mile-long (24km) island of Raasay. Sligachan, 9 miles (14.5km) south, and Glenbrittle, 7 miles (11km) farther southwest, are centers for climbing the Cuillin Hills.

### ACCOMMODATIONS

**Bosville Hotel.** Bosville Terrace, Portree, Isle of Skye IV51 9DG. ☎ **01478/612-846.** Fax 01478/613-434. www.taste-of-scotland.com/bosville-hotel.html. E-mail: basville@macleoudhotels. co.uk. 15 units. TV TEL. £76 ($129.20) double; £95–£110 ($161.50–$187) family unit. Rates include breakfast. AE, MC, V.

This well-established hotel stands in the center of Portree and commands panoramic views of the harbor and the Cuillin Mountains. It's a bright, welcoming, and well-maintained inn known equally for its cuisine (see The Chandlery Restaurant, below) and for its bedrooms. Accommodations are generally spacious and well decorated, with such amenities as beverage makers, hair dryers, and irons.

○ **Cuillin Hills Hotel.** Portree, Isle of Skye IV51 9LU. ☎ **01478/612-003.** Fax 01478/613-092. www.cuillinhills.demon.co.uk. E-mail: office@cuillinhills.demon.co.uk. 29 units. TV TEL. £76–£150 ($129.20–$255) double. Rates include breakfast. AE, DC, MC, V.

Half a mile (almost 1km) north of Portree's center, this stone-sided manor was built in the 1820s as a hunting lodge for the MacDonald clan. Today it's a comfortable hotel that appeals to hikers and bird watchers. Views from all the good-sized guest rooms encompass the unspoiled Cuillin Hills, Portree's harbor, and/or the sea, and each is outfitted with reproductions of old-fashioned furniture and some kind of flowered wallpaper. Rather expensive dinners are available to both guests and nonguests who phone in advance. Menu items change virtually every night but might include Highland terrine of game on a pool of wild rowan and juniper berry jelly or roasted grouse with bacon and mushrooms.

**Rosedale Hotel.** Beaumont Crescent, Portree, Isle of Skye IV51 9DF. ☎ **01478/613-131.** Fax 01478/612-531. 23 units. TV TEL. £76–£98 ($129.20–$166.60) double. Rates include Scottish breakfast. MC, V.

In one of the more secluded parts of Portree, on the harbor 100 yards (91m) from the village square, the Rosedale opens directly onto the sea. It was created from a row of dwellings dating from the reign of William IV. The midsize guest rooms in this warm and welcoming place are decorated in modern style and have radios, hair dryers, and other amenities. The award-winning dining room serves expensive Scottish fare with the requisite seafood; there's also a coffee shop and guest lounge.

**Royal Hotel.** Bank St., Portree, Isle of Skye IV51 9BU. ☎ **01478/612-525.** Fax 01478/613-198. www.royal-hotel-demon.co.uk/hotel.html. E-mail: info@royal-hotel. 25 units. TV TEL. £79–£88 ($134.30–$149.60) double. Rates include Scottish breakfast. MC, V.

The Royal stands on a hill facing the water and is said to have extended hospitality to Bonnie Prince Charlie during his 1746 flight. In less dramatic circumstances, you can book one of its comfortable, small-to-midsize guest rooms; the preferred ones open onto the sea, and all have hair dryers and tea/coffeemakers. Formal meals and bar snacks are offered.

# DINING

**The Chandlery Restaurant.** In the Bosville Hotel, Bosville Terrace. ☎ **01478/612-846.** Reservations recommended. Main courses £12.75–£21.50 ($21.70–$36.55). AE, MC, V. Daily 11am–10pm. SCOTTISH/SEAFOOD.

This restaurant attracts visitors and locals alike. Chef John Kelly is highly skilled and creates delicious, innovative dishes. Fresh seafood is a specialty and includes items like langoustine tails in thermidor sauce, and king scallops with green garlic butter and crispy bacon. Other favorites are medaillons of Aberdeen Angus; or Highland venison grilled and served with red-currant jelly. A tasty way to complete your meal is with the ripe pear, poached in port and flavored with cinnamon, served with a tartlet of whisky, honey, and oatmeal ice cream.

# UIG

The village of Uig is on Trotternish, the largest Skye peninsula. The ferry port for Harris and Uist in the Outer Hebrides, it's 15 miles (24km) north of Portree and 49 miles (79km) from the Kyle of Lochalsh. Many people like to anchor here because it's convenient for early departures. Uig is also one of the most beautiful places in Skye to spend the night, as it opens onto Uig Bay set against a backdrop of green hills and is known for its beautiful sunrises and sunsets.

Now a virtual ruin and only of passing interest, **Monkstadt House,** 1½ miles (2.5km) north, is where Flora MacDonald brought Bonnie Prince Charlie after their escape from Benbecula. This famous Scottish heroine lived with her family in North Carolina for several years before returning to her beloved Skye, where she died at age 68 and was buried in **Kilmuir churchyard,** 5 miles (8km) north. Flora was wrapped in a sheet used by the prince, and her grave is marked by a Celtic cross. When Dr. Samuel Johnson visited, he wrote, "Flora MacDonald, a name that will be mentioned in history, and if courage and fidelity be virtues, mentioned with honor. She is a woman of middle stature, soft features, gentle manners and elegant presence."

While on the Trotternish peninsula, you can also visit the **Skye Museum of Island Life** (☎ 01470/552-206) at Kilmuir. At this museum the old way of island life is preserved, along with artifacts based on farming on the crofts. Some interiors from the 18th and 19th centuries have been reconstructed, and ways of former Skye life are depicted in photographs. Admission is £1.75 ($3), and Easter to October, the museum is open Monday to Saturday 9:30am to 5:30pm.

## ACCOMMODATIONS

**Ferry Inn.** Uig, Isle of Skye IV51 9XP. ☎ **01470/542-242.** 6 units. TV. £50–£60 ($85–$102) double. Rates include Scottish breakfast. MC, V.

This building was first a bank and later a post office, but today this hotel's main focus is its popular pub, serving affordable meals. There are a handful of cozy guest rooms upstairs, each comfortably furnished, plus a modern TV lounge. You'll recognize this place in the town center by its roadside design of late-Victorian gables.

### A Great Road Trip

Skye is full of gorgeous scenery and stunning views. One particularly scenic drive is the **northeastern loop road** that begins and ends at Portree and passes through villages like Culnaknock, Staffin, and Uig. A perfect spot is near the ruined base of Duntalem Castle, close to the peninsula's most northerly tip; from here, views stretch out as far as the neighboring islands of Harris and North Uist, over waters that are striking at sunset.

# DUNVEGAN

The village of Dunvegan, northwest of Portree, grew up around Skye's principal sight: ✪ **Dunvegan Castle** (☎ 01470/521-206), the seat of the chiefs of Clan MacLeod, who have lived here for 750 years. The castle, standing on a rocky promontory and said to be Britain's oldest inhabited castle, was once accessible only by boat, but now the moat is bridged and the castle open to the public. It holds many relics, like a "fairy flag" reputed to have brought good luck to the MacLeod clan leaders who carried it defiantly into battle; it's a tattered khaki-colored standard believed to have been given to the MacLeods by woodland spirits, bringing with it all the mystical powers of their fairy tribe. The castle is open daily: March to October 10am to 5:30pm and November to February 11am to 4pm. Admission to the castle and gardens is £5.50 ($9.35) adults, £4.80 ($8.15) seniors, £3 ($5.10) children, £15 ($25.50) family ticket. Admission to the gardens only is £3.80 ($6.45) adults/seniors and £2 ($3.40) children; free for children under 5.

Boats leave the castle jetty at frequent intervals daily May to the end of September for the **seal colony.** The seals in Loch Dunvegan, both brown and gray varieties, aren't bothered by the approach of people in boats and can be studied at close range. The 25-minute round-trip is £4 ($6.80) adults/seniors and £2.50 ($4.25) children.

At **Trumpan,** 9 miles (14.5km) north of Dunvegan, are the scant but still recognizable remains of a church that was set afire in 1597 by MacDonald raiders while the congregation, all MacLeods, were inside at worship. Only one woman survived. The MacLeods of Dunvegan rushed to the defense, and only two MacDonalds escaped death.

## ACCOMMODATIONS

**Atholl House Hotel.** Dunvegan, Isle of Skye IV55 8WA. ☎ **01470/521-219.** Fax 01470/521-481. www.athollhotel.demon.co.uk. E-mail: reservations@athollhotel.demon.co.uk. 8 units, 7 with private bathroom. TV. £64–£80 ($108.80–$136) double; £80–£90 ($136–$153) double with 4-poster bed; from £85 ($144.50) per person family room. Rates include Scottish breakfast. AE, MC, V.

Opposite the post office and near Dunvegan Castle, this hotel rents well-furnished midsize guest rooms with tea/coffeemakers and hair dryers (the single doesn't have a bathroom). Two rooms have four-poster beds along with the best views of the mountain moorland and Loch Dunvegan. In addition, a family room accommodates an extra three cots. The chef prepares quality cuisine using an abundance of locally caught seafood, plus lamb, venison, and fresh-grown produce.

## DINING

✪ **Three Chimneys Restaurant.** Hwy. B884, Colbost. ☎ **01470/511-258.** Fax 01470/511358. www.threechimneys.co.uk. Reservations required at dinner, recommended at lunch. Fixed-price menu £12.95 ($22) for 2 courses, £17.95 ($30.50) for 3 courses; fixed-price dinner £24 ($40.80) for 2 courses, £30 ($51) for 3 courses, £34.95 ($59.40) for four courses. MC, V. Mon–Sat 12:30–2:30pm (last order) and 6:30–9:30pm (last order). Drive 4 miles (about 6.5km) west of Dunvegan on B884. SCOTTISH.

The Three Chimneys, in a stone crofter's house, is the winner of multiple awards. Two of the three chimneys funnel smoke from a pair of blazing fireplaces during cold and foggy weather. The food is prepared by Edinburgh-born Shirley Speare and served by her London-born husband, Edward. An exceptionally good starter is the wild duck pâté, with wafer-thin grilled potato scones. Specialties are fresh seafood and shellfish and Highland game, with examples like roasted wild salmon Filet with warm lime-and-peppercorn vinaigrette and a trio of Highland game (venison, wild hare, and

# The Young Pretender

He was called **Bonnie Prince Charlie,** and he blazed across the pages of British history in his gallant but ill-fated attempt to regain the British crown for the Catholic Jacobite dynasty. Born in 1720 in exile in Rome, Charles Edward Stuart had a direct claim to the throne of Britain but had lost the succession to the German Protestant House of Hanover.

On July 23, 1745, when the prince landed on the Isle of Eriskay from France, islanders advised the 25-year-old pretender to return home. Within 2 days, he crossed to the mainland at Loch nan Uamh in Arisaig to rally support and on August 19 raised his royal standard at Glenfinnan. Many clans rallied to his call, and backed by 1,200 troops he marched south, gathering an ever larger army as he went.

Amazingly, he took Edinburgh by stealth on September 17. And on September 21, the prince's army crushingly defeated the English at the Battle of Prestonpans. The prince proclaimed his father as James VIII, king of Scotland, with himself as regent. For a few weeks, he held court at the Palace of Holyroodhouse in Edinburgh.

On November 8, he directed his army south, crossing into England and capturing the town of Carlisle. His invading armies took Kendal, Penrith, Lancaster, and Preston. Even Manchester fell, as the Scots were joined by English Jacobites. By December they were only 120 miles (193km) from London. There was panic in the streets of the English capital, and King George planned an escape to Hanover.

Charles wanted to press forward, but his military advisers warned him to turn back. Slowly they retreated to Scotland and settled down for the winter in Inverness. In the meantime, the duke of Cumberland's army was moving up to challenge the prince's forces. Charles decided to confront them on the desolate Moor of Culloden, an ill-fated choice. On the morning of April 16, 1746, backed by anti-Jacobite Scots, the English army crushed the Scottish forces and earned for its general the name of "Butcher Cumberland." The Battle of Culloden ended in notorious atrocities, including the burning alive of injured prisoners and the killing of women and children.

The prince began 5 long months of wandering across the Highlands and islands. He had a £30,000 ($51,000) price tag on his head—unbelievable wealth in those days—but no one turned him in. Finally, in the words of the song, he went "over the sea to Skye" disguised as the servant girl of Flora MacDonald, the Highland heroine. On September 20, 1746, Bonnie Prince Charlie returned to France secretly on the vessel *L'Heureux*. There he drifted and drank, eventually ending in Rome, where he died, all but forgotten by the world. A piper played "Lochaber No More" outside the window of his death chamber.

His brother assumed the Jacobite mantle, and—believe it or not—there's still a claimant to the throne today. His name is Prince Michael Stuart. He lives in exile in Paris but stays abreast of events in Scotland and even has plans of what he'll do "when [he's] restored to the throne, as [he] inevitably will be."

pigeon) with a sauce of beet root and black currants. The dessert menu includes scrumptious treats like marmalade pudding and Drambruie custard. More than 100 vintages from one of the most complete wine lists on Skye is available to accompany your meal.

The newest addition to Three Chimneys are the six luxurious bedroom suites located a few steps away from the restaurant. The House Over-By boasts a panoramic view of the sea, and each suite is fully equipped with amenities such as a TV, VCR, CD player, telephone, minibar, hair dryer, and coffee maker. The cost for bed-and-breakfast is £140 ($238) per couple per night. Family suites begin at £190 ($323). Both the restaurant and the suites have been given a 5-star grading by the Scottish Tourist Board.

## SKEABOST BRIDGE

Eastward from Dunvegan, Skeabost Bridge has an island cemetery of great antiquity. The graves of four Crusaders are here.

### ACCOMMODATIONS

✪ **Skeabost House Hotel.** Skeabost Bridge, Isle of Skye IV51 9NP. ☎ **01470/532-202.** Fax 01470/532-454. www.sol.co.uk/s/skeabost. E-mail: skeabost@sol.co.uk. 26 units. TV TEL. £68–£118 ($115.60–$200.60) double. Rates include Scottish breakfast. MC, V. Closed Dec–Mar.

This is one of the most inviting country homes on Skye, 35 miles (56km) west of the Kyle of Lochalsh and 6 miles (10km) north of Portree. Built in 1870 as a private estate, it has been converted into a lochside hotel boasting dormers, chimneys, tower, and gables. The hotel owns 8 miles (13km) of the bank of the River Snizort, so it attracts many sports people who come to pull trout and salmon from the waters. In addition, guests can play the hotel's par-3 golf course. The guest rooms come in a variety of shapes and sizes, each comfortably appointed. The Conservatory restaurant focuses on an extensive buffet bar with a variety of cold salads, and the main dining room offers expensive table d'hôte menus focusing on seafood.

## SLEAT PENINSULA

A lot of Skye can look melancholy and forlorn, especially in misty weather. For a change of landscape, head for the **Sleat Peninsula,** the southeastern section of the island. Because of the lushness of its vegetation (the shores are washed by the warmer waters of the Gulf Stream), it has long been known as the "Garden of Skye." Although there are no actual gardens open to the public, the climate is warmer and less bleak than in many other parts of Skye. As you drive along, you'll note the intense green of the landscape and the well-kept grounds of locals' homes.

### SEEING THE SIGHTS

A ruined stronghold of the MacDonalds, **Knock Castle** is off A851 some 12 miles (19km) south of Broadford. Another MacDonald stronghold, **Dunsgiath Castle** has some well-preserved ruins open to view. They're found at Tokavaig on an unclassified road (a sign directs you) at a point 20 miles (32km) south and southwest of Broadford. You can visit both these evocative ruins for free day or night. Inquire at the number given below for the Armadale Castle Gardens & Museum of the Isle.

**Armadale Castle Gardens & Museum of the Isles.** Armadale. ☎ **01471/844-305.** Admission £3.85 ($6.55) adults, £2.60 ($4.40) seniors/ages 5–15; free for ages 4 and under. Apr–Oct daily 9:30am–5:30pm.

At Armadale, you don't have to have MacDonald as your last name to enjoy a visit to Skye's award-winning Clan Donald Visitor Centre, with its historical exhibit "The Headship of the Gael," woodland gardens, restaurant, and gift shop. From Broadford, travel along a winding seaside road to the recently restored grounds surrounding the sculptured ruins of Armadale Castle and the rebuilt baronial stables. The multimedia exhibit is in part of the castle and tells of the lost culture of the ancient Gaelic world under the MacDonalds as lords of the Isles. The countryside ranger service offers a full summer program of guided walks and talks to introduce you to several miles of trails and the history and workings of the Highland estate. The licensed restaurant in the stables offers home baking and good local food, from teas and coffees to a full meal. The drive from the ferry at Kyleakin is about 30 minutes, and the center is along A851 (follow the signs) near the Armadale–Mallaig ferry.

## ACCOMMODATIONS

✪ **Ardvasar Hotel.** Ardvasar, Isle of Skye IV45 8RS. ☎ **01471/844-223.** www.ardvasarhotel. com. 10 units. TV. £80 ($136) double; from £110 ($187) family room. Rates include Scottish breakfast. MC, V.

The oldest part of this 250-year-old coaching inn is a stone-trimmed pub in what was a stable. In 1990, a major renovation added bathrooms to each of the guest rooms and a cottage-cozy decor that includes pastels, flowered chintz, and pinewood furniture. Guests are free to congregate in the lounge, which contains a fireplace and separate sections for TV watching and reading. Today virtually everyone in the area heads here for a mug of lager and a taste of the fine cuisine prepared by chef David Evany. Menu items include starters like peppered mushrooms with hot brandy sauce, followed by smoked chicken with cranberry sauce, although seafood is the specialty. Less formal bar meals are available, too.

**Fiordhem.** Ord, Sleat, Isle of Skye IV44 8RN. ☎ **01471/855-226.** www.host.co.uk. 3 units. £38–£42 ($64.60–$71.40) per person. Minimum stay 3 nights. Rates include half-board. MC, V. Closed Oct–Easter. Take A852 south along the eastern coast of Skye, but cut west along an unclassified road toward Ord to the west coast of the island.

Some kind of stone-sided house has stood in this spot for hundreds of years. The present version is a rebuilt fisherman's cottage, enlarged in 1990, within 20 feet (about 6m) of the edge of Loch Eishort; it's a place to stop and linger a bit. The small but comfortable guest rooms are on the upper floor, with panoramic views of the Cuillin Hills and the islands of Canna and Rhum. The dining room is pleasantly furnished with antiques, and the welcome is warm and hearty. Fresh fish and seafood, along with lamb and venison, are featured on the menu. In the sitting room are comfortable armchairs, gleaming copper and brass, and an open fireplace for peat and log fires.

**Kinloch Lodge.** Isleornsay, Sleat, Isle of Skye IV43 8QY. ☎ **01471/833-333.** Fax 01471/833-277. www.kinloch-lodge.co.uk. 15 units. TEL. £110–£180 ($187–$306) double. Rates include Scottish breakfast. AE, MC, V.

The white-stone walls of this manor are visible from across the scrub- and pine-covered hillsides bordering the edges of this property. When it was built in 1680, it was a hunting lodge for the MacDonald estates. Today, after much rebuilding and expansion, the linden-flanked house is the residence of Lord and Lady MacDonald, who welcome you into their elegant home. Portraits of the family's 18th-century forebears are a striking feature of the reception rooms, as are the open fireplaces and the scores of antiques. Many of the guest rooms, which come in various shapes and sizes, have been freshly papered and painted. From the windows of some, you can sometimes glimpse the sea, which washes up to the edge of the property's sloping gardens. Every evening, you enjoy drinks in a drawing room before dining on one of the upscale meals for which Lady MacDonald is famous. The author of 13 cookbooks, she applies her imaginative recipes to ingredients shot, trapped, netted, or grown on Skye.

## 3 Rhum (Rum)

9 miles (14.5km) SW of the Isle of Skye

The enticingly named island of Rhum is only about 8 miles (13km) wide and 8 miles long. There are those who'll tell you not to go: "If you like a barren desert where it rains all the time, you'll love Rhum," a skipper in Mallaig recently told us. It's stark all right. And very wet. In fact, with more than 90 inches (229cm) of rainfall recorded annually, it's said to be the wettest island of the Inner Hebrides.

Since the mid-1950s, Rhum has been owned by the Edinburgh-based Nature Conservancy Council, an ecological conservation group. Conservation is of paramount importance, and attempts are being made to bring back the sea eagle, which inhabited the island in Queen Victoria's day. On this storm-tossed outpost in summer, mountain climbers meet challenging peaks and anglers go for its good trout fishing. Bird-lovers seek out the Manx shearwaters that live on the island in great numbers. Red deer and ponies, along with the wildflowers of summer, add color to an otherwise bleak landscape.

### ESSENTIALS

**GETTING THERE**    A passenger **ferry** from Mallaig, on the western coast of Scotland, leaves about four times a week. No cars are allowed on the island. For information, contact **Caledonian MacBrayne** (☎ **01687/462-403** in Mallaig). Sailings are May to September only, on Monday and Wednesday at 10:30am, Friday at 6am, and Saturday at 5am and 12:30pm. A round-trip is £12 ($20.40) adults and £6 ($10.20) children. *Murdo Grant* (☎ **01687/450-224**) sails from Airsaig to Rhum on Tuesday, Thursday, Saturday, and Sunday at 11am. A round-trip ticket is £17 ($28.90) adults, £6 ($10.20) ages 12 to 16, and £3 ($5.10) for those under age 12. Schedules can vary, so it's best to call for confirmations. It takes about 2 hours to reach Rhum from one of these ports.

### ACCOMMODATIONS & DINING

**Kinloch Castle.** Kinloch, Isle of Rhum PH43 4RR. ☎ /fax **01687/462-037.** 27 units, none with private bathroom; 52 hostel beds. Rooms £60 ($102) double; hostel £12 ($20.40) per person, in rooms with 2 to 5 beds. MC, V.

You'll be astonished that in such a forbidding place you can come on a hotel that has been called "Britain's most intact example of an Edwardian Country House." On the seafront in the center of Rhum's biggest hamlet, Kinloch, this mansion was completed in 1901 for Sir George Boullough, a wealthy Lancashire textile magnate, and decorated under the direction of his wife, Lady Monica (both are buried in the family mausoleum on the west coast). The castle still contains their ballroom, with its gold curtains and upholstery, a massive inglenook Adam-style fireplace, and the monumental paintings and stuffed animals that were de rigueur when Kinloch Castle was in its heyday. The former servants' quarters are now a simple and functional hostel, and the more elegant and much more private rooms are furnished with heavy four-poster oak beds and share spacious bathrooms. Because guests spend their days

### Before You Go . . .

Before traveling to Rhum, you must contact **Denise Reed,** the reserve manager at the Scottish Natural Heritage Nature Reserve, by calling ☎ **01687/462-026.** The office will assist you in organizing accommodations on the island.

trekking around the island, all lunches are packed picnics at £4.50 ($7.65) per person. The bistro-style restaurant serves breakfasts and hearty dinners for reasonable prices.

# 4  Eigg & Muck

Eigg: 4 miles (6.5km) SE of Rhum; Muck: 7 (11km) miles SW of Eigg

The tiny islands of Eigg and Muck lie in the Sea of the Hebrides, which separates the Inner from the Outer Hebrides. If you're doing the whirlwind tour of Europe, Eigg and Muck will hardly top your agenda. They appeal only to nature lovers seeking a variety of Hebridean scenery and a chance to look at life of long ago—a true feeling of getting away from it all. If your time is limited and you can visit only one isle, make it Eigg, with the most dramatic scenery.

## ESSENTIALS FOR THE ISLANDS

**GETTING THERE**    Before venturing to either Eigg or Muck, confirm the schedule of the ferry's return. Since service isn't every day, you may find yourself staying at least 2 nights on either island. **Caledonian MacBrayne** ferries (☎ **01687/462-403** in Mallaig) sail from Mallaig to Eigg on Monday, Tuesday, and Thursday at 10:30am, on Friday at 6am, and on Saturday at 5am and 12:30pm. The round-trip ticket is £8.05 ($13.70) adults and £4 ($6.80) children. From Airsaig, another ferry line, **Murdo Grant** (call ☎ **01687/450-224** for schedules), sails to Muck on Monday, Wednesday, and Friday (but departure days and times can vary). Sailings to Eigg are Friday to Wednesday. Most departures are at either 11 or 11:30am (subject to change, based on weather conditions). The round-trip fare for either is £13 ($22.10) adults, £6 ($10.20) ages 12 to 16, and £3 ($5.10) those under 12.

**VISITOR INFORMATION**    For assistance in finding accommodations on Eigg or for any general information, contact **Mrs. Mairi Kirk,** 7 Cleadane, Isle of Eigg PH42 4RL (☎ **01687/482-416**). Rates range from £26 to £35 ($44.20 to $59.50) per person, double occupancy, and include dinner, breakfast, and a packed lunch for hill-trekking the next day.

## EIGG

Eigg, about 4½ miles by 3 miles (7km by 5km), is some 12 miles (19km) out in the Atlantic. The island is owned by the Isle of Eigg Heritage Trust, consisting of about 70 island residents and the Highland Council and Scottish Wildlife Trust. The farmers, shepherds, fishermen, and guesthouse keepers who live there raised $2.4 million through a worldwide public appeal over the Internet to buy their island.

You can see the **Sgurr of Eigg,** a tall column of lava, said to be the biggest such pitchstone (volcanic rock) mass in the United Kingdom. Climbers on its north side try to attain its impressive height of 1,300 feet (394m). It's said that the last of the pterodactyls roosted there—the bones of this towering bat-winged and beaked flying dinosaur were discovered in the 7th century, or so it's reported, by St. Donnan, a Christian missionary.

After your arrival at **Galmisdale,** the principal hamlet and pier, you can take an antique bus to Cleadale. Once there, you walk across moors to **Camas Sgiotaig,** with its well-known beach of the Singing Sands (its black-and-white quartz grains are decidedly off-key). Since the island is crisscrossed with paths and tracks, and access isn't restricted, you can walk in any direction that captures your fancy. However, much of this land is privately owned, so don't litter or damage anything.

You come to Eigg for the remoteness and the sense of living in the 19th century. The island is known for its plant, animal, and bird life, including golden eagles flying overhead and seals basking on the rocks. In summer you can sometimes see minke whales and porpoises in the offshore waters. The island's resident warden leads guided walks of Eigg once a week in summer. Call ☎ **01687/482-477** for details.

## MUCK

Lying 7 miles (11km) southwest of Eigg, Muck has such an unappetizing name that visitors may turn away. However, the name of this 2½-square-mile (6.5sq km) island was originally a Gaelic word, *muic,* meaning "island of the sow." Naturalists come here to look for everything from rare butterflies to otters. Large colonies of nesting seabirds in can be viewed in May and June.

Muck is actually a farm. There are hardly more than 30 people, and all are concerned with the running of the farm. Visitors are welcome. The entire island is owned by two brothers: the Laird of Muck, Lawrence MacEwan, and his younger brother, Ewen MacEwan. There are no vehicles on the island except for bicycles and tractors.

What's the real reason to come? To see and explore a tiny fragile Hebridean community that has survived, sometimes at great odds. That it carries on, and that its locals still eke out a living from farmland and the sea, is reason enough to go. The scenery and the solitude are wonderful, and so are the cattle, sheep, hens, house cats, and ducks roaming with relative freedom. If you walk to the top of the highest hill, **Ben Airean,** at 451 feet (137m), you'll have a panoramic view of Muck and its neighbor islands of Rhum and Eigg.

### ACCOMMODATIONS & DINING

**Port Mhor House.** Port Mhor (a few steps from the ferry landing), Isle of Muck PH42 4RP. ☎/fax **01687/462-365.** 8 units, none with private bathroom. £68 ($115.60) double. Rates include half-board. No credit cards. Closed Sept 15–May 15.

This solidly weatherproof hotel with its varnished planks of Scots pine was built by Ewen MacEwan. Its construction required 5 years (1975–80), and most of its building materials were barged in from the mainland. The small guest rooms are functional, well maintained, and comfortable, with lots of pinewood trim. Almost everyone checks in on the half-board plan, with breakfast and dinner; vegetarian dishes are available on request. Guests can get a drink in the sitting room, and during cold weather a log fire blazes. The kitchen uses produce from the island's farm for plain and wholesome fare well suited to the brisk climate.

## 5 Coll & Tyree

90 miles (145km) NW of Glasgow, 48 miles (77km) W of Fort William

If you like your scenery stark and tranquil, try tiny Coll and Tyree. The outermost of the Inner Hebrides, they're sibling islands, exposed to the open Atlantic, said to have the highest sunshine records in Britain. On Tyree (also spelled Tiree), the shell-sand *machair* (sand dunes) increase the arable area, differentiating it from the other inner isles.

Trees are rare on either island, but that doesn't mean they're bleak. Both are rich in flora, with some 500 species, along with bird life. It's estimated that some 150 bird species are found here, including Arctic skuas and razorbills. Both common and gray seals have breeding colonies on the islands. Boat rentals and sea angling can be arranged on both Coll and Tyree. Many visitors bicycle around the island, and there are a few cars for rent. Tyree has the least expensive method of transport: A mail bus serves most of the island.

## GETTING TO THE ISLANDS

**British Airways** (☎ 0345/222-111 in Glasgow) flies directly to Tyree from Glasgow, with about six scheduled flights weekly (none on Sunday) lasting 90 minutes.

A **car ferry** sails from Oban to Coll (a 3-hour trip, costing £18.85/$32.05 round-trip) and Tyree (an extra 45 minutes, costing an extra £7/$11.90 round-trip), but in very rare instances gales may force cancellation of the trip. If the gale is very strong, you might be stranded on an island for a while, waiting for the next departure. Details and bookings, essential for cars, are available from **Caledonian MacBrayne** (☎ 0990/650-000).

## COLL

Lying in the seemingly timeless world of the Celtic west, the island of Coll, with a population of some 130 hearty souls, is rich in history, even prehistory. Distances from one place to another are small on Coll, since the island averages about 3 miles (5km) in breadth; at its longest point, it stretches for some 13 miles (21km).

Coll has a partially restored castle rising majestically from its southeastern side, **Breacachadh,** a stronghold of the Macleans in the 15th century. This is a private residence but also a center for Project Trust, which prepares young people for voluntary service overseas. On some occasions it's open to the public. Immediately adjacent is the so-called **New Castle,** built for Hector Maclean in 1750. It provided shelter for Samuel Johnson and James Boswell when they were stranded on the island for 10 days because of storms at sea. The castle, still a private home, was altered considerably in the 19th century and embellished with pepper-pot turrets and parapets.

In the western part of the island at Totronald are two standing stones called **Na Sgeulachan** ("Teller of Tales"). The stones predate the Druids and are thought to have been the site of a temple. It's also been suggested they may have been an astronomical laboratory, recording the movements of the sun and moon. The highest point on Coll is **Ben Hogh** (340 feet/103m), which you can climb for a panoramic view. The boulder on the hill, supported by smaller stones, is believed to have been left that way from the Ice Age.

On the road to Sorisdale, at **Killunaig,** stand the ruins of a church from the late Middle Ages and a burial ground. Going on to **Sorisdale,** you'll see the ruins of houses occupied by crofters earlier in this century. Hundreds of families once lived here. Some were chased away in the wake of the potato famine and many were forced out in Land Clearance programs. Enduring great hardships at sea, including disease, they went to Canada, Australia, the United States, and New Zealand.

### ACCOMMODATIONS

**Isle of Coll Hotel.** Arinagour, Isle of Coll PA78 6SZ. ☎ **01879/230-334.** Fax 01879/230-317. www.collhotel.freeserve.co.uk. E-mail:joliphotel@aol.com. 6 units, 3 with private bathroom. TV. £50 ($85) double without bathroom; £60 ($102) double with bathroom. Rates include Scottish breakfast. MC, V.

This hotel enjoys the dubious honor of being immediately rejected by Samuel Johnson and James Boswell as an inappropriate place to spend the night during their 18th-century tour of Scotland (they eventually succeeded in securing lodgings with the laird of Coll). Today the small to midsize guest rooms are far more comfortable, with electric blankets, hair dryers, tea/coffeemakers, and simple but functional furniture. A good dinner is rather expensive in the dining room. The hotel contains the town's only pub, so you're likely to meet locals over a pint of ale and a platter of more affordable bar food. The hotel sits on a hilltop at the end of the Arinagour estuary about a 10-minute walk north of town, beside B8071. Its facilities include a sauna, children's play area, and a garden.

## TYREE (TIREE)

A fertile island, one of the richest in the Hebrides, flat Tyree earned the Gaelic nickname the "land below the wave tops." Tyree has a population of some 800 residents, mostly in farming communities, who enjoy its gentle landscape, sandy beaches, and rolling hills. At Vaul is a nine-hole golf course open to visitors. The best way to see the island is by bike, and you can rent one at the Tiree Lodge Hotel (see below) at £8 ($13.20) per day.

As you travel about the island, you'll see many Hebridean **crofter's houses** with thatched roofs built in the early 1800s. In 1886, the duke of Argyll caused a scandal when he sent in marines and police to clear the crofters off the land. Many were sent destitute to Canada. But today crofters once again occupy the land.

Most of the population is centered around **Scarinish,** with its little stone harbor where lobster boats put in. Fishing isn't what it used to be; the appearance of fast and dangerous squalls and storms are said to scatter the fishing fleet as far as the shores of North America. Bird watchers are drawn to the shores of **Loch Bhasapoll,** a favorite gathering place of wild geese and ducks, and to a cave on the coast at **Kenavara,** where many seabirds can be observed. The Reef was an important air base for the Royal Air Force in World War II and is still in use.

Ancient duns and forts are scattered around Tyree. The best of these is a broch at **Vaul Bay,** with walls more than 12 feet (3.5m) thick. It's 30 feet (9m) in diameter. At **Balephetrish,** on the northern rim of the island, stands a huge granite boulder. Locals call it the Ringing Stone, because when struck it gives off a metallic sound. In the western part of the island, at Kilkenneth, are the ruins of the **Chapel of St. Kenneth,** a comrade of St. Columba.

### ACCOMMODATIONS & DINING

**Tiree Lodge Hotel.** Kirkatol, Isle of Tiree PA77 6TW. ☎ **01879/220-368.** Fax 01879/220-884. 11 units, 9 with private bathroom. TV. £44 ($74.80) double without bathroom; £49 ($83.30) double with bathroom. Rates include Scottish breakfast. MC, V.

Built as a simple hunting lodge around 1790 for the duke of Argyll, this place was greatly enlarged in the 1970s with a modern addition, and the interior was brought up-to-date. A mile (1.5km) east of the island's only ferry landing, the hotel, run by Kenneth and Irene Hutchinson, contains one of the island's two pubs (the other is almost 3 miles/5km away). Because of the crowd of locals and visitors who keep the place packed, renovations have expanded both the bar and restaurant. Meals are served in both places. The small guest rooms are well maintained and comfortable and have tea/coffeemakers.

## 6 Mull

121 miles (195km) NW of Edinburgh, 90 miles (145km) NW of Glasgow

The third-largest island in the Hebrides, Mull is rich in legend and folklore, a land of ghosts, monsters, and the wee folk. The island is wild and mountainous, characterized by sea lochs and sandy bars. Be sure to bring a raincoat to Mull: It's known as one of the wettest islands in the Hebrides, a fact that upset Dr. Johnson, who visited in 1773. Actually, Dr. Johnson was a latecomer to Mull, which has an ancient history. It was known to the classical Greeks, and its prehistoric past is recalled in forts, duns, and stone circles.

Many visitors consider Mull more beautiful than Skye, a controversy we don't choose to get involved in, since we love them both. Mull has varied scenery with many

## A Driving Warning

If you're driving along any of Mull's single-track roads, remember to take your time and let the sheep and cattle have the right-of-way. Also, a car coming downhill toward you has the right of way, so look for a spot to pull off.

waterfalls, and the wild countryside was the scene of many of David Balfour's adventures in *Kidnapped* by Robert Louis Stevenson. Its highest peak is **Ben More** at 3,169 feet (961m), but it also has many flat areas. The island's wildlife includes roe deer, golden eagles, polecats, seabirds, and feral goats. Mull is also a jumping-off point to visit Iona and Staffa (see "Iona & Staffa: An Abbey & a Musical Cave," below).

Guarding the bay (you'll see it as you cross on the ferry) is **Duart Castle,** restored just before World War I. It was once the seat of the fiery Macleans, who shed much blood in and around the castle during their battles with the lords of the Isles. In the bay—somewhere—lies the *Florencia,* a Spanish galleon that went down laden with treasure. Many attempts have been made to find it and bring it up, but so far all have failed. To the southeast, near Salen, are the ruins of **Aros Castle,** once a stronghold of the MacDonalds, lords of the Isles. Its ruins date from the 14th century, and it was last occupied in the 17th century. On the far south coast at Lochbuie, **Moy Castle** has a water-filled dungeon.

At the end of the day, you might enjoy a dram of malt whisky from the **Tobermory Malt Whisky Distillery** (☎ 01688/302-647), which has had a troubled history but is now back in business. You're welcome to visit the distillery in Tobermory, opened in 1823. Tours are Monday to Friday 10:30am to 4pm and cost £2.50 ($4.25) adults and £1 ($1.70) seniors (ages 17 and under free). Be sure to call to arrange a tour in advance, as the distillery seems to shut down from time to time.

## ISLAND ESSENTIALS

**GETTING THERE**    It's a 45-minute **car-ferry** trip from Oban to Craignure on Mull. For times of departure, contact **Caledonian MacBrayne** (☎ 0990/650-000). It's a roll-on/roll-off operation for your car. From Oban, there are about five or six sailings per day at a cost of £5.75 ($9.80) adults and £2.90 ($4.95) children. To transport your car to the island, the cost is £40 ($68) for a 5-day return ticket.

**GETTING AROUND**    Take the ferry to get here, then use **Bowmans Coaches Mull** to go around the island (☎ 01680/812-313). Coaches connect with the ferry at least three times per day and will take you to Fionnphort or Tobermory for £7 ($11.90) or £4.50 ($7.65) round-trip; children are half price. Another option is to buy a tour ticket combining the cost of the ferry with a guided bus tour to Fionnphort and Iona. The tour begins when you board the 10am ferry from Oban and ends at about 5:40pm, once again at Oban. The cost is £19 ($32.30) adults and £12 ($20.40) children.

**VISITOR INFORMATION**    The **tourist office** is on Main Street in Tobermory (☎ 01688/302-182). Easter to October, it's open Monday to Friday 9am to 5pm (to 6pm July and August).

**SPECIAL EVENTS**    The **Mull Highland Games** are held annually in July, filled with all the traditional events such as bagpipes, caber tossing, and dancing. The **Tour of Mull Rally** is held in early October of every year. Ask at the tourist office for exact dates.

## FUN IN THE OUTDOORS AROUND THE ISLAND

**BIKING**    Its combinations of heather-clad, rock-strewn moors and sylvan forests make Mull especially appropriate for cycling. To rent a bike, try **On Yer Bike,** The Pierhead, in Craignure (☎ 01680/812-487), 22 miles (35.5km) from Tobermory. In Tobermory itself, consider **Brown's,** High Street (☎ 01688/302-020). Both charge £12 to £14 ($20.40 to $23.80) a day, depending on the model you choose, with discounts for multiple-day rentals paid in advance. Both are open daily 10am to around 7pm.

**ECO-CRUISES**    Several operators will take you out to see whales, dolphins, and seals. Two of the best-recommended are **Sea Life Surveys,** Beadoun, Breidwood, Tobermory (☎ 01688/400-223), and a hardworking entrepreneur named **Mr. Liverty,** High Street (☎ 01688/302-048), who maintains midsized boats for 6 to 12 passengers each. At both, you pay £15 ($25.50) for a half-day excursion that will offer sweeping views of the Mull coast and active colonies of seals and sea birds.

Mull is rich in wildlife and visitors can experience the natural habitat with **Island Encounters** (☎ 01680/300-441). Guided by a local expert, you can spend the day on a safari, exploring the remote and most scenic areas of the island in a comfortable 8-seat vehicle. The cost for the day is £23 ($39.10) for adults and £19 ($32.30) for children 14 and under. Binoculars and lunch are included in the price, and pick-up can be arranged at all ferry terminals on Mull.

**GOLF**    Golf isn't exactly as grand and elaborate out here as on the fabled courses elsewhere in Scotland. The best of the lot is the nine-hole **Western Isles Golf Course,** about a quarter mile (about .5km) north of Tobermory. You're likely to not even see another player or employee if you head there most times of the year: The golf course's agent/administrator is **Brown's Hardware Store,** High Street, Tobermory (☎ 01688/302-020), where you pay the greens fees of £13 ($22.10) per person per day and the rental fee for clubs of £5 ($8.50) per set per day. Twenty-two miles (35.5km) west of Tobermory, is the **Craignure Golf Course,** an isolated nine-hole course with an honesty box into which you deposit the greens fees of £11 ($18.70) per person per day. For information about this course, contact its secretary, D. Howitt, at ☎ 01680/812-487.

**HIKING**    The island is wonderful for hiking. You'll probably drive off to a trailhead, park your car beside the road (most residents boast they haven't locked their car in decades), and then set off on foot in total isolation. The tourist office sells two books, each costing £2.95 ($5): *Walks in North Mull* and *Walks in South Mull.* They provide detailed options for specific routes with historic, ethnographical, scenic, or geological interest. Dress in layers, and wear something waterproof.

## CRAIGNURE

Even passengers who arrive on Mull with a car might want to take an excursion on the **Mull Railway,** Old Pier Station, Craignure (☎ 01680/812-494), the only passenger rail in the Hebrides. It was inaugurated in 1983, but its puffing engine and narrow-gauge tracks are thoroughly old-fashioned. The tracks begin at the Old Pier in Craignure, running 1½ miles (2.5km) to Torosay Castle and its famous gardens. Some of the engines are powered by steam, others by diesel. The view is one of unspoiled mountains, glens, and seaside; you can sometimes see otters, eagles, and deer in the course of the 20-minute journey. The trains operate Easter to mid-October: The most frequent service is June to mid-September, when daily trips begin around 11am. One-way fares are £2.30 ($3.90) adults and £1.40 ($2.40) children. A special ticket is available for families with two parents and two children at £6 ($10.20) one way or £8.75

($14.90) round-trip. For more details, call the Mull & West Highland Railway Company in Craignure at ☎ **01680/300-389.**

A good way to see the sights of Mull is to book a ticket for "The Mull Experience," a tour offered by **Caledonian MacBrayne.** For information, call **Torosay Castle** at ☎ **01680/812-421.** The tour begins in Oban, where you board a ferry for Craignure. Once in Craignure, you catch the train to Torosay Castle, where you'll spend a few hours exploring the Victorian structure and its gardens. The next stop is the castle of Duart, the 13th-century home of the chief of Clan Maclean. You then return to Oban by ferry. The tour is offered May to September, three times a day Sunday to Thursday and twice on Friday. The cost is £17 ($28.90) adults and £8.50 ($14.45) children.

✪ **Torosay Castle and Gardens.** 1½ miles (2.5km) south of Craignure on A849. ☎ **01680/812-421.** Admission to castle and gardens £4.50 ($7.65) adults, £3.50 ($5.95) seniors/students, £1.50 ($2.55) ages 6–16, £10 ($17) families; free for ages 5 and under. Admission to gardens and tearoom only £3.50 ($5.95) adults, £2.75 ($4.70) seniors/students, £1 ($1.70) children. Easter–mid-Oct daily 10:30am–5:30pm.

This Victorian mansion was built in the mid–19th century by David Bryce, a famous Scottish architect. It's set in early-1900s gardens attributed to Sir Robert Lorimer. In his early years, Winston Churchill was a frequent visitor. One writer said a visit here is like returning to the "Edwardian age of leisure," and so it is. To the surprise of hundreds of visitors, the armchairs are labeled PLEASE SIT DOWN instead of PLEASE KEEP OFF. This is very much a family place, the only privately occupied castle and garden in the western Highlands open daily to the public. The family portraits are by such famous artists as Sargent. Its numerous exhibits include evidence for the existence of the Loch Ness monster. You can wander through 12 acres of Italian-style terraced gardens, a water garden with shrubs that grow in the Gulf Stream climate, and a Japanese garden with life-size figures by Antonio Bonazza. You can enjoy extensive views of the Appin coastline from Ben Nevis to Ben Cruachen.

**Duart Castle.** Off A849, on the eastern point of Mull. ☎ **01680/812-309.** Admission £3.50 ($5.95) adults, £3 ($5.10) seniors/students, £1.75 ($3) ages 3–15, £8.75 ($14.90) families; free for ages 2 and under. May to mid-Oct daily 10:30am–6pm.

You can visit both Torosay Castle (see above) and Duart Castle on the same day. Located 3 miles (5km) west of Torosay, this castle dates from the 13th century and was the home of the Maclean clan. A majestic structure, it was sacked in 1791 by the dukes of Argyll in retaliation for the Macleans' support of the Stuarts in 1715 and 1745. It was allowed to fall into ruins. However, Sir Fitzroy Maclean, the 26th chief of the clan and grandfather of the present occupant, began a restoration in 1911 when he was 76, spending a considerable fortune. It had been his ambition since he was a boy to see his ancestral home restored (he lived until he was 102). Visitors can wander about, taking

---

### A Stunning View

Even locals sometimes drive out of their way to catch the sunset over the **Gribun Rock,** a large peninsula midway along the island's western coast, whose centerpiece is the windy uplands of Ben More. The entire stretch of single-lane highway on the western flank of Ben More is a particularly spectacular highlight. To reach it from Tobermory or Craignure, follow the signs to the hamlet of Salen, then drive west to Gribun. En route, you'll pass through the hamlets of Knock, Balnahard, and Balevuin. From dozens of points en route, views stretch over the clifftops, encompassing the setting sun (if your timing is right) as well as the Isles of Staffa, Coll, and Tiree.

in such rooms as the Banqueting Hall, which is in the keep, the great tower that's the heart of the castle.

## ACCOMMODATIONS & DINING

**Isle of Mull.** Craignure, Isle of Mull PA65 6BB. ☎ **01680/812-351.** Fax 01680/812-462. 87 units. TV TEL. £60–£90 ($102–$153) double. Rates include Scottish breakfast. MC, V. Closed mid-Oct to mid-Mar.

The Isle of Mull stands near the ferry and the meeting point of the Sound of Mull and Loch Linnhe. From the picture windows of its public rooms you'll have panoramic vistas of mountains and the island of Lismore. The small guest rooms are handsomely furnished and come with tea/coffeemakers. The chef serves British and continental food in the attractive dining room, which faces both sea and hills. Other facilities include a cocktail bar and a lounge.

## SALEN

Near Salen are the ruins of **Aros Castle,** once a stronghold of the lords of the Isles, the MacDonalds. It dates from the 14th century and was last occupied in the 17th century. Most of the former castle has been carted off, but the site is still visible 11 miles southeast of Tobermory.

## ACCOMMODATIONS

**Glenforsa Hotel.** By Salen, Aros, Isle of Mull PA72 6JN. ☎ **01680/300-377.** Fax 01680/300-535. www.glenforsa.com. 13 units, 12 with private bathroom. £55–£70 ($93.50–$119) double. Rates include Scottish breakfast. MC, V.

This 1968 Norwegian pine log construction, in secluded grounds by the Sound of Mull and the River Forsa 11 miles (18km) southeast of Tobermory, is known in late summer for its seafront and salmon. The guest rooms are well appointed and spacious. The bar serves an array of tempting pub food, with venison, trout, and salmon offered in season for guests and nonguests alike. The dining room serves much the same fare at higher prices. The hotel has an adjacent grass airstrip, at which Dakotas and other private and charter planes can land from dawn to dusk.

## TOBERMORY

The **Mull Museum** (☎ 01688/302-208) has local exhibits relating to the island, displayed in an old bakery building on Main Street. Easter to mid-October, it's open Monday to Friday 10am to 4pm and Saturday 10am to 1pm, charging £1 ($1.70) adults and 20p (35¢) children. The **Western Isle Golf Course** dates from the 1930s and is said to have possibly the best views of any golf course in the world.

Isle of Mull Silver, Main Street (☎ 01688/302-345), stocks jewelry made by a number of Scottish designers. This shop, open since 1975, also produces some of the silver and gold pieces available here. Among the unique items made on the premises are traditional Scottish silver *quaich* (drinking vessels) and christening spoons. **Mull Pottery,** Main Street (☎ 01688/302-057), is the domain of potter Pete Walker, who produces tableware, ovenware, and lamps in seashore, seagull, and turquoise patterns. Among the more unusual items is a large crock designed for bread storage. The shop also stocks the wares of other Scottish potters.

Sgriob Ruadh Dairy/Isle of Mull Cheese, Glengorm Road (☎ 01688/302-235), a family-run farm, half a mile (almost 1km) outside Tobermory, has been producing cheeses for more than 20 years. You're welcome to watch the cheesemaking process and check out the farm. The shop itself is an attractive glass house where you'll find Isle of Mull cheese, a softer washed-curd cheese, and flavored variations of both. The flavor of the cheese is unique for much the same reason Scottish malt whiskies are unique—the naturally occurring qualities of the water and the natural grazing, supplemented with a feed made of grains used in producing malt whiskies, which feed the cattle. There's a simple country restaurant on the premises, where good, inexpensive home-cooked meals are available 10am to 4pm. Especially popular are the hearty soups served with as much freshly baked bread as you care to eat—a meal in itself for £1.80 ($3.05). You can also get an Isle of Mull cheese board with a salad and as much bread as you want for £3.50 ($5.95).

   **Tackle & Books,** Main Street (☎ 01688/302-336), as the name suggests, carries fishing gear, bait, and an impressive array of reading materials. The shop sells anything in print about Mull and works by local authors. There's also a decent selection of contemporary fiction and publications about Scottish history, regional folklore, all things Celtic, and natural history, including books on bird watching and whale watching on the island.

## ACCOMMODATIONS

**Tobermory Hotel.** 53 Main St., Tobermory, Isle of Mull PA75 6NT. ☎ 01688/302-091. Fax 01688/302-254. www.tobermoryhotel.com. 16 units. TV. £70–£90 ($119–$153) double. Rates include Scottish breakfast. MC, V. Parking available on nearby streets.

On the upper end of the town's main street, this hotel has a sense of privacy and intimacy. It has recently undergone major renovations, with the guest rooms getting special attention. Thirteen of the rooms have views of the fishing boats bobbing at anchor in the harbor just off the road; the remaining four have views of the steep and tree-dotted cliff that rises abruptly behind the hotel. The dining room serves dinner nightly; prices are on the high side of moderate, and the selections include seafood and seasonal game.

**Western Isles Hotel.** Tobermory, Isle of Mull PA75 6PR. ☎ 01688/302-012. Fax 01688/302-297. www.mollhotel.com. 25 units. TV TEL. £78–£160 ($132.60–$272) double; £190 ($323) suite. Rates include Scottish breakfast. AE, MC, V. Closed Dec 18–28.

In a scenic location on a bluff above the harbor, the Western Isles is a large gray-stone country inn. It was constructed by the Sandeman sherry company in the late 1880s as a hunting/fishing lodge for their top-level staff and customers. The current owners welcome guests to rooms decorated in a mix of styles that are homelike and spotless, with electric heaters, hair dryers, and tea/coffeemakers. The hotel has a conservatory bar as well as an upscale restaurant.

## DINING

**Gannet's Restaurant.** 25 Main St. ☎ 01688/302-203. Main courses £5.50–£10.95 ($9.35–$18.60). MC, V. Easter–Oct daily 10am–10pm; Nov–Easter daily 10am–3:30pm. REGIONAL.

This place enjoys a quayside setting in one of the stone-fronted 200-year-old buildings along Main Street. It's one of the best independent restaurants here. You get fresh seafood, much of it caught locally, along with salads, tender and juicy steaks, and some fine vegetable dishes, finished off by creamy desserts. During the day you might stop in for sandwiches and fresh coffee.

## TOBERMORY AFTER DARK

**Macgochan's Pub,** Ledag (☎ 01688/302-350), is an old traditional pub that has free Scottish music most nights 8pm to 1am. On tap you can choose from beers that include Guinness and McEwan's or Tennant's 60 Shilling. There's also a separate games room with a pool table. The **Mishnish Hotel,** Main Street (☎ 01688/302-009), is faux traditional pub style, which fits the Scottish music featured here nightly just fine.

Real ales on tap change weekly, and standard lagers include McEwan's 70 and 80 Shilling. In pleasant weather, you can step into the beer garden for a breath of fresh air.

# DERVAIG

The loveliest village of Mull, Dervaig (Little Grove) is an 8-mile (13km) drive west from Tobermory. A Maclean built the town in the closing year of the 18th century.

The **Old Byre Heritage Centre,** Dervaig (☎ 01688/400-229), houses one of the most charming museums you could hope to find. The main exhibit features 25 scale models, painstakingly researched and made by a local historian, showing the history of Mull from the first settlers to the Highland clearances. The models are also featured in a film shown on the hour and half hour (last show at 5:30pm). A fully licensed tearoom serves light meals 10:30am to 6pm. Admission is £3 ($5.10) adults, £2 ($3.40) seniors/students, and £1.50 ($2.55) ages 5 to 12; ages 4 and under are free. Easter to October, it's open daily 10:30am to 6:30pm. Take the twice-daily bus from Tobermory.

Just outside Dervaig is the **Mull Little Theater,** founded in 1966, seating 43 viewers. According to the *Guinness Book of World Records,* this makes it the smallest professional theater in Great Britain. See "Dervaig After Dark," below, for details.

From Dervaig, you can cruise to the lonely **Treshnish Isles,** a sanctuary for seabirds and seals. These islands form a group unto themselves, including Fladda ("is flatter") and Lunga ("is longer"), along with the well-named Bac Mor ("Dutchman's Cap"). April to September, a local entrepreneur operates the *Turus Mara* (☎ 01688/400-242), carrying up to 60 passengers on half-day visits at £12 ($20.40) or full-day visits at £27 ($45.90). Scheduling is erratic, depending on business, the weather, and the season. The boat departs from the Ulva Ferry Piers, on the west side of Mull, opposite the isle of Ulva. The Treshnish Isles are murky, muddy, and boggy, so bring dry clothes, boots, and a sense of humor.

## ACCOMMODATIONS

**Druimard Hotel.** Dervaig, Isle of Mull PA75 6QW. ☎ **01688/400-345.** Fax 01688/400-345. www.smoothound.co.uk/hotels/druimard.html. E-mail: druimard@talk21.com. 5 units. TV TEL. £62–£74 ($105.40–$125.80) double. Rates include breakfast and dinner. MC, V. Closed Nov–Mar. Follow signs to Mull Little Theatre.

In the northwest of the island, this restored Victorian country house opens to views of an idyllic glen and the River Bellart where it flows into Loch Cuin and out to sea. For old-fashioned Scottish comfort and a relaxed, tranquil atmosphere, this homelike choice is the place to be. With its period furnishings and blazing fireplace, it is a cozy retreat. The medium to spacious bedrooms are tastefully furnished, with excellent mattresses, beverage makers, and hair dryers. Your hosts, Wendy and Haydn Hubbard, are on hand to tend to your needs and are a font of information about Mull itself. They'll arrange cruises to remote isles, wildlife expeditions, and even whale-watching jaunts. Even if you don't stay here, consider a visit to their winning restaurant (see below).

**Druimnacroish Hotel.** Dervaig, Isle of Mull PA75 6QW. ☎/fax **01688/400-274.** www.druimnacroish.co.uk. E-mail: info@druimnacroish.co.uk. 6 units. £70–£84 ($119–$142.80) double; £225–£275 ($382.50–$467.50) self-catering apt for a week. Room rates include Scottish breakfast. AE, MC, V.

Neil Hutton and Margriet Van de Pol have recently refurbished and upgraded this hotel as a haven of escape from the stress of modern life. TVs and phones are purposely not included in the rooms (although they are available if requested). There's one self-catering apartment rented for weekly stays. The moderately priced meals are simple modern Scottish cuisine taking full advantage of the availability of fresh local produce.

## DINING

**Druimard Hotel Restaurant.** In the Druimard Hotel, Dervaig. ☎ **01688/400-345.** Reservations recommended. Set-price 5-course dinner £26.50 ($45.05). MC, V. Daily 6:30–8:30pm. Closed Nov–Mar. SCOTTISH.

This acclaimed restaurant offers a varied, well-prepared menu based on the use of local produce and supplies, ranging from the freshest of fish to tender Scottish beef. The cuisine is skillfully prepared, often with unusual sauces. You'll be won over by the potato pancake topped with spring onion crème fraîche and a basil oil dressing. Meat eaters dig into the fillet of Aberdeen Angus topped with local oysters and parsley pesto on a bed of celeriac, wild mushrooms, and baby spinach with caramelized shallots and red wine sauce. You might begin with a real Scottish creation: creamy smoked haddock soup. The desserts are sumptuous, including "sinful" chocolate truffle terrine with a strawberry coulis or steamed lemon pudding with crème Anglaise and marmalade ice cream.

## DERVAIG AFTER DARK

Located 8½ miles (14km) west of Tobermory, the **Mull Little Theatre,** Tobermory-Dervaig Rd. (☎ **01688/400-377**), is indeed quite small, with an audience capacity of 43 people for the dramas and comedies housed inside a stone-built byre (stable) turned theater. Productions are staged Easter to September, with visiting companies filling the bill early on and the small-but-capable Mull Theater Company staging plays later in the season. On performance nights, the doors open at 8pm, and the curtain goes up 30 minutes later. Adult tickets run £10 ($17); seniors, students, and children pay £6 ($10.20). Because of the size of the facility, tickets should be reserved in advance. There's no seat allocation, so arrive early. Some of the more popular performances are actually held in larger venues in Tobermory.

# FIONNPHORT

At the western tip of the Ross of Mull, Fionnphort is a tiny port that sees a lot of traffic. This is where the road ends and regular ferry passage is available across the mile-long (1.5km) Sound of Iona to the Isle of Iona, one of the most visited attractions in Scotland. Iona is clearly visible from Fionnphort. Less than 2 miles (3km) to the south is the tidal island of Erraid, where David Balfour had adventures in Stevenson's *Kidnapped*.

## ACCOMMODATIONS

**Achaban House.** Fionnphort, Isle of Mull PA66 6BL. ☎ **01681/700-205.** Fax 01681/700-649. www.achabanhouse.co.uk. 6 units. £22 ($37.40) per person; family room £50–£60 ($85–$102). Rates include Scottish breakfast. No credit cards.

Its almost indestructible walls (3 feet/1m thick in many places) were built in 1820 of pink granite for the supervisor of the local quarry. Shortly after, the building was converted into the manse (pastor's residence) for the local church. Today it sits beside the town's only highway, a 10-minute walk (or 1-minute drive) east of the ferry landing. Thirty feet (9m) from the hotel entrance is a 10-foot-tall (3m) Druidic dolmen built by prehistoric inhabitants several thousand years ago. Recent refurbishments have upgraded all the guest rooms. Two doubles have bathrooms in the rooms; two have private facilities across the hall. One family room is available and sleeps up to five.

Enticing aromas invite you to sample the cuisine of German-born Camilla Baigent and her husband, Chris. Fixed-price dinners are available on request and might include excellent preparations of poached local salmon wrapped in a sheath of herbs and such local game dishes as wild hare or venison. If you choose to have dinner here, it'll be moderately priced, and you should notify Camilla in the morning.

## DINING

**Keel Row.** At the harborfront, at the end of A849. ☎ **01681/700-458.** Main courses £5.85–£10.25 ($9.95–$17.45); sandwiches and burgers £1.75–£3.25 ($3–$5.50). MC, V. Restaurant summer only, daily noon–2:30pm and 6–9pm; snacks and drinks year-round, daily noon–9pm; meals served in the bar during winter, daily 6–8:30pm. REGIONAL.

The undisputed leader in providing food and drink to passengers waiting for a ferry to Iona, this efficient and friendly place is in two connected buildings near the pier. Food is served in a box-shaped cedar-sided building with big windows overlooking the waterfront, and drinks are offered in a 19th-century stone cottage whose rustic walls and blazing fireplace add cheer to many a gray day. Meals include spicy fried crab with coriander, onions, tomatoes, and spices served with turmeric rice and salad or the national dish of haggis with *neeps* and *tatties* (turnips and mashed potatoes). Lighter fare includes sandwiches, steaming pots of tea, and pastries.

## 7  Iona & Staffa: An Abbey & a Musical Cave

Iona: ⅛ mile (about 20m) W of Mull; Staffa: 6 miles (10km) NE of Iona

A remote, low-lying, and treeless green island with high cliffs and rolling meadows, Iona is off the southwestern coast of Mull across the Sound of Iona. It's only 1 mile by 3½ miles (1.5km by 5.5km). Staffa, with its famous musical cave, is a 75-acre island in the Inner Hebrides, lying to the west of Mull.

## IONA

Someone once said, "When Edinburgh was but a barren rock and Oxford but a swamp, Iona was famous." It has been known as a place of spiritual power and pilgrimage for centuries and was the site of the first Christian settlement in Scotland, preserving the learning that was nearly lost in the Dark Ages.

The island was owned by the dukes of Argyll from 1695, but to pay £1 million ($1.7 million) in real estate taxes, the 12th duke was forced to sell it to Sir Hugh Fraser, former owner of Harrods. He secured Iona's future and made it possible for money raised by the National Trust for Scotland to be turned over to the trustees of the restored abbey. The only village on Iona, **Baille Mor,** sits in the most sheltered spot, allowing some trees and garden plots to be cultivated. The best way to get around Iona is to walk. If that's not for you, you can take horse-drawn carriage tours given by **Island Carriages** (☎ **01681/704-230**).

Iona is accessible only by passenger ferry from the Island of Mull (cars must remain on Mull). Service is informal but fairly frequent in summer. The ferry makes the 5-minute crossing about every half hour 8:45 to noon, and then every 15 minutes daily noon to 4pm in summer; less frequent crossings are made daily 8:45 to 11:45am and 4:30 to 6:15pm. The round-trip fare is £3.20 ($5.45). In the off-season, transport depends entirely on the weather but is usually every 30 minutes daily 10am to 5pm. Call **Caledonian MacBrayne** in Tobermory (☎ **01688/302-017**) for exact times, as schedules are subject to change.

Today, the island attracts nearly 1,000 visitors a week in high season. Most come to see the impossible-to-miss Benedictine ✪ **Iona Abbey,** part of which dates from the 13th century. Its major restorations occurred in 1909 and in stages between 1938 and 1965. People also come to visit relics of the settlement founded here by St. Columba in 563, from which Celtic Christianity spread through Scotland and beyond to Europe. The abbey has been restored by the Iona Community, which leads tours and runs a coffee shop daily 10am to 4:30pm; a voluntary contribution of £2 ($3.40) is requested. The community also offers room and board to interested visitors, conducts

# Staying at Iona Abbey

Some people consider a visit to Iona the highlight of their trip to Scotland. Besides feeling impressed by the unusual historical and archaeological site, many gain a renewed interest in the power of religion. If that's what you're seeking, you can contact the **Iona Community** (☎ 01681/700-404), an ecumenical religious group that maintains a communal lifestyle in the ancient abbey and offers full board and accommodation to visitors who want to share in the community's daily life. The only ordained members of the group are its two wardens, who are members of either the Presbyterian Church of Scotland or the Scottish Episcopal Church.

March to October, the community leads a series of discussion seminars, each stretching from Saturday to Saturday. A recent example focused on the role of the Christian Church in the United Europe of the 21st century. The cost of a week's full board during one of these seminars is £185 ($314.50) per person. The abbey also opens to guests late November to mid-December, although no seminars are offered then. The per-week price is the same as in summer. Guests are expected to contribute about 30 minutes per day to the execution of some kind of household chore. The daily schedule involves a wakeup call at 8am, communal breakfast at 8:20am, a morning religious service, and plenty of unscheduled time for conversation, study, and contemplation. Up to 44 guests can be accommodated at one time in bunk-bedded twin rooms without bathrooms. In addition to the abbey, there's the Iona Community's center for reconciliation, the **MacLeod Centre,** built for youth, people with disabilities, and families. It accommodates up to 50 guests, during summer only. For further details, phone ☎ 01681/700-404.

workshops on Christianity, sponsors a youth camp, and each Wednesday leads a 7-mile (11km) hike to the island's holy and historic spots. The **Abbey Shop** (☎ 01681/700-404) features numerous books of Christian literature, along with locally made pottery and Celtic crosses and jewelry.

Iona is also known for its **"Graves of the Kings,"** adjacent to the abbey. A total of 48 Scottish kings, including (according to legend) Macbeth and his supposed victim, Duncan, were buried on Iona. Also here (again according to legend, with some justification from historical texts) are the graves of four Irish kings and eight Norwegian kings. Be aware, however, that the individual graves are unmarked—because of horrendous erosion (some were illegible even in 1909), most of the actual headstones have been removed to the abbey.

Despite the many visitors, the atmosphere on the island remains peaceful and spiritual. You can walk off among the sheep and cows that wander freely everywhere to the top of **Dun-I,** a small mountain, and contemplate the ocean and the landscape as though you were the only person on earth.

One reader, Capt. Robert Haggart of Laguna, California, described his experience this way: "I was enchanted by the place. It really has a mystic atmosphere—one feels something ancient here, something spiritual, sacred, long struggles, and wonderment about the strength of religion."

## ACCOMMODATIONS & DINING

Most of the islanders live by crofting and fishing and supplement their income by taking in paying guests in season, usually charging very low or at least fair prices. You can, of course, check into the hotels below, but a stay in a private home may be an altogether rewarding adventure. If you don't stay on Iona, you must catch one of the ferries back to Mull.

**Argyll Hotel.** Isle of Iona PA76 6SJ. ☎ **01681/700-334.** Fax 01681/700-510. www. argyllhoteliona.co.uk. E-mail: reception@argyllhoteliona.co.uk. 15 units, 14 with private bathroom. £86–£94 ($146.20–$159.80) double with bathroom. Rates include Scottish breakfast. MC, V. Closed early Oct–Mar.

Housed in an 1868 Victorian, this famous hotel, well run by Daniel Morgan and Claire Bachellerie, stands 200 yards (182m) from the ferry dock, overlooking the Sound of Iona and Mull. The small guest rooms, including one single without bathroom, are attractive. You get good home cooking and baking, and vegetarian meals are available; on their à la carte menu. In summer, the vegetables are home-grown. There's a nice selection of wines, and the hotel is licensed to serve alcohol to guests.

**St. Columba Hotel.** Isle of Iona PA76 6SL. ☎ **01681/700-304.** Fax 01681/700-688. www.stcolumba-hotel.co.uk. 27 units. £100–£150 ($170–$255) double. Rates include half-board. MC, V. Closed Oct 17–Easter.

This hotel, built of clapboard and white stone, is just uphill from the village about a quarter of a mile (5km) from the jetty. Built as a manse for Presbyterian clergy in 1847, it was transformed into a hotel in 1868. The guest rooms are rather basic and monastic but clean and reasonably comfortable for the price. Try to get one overlooking the sea, but keep in mind it's virtually impossible to secure a room in summer without a reservation made well in advance. A set dinner is served nightly at 7pm, with hearty and wholesome food—the fish dishes are especially good. Vegetarian meals are available on request.

Across from the hotel is the **Old Printing Press Bookshop** (☎ 01681/700-699), specializing in antiquarian books about and from the west of Scotland, with selections ranging back to the mid-18th century.

## STAFFA

The attraction of the island of Staffa, 6 miles (10km) north of Iona, is ✪ **Fingal's Cave,** a lure to visitors for more than 200 years and the inspiration for music, poetry, paintings, and prose. Its Gaelic name, *An Uamh Ehinn,* means "musical cave." It's the only such formation known in the world that has basalt columns; over the centuries, the sea has carved a huge cavern in the basalt, leaving massive hexagonal columns. After a visit, Queen Victoria stated: "The effect is splendid, like a great entrance into a vaulted hall. The sea is immensely deep in the cave. The rocks under water were all colors—pink, blue, and green." The sound of the crashing waves and swirling waters (the music) caused Mendelssohn to write the *Fingal's Cave Overture.* Turner painted the cave on canvas, and Keats, Wordsworth, and Tennyson all praised it in their poetry.

Staffa has been uninhabited for more than 170 years, but you can still explore the cave, which is strictly protected by the National Trust from development. Entrance is free, requiring only payment for boat passage from Mull or Iona at £12.50 ($21.25) adults and £5 ($8.50) children. You're taken to Staffa's only pier, which was enlarged in 1992 near a lesser attraction known as Clamshell Cave. You then walk along a basalt path into Fingal's Cave, where a guardrail separates you from the water and waves below. The noise of the pounding surf is deafening. The boat carries 67 passengers and runs twice daily from Iona and Mull between March and October, departing from Iona at 9:45am and 1:45pm, stopping briefly at Fionnphort, on Mull, to pick up more passengers. Return tours last about 3 hours, depending on weather conditions.

During violent storms no tours are possible. Rubber-soled shoes and warm clothing are recommended. Reservations are important: Call **Mrs. Carol Kirkpatrick,** whose husband, David, operates the boat, at *Tigh-na-Traigh* (House by the Shore), Isle of Iona (☎ **01681/700-358**), or visit their Web site at www.staffatrips.fg.co.uk.

# 8  Isle of Colonsay

15 miles (24km) S of the Isle of Mull

The most remote of the islands of Argyll, Colonsay, with **Oransay** its tidal neighbor, shares some of the same characteristics as Iona, Tyree, and Coll. To the west it faces nothing but the open Atlantic—only a lighthouse stands between Colonsay and Canada. The island encompasses 20 square miles (52sq km), enjoying an equable climate because of the warming waters of the Gulf Stream. It's more tranquil than Mull and Skye because it doesn't accommodate day-trippers.

A ferry, operated by **Caledonian MacBrayne** (☎ **0990/650-000** for schedules), sails between Oban and Colonsay three times a week. The 37-mile (59.5km) crossing takes 2½ hours.

## SEEING THE SIGHTS

You can explore all parts of the island along its one-lane roads. Many visitors prefer to rent a bike rather than drive (go to the Isle of Colonsay Hotel, which charges £5/$8.50 per day or £15/$25.50 per week). You can also rent sailing dinghies and rowboats and sail around the island, following in the grand tradition of the Vikings. Go to the Isle of Colonsay Hotel, whose staff will put you in touch with local fishermen and entrepreneurs; the boat should cost around £15/$25.50 per hour (see "Accommodations & Dining," below). The Vikings also held several ship burials on the island. Some of the sites have been excavated, but, regrettably, the ships have decayed.

Wildlife abounds, including golden eagles, falcons, gray seals, otters, and wild goats with elegant horns and long shaggy hair. Prehistoric forts, stone circles, and single standing stones attest to the antiquity of Colonsay, which has been occupied since the Stone Age.

It's estimated there are some 500 species of flora on the island. The gardens of the 1722 **Colonsay House** (seat of the laird, Lord Strathcona, and not open to the public) are filled with rare rhododendrons, magnolias, and eucalyptus, even palm trees; April to October, you can visit Wednesday noon to 5pm and Friday 2 to 5pm for £3 ($5.10). There's also an 18-hole golf course.

The little island of **Oransay** was named for Oran, a disciple of St. Columba. It's joined at low tide by the Strand, and you can wade across the sands during a 2-hour period. The ancient monastic ruins here date from the 6th century, and tradition has it they were founded by St. Columba. You can see some tombstones of carved stone, the most notable being the **Great Cross of Prior Colin,** from the early 16th century.

## ACCOMMODATIONS & DINING

**Isle of Colonsay Hotel.** Isle of Colonsay PA61 7YP. ☎ **01951/200-316.** Fax 01951/200353 www.colonsay.org.uk/hotel.html. E-mail: colonsay.hotel@pipemedia.co.uk. 12 units, 9 with private bathroom. TV. £69–£85 ($117.30–$144.50) per person double. Rates include half-board. MC, V.

This is Great Britain's most isolated hotel and Colonsay's social center. Solidly constructed 18th-century gables and chimneys rise above surrounding herb and vegetable gardens. The guest rooms are small and decidedly informal, with rather basic but still comfortable furnishings. Guests who want to get close-up views of the island's abundant flora and fauna can ask to be dropped off by courtesy car to go on rambles. A meal in the tongue-and-groove-paneled dining room is an event for locals, who appreciate the ambience of the cocktail lounge and the bar. The inn serves lunch and rather expensive fixed-price dinners daily, with selections like homemade soup, fresh mussels, trout, scallops, and prawns, with vegetables from the garden.

## 9  The Isle of Lewis: Island of Heather

209 miles (336.5km) NW of Edinburgh, 213 miles (343km) NW of Glasgow

The most northerly of the Outer Hebrides and also the largest at 60 miles (100km) long and 18 to 28 miles (29 to 45km) across, Lewis is easily reached by ferry from Ullapool (see chapter 10, "Inverness & the West Highlands"). The island was once known as Lews, or more poetically, the "island of heather"—the sweetness of the lamb raised here is said to come from their heather diet. Lewis and Harris (see "Harris," below) form part of the same island, stretching for a total of 95 miles (153km). Filled with marshy peat bogs, Lewis's landscape is relatively treeless, thanks in part to Norse raider Magnus Barelegs: There used to be trees, but Barelegs and his Viking warriors burned most of them, leaving Lewis as bare as his shanks. Reforestation efforts have been unsuccessful.

Even though the whole world has heard of Harris tweed, it might as well be called Lewis tweed, as Stornoway has taken over the industry. On the eastern side of the island and with a population of some 5,000 souls, **Stornoway** is the only real town in the Outer Hebrides; it's a landlocked harbor where you can see gray seals along with fishing boats setting out. There are some 600 weavers on the island, and one of the attractions of this rather bleak port is visiting a mill shop or a weaver's cottage.

### ESSENTIALS

**GETTING THERE**   An **airport,** which doubles as an RAF base, is 3½ miles (5.5km) from the center of Stornoway. Stornoway receives flights from Glasgow and Inverness every day except Sunday, as well as frequent service from Benbecula. Phone **British Airways** at ☎ **0345/222-111** in Glasgow to confirm schedules or to make reservations.

Monday to Saturday, **Caledonian MacBrayne** operates two or three ferries from Ullapool to Stornoway. One-way passage costs £12.70 ($21.60). For reservations, check with Caledonian MacBrayne (☎ **0990/650-000** at the ferry terminal in Gourock). Cars can be transported as well. Trip time is 3½ hours.

**VISITOR INFORMATION**   The **Western Isles Tourist Board,** which has information about all the Outer Hebrides, is at 26 Cromwell St., Stornoway (☎ **01851/703-088**). April to October, it's open Monday, Tuesday, Thursday, and Saturday 9am to 6pm and 8 to 9pm and Wednesday and Friday 9am to 8pm; October to April, it's open Monday to Friday 9am to 5pm.

### EXPLORING THE ISLAND

The major attraction is the Neolithic temple of Callanish, called the ✪ **Standing Stones of Callanish.** Off A858, 16 miles (26km) west of Stornoway, this unique cruciform setting of megaliths is outranked in prehistoric archaeological splendor only by Stonehenge. From a circle of 13 stones, a road of 19 monoliths leads north. Branching off to the south, east, and west are rows of more stones. A tiny chambered tomb is inside the circle. You can wander among the ruins for free day or night. The "visitors center" provides some historical background and charges £1.50 ($2.50) if you

## A Great Road Trip

The entire outer archipelago offers sweeping panoramas over land, sea, and sky, usually with very few signs of modern civilization. But for a drive that doesn't require any inconveniently scheduled ferry connections, consider exploring the **Uig region,** on the northwestern coast of Lewis. Between the villages of Arnol and Miaveig, you can spend two hours reveling in glorious scenery, looking at ancient dolmen, ruined medieval fortresses, deep heather that probably hasn't been trampled over in several generations, and a poetically uplifting view of sea and sky—wild Scotland at its best.

---

want to see some videos on the site. It's open Monday to Saturday 10am to 4pm (July and August, 9am to 6:30pm). Also here are a gift shop and a cafe.

Just west of the harbor at Stornoway, you can visit the grounds of 1818 **Lews Castle** (which uses the old spelling). The castle itself is closed to the public, but you can wander through the garden at its flowery best in May.

At Arnol, 15 miles (24km) northwest of Stornoway off A858, is the thatched **Lewis Black House** (☎ 01851/710-395), constructed without mortar and preserved to show what a typical Hebridean dwelling looked like. It's called a "black house" because it was believed the smoke from the open peat fires was good for the thatched roof—the Leodhasach (as the islanders are called) built their houses with no chimneys so the smoke could pass through the thatch. Many of the original furnishings are intact. April to September, it's open Monday to Saturday 9:30am to 6pm (to 4pm October to March). Admission is £2.50 ($4.25) adults, £1.90 ($3.25) seniors, and £1 ($1.70) children.

For the serious student of history and ancient monuments, the **Steinacleit Cairn and Stone Circle** are the ruined fragments of what was once a substantial house built in the mists of prehistory. The house was found beneath huge layers of peat. It's at the southern end of Loch an Duin, Shader, 13 miles (21km) north of Stornoway, and you can visit throughout the day for no fee.

At 19 feet (6m) tall and 6 feet (2m) wide, the **Clach an Trushal** at Balanthrushal, Barvas, is the largest single monolith in northern Scotland. It's signposted beside the main highway leading north from Stornoway. Near this site was the field of the last battle fought between the Macaulays of Uig and the Morrisons of Ness.

Along A858, 20 miles (32km) northwest of Stornoway, stands **Dun Carloway Broch,** a 30-foot-high (9m) broch tower (a once-fortified round-sided stone tower) left over from the Iron Age. You can visit anytime day or night for no fee. At Arnish, near Stornoway, is the **Bonnie Prince Charlie Monument**—no more than a commemorative plaque set into a rock that extols the tragic life and dubious accomplishments of Scotland's most ambitious monarch.

At Dun Borranish, near the village of Ardroil, the famous **Lewis Chessmen** were dug up in 1831 outside Uig Sands. Made of walrus tusks and reputed to have been carved around A.D. 500, they now form an outstanding exhibit in the British Museum in London. If you're a chess player, you may want to purchase a reproduction set in Lewis.

Once the burial grounds of the MacLeods of Lewis, **Ui Church,** off A866 at Aignish, 2 miles (3km) east of Stornoway on the Eye Peninsula (also known as The Point), is now in ruins. You can see their carved tombs.

At Ness, toward that northerly outpost, the Butt of Lewis, is **St. Moluag's Church,** a Scottish Episcopal church. You can attend an occasional service here. The chapel, known in Gaelic as *Teampull Mhor* ("big temple"), is from about the 12th century, founded by Olav the Black during the Norse occupation. The original church is said to have been founded in the 6th century by a companion of St. Columba.

**Borge Pottery,** on A857 at Borve, 17 miles (27km) from Stornoway on the road to Ness (☎ **01851/850-345**), has been in business for more than 20 years, producing hand-thrown stoneware pieces for kitchen and table use, available in pink, blue, red, green, black, and cream. Its name is spelled with a *g,* the Gaelic spelling of Borve.

If you'd like to rent a bike and explore the island on two wheels, head for **Alex Dan's Cycle Centre,** 67 Kenneth St., Stornoway (☎ **01851/704-025**).

The Isle of Lewis's contribution to the world of golf is the 18-hole **Golf Club,** Willow Glen Road, about a mile (1.5km) from Stornoway (☎ **01851/702-240**), charging £20 ($34) greens fees. It's a windswept, isolated course carved out of the moors.

## ACCOMMODATIONS

You can also stay at the **Park Guest House** (see "Dining," below).

**Cabarfeidh Hotel.** Manor Park, Stornoway, Lewis, Outer Hebrides H51 2EU. ☎ **01851/ 702-604.** Fax 01851/705-572. 46 units. TV TEL. £92 ($156.40) double. Rates include Scottish breakfast. AE, DC, MC, V.

About a mile (1.5km) north of Stornoway, midway between Laxdale and Newmarket, the Cabarfeidh is one of the best hotels on Lewis and even in the Outer Hebrides, designed as a contemporary arrangement of cubes. It was built by a Mackenzie, who named it after the battle cry of his fighting clan, "stag antlers," and the decor includes a collection of just that. It was completely renovated in 1990. The small but pleasant guest rooms have trouser presses and hair dryers along with other amenities. The dining room offers the best local produce, fresh fish (especially trout and salmon), local beef and lamb, and scallops, with prices on the high side of moderate. The convivial bar is shaped like a Viking longship.

**Seaforth Hotel.** 9 James St., Stornoway, Lewis, Outer Hebrides HS1 2QN. ☎ **01851/ 702-740.** Fax 01851/703-900. 70 units. TV TEL. £79 ($134.30) double. Rates include Scottish breakfast. AE, MC, V.

A 5-minute walk from the town center, the Seaforth is one of the most modern hotels in the Outer Hebrides. The midsize guest rooms are well equipped; all contain tea/ coffeemakers and trouser presses, and some have hair dryers. The public rooms have several full-size snooker tables; there's a bar/lounge as well as a basement nightclub

### Watersports in the Outer Hebrides

The seas and tortuous inlets around the Outer Hebrides are dotted with scenic coves and underwater shipwrecks. The best way to view some of the wreckage close up is through the diving tours by **Scalpay Diving Services,** 34 Out End, Isle of Scarpay (☎ **01859/540-328**), midway between Harris and Lewis (it's easily accessible from both by bridges).

If you prefer the quiet and calm paddling of a sea kayak, contact **Hebridean Explorations,** 19 West View Terrace, Stornoway, Isle of Lewis (☎ **01851/ 705-655**), which offers rentals, guided tours, and advice about how best to view the flora and fauna.

And if you'd rather just be a passenger, you might take a day cruise with **Sea Trek,** 16 Uigen, Miavaig, Isle of Lewis (☎ **01851/672-464**); **Island Cruising,** 1 Erista, Uig, Isle of Lewis (☎ **01851/672-381**); or **Strond Wildlife Charters,** 1 Strond, Isle of Harris (☎ **01859/520-204**). All specialize in full- and half-day cruises that focus on the wildlife, bird life, and ecology of the Hebridean archipelago, usually with special emphasis on approaching the seal colonies that thrive offshore.

open Friday and Saturday. The restaurant offers a reasonably priced three-course dinner menu. The fare is rather plain but hearty and filling.

## DINING

**Park Guest House.** 30 James St., Stornoway, Lewis, Outer Hebrides H51 2QN. ☎ **01851/ 702-485.** Reservations required. Main courses £13–£20 ($22.10–$34); fixed-price 2-course early-bird dinner (only 5:30–6:45pm) £11.95 ($20.30). MC, V. Tues–Sat 5:30–9pm. BRITISH.

In a century-old stone house about a 10-minute walk north of the ferry terminal, this is one of the best dining rooms in town. Owned and operated by island-born Roddy and Catherine Afrin, it contains a fireplace in the style of Charles Rennie Mackintosh and a country-house decor designed by Catherine, a graduate of the Glasgow School of Art. Menu items feature seasonal game, such as venison Filets in port-wine sauce, and choices from the bounties of the nearby seas. They might include grilled lobster thermidor style with brandy sauce, oysters either raw or au gratin, pan-fried scallops in lemon butter and herbs, and turbot fillet grilled with herb butter. The restaurant is fully licensed and at its most elegant between 7 and 9pm.

The Afrins also offer nine simple guest rooms. Including breakfast, rates range from £42 to £58 ($71.40 to $98.60) for a double and £72 ($122.40) for a family room sleeping up to four.

## STORNOWAY AFTER DARK

Most of the pubs lining the waterfront have live music on weekends, usually traditional Celtic or Scottish performers. There's generally no cover charge, so for the price of a pint the sounds of the region are available for your listening pleasure.

**An Lanntair Gallery,** Town Hall, South Beach Street (☎ **01851/703-307**), produces and stages musical and theatrical events with a strong emphasis on Gaelic culture. The center also has jazz, folk, and traditional music concerts, plus classic and contemporary drama and comedy and children's shows. Shows start at 8pm, and tickets are £6 to £7 ($10.20 to $11.90) adults and £4 ($6.80) seniors/students/children. Productions take place in either the gallery space, which seats 55, or the town hall, which holds 350.

**Clachan Bar,** North Beach Street (☎ **01851/703-653**), is split into a public bar and a lounge bar. It boasts none of the quaintness of a traditional pub, but locals and visitors alike come on Friday and Saturday for live bands, which play downstairs, or for the disco upstairs. A range of Tennant's beers is available on tap.

Another updated bar that features live music is **Lewis Bar,** South Beach Street (☎ **01851/704-567**). On Saturday the stage might hold anything from a rock band to a traditional Scottish group. The free music starts at 9pm, and there's a selection of Tennant's products on tap.

## 10  Harris

218 miles (351km) NW of Glasgow, 56 miles (90km) NW of Mallaig, 246 miles (396km) NW of Edinburgh, 34 miles (55km) S of Stornoway

Harris, south of Lewis but really part of the same island, has a different geography. North Harris is full of mountains, dominated by the **Clisham,** which at 2,600 feet (789m) is the highest peak in the Outer Hebrides. Harris may not have as many ancient relics as Lewis, but most visitors agree that the mountains, beaches, and scenic vistas make up for it. The beaches in the west are good for strolling, swimming (if you're hearty) or camping; the bays in the east are ideal for fishing and sailing.

The locals, some 3,000 in all, are called Hearach, and they're different from the people of Lewis, even speaking with a different accent. If you've arrived in Lewis, you can drive to Harris, as the two islands are connected by a small single-lane road, going from pass to pass. As you go along the rugged terrain, you might see a fell walker. Occasionally you'll meet another car. If you do, "passing places" have been provided. In any case, you should drive slowly, because sheep might suddenly scamper in front of your wheels. The distance from Stornoway, the capital of Lewis, to Tarbert, the capital of Harris, is 34 miles (55km).

Many visitors, however, prefer to take the ferry from the little port of Uig on the Isle of Skye that heads for Harris daily except Sunday. Even in the busiest season Harris isn't overrun. From Harris you can also make connections to Lochmaddy on North Uist (see "North & South Uist," below).

Harris has long been known for its hand-weaving and tweed. Although that industry has now passed to Stornoway (see "The Isle of Lewis: Island of Heather," above), you can still buy Harris tweed jackets in Harris. In summer, you'll see them displayed on the walls of corrugated iron sheds along the road selling for very good prices.

The main village is one-street **Tarbert.** The island is bisected by two long sea lochs that meet at Tarbert, which is surrounded by rocky hills. Whatever you need in the way of supplies, you should pick up here—otherwise you'll be out of luck. If you're touring by car, also fill up with petrol (gas) here. Ask at the info center about the bus tours conducted in summer around Harris. For an adventure, take the car ferry running regularly across the sound to the little fishing community of **Scalpay,** an offshore island.

## ESSENTIALS

**GETTING THERE**   You can take a **ferry** to Tarbert, capital of Harris, from Uig on the Isle of Skye, Monday to Saturday. There are one or two ferries per day, and a one-way ticket for the 1¾-hour trip is £8.30 ($14.11). Contact **Caledonian MacBrayne** at ☎ **0990/650-000** for schedules.

**Buses** run from Stornoway to Tarbert daily (a 70-minute trip). Call **Harris Coaches** at ☎ **01859/2441** for schedules. At least five buses per day make the run Monday to Saturday.

From Stornoway on Lewis in the north, **drive** south along A859 to reach Tarbert.

**VISITOR INFORMATION**   A **tourist office** operates from the port at Tarbert (☎ **01859/502-011**). April to October, it's open Monday to Saturday 9am to 5pm; November to March, it's open Monday to Saturday 10am to 2pm.

## EXPLORING THE ISLAND

Because of the lack of roads, you can't make a circular tour of the island. However, using Tarbert as your base, you can set out northwest along the coast of **West Loch Tarbert,** with the Forest of Harris to your north. Or you can go south from Tarbert, hugging the western coast road along the Sound of Taransay, with Rodel as your final destination.

Taking the northwesterly route first, you come to an **Old Whaling Station** at Bunavoneadar. Norwegians set up a whaling station here in the early 20th century, but because of dwindling profits it was abandoned in 1930. You can still see slipways and a chimney. Continuing north along B887, you'll arrive at the **Amhuinnsuidhe Estate,** a Scottish baronial castle built for the earl of Dunmore in 1868. Sir James Barrie stayed here while working on *Mary Rose.* The river to the left has one of the most beautiful salmon leaps in Scotland.

The road beyond the castle continues to **Hushinish Point,** where you can see the little island of Scarp, which was once inhabited. Returning to Tarbert, you can take A859 south. Some of the South Harris coastline will remind you of Norway, with its sea lochs and fjord fingers. The main road to Rodel is mostly two lanes and well surfaced; however, if you take the east-coast road, you'll find it not only single lane but also tortuous and winding. Along the way you'll pass the **Clach Mhicleoid** ("standing stone"). Locals call it MacLeod's Stone. This monolith, placed above the Nisabost Sands, stands as a lonely sentinel at night, a silent witness to what it has seen over the centuries.

From here you can look out across the Sound of Taransay to the **Island of Taransay,** named after St. Tarran. It has several ancient sites, including the remains of St. Tarran's Chapel. Like Scarp, it was once populated, but now its grazing fields have been turned over to sheep. Continuing on the coastal road along the wild Atlantic—actually the Sound of Taransay—you'll see another ancient stone, the **Scarista Standing Stone.** But before reaching it you'll pass **Borve Lodge,** the former home of Lord Leverhulme, the soap tycoon.

The road south passes the little promontory of Toe Head jutting into the Atlantic. An ancient chapel, **Rudhan Teampull,** stands about three-quarters of a mile (1.2km) west of Northton, reached by a sand track. Many prehistoric sites were uncovered and excavated on the tiny machair-studded peninsula of Toe Head. Bone tools and Neolithic pottery were found, the earliest recorded habitations of the Western Isles.

The next village is **Leverburgh,** named after Lord Leverhulme, the soap magnate. He's credited with trying to bring the people of the area into the 20th century, but his efforts to rejuvenate the economy largely failed. From here you can take a small passenger ferry to North Uist and Berneray.

Finally, you drive east to Rodel, where ✪ **St. Clement's Church** stands high in the village. Overlooking Loch Rodel, this church is one of the most important monuments in the Western Isles. Cruciform in plan, it has a western tower, a nave, and two cross aisles. Some of the masonry work in freestone is similar to that used at Iona Abbey. The church is believed to have been built around the closing years of the 15th century or the very early years of the 16th century. There are three tombs inside, including one that's among the finest in the islands. The tomb contains part of the MacLeod coat-of-arms.

In the Sound of Harris, separating Harris from North Uist, lie the islands of **Ensay, Killegray,** and **Pabbay.** Once they were populated, but now they've been turned over to grazing sheep.

The island has the nine-hole **Golf Club,** Sgarasta (☎ **01859/520-214**), an isolated, windswept course carved into the Hebridean moors. You can rent clubs for around £5 ($8.25).

## ACCOMMODATIONS & DINING

✪ **Ardvourlie Castle.** Hwy. A859, Tarbert, Harris, Outer Hebrides HS3 3AB. ☎ **01859/ 502-307.** Fax 01859/502-348. 4 units. £180–£220 ($306–$374) double. Rates include breakfast and dinner. No credit cards. Closed Oct–Mar. Drive 10 miles (16km) north of Tarbert or 27 miles (43.5km) south of Stornaway along A859.

In 1860, the earl of Dunmore commissioned a substantial-looking hunting lodge here. In the early 1980s, after the building had lain empty for at least 40 years, London-born chef Derek Martin bought it, chased out the cobwebs and the sheep foraging inside, and upgraded everything admirably. He even planted 7,000 trees that are finally taking on recognizable forms. You'll now find an elegant house filled with English and Scottish antiques, and nary a hint that a decorator fussed too much with the coordinated fabrics. The lovely guest rooms overlook the Loch of Seaforth or an evocative tundra leading up to Harris's highest mountain.

**Dining/Diversions:** The dining room is presided over by Derek's sister, Pamela, who serves splendid food with ultrafresh ingredients. Examples are honey-marinated crisp duck with orange-flavored Drambuie sauce and garlic potatoes, prawns with orange segments and celery-Tabasco sauce, halibut in mushroom sauce, and desserts like Tipsy Laird (trifle with Drambuie and sherry) and baked apples with sultanas and hot whisky sauce. There's also a cocktail lounge and interesting libraries full of books.

**Harris Hotel.** Tarbert, Harris, Outer Hebrides HS3 3DL. ☎ **01859/502-154.** Fax 01859/502-281. E-mail: cameronharris@btinternet.com. 24 units, 16 with private bathroom. TV. £67 ($113.90) double without bathroom; £77 ($130.90) double with bathroom. Rates include Scottish breakfast. MC, V.

This Queen Anne hotel, a landmark since it opened in 1904, is one of the most popular places in the Outer Hebrides. Each guest room has hot and cold running water, lots of old-fashioned comfort, and modern amenities like hair dryers. Some family rooms are available, many looking out over the garden, one of the largest in Harris. The pub is the social center for locals, including the ghillies who show guests who come for fishing holidays how it's done. You can order pub grub throughout the day and evening, or there's a more formal restaurant offering moderately priced dinners.

**Leachin House.** Tarbert, Isle of Harris HS3 3AH. ☎/fax **01859/502-157.** www.leachinhouse.com. E-mail: leachin.house@virgin.net. 2 units, 1 with private bathroom. £86 ($146.20) double with or without bathroom. MC, V. From Tarbert, follow A859 for a mile (1.5km), signposted to Stornoway.

On the north shore of the loch, with big windows and Victorian gingerbread trim, this house was built from Berneray granite (a form of gneiss) in 1898 by Norman McLeod, the fisherman/entrepreneur credited as the father of the Harris tweed industry. (From this house he conducted one of his most famous lawsuits, defending the authenticity of the marketing logo "Harris tweed.") It's loaded with antiques and unusual paintings, many of them collected during the frequent travels of owners Diarmuid and Linda Wood. The high-ceilinged guest rooms are comfortably furnished and make you feel as if you're staying in a friend's home.

**Dining:** The rather expensive dinners here, served for a fixed price that includes wine, will make you feel like you're attending a private dinner party. The food is based on modern Scottish cuisine as interpreted by Linda and may include wild-venison filets with cassis sauce, various preparations of lamb and salmon, and mussels in garlic-cream sauce.

**Amenities:** Laundry. The staff will arrange nearby fishing, sea trips, hill walking, private tours, and golf.

✪ **Scarista House.** On A859, about 15 miles (24km) southwest of Tarbert, Scarista, Harris, Outer Hebrides HS3 3HX. ☎ **01859/550-238.** Fax 01859/550-277. www.scaristahouse. demon.co.uk. 5 units, 2 apts. TEL. £116 ($197.20) double; £275–£550 ($467.50–$935) apt. Room rates include Scottish breakfast. MC, V. Closed Oct–Apr.

Built long ago as a Georgian vicarage, this is a lovely hotel. The handsome midsize guest rooms are comfortable, as are the two self-catering apartments (one accommodates two people, the other up to six). Some summer guests enjoy a bracing dip in the icy water of Scarista Beach, while others prefer to read in the well-stocked library.

**Dining:** Here you get the best breakfast around: freshly squeezed orange juice, compote of fresh and dried fruits, organic oatmeal porridge with cream, Lewis kippers, Stornoway black pudding, bacon, sausage, fresh eggs, and fresh herring rolled in oatmeal. There's also homemade whole-wheat bread and a variety of other baked items.

If you plan to burn off this morning feast, a packed lunch will be provided that you can take along on your hikes. Most guests return for a drink near the fireplace of the beautiful drawing room, then at 8:15pm enjoy an upscale four-course dinner featuring local shellfish and heather-fed lamb among other ingredients.

**Amenities:** Room service. The staff will arrange tee times nearby.

## 11  North & South Uist

90–100 miles (145–161km) NW of Glasgow

Standing stones, chambered cairns, ruins, and fortresses tell of a history-rich past on North Uist and South Uist, connected by the smaller island of Benbecula.

## ESSENTIALS

**GETTING THERE**    British Airways flies daily except Sunday between **Benbecula Airport** (the nearest connection for North Uist) and Glasgow (a 1-hour trip). Phone ☎ **0141/887-1111** at the Glasgow Airport for flight information.

For information about **car-ferry** services, consult **Caledonian MacBrayne** (☎ **01876/500-337** in Lochmaddy). Lochboisdale is the site of the ferry terminal providing a link between South Uist and the mainland at Oban, taking 5½ hours. Monday to Saturday, one ferry per day runs from Oban to Lochboisdale, costing £18.25 ($31.02) one way. Some of these ferries stop at Castlebay on Barra. Other ferries run from Uig on the Isle of Skye to Lochmaddy once or twice daily. The most popular connection, this ferry trip takes anywhere from 2 to 4 hours and costs £8.30 ($14.11) one way.

North Uist is linked to Benbecula and South Uist by causeways and bridges, so you can **drive** to or from either of these islands along A867, which becomes A865.

**VISITOR INFORMATION**    Consult with the Western Isles Tourist Board in Stornoway (see "The Isle of Lewis: Island of Heather," above). There's also a **tourist office** at the pier in Lochmaddy (☎ **01876/500-321**), open Monday to Friday 9am to 5pm, Saturday 9:30am to 1pm and 2 to 5:30pm, and Monday, Wednesday, and Friday 8 to 9pm. The staff can arrange accommodations if you've arrived without a reservation.

At Lochboisdale, the **tourist office** is found at the pier (☎ **01878/700-286**), open Easter to October only, Monday to Saturday 9am to 5pm. It's also open for late ferry arrivals, usually Monday to Thursday and Saturday 9 to 10pm and Friday 7:30 to 8:30pm. Accommodations can be arranged through this office.

## NORTH UIST

A real bogland where hardy crofters try to wrestle a living from a turbulent sea and disappointing ground, **North Uist** is one of the lesser-known islands in the Outer Hebrides, but it's beautiful. Its antiquity is reflected in the brochs, duns, wheelhouses, and stark monoliths, all left by the island's prehistoric dwellers.

The population of North Uist is about 2,000, and the island is about 12½ miles (20km) wide by 35 miles (56km) at its longest point. North Uist is served by a circular road, most often the single-lane variety with "passing places," and several feeder routes branch east and west. The road surfaces are usually good.

The main village is **Lochmaddy,** on the eastern shore. Whatever you need, you're likely to find it here (if it's available on North Uist at all), from a post office to a petrol station. Lochmaddy is the site of the ferry terminal. In addition to the ferries from Oban and Uig, a small private ferry runs from Newton Ferry, north of Lochmaddy, to Leverburgh on Harris. This isn't a car ferry, but it does allow small motorcycles or bikes. A small vehicular ferry will take you to the island of Berneray. In keeping with the strict religious tradition of these islands, the ferry doesn't operate on Sunday—and neither, seemingly, does anything else.

## EXPLORING THE ISLAND

North Uist may be small, but its scenery is extremely varied. The eastern shores possess an untamed beauty. The coastline is dotted with trout-filled lochs, and everything is set against a backdrop of darkened, rolling heather-clad hills. Nights come on fast in winter; sunsets linger in summer. The western side of North Uist is a land of rich meadows filled with wildflowers. Here you find long white beaches, where Atlantic rollers attract the hardier surfers.

Heading northwest from Lochmaddy for 2½ miles (4km), you come to the hamlet of **Blashaval,** where you'll find the **Three Standing Stones of the False Men.** (The stones are almost buried, but a sign indicates their position.) Local tradition has it that this trio of stones, known in Gaelic as *Na Fir Bhreige,* actually were men, wife deserters from Skye turned into stone by a witch.

Continuing along the road for 4 miles (6.5km), you approach uninhabited **Dun Torcuill** island, rising above the west side of **Loch an Duin.** Access to the island is possible on foot only at periods of low tide. Exercise caution. On the island is a ruined but still fine example of a *broch* (circular fortified tower) that provided defense during the Middle Ages. Most visitors prefer to admire it from across the water, not actually braving the tidal flats on foot.

Turning north on B893, you come to **Newton Ferry** (see above). A 15-minute crossing will take you to the little offshore island of **Berneray,** which has some ancient sites, including the **Borve Standing Stone,** a mysterious-looking monolith rising starkly. There's a privately run hostel here. The 140 or so people who live on the island are mainly engaged in crofting and fishing and may regard *you* as a sightseeing attraction. After you return to Newton Ferry, head south on the same road. A left-hand fork takes you to **Trumisgarry** to see the ruins of an old chapel where an early Christian settlement was founded. **St. Columba's Well** (*Tobar Chaluim Chille* in Gaelic) is named after the saint.

Return to the main road and head west toward Sollas. On both sides of the road are cairns and standing stones, many from 2000 B.C.—some hard to reach, including those on uninhabited islands. Pass through **Hosta,** site of the Highland Games, heading for the **Balranaid Nature Reserve,** 3 miles (5km) northwest of Bayhead. At a reception cottage at **Goulat,** near Hougharty, you can learn more about the birds inhabiting the Outer Hebrides. You can walk through the reserve at any time at no charge, but guided tours are given at 2pm Tuesday and Friday. The cost is £2.50 ($4.25) adults and £1 ($1.70) children.

Back on the main road, you'll pass through **Bayhead** heading southeast. Again, the area is filled with an astonishing number of ancient monuments; many more have disappeared since the 1920s, reclaimed by the Atlantic. At the junction, take A867 back toward Lochmaddy. You'll see a sign pointing to **Ben Langass.** On the slopes of a mountain is a chambered cairn thought to be at least 3,000 years old, one of the best preserved on the island. Some historians believe a warrior chieftain was buried here, but others suggest it was a communal burial ground. Bones and pottery fragments removed from excavations here were sent to the National Museum in Edinburgh.

Returning to the main road again, retrace your trail and head south for Carinish, a hamlet known for the **Carinish Stone Circle** and the **Barpa Carinish,** the site of the major attraction on the island, **Trinity Temple** (*Teampull na Trionad* in Gaelic), off

A865 some 8 miles (13km) southwest of Lochmaddy. Admission is free and it's open at all times. The monastery is said to have been founded in the 13th century by Beathag, the first prioress of Iona, daughter of Somerland, an Irish mercenary and the founding father of the MacDonalds. In the Middle Ages, on this site was a great college that the Franciscan scholar, Duns Scotus (1265–1308), was said to have attended. He later became one of the most influential medieval philosophers and theologians.

Nearby is the **Teampull Clann A'Phlocair,** the chapel of the MacVicars. You can see a number of ancient cup and ring markings. The site of a clan battle is also nearby. Appropriately called the "Field of Blood," it's where the MacLeods of Harris and the MacDonalds of Uist met in 1601.

You can continue southeast to the island of **Grimsay,** connected by a causeway and known for its lobster ponds. You'll also find the remains of **Michael's Chapel** and the ruins of **Dun Bay Grimsay,** an ancient fortification.

## ACCOMMODATIONS & DINING

**Langass Lodge.** Locheport, North Uist, Outer Hebrides HS6 5HA. ☎/fax **01876/580-285.** E-mail: langass@aol.com. 6 units. TV TEL. £60 ($102) double. Rates include Scottish breakfast. MC, V. Closed Feb.

This hotel's spaciousness and comfort comes as a welcome surprise after the miles of windswept barren countryside you traverse before reaching it. Its multiple chimneys and mint-green facade are softened by the half a dozen nearby sycamores, cited by the staff as among the few trees on all North Uist. Built as a hunting lodge in 1876, the hotel has been comfortably modernized and today attracts hunters, anglers, and nature lovers from Britain, Europe, and North America. The guest rooms were completely refurbished in 1996 and 1997, with solid furnishings, a pleasant decor, hair dryers, and tea/coffeemakers. They open onto views of the nearby loch. You can order meals in either the dining room or the bar.

**Lochmaddy Hotel.** Lochmaddy, North Uist, Outer Hebrides HS6 5AA. ☎ **01876/500-331.** Fax 01876/500-210. 15 units. TV TEL. £65–£80 ($110.50–$136) double. Rates include Scottish breakfast. AE, MC, V.

You can't miss the peaked gables of this white-walled hotel a few steps from the ferry terminal. Those who come to fish for the area's brown trout, sea trout, and salmon often stay here (anyone who wants to weigh his or her catch of the day is welcome to use the hotel's scales). This is one of the few places on the island where you can buy fishing permits; prices are £6 to £40 ($10.20 to $68) a day, according to what kind of fish you're seeking and the season. The guest rooms are uncluttered and tasteful, having benefited from a 1997 renovation. There's an accommodating pub, a cocktail bar offering about the best collection of single-malt whiskies in the Outer Hebrides, and a dining room. At dinner you're likely to be offered fresh local produce, lobster, king prawns, venison, or salmon, and bar meals are served at lunch and dinner.

## SOUTH UIST

You can find a rich treasure trove of antiquity on South Uist. A number of ecclesiastical remains are scattered along its shores, and Clan Ranald, which ruled the island, left many ruins and fortresses known as *duns.* Ornithologists and anglers are attracted here. Part bogland, the island is 20 miles (32km) long and 6 miles (10km) wide at its broadest point. A main road, A865, bisects the island, with feeder roads—single-track lanes with "passing places"—branching off east and west. Some of the most interesting sights, all ruins, lie off these little roads.

## EXPLORING THE ISLAND

The biggest village in South Uist is **Lochboisdale,** at the head of a deep-sea loch in the southeastern part of the island. It was settled in the 19th century by crofters who had been forced off their land in the notorious Land Clearances of those troubled years. However, the ruins of a small medieval castle can also be seen at the head of the loch on the island of Calvay, one of the many places where Bonnie Prince Charlie hid out.

Leaving Lochboisdale, A865 goes west for 3 miles (5km) to Daliburgh, where you can pick up B888 south to Pollachar on the southern shore, a distance of 6 miles (10km)—the village is named for the **Pollachar Standing Stone,** a jagged dolmen rising a few paces from the hamlet's center. Continue east along a minor road for 2½ miles (4km) to the Ludag jetty, where a private ferry goes to Eriskay and Barra. Then head north again in the direction of Daliburgh to visit the contemporary **Church of Our Lady of Sorrows,** at Garrynamonie, a short drive north of Pollachar. Consecrated in 1964, it has a mosaic of Our Lady and can be visited daily at any time.

The next stop is at the **Klipheder Wheelhouse,** 2 miles (3km) west of A865, the meager ruins of a circular building from A.D. 200. Back on the main road again, you come to Askernish, site of a nine-hole **golf course.** At Mingarry are the remains of a big chambered cairn.

Three miles (5km) north from Daliburgh, at Airidh Mhuilinn, is a **Flora MacDonald memorial.** West of A865, about 200 yards (182m) up a little farm track half a mile (about 1km) north of Milton, a cairn atop a little hill marks the spot where this woman, so revered in legend, was born in 1722. Staying on the minor roads, you'll see the dramatic machair-fringed shoreline and pass through the hamlets of Bornish, Ormiclete, and Stoneybridge. At Ormiclete are the ruins of **Ormiclete Castle,** constructed by the Clan Ranald chieftains in the early 18th century.

Rejoin the main road at Howbeg. The part of the island directly north of Howbeg is rich in archaeological remains. Ruins of several **medieval chapels** are all that's left of a major South Uist ecclesiastical center. An ancient **graveyard** nearby was the burial ground of the Clan Ranald chieftains.

Farther north, A865 passes the **Loch Druidibeg National Nature Reserve,** the most significant breeding ground for the native grayleg goose in the country. Attracting the dedicated bird watcher, it's a setting of machair and brackish lochs. At Drimsdale lie the ruins of a big dun, a fortification in a loch where the villagers retreated when under attack. It continued as a stronghold for the Clan Ranald until the early 1500s.

The road continues past the Royal Artillery Rocket Range (heed those warning signs). On the flank of Reuval Hill, called the "mountain of miracles," stands **Our Lady of the Isles,** a 30-foot (9m) statue of the Virgin and Child. Erected in 1957, the statue was the creation of artist Hew Lorimer, and Catholic contributions from around the world financed the project. It's the largest religious statue in Britain.

**Loch Bee,** inhabited by mute swans, nearly bisects the northern part of South Uist.

You'll find **Hebridean Jewelry,** Garrieganichy, Iochdar (☎ **01870/610-288**), signposted on the north end of the Iochdar Road. The shop produces silver and gold pendants and brooches featuring Celtic patterns. The artists here can create custom pieces on request.

If you'd like to explore the island on two wheels, head for **Rothan Cycles,** 9 Howmore (☎ **01870/620-283**).

## ACCOMMODATIONS & DINING

**Borrodale Hotel.** Daliburgh, South Uist, Outer Hebrides HS8 5SS. ☎ **01878/700-444.** Fax 01878/700-446. www.witb.co.uk. 14 units, 13 with private bathroom. TV TEL. £60–£85 ($102–$144.50) double with bathroom. Rates include Scottish breakfast. MC, V.

Near the center of the island, 2½ miles (4km) west of Loch Boisdale along A865, this hotel stands in a landscape of freshwater lakes, heather, and gorse. A row of gables runs across the building's second floor, and the interior contains a cocktail bar, a pub, and an upscale restaurant. The hotel underwent extensive renovations in 1997, updating the guest rooms and common rooms. The owners will assist in arranging fishing and golf expeditions.

**Lochboisdale Hotel.** Lochboisdale, South Uist, Outer Hebrides HS8 5TH. ☎ **01878/ 700-332.** Fax 01878/700-367. 18 units, 17 with private bathroom. £72–£84 ($122.40– $142.80) double with bathroom. Rates include Scottish breakfast. MC, V.

This is the quintessential anglers' refuge. Solidly built of local stone in 1892, it's in the center of town a half-minute walk from the ferry terminal and proudly displays tile-covered tables and scales near its entrance for weighing and preparing the daily catch of its guests. Trophies and memorabilia decorate the half-paneled walls of the cocktail lounge and restaurant. Both have blazing fireplaces and a feeling of conviviality. The midsize guest rooms are outfitted in English country-house style, with chintz curtains and solidly comfortable furniture. One single doesn't have its own bathroom. Meals are moderately priced in the restaurant; the hotel's public bar is the only one within 4 miles (6.5km) and is frequented by locals.

## 12 Barra: Garden of the Hebrides

118 miles (190km) NW of Edinburgh, 88 miles (142km) NW of Glasgow

Called the "garden of the Hebrides," Barra lies at the southern end of the Outer Hebrides. Locals claim it has some 1,000 varieties of wildflowers. The island is one of the most beautiful in the Hebridean chain, with heather-clad meadows, beaches, sandy grasslands, peaks, rocky bays, and lofty headlands. Since the days of the conquering Vikings, it has been associated with the Clan MacNeil.

A circular road of 10 miles (16km) will take you around Barra, which is about 4 by 8 miles (6.5 by 13km) in size. **Cockle Strand,** the airport, is a long and wide beach of white sand, the only runway in Britain washed twice daily by sea tides.

Most of the 200 inhabitants of Barra are centered at **Castlebay,** its capital, a 19th-century herring port and the best place to stock up on supplies. In the background of the port is **Ben Heaval,** at 1,250 feet (379m) the highest mountain on Barra.

### ESSENTIALS

**GETTING THERE**   At the northern end of Barra is **Cockle Strand,** the airport. Loganair, the Scottish airline, flies here from Glasgow or from Benbecula on Lewis. Phone **British Airways** (☎ 0345/222-111) in Glasgow for flight information.

From the mainland at Oban, Barra can be reached by **Caledonian MacBrayne** car ferry, which docks at Castlebay. Subject to weather conditions, departures from Oban are on Monday, Wednesday, Thursday, and Saturday, with a return on Tuesday, Thursday, Friday, and Sunday. Sailing time is 5 hours, and a one-way ticket is £18.25 ($31.05). Call ☎ 0990/650-000 for sailing information.

From South Uist, you can also take a car ferry from Lochboisdale to Castlebay. A privately operated 12-passenger ferry will take you from Eoligarry, north of the Cockle Strand airport, to Ludag on South Uist. It operates Monday to Saturday (☎ 01878/ 720-265 in the morning or ☎ 01878/720-238 in the afternoon for schedules). A one-way ticket is £5 ($8.50).

**VISITOR INFORMATION**   The **Castlebay Tourist Information Centre** (☎ 01871/810-336) is near the pier where the ferry docks. Easter to mid-October, it's open Monday to Saturday 9am to 5pm. The staff will help you locate a room should you arrive on Barra without a reservation.

## EXPLORING THE ISLAND

The most important attraction is in the bay: **Kismul Castle** (☎ **01871/810-336**) was built for strategic purposes on a small islet, the longtime stronghold of the notorious MacNeils of Barra, a clan known for piracy and lawlessness. Their 35th chief, Ruari the Turbulent, was even so bold as to seize a ship of a subject of Elizabeth I. When the direct male line died out in 1863, leadership of the clan reverted to the Canadian branch.

The oldest part of the castle is an 1120 tower. An accidental fire swept through the 15th- and 16th-century part of the structure in 1795. In 1938, the 45th chieftain, the late Robert Lister MacNeil of Barra, an architect, began restoration work on his ancestral home. After many interruptions, including World War II, the job was completed in 1970. April to October, you can visit on Monday, Wednesday, and Saturday afternoons. A boatman will take you over and back from 2 to 4 or 5pm. Entrance is £3 ($5.10) adults and 50p (85¢) children, including the boat ride.

To drive around the island, head west from Castlebay until you reach Kinloch. On the left is **Loch St. Clair,** reached by a tiny track road. In the loch, on an islet, stand the ruins of St. Clair Castle, called **MacLeod's Fort.** Also nearby you can see **St. Columba's Well,** named for the saint.

Continuing north to Borve, you'll see the **Borve Standing Stones** on your left. At Borve, the north fork leads to a chambered cairn and the hamlet of **Craigston,** which has a church dedicated to St. Brendan, the Irish navigator who many cite as the discoverer of America. In the area are two interesting ruins: **Dun Bharpa,** a collection of stones encircled by standing stones, and **Tigh Talamhanta,** a ruined wheelhouse.

Continue north to Allasdale. **Dun Cuier** is one of the few excavated Hebridean Iron Age forts, better preserved than most. Opposite Allasdale is **Seal Bay,** a beauty spot where the seals do as much inspection of you as you do of them.

At **Northbay** at Loch an Duin, the remains of an old dun protrude from the water. Continue north to Eoligarry, site of a small ferry terminal taking passengers to Ludag on South Uist. Eoligarry's proud possession is **St. Barr's Church,** named after St. Findbarr of Cork (A.D. 550–623), who's said to have converted the islanders to Christianity after finding many of them practicing cannibalism when he arrived. The original 12th-century chapel was restored by Fr. Callum MacNeil. The Celtic stones in the churchyard are called Crusader stones. This was the old burial ground of the MacNeil chieftains. Novelist Compton MacKenzie is buried here. Near Eoligarry, on the summit of a small hill, is **Dun Scurrival,** another ruined fort, this one measuring 39 by 52 feet (12 by 16m).

For bike rentals and advice on scenic routes, head for **Barra Cycle Hire,** 29 St. Brendans Rd. (☎ **01871/810-284**).

## ACCOMMODATIONS & DINING

**Castlebay Hotel.** Castlebay, Barra, Outer Hebrides HS9 5XD. ☎ **01871/810-223.** Fax 01871/810-455. 13 units. TV TEL. £65 ($110.50) double. Rates include Scottish breakfast. MC, V. Closed Dec 22–Jan 5.

Built around 1890, this hotel with gables overlooks the bay and the ferry terminal where most of the island's visitors disembark. The small guest rooms are simply but comfortably furnished and come with tea/coffeemakers. Its cocktail bar has a quiet corner reserved for dining. Adjacent to the hotel and under the same management is the Castlebay Bar, the island's most popular gathering place.

**Isle of Barra Hotel.** Tangusdale, Castlebay, Barra, Outer Hebrides HS9 5XW. ☎ **01871/ 810-383.** Fax 01871/810-385. www.isleofbarra.com/lob.html. 30 units. TV. £78 ($132.60) double with breakfast; £110 ($187) double with half-board. Rates include Scottish breakfast. MC, V. Closed Oct 18–Mar 20.

This low-slung seashore hotel is architecturally striking, and for the Outer Hebrides, it's a luxury selection. Its brick walls are adorned with nautical paraphernalia and contemporary tapestries. It commands a view of the tranquil less-populated western shore of the island, and its pub, the most westerly in Scotland, is widely touted as the "last dram before America." From the dining room and many of the well-furnished guest rooms, you can see everything that's coming and going at sea. At the suggestion of their Scottish nanny, the shah of Iran used this hotel as a safe haven for his children when a revolution was knocking at his door. The shah and his retinue are long gone, but the hotel remains a favorite with the yachting crowd. Some of the best food on Barra is served here.

# 12

# The Orkney & Shetland Islands

**N**orthern outposts of civilization, the Orkney and Shetland archipelagos consist of around 200 islands, about 40 of which are inhabited. "Go to Shetland for scenery, Orkney for antiquities"—or so the saying goes. That doesn't mean the Orkneys don't have scenery too. They do, in abundance.

These far-flung and scattered islands are rich in a great Viking heritage. Ceded to Scotland by Norway as part of the 1472 dowry of Princess Margaret when she married James III, the islands were part of the great Norse earldoms. They were a gathering place for Norse fleets and celebrated in the *Orkneyinga Saga,* which detailed the exploits of the Viking warriors.

Before the Vikings, however, tribes of Stone Age people occupied both the Shetlands and the Orkneys. The Picts came later, and you can still see ruins of their round forts dotting the coastlines. The island chains aren't part of the Highlands and totally differ from both the Inner and the Outer Hebrides. Clans, Gaelic, and kilts were unfamiliar to the Orcadians and the Shetlanders—until the Scots arrived. At first these merchants and newcomer landlords were bitterly resented. Even today the islanders are fiercely independent. They speak of themselves as Orcadians and Shetlanders instead of as Scots. Not only are Orkney and Shetland different from the Highlands, they're different from each other, as you'll soon see.

Change, as was inevitable, has come to the Orkneys and Shetlands by the way of oil and modern conveniences, but tradition is still strong. It has a lot to do with climate and with ancestry.

**P&O Ferries** (☎ **01856/850-655**) provides service from Scrabster (near Thurso) on Scotland's north coast to the Orkneys. Trips are made two to three times per day (only once a day on Sunday) in summer, each taking 2 hours; in winter, service drops to one to two trips per day. While P&O accommodates both vehicles and individuals on foot, a **John o' Groats** ferry (☎ **01955/611-353;** www.johnferry.co.uk) accepts passengers only and operates Easter to September two to four times daily; the trip takes about 45 minutes. **British Airways** (☎ **0345/222-111;** www.britishairways.co.uk) flies into the Orkneys, as it does to Sumburgh, 26 miles (42km) south of Lerwick, the most important center on the Shetlands. P&O Ferries provides overnight ferry service once daily, Monday to Friday between Aberdeen in northeast Scotland and Lerwick. They also provide a twice-weekly service from the Orkneys to Lerwick. Book in advance during July and August.

# 1  The Orkney Islands: An Archaeological Garden

6 miles (10km) N of John o' Groats (mainland Scotland) across Pentland Firth, 280 miles (451km) N of Edinburgh

To visit the Orkney Islands, an archipelago extending for about 50 miles (80.5km) north and northeast, is to look at 1,000 years of history. Orkney is a virtual archaeological garden. Some 100 of the 500 known brochs—often called the "castles of the Picts"—are found here. Built by Orkney chiefs, they were fortified structures where islanders could find refuge from invaders, and wells inside provided water. The *Orkneyinga Saga,* written in the 9th or 10th century, is the record of the pomp and heraldry of Orkney's "golden age."

Covering a land area of 376 square miles (977.5 km²), the islands lie 6 miles (10km) north of the Scottish mainland. The terrain has lots of rich and fertile farmland but also dramatic scenery: Britain's highest perpendicular cliffs rise to 1,140 feet (346m). The population of the entire chain is less than 20,000, spread sparsely across about 29 inhabited islands. The people are somewhat suspicious of strangers, and if you meet an Orcadian in a local pub you'll have to break the ice. The climate is far milder than the location would suggest because of the warming currents of the Gulf Stream. There are few extremes in temperature. May to July, you'll be astonished by the sunsets, with the midsummer sun remaining over the horizon for 18¼ hours a day. The Orcadians call their midsummer sky "Grimlins" from the Old Norse word *grimla,* which means to "twinkle" or "glimmer." There's enough light for golfers to play at midnight.

Who comes here other than golfers? Archaeologists, artists, walkers, climbers, bird watchers, and more. Divers are often drawn by the remains of the German Imperial Navy warships scuttled here on June 21, 1919, on orders of Rear Adm. Ludwig von Reuter. Most of the vessels have been salvaged, but there are still plenty down there in the deep. Mid-March to the first week in October, anglers come in droves. Unlike other parts of Scotland, fishing is free in Orkney because of Old Norse law and ancient Udal tradition. The wild brown trout is said to be the best in Britain.

A large percentage of the world's gray seal population visits the Orkneys to breed and molt. The islanders call the seal a "selkie." Wildfowl migrate from Iceland and northern Europe in winter, including the goldeneye, the red-throated diver (known locally as the "rain goose"), and the short-eared owl ("cattieface"), as well as such breeding seabirds as kittiwakes, puffins ("tammie-honies"), and guillemots. The resident bird of prey is the hen harrier. Some 300 species have been identified on the islands.

The Orkneys are also known for their flora, including the Scottish primrose, which is no more than 2 inches (5cm) in height and is believed to have survived the Ice Age by growing in small ice-free areas. The amethyst, with a pale-yellow eye, is found only in the Orkneys and parts of northern Scotland.

## ORKNEY ESSENTIALS

**GETTING THERE**   British Airways offers service to **Kirkwall Airport** on Mainland Orkney every day except Sunday. British Airways flies from Glasgow, Inverness, and Aberdeen, with connections from London and Birmingham. Call ☎ **0345/ 222-111** for schedules.

If you aren't driving, it's faster and cheaper to go from "end-of-the-line" John o' Groats to Burwick. The daily ferries operate May to September, with ferries leaving twice daily. Round-trip fares are £25 ($42.50) per person. **John o' Groats Ferries Ltd.**

can be reached at ☎ **01955/611-353. P&O Ferries** (☎ **01856/850-655**) schedules departures from Scabster at noon daily with additional ones from Monday to Saturday at 6am and Monday, Friday, and Saturday at 5:45pm. A passenger 5-day round-trip fare is £22 ($37.40) per person, £55 ($93.50) per car.

If you're driving over, head for Scrabster, near Thurso, in the northern province of Caithness. Here, P&O's *St. Ola* operates a roll-on/roll-off ferry service with 2-hour sailings to Stromness on Mainland Orkney. The ferry sails two or three times a day in summer. A 5-day round-trip fare is £55 ($93.50) for a car. For more information, check with **P&O Ferries** (☎ **01856/850-655** in Stromness).

**GETTING AROUND**   Island-hopping is common in the north of Scotland. Loganair operates scheduled flights from **Kirkwall Airport** on Mainland to the isles of Sanday, Stronsay, Westray, Eday, North Ronaldsay, and Papa Westray. For information and reservations, call **British Airways** at ☎ **0345/222-111.**

The **Orkney Ferries Limited** operates scheduled ferry service from Kirkwall to Orkney's north and south islands: Eday, Papa Westray, Sanday, Stronsay, Westray, North Ronaldsay, and Shapinsay. From Houton there's service to the south isles: Flotta, Graemsay, and Hoy at Longhope and Lyness, and from Tingwall to Rousay, Egilsay, and Wyre. Contact the shipping line in Kirkwall at ☎ **01856/872-044.** There's also a private ferry service to take you to Hoy, departing from Stromness. The tourist office will have the latest details on departures.

The Churchill barriers, erected to impede enemy shipping in World War II, have been turned into a road link between the islands of Mainland and South Ronaldsay.

**VISITOR INFORMATION**   If you want to know what's taking place during your visit, consult *The Orcadian,* a weekly published since 1854. There are tourist offices in Kirkwall and in Stromness (see below). You can also read up on the Web before you leave home by logging into **www.orkney.com.**

**SPECIAL EVENTS**   These sparsely populated islands generate quite a bit of cultural activity, especially in celebrating the region's music. A number of festivals draw both curious visitors and fans of Scottish and, more specifically, Orkney music. Information, including schedules and ticket prices, for all events is available through the Kirkwall tourist office (see "Exploring Mainland from Kirkwall to Stromness," below). This office publishes the yearly *Orkney Diary,* listing annual events and dates, as well as monthly events.

The festival season kicks off in February with the **Drama Festival,** which hosts traveling stage companies presenting an array of productions in venues spread across the islands. Ticket prices hover around £3 to £5 ($5.10 to $8.50). Early May brings the **Country and Irish Festival,** and late May finds the **Orkney Traditional Folk Festival** in full swing. Both feature ceilidhs and concerts of traditional music spread throughout the parish halls, and tickets to most events are £4 to £6 ($6.80 to $10.20). June brings a change of pace in the form of the **St. Magnus Festival,** which celebrates classical music and the dramatic arts, as well as music and drama workshops. These productions are spread throughout the different venues as well, and tickets average £10 to £15 ($17 to $25.50).

**TOURS**   Bus tours operate throughout the year, but with limited schedules over the winter. One reliable operator is **Wildabout Tours,** 5 Clouston Corner, Stenness (☎ **01856/851-011;** www.orkneyislands.co.uk/wildabout). It offers minibus tours of the island, of no more than 15 passengers, which take in prehistoric and Neolithic monuments and local wildlife. The tours are full or half day and range from £10.50

# The Orkney Islands

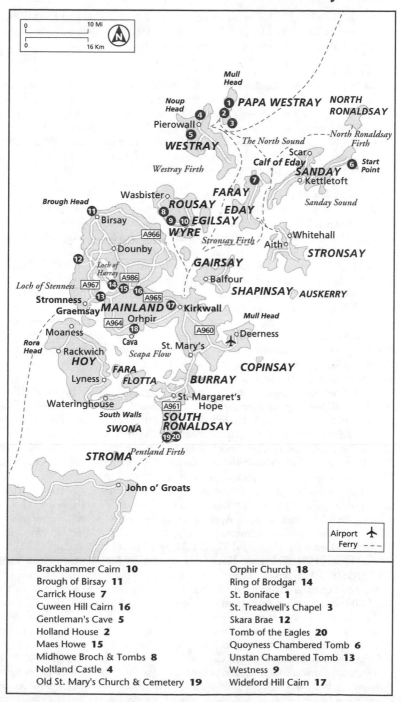

Brackhammer Cairn **10**
Brough of Birsay **11**
Carrick House **7**
Cuween Hill Cairn **16**
Gentleman's Cave **5**
Holland House **2**
Maes Howe **15**
Midhowe Broch & Tombs **8**
Noltland Castle **4**
Old St. Mary's Church & Cemetery **19**

Orphir Church **18**
Ring of Brodgar **14**
St. Boniface **1**
St. Treadwell's Chapel **3**
Skara Brae **12**
Tomb of the Eagles **20**
Quoyness Chambered Tomb **6**
Unstan Chambered Tomb **13**
Westness **9**
Wideford Hill Cairn **17**

to £11.50 ($17.85 to $19.55) for morning tours and £9 to £10 ($15.30 to $17) for afternoon tours. There's a £2 ($3.40) discount for students. The tours are popular, particularly in summer, so it's wise to book seats in advance.

# KIRKWALL

On the island called Mainland, Kirkwall, established by Norse invaders, has been the capital of the Orkney Islands for at least 900 years. It used to be called Kirkjuvagr ("church bay"), after a church built around 1040 honoring the memory of King Olaf Harraldsson, later the patron saint of Norway. That church no longer stands.

The Old Norse streets of Kirkwall are very narrow, to protect the buildings from galelike winds. But don't get the idea they're pedestrian walkways. That myth is dispelled when a car comes roaring down the street.

## SEEING THE SIGHTS

For the most scenic walk in town, providing views over Kirkwall and the North Isles, head up **Wideford Hill,** about 2 miles (3km) west of town. On the western slope of this hill, 2½ miles (4km) west of Kirkwall, is the **Wideford Hill Cairn,** a trio of concentric walls built around a passage and a megalithic chamber.

The "Pride of Orkney" is ✪ **St. Magnus Cathedral** on Broad Street (☎ **01856/ 874-894**). Jarl Rognvald, nephew of the martyred St. Magnus, the island chain's patron saint, founded the cathedral to honor him in 1137, and the remains of the saint and Rognvald were interred between the two large East Choir piers. The cathedral is a "Norman" building, constructed of gray and pinkish rose sandstone. Work went on over centuries, and additions were made in the transitional and very early Gothic styles. It's still in regular use as a church. April to September, you can visit Monday to Saturday 9am to 6pm and Sunday 2 to 6pm; October to March, hours are Monday to Saturday 9am to 1pm and 2 to 5pm.

Across from the cathedral are the ruins of a 12th-century **Bishop's Palace** (☎ **01856/87546**), Broad Street, with a round tower from the 16th century. King Haakon came here to die in 1263, following the Battle of Largs and his attempt to invade Scotland. The palace was originally constructed for William the Old, a bishop who died in 1168. An easy scenic walk will take you to the impressive ruins of ✪ **Earl Patrick's Palace** (☎ **01856/87546**), on Watergate. Built in 1607, it has been called "the most mature and accomplished piece of Renaissance architecture left in Scotland." Earl Patrick Stewart was the son of the illegitimate brother of Mary Queen of Scots, and the palace figured in Sir Walter Scott's *The Pirate.* Both the Bishop's Palace and Earl Patrick's Palace are open April to September, Monday to Saturday 9am to 6pm and Sunday 2 to 6pm. Admission covering both palaces is £1.80 ($3.05) adults, £1.30 ($2.20) seniors/students, and 75p ($1.30) ages 5 to 16; age 4 and under are free.

Nearby is the 1574 **Tankerness House** (aka the **Orkney Museum**), on Broad Street (☎ **01856/873-191**), an example of a merchant laird's mansion, with crow-stepped gables, a courtyard, and gardens. A museum here depicts life in the Orkneys over the past 5,000 years. Exhibits range from the bones of the earliest prehistoric inhabitants to Neolithic pottery to bronze jewelry to Pictish stone symbols to farming and domestic utensils. It's open Monday to Saturday 10:30am to 12:30pm and 1:30 to 5pm (May to September, also Sunday 2 to 5pm). Admission is free.

**Orkney Wireless Museum,** Kiln Corner, Junction Road (☎ **01856/874-272**), is a museum of wartime communications used at Scapa Flow, which was a major naval anchorage in both World War I and World War II. Today this sea area, enclosed by Mainland and several other islands, has developed as a pipeline landfall and tanker terminal for North Sea oil. You can also see a large collection of early domestic radios.

April to September, it's open Monday to Saturday 10am to 4:30pm and Sunday 2:30 to 4:30pm. Admission is £2 ($3.40) adults and £1 ($1.70) children.

In the environs, you can visit the **Grain Earth Houses** at Hatson, near Kirkwall. This is an Iron Age souterrain (underground cellar), with stairs leading down to the below-ground chamber. Another Iron Age souterrain, **Rennibister Earth House,** is about 4½ miles (7km) northwest of Kirkwall. This excavation also has an underground chamber that has supporting roof pillars.

## SHOPPING

**The Longship,** 7–9 Broad St. (☎ 01856/873-251), is the retail outlet of Ola Gorie, for Orkney jewelry in Kirkwall. Now in its third decade, this family business has a wide range of high-quality jewelry, including some inspired by stone carvings found at archaeological digs and others by the rich flora and fauna of the islands. A collection based on Charles Rennie Mackintosh designs has proved popular. The Longship also offers a variety of gifts, including fashion and furnishing accessories by Orkney-based Tait & Style.

**Ortak Jewelry,** 10 Albert St. (☎ 01856/873-536), is the main shop of the famous jewelry studio that produces a wide range of silver and gold pieces featuring Celtic, traditional Arcadian, Victorian, and art nouveau designs. The shop also sells items like pottery, barometers, and crystal made by other local artists. The **Ortak Factory Shop,** Hatston Industrial Estate (☎ 01856/872-224), is adjacent to the Ortak factory, and it's the only shop that carries the complete Ortak line. A visitor center here features videos about jewelry making, and factory tours are offered free Monday to Friday 9am and 5pm in July and August. In winter, the shop and visitor center are open by appointment only.

**Judith Glue,** 25 Broad St. (☎ 01856/874-225), produces and sells hand- and machine-made knitwear for the entire family. The artisans tend to favor old-fashioned island patterns, handed down over the generations. Also available are wares of other local artists, and you'll find an interesting selection of handmade pottery, jewelry, greeting cards, soaps, and island music CDs.

## ACCOMMODATIONS

You can also rent rooms at the **Foveran Hotel** (see "Dining," below).

**Ayre Hotel.** Ayre Rd., Kirkwall, Orkney KW15 1QX. ☎ **01856/873-001.** Fax 01856/ 876-289. www.ayrehotel.co.uk. 33 units. TV TEL. £88–£126 ($149.60–$214.20) double. Rates include Scottish breakfast and dinner. AE, MC, V.

Midway between the town's copper-spired church and the harborfront, this white-sided hotel consists of a 1792 stone core and a 1970s sprawling uninspired addition. When it was first built, it was a social center for the town, hosting dances and bridge parties. Today, guests congregate in the popular bar. The small guest rooms are functionally modern and well appointed, with tea/coffeemakers and hair dryers. There's a restaurant offering moderately priced meals, plus a bar, which also serves affordable food.

**Royal Hotel.** Victoria St., Kirkwall, Orkney KW15 1DN. ☎ **01856/873-477.** Fax 01856/872-767. 28 units, 22 with private bathroom. TV. £60 ($102) double without bathroom; £80 ($136) double with bathroom. Rates include Scottish breakfast. MC, V.

Although this hotel has been fully refurbished and the guest rooms modernized (with amenities like tea/coffeemakers and hair dryers), the overall style is traditional. The Royal's restaurant offers a moderately priced table d'hôte menu nightly as well as an extensive à la carte selection. There are also two well-stocked bars, the Public Bar and the Lounge Bar, both offering affordable food.

**West End Hotel.** 14 Main St., Kirkwall, Orkney KW15 1BU. ☎ **01856/872-368.** Fax 01856/876-181. www.orkneyishes.co.uk/westendhotel. 16 units. TV TEL. £58 ($95.70) double. Rates include Scottish breakfast. AE, MC, V.

This hotel just outside town was built in 1837 by a retired sea captain who had made his fortune running contraband between Britain and the Baltics. Today, Jimmy and Isabelle Curry own the place, offering a warm welcome and comfortable guest rooms with tea/coffeemakers and hair dryers; irons are provided on request. The hotel has been refurbished in the past few years and is fresh and inviting. Affordable meals are served in a small restaurant or the hotel's bar. The hotel is fully licensed, attracting both locals and visitors.

## DINING

**Foveran Hotel.** St. Ola, Kirkwall, Orkney KW15 1SF. ☎ **01856/872-389.** Fax 01856/876-430. Reservations recommended. Main courses £7.50–£15 ($12.75–$25.50). AE, DC, MC, V. Daily 7–9pm. SCOTTISH.

Located 2 miles (3km) west of Kirkwall, overlooking the Scapa Flow, where the German Imperial Fleet was sunk in 1919, the Foveran looks like a modern hotel of Scandinavian design. Fully licensed, its restaurant offers the best cuisine in the area and emphasizes "Taste of Scotland" menus. The catch of the day might turn out to be lobster, grilled salmon, deep-fried squid, giant crab claws (known locally as "partan toes"), or brown trout. Vegetarian meals are also offered, as well as succulent portions of Orkney Island beef, lamb, and farm-made cheeses.

The hotel also rents eight pleasant guest rooms; seven are doubles with bathrooms going for £70 ($119), breakfast included.

## EXPLORING MAINLAND FROM KIRKWALL TO STROMNESS

There's a **tourist office** at Kirkwall, 6 Broad St. (☎ **01856/872-856;** www.orkney. com), open in April, Monday to Saturday 9am to 5pm and Sunday 10am to 4pm; May to September, daily 8:30am to 8pm; October to March, Monday to Saturday 9:30am to 6pm.

Heading south from Kirkwall along the southern coastal road toward Stromness, you come first to the hamlet of Orphir. **Orphir Church,** along A964, is 6 miles (10km) southwest of Kirkwall. The ruins are of the country's only circular medieval church, built in the first part of the 1100s and dedicated to St. Nicholas. At Orphir, you can see vast tracts of land set aside for **bird watching.** This area is also ideal for **scenic walks** even if you aren't a "birdie." If you're an angler, the **fishing** is free on Kirbister Loch. Ferries leave the Houton Terminal for Hoy and Flotta five or six times a day.

In the area is the **Cuween Hill Cairn,** along A965, half a mile (about 1km) south of Finstown and 6 miles (10km) northwest of Kirkwall. The owner of a nearby farmhouse (look for the signs) has the key that opens a door to reveal a low mound over a megalithic passage tomb, probably dating from the 3rd millennium B.C. Ancient human bones, along with those of their oxen and dogs, were excavated here.

Bypassing Stromness for the moment, you can continue with a circular tour of the island. Near Stromness, lying off A965, is **Maes Howe,** 10 miles (16km) west of Kirkwall. Dating from 2700 B.C., this is a superb achievement of prehistoric architecture, constructed from single slabs more than 18 feet (5.5m) long and some 4 feet (1.2m) wide. There's a passageway the sun shines through only at the winter solstice. It also contains the world's largest collection of Viking rune inscriptions, the work of marauding Norsemen who broke into the chambered cairn in search of buried treasure.

The ✪ **Ring of Brodgar,** between Lochand Stenness and Loch of Harray, is 5 miles (8km) northwest of Stromness. Dated to 1560 B.C., a circle of some 36 stones is surrounded by a deep ditch carved out of solid bedrock. While it has been suggested it was a lunar observatory, like Stonehenge, its exact purpose remains a mystery. In the vicinity, the **Stenness Standing Stones** are a quartet of four upright stones, all that's left from a stone circle from 3000 B.C.

The ✪ **Unstan Chambered Tomb,** 2 miles (3km) northeast of Stromness along A965, 10 miles (16km) west of Kirkwall, is a big (115 feet/35m in diameter) burial mound dating from 2500 B.C. For its type, it's unsurpassed in Western Europe. There's a chambered tomb more than 6 feet (2m) high. It's open throughout the day, and admission is free. For information, call the **Tankerness House** at ☎ **01856/873-191.** Unstan Ware is the name given to pottery discovered in the tomb.

Last occupied about 2500 B.C., ✪ **Skara Brae** (☎ **1856/841-815**), 7½ miles (12km) north of Stromness, was a collection of Neolithic village houses joined by covered passages. This colony was believed to have sheltered farmers and herders and remained buried in the sands for 4,500 years, until an 1850 storm revealed the ruins. You can see the remains of six houses and a workshop. Once there were 10 dwellings. The walls were made from flagstone rock and the roofs were skins laid on wooden or whalebone rafters. A fireplace was in the center; beds were placed against the side walls. The bed "linen" was bracken or heather, and the "quilts" were animal skins. This prehistoric village is the best preserved of its type in Europe. April to September, it's open daily 9:30am to 6:30pm; October to March, hours are Monday to Saturday 9:30am to 4:30pm. Admission is £4.50 ($7.65) adults, £3.30 ($5.60) seniors, and £1.30 ($2.20) children.

The **Brough of Birsay,** in Birsay at the northern end of Mainland about 11 miles (18km) north of Stromness, is the ruin of a Norse settlement and Romanesque church on an islet that you can reach only at low tide. You can see a replica of a Pictish sculptured stone (the original was removed to a museum for safekeeping). The site is open daily year-round, and admission is free. Nearby are the ruins of the **Earls' Palace** at Birsay, a mansion constructed in the 16th century for the earls of Orkney.

**Click Mill,** off B9057, 2 miles (3km) northeast of Dounby, is the only still-functioning example of an old horizontal water mill on the island.

If you'd like to explore the region described above on two wheels, stop by **Patterson's Cycle Hire,** Kirkwall (☎ **01856/873-097**), which doesn't charge a deposit and has rates of £8 ($13.60) daily or £60 ($102) weekly. It's open Monday to Saturday 9am to 5:30pm.

Every Wednesday night, the **Ayre Hotel** (☎ **01856/873-001**) in Kirkwall hosts the weekly **Accordian and Fiddle Club,** and on Thursday night over the winter locals gather at the Town Hall to enjoy the music of the **Reel and Strathspey Society.** Admission to these events is about £3 to £5 ($5.10 to $8.50). Parish halls in the different communities host an erratic schedule of ceilidhs and concerts throughout the year. Check with the Kirkwall tourist office for details.

## DINING

**Scorrabrae Inn.** Orphir. ☎ **01856/811-262.** Reservations recommended. Main courses £5–£9 ($8.50–$15.30). No credit cards. May–Aug Mon–Thurs 6–11pm, Fri 5pm–1am, Sat noon–2pm and 5pm–1am, and Sun 12:30–10pm; Sept–Apr Mon–Sat 6–10pm, Sat noon–2pm, Sun noon–10pm. Bar open year-round to at least 11:30pm. BRITISH.

In an extension attached to a 19th-century grocer's shop, this simple but convenient restaurant also contains the town's only pub. The bar features whiskies distilled in the

Orkneys, as well as beers. The à la carte menu offers a wide variety of choices, including several fish and chicken dishes, lasagna, salads, and vegetarian meals.

## STROMNESS

Set against a hill, Brinkie's Brae, on the west coast of Mainland, Stromness was once known as *Hamnavoe* ("haven bay") in Old Norse. With its sheltered anchorage, it's the main port of Orkney, and the stone-flagged main street is said to "uncoil like a sailor's rope." The ferry *St. Ola* arrives from the mainland, having left from Scrabster. Fishing boats find shelter here from storms in the North Atlantic.

With its waterfront gables, nousts (slipways), and jetties, Stromness strikes many visitors as more interesting than Kirkwall. It's an ideal place to walk about, exploring whatever captures your fancy. In the old days you could see whaling ships in port, along with vessels belonging to the Hudson's Bay Company. Some young men of Orkney left with them to man lonely fur stations in the far outposts of Canada. For many transatlantic vessels, Stromness was the last port of call before the New World. At Login's Well, many ships were outfitted for Arctic expeditions.

Stromness has a **tourist office** in the ferry terminal building (☎ 01856/850-716), open April to October, Monday to Friday 8am to 6pm, Saturday 9 to 6pm, and Sunday 10am to 3pm (also opens to greet all incoming ferries, to as late as 9pm; July and August, also open Sunday 9am to 4pm); November to March, Monday to Friday 8am to 5pm and Saturday 9am to 4pm.

A small but well-planned bookshop, **Stromness Books and Prints,** 1 Graham Place (☎ 01856/850-565), specializes in books about Orkney and has in-stock copies of the *Orkneyinga Saga.* It's open Monday to Saturday 10am to 6pm and sometimes during ferry arrival times in the evening. The **Pier Arts Centre,** Victoria Street (☎ 01856/850-209), has dazzled Orcadians with its "St. Ives school" of art, including works displayed by Barbara Hepworth and Ben Nicholson. Admission is free, and it's open Tuesday to Saturday 10:30am to 5pm (closed 12:30 to 1:30pm in winter).

At the **Stromness Museum,** 52 Alfred St. (☎ 01856/850-025), you can see a collection of artifacts relating to the history of the Orkneys, especially a gallery devoted to maritime subjects, such as the Hudson's Bay Company and the story of the sinking of the German Imperial Fleet. Founded in 1837, the year Victoria became queen, the museum has been much changed over the years. There's a natural history section, with excellent collections of local birds and their eggs, fossils, shells, butterflies, and moths. May to September, it's open daily 10am to 5pm; October to April, hours are Monday to Saturday 10:30am to 12:30pm and 1:30 to 5pm. Admission is £2.50 ($4.25) adults, £2 ($3.40) students, 50p (85¢) age 13 and under, and £5 ($8.50) families.

If you want to rent a bike, head for **Orkney Cycle Hire,** 52 Dundas St., Stromness (☎ 01856/850-255), which rents bikes for £5 to £6.50 ($8.50 to $11.05) daily and £30 to £35 ($51 to $59.50) weekly. No deposit is required. Summer hours are daily 8:30am to dusk.

### ACCOMMODATIONS & DINING

**Ferry Inn.** John St., Stromness, Orkney KW16 3AA. ☎ 01856/850-280. Fax 01856/851-332. www.ferryin.com. 17 units, 16 with private bathroom. TV. £42 ($71.40) double without bathroom; £50 ($85) double with bathroom. AE, MC, V. Metered daytime parking available.

As its name implies, this modernized hotel is close to the ferry. The small guest rooms are simple and a bit utilitarian but adequate, with tea/coffeemakers; some have trouser presses. Afffordable meals are served from either a pub menu or an à la carte menu at lunch and dinner; look for typical Scottish fare like haggis, smoked salmon, and steak pie. To finish, try a clootie dumpling with cream.

**Stromness Hotel.** Victoria St., Stromness, Orkney KW16 3AA. ☎ **01856/850-298.** Fax 01856/850-610. 40 units. TV TEL. £60 ($102) double. Rates include Scottish breakfast. MC, V.

Behind an elaborate Victorian facade of symmetrical bay windows and beige sand-stone blocks, this is the most important hotel in the Orkneys' second most important community, about 100 yards (91m) from the ferry terminal. It was once a bit dowdy but was extensively renovated in 1996 and 1997. The small guest rooms are outfitted with old-fashioned furniture and have tea/coffeemakers; many offer views of the water. Lunch and dinner, simple but hearty, are served in the cocktail lounge; the moderately priced restaurant has a lunch and dinner menu focusing on seafood and steaks from Orkney.

# BURRAY

Burray and South Ronaldsay (see below) are two of the most visited of the southeast-ern isles, lying within an easy drive of Kirkwall on Mainland. Both are connected to Mainland by the Churchill Barriers causeway linking the islands of Glims Holm, Bur-ray, and South Ronaldsay. The Vikings called the island Borgarey ("broch island").

You come to Burray for scenic drives, to enjoy coastal views, lush pastures, and rugged grandeur. A center for watersports in summer, it also boasts several sandy beaches. You can inquire locally about the possibilities, as everything is casually run. But many Scots come here for canoeing, diving, sailing, swimming, and water-skiing.

The island is an ornithologist's delight, with a **bird sanctuary** filled with a wide range of species, including grouse, lapwing, curlew, and the Arctic tern. Look also for the puffin, the cormorant, and the oystercatcher. You can see gray seals along various shorelines. Their breeding ground is Hesta Head.

Burray is one of the major dive centers of the Orkneys. **Scapa Flow** is the best dive site in the northern hemisphere, for here lie the remnants of the German High Seas fleet scuttled on June 21, 1919. Seven warships range from battleships to light cruis-ers. Many block ships were sunk before the building of the Churchill Barriers, which were constructed to prevent enemy ships from coming into British waters. Marine life, including some rare sponges, enhance the variety of the dives. If you'd like a diving adventure, call **Dolphin Scuba Services,** Garlise, Burray ( ☎ **01856/731-269**). They also offer tours for £30 ($51).

## ACCOMMODATIONS & DINING

**Watersound Restaurant/Sands Motel.** Burray Village, Burray, Orkney KW17 2SS. ☎ **01856/731-298.** Fax 01856/731-298. 4 units. TV. £280–£300 ($476–$510) per week for 1 to 6 occupants. MC, V.

One of the island's most prominent structures, this stone-fronted building was origi-nally a fish-processing plant. Today, it contains a reputable restaurant, the Water-sound. The hostelry sits in the center of Burray Village, 8 miles (13km) north of the passenger ferry at Burwick, on South Ronaldsay. There are four upper-story flats with kitchens. Each contains three rooms and a kitchenette and can be rented (most likely in low season) for less than a week if not fully booked.

The Watersound Restaurant contains the island's only pub, serving lunch and din-ner. Main courses may include preparations of local trout as well as other Orkney pro-duce. On Sunday, specials are offered; a favorite is the full roast beef lunch, which includes generous servings of meat and vegetables.

# SOUTH RONALDSAY

Also joined by the Churchill Barriers, the island of South Ronaldsay is unspoiled fertile countryside. **St. Margaret's Hope,** a hamlet, was named after the young Norwegian princess, the "Maid of Norway," who was Edward II's child bride. Had she lived, she was slated to become queen of England, which at the time laid claim to Scotland. South Ronaldsay is the nearest Orkney island to mainland Scotland, 6½ miles (10.5km) north of the port of John o' Groats. It's separated from the British mainland by the waters of Pentland Firth.

The island offers some of the best **sea angling** waters in the world. Record-breaking catches, particularly in halibut and skate, have been caught, and you can hire local boats on a daily basis. There's also excellent shore fishing from local shores and rocks.

**Tomb of the Eagles,** south of Windwick Bay at the southern tip of the island, is a fine chambered tomb dating from 3000 B.C. The name comes from the many sea-eagles' claws found among the burial grounds. Nearby is a recently excavated mound dating from 1500 B.C. Mr. R. Simison of Liddle Farm, who has excavated the area, will be happy to explain to you about the mound and tomb. Please call at the farm before visiting the tomb and mound (☎ **01856/831-339**). Admission is £3 ($5.10) adults, £2.50 ($4.25) seniors, and £1.50 ($2.55) children 12 and under. Open daily 10am to 8pm.

In the southwest corner of the island, on the opposite side from the Tomb of Eagles, stands **Old St. Mary's Church and Cemetery.** This ancient church is stone-carved with the shape of two feet. Other stones of similar type have been found, and they're thought to be coronation stones for tribal chiefs or petty kings.

**The Workshop,** Front Road (☎ **01856/831-587**), is a craft producers' cooperative in the center of the village of St. Margaret's Hope. It sells a wide range of locally produced crafts, including pottery, jewelry, baskets, rugs, and fine-quality handknits.

## DINING

✪ **Creel Restaurant.** Front Rd., St. Margaret's Hope, Orkney KW17 2SL. ☎ **01856/ 831-311.** Reservations recommended. All main dishes £15.60 ($26.50). MC, V. Apr–Sept daily 7–9pm; open some weekends during winter. Call first. SCOTTISH.

This cozy restaurant, a winner of the "Taste of Scotland" award, overlooks the bay and uses fresh local produce and a large selection of local products. Specialties include Orkney crab soup, followed by fillet steak with onion-and-chile marmalade. You might also try the pan-fried seafood assortment presented on a thick tomato, basil, and leek stew or the roasted monkfish tails with sweet-pepper dressing. For a change from the traditional clootie dumpling you may have sampled elsewhere, the clootie dumpling parfait is a lighter version. The strawberry shortcake, made with homemade shortbread, cream, and fresh Orkney strawberries in season, is also a treat.

The restaurant also rents three guest rooms costing £75 ($127.50) double, including a Scottish breakfast.

# SHAPINSAY

Visitors come here mainly for the secluded beaches, the many walking trails, and the wildlife, including seals.

Getting here is fairly easy if you're based on Kirkwall, for the **Orkney Ferries Ltd.,** Shore Street (☎ **01856/872-044**), goes there six times a day. The round-trip passage is £15 ($25.50) vehicles, £5 ($8.50) adults, and £3 ($5.10) children.

The island was the seat of the Balfours of Trenabie. John Balfour was a nabob, making his fortune in India before becoming the member of Parliament for Orkney and Shetland in 1790. He launched the Scottish baronial castle Balfour. Washington

Irving's father was born on Shapinsay. There are several Neolithic sites on the island, but most remain unexcavated.

## ACCOMMODATIONS & DINING

✪ **Balfour Castle.** Balfour Village, Shapinsay, Orkney KW17 2DY. ☎ **01856/711-282.** Fax 01856/711-283. www.balfourcastle.co.uk. E-mail: balfourcastle@btinternet.com. 6 units. £94 ($159.80) per person. Rates include three meals. 30% discount for age 12 and under. DC, MC, V.

The region's most important benefactors were the worldwide shipping magnates, the Balfour family. John Balfour began work on this castle in the southwest corner of Shapinsay, but it was completed by his heir in 1847. In the 1950s, when the last Balfour died without an heir, the castle and estate were bought by a former Polish officer, Tadeusz Zawadski, and his Scottish wife, Catherine. Today, the place is run by the widow Catherine and her family. It accepts no more than 12 guests at a time, and the family treats them to conversation and entertainment. The guest rooms boast antique or semi-antique furniture and lots of character.

The cuisine relies on such tempting ingredients as local wild duck and fresh scallops, crabmeat, and lobster. Guests who catch their own dinner will have it cheerfully prepared for them.

The estate shelters the only forest in the Orkney Islands, planted in the 19th century by the Balfours and composed chiefly of sycamores. In its center, a 12-foot (3.5m) stone wall surrounds the kitchen gardens, where greenhouses produce peaches, figs, and grapes; strawberries, cabbages, and salad greens grow well within the shelter of the wall. The estate is still a working farm, involved with beef cattle, sheep, and grain production. The hosts will take the time to tour the property with guests and also arrange fishing trips or bird-watching tours, as well as photographic and ornithological trips with guide and boat. Between May and July the bird life is unbelievably profuse. Guests may also be taken to the family's 100-acre uninhabited island where colonies of gray seals and puffins like to say hello.

## ROUSAY

Called the "Egypt of the North," the island of Rousay lies off the northwest coast of Mainland. Almost moon-shaped and measuring about 6 miles (10km) across, the island is known for its trout lochs, which draw anglers from all over Europe. Much of the land is heather-covered moors. Part of the island has hills, including **Ward Hill,** which many people walk up for a panoramic sweep of Orcadian seascape. In the northwestern part of the island is **Hellia Spur,** one of Europe's most important seabird colonies. Here as you walk about you can see the much-photographed puffin.

But where does the bit about Egypt come in? Rousay boasts nearly 200 prehistoric monuments, including one of the most significant, the Iron Age ✪ **Midhowe Broch and Tombs,** in the west of the island, excavated in the 1930s. The walled enclosure on a promontory is cut off by a deep rock-cut ditch. The cairn is more than 75 feet (23m) long and was split among a dozen stalls or compartments. The graves of some two dozen settlers, along with their cattle, were found inside. One writer called the cairn the "great ship of death." The other major sight, the **Blackhammer Cairn,** lies north of B9064 on the southern coast. This megalithic burial chamber is believed to date from the third millennium B.C. It was separated into about half a dozen compartments for the dead.

Excavation began in 1978 on a Viking site at **Westness,** which figured in the *Orkneyinga Saga.* A farmer digging a hole to bury a dead cow came across an Old Norse grave site. Three silver brooches, shipped to the National Museum of Scotland at Edinburgh, were discovered among the ruins. The earliest one dated from the 9th century. Die-hard archaeology buffs might like to know that a mile-long (1.5km) archaeological trail begins here; a mimeographed map (not very precise) of it is sometimes available from the tourist office. The trail is clearly marked with placards and signs describing the dusty-looking excavations that crop up on either side.

To reach Rousay, you can rely on the service provided by the **Orkney Ferries Ltd.** (☎ **01856/872-044**), in Kirkwall. The trip is made six times daily; round-trip passage for vehicles is £15 ($25.50). For passengers, the ticket is £5 ($8.50) adults and £3 ($5.10) children.

## ACCOMMODATIONS & DINING

**Taversoe Hotel.** Frotoft, Rousay, Orkney KW17 2PT. ☎/fax **01856/821-325.** 3 units, 1 with private bathroom. £35 ($59.50) per person. Rates include Scottish breakfast. No credit cards.

On a treeless landscape, this little guesthouse provides small but clean and comfortable guest rooms—two rooms overlook the sea (the occupants share a bathroom); the third has no view but does have a private bathroom. The hotel dining room is open for lunch and dinner. Guests and nonguests alike enjoy what the proprietor calls "peasant cooking" prepared with fresh fish and local produce. Despite this rather humble description and the affordable prices, the restaurant has been widely acclaimed.

# EDAY

Called the "Isthmus Isle of the Norsemen," Eday is the center of a hardworking and traditional crofting community that ekes out a living among the heather and peat bogs of this isolated island. Life isn't easy here, for most of this north isle is barren, with heather-clad and hilly moorlands that often lead to sheer cliffs or give way to sand dunes with long sweeping beaches. Chambered cairns and standing stones speak of ancient settlements. In the 18th and 19th centuries, the island was a major supplier of peat.

Today, most of the population derives its income from cattle and dairy farming, although other products include handknit sweaters, cheese, and a highly rated beer brewed in individual crofts by local farmers and their families.

People come to this almost-forgotten oasis today for **bird watching, beachcombing,** and **sea angling.** Others prefer the peaceful **scenic walks** to the Red Head cliffs, likely to be filled with guillemots and kittiwakes. The cliffs rise to a height of 200 feet (61m), and on a clear day you can see Fair Isle.

On its eastern coastline, Eday opens onto Eday Sound, where pirate John Gow was captured. After a trial in London, he was hanged in 1725; his exploits are detailed in *The Pirate* by Sir Walter Scott. Following his capture, Gow was held prisoner at **Carrick House,** discreetly signposted on the northern part of the island. Carrick House was built in 1633 by James Stewart, the second son of Robert Stewart, who had been named earl of Carrick. It's now the home of Mrs. Joy (☎ **01857/622-260**), but if you're polite and have a flexible schedule, she might open her house to a visit. There may or may not be a fee—about £5 ($8.50) per person "feels right." She's most amenable to visitors between late June and mid-September, and Sundays are an especially good time to test your luck. Despite the sale of various parcels of land to the island's 130 to 140 inhabitants, most of the island is owned by the laird of Eday, Mrs. Rosemary Hebdon Joy, whose link to the island dates to around 1900, when her grandfather bought it from his London club. Interestingly, since then the circumstances surrounding the island's inheritance have made it one of the few matriarchal lairdships in Scotland—its ownership has passed from mother to daughter for several generations. Mrs. Joy and her husband, retired from Britain's diplomatic corps, spend their winters in Worcestershire and the warm-weather months on Eday.

Because of limited accommodations, Eday is most often visited on a day trip. **Loganair** in Kirkwall offers service to Eday one time per week on Wednesday. Call **British Airways** at ☎ **0345/111-222** for reservations. The **Orkney Ferries Ltd.,** Shore Street in Kirkwall (☎ **01856/872-044**), crosses to Eday about twice daily. Vehicles pay £22.40 ($38.10) round-trip, and passengers pay £10 ($17). Children's fares are half price.

## ACCOMMODATIONS

There's no formal tourist office in Eday. However, **Mrs. Popplewell** (☎ **01857/622-248**) from Little Croft House (see "Dining," below) provides an information service and can assist you with finding accommodation or organizing any activities on the island.

✪ **Skaill Farm.** Skaill, Eday, Orkney KW17 2AA. ☎/fax **01857/622-271.** 2 units, none with bathroom. £56 ($95.20) double. No credit cards. Rates include half-board.

Operated by a pair of English expatriates fleeing the congestion of the London suburbs, Skaill is the centerpiece for the island's third-largest farm. Set on 800 acres of windswept grazing land, midway along the length of the island near its narrowest point, 5 miles (8km) from both Calfsound and Backaland, it's in a stone building whose 18th-century core was constructed on the foundations of the island's medieval skaill. (A skaill is the honorific home of an earl, designed to shelter him during his visits from other parts of his realm.) Part of the farmstead dates from 1850, when it was nearly doubled in size. Michael and Dee Cockram welcome you to their home, providing well-prepared dinners and comfortable but simple guest rooms. Meals might include fresh vegetables from the family garden, lobsters, scallops, lamb, and beef.

## DINING

✪ **Little Croft House.** Isle of Eday, Orkney KW17 2AB. ☎ **01857/622-248.** Reservations required as far in advance as possible. About £10 ($17) per person. No credit cards. Time to be arranged when making reservations. SCOTTISH.

One of the most charming possibilities for a meal on Eday is provided by Yorkshire-born Mrs. Emma Popplewell, who, if notified in advance, will prepare fixed-price lunches and dinners. Meals are often served to a loyal following of "off-island" yacht owners enjoying the nautical challenges of the local waters. The setting is a croft cottage whose 30-inch-thick (76cm) stone walls were built around 1900. Its flower and vegetable gardens slope down to the edge of the sea, source of some of the kelp and seaweed Mrs. Popplewell uses to flavor her succulent versions of Orkney lamb. Depending on what's available that day, menu items may include grilled halibut with scallops and local dill and fennel, salads made with wild greens gathered from the hills, homemade versions of raspberry bramble sorbet, locally made cheeses and beers, and aromatic crusty bread that's freshly baked every morning.

In one of the croft's outbuildings (a former boathouse), Mrs. Popplewell sells sweaters, accessories, and caftans that are handknit on Eday by local women. (In recent years, this merchandise has found an enthusiastic market in such places as Colorado, New Hampshire, and Texas.) Also for sale are paintings and sculpture by island artists, among which are included the watercolors by Mrs. Popplewell's recently deceased husband, Geoffrey.

Mrs. Popplewell also rents four comfortably furnished rooms containing TVs; the two doubles are £48 ($81.60), including half-board.

# SANDAY

The name of Sanday means "sand island," which is appropriate; the island's long white beaches have grown as tides have changed over the last century. With few residents or visitors, the stretches of seashore are often deserted—perfect for long solitary walks. One of the largest of the North Isles, some 16 miles (26km) in length, Sanday is part of the eastern archipelago.

On the Elsness Peninsula, jutting southeast from the bulk of Sanday Island, you'll find one of the most spectacular chambered cairns found in the Orkneys: the ✪ **Quoyness Chambered Tomb.** The tomb and its principal chamber date from around 2900 B.C., reaching a height of some 13 feet (almost 4m). Access is by key, which is available at the local post office in Lady Village. Other ancient monuments, including Viking burial grounds and broch sites, have been found on Sanday.

You can see rare migrant birds and terns at the **Start Point Lighthouse,** near the extreme tip of Start Point, a tidal peninsula jutting northward from the rest of Sanday. The early 19th-century lighthouse is one of the oldest in the country, but since the early 1960s it has been on "automatic pilot," without a permanent resident to tend the machinery except for a part-time warden (☎ **01857/600-385**) who may or may not be there at the time of your visit. The number of ships wrecked off Sanday's shore is topped only by North Ronaldsay; you can see the wreck of a German destroyer on the Sand of Langamay. If you want to see this monument, know that only specialized vehicles can drive across the tidal flats and only at low tide. Locals, however, are aware of the times when a trekker can safely walk across the kelp-strewn sandy flats. If you feel adventurous, ask a local how to get there or phone the warden (see above) for advice.

While on the island, you may visit the **Isle of Sanday Knitters,** which has a large selection of high-quality knitwear in both classic and modern design. A display and a sales room are found in the Wool Hall at Lady Village. This cooperative, the largest of its kind in the North Isles, employs more than 100 women. At this writing, however, its future was doubtful, and it may or may not be in existence by the time of your visit.

**Loganair** flies in from the Kirkwall Airport (☎ **01856/872-494**) twice a day Monday to Friday, and Saturday once a day for a cost of £31 ($52.70). Also the **Orkney Ferries Ltd.,** Shore Street in Kirkwall (☎ **01856/872-044**), crosses to the island about two times daily. Round-trip fare for passengers is £10 ($17) adults and £5 ($8.50) children. If you're driving, the cost for vehicles is £22.40 ($38.10).

## ACCOMMODATIONS & DINING

Accommodations are extremely limited, so arrive with a reservation if you're planning to stay over.

**Belsair Hotel.** Kettletoft, Sanday, Orkney KW17 2BJ. ☎ **01857/600-206.** 6 units, 3 with private bathroom. TV. £45 ($76.50) double without bathroom; £52 ($88.40) double with bathroom. Rates include full Scottish breakfast. No credit cards.

In the village of Kettletoft, site of about 15 buildings and the most central of the island's four communities, this hotel contains one of the island's two pubs and its only restaurant. The ancestors of its present owners built it of stone and clapboards in 1879. The functionally furnished guest rooms were upgraded and renovated in 1992. The owner/manager, Mrs. Joy Foubister, is the island's postmistress, and her husband, Kenneth, is the postman. The hotel is about 8 miles (13km) northeast of Sanday's roll-on/roll-off ferry pier.

Gardens across the road produce many of the vegetables served in the hotel's dining room, where moderately priced dishes include straightforward but flavorful preparations of fish, beef, and lamb. You can also enjoy affordable bar meals at lunch and dinner.

# WESTRAY

One of the biggest of the North Isles, Westray is a fertile island with a closely knit community, many of whom are said to have Spanish blood, owing to shipwrecks of the Armada off its stormy shores. The western shoreline is the steepest, rising in parts to some 200 feet (61m), from which you can enjoy panoramic vistas as you walk about. You can see seabirds like guillemots around Noup Head, with its red-sandstone cliffs. The island is a bird watcher's paradise. Along the lochs are many sandy beaches.

Below the cliffs is the so-called **Gentleman's Cave.** A Balfour of Trenabie is said to have found refuge in this cave, along with his comrades, after the defeat at Culloden in 1746. As winter winds howled outside, they drank to the welfare of the "king over the water," Bonnie Prince Charlie. A hike to the cave is recommended only for the hardy and only after you've talked to locals first about how to access the remote site. A knowledgeable guide is Mr. Alex Costie (☎ **01857/677-355**), who gives hiking tours of the island for around £22 ($37.40) per person; these tours usually include a visit to the caves and soup and sandwiches for lunch.

At **Pierowall,** the major hamlet, you can see **Pierowall Church,** a ruin with a chancel and a nave. There are also some finely lettered grave slabs.

The most famous attraction is **Noltland Castle,** a former fortress overlooking Pierowall. A governor of the island, Thomas de Tulloch, had this castle built in 1420. Eventually it was occupied by Gilbert Balfour of Westray, who had it redesigned as a fortress in a "three-stepped" or Z plan, providing complete all-round visibility against attack. But it was never finished. (One of John Knox's "men without God," Balfour was involved in many intrigues around Mary Queen of Scots—he was perhaps implicated in the murder of Lord Darnley. Eventually he fled to Sweden, but more intrigues there led to his hanging in 1576.) The castle's present ruins date from around the mid-1500s. It was destroyed in part by a fire in 1746. A kitchen, a stately hall, and a winding staircase are still standing.

**Orkney Ferries Ltd.** (☎ **01856/872-044** in Kirkwall) sails to Pierowall, Westray, two to three times daily. Bookings are required for cars; the cost is £22.40 ($38.10) round-trip. Passengers for round-trips pay £10 ($17) adults and £5 ($8.50) children and seniors. **Loganair** flies to Westray one to two times daily except Sunday throughout the year. Phone ☎ **01856/872-494** in Kirkwall for information; for reservations, call **British Airways** at ☎ **0345/222-111.**

## ACCOMMODATIONS & DINING

Since accommodations are very limited, always make reservations in advance.

**Pierowall Hotel.** Pierowall Village, Westray, Orkney KW17 2BZ. ☎ **01857/677-208.** Fax 01857/677-707. 5 units, 2 with private bathroom. TV. £29 ($49.30) double without bathroom; £50 ($85) double with bathroom. Rates include Scottish breakfast. No credit cards.

Built a century ago as a manse (clergyman's residence) for a nearby Presbyterian church, this cozy hotel is the domain of Mrs. Jean Fergus, 7¼ miles (12km) north of the roll-on/roll-off ferry terminal. The hotel was refurbished in 1997, when bathrooms were added to two rooms—one double, one twin. The other five rooms have benefited from new furnishings and carpeting as well as redecorations. The hotel pub offers affordable food and drink to anyone who stops in.

## PAPA WESTRAY

Both bird watchers and students of history are drawn to Papa Westray, which was believed to have been settled at least by 3500 B.C. One of the most northerly isles in the Orkneys, it's rich in archaeological sites. In the fertile farmland around Holland, the **Knap of Howar** was discovered, the earliest standing dwelling house in north-western Europe, dating from before 3000 B.C.

On the eastern shore of Loch Treadwell, on a peninsula jutting southeast from the bulk of Papa Westray, you can visit the ruins of **St. Treadwell's Chapel,** believed to have marked the arrival of Christianity in the Orkney Islands. The chapel, now in ruins, was dedicated to Triduana, a Celtic saint. When a Pictish king, Nechtan, admired her lovely eyes, she is said to have plucked them out and sent them by messenger to the king—she hoped he'd learn it was foolish to admire physical beauty. After that she went to a nunnery. For many decades the chapel was a place of pilgrimage for those suffering from eye problems.

On the island's western edge, about 2 miles (3km) from St. Treadwell's Chapel, north of the island's airport, is **St. Boniface Church,** also a Celtic site. Stone Celtic crosses were found here, as well as a series of much-eroded grave slabs carved from red sandstone. This is believed to have been a Christian Viking burial ground, now exposed to the howling winds and bleak sunlight of this rocky peat-clad island.

A major attraction here is **Holland House,** formerly the home of the Traills of Holland. Dating from the 17th century, the house is a fine example of a circular "Horse Engine House," which was driven by 11 horses and a dovecote. At one time the Traills owned most of Papa Westray. The house is now owned by farmer John Rendall (☎ **01857/644-251**); you might be able to see inside if you're polite and Mr. Rendall is feeling sociable.

The northern end of the island has been turned into a **nature reserve,** which is the best place to go for scenic walks. Along with colonies of guillemots and kittiwakes, **North Hill** is the site of one of the largest breeding colonies of the Arctic tern. Once the great auk flew over this island, but the last male was shot in 1813. If you'd like to see what an auk looked like, you'll find a typical one stuffed in the British Museum in London.

Twice-daily flights to Papa Westray from Kirkwall on Mainland are offered by **Loganair** (☎ **01856/872-494**). You can also call **British Airways** at ☎ **0345/222-111** for reservations. **Orkney Ferries Ltd.,** Shore Street in Kirkwall (☎ **01856/872-044;** www.orkneyferry.com), sails to Papa Westray direct on Tuesdays and Fridays, and on the other days, the ferry stops at Westray, where you catch a smaller ferry service on to Papa Westray. If there's no stopover in Westray, this additional ferry service is included in the fare. Round-trip fares are £22.40 ($38.10) vehicles and £10 ($17) adults and £5 ($8.50) children and seniors.

## ACCOMMODATIONS & DINING

**Beltane House.** Papa Westray, Orkney KW17 2BU. ☎ **01857/644-267.** 4 units. £70 ($119) double. Rates include Scottish breakfast and dinner. Prices for youth hostel: £8.50 ($14.45) per person for those 18 and over; £7 ($11.90) per person for those 17 and under. (Rates are set by the Scottish Youth Hostel Association and change frequently.) MC, V.

Built in 1983 about 2 miles (3km) from the island's main pier, this all-purpose accommodation was developed by the local farm cooperative. A row of stone-sided farmworkers' cottages was renovated to form a complex of shops, a guesthouse (the price of which is quoted above), and a bare-bones youth hostel containing two dorms (male and female) with bunk beds. June and July are the busiest months, requiring advance reservations. No meals are provided in the hostel, but there's a self-catering kitchen. Hostel guests sometimes choose to join the guests of the main house for the affordable nightly set-price dinner.

## 2 Fair Isle

27 miles (43.5km) S of Lerwick, Shetland Islands

Called the "most isolated inhabited part of Britain," Fair Isle lies on the same latitude as Bergen, Norway. It measures only about 1 mile by 3½ miles (1.5km by 6km) and sits in the lonely sea, about midway between the Orkneys and the Shetlands, administered by the latter. Relentless seas pound its 20-mile (32km) coast in winter and powerful westerly winds fling Atlantic spray from one side of the island to the other. It's home to fewer than 100 hearty, rugged, and self-reliant souls.

An important staging point for migrating birds, Fair Isle is even better known for the patterned pullovers produced here. They came into fashion again in the 1970s, and greatly aid the island's economy. In stores around the world, you'll see these intricately patterned garments retailing at high prices. But the homegrown product is sold on Fair Isle at half the price. Fair Isle knitting is even a part of the curriculum at all primary schools, and many jobless men have turned to knitting.

Originally the fame of the sweaters was spread in the 1920s by the then Prince of Wales. The pattern is of mysterious origin. Some suggest it was derived from Celtic sources; others that it came from the island's Viking heritage. A more daring theory maintains the themes were Moorish, learned from Spanish sailors shipwrecked off Fair Isle from the Armada in 1588.

In 1954, the island was acquired by the National Trust for Scotland. The bird observatory installed here is the most remarkable in the country. Since work began in 1948, some 200 species have been ringed. Fair Isle is an important breeding ground for everything from the puffin to the Arctic skua, from the razorbill to the storm petrel.

### GETTING THERE

**Loganair** operates scheduled service in a seven-seat "Islander" (flight time: 25 min.). From Sumburgh Airport, there's a flight on Saturday only, which links with incoming Loganair flights from both Glasgow and Edinburgh. From Lerwick Airport, flights are once or twice a day from Monday to Saturday. Call **Loganair** at ☎ **01856/872-494** or **British Airways** at ☎ **0345/222-111** for more information.

The mailboat *Good Shepherd* sails on Tuesday, Thursday, and Saturday from Grutness Pier, Sumburgh Head, on Shetland. It's advisable to check sailing times from Grutness by phoning before 9:30am on the morning of the scheduled departure for Fair Isle, in case of weather delay, which is frequent. Bookings for the trips to Fair Isle can be made through **J. W. Stout**, Skerryholm, Fair Isle (☎ **01595/760-222**). A one-way fare is £2.15 ($3.65), and the trip takes 2½ hours.

### ACCOMMODATIONS & DINING

**Fair Isle Lodge and Bird Observatory.** Fair Isle, Shetland ZE2 9JU. ☎/fax **01595/760-258.** www.fairislebirdobs.co.uk. 17 units, none with private bathroom. £70 ($119) double; £25 ($42.50) dorm bed. Rates include full board. MC, V. Closed Nov to mid-Apr.

Even if you're not a bird watcher, you might stay at this low-slung, big-windowed building in the shelter of treeless hillsides, near the sea at the northern end of the island. It was the dream of a well-respected ornithologist, George Waterston, who bought the lodge in 1948 and created the observatory. It's now administered by the Fair Isle Bird Observatory Trust. The place is most popular during the spring and autumn bird migrations. It's always wise to reserve well in advance, especially during those seasons. On the premises you'll find an extensive collection of reference books on birds. Sometimes, the wardens will take guests on before-breakfast tours of bird traps, which, for tagging purposes, are placed in strategic points along the stone dikes surrounding the island.

Adjacent accommodations were constructed to provide housing for visitors. There are 33 beds for rent. It's also possible to stay here in a dorm room, with four or five or maybe even six beds.

# 3 The Shetland Islands: A Land of Stark Beauty

60 miles (97km) N and NE of the Orkneys

The northernmost part of the British Isles, the archipelago of the Shetland Islands includes some 100 islands that make up 50 square miles (130sq km) of land. Many are merely islets or rocks, but 17 are inhabited. The major island is called **Mainland,** as in the Orkneys. This island, on which the capital, **Lerwick,** is located, is about 55 miles (88.5km) long and 20 miles (32km) wide. It has been turned into what some critics have called "a gargantuan oil terminal." The Shetlands handle about half of Britain's oil.

The islands have been called that "long string of peat and gneiss that stands precariously where three seas—the Atlantic Ocean, the North Sea, and the Arctic Ocean—meet." Shetland's fjordlike *voes* (sheer rock cliffs) make the islands beautiful in both seascape and landscape. But it's a stark beauty, wild and rugged, with windswept moors. Because there are few trees, the landscape at first looks barren. But after a while it begins to take on a fascination, especially when you come on a typical Shetlander, in his sturdy Wellington boots and thick woolen sweater, cutting peat along a bog as his ancestors did before him. Shetlanders are proud, warm, and often eager to share the treasures of their island chain with you. At no point in Shetland are you more than 3 miles (5km) from the sea—the coastline stretches for some 3,000 miles (4,830km).

The major airport is at **Sumburgh,** on the southern tip of the southernmost island of Mainland. The far-northern outpost is **Muckle Flugga Lighthouse,** an advanced achievement of engineering. Standing poised on near-vertical rock, it's "the last window on the world" through which Great Britain looks out to the north. It's not as cold here as you might think: The Shetland archipelago benefits from the warming influence of the Gulf Stream, but even in summer the weather tends to be chilly, and Shetland has less than half the annual rainfall recorded in the western Highlands. In summer there's almost continuous daylight. The Shetlanders call it "Simmer Dim." In midwinter there are no more than 5 hours of daylight.

Civilization here dates back some 5,000 years. The Shetlands were inhabited more than 2,000 years before the Romans, who called them "Ultima Thule." Through these islands paraded Neolithic people, followed by the people of the Iron and Bronze Ages, who gave way to the Picts and the Celts. But the most enduring influence came from the Vikings, who ruled the Shetlands until some 500 years ago. The Norse established an influence that not only lasted for centuries, but which is still evident today in language, culture, and customs.

The Vikings held the islands from A.D. 800 until they were given to Scotland in 1469 as part of the wedding dowry of Princess Margaret of Norway when she married James III. Scotland's takeover of the Shetlands marked a sad period in the life of the islanders, who found themselves under the sway of often cruel and unreasonable feudal barons. One of the most hated of rulers was Earl Patrick Stewart, who was assigned the dubious task of imposing Scottish customs on a people who had known only

# The Shetland Islands

Broch of Mousa **6**
Clickhimin Broch **5**
Jarlshof **9**
Kirk of Lund **1**
Muness Castle **2**
Shetland Croft House Museum **8**
St. Ninian's Island **7**
Staneydale Temple **3**
Tingwall Agricultural Museum **4**

Muckle Flugga
Lamba Ness
Herma Ness
*UNST*
Haroldswick
Baltasound
Cullivoe
**1**
A968
**2**
Belmont
*Point of Fethaland*
Gutcher
*YELL* *HASCOSAY*
*FETLAR*
A968
Mid Yell
A970
*Yell Sound*
*Colgrave Sound*
Burravoe
Stenness
*Esha Ness*
Hillswick
*OUT SKERRIES*
*Saint Magnus Bay*
A970
A968
Brae
*WHALSAY*
Vidlin
*MUCKLE ROE*
Voe Laxo
Symbister
*PAPA STOUR* *PAPA LITTLE*
A970
Melby Ho
Kergord
*Wats Ness*
A971
*MAINLAND*
Bridge of Walls
Walls **3**
A971
Whiteness
*North Sea*
*VAILA*
**4**
*The Deeps* Lerwick
*ISLE OF NOSS*
Scalloway **5**
*BRESSAY*
*FOULA*
Ham
Hamnavoe
*Bard Head*
*WEST BURRA*
Ferry to Bergen →
*Kettle Ness*
*MOUSA*
Sandwick **6**
*ST. NINIAN'S ISLAND* **7**
Ferry to Westray (Orkney Islands)
*Fitful Head*
**8**
Ferries to Fair Isle & Aberdeen
**9**
Sumburgh

Airport ✈
Ferry - - - -

Viking law. His son matched him in cruelty, and eventually both earls were executed in Edinburgh for their crimes. Shetlanders still think of themselves as separate from Scots.

The impact of the North Sea oilmen on this traditionally straitlaced community is noticeable, in overcrowding and other ways. However, away from all the oil activity, life in the Shetlands goes on much as it always did, except for the profusion of modern conveniences and imported foodstuff—you'll notice that food on Shetland tastes better when it's from Shetland; for example, try the Reestit mutton, salted and smoked, with a distinctive flavor.

The islands are famous for their ponies and wool. Shetland ponies roam freely among the hills and common grazing lands in the island chain. Some are shipped south to England where they're popular as children's mounts. The Shetlands also have 10% of all the seabirds in the British Isles, and several of the smaller islands or islets have nature reserves. There are 300 recorded species. Seals are protected and welcomed here. You can see them drifting among the waves, sliding down in pursuit of a fish dinner, or lounging about on the rocks and beaches. You'll recognize most of them as the Atlantic gray seal, with its big angular head. The common seal, with a dog-shaped head, is most often found on the islet of Mousa. If you want to see the otter, you have a better chance in Shetland than anywhere else in Britain.

Anglers find some 200 freshwater lochs in Shetland, and deep-sea angling makes for a memorable sport. Many world fishing records have been set in Shetland. "Ton-up" fish are common.

The island craftspeople are noted for their creativity, reflected in their handcrafts, jewelry, and knitware. In some places you can watch these items being made in the workshops of the artists. Handknitted sweaters are still produced in great numbers on the island, and anyone contemplating a visit might want to return with at least one.

It's imperative to have advance reservations if you're considering a trip to the Shetlands, especially in midsummer.

## SHETLAND ESSENTIALS

**GETTING THERE**   It's a 2½-hour flight from London. By air or sea, Aberdeen is the major departure point from Scotland. **British Airways** (for flight information, call ☎ 800/247-9297 in the U.S. or 0345/222-111) flies four times per day to Shetland from Aberdeen between 9:30am and 5pm, with reduced service on Saturday and Sunday. The flight takes less than an hour.

Roll-on/roll-off car ferries operate to Shetland from Aberdeen Monday to Friday, carrying up to 600 passengers and 240 autos. On-board facilities include restaurants, cafeterias, bars, lounges, and gift shops. The trip takes about 14 hours and costs £116 to £160 ($197.20 to $272) per person. For more information, get in touch with **P&O Ferries,** Jamieson's Quay in Aberdeen (☎ 01224/572-615).

**P&O** offers ferry service once a week, departing on Sunday at noon and Tuesday at 10pm from Stromness, Orkney, heading for Lerwick in the Shetlands. Service is in both summer and winter. For information in Stromness, call ☎ 01856/850-655.

**GETTING AROUND**   If you have a problem with transportation either to or around the islands, you can always check with the tourist office in Lerwick (see below).

**Loganair** (☎ 01595/840-246) provides daily and weekly service to the islands of Whalsay, Fetlar, Foula, and Out Skerries. Although flying is a bit more expensive than taking a ferry, the bonus is that you can go and return on the same day as opposed to spending 2 or possibly 3 days on a rather small island.

Most of the inhabited islands are reached from the Shetland Mainland, and passenger fares are nominal since they're heavily subsidized by the government. Service is 13 to 16 times a day to the islands of Unst, Yell, Whalsay, Fetlar, and Bressay. Passenger/cargo vessels service the islands of Fair Isle, Foula, the Skerries, and Papa Stour. Scheduled services to the little-visited places operate only once or twice a week, however. Boat trips to the islands of Mousa and Noss can be arranged in summer. Call the Shetland Island Tourism office at ☎ 01595/693-434 for more information.

In summer, buses travel around Mainland to all the major places of interest. Call the leading bus company, **John Leask & Son** at ☎ 01595/693-162 or pick up a copy of the "Inter-Shetland Transport Timetable," costing 75p ($1.30) at the tourist office.

It's easier to drive around the Shetlands than you'd think, as there are some 500 miles (805km) of passable roads—no traffic jams, no traffic lights. Many of the islands are connected by road bridges, and for those that aren't, car ferries provide service. Renting a car might be the best solution if you want to cover a lot of ground in the shortest time. You can either bring a car from mainland Scotland or pick one up in

Lerwick. No major international car-rental firm as yet maintains an office in the Shetlands. However, Avis and Europcar have as their on-island agents **Bolts Car Hire,** 26 North Rd. in Lerwick (☎ **01595/693-636**); a competitor is **Grantsfield Garage,** North Road (☎ **01595/692-709**).

If you want to bike your way around, **Grantsfield Garage,** North Road (☎ **01595/692-709**), rents bikes in Lerwick for £7 ($11.90) per day, £30 ($51) per week. If you're planning on renting a bike for several days, call at least a day in advance so one will be reserved for you.

**VISITOR INFORMATION**    The **Shetland Islands Tourism office** is at the Market Cross in Lerwick (☎ **01595/693-434;** www.shetland-tourism.co.uk). The helpful staff does many things, such as arranging rooms and providing information about ferries, boat trips, car rentals, and local events—they even rent fishing tackle. April to September, it's open Monday to Saturday 8am to 6pm and Saturday 8am to 4pm (May to August also Sunday 10am to 1pm); October to March, hours are Monday to Friday 9am to 5pm.

**SPECIAL EVENTS**    Festivals and a festive atmosphere surround the communities of these remote islands, where the slightest excuse will kick off music and revelry. Pubs and community centers regularly schedule music and dancing, and during most weekend nights all you have to do is go in search of a pint of beer to find one of the many live traditional music options.

The **Shetland Folk Festival** takes place at Lerwick around the end of April and the beginning of May. Young fiddlers on the island take part, and international artists fly in for 4 days of concerts, musical workshops, and informal jam sessions, climaxed by what they call their "Final Foy." Concerts, usually incorporating dinner and dancing, are held in local halls throughout the islands, with most events costing about £12 to £15 ($19.80 to $24.75). Often festival entertainers will convene at the pubs and join local performers in jam sessions celebrating the local musical tradition. For information, call ☎ **01595/694-757.**

**Up Helly Aa,** a Viking tradition left over from pagan days, is celebrated at Lerwick with great relish on the last Tuesday in January. Blazing torches light up the dark winter sky as a replica of a Viking longboat is paraded through the streets of Lerwick, then ceremonially burned (see the box below).

January finds Lerwick hosting its famous **Fire Festival** on the last Tuesday of the month, where a thousand locals, torches held high, are cheered on as they storm an effigy of a Viking longboat and set it aflame. These heroes and their witnesses follow this with 2 straight days of eating, drinking, playing music, and dancing. The celebrations spread out from here, and more remote communities hold their local versions of the event over the next 3 months.

Summer months are marked by artistic and cultural **exchange programs** with Norway, Holland, and Sweden. Highlights during these events are musical and dramatic performances by the visiting artists. You can get information about the varying dates, venues, and prices by contacting the tourist office in Lerwick (☎ **01595/693-434**). Summer weekends also bring regularly scheduled **local regattas,** where different communities compete in sailing and rowing competitions. Afterward, there are celebratory dinners, music, and dancing in local venues.

# LERWICK

The capital of the Shetlands since the 17th century, Lerwick, on the eastern coast of Mainland, is sheltered by the little offshore island of Bressay. In the 19th century it was the herring capital of northern Europe, and before that, a haven for smugglers.

The fishing fleet of the Netherlands put in here after combing the North Sea. Even before Victoria came to the throne in 1837, Lerwick had a bustling, cosmopolitan atmosphere. That's even truer today, with the influx of foreign visitors.

Believe it or not, Lerwick is sometimes the sunniest place in Britain, experiencing some 12 hours of sunshine a day in early summer. Commercial Street is the town's principal artery, and it's said that beneath the steep and narrow lanes runs a network of passages used by smugglers. Lerwick today is the main port and shopping center of Shetland.

## EXPLORING THE TOWN

Your first stop should be at the **tourist office** (see above). The helpful staff does everything from arranging for rooms and providing info about ferries, boat trips, and local events to renting fishing tackle there. They're used to unusual requests: Sometimes visitors from Canada or America drop in here wanting their ancestors traced.

The **Shetland Library and Museum,** Lower Hillhead Road, a 5-minute walk west of Lerwick's center (☎ **01595/695-057;** www.shetland/museum.org.uk), has, in addition to a reading room, four galleries devoted to exhibits covering art and textiles, shipping, archaeological digs, and oil exploration. Admission is free. It's open Monday, Wednesday, and Friday 10am to 7pm and Tuesday, Thursday, and Saturday 10am to 5pm.

Entered via both Market Street and Charlotte Street, pentagonal **Fort Charlotte** (☎ **01595/693-434**), built in 1665, contains high walls with gun slits pointing, naturally, at the sea. Eight years after it was constructed, it was burned by the Dutch. Restoration came in 1781. It's open daily 9am to 10pm, and admission is free.

**Clickhimin Broch,** about a quarter of a mile (1.6km) southwest of Lerwick beside A970, was fortified at the beginning of the Iron Age. Excavated in the 1950s, the site revealed 1,000 years of history. It was at one time turned into a broch, rising 17 feet (5m) and built inside the fort. Admission is free, and it's open daily with no set hours. It's a great place to go for a scenic walk.

A 40-foot (12m) replica of a Viking longboat, *Dim Riv* (**"Morning Light"**), anchored in the harbor of Lerwick, is available for a tour of the harbor on summer evenings. The boat was constructed by Lerwick craftsmen in 1980 and has been a popular attraction ever since. Ask at the tourist office (see above).

Of the many shops in Lerwick, you may want to drop in at **Anderson & Co.,** Shetland Warehouse, Commercial Street (☎ **01595/693-714**), which sells handmade crofter and designer sweaters as well as other cottage-industry goods. Selling the wares of the local Judane factory, **Miller's,** 116 Commercial St. (☎ **01595/692-517**), features machine-knit clothing items, including sweaters and capes and rugs. A variety of solid tones and patterns is available, with Argyle being predominant.

**J. G. Rae,** 92 Commercial St. (☎ **01595/693-686**), sells silver and gold jewelry featuring Celtic motifs and images based on Norse mythology and Shetland tales and legends. Gold- and silversmith Rosalyn Thompson produces the jewelry sold at **Hjaltasteyn,** 161 Commercial St. (☎ **01595/696-224**), where you'll find a selection of sterling silver and 9-carat gold items, some of which are set with garnets and amethysts.

## ACCOMMODATIONS

**Glen Orchy Guest House.** 20 Knab Rd., Lerwick, Shetland ZE1 0AX. ☎/fax **01595/ 692-031.** www.guesthouselerwick.com. E-mail: glenorchy@virgin.net. 22 units. A/C TV. £66 ($112.20) double. Rates include Scottish breakfast. V.

Near the top of a brae (gently sloping hill) and not far from a nine-hole golf course that's free to the public, Glen Orchy House is a 4-minute walk from the center of

# Up Helly Aa!

The farther north you travel in Scotland, the stronger are the undercurrents of pagan myth and pageantry, culminating in the vivid Norse traditions of the Shetlands. On the moss-covered rocky surface of the 100-or-so islands, the collective unconscious of the locals is sometimes startlingly revealed as something other than Anglo-Saxon or Celtic.

Ask anyone in a local pub, and he or she will tell you the islands are Scottish only because of the fiscal embarrassment of a Norwegian king who sold the Shetlands to the Scottish monarchs in 1469 with the tacit understanding they'd eventually be returned to Scandinavia. Although for many generations the Shetlanders retained their Norse dialect and allegiance to Viking ways, the switch back to Norway never happened. Perhaps in reaction to their medieval role as bartered chattel between the two northern kingdoms, the Shetlands remained dourly outside Scottish culture, with a populace who referred for many generations to the provincial capital of Lerwick as "the mainland," and not to the mainland of Scotland.

How do the Shetlanders celebrate their Nordic heritage? By brightening up the midwinter darkness with the **Up Helly Aa festival,** held—in fair weather, snow, or storm—every year on the last Tuesday in January. The festival's centerpiece is a meticulously crafted re-creation of a Viking longboat. The people of Lerwick parade by torchlight through the streets in Viking costume, and the highlight of the evening comes when the longboat is set alight and its dragon-head prow is engulfed in flames. Presiding over the ritual is an elected master of ceremonies, the Guizer Jarl (a significant honor bestowed only on a longtime resident male of proven civic worth and integrity).

This ancient ritual celebrates the death of winter and the return of the sun and the earth's rebirth with the coming of spring. The ceremony is based on an ancient Viking death ritual when the body of a dead earl (Jarl) would be set ablaze at sea. An essential part of the ritual is the almost immediate removal of all traces of the burned-out hulk of the longboat after the cremation is over. The morning after the ceremony, even the ashes of the celebration have been carted off, and Lerwick resumes its outwardly Christian and Scottish demeanor—until the Viking tradition of the Up Helly Aa is revived again the following year.

town. The building was constructed in 1904 as an Episcopalian nunnery; the most recent modifications to it were in 1996 and 1997, when Trevor and Joan Howarth added a new wing and upgraded the existing guest rooms. In addition to single and doubles, there are now three family rooms with single beds or bunk beds. All rooms have central heating and air-conditioning, as well as hair dryers and tea/coffeemakers. Trevor and Joan will provide an affordable evening meal to those who request it.

**Grand Hotel.** 149 Commercial St., Lerwick, Shetland ZE1 0AB. ☎ **01595/692-826.** Fax 01595/694-048. 24 units. TV TEL. £90 ($153) double; £120 ($204) family room. Rates include Scottish breakfast. AE, DC, MC, V. Free parking in nearby public lot.

A grander hotel would be hard to find anywhere in Shetland. With pointed turrets, weather vanes, crow's-step gables, and solid stone walls, it lies a block from the waterfront, in the town center. All the guest rooms, conservative yet comfortable, have tea/coffeemakers. The extensively modernized hotel has two lounge bars, a dining room, and a nightclub (Poser's Disco) open Wednesday, Friday, and Sunday to every night owl in Lerwick. The Grand shares its reservations facilities and some of its staff with the Queens Hotel (see below).

**Lerwick Hotel.** South Rd., Shetland ZE1 0RB. ☎ **01595/692-166.** Fax 01595/694-419. www.nes.co.uk/lerwickhotel. 35 units. TV TEL. £89.75 ($152.55) double; £115 ($195.50) suite. Rates include Scottish breakfast. AE, MC, V. Take Scalloway Rd. west from the center for 5 minutes.

This is one of the biggest and most up-to-date hotels in the Shetlands, sprawling beside a gravel- and kelp-covered beach. Its simply furnished, streamlined guest rooms offer various amenities, including hair dryers; about half have views over the water toward Bressay. There's a full-service, upscale restaurant, where the main dishes are likely to include at least one seafood and one vegetarian choice as well as chicken or wild game. In summer, dinner dances that combine hearty meals with traditional Scottish fun are frequently held. There's also a brasserie serving more affordable meals.

**Queens Hotel.** 24 Commercial St., Lerwick, Shetland ZE1 0AB. ☎ **01595/692-826.** Fax 01595/694-048. www.kgqhotels.co.uk. 26 units. TV TEL. £90 ($153) double; £120 ($204) family room. Rates include Scottish breakfast. AE, DC, MC, V.

Its foundations rise directly from the sea at the harborfront, so on blustery nights fine sprays of saltwater sometimes coat the windowpanes of the lower floors. Built of natural stone around 1900, the Queens rivals the nearby Grand Hotel (see above) as the most prestigious hotel in Lerwick. They share the same reservations staff. Inexpensive bar lunches are offered in the cocktail lounge, and more formal dinners are served in the dining room. The small guest rooms are conservatively and comfortably furnished.

**Shetland Hotel.** Holmsgarth Rd., Lerwick, Shetland ZE1 0PW. ☎ **01595/695-515.** Fax 01595/695-828. www.nes.co.uk/shetlandhotel. E-mail: reception@shetlandhotel.co.uk. 67 units. TV TEL. £92 ($156.40) double; £99.75 ($169.60) suite. Rates include Scottish breakfast. AE, DC, MC, V.

Built in 1984, this brick, stone, and concrete structure with square windows is one of the most modern hotels in the Shetlands. It's opposite the ferry terminal, with a good view of the harbor. The guest rooms are well furnished and contain trouser presses and tea/coffeemakers. For a fee, the hotel provides laundry service. The building also houses a public bar, a cocktail lounge, and two restaurants (one serving an upscale fixed-price menu, the other serving from an à la carte menu, and both offering local fish and vegetarian items).

## DINING

**Golden Coach.** 17 Hillhead. ☎ **01595/693-848.** Reservations required Sat–Sun. Main courses £6.80–£8 ($11.55–$13.60); fixed-price lunch £5 ($8.50); dinner menu £18 ($30.60). MC, V. Mon–Fri noon–2pm and 5:30–11pm; Sat–Sun noon–11pm. CHINESE.

One of the two Chinese restaurants in the Shetlands, this intimate place is softly lit and contemporary in decor. Try the barbecued Peking duck or deep-fried shredded beef in hot sweet-and-sour sauce. Malaysian chicken comes in a peanut sauce, or you can order king prawns Peking with garlic sauce.

**Oasis Bistro.** In the Shetland Hotel, Holmsgarth Rd. ☎ **01595/695-515.** Main courses £6–£13 ($10.20–$22.10). AE, DC, MC, V. Daily 11am–9:30pm; hot meals noon–2pm and 5–9:30pm. SCOTTISH.

On the second floor of the four-story Shetland Hotel, this eatery is a good choice for a light snack at odd hours; salads and sandwiches are served all day. The restaurant also offers hot meals at lunch and dinner. Emphasis is on fresh local produce, including fresh fish and vegetarian fare straight from Shetland gardens.

**Queens Hotel.** 24 Commercial St. ☎ **01595/692-826.** Reservations recommended. Main courses £9.50–£12.50 ($16.15–$21.25); fixed-price 3-course dinner £15.25 ($25.95). AE, DC, MC, V. Daily noon–2pm and 6–9:30pm. BRITISH.

On the lobby level of this previously recommended hotel, this restaurant's pink-and-white premises overlook the sea, the wharves, and the many fishing boats bobbing at anchor. It caters to families, many of whom seem to arrive in groups as part of reunions. Many locals consider it the best restaurant in Lerwick, a staple on the island's culinary scene. Menu specialties include goujons of haddock with tartar sauce, roast beef sirloin with Yorkshire pudding, chicken Caribbean with pineapple sauce, braised lamb cutlets, surf and turf, and conservative preparations of fish dishes.

### LERWICK AFTER DARK

May to September, the **Islesburgh Community Centre,** King Harold Street (☎ **01595/692-114**), hosts dancing to Shetland fiddle music called the Summer Exhibition on Wednesday and Friday 7 to 9:30pm. Admission is £2.50 ($4.25) adults and £1.50 ($2.55) seniors/students/children. Another place to hear fiddle music, the **Lounge Bar,** Mounthooly Street (☎ **01595/692-231**), hosts an informal evening of traditional music on Wednesday, usually starting around 9:30pm. They also have live music on Friday night and often on Saturday afternoon. There's no admission fee to this old traditional pub, and Belhaven and Tennant beers, along with Guinness, are available on tap.

## SCALLOWAY

On the western coast, 6 miles (10km) west of Lerwick, Scalloway was once the capital of Shetland. This town was the base for rescue operations in Norway during the darkest days of World War II. Still an important fishing port, Scalloway has changed because of the oil boom. New businesses have opened, attracting more and more people to the area, which has emerged after a long slumber into a prosperous and lively place in this remote corner of the world.

Dominating the town are the ruins of corbel-turreted medieval **Scalloway Castle** (☎ **01595/880-243**), commissioned by the dreaded Earl Patrick Stewart at the beginning of the 17th century and built with forced (slave) labor culled from the island's residents. After it was built, he imposed exorbitant taxes and fines on the islanders. In 1615, the Earl and all his sons were executed in Edinburgh, partly as a means of placating the islanders, partly because he rebelled against the powers of the central Scottish/British government. The castle was allowed to deteriorate after this (no one in Scalloway wanted to perpetuate the earl's memory). Admission is free and hours are those of the Shetland Woollen Company (see below), from which you must get the key to enter.

The **Shetland Woollen Company** (☎ **01595/880-243**) is open to visitors Monday to Friday 9am to 5pm (in summer, also Saturday 9am to 5pm). You can see the processing and finishing of Shetland knitware, then visit the showroom where a selection of garments made locally is sold, along with Icelandic knitwear.

To escape to a beautiful area, ideal for long walks or drives, follow B9075 east off A970 to the top of a small sea inlet that'll lead you to the lushly green **Kergord.** This surprisingly lush valley contains forests ideal for long strolls. The particular greenery of the spot, so familiar on the Scottish mainland, comes like an oasis in this far northern part of the world.

## WEST MAINLAND

It's said you can see more of Shetland from the **Scord of Weisdale** than from any other vantage point in the archipelago.

Shetland's only stone-polishing business operates at **Hjaltasteyn,** Whiteness, 9 miles (14.5km) west of Lerwick. Here gemstones are turned out from raw materials in fetching hand-wrought silver settings. Alas, the workshop isn't currently open to visitors. You can, however, visit the showroom at 161 Commercial St. in Lerwick (☎ **01595/696-224**) to see what's been made. It's open summer only, Monday to Tuesday and Thursday to Saturday 9:15am to 4:45pm, and Wednesday 10am to 4pm (closes 1 to 2pm for lunch).

Continuing north, you can watch high-quality jewelry being made at **Shetland Jewelry,** Soundside, Weisdale (☎ **01595/830-275**), where the artisans base many of their designs on ancient Celtic and Viking patterns. You may go through the workrooms and later stop in for an inspection of the stocks available in the showroom. It's open Monday to Friday 9am to 1pm and 2 to 5pm.

### DINING

**Norseman's Inn.** Voehead, Weisdale Parish. ☎ **01595/830-304.** Main courses £4–£7 ($6.80–$11.90). MC, V. Pub Mon–Fri 11am–2pm and 5pm–midnight; Sat–Sun 11am–1am. Food service May–Sept Wed–Mon 5–10pm. SCOTTISH.

This is your basic Scottish pub on the main A970 highway, 12 miles (19km) northwest of Lerwick. Built in 1981 at the head of one of the most dramatic estuaries in the Shetlands, it's a popular place for both locals and visitors. Only in the high season, the pub serves a variety of hot dishes to accompany the spirits. Shrimp scampi, lasagna, sweet-and-sour chicken, and baked fresh fish are a few house favorites. The atmosphere is rustic and inviting.

### AROUND WALLS

You can continue your tour of West Mainland by heading west along A971 toward Walls. You come first to **Staneydale Temple,** 2¾ miles (4.5km) outside Walls. This early Bronze Age (perhaps Neolithic) hall once had a timbered roof. It's called a temple because it bears a remarkable resemblance to similar sites on Malta, lending support to the theory that the early settlers of Shetland came from the Mediterranean.

Continuing past several lochs and sea inlets, you come to **Walls,** a hamlet built on the periphery of two voes (a local term for inlet). Its natural harbor is sheltered by the offshore islet of Vaila.

#### Accommodations & Dining

✪ **Burrastow House.** Walls, West Mainland, Shetland ZE2 9PD. ☎ **01595/809-307.** Fax 01595/809-213. www.users.shetland.co.uk/burrowstow-hotel. 6 units. £170 ($289) double; £85 ($144.50) per person family room. Rates include half-board. AE, MC, V. Closed Jan–Feb.

About 3 miles (5km) southwest of Walls, a 40-minute drive northwest of Lerwick, this simple but comfortable building was constructed in 1759 as a *haa* (home of the farm manager of a laird's estate). Set amid lands still used in summer for grazing sheep, it lies at the widest section of a windswept peninsula with views of a cluster of rocky and sparsely inhabited islands. The guest rooms are well furnished and evoke country-house living. One family suite, consisting of a double room and a twin room connected by a bath, is available.

**Dining:** The food is the best on the island, and the daily menu in the oak-paneled dining room is likely to include nettle-and-oatmeal fritters, mussel brose (a stew of mussels thickened with oatmeal), monkfish with anchovy stuffing, lamb, and Scottish beef. Lunch, high tea, and upscale dinners are served daily. The proprietors ask that you call ahead if you want a hot meal, but they'll accommodate you with fresh-baked bread, cheese, and homemade soup if you just drop in. They offer a good vegetarian selection. The restaurant is closed all day Sunday and Monday to nonguests.

## PAPA STOUR

The "great island of priests," in the shape of a large starfish, Papa Stour lies off the west coast of Mainland, 25 miles (40km) northwest of Lerwick. As its name indicates, it was an early base for monks. Two centuries ago there was a leper colony here on the little offshore islet of Brei Holm.

Legend has it that its profusion of wildflowers had such a strong scent that old fishermen could use the perfume—borne far out on the wind—to fix their positions. Papa Stour is very isolated, and once it was feared the island might be depopulated, but about 26 settlers live here now.

In the darkest days of winter, bad weather can cut it off for days. But if you see it on a sunny day, it's striking. Encircled by pillars of rock and reefs, its sea caves, sculpted by turbulent winds and raging seas, are among the most impressive in Britain. The largest of these is **Kirstan's Hole,** extending some 80 yards (73m).

Boats go to Papa Stour about seven times per day, 5 days a week, from West Burrafirth on Mainland, at a cost of £5 ($8.50). Call Mr. Clark at ☎ **01595/810-460** for information about these constantly changing details.

### ACCOMMODATIONS & DINING

**Northouse.** North-house, Papa Stour, Shetland ZE2 9PW. ☎ **01595/873-238.** 4 units, 1 with bathroom. £55 ($93.50) double. Rates include full board. No credit cards.

Within walking distance of the island's only pier, just outside Housa Voe (the only hamlet, with seven buildings), this stone croft is an unusual building. The foundations are Viking, and Dutch coins from the 1620s have been unearthed here. It's the domain of Andrew and Sabina Holt-Brook, who moved from the mainland of Scotland more than 20 years ago in search of affordable land. Now owners of 30 acres of windswept peninsula (which geologists define as an ancient Devonian fish bed), they offer the only accommodations and/or meals on the island. The rooms are comfortable and inviting, and the "garden room" has its own entrance. Meals are served to both guests and nonguests, but for just a meal, call in advance. The working farm also supplies the Holt-Brooks with free-range eggs and fresh vegetables. The inexpensive lunches are brown-bag affairs (homemade sandwiches and cakes) to be taken along while you enjoy the island's wild landscapes.

## FOULA

This tiny remote island—only 3 miles (5km) wide by 5 miles (8km) long—with five high peaks is an "Edge of the World" place. Called the "Island West of the Sun," Foula may have been the Romans' legendary Thule. In local dialect, *foula* means "bird island"—and the name fits. Uncountable numbers of birds haunt the isle. Its towering sea cliffs include the second-highest cliff face in Britain, the **Kame,** at 1,220 feet (370m). About 3,000 pairs of the world's great skuas, known as "bonxie," live here. On the island, you'll hear many stories about the rock-climbing prowess of locals who go in search of gulls' eggs.

The island lies 27 miles (43.5km) west of Scalloway on the west coast of Mainland, where the locals are vastly outnumbered by sheep. Until the beginning of the 19th century, Old Norse was the language spoken. Its 400 people remain very traditional. If you're very lucky you might see them dance the Foula reel, a classic dance in Shetland.

If the weather's right, a weekly mailboat sails to Foula from Walls on Mainland. Even in summer, the seas are likely to be turbulent, and in winter Foula has been known to be cut off from the rest of Britain for weeks. The trip takes 2½ hours. Loganair also operates a summer service from Tingwall on Monday, Wednesday, and Friday (trip time: 15 min.).

## ACCOMMODATIONS & DINING

Because of the interest by visitors in recent years, some islanders have taken to offering accommodations that include half-board.

**Mrs. Marion Taylor.** Leraback, Isle of Foula, Shetland ZE2 9PN. ☎ **01595/753-226.** 3 units, none with private bathroom; 1 cottage. £48 ($81.60) double; £24 ($40.80) cottage for up to 4. Rates include half-board in a double. No credit cards.

Owners Bryan and Marion Taylor emigrated from Edinburgh 14 years ago. Their cozy modern farmhouse is near the geographical center of the island, within walking distance of everything. The comfortable rooms in the main house have easy access to the large kitchen whose brick hearth is the focal point of the farm. The cottage has two bedrooms, a sitting room, and kitchen. There are no food shops on the island, so you'll have to bring your own supplies, as the rates for the cottage don't include meals. The Taylors' 7 acres is a sheep farm, and they extend their income by knitting and spinning—you can order a custom-made handknit sweater.

# NORTH MAINLAND

The most rugged scenery Shetland has to offer is in the northern part of the island of Mainland. Some visitors have found the area reminds them of Norway, and we agree. That's especially true in the tiny village of **Voe,** with its little wooden houses.

## VIDLIN

Heading north from Voe along A970, you'll reach the eastern junction of B9071, which will take you to **Vidlin,** where the **Lunna Kirk,** one of the oldest churches in the archipelago, is still used by its congregation. Construction began in 1753. The church has a "leper hole," from which the poor victims could listen to the sermon without being seen.

## BRAE & BUSTA

Heading west back to A970, continue north to **Mavis Grind,** a narrow isthmus marking the point where the North Mainland is at its most narrow. The touristy thing to do in North Mainland is to pause at Mavis Grind, take a couple of stones, and throw one to your right into the North Sea and the other to your left into the Atlantic Ocean.

Near the villages of Brae and Busta, you'll find some of the best food and hotels in Shetland. Oil contractors, helicopter pilots, and shipping executives sent by mainland companies to service the nearby Sullom Voe, site of the largest oil terminal in Europe, often stay in this area.

### Accommodations & Dining

**Brae Hotel.** Brae, North Mainland, Shetland ZE2 9QJ. ☎ **01806/522-456.** Fax 01806/522-459. 36 units. TV TEL. £55 ($93.50) double. Rates include Scottish breakfast. Discounts offered for stays of 4 or more days. AE, DC, MC, V.

Built in 1979, this modern building lies in the center of the village, 28 miles (45km) north of Lerwick beside A970 about a mile (1.5km) south of the narrow isthmus that separates North from South Mainland. The small guest rooms are wallpapered and painted in pastels and reassuringly warm. The restaurant serves affordable meals in generous portions. On the premises are a bank, a billiard room, and a unisex hair salon.

✪ **Busta House**. Busta, near Brae, North Mainland, Shetland ZE2 9QN. ☎ **01806/ 522-506.** Fax 01806/522-588. www.mes.co.uk/busta. E-mail: busta@mes.co.uk. 20 units. TV TEL. £91 ($154.70) double. Rates include Scottish breakfast. Discounts offered for stays of 5 days or more. AE, DC, MC, V.

Busta House is the oldest continuously inhabited house in the Shetlands. Built in 1580, with ample extensions added in 1714 and 1983, it was the original *busta* (homestead) of the medieval Norwegian rulers of the island. Later inhabited by the island's laird, it once welcomed Elizabeth II at tea during her tour of the Shetlands on the royal yacht *Britannia*. The estate's long and tormented history includes episodes of multiple drownings, a handful of resident ghosts, and some of the most famous lawsuits in Britain. Some literary enthusiasts claim the house in all its drama was the inspiration for Dickens's *Bleak House.*

In recent times, the important economic agreement that paved the way for the construction of the massive Sullom Voe oil terminal (the Busta House Agreement) was signed here between the local government and Britain's multinational oil companies.

Rising above its own small harbor a short drive from A970, a 10-minute drive south of the village of Sullom, 1½ miles (2.5km) from Brae, the hotel has crow's-foot gables, stone walls measuring 6 feet (2m) thick, and an appearance of a fortified manor house. Peter and Judith Jones, the resident proprietors, maintain the antique charm of the public rooms and the chintz-filled guest rooms (each with a trouser press, hair dryer, and tea/coffeemaker); same-day laundry facilities are available. They prepare upscale dinners (there's also a more affordable bar menu), and there's a cocktail lounge with an impressive array of malt whiskies, as well as a quiet library.

## HILLSWICK

If you head north along A970, we suggest you take the secondary road going west to **Esha Ness,** where you'll come on the most dramatic cliff scenery not only in Shetland but in all Britain. This is simply a gorgeous area for hiking. On the way, 15 miles (24km) northwest of Brae, you'll pass the little fishing hamlet of **Hillswick,** opening onto the bay in Ura Firth.

### Accommodations & Dining

**St. Magnus Bay Hotel.** Hillswick, Shetland ZE2 9RW. ☎ **01806/503-372.** Fax 01806/ 503-373. 26 units. TV TEL. £60–£80 ($102–$136) double. Rates include Scottish breakfast. MC, V.

Isolated at the head of St. Magnus Bay, this hotel was prefabricated of solid pine in Norway, barged across the North Sea, and assembled as part of Glasgow's Great Exhibition of 1896. In 1900, it was floated to Hillswick and reassembled as one of the terminals for the old North of Scotland Shipping Co. Despite its black-with-white-trim and double-gabled severity, it's one of the most lavish Edwardian buildings in the Shetlands, with a boisterously popular pub offering affordable bar meals. There's also a pleasingly old-fashioned dining room serving lunch and dinner daily, with a Sunday carvery 1 to 2pm. Specialties are fresh lobster in season, fresh haddock, sea trout, Aberdeen Angus beef, local salmon, distinctively flavored Shetland lamb, and a traditional Scottish version of cullen skink.

## SOUTH MAINLAND

This part of Shetland, reached by heading south along A970, is both ancient and modern. On the one hand there's the gleaming **Sumburgh Airport,** which has played a major role in the North Sea oilfields development and services many of the offshore rigs today. On the other hand, you stumble on the ruins of Jarlshof (see below), which may have been inhabited for some 3,000 years.

## EXPLORING THE AREA

As you go down the "long leg" of Shetland, as it's called, heading due south, passing a peaty moorland and fresh meadows, the first attraction is not on Mainland at all but on an offshore island called Mousa: the famous ✪ **Broch of Mousa,** a Pictish defense tower that guarded the islet for some 2,000 years. It reached the then-incredible height of some 40 feet (12m) and was constructed of local stones, with two circular walls, one within the other. They enclosed a staircase leading to sleeping quarters. It's the best-preserved example of an Iron Age broch in Britain. The village of **Sandwick,** 7 miles (11km) south of Lerwick, is the ferry point for reaching Mousa. There's daily bus service between Lerwick and Sandwick. A local boatman, Mr. Jamieson, will take you across to Mousa. It takes about 15 minutes. April to September only, you can visit Mousa Monday to Saturday. The cost is £7 ($11.90) adults and £3.50 ($5.95) children. For boat schedules, call the tourist office in Lerwick at ☎ **01595/693-434.**

South of Sandwick, you reach the parish of Dunrossness. At Boddam is the **Shetland Croft House Museum** (☎ **01595/695-057**), east of A970 on an unmarked road 25 miles (40km) south of Lerwick. Rural Shetland life comes alive here in this thatched croft house from the mid-1800s. The museum also has some outbuildings and a functioning water mill. It's open from May to September from 10am to 1pm and from 2 to 5pm. Admission is £2 ($3.30) for adults and £1.50 ($2.45) for seniors and children.

Continuing south, you reach the outstanding man-made attraction in Shetland, ✪ **Jarlshof,** Sumburgh (☎ **01950/460-112**), near the Sumburgh Airport. It has been called "the most remarkable archaeological discovery in Britain." A violent storm in 1897 performed the first archaeological dig. Washing away sections of the large mound, it revealed huge stone walls. Excavations that followed turned up an astonishing array of seven distinct civilizations. The earliest was from the Bronze Age, but habitation continued at the site through the 1500s, from wheelhouse people to Vikings, from broch builders to medieval settlers. A manor house was built here in the 16th century by the treacherous earl, Patrick Stewart, but it was sacked in 1609. The site is open April to September, daily 9:30am to 6:30pm. Admission is £2.50 ($4.25) adults, £1.90 ($3.25) seniors, and £1 ($1.70) children.

Also nearby is the **Sumburgh Lighthouse,** one of the many Scottish lighthouses constructed by the grandfather of novelist Robert Louis Stevenson. The lighthouse is now fully automated. The property offers a self-catering four-bedroom cottage, costing £350 ($595) per week. Built in 1821, it can be visited by the public, but you must phone the Lerwick tourist office (☎ **01595/693-434**) for an appointment; reservations for the cottage can also be made with the owner, Mr. Johnston-Ferguson, at ☎ **01387/372-240.** Reserve at least 3 months in advance.

On the coast at the tip of Scatness, about a mile (1.5km) southwest of Jarlshof at the end of the Mainland, is the **Ness of Burgi,** which was a defensive Iron Age structure related to a broch.

Heading back north toward Lerwick, you can veer west for a trip to **St. Ninian's Island** in the southwestern corner of Shetland. It's reached by going along B9122. The island is approached by what's called a *tombolo* (bridging sandbar). An early monastery once stood on this island, but it wasn't uncovered until 1958. Puffins with their orange beaks often favor the islet, which has a pure white sandy beach on each side. The island became famous in 1958 when a group of students from Aberdeen came upon a rich cache of Celtic artifacts, mainly silverware, including brooches and other valuable pieces. Monks are believed to have hidden the treasure trove, fearing a Viking attack. The St. Ninian treasure is in the National Museum of Scotland at Edinburgh.

## Accommodations & Dining

**Sumburgh Hotel.** Sumburgh Head, Virkie Parish, Shetland ZE3 9JN. ☎ **01950/460-201.** Fax 01950/460-394. 32 units. TV TEL. £60 ($102) double. Rates include Scottish breakfast. AE, MC, V.

Its turrets and towers were built in 1857 of local stone for the laird of Virkie, the Victorian descendant of Robert the Bruce. Set on 12 barren acres of land jutting dramatically out to sea, it lies at the southernmost end of the Shetland Islands, at the end of A970. A modern addition completed in the 1960s doubled the size of the place, which contains the Voe Room restaurant (offering an affordable fixed-price dinner nightly) and two very popular bars. Recent refurbishments to the guest rooms have brightened them up and made them more inviting.

# UNST

The northernmost point of Britain, remote and beautiful **Unst** is easy to reach. After crossing over to Yell, you can drive along A968 to the little harbor at Gutcher in the northeast of Yell. The **Shetland Island Coastal Marine Operations** operates a ferry crossing from here fairly frequently every day. The cost of a car and driver is £3 ($5.10), £1.20 ($2.05) for each extra adult, and 20p (35¢) per child. For schedules, call ☎ **01957/722-259. Loganair** (☎ **01595/840-246**) also flies to Unst from both Lerwick and Sumburgh, once a day from Monday to Friday.

## Exploring the Island

Robert Louis Stevenson stayed here for a time. His father, Alan Stevenson, was designing and building the Muckle Flugga lighthouse on an outermost skerry, which is even farther north than Labrador.

Unst is steeped in folklore and legend. An **Old Norse longhouse,** believed to date from the 9th century, was excavated at Underhoull. The best beach is at **Skaw,** set against the backdrop of **Saxa Vord,** legendary home of the giant Saxi. A drive to the top will reward you with a view of the Burra Firth. Visitors go to Haroldswick to mail their cards and letters in the northernmost post office in the British Isles.

The roll-on/roll-off car ferry from Yell comes into Belmont. Nearby is **Muness Castle,** constructed in 1598 by Laurence Bruce, a relative of the notorious Earl Patrick Stewart who ruled Shetland so harshly. Adam Crawford, who designed Scalloway Castle for the ruling earls on Mainland, also drew up the plans for Muness. Built with rubble and known for its fine architectural detail, the castle was inhabited for less than a century. Normally it's open April to September, daily 9am to 7pm; if it's closed, ask for the key at Mrs. Peterson's cottage across the way. For information, call ☎ **01957/755-215.**

The ruins of the **Kirk of Lund,** dating from the Middle Ages, can also be seen on Unst. Like Lunna Kirk in Vidlin, it, too, had a "leper hole" through which victims could hear the service.

Unst is home of the **Hermaness Bird Reserve,** one of the most important ornithological sites in Britain. Ideal for scenic walks, its 600-foot (182m) cliffs are filled with kittiwakes, razorbills, guillemots, and the inevitable puffins.

## Accommodations & Dining

**Baltasound Hotel.** Baltasound, Unst, Shetland ZE2 9DS. ☎ **01957/711-334.** 25 units, 22 with private bathroom. TV TEL. £59 ($100.30) double with or without bathroom. Rates include Scottish breakfast. MC, V.

Built 150 years ago for the family of the local laird and converted into a hotel in 1939, this granite house sits in isolation beside the sea about a quarter mile (.5m) from the hamlet of Baltasound. Many of the guests are bird watchers and geologists. Its guest rooms are in what locals call a "Scandinavian extension" jutting out to the building's side, sheathed with blackened wood siding. It contains simple and uncluttered rooms. Late in 1992 the hotel was enlarged with a series of motel-like "chalet" rooms attached to the main building. The two bars serve lunch and inexpensive dinners daily; the restaurant offers moderately priced main courses, and you should book in advance.

# Appendix:
# Scotland in Depth

A small nation ("Tis a wee country, aye—but a bonny one"), Scotland is only 275 miles (443km) long and some 150 miles (241.5km) wide at its broadest. No Scot lives more than 40 miles (64.5km) from saltwater. But despite the small size of their country, the Scots have extended their influence around the world. And in this land of bagpipes and clans and kilts, you'll find some of Europe's grandest scenery.

Inventor Alexander Graham Bell and explorers Mungo Park and David Livingstone came from Scotland. This country gave the world entrepreneur Andrew Carnegie, poet Robert Burns, novelist Sir Walter Scott, actor Sean Connery, singer Sheena Easton, and comedian/actor Billy Connelly. But, curiously, for a long time its most famous resident has been neither man nor woman but Nessie, the Loch Ness Monster.

The border is just a line on a map; you'll hardly be aware of crossing out of England into Scotland. Yet even though the two countries have been joined constitutionally since 1707, Scotland is very different from England and is very much its own country. (In fact, on July 1, 1999, Scotland was granted greater independence when a reform instituted by Prime Minister Tony Blair brought back regional government and a new Scottish Parliament was opened by Queen Elizabeth in Edinburgh.)

In Scotland you'll discover mountains and glens, lochs and heather-covered moors, skirling bagpipes and twirling kilts, pastel-bathed houses and gray stone cottages, and rivers and streams filled with trout and salmon. Eagles soar and deer run free. Lush meadowlands are filled with sheep, and rocky coves and secret harbors wait for the adventurous. You can hear the sound of Gaelic, admire the misty blue hills, and attend a Highland gathering. You'll find quiet contemplation or you can enjoy an activity-filled calendar. And in Scotland you'll find one of Europe's biggest welcomes.

## 1 History 101

Much of the history of the Scots has been shaped by their country's location in a remote corner of northwestern Europe. Amazingly, Scotland encompasses 787 islands (although only about one fourth are established). Its some 6,214 miles (10,004km) of coastline is deeply penetrated by the Atlantic Ocean on the west and the often turbulent North Sea on the east. Most places lie only 60 miles inland. In fact, the

**Dateline**

- **6000 B.C.** The earliest known residents of Scotland establish settlements on the Argyll Peninsula.
- **3000 B.C.** Celtic tribes invade, making the use of Gaelic widespread.
- **A.D. 82** Roman armies directed by Agricola push into southern Scotland; the Roman victories, however, are short-lived.
- **A.D. 90** Romans abandon the hope of conquering Scotland, retreating to England and the relative safety of Hadrian's Wall.
- **500** Newcomers from Ireland, identified as Scots, invade from the west, mingling their bloodlines with Norse, Pictish, Celtic, and Teutonic tribes.
- **563** St. Columba establishes a mission on Iona, accelerating the movement established by earlier ecclesiastics to Christianize Scotland.
- **843** Kenneth MacAlpin unifies the Picts and the Scots.
- **1005–34** Malcolm II unites the four major tribes of Scotland into one roughly cohesive unit.
- **1124–53** David I builds monasteries, consolidates royal power and prestige, and imports clearly defined Norman values.
- **1266** The Hebrides and the coast of western Scotland are released from Norse control; the Donald clan consolidates power here into a semi-autonomous state within Scotland.
- **1272** Edward I of England embarks on an aggressive campaign to conquer both Wales and Scotland but is deflected by Robert the Bruce, among others.
- **1314** The victory of the Scots over the English armies at Bannockburn leads to the

*continues*

sea has shaped Scotland's destiny more than any other element and bred a nation of seafarers, many of whom still earn their living from the sea.

Scotland is a world apart, a distinctly unique nation within the United Kingdom. Just more than half the size of England, with only a tenth of England's population, it boasts more open spaces and natural splendor than England ever did. The Scots are hard to classify: They're generous yet have the reputation for stinginess, eloquent yet dour at times, and romantic at heart yet brutally realistic in their appraisals (especially of the English). Even the Romans couldn't subdue these Caledonians, and they remain Braveheart proud and fiercely independent.

But how did it all begin?

## EARLY HISTORY

Scotland was a melting pot in its early history. Standing stones, brochs, cromlechs, cairns, and burial chambers attest to its earliest occupation, but we know little about these first tribes and invaders. By the time the Roman armies decided to invade in A.D. 82, the land was occupied by a people the Romans called the Picts (Painted Ones). Despite spectacular bloodletting, the Romans were unsuccessful, and the building of Hadrian's Wall effectively marked the northern limits of their influence.

Parts of Hadrian's Wall still stand, but in England, not Scotland. The wall extends for 73 miles (117.5km) across the north of England, from the North Sea to the Irish Sea, its most interesting stretch consisting of 10 miles (16km) west of the town of Housesteads. If you're driving north from England into Scotland, you might want to stop and see the remains of this wall before penetrating the Border country of Scotland.

By A.D. 500, the Picts were again attacked, this time by the Dalriad Irish called Scots, who were successful. They established themselves on the Argyll Peninsula and battled and intermarried with the Picts. Britons emigrated from the south and Norsemen from the east, creating new bloodlines and migratory patterns. Druidism, a little-understood mystical form of nature worship whose most visible monuments are runic etchings and stone circles, flourished at this time. Languages of the era included a diverse array of Celtic and Norse dialects with scatterings of Low German and Saxon English.

The power of the Scotians, entrenched in western Scotland, was cemented when a missionary named Columba (later canonized) arrived from Ireland in 563. The rocky Hebridean island of Iona became the base for his Christian mission. Christianity, already introduced by Sts. Ninian and Mungo to Strathclyde and Galloway, became widespread.

If you have an interest in this early part of Scottish history, visit remote Iona, part of the Hebrides (see chapter 11, "The Hebridean Islands"). More than any dull recitation of history, a visit here, especially to Iona Abbey, can recapture some of this land's dim, often unrecorded history.

## THE MIDDLE AGES

The Scots and the Picts were united in 843 under the kingship of an early chieftain named Kenneth MacAlpin, but it was the invasionary pressures from England and Scandinavia and the unifying force of Christianity that molded Scotland into a relatively coherent unit. Under Malcolm II (1005–34), the British and the Angles, who occupied the southwest and southeast of the Scottish mainland, merged with the Scots and the Picts. Malcolm's son and heir, Duncan, was murdered by Macbeth of Moray, and this event fueled the plotline of Shakespeare's famous "Scottish play." Glamis Castle, in the village of Glamis outside Dundee, contains Duncan's Hall, where the Victorians imagined Macbeth killed Duncan. See chapter 9, "Aberdeen & the Tayside & Grampian Regions," for details on Glamis.

Malcolm III's marriage to an English princess, Margaret, furthered the Anglicization of the Scottish Lowlands. A determined woman of strong ideas, she imported English priests into Scotland and carried out church reforms that soon replaced St. Columba's Gaelic form of Christianity. Her Anglicization efforts and introduction of the English language as a teaching tool laid important groundwork for making Scotland into a potential English kingdom. She led a life of great piety and was canonized as St. Margaret in 1251.

While Europe's feudal system was coming to full flower, Scotland was preoccupied with the territorial battles of clan allegiances and the attempt to define its borders with England. Cultural assimilation with England continued under David I (1081–1153), who made land

Treaty of Arbroath (1320), formally recognizing Scotland's independence from England.

- **1468** The Orkney and the Shetland Islands are given to Scotland as part of the marriage dowry of a Norse princess to a Scottish king.
- **Late 1400s** The Auld Alliance with France, a cynical arrangement based mostly on mutual distrust of England, is born.
- **1535** At the urging of Henry VIII of England, Parliament officially severs all ties with the Catholic Church, legally sanctioning the Reformation.
- **1559–64** John Knox lays out the rough outline of the Scottish Presbyterian Church.
- **1561** Queen Mary returns to Scotland from France.
- **1568** Mary is defeated and flees to England.
- **1572** John Knox dies; his work is continued by Andrew Melville.
- **1587** Mary Queen of Scots is executed.
- **1603** Mary's son, James VI of Scotland, accedes to the throne of England as James I and unifies the two countries.
- **1689** Parliament strips the uncompromising Catholic James II of his crown and imports the Protestant William and Mary from Holland to replace him.
- **1746** Bonnie Prince Charlie's attempt to reclaim his grandfather's throne ends in defeat at the Battle of Culloden, destroying any hope of a Stuart revival.
- **1750–1850** England and Scotland experience rapid industrialization; the Clearances strip many crofters of their farms, creating epic bitterness and forcing new patterns of Scottish migrations.

*continues*

**477**

Scotland in Depth

- **1789** The French Revolution ignites; British monarchists tighten their grip on civil unrest in Scotland.
- **Late 19th century** An astonishing success in the sciences propels Scotland into the role of arbiter of industrial know-how around the globe.
- **Mid-20th century** The decline of traditional industries, especially shipbuilding, painfully redefines the nature of Scottish industry.
- **1970** The discovery of North Sea oil deposits brings new vitality to Scotland.
- **1973** Scotland, as part of the United Kingdom, becomes a member of the Common Market.
- **1974** The old counties or shires are reorganized; many regions are renamed.
- **1979** Scots vote on devolution (separation from England): 33% vote yes, 31% vote no, and 36% don't vote at all.
- **1981** The largest oil terminal in Europe is launched at Sullom Voe in the Shetland Islands.
- **1988** Scottish nationalism revives under the marching cry of "Scotland in Europe"; Pan Am Flight 103 from London crashes at Lockerbie, killing all passengers and some locals.
- **1992** The Scots continue to express dissatisfaction with English rule: Polls show one of two favor independence.
- **1996** A psychopath guns down 16 kids and a teacher in one of Britain's greatest mass-murder sprees.
- **1997** A sheep is cloned for the first time; Scotland votes to establish a legislature of its own for the first time since 1707.
- **1999** British Prime Minister Tony Blair holds off threats

*continues*

grants to many Anglo-Norman families, providing Scotland with a feudal aristocracy and bringing in ancient names like Fraser, Seton, and Lindsay. He also embarked on one of the most lavish building sprees in Scottish history, erecting many abbeys, including Jedburgh, Kelso, Melrose, and Dryburgh. You can still see these abbeys or their ruins. This extravagance, although giving modern visitors lots of photogenic medieval monuments, almost bankrupted his treasury.

In 1266, after about a century of Norse control, the foggy and windswept Western Isles were returned to Scotland following the Battle of Largs. Despite nominal allegiance to the Scottish monarch, this region's inhabitants quickly organized themselves around the Donald (or MacDonald) clan, which for nearly 100 years was one of the most powerful and ruled its territory almost as an independent state. The honorary title of their patriarch, Lord of the Isles, is still one of the formal titles used on state occasions by Britain's Prince of Wales. To learn more about what may be the most important clan in Scottish history, you can visit the Clan Donald Visitor Centre at Armadale on the island of Skye (see chapter 11).

In the meantime, real trouble was brewing in the south. Edward I, ambitious Plantagenet king of England (also known as Longshanks and then the Hammer of the Scots), yearned to rule over an undivided nation incorporating England, Scotland, and Wales. Successful at first, he set up John de Balliol as a vassal king to do homage to him for Scotland. Many of Scotland's legendary heroes lived during this period: Sir William Wallace (1270–1305), who drove the English out of Perth and Stirling; Sir James Douglas (the Black Douglas; 1286–1330), who terrorized the English borders; and Robert the Bruce (1274–1329), who, with skill and courage, finally succeeded in freeing Scotland from England. Crowned Robert I at Scone in 1306 in defiance of the English, Robert the Bruce defeated Edward II of England decisively at the 1314 Battle of Bannockburn. Scotland's independence was formally recognized in the 1328 Treaty of Northampton, inaugurating a heady but short-lived separation from England.

For more legend and lore about those towering Scottish heroes, William Wallace and Robert the Bruce, see chapter 8. You can also visit Stirling Castle, which loomed so large in

Scottish history. If you'd rather see where the crucial Battle of Bannockburn took place, you can visit the Bannockburn Heritage Centre outside Stirling, whose audiovisual presentation makes these stirring events come alive (see chapter 8, "Fife & the Central Highlands").

from the nationalist party as his own Labour Party triumphs in national elections; on July 1, Queen Elizabeth opens a new Scottish Parliament for the first time in 300 years.

In 1468, the Orkneys and the Shetlands, Norse to the core, were brought into the Scottish web of power as part of the marriage dowry of the Norse princess Margaret to James III. This acquisition was the last successful expansion of Scottish sovereignty during the period when Scottish power and independence were at their zenith. It was at this time the Scots entered with the French into an alliance that was to have far-reaching effects. The line of Stuart (or Stewart) kings, so named because the family had become powerful as stewards of the English king, were generally accepted as the least troublesome of a series of potential evils. Real power, however, lay with Scotland's great lords, patriarchs of the famous clans. Jealous of both their bloodlines and their territories, they could rarely agree on anything other than their common distrust of England.

## THE REFORMATION

The passions of the Reformation burst on an already turbulent Scottish scene in the person of John Knox, a devoted disciple of the Geneva Protestant John Calvin and a bitter enemy of both the Catholic Church and the Anglican Church. Knox became famous for the screaming insults he heaped on ardently Catholic Queen Mary and for his absolute lack of a sense of humor. His polemics were famous—in his struggle against Queen Mary, he wrote his *First Blast of the Trumpet Against the Monstrous Regiment of Women*. His was a peculiar mixture of piety, conservatism, strict morality, and intellectual independence that's still a pronounced feature of the Scottish character.

Knox's teachings helped shape the democratic form of Scottish government and set the Scottish Church's austere moral tone for generations to come. He focused on practical considerations as well as religious ones: church administration and funding, and the relationship between church and state. Foremost among the tenets were provisions for a self-governing congregation and pure allegiance to the Word of God as contained in meticulous translations of the Old and New Testaments. In Edinburgh, you can still visit the John Knox House, where the reformer lived (see chapter 4, "Edinburgh & the Lothian Region").

On Knox's 1562 death, his work was continued by Scots-born, Geneva-trained Andrew Melville, who hated ecclesiastical tyranny even more (if that were possible) than Knox himself. Melville reorganized the Scottish universities and emphasized classical studies and the study of the Bible in its original Hebrew and Greek. Under his leadership emerged a clearly defined Scottish Presbyterian Church whose elected leaders were responsible for practical as well as spiritual matters.

Later, the Church of Scotland's almost obsessive insistence on self-government led to endless conflicts, first with the Scottish and then, after unification, with the British monarchs.

## MARY QUEEN OF SCOTS

When Mary Stuart, Queen of Scots (1542–87), took up her rule, she was a Roman Catholic of French upbringing trying to govern an unruly land to which she was a relative newcomer. Daughter of Scotland's James V and

France's Mary of Guise, she became queen when 6 days old. She was sent to be educated in France and at age 15 married the heir to the French throne; she returned to Scotland only after his death. Mary then set out on two roads that were anathema to the Scots—to make herself absolute monarch in the French style and to impose Roman Catholicism. The first alienated the lords who held the real power, and the second made her the enemy of John Knox and the Calvinists. After a series of disastrous political and romantic alliances and endless abortive episodes of often indiscreet intrigue, her life was ended by the headsman's ax in England. The execution order was reluctantly issued by her cousin, Elizabeth I, who considered Mary's presence an incitement to civil unrest and a threat to the stability of the English throne.

Of all the towering figures in Scottish history, only Mary Queen of Scots left an extensive trail of palaces and castles you can still visit to see where she lived and played out the tragic events of her life. Begin in the Borders (chapter 4) at Mary Queen of Scots House and go on to the Palace of Holyroodhouse in Edinburgh (see chapter 4) where her Italian secretary, David Rizzio, was stabbed 56 times in front of her.

The queen used to come to Falkland Palace (see chapter 8) for hunting and hawking and lived at Stirling Castle (also chapter 8) as an infant monarch for the first 4 years of her life.

The power of the great lords of Scotland was broken only in 1603, when Mary's son, James VI of Scotland, assumed the throne of England as James I, Elizabeth's heir. James succeeded where his doomed mother had failed. He was the first of the Stuarts to occupy the English throne, and his coronation effectively united England and Scotland.

## UNION WITH ENGLAND

Despite the hopes for peace that accompanied the union, religion almost immediately became a prime source of discontent. From their base in England, the two Stuart kings attempted to promote a Church of Scotland governed by bishops, in opposition to the Presbyterian Church's self-ruling organization. So incensed were the Scots that in 1638 they signed the National Covenant, which not only reasserted the Reformation's principles but also questioned the king's right to make laws, a role the Covenanters believed should be filled by Parliament. However, the monarch was still allowed a role, unlike the position the Puritans took in England.

Charles I, king of England from 1625 to 1649, believed strongly in the divine right of kings. When Parliament stripped away much of his authority in 1642, Charles fled north to organize an army against the Parliamentary forces centered in London. A civil war ensued, and the forces of Parliament were led to victory by Oliver Cromwell (1599–1658). Charles fled to Scotland, but the Scots turned him over to Parliament, and in 1649 he was convicted of treason and beheaded. Under the Commonwealth set up, Cromwell assumed a dominant political role and became Lord Protector in 1653. King in all but name, he ruled England until his death.

### A Scot Is Not a Scotch

Remember one thing: Scotch is a whisky and not the name of the proud people who inhabit the country. They're called **Scots,** and the adjective is **Scottish.**

Even if you forget and call them Scotch, they'll forgive you. What they won't forgive is calling them English.

But trouble brewed in Scotland. The death of Charles I led to deep divisions in the country, which finally openly defied Cromwell, proclaiming Charles II king. The Scots even launched abortive invasions of England. Cromwell's forces finally defeated the Scots at Dunbar in 1650. For nearly 9 years (1651–60), Scotland was under Commonwealth military occupation, although the result of that invasion had virtually nothing to do with what you'll see as a visitor today. Religious friction continued, however, after the restoration of Charles II to the English throne.

## THE JACOBITES

In 1689, when the English Parliament stripped Catholic James II of his crown and imported Protestant monarchs William and Mary from Holland, the exiled ex-king and then his son James Edward (the Old Pretender) became focal points for Scottish unrest. The Jacobites (the name comes from *Jacobus,* the Latin form of James) attempted unsuccessfully in 1715 to place the Old Pretender on the English throne and restore the Stuart line. Although James died in exile, his son Charles Edward (the Young Pretender), better known as Bonnie Prince Charlie, carried on his father's dream. Charismatic but with an alcohol-induced instability, he was the central figure of the 1745 Jacobite uprising. For more legend and lore about Bonnie Prince Charlie, see chapter 11.

Although the revolt was initially promising because of the many Scottish adherents who crossed religious lines to rally to the cause, the Jacobite forces were crushed at the Battle of Culloden, near Inverness, by a numerically superior English army led by the duke of Cumberland. Many supporters of the Pretender's cause were killed in battle, some were executed, and others fled to the United States and other safe havens. Fearing a rebirth of similar types of Scottish nationalism, the clan system was rigorously suppressed, clans that supported the Jacobite cause lost their lands, and, until 1782, the wearing of Highland dress was made illegal. Six miles southeast of Inverness, you can still visit the historic battlefield at Culloden, at Culloden Moor (see chapter 10, "Inverness & the West Highlands").

The Young Pretender himself was smuggled unglamorously out of Scotland, assisted by a resident of the obscure Hebridean island of South Uist, Flora MacDonald. One of the era's most visible Scottish heroines, she has ever since provided fodder for the Scottish sense of romance. The Bonnie Prince dissipated himself in Paris and Rome, and the hopes of an independent Scotland were buried forever.

## ECONOMIC GROWTH & THE INDUSTRIAL REVOLUTION

During the 18th century, the Scottish economy underwent a radical transformation of growth and diversification. The British government, fearing civil unrest, commissioned one of its most capable generals to build roads and bridges throughout the country, presumably to increase military access from London in the event of a revolt—however, they actually encouraged business and commerce.

As trade with British overseas colonies, England, and Europe increased, the great ports of Aberdeen, Glasgow, and Leith (near Edinburgh) flourished. The merchants of Glasgow grew rich on a nearly monopolistic tobacco trade with Virginia and the Carolinas, until the outbreak of the Revolution sent American tobacco elsewhere. Other forms of commerce continued to enrich a battalion of shrewd Scots.

The 1789 outbreak of the French Revolution engendered so much sympathy in Scotland for the cause that a panicked government in London became

# The Stone of Destiny, Home at Last

After a rocky journey, the Stone of Scone or Stone of Destiny has finally been returned to Scotland. The stone is physically only a block of sandstone, measuring 26 inches long and 16 inches wide and weighing 336 pounds. But it's not just a stone: Revered for centuries as a holy relic, it allegedly came from the Middle East, and in biblical times Jacob is said to have used the stone as a pillow.

The stone was used at Dunadd, Iona, and Dunstaffnage for enthroning the Dalriad Irish Monarchs called Scots. Later it was moved to Scone, and in 1292 John Balliol became the last king to be crowned on the stone in Scotland. So powerful was its legend that Edward I took it to England in 1296, believing possession of the stone gave him sovereignty over Scotland. There it stayed, under the coronation chair in Westminster Abbey. In 1328, the Treaty of Northampton recognizing Scotland's independence returned the stone to Scotland, but the English reneged on the promise and the stone never moved from Westminster Abbey.

On Christmas Day 1950, the stone was taken from the abbey by a group of Scottish Nationalists. No one knows where it went then, but it was found about 4 months later in Arbroath Abbey and returned to Westminster. A rumor went around that the found stone was actually a replica and that the replica—and not the real stone—was carted back to London, but this has never been proved.

In 1996, the Stone of Destiny left Westminster Abbey by Land Rover, crossing from England into Scotland at the border town of Coldstream, where a small but moving ceremony was held. On November 30 of that year, the stone proceeded with pomp and circumstance up the Royal Mile in Edinburgh to its permanent home beside the Scottish Crown Jewels in Edinburgh Castle, where you can see it today (see chapter 4). Scots hailed the return of the stone after 700 years in English captivity.

"Thank God it's back where it belongs," said Andrew McGregor, an Edinburgh office worker. Yet not all Scots are pleased with the return of the stone. Some have denounced it as a "cheap political ploy," especially as the Queen claims she's "lending" it to her Scottish subjects—the idea is that after 7 centuries possession is nine-tenths of the law, and it can be called back to London for a future coronation.

Some Scots want to see the stone returned to Scone. "Edinburgh has no claim, legally, morally, or whatever, to the Stone of Scone," said Andrew R. Robinson, administrator of Scone Castle. "It's not called the Stone of Edinburgh, is it?"

more autocratic than ever in its attempts to suppress Scottish antimonarchical feelings.

The infamous Clearances (1750–1850) changed forever Scotland's demographics. Small farmers, or crofters, were expelled from their ancestral lands to make way for sheep-grazing. Increased industrialization, continued civil unrest, migration into urban centers, and a massive wave of emigration out of Scotland into the United States, Canada, Australia, South Africa, and New Zealand all contributed to a changing national demographic and a dispersal of the Scottish ethic throughout the world.

Meanwhile, rapid progress in the arts, science, and education and the new industrial age meshed neatly with the Scottish genius for thrift, hard work, shrewdness, and conservatism. The 19th century produced vast numbers of prominent Scots who made broad and sweeping contributions to all fields of endeavor. Many of the inventions that altered the history of the developing world were either invented or installed by Scottish genius and industry.

## THE 20TH CENTURY

Scotland endured bitter privations during the Great Depression and the two world wars. In the 1960s and 1970s, Scotland found that, like the rest of Britain, its aging industrial plants couldn't compete with more modern commercial competition from abroad. The most visible decline occurred in the shipbuilding industries. The vast Glasgow shipyards that once produced some of the world's great ocean liners were now bankrupt. The companies that produced automobiles were wiped out during the 1930s. Many commercial enterprises once controlled by Scots had been merged into English or multinational conglomerates.

However, all wasn't bleak on the Scottish horizon. The 1970 discovery of North Sea oil by British Petroleum boosted the economy considerably and provided jobs for thousands of workers. Oil has continued to play a prominent role in the Scottish economy. In 1981, the largest oil terminal in Europe opened at Sullom Voe in the remote Shetland Islands.

As part of the United Kingdom, Scotland became a member of the European Common Market in 1973, although many Scots—perhaps owing to their longtime isolationism—opposed entry. Some voters expressed a great fear that membership would take away hunks of their rights of self-government and determination. In 1974, it underwent a drastic revision of its counties. Many regions were renamed. For example, Tayside was carved out of the old counties of Perth and Angus.

A landmark scientific breakthrough occurred in 1997. The Scots have always contributed almost disproportionately to the world's science and technology. Now the land that gave us Sir Alexander Fleming, Nobel Prize winner as discoverer of penicillin, has given us the first cloned sheep. The issue of *Nature* for February 27, 1997, reported the event, the work of scientists in Roslin. Dolly was the first lamb to be produced by cloning the udder cells of an adult sheep. In the summer of 1997, another major step was taken, and Polly was created, a lamb that has a human gene in every cell of its body. The work was hailed as a milestone. Animals with human genes (at least in theory) could be used to produce hormones or other biological products to treat human diseases or even to produce organs for human transplant.

In May 1999, national election results gave Prime Minister Tony Blair a victory over the nationalist party of Scotland. Labour, however, failed to win outright control of the Scottish Parliament; but Blair said he felt the results represented an endorsement of his reform of British politics. Because it came in 9 seats short of a majority in the new 129-seat Parliament (the first legislature Scotland has had since its 1707 union with England), Labour became obliged to enlist the centrist Liberal Democrats in a coalition, a form of governing not seen in Britain since World War II.

The new Scottish legislature will have authority to pursue such matters as health, education, public transportation, and public housing. Unlike the new Welsh Parliament, the Scottish Parliament will also have taxing powers and can make laws. The main Parliament, of course, will remain in London, where Scotland will be widely represented. The country will bow to the greater will of Britain in matters like foreign policy, national defense, and economic and fiscal policies and may one day become part of euro-land, the new umbrella of single-currency countries (France, Germany, Italy, and so on). So far, Britain has decided to stick with the pound sterling as its time-honored form of currency.

This doesn't mean the Scottish Nationalist Party is now more relevant to Brigadoon than to Britain. Determined leaders of the Independence movement will continue to press for total separation from England. "We are not just provincial mischief-makers in kilts," one nationalist said. "We will one day gain independence. England will lose a surly lodger and gain a good neighbor."

On a more optimistic front, Scotland is turning a strong face to the world, with its abundant natural resources in oil, water, gas, and coal. Its high-tech industries have played an important role in the technological revolution, and today the country produces 13% of Europe's personal computers, 45% of Europe's workstations, and 50% of Europe's automated banking machines. Everything in the country is loosening up—blue laws are giving way, later hours are being kept, nightlife is looking up, and eco-tourism is being developed. Scotland's time-tested crafts (woolen tweeds and knitwear) are thriving, the market for scotch whisky has burgeoned all around the world, and tourists are visiting in record numbers.

As Scotland goes into the 21st century, there's a new esprit in the land. The question of national identity fills the press. Scots are on a roll, declaring that their country is not a mere tartan theme park.

And speaking of tartans, nothing has shaken up the identity of Scotland more than the new kilts designed by Howie Nicholsby of Edinburgh. To model his new kilt design, Howie secured tough rugby star Chris Capaldi. The kilt is transparent—and in pink no less.

Is nothing sacred?

## 2  A Portrait of the Scots

### LANGUAGE

In Scotland's earliest history, its prevailing tongue was the Celtic language, Gaelic, along with a smattering of Norse dialects. When English was introduced and Scottish English developed, it borrowed heavily not only from Gaelic but from Scandinavian, Dutch, and French. In the 15th and 16th centuries, when Scotland had close ties to France, French was a literary language of precision and grace, and it was the language of Mary Queen of Scots, who spoke no Gaelic at all. After the Scottish court moved to England in 1603, Scottish English was looked on as a rather awkward dialect.

As the centuries progressed, ancient and complex Gaelic diminished in importance, partly because the British government's deliberate policy was to make English the language of all Britain. By the 1980s, less than 2% of the Scottish population understood Gaelic. Most of those who still speak it live in the northwestern Highlands and in the Hebridean Islands—especially the Isle of Skye, where about 60% of the population still uses the Gaelic language.

Scottish English never developed the linguistic class divisions that still exist so strongly in England between upper-, middle-, and lower-class speech patterns. Throughout most of its English-speaking history, the hardships of Scotland were suffered in common by a society that was well knit and had few barriers between the classes. Social snobbery was relatively unknown and the laird (estate owner) and his man conversed as equals.

At the end of the 20th century, the great leveling effects of TV and radio have begun to even out some of the more pronounced burrs and lilts of the Scottish tongue. However, the dialect and speech patterns of the Scots are still rich and evocative.

Today, after years of struggle, Scottish students are rewarded with approval by pro-Scots educators when they say, "Whos all comin tae the jiggin?" ("Who's coming to the dance?"). This increasing pride in the Scottish language is in direct contrast to what happened in classrooms back in, say, the 1950s. At that time, students were under a constant threat of a whack from a tawse (leather strap) if they blurted out a single *aye*.

## HIGHLAND GAMES & GATHERINGS

Highland gatherings or games have their origins in the fairs organized by the tribes or clans for the exchange of goods. At these gatherings there were often trials of strength among the men, and the strongest were selected for the chief's army.

The earliest games were held more than 1,000 years ago. The same tradition is maintained today: throwing hammers, putting rounded stones found in the rivers, tossing tree trunks, running in flat races and up steep hillsides. Playing the bagpipes and performing dances have always been part of the gatherings. The Heavies, a breed of gigantic men, always draw the most attention with their prowess. Of all the events, the most popular and most spectacular is the tossing of the caber (the throwing of a great tree trunk).

Queen Victoria, who had a deep love for Scotland (which was dramatized in the film *Mrs. Brown*) popularized the Highland games, which for many decades had been suppressed after the failure of the 1745 rebellion. In 1848, the queen and her consort, Prince Albert, attended the Braemar Gathering and saw her ghillie, Duncan, win the race up the hill of Craig Choinnich, as she recorded in her journal.

The most famous gathering nowadays is at Braemar, held in early September each year and patronized by the royal family. When that chief of chiefs takes the salute, Queen Elizabeth is fulfilling a role assumed by a predecessor of hers in the 11th century.

Other major games are held at Ballater (Grampian), Aberdeen, Elgin, and Newtonmore.

## CLANS, TARTANS & KILTS

To the outsider, Scotland's deepest traditions appear to be based on the clan system of old with all the familiar paraphernalia of tartans and bagpipes. However, this is a romantic memory, and in any case, a good part of the Scots—the 75% of the population that live in the central Lowland, for example—have little or no connection with the clansmen of earlier times.

The clan tradition dates from the tribal units of the country's earliest Celtic history. Power was organized around a series of chieftains who exacted loyalties from the inhabitants of a particular region in exchange for protection against exterior invasions. The position of chieftain wasn't hereditary, and land was owned by the clan, not by the chieftain. Clan members had both rights and duties. Rigidly militaristic and paternalistic—the stuff with which Scottish legend is imbued—the clan tradition is still emphasized today, albeit in a much friendlier fashion than when claymores and crossbows threatened a bloody death or dismemberment for alleged slights on a clan's honor.

Chieftains were absolute potentates, with life and death power over members and interlopers, although they were usually viewed as patriarchs actively

# How the Scots Say It

| | |
|---|---|
| aber | river mouth |
| ach | field |
| aird | promontory |
| alt | stream |
| auch | field |
| auld | old |
| baillie | magistrate |
| bal | hamlet or tiny village |
| ben | peak, often rugged |
| birk | birch tree |
| brae | hillside, especially along a river |
| brig | bridge |
| broch | circular stone tower |
| burn | stream |
| cairn | heap of stone piled up as memorial or landmark |
| ceilidh | Scottish hoedown with singing, music, tall tales |
| clach | stone |
| clachan | hamlet |
| close | narrow passage leading from the street to a court or tenement |
| craig | rock |
| creel | basket |
| croft | small farm worked by a tenant, often with hereditary rights |
| cromlech, dolmen | prehistoric tomb or monument consisting of a large flat stone laid across upright stones |
| dram | ⅛ fluid ounce |
| drum | ridge |
| dun | fortress, often in a lake, for refuge in times of trouble |
| eas | waterfall |
| eilean | island |
| factor | manager of an estate |

engaged in the perpetuation of the clan's bloodlines, traditions, and honor. The entourage of a chieftain always included bodyguards, musicians (harpers and pipers), a spokesman (known as a tatler), and—perhaps most important to latter-day students of clan traditions—a bard. The bard's role was to sing, to exalt the role of the clan and its heroes, to keep a genealogical record of births and deaths, and to compose or recite epic poems relating to the clan's history.

Most of the clans were organized during two distinctly different eras of Scottish history. One of the country's oldest and largest is Clan Donald, whose original organization occurred during the early mists of the Christianization of Scotland and whose headquarters has traditionally been Scotland's

| | |
|---|---|
| fell | hill |
| firth | arm of the sea reaching inland |
| gait | street (in proper names) |
| gil | ravine |
| glen | a small valley |
| haugh | water meadow |
| how | burial mound |
| howff | meeting place |
| inver | mouth of a river |
| kil, kin, kirk | church |
| kyle | narrows of ancient or unknown origin |
| land | house built on a piece of ground considered as property |
| larig | mountain pass |
| links | dunes |
| loch | lake |
| machair | sand dune, sometimes covered with sea grass |
| mon | hill |
| muir | moor |
| mull | cape or promontory |
| ness | headland |
| neuk | nose |
| pend | vaulted passage |
| provost | mayor |
| reek | smoke |
| ross | cape |
| schist | highly compact crystalline rock formation |
| strath | broad valley |
| tarbert | isthmus |
| tolbooth | old town hall (often with prison) |
| uig | sheltered bay |
| uisge | water |
| uisge beatha | water of life, whisky |
| way | bay |
| wynd | alley |

northwestern coast and western islands. The fragmentation of Clan Donald into subdivisions (which include the Sleat, the Dunyveg, the Clanranald, and the Keppoch clans) happened after the violent battles of succession over control of the clan in the 1400s. These feuds so weakened the once powerful unity of the MacDonalds that a new crop of former vassal tribes in northwestern Scotland declared their independence and established new clans of their own. These included the Mackintoshes, the Macleans, the MacNeils, the Mackinnons, and the MacLeods.

Meanwhile, the giant Celtic earldoms of eastern Scotland disintegrated and Norman influences from the south became more dominant. Clans whose earliest makeup might have been heavily influenced by Norman bloodlines

# Garb o' the Gods

*"A memorable photograph from the handover of Hong Kong may spare the First Battalion of the Black Watch from having to answer the question most frequently put to men in kilts. As the flags were being lowered at the Cenotaph, a rush of wind lifted the tartan fabrics from the backside of Lance Cpl. Lee Wotherspoon and revealed nothing at all but his backside. He received a lot of mail and an admiring review from a gay publication in France."*

—Warren Hoge, *New York Times* (1998)

Although not every visitor to Scotland is descended from a clan, almost all are familiar with plaids and the traditions associated with them. Over the centuries, each clan developed a distinctive pattern to be worn by its members, presumably to better identify its soldiers in the heat of battle. (Today, *tartan* is used interchangeably with *plaid,* but the word *tartan* originally referred specifically to a mantle of cloth draped over the back and shoulders.)

Kilts enjoy an ancient history. Checkered tartans were first mentioned in a 1471 English inventory. The clans developed special dyeing and weaving techniques, with colors and patterns reflecting their flair and imagination. The craft of dyeing was raised to an art that was a point of pride for the clan: Alder bark, steeped in hot water, produces a black dye; gorse, broom, and knapweed produce shades of green; cup moss produces purple; dandelion leaves produce magenta; bracken and heather produce yellow; white lichens produce red; and indigo had to be imported for blue.

When Bonnie Prince Charlie launched his abortive rebellion in 1745, he used tartans as a symbol of his army, and this threatened the English enemy so much that public display of tartans was banned for a period after his defeat. Tartans came into high fashion in Queen Victoria's day

include Clan Frasier (from the French *des fraises,* because of the strawberry leaves on the family's coat of arms), de Umfraville, and Rose. Other clans adapted their Celtic names, like Clan Robertson (Celtic Clan Donnachaidh) and Clan Campbell (Celtic Diarmid).

Simultaneously, in the Borders region between England and Scotland, families and clans with differing sets of traditions and symbols held a precarious power over one of Britain's most heavily contested regions, enduring or instigating raids on their territories from both north and south. But despite the rich traditions of the Lowland and Border clans, it's the traditions of the Highland clans with their costumes, bagpipes, speech patterns, and grandly tragic struggles that have captured the imagination of the world.

The clans had broken down long before Sir Walter Scott wrote his romantic novels about them and long before Queen Victoria made Scotland socially fashionable. The clans today represent a cultural rather than a political power. The best place to see the remnants of their tradition in action is at any traditional Highland gathering, although battalions of bagpipers seem to show up at everything from weddings and funerals to political rallies, parades, and civic events throughout Scotland.

when she and her kilt-wearing German consort, Albert, made all things Scottish popular.

Today, there are at least 300 tartans, each subtly distinct from its neighbor and all available for sale in Scotland's shops and markets. If you're not fortunate enough to be of Scottish extraction, Queen Victoria long ago authorized two Lowland designs as suitable garb for Sassenachs (the English, and more remotely, the Americans).

Few people realize that from 7 to 10 yards of tartan wool cloth goes into the average kilt. Even fewer non-Scots know what's actually worn beneath those folds strapped over the muscular thighs of a parading Scotsman. For a Highlander, the answer to that question is nothing, an answer that goes along with such defenders of ancient tradition who hold that only a Stewart (MacPherson and the like) can wear a Stewart (MacPherson and the like) tartan, only a Scotsman looks good in a kilt, and only a foreigner would stoop to wearing anything under it.

Alas, commercialism has reared its head with the introduction of undershorts to match the material making up bagpipe players' kilts. A story is told of a colonel who heard a rumor that the soldiers of his elite Highland Light Infantry regiment were mollycoddling themselves with undershorts. The next day, his eyebrows bristling, he ordered the entire regiment to undress in front of him. To his horror, half a dozen of his soldiers had disgraced the regiment by putting on what only an Englishman would wear. He publicly ordered the offending garments removed, and when he gave the order the next day to drop your kilts, not a soldier in the regiment had on the trews (close-cut tartan shorts).

Even in today's general decline of standards, the mark of a man in the Highlands is still whether he can abide the drafts up his thighs and the feel of wool cloth against his tender flesh.

## 3 A Taste of Scotland

### FROM ANGUS BEEF TO HAGGIS

For many years, restaurants in Scotland were known mainly for their modest prices, watery overcooked vegetables, and boiled meats. But you need no longer expect a diet of oats, fried fish, and greasy chips—in the past 20 or so years there has been a significant improvement in Scottish cookery. There was a time that the Scot going out for dinner would head for the nearest hotel, but independent restaurants are now opening everywhere, often by newly arrived immigrants, along with bistros and wine bars.

More and more restaurants are offering "Taste of Scotland" menus of traditional dishes prepared with the freshest local ingredients, a culinary program initiated by the Scottish Tourist Board. Scotland's culinary strength is in its fresh raw ingredients, ranging from seafood, beef, and game to vegetables and native fruits.

One of Scotland's best-known exports is pedigree **Aberdeen Angus beef.** In fact, the famous ye olde roast beef of England often came from Scotland. Scottish **lamb** is known for its tender, tasty meat. A true connoisseur can taste the difference in lamb by its grazing grounds, ranging from the coarse pastureland and seaweed of the Shetlands to the heather-clad hills of the mainland.

**Game** plays an important role in the Scottish diet, from woodcock, red deer, and grouse to the rabbit and hare in the crofter's kitchen. And **fish** in this land of seas, rivers, and lochs is a mainstay, from salmon to the pink-fleshed brown trout, to the modest herring that's transformed into the elegant kipper (the best are the Loch Fyne kippers). Scottish smoked salmon is, of course, a delicacy known worldwide.

One of the joys of traveling around Scotland is finding a small-town restaurant where perfection is sought in the kitchen. The best example is **La Potinière** at Gullane, where David and Hilary Brown maintain the Auld Alliance, using French culinary techniques on Scottish ingredients. Another gastronomic surprise comes at the **Peat Inn,** 6 miles (10km) southwest of St. Andrews, where David and Patricia Wilson pay homage to the best from field, sky, and stream. They've even encouraged locals to form cottage industries to supply only the best herbs, vegetables, salads, and game. Sample the deep, rich flavors of their pan-fried venison, kidney, and liver or their pigeon breast with wild mushrooms in truffle sauce. **Braeval** at Aberfoyle is typical of the changing state of Scottish cuisine. Chicken livers with baby leeks wasn't an unknown dish in the days of yore, but today it's likely to appear with pesto dressing, and roast lamb is likely to be served with couscous from the kitchens of North Africa.

**Silver Darling,** a restaurant in Aberdeen, calls itself a barbecued seafood restaurant, cooking the day's catch over charcoal. Oysters are likely to appear with spicy Cajun flavoring, and roasted monkfish might be awakened with roasted garlic, cumin, and coriander. Smoked salmon is still on the menu, of course, but chances are it might be whipped into a Swiss cheese soufflé. Tradition is still respected—red-deer fillet marinated in whisky and juniper with black-currant sauce still gets the vote of the traditionalist.

There was a time when no serious gourmet would patronize a hotel dining room. Nowadays you can order some of your best cuisine in hotels, notably **Airds Hotel** in Port Appin, where that grand delight of Scottish cuisine, Aberdeen Angus beef, is in partnership with roasted shallots, morels, leek confit, and red-wine sauce.

Finally, the good news is that the word *eclectic* now describes many restaurants in Scotland. To cite only an example or two, fresh salads often are given a Thai kick with lime leaves and chile, and stir-fry and chargrill are standard features. Scots today can eat better than ever in their history. Robert Burns would be shocked at some of the new taste sensations creative chefs are devising. But he would be happy to learn that alcohol—especially whisky—is still a favored ingredient in many dishes and sauces.

## Impressions

*It is not exactly true that you have to have grown up eating haggis—sheep's offal cooked in a sheep's stomach—to enjoy it. Not when it has been taken out of the sheep's stomach (the major turnoff) and turned into a tiny layer cake with puréed turnips and mashed potatoes and given the hilariously over-the-top name of gateaux of haggis, neeps, and tatties with whisky butter sauce. I licked my plate.*

—Marian Burros, *In Britain* (1997)

Of course, it takes a wise chef to leave well enough alone, and many Scottish cooks know the simplest dishes have never lost their appeal, especially if that means Lismore oysters or Loch Etive mussels. The Scots have always been good bakers, and many small tearooms still bake their own scones, buttery shortbread, and fruity breads. Heather honey is justly celebrated, and jams make use of Scotland's abundant harvest of soft fruit. Scottish raspberries, for example, are said to be among the finest in the world.

You'll most definitely want to try some of Scotland's excellent **cheeses.** The mild or mature cheddars are the best known. A famous hard cheese, Dunlop, comes from the Orkney Islands as well as Arran and Islay. One of the best-known cheeses from the Highlands is Caboc, creamy and rich, formed into cork shapes and rolled in pinhead oatmeal. Many varieties of cottage cheese are flavored with herbs, chives, or garlic.

And, yes, **haggis** is still Scotland's national dish—it's perhaps more symbolic than gustatory. One wit described this dish as a "castrated bagpipe." Regardless of what you might be told facetiously, haggis isn't a bird. Therefore, you should turn down invitations (usually offered in pubs) to go on a midnight haggis hunt. Cooked in a sheep's paunch (nowadays more likely a plastic bag), it's made with bits and pieces of the lung, liver, and heart of sheep mixed with suet and spices, along with onions and oatmeal. Haggis is often accompanied by single-malt whisky—then again, what isn't?

## SINGLE MALT OR BLEND?

"It's the only liquor fit for a gentleman to drink in the morning if he can have the good fortune to come by it . . . or after dinner either." Thus wrote Sir Walter Scott of the drink of his country—**scotch whisky.** Of course, if you're here or almost anywhere in Britain or Europe, you don't have to identify it as *scotch* whisky when you order. That's what you'll get. In fact, in some parts of Scotland, England, and Wales, they look at you oddly if you order scotch as you would in the States.

The true difference in the scotch whiskies you may have become accustomed to seeing on bars or shelves of liquor stores at home is whether they're blends or single-malt whiskies. Many connoisseurs prefer single malts, whose tastes depend on their points of origin: Highlands, Lowlands, Islay, or Campbeltown on Kintyre. These are usually seen as sipping whiskies, not to be mixed with water (well, maybe soda) and not to be served with ice. Many have come to be used as after-dinner drinks, served in a snifter like cognac.

The blended scotches came into being both because the single malts were for a long time too harsh for delicate palates and because they were expensive and time consuming to produce. A shortcut was developed: The clear and almost tasteless alcohol produced in the traditional way could be mixed with such ingredients as American corn, Finnish barley, Glasgow city tap water, and caramel coloring with a certain percentage of malt whiskies that flavored the entire bottle. Whichever you prefer, both the single malts and the blends must be made within the borders of Scotland and then aged for at least 3 years before they can legally be called scotch whisky.

Two after-dinner drinks are scotch-based liqueurs—**Drambuie** and **Glayva.** The recipe for Drambuie, better known to Americans than Glayva, is supposed to have been given to its first producers, the Mackinnons of Strath on the Isle of Skye, by an impecunious guest, Bonnie Prince Charlie. The name of the drink is derived from the Gaelic *an dram buidheach,* meaning "a dram that satisfies."

*Despite the beauty of the land and the indomitable spirit of its people, take whisky away from Scotland and you take away the heart.*
—Laura Latham, *In Britain* (1997)

The making of Scottish **beer**—the ales drunk by the common folk in earlier days—almost died out when palates became more adapted to scotch whisky and when a malt tax was levied in the 18th century, followed in the 19th century by beer duty. The brewing industry has made a comeback in the last quarter of a century, and Scottish beer, or scotch ale, is being produced. Real **ale** is beer made from malted barley, hop flowers, yeast, and water, with a fining process (use of an extract from the swim bladders of certain fish) to complete the brewing. Ales are fermented in casks in a series of steps. Scottish ale, either dark or light, is malty and full of flavor.

## 4 Recommended Books

### BIOGRAPHY & AUTOBIOGRAPHY

*Burns: A Biography of Robert Burns,* by James MacKay, is one of the best works devoted to Scotland's national poet (1759–96), in that it relies often on primary source materials and not previously published information. The life of Burns is portrayed against the historical framework of 18th-century Scotland. A Burns scholar, MacKay defends the author of *Tam O'Shanter* and "Auld Lang Syne" against previously published charges that he was a drunkard and a rake.

Today's most famous Scot is revealed in a biography, *Sean Connery: From 007 to Hollywood Icon,* by Andrew Yule. It traces the legendary actor's rise from humble origins in Edinburgh to later success "escaping bondage" in such films as *Rising Sun.* Like all true Scotsmen, Connery is said to have a fascinated interest in golf (playing it) and money (not spending it). Scottish-American readers may find the early years of growing up in Edinburgh during the Depression the most interesting.

*Curriculum Vitae,* an autobiography by Muriel Spark, is a book in which this gifted writer sets the record straight about her first 39 years, up to 1957 and the publication of her novel *The Comforters.* The best parts are about her life as a child in Edinburgh. She tells how at 5 she was sent to Gillespie's, an Edinburgh day school, where she became a pupil of Miss Christina Kay—in time, she'd appear in Ms. Spark's fiction as the immortal Miss Jean Brodie.

*Robert Louis Stevenson: A Biography,* by Frank McLynn, maintains that the frail adventurer and author of *The Strange Case of Dr. Jekyll and Mr. Hyde* was Scotland's greatest writer. The book documents the tragic life of the writer who suffered from "bloody jack" (a hemorrhaging consumptive) and died at 44. He'd ended up a squire in Samoa, with 14 household servants he couldn't really afford. The Samoan servants intensely disliked Stevenson's wife, Fanny, whom they labeled the "Witch Woman of the Mountain." At least part of their allegations might have been true, as his wife complained so much about the first draft of *Dr. Jekyll and Mr. Hyde* that Stevenson destroyed it in a fire; later he came to believe it was the best work he'd ever done.

For true Stevenson readers, *The Letters of Robert Louis Stevenson* (vols. 1 and 2), edited by Bradford A. Booth and Ernest Meh, offers more insight into this often mysterious writer. Volume 1 covers 1854 to April 1874, and volume 2 takes up from there and goes through July 1879.

# FICTION & POETRY

Scotland's most celebrated literary figure remains Robert Burns (1759–1796), whose **"Auld Lang Syne"** is still sung the world over on New Year's Eve. At all bookstores in Scotland today you can pick up volumes of his poems, plus numerous biographies. Although not read with the fervor as in days of yore, poet/novelist Sir Walter Scott (1771–1832) was one of Scotland's top literary figures. The list of his works is so long it would take up a full printed page, everything from *Ivanhoe* in 1820 to *The Fair Maid of Perth* in 1828.

Another great name in Scottish literature, poet/novelist Robert Louis Stevenson (1850–94) became famous in 1883 after the publication of his first novel, *Treasure Island.* He went on to produce memorable works like *Kidnapped* in 1885 and *The Strange Case of Dr. Jekyll and Mr. Hyde* in 1886. (The story was based on an Edinburgh man, Deacon Brodie, but set in London.)

In modern times, Scotland hasn't turned out the big names in literature that it had previously. A Communist, poet Hugh MacDiarmid (1892–1978), produced an enormous output of poetry and essays as his international stature grew. His *Complete Poems* was published in two volumes in 1978. *Morning Tide,* by Neil Gunn, was written in the 1930s and helps explain why Gunn (1891–1973) is considered the master of modern Scottish fiction. It's a straightforward account of a boy's coming of age in a small fishing village in Scotland in the last years of Victoria's reign.

Glaswegian Alistair MacLean (1922–1987) has also achieved acclaim. His novel *HMS Ulysses,* drawing heavily on his experiences with Russian convoys, became one of the most successful British novels of all time and was followed by *The Guns of Navarone,* which earned a worldwide audience. Many readers became familiar with the works of Muriel Spark (b. 1918) through her most famous book, *The Prime of Miss Jean Brodie,* which was made into a successful film starring Maggie Smith. With numerous works still in print, including *Symposium* and *The Ballad of Peckham Rye,* Ms. Spark remains a giant of 20th-century fiction.

The 1995 film *Braveheart* inspired a book of the same name by Randall Wallace, who also wrote the screenplay. Critics mostly found it an entertaining read "if you don't mind the complete bastardization of Scottish history."

# HISTORY

Good historical overviews of Scotland, beginning with its earliest prehistory, are provided by Michael Jenner's *Scotland Through the Ages,* Rosalind Mitchison's *A History of Scotland,* and W. Croft Dickinson and George S. Pryde's *A New History of Scotland.* Also insightful, perhaps because of its authorship by a famous Scots novelist, is Alistair Maclean's *Alistair Maclean Introduces Scotland.*

Dealing in detail with the famous personalities of the 16th century is Alison Plowden's *Elizabeth Tudor and Mary Stewart: Two Queens in One Isle.* Antonia Fraser's *Mary, Queen of Scots* is a highly readable biography. Also by Antonia Fraser is a short, subjective, and exceedingly charming anthology, *Scottish Love Poems: A Personal Anthology.*

Other historical eras are analyzed by Iain Moncreiffe in *The Highland Clans* and by Richard B. Sher and Jeffrey R. Smitten in *Scotland and America in the Age of Enlightenment.* Also interesting are David Daiches's *A Hotbed of Genius: The Scottish Enlightenment 1730–1790,* and Henry Hamilton's *The Industrial Revolution in Scotland.* For U.S. citizens of Scots descent, a richly evocative book, much applauded in the American South, is Duane Gilbert Meyer's *The Highland Scots of North Carolina.*

James Kerr's *Fiction Against History: Scott as Storyteller* explores the fiction as well as the sense of historical destiny of Scotland's "national troubador," Sir Walter Scott. In her book *Burns and Tradition,* Mary Ellen Brown explores the values of Robert Burns and the influence of Scotland's lore and history on him.

The more recent Scottish experience, particularly the events engendered by the flow of black gold from the North Sea, is carefully described in T. M. Lewis and J. H. McNicoll's *North Sea Oil and Scotland's Economic Prospects.* In the same vein is Charlotte Lythe and Madhavi Mamjudar's *The Renaissance of the Scottish Economy.* Appropriate for anyone interested in European history just before, during, and after World War II is T. Christopher Smout's *A History of the Scottish People 1930–1950.*

## CLANS & THEIR SYMBOLS

Finally, on a purely decorative and symbolic level, but with rich interest for anyone tracing genealogical roots, is Robert Bain's *The Clans and Tartans of Scotland,* enlarged and re-edited by Margaret MacDougall, with heraldic advice supplied by P. E. Stewart-Blacker. Somewhat shorter and more succinct is *Tartans,* edited and published by the Belvedere Editions of Rizzoli International.

# Index

Index

Index

Index

Index